C0-AVY-390

GARY DONELL

Study Guide
to accompany

Byrd & Chen's
Canadian
Tax
Principles

2021–2022 EDITION

Please contact https://support.pearson.com/getsupport/s/contactsupport with any queries on this content.

Pearson Canada Inc., 26 Prince Andrew Place, North York, Ontario M3C 2H4.

Copyright © 2022, 2021, 2020 Pearson Canada Inc. All rights reserved.

Printed in the United States of America. This publication is protected by copyright, and permission should be obtained from the publisher prior to any prohibited reproduction, storage in a retrieval system, or transmission in any form or by any means, electronic, mechanical, photocopying, recording, or otherwise. For information regarding permissions, request forms, and the appropriate contacts, please contact Pearson Canada's Rights and Permissions Department by visiting www.pearson.com/ca/en/contact-us/permissions.html.

PEARSON and ALWAYS LEARNING are exclusive trademarks owned by Pearson Canada Inc. or its affiliates in Canada and/or other countries.

Unless otherwise indicated herein, any third-party trademarks that may appear in this work are the property of their respective owners and any references to third-party trademarks, logos, or other trade dress are for demonstrative or descriptive purposes only. Such references are not intended to imply any sponsorship, endorsement, authorization, or promotion of Pearson Canada products by the owners of such marks, or any relationship between the owner and Pearson Canada or its affiliates, authors, licensees, or distributors.

If you purchased this book outside the United States or Canada, you should be aware that it has been imported without the approval of the publisher or the author.

ISBN 978-0-13-737777-0

ScoutAutomatedPrintCode

CONTENTS

PREFACE

Complete Preface In Volume I

The complete preface to this three volume set of *Byrd & Chen's Canadian Tax Principles* can be found in Volume I.

This Study Guide

Contents

Your two volume textbook is accompanied by this Study Guide. The chapters of this Study Guide correspond to the chapters of *Byrd & Chen's Canadian Tax Principles.* Each of these Study Guide chapters contains the following:

- A list of learning objectives for the material in the chapter.
- Detailed guidance on how to work through the text and problems in the chapter.
- Detailed solutions to the Exercises in the textbook for the chapter and the Self-Study Problems available online.
- Two sample personal tax returns and two Self-Study Tax Software Problems in Chapters 4 and 11.
- A sample corporate tax return in Chapter 13.

Glossary

At the back of this Study Guide, the comprehensive glossary defines more than 500 tax terms used throughout the text. Tied to this important resource, at the end of each chapter you will find a list of the Key Terms, without definitions, that were used in that chapter. Glossary Flashcards are also available on MyLab.

Using the Solutions

We encourage you to try to solve each Exercise and Self-Study Problem before consulting these solutions. It is our opinion that one of the most unfortunate misconceptions that many students have is the belief that simply reading through a solution is a good learning experience. It is not!

MyLab Accounting

MyLab Accounting for *Byrd & Chen's Canadian Tax Principles* contains a great deal of additional material that will provide significant assistance to users of this text. Instructions on how to access MyLab can be found on the access card provided with this package. Learn more about MyLab at https://mlm.pearson.com/northamerica/myaccountinglab/.

CHAPTER 1

Learning Objectives

After completing Chapter 1, you should be able to:

1. Describe the purpose of the Canadian income tax system, the principal questions answered by the *Income Tax Act* (ITA) pertaining to Canadian resident individuals and corporations, and the four-step process used to determine one's income tax liability or refund (Paragraph [P hereafter] 1-1 to 1-9).
2. Explain the role that accounting plays in income tax (P 1-10 to 1-11).
3. List some of the different tax bases used by various levels of government to raise tax revenue (P 1-12 to 1-15)
4. List and describe the four principal entities referred to in the ITA (P 1-16 to 1-22).
5. Describe the three main ways that business is carried on and identify who is subject to income tax in each case (P 1-23 to 1-24).
6. Describe those entities that are exempt and those that are taxable (not exempt) (P 1-25 to 1-26).
7. Explain how the GST/HST differs from income tax in terms of how it is collected together with the entities that are accountable for GST/HST (P 1-27 to 1-28).
8. Explain the relationship between the assessment of taxes at the federal level and the assessment of taxes at the provincial level (P 1-29 to 1-40).
9. List some of the ways that taxation is used to achieve economic objectives (P 1-41).
10. Describe the differences between progressive, regressive, and flat tax systems, including some of the advantages and disadvantages of each (P 1-42 to 1-50).
11. Discuss the issue of who ultimately pays the cost of various types of taxes (P 1-51 and 1-52).
12. Explain the nature of tax expenditures (P 1-53 to 1-56).
13. Evaluate issues in tax policy on the basis of the qualitative characteristics of tax systems (P 1-57 to 1-59).
14. Describe the reference materials that are available on income tax databases (P 1-60 to 1-64).
15. Describe the general structure of the *Income Tax Act* (P 1-65 to 1-77).
16. List and explain the nature of other sources of income tax legislation (P 1-78 to 1-88).
17. Describe other sources of *income tax information* (P 1-89 to 1-93).
18. Describe the charging provisions of the ITA for residents and non-residents (P 1-94 to 1-110).
19. Identify the three types of residency and be able to determine the residence of an individual based on an evaluation of the facts (P 1-111 to 1-124).
20. Evaluate the residency status of an individual who is temporarily absent from Canada or is only resident for part of the year (P 1-125 to 1-143).
21. Explain how residency determinations are made for dual resident individuals and the impact of citizenship versus residency (P 1-144 to 1-150).
22. Explain and be able to apply the residency analysis for individuals (P 1-151).
23. Explain how residency is determined for corporations, deemed corporate residency, and how dual residency issues occur and how they are resolved (P 1-152 to 1-159).
24. Explain and be able to apply the residency analysis for corporations (P 1-160).

---

25. Explain how residency determinations are made for trusts (P 1-161 to 1-163).
26. Describe, in general terms, the various views of income that are held by economists and accountants (P 1-164 to 1-169).
27. Explain the source concept of income for income tax purposes and identify the specific types of other income that are subject to income tax in Canada (P 1-170 to 1-177).
28. Calculate net income by applying the rules found in ITA 3 (P 1-178 to 1-186).
29. Explain how net income is converted to taxable income (P 1-187 to 1-188).
30. Explain the principles of tax planning (P 1-189 to 1-192).
31. Explain and provide examples of tax avoidance or reduction and tax deferral (P 1-193 to 1-200).
32. Explain and provide examples of income splitting (P 1-201 to 1-207).

How to Work through Chapter 1

Visit pearsonmylabandmastering.com to access MyLab Accounting for this text. Once there, you can access student resources such as Self-Study Problems, Practice Exams, Flashcards, updates, and more.

We recommend the following approach in dealing with the material in this chapter:

The Canadian Tax System and Taxable Entities in Canada
- Read paragraph 1-1 to 1-28 (in the text).
- Do Exercises 1-1 and 1-2 (in the text) and check the solutions in this Study Guide. All solutions to Exercises and Self-Study Problems can be found in this Study Guide; the page numbers all start with the prefix S-.
- Read paragraph 1-29 to 1-33.
- Do Exercise 1-3 and check the solution in this Study Guide.
- Read paragraph 1-34 to 1-40.

Tax Policy Concepts and Qualitative Characteristics of Tax Systems
- Read paragraph 1-41 to 1-42.
- Do Exercise 1-4 and check the solution in this Study Guide.
- Do Self-Study Problem 1-1, which is available on MyLab, and check the solution in this Study Guide.
- Read paragraph 1-43 to 1-50.
- Do Self Study Problem 1-2 and check the solution in this Study Guide.
- Read paragraph 1-51 to 1-59.
- Do Self Study Problem 1-3 and check the solution in this Study Guide.

Income Tax Reference Materials
- Read paragraph 1-60 to 1-93.
- Do Self Study Problems 1-4 and 1-5 and check the solution in this Study Guide.

Liability for Income Tax
- Read paragraph 1-94 to 1-110.
- Do Exercise 1-5 and check the solution in this Study Guide.

Residence of Individuals, Including Part-Year, Sojourner, and Deemed Residents
- Read paragraph 1-111 to 1-124.
- Do Exercise 1-6 and check the solution in this Study Guide.
- Read paragraph 1-125 to 1-129.
- Do Exercise 1-7 and check the solution in this Study Guide.
- Read paragraph 1-130 to 1-135.
- Do Exercises 1-8 and 1-9 and check the solutions in this Study Guide.
- Read paragraph 1-136 to 1-143.
- Do Exercise 1-10 and check the solution in this Study Guide.

Individuals with Dual Residency
- Read paragraph 1-144 to 1-151.
- Do Exercise 1-11 and check the solution in this Study Guide.
- Do Self-Study Problems 1-6 to 1-8 and check the solutions in this Study Guide.

Residence of Corporations and Trusts
- Read paragraph 1-152 to 1-160.
- Do Exercises 1-12 to 1-14 and check the solutions in this Study Guide.
- Do Self-Study Problems 1-9 and 1-10 and check the solutions in this Study Guide.
- Read paragraph 1-161 to 1-163.
- Do Self Study Problem 1-11 and check the solution in this Study Guide.

Alternative Concepts of Income
- Read paragraph 1-164 to 1-177.
- Do Exercise 1-15 and check the solution in this Study Guide.

Net Income
- Read paragraph 1-178 to 1-188.
- Do Exercises 1-16 to 1-18 and check the solutions in this Study Guide.
- Do Self-Study Problems 1-12 to 1-14 and check the solutions in this Study Guide.

Principles of Tax Planning
- Read paragraph 1-189 to 1-207.
- Do Exercises 1-19 and 1-20 and check the solutions in this Study Guide.

To Complete This Chapter
- Visit MyLab Accounting for more practice problem material, and test yourself with the glossary flashcards.
- Review the Key Terms at the end of the chapter, and consult the glossary for definitions.
- Ensure you have achieved the Chapter 1 Learning Objectives listed in this Study Guide.
- As a review, view the PowerPoint presentations available on MyLab.

Practice Examination
- Available on MyLab, write the Practice Examination for this chapter, and mark it using the solutions provided.

Exercise Solutions

Exercise 1-1 Solution
Max Jordan, the Jordan family trust, and Jordan Enterprises Ltd. are all taxable entities and therefore could be required to file income tax returns. Jordan's Hardware store is a sole proprietorship and not an entity, therefore no separate tax return would be required to be filed. Jordan & Jordan is a partnership and not a taxable entity, therefore no tax return is required for the partnership (although the partnership could be required to file an information return). Finally, the Jordan Foundation is a corporate entity, but it is not a taxable entity because, as a registered charity, it is exempt from Part I tax by ITA 149.

Exercise 1-2 Solution
Under the ETA, all of the listed entities, with the exception of Jordan's Hardware store, could be required to file a GST/HST return. The hardware store is operated as a sole proprietorship, which is not an entity nor is it specifically mentioned in the ETA. The sole proprietor would be the person identified by the ETA as responsible for filing a GST/HST return.

Where only individuals, corporations, and trusts are taxable entities for income tax purposes that can be required to file an income tax return, the definition of a person (i.e., taxable entity) is much broader for GST/HST purposes.

Exercise 1-3 Solution

Federal tax payable [(15%)($27,000)]	$4,050
Provincial tax payable [(7.5%)($27,000)]	2,025
Total tax payable [(15% + 7.5%)($27,000)]	$6,075

Exercise 1-4 Solution

Margie's HST paid totals $22,360 [(13%)($172,000)]. Based on her taxable income of $895,000, this would represent an effective rate of 2.5% ($22,360 ÷ $895,000).

Jane's HST paid totals $3,575 [(13%)($27,500)]. On her taxable income of $18,000, this would be an effective rate of 19.9% ($3,575 ÷ $18,000).

Exercise 1-5 Solution

She is not correct. As a non-resident of Canada, she would be subject to Canadian taxes on employment income earned in Canada as a result of ITA 2(3).

Exercise 1-6 Solution

While the situation is not completely clear, it is likely that the CRA would conclude that Simon is no longer a Canadian resident. By retaining his residence, he has maintained one of the primary residential ties. However, the fact that he was not able to sell the property, accompanied by the long-term lease to a third party, would probably be sufficient evidence that this is not a significant residential tie. The retention of his membership in the CPA would be viewed as a secondary residential tie. However, S5-F1-C1 indicates that it would be unusual for a single secondary tie to be sufficient for an individual to be considered a Canadian resident.

Exercise 1-7 Solution

Jane's actions, which include severing both primary and secondary residential ties, support a finding that she intended to establish residency in the United States and end her residency in Canada. This would mean that she was a non-resident of Canada throughout the 26-month period. The return to Canada would result in re-establishing residency in Canada at that time. The fact that she returned frequently to visit her boyfriend would not likely change this conclusion, although it would be prudent to determine her intentions with respect to the relationship, including future plans.

Exercise 1-8 Solution

Mark would be taxed on his worldwide income for the part of the year that he was resident in Canada. This would be the period January 1 through June 15, the date that his wife and children fly to the United States. June 15 would be latest of the date that Mark leaves Canada (February 1), the date that Mark establishes U.S. residency (February 1), and the date that his wife and children depart Canada (June 15). It is unlikely that the fact that his house was not sold until a later date would influence his residence status.

Exercise 1-9 Solution

Mr. Kirsh will be a part-year resident and liable for Canadian taxes on his worldwide income, including any income on the U.S. bank accounts, for the period September 1 through December 31 of the current year.

Exercise 1-10 Solution

While Ms. Blakey is the child of a Canadian high commissioner, she is clearly no longer dependent on this individual. In addition, her income is in excess of the base for the basic personal tax credit for 2021 of $13,808. As a consequence, she would not be considered a deemed resident under ITA 250(1)(f) (point 5 of Paragraph 1-139). She would also not be considered a deemed resident as a result of ITA 250(1)(g) (point 6 of Paragraph 1-139) because none of her income in London is exempt from income tax in London as a result of her father's role as Canadian high commissioner in France.

Exercise 1-11 Solution
Case 1
Step 1   Dizzy is not a factual resident but is a deemed resident as a result of the sojourner rule because he was in Canada for 183 days or more.
Step 2   Dizzy is a resident of the United States.
Step 3   Canada has a tax treaty with the United States.
Step 4   Dizzy has a permanent home in the United States but only a temporary home in Canada. As a result he is considered a resident of the U.S. only.
Step 5   Dizzy is deemed to be a non-resident of Canada.

Case 2
Step 1   Donna is not a factual resident but is a deemed resident as a result of the sojourner rule because she was in Canada for 183 days or more.
Step 2   Donna is a resident of the United States.
Step 3   Canada has a tax treaty with the United States.
Step 4   Donna does not have a permanent home in the United States as she gave up the lease. The month-to-month lease in Canada would not appear to meet the level of continuity required and would therefore not be considered a permanent home. The next step requires looking to the "Centre of Vital Interests," which appears to be in the United States. As a result she would be considered a resident of the U.S. only.
Step 5   Donna is therefore deemed to be a non-resident of Canada.

Exercise 1-12 Solution
Step 1   Roswell is a factual resident of Canada because its CMC is exercised in Canada where the board meetings are held. The fact that it carries on business in Canada and the United States is irrelevant.
Step 2   Roswell is a resident of the U.S. because it was incorporated in the U.S.
Step 3   Canada has a tax treaty with the U.S.
Step 4   The tie-breaker rule applies in favour of the U.S.; because it was incorporated in the U.S. the company is deemed to be a resident of the U.S. only.
Step 5   ITA 250(5) deems the company to be a non-resident of Canada.

Exercise 1-13 Solution
Step 1   Sateen is a deemed resident of Canada because it was incorporated in Canada after April 26, 1965. The fact that it carries on business outside Canada is irrelevant.
Step 2   There is insufficient information to determine if it is resident in another country.
Step 3   Not applicable (N/A)
Step 4   N/A
Step 5   N/A

Exercise 1-14 Solution
Case 1
Step 1   Taxco is a deemed resident of Canada because it was incorporated in Canada after April 26, 1965. The company's purpose, the nature of its assets, and whether it carried on business in or outside Canada is irrelevant to the determination of residency.
Step 2   Taxco is a factual resident of the United States because CMC is exercised in the U.S.
Step 3   Canada has a tax treaty with the United States.
Step 4   The tie-breaker rule applies in favour of Canada because it was incorporated in Canada. The company is deemed to be a resident of Canada only.
Step 5   N/A

Case 2
Step 1   Junkco is a factual resident of Canada because its CMC is exercised in Canada. The company's purpose, the nature of its assets, and whether it carried on business in or outside Canada is irrelevant to the determination of residency.

Step 2 Junkco is a resident of the United States because it was incorporated in the U.S.
Step 3 Canada has a tax treaty with the United States.
Step 4 The tie-breaker rule applies in favour of the U.S. because it was incorporated in the U.S.. The company is deemed to be a resident of the U.S. only.
Step 5 ITA 250(5) deems the company to be a non-resident of Canada.

Exercise 1-15 Solution

None of the four amounts are specifically required to be included in income; therefore, since they are not considered sources of income they would not be subject to Part I tax.

(1) Not a source of income. It is not an activity attributable to one's labour, capital, or property, nor is it continuous. If it were an activity attributable to one's labour it would not be capable of producing a positive return.

(2) Not a source of income. The same reasons as #1.

(3) This is a source of income. The cash deposit is your property from which you have earned the income.

(4) Not a source of income. While this is an activity attributable to labour and capital (e.g., invested funds), it is not likely an activity that is capable of producing a positive return given its primary personal motivation.

(5) This is a source of business income. The activity is attributable to labour, capital, and property (e.g., the 10 acres of land). While there is a minor personal motivation, it appears to be conducted in a manner similar to what one would expect with a person engaged in farming.

(6) Not a source of income. Same reasons as #1.

Exercise 1-16 Solution

Mr. Blanton's net income is calculated as follows:

Income under ITA 3(a):		
Net employment income		$42,000
Income under ITA 3(b):		
Taxable capital gains	$24,000	
Allowable capital losses	Nil	24,000
Balance from ITA 3(a) and (b)		$66,000
Subdivision e deductions		(13,000)
Balance under ITA 3(c)		$53,000
Deduction under ITA 3(d):		
Business loss		(15,000)
Net Income (Division B income)		**$38,000**

Exercise 1-17 Solution

Ms. Stodard's net income would be calculated as follows:

Income under ITA 3(a):		
Interest income		$33,240
Income under ITA 3(b):		
Taxable capital gains	$24,750	
Allowable capital losses	(19,500)	5,250
Balance from ITA 3(a) and (b)		$38,490
Subdivision e deductions		Nil
Balance under ITA 3(c)		$38,490
Deduction under ITA 3(d):		
Rental loss		(48,970)
Net income (Division B income)		**Nil**

She would have a non-capital loss carry over of $10,480 ($48,970 – $38,490).

Exercise 1-18 Solution

Mrs. Bergeron's net income would be calculated as follows:

Income under ITA 3(a):		
Net employment income		$42,680
Income under ITA 3(b):		
Taxable capital gains	$27,400	
Allowable capital losses	(33,280)	Nil
Balance from ITA 3(a) and (b)		$42,680
Subdivision e deductions		(8,460)
Balance under ITA 3(c)		$34,220
Deduction under ITA 3(d):		
Business loss		(26,326)
Net income (Division B income)		**$ 7,894**

She would have a net capital loss carry over of $5,880 ($33,280 – $27,400).

Exercise 1-19 Solution

Mr. Chung is involved in acceptable income splitting, tax deferral, and possibly tax avoidance. He is taking advantage of a deduction from income that will allow him to reduce his current taxes in favour of his spouse obtaining the rights to that income in the future, which may, at that time, be taxed at much lower tax rates. All RRSP contributions usually create a tax deferral. The contribution will be deductible to the contributor, and income earned on the contribution within the RRSP (e.g., a trust) are allowed to accumulate tax free. However, the contributions plus the earnings will become taxable when they are withdrawn from the plan by the spouse (Mrs. Chung). There may also be tax avoidance in the sense of a permanent reduction or tax savings compared to the taxes that would have been paid had Mr. Chung not made the RRSP contribution. This will happen if Mrs. Chung is taxed at a lower rate than Mr. Chung's tax rate at the time of the contribution.

Exercise 1-20 Solution

As the dental plan is a benefit received by Mr. Green without being taxed (private health services plan), acceptable tax avoidance is illustrated.

Self-Study Problem Solutions

Self-Study Problems are available to download from MyLab Accounting.

SSP 1-1 Solution

The HST is based on certain specified expenditures, not on the income level of the individual making the expenditure. In most cases, the proportion of an individual's income that is spent declines as the individual's level of income increases. This means that when a flat rate of tax is applied to a decreasing portion of the individual's income, the rate of taxation as a percentage of that income will decline.

For example, a 13% HST applied to $150,000 in expenditures made by a person with $250,000 in income would amount to only 7.8% of that person's income ($19,500 ÷ $250,000).

In contrast, that same 13% HST applied to $25,000 in expenditures made by a person with $20,000 in income would reflect a tax rate of 16.25% ($3,250 ÷ $20,000) of that person's income.

SSP 1-2 Solution

Canada's income tax system is complex as a result of having to keep current with the variety of ways income is earned throughout the world, the multiple entities used, and the fact that it also serves to distribute many social and economic benefits. A flat tax rate simply revises the tax rate structure, which is but one small piece of a much larger puzzle, meaning that a flat rate system has little if any impact on simplifying a tax system.

In terms of certain qualitative characteristics of a tax system, a flat rate introduces policy concerns. For example, it would almost certainly be in conflict with the objective of fairness in that it would not provide for treating different types of income (capital gains vs. employment income) or people (the poor vs. the rich) in a suitable manner. Such a system would also conflict with other objectives, such as the goal of equity and after-tax income stability and the need for redistribution of income. In other words Mr. Right's system would ignore other possible economic and social objectives of a taxation system.

SSP 1-3 Solution

Note The descriptions of these tax measures are significantly simplified. The objective of this problem is to present the basic ideas so they can be understood without a detailed knowledge of tax, while still providing a basis for discussion. The following analysis is intended to be no more than suggestive of possible points that could be made. There are, of course, many alternative solutions.

Increase in Lifetime Capital Gains Deduction
Possible comments here would be as follows:

Neutrality The increase in the amount of the deduction for farmers and fishers is not neutral. It favours farmers and fishers with no benefits for any other group.

Simplicity The determination of what properties are considered to be qualified for this deduction involves some very complex legislation.

Home Accessibility Tax Credit
Possible comments here would be as follows:

Neutrality This provision is not neutral. Its benefits accrue exclusively to seniors, individuals with disabilities, and their families. Other individuals do not benefit from this provision.

Equity or Fairness Seniors with disabilities face accessibility challenges that are not present for most other individuals. Given this, it can be argued that helping this particular group involves fairer treatment of these individuals.

Increase in Tax-Free Savings Account Limits
Possible comments here would be as follows:

Equity or Fairness It was clear that this change would not benefit low-income individuals. If an individual is making $20,000 per year, it is highly unlikely that he would have the first $5,500, much less an extra $4,500, to contribute. The reversal of the increase in 2016 was due in large part to its lack of fairness.

Simplicity This change gets high marks for simplicity. Amounts earned on the assets in the account are not subject to tax, either while the assets are in the plan or when the earnings are removed from the plan.

SSP 1-4 Solution
The principal other sources of information can be described as follows:

1. **Draft Legislation** This legislation often provides the only information available with respect to announced budget changes that require application in the current taxation year. Explanatory notes are included with released draft legislation but are always set out separately.

   Note: When legislation is passed and becomes law the explanatory notes continue to be of considerable value in understanding the reasoning behind the legislation.

2. **Income Tax Regulations**   These regulations provide detailed guidance with respect to the implementation and administrative enforcement of the provisions of the ITA.

3. **International Tax Treaties**   These are bilateral tax treaties between Canada and other countries. They are designed to avoid double taxation and provide relief where taxpayers may be liable for taxes on the same income in more than one jurisdiction. They also provide a sharing of information to prevent international tax avoidance and evasion.

4. **Income Tax Folios**   Income tax folios are a series of publications, introduced in 2013, that deal with technical issues. They are scheduled to replace existing interpretation bulletins (see item 5). The publications are organized into seven series, with each series divided into folios that contain chapters on specific topics. As new folios are introduced, the interpretation bulletins and income tax technical newsletters they replace are being canceled.

5. **Interpretation Bulletins**   These bulletins give the CRA's interpretations of particular sections of the law that it administers and provide a vehicle for announcing significant changes in interpretation of a general interest. These bulletins are being replaced by income tax folios (see item 4). Currently all interpretation bulletins are either "canceled" or "archived." Only archived bulletins continue to have any usefulness.

6. **Income Tax Application Rules, 1971 (ITARs)**   These are a set of transitional rules that were introduced when the ITA amended at the end of 1971. The rules were largely designed to ensure that the provisions of the new Act were not applied retroactively. Although they continue to be of some significance in a limited number of situations, their general importance has been greatly diminished over time.

7. **Income Tax Technical News**   These newsletters were an occasional publication of the CRA that provided detailed guidance on various current issues often presented at national tax conferences. Existing newsletters have all been archived with no new releases since 2011.

8. **Information Circulars**   These circulars provide information with respect to procedural matters related to both the ITA and the Canada Pension Plan. ICs continue to be of use.

9. **CRA News Releases, Tax Tips, and Fact Sheets**   The CRA provides news releases, tax tips, and fact sheets on a variety of current subjects on its website. These also continue to be periodically released.

10. **Guides and Pamphlets**   These non-technical publications provide current yearly guidance for the public on a variety of income tax issues (e.g., treatment of rental income).

11. **Advance Income Tax Rulings**   For a fee, the CRA will provide an Advance Income Tax Ruling on how it will tax a proposed transaction, subject to certain limitations and qualifications. These are rulings that are provided in response to requests from taxpayers and are only relevant to the taxpayer for whom they were written.

12. **Technical Interpretations**   The CRA provides both written and telephone technical interpretations to the public free of charge. These interpretations provide ongoing technical information on various current issues.

13. **Court Decisions**   Decisions by the Tax Court of Canada, the Federal Court, and the Supreme Court on income tax cases serve to establish precedents for dealing with particular tax issues.

SSP 1-5 Solution

Note to students: The purpose of this problem is to give you some practical examples of how to identify the part of the ITA where you are likely to find guidance on the income tax outcome. Specific references have been added for information purposes only. You will not be required to reference any provisions of the ITA in this tax course, although we will continue to provide income tax references.

(a) You spent $15,000 to landscape around the building in which you carry on your business. **Answer:** Subdivision b (Paragraph 20(1)(aa))

(b) Someone told you that you could only deduct 50% of any business-related meals. **Answer:** Subdivision f (Section 67.1)

(c) You became a member of a partnership this year and want to contribute to it some land you own. **Answer:** Subdivision j (Section 97)

(d) Your employer advises you that you now qualify for the company stock option plan. **Answer:** Subdivision a (Section 7)

(e) Your spouse was unemployed and received employment insurance payments. **Answer:** Subdivision d (Subparagraph 56(1)(a)(iv))

(f) One of your parents passed away and you have been named as the executor. **Answer:** Subdivisions f (Section 70) and k (Section 104)

(g) Your employer provides you with a company-owned car for you to use in your employment duties. **Answer:** Subdivision a (Paragraphs 6(1)(e) and (k) and Subsection 6(2))

(h) You sold the home you have lived in for the last 10 years and purchased another one. **Answer:** Subdivision c (Paragraph 40(2)(b) and the definition of "principal residence" in Section 54)

(i) You were audited by the CRA. It cost you $2,000 to have advisors represent you in dealing with the CRA. You wonder if you can deduct the fees. **Answer:** Subdivision e (Paragraph 60(o))

(j) You purchased some shares of a major Canadian public company last year and made money selling them this year. You also received dividends from the company earlier this same year. **Answer:** Subdivision b and h for the dividends received (Paragraph 12(1)(j) and Section 82) and Subdivision c for the sale of the shares (Sections 38, 39, and 40)

(k) Your parents created a family trust years ago and named you a beneficiary. You received a cheque from the trust this year for your part of the trust income. **Answer:** Subdivision b and k (Paragraph 12(1)(m) and Section 104)

(l) You own shares in a family operated company. The company redeemed (bought back) half of your shares this year. **Answer:** Subsection b and h (Paragraph 12(1)(j) and Subsection 84(3))

(m) You paid $4,500 in child care expenses this year for your four-year-old daughter. **Answer:** Subdivision e (Section 63)

(n) You received $6,000 in Canada Child Benefit payments from the federal government. **Answer:** You would look to Subdivision d. If the Canada Child Benefit is to be included in income and taxed, it must be found in that subdivision. Since it is not in that subdivision, the amount is not required to be included in income.

(o) A family friend lost her job after 10 years of service but had been given a large cheque in recognition of those years of service. **Answer:** Subdivision d (Subparagraph 56(1)(a)(ii))

SSP 1-6 Solution

S5-F1-C1 indicates that, in general, the CRA will view an individual as becoming a non-resident on the latest of three dates:

- The date the individual leaves Canada
- The date the individual's spouse or common-law partner and dependants leave Canada
- The date the individual becomes a resident of another country

This general position of the CRA, however, is used as a guideline only, as the determination of the time that residency has been severed is always a question of fact. Based on the facts it is clear that Paul had the intention of permanently departing from Canada—he quit his job in Canada, purchased a home in the U.S. after accepting a full-time position, and severed some other ties. In addition, his family will join him in the U.S. when his daughter's school has ended.

The facts indicate that Paul severed Canadian residency and became a resident of the U.S. at the same point in time when he purchased a home in preparation for the employment he had accepted. Given the facts, at no time would Paul be considered a resident of both Canada and the U.S. (e.g., a dual resident), with the result that the Canada/U.S. tax treaty is irrelevant in this case.

SSP 1-7 Solution
Mr. Aiken and Mr. Baker
Assuming that their respective moves were permanent in nature, both Mr. Aiken and Mr. Baker would be treated as part-year residents. This means that they would be considered residents of Canada only for that portion of the year that they were actually in Canada. As a result, they will be liable for Canadian taxes only for a part of the current year. The fact that they both were physically present in Canada for 183 days or more is only relevant for the deemed residency "sojourner" rule if those days represented a temporary stay in Canada only. Since those days were not temporary stays they are not relevant, and the sojourner rule would not apply.

Mr. Chase
Mr. Chase was also physically present in Canada for 192 days, however the relevant question for purposes of the sojourner rule that deems an individual to be resident is whether or not those days were temporary stays. Sojourning requires establishing a temporary residence for a short duration. If Mr. Chase attends games in Canada and then returns home to the U.S., then those stays would not count toward the sojourner rule (see Paragraph 1.33 of Folio S5-F1-C1) because those days would be considered commuting for work purposes. In this case if there are 10 or more such days then the 183-day test would not be met.

If Mr. Chase was unable to prove that the days were not temporary stays then he would be a sojourner and therefore a dual resident. The dual residency status would be resolved by the tie-breaker rules in the Canada/U.S. tax treaty. As he only has a permanent home in the U.S., the tie-breaker rules would consider Mr. Chase to be a resident of the U.S. only. ITA 250(5) would then deem him to be a non-resident of Canada.

Note to Instructors: There are no reported cases of athletes being considered sojourners of Canada. The important income tax issues with athletes playing games in both Canada and the U.S. is that if they are non-residents the employment income earned while in Canada would be subject to Canadian tax as a result of ITA 2(3)(a) (employed in Canada).

SSP 1-8 Solution
A. Jane Smith would be deemed a Canadian resident because she is a dependent child of a Canadian ambassador [ITA 250(1)(f)].

B. Marvin Black would not be considered a resident of Canada as he does not live in Canada. He would not be a deemed resident as S5-F1-C1 makes it clear that days spent commuting to Canada to earn employment income do not count as sojourning in Canada. However, he would be subject to Canadian taxation on the employment income earned in Canada [ITA 2(3)(a)].

C. John Leather would be considered a resident of Canada for the part of the year until September 12. As his presence in Canada during the first part of the year was not on a temporary basis, he would not fall under the sojourning rules.

D. Members of the Canadian Armed Forces are deemed to be Canadian residents without regard to where they actually live. As Francine Donaire is exempt from French taxation due to her relationship to a deemed resident, she is a deemed resident of Canada [ITA 250(1)(g)].

E. More information would be required here. Depending on the nature of his stay in Canada, Robert could either be a part-year resident of Canada or, alternatively, a non-resident earning employment income in Canada. If he established sufficient residential ties in Canada, it is possible that he would be viewed as a resident during his short stay. The importance of this is that, under this interpretation of the facts, he would be subject to Canadian income tax on his worldwide income during his stay. Alternatively, if he is not considered a resident during his stay in Canada, he is likely to be subject to Canadian tax on only his Canadian employment income.

F. The fact that Susan Allen is a Canadian citizen is irrelevant to the determination of residency. The absence of facts makes it impossible to assess whether she is a non-resident of Canada. If she has no connections to Canada whatsoever then the facts weigh in favour of her being a non-resident. This case illustrates the importance of understanding the facts.

SSP 1-9 Solution

A. As AMT Ltd. was incorporated prior to April 27, 1965, it is not automatically considered to be a deemed resident of Canada. However, under Canadian legislation the company would be deemed a Canadian resident based on the fact that the mind and management was in Canada subsequent to that date. [ITA 250(4)(a) and(c)].

   As the mind and management is currently in the U.S., it would be considered a factual resident of the U.S. Given this dual residency, the tie-breaker rules in the Canada/U.S. tax treaty resolve the situation by considering the company to be a resident of the U.S. only since it was incorporated in the U.S. This would result in AMT being considered a deemed non-resident of Canada.

B. UIF Inc. is neither a deemed nor factual resident of Canada because it was not incorporated in Canada and its mind and management are not currently in Canada. Therefore, UIF Inc. would be a non-resident of Canada.

C. BDT Ltd. would be deemed a Canadian resident because it was incorporated in Canada subsequent to April 26, 1965. [ITA 250(4)(a)]. However, as the mind and management is now in the U.S., it would also be considered a factual resident of the U.S. Given this dual residency, the tie-breaker rules in the Canada/U.S. tax treaty resolve the situation by making the company a resident of the country in which it was incorporated. This would result in BDT being considered a resident of Canada and a non-resident of the U.S.

D. While QRS Inc. was not incorporated in Canada, its mind and management are located in Ontario, making the company a factual resident of Canada. However, as it was incorporated in New York state, it will also be considered a resident of the U.S. As noted previously, in such cases, the tie-breaker rules in the Canada/U.S. tax treaty would make the company a resident of the U.S. as that is the country of incorporation. ITA 250(5) would therefore deem the company to be a non-resident of Canada.

SSP 1-10 Solution
Case A

Mr. Salazar is not a resident of Canada. Commuting across the border for employment purposes is not considered sojourning (S5-F1-C1). However, unless he is exempted by the Canada/U.S. tax treaty, he would be subject to Canadian taxation on the employment income he earns in Windsor.

With respect to the treaty exemption, his employment income exceeds $10,000 and is paid by a resident of Canada and he is physically present in Canada for more than 183 days in the year. Given these facts, he would not qualify for the treaty exemption.

Case B

The information suggests that Mr. Wills made a clean break with Canada on September 1 of the current year. As a consequence, he would be considered a Canadian resident for the portion of the current year prior to his departure and would be taxed on his worldwide income for this period. For the portion of the year subsequent to his departure, he would be considered a non-resident of Canada.

Case C

Joan Brothers would be deemed to be a Canadian resident under ITA 250(1)(f) because she is a dependent child of an officer or servant of Canada who is deemed to be a resident of Canada under ITA 250(1)(c)(i). Her worldwide income, if she had any, would be subject to tax in Canada.

Case D

Brogan Inc. is neither a factual nor deemed resident of Canada as it was not incorporated in Canada and its mind and management are not currently in Canada. As a result, the company is a non-resident of Canadian. It would only be taxable on Canadian source income.

Case E

Mercer Ltd. was incorporated prior to April 27, 1965, and, if it had not resided in or done business in Canada subsequent to that date, it would not be considered a resident of Canada. However, the fact that directors' meetings were held in Canada until May 1997 makes it a deemed resident of Canada. As the mind and management are now in the U.S., it would be considered a factual resident of the U.S.

In cases of dual residency for corporations, where a corporation could be considered a resident of both countries, the Canada/U.S. tax treaty considers a corporation to only be a resident of the country in which it was incorporated. Mercer Ltd. would therefore be a resident of Canada and its worldwide income would be subject to tax in Canada.

Case F

The Booker Manufacturing Company would be considered a factual resident of Canada because of the location of its mind and management. However, as Booker was incorporated in the U.S., it would also be considered a U.S. resident. In cases of dual residency for corporations, where a corporation could be considered a resident of both countries, the Canada/U.S. tax treaty considers the corporation to be a resident only of the country in which it was incorporated. As a result, the company is deemed to be a non-resident of Canada. It would only be subject to tax in Canada on Canadian source income.

SSP 1-11 Solution
Solution to Case 1

Jim is a factual resident of the U.S. since his current family, home, social, and economic life is in the U.S. However, because of the 183-day sojourner rule of ITA 250(1)(a), Jim is also initially considered a deemed resident of Canada. This deemed residency status results in Jim being considered a dual resident of both Canada and the U.S. When this occurs you need to consider the tax treaty between the two countries. One of the purposes of the treaty is to determine which country has the priority to tax that individual. The tie-breaker rule was briefly discussed in Paragraph 1-116 and is easily resolved in this case using the first criteria of the "permanent home." Since Jim has a permanent home in the U.S. and none in Canada, the tax treaty resolves the dual residency problem in favour of the U.S. ITA 250(5) (discussed in Paragraph 1-117 and 1-146) applies when a tax treaty resolved dual residency in favour of another country by then deeming the person to be a non-resident of Canada. This final step of the analysis overrides the sojourner rule. It is important to add that if Jim demonstrates that he is in Canada for temporary stays less than 183 days that the sojourner rule would not apply. This would require an evaluation of each stay. Each work-related stay in which he returned to the U.S. without seeing his children would likely be considered commuting and would therefore not count toward the sojourner rule.

Conclusion—Case 1

Jim is a deemed non-resident of Canada.

Solution to Case 2

U.S. federal tax law considers any corporation incorporated in the U.S. to be a resident of the U.S. Therefore, Sitcom will be a factual resident of the U.S. For Canadian tax purposes a corporation will be considered a deemed resident of Canada by either (1) incorporating in Canada after April 26, 1965 (ITA 250(4)(a)) or (2) by being factually resident in Canada, which can only occur if the majority of the members of the board of directors actually make decisions on behalf of the company in Canada. Since the majority of the directors meet in Canada to make decisions, the corporation is initially considered to be factually resident in Canada. We refer to this factual concept as the "mind and management" rule.

Based on the facts, Sitcom Inc. is a dual resident—both a factual resident of the U.S. and Canada. When this occurs we must turn to the tax treaty. The tie-breaker rule in the Canada/U.S. tax treaty resolves residency in favour of the country in which the company was incorporated. As a result, Sitcom is considered a resident of the U.S. Since the tax treaty treats the company as only a resident of the U.S., ITA 250(5) once again applies to deem Sitcom to be a non-resident of Canada, overriding the mind and management factual residency determination.

Conclusion—Case 2

Sitcom Inc. is a deemed non-resident of Canada.

Solution to Case 3

There are no deemed residency rules in Canada for trusts except for certain non-resident trusts. The determination of trust residency has been somewhat of a grey area until the 2012 decision of the Supreme Court of Canada in Fundy Settlement. In that decision the Supreme Court applied a factual residency test to trusts that is comparable to that of corporations. The test looks to where the important decisions are made, which is where the mind and management actually takes place.

With corporations you look to the board of directors, and with trusts you look to the trustee or trustees where there are more than one. The creation of a trust outside Canada may result in the trust being considered a resident of that country and potentially liable to its tax subject to a tax treaty. Most tax treaties do not contemplate trust residence, meaning that decisions to determine which country has priority to tax are made by the competent authority. If no tax treaty exists then a trust could potentially be resident in both countries.

In this case the sole trustee clearly has no real authority to make decisions with regard to the trust as they are made by Jan and Dean. Since Jan and Dean reside in Canada and direct the trustee from Canada the trust would be considered a factual resident of Canada.

Conclusion—Case 3

The family trust is a factual resident of Canada.

Note for Case 3: We have purposefully avoided discussion of the non-resident trust rules of ITA 94, which is well beyond the scope of an introductory course on federal income taxation.

Those complex rules, however, would only apply if the trust were a non-resident of Canada. Since our analysis has concluded that the trust is a resident of Canada, those rules would not have applied in any case.

Note on new trust reporting: Beginning in 2021, trusts will be required to disclose the identity of beneficiaries, trustees, and those other persons who can make or influence decisions. This is discussed in Chapter 2.

SSP 1-12 Solution
Case A
The Case A solution would be calculated as follows:

Income under ITA 3(a):		
Employment income	$50,000	
Interest income	12,000	$62,000
Income under ITA 3(b):		
Taxable capital gains	$95,000	
Allowable capital losses	(73,000)	22,000
Balance from ITA 3(a) and (b)		$84,000
Subdivision e deductions		(8,000)
Balance from ITA 3(c)		$76,000
Deductions under ITA 3(d):		
Business loss	(23,000)	
Rental loss	(5,000)	(28,000)
Net income (Division B income)		$48,000

In this case, Mr. Dorne has no carry overs available.

Case B
The Case B solution would be calculated as follows:

Income under ITA 3(a):		
Employment income	$45,000	
Interest income	23,000	$68,000
Income under ITA 3(b):		
Taxable capital gains	$25,000	
Allowable capital losses	(46,000)	Nil
Balance from ITA 3(a) and (b)		$68,000
Subdivision e deductions		(10,500)
Balance from ITA 3(c)		$ 57,500
Deduction under ITA 3(d):		
Business loss		(51,000)
Net income (Division B income)		$ 6,500

In this case, Mr. Dorne has a net capital loss carry over of $21,000 ($46,000 - $25,000). The lottery prize is not considered to be a source of income and therefore is not included.

SSP 1-13 Solution
Case A

Income under ITA 3(a):		
Employment income	$73,300	
Interest income	8,300	$ 81,600
Income under ITA 3(b):		
Taxable capital gains	$42,400	
Allowable capital losses	(18,600)	23,800
Balance from ITA 3(a) and (b)		$105,400
Subdivision e deductions		(6,200)
Balance from ITA 3(c)		$ 99,200
Deduction under ITA 3(d):		
Business loss		(14,700)
Net income (Division B income)		$ 84,500

In this case, Mr. Marks has no loss carry overs at the end of the year.

Case B

Income under ITA 3(a):		
Employment income	$41,400	
Interest income	5,900	$47,300
Income under ITA 3(b):		
Taxable capital gains	$ 7,800	
Allowable capital losses	(11,600)	Nil
Balance from ITA 3(a) and (b)		$47,300
Subdivision e deductions		(2,800)
Balance from ITA 3(c)		$44,500
Deduction under ITA 3(d):		
Business loss		(4,700)
Net income (Division B income)		$39,800

In this case, Mr. Marks has a net capital loss carry over of $3,800 ($7,800 - $11,600).

Case C

Income under ITA 3(a):		
Employment income	$89,400	
Interest income	5,300	$ 94,700
Income under ITA 3(b):		
Taxable capital gains	$23,700	
Allowable capital losses	(21,200)	2,500
Balance from ITA 3(a) and (b)		$ 97,200
Subdivision e deductions		(22,400)
Balance from ITA 3(c)		$ 74,800
Deduction under ITA 3(d):		
business loss		(112,600)
Net income (Division B income)		$ Nil

In this case, Mr. Marks would have a non-capital loss carry over in the amount of $37,800 ($74,800 - $112,600).

Case D

Income under ITA 3(a):		
Employment income		$34,300
Income under ITA 3(b):		
Taxable capital gains	$24,700	
Allowable capital losses	(26,300)	Nil
Balance from ITA 3(a) and (b)		$34,300
Subdivision e deductions		(6,400)
Balance from ITA 3(c)		$27,900
Deduction under ITA 3(d):		
Business loss		(47,800)
Rental loss	(20,100)	(67,900)
Net income (Division B income)		$ Nil

Mr. Marks would have a non-capital loss carry over in the amount of $40,000 ($67,900 - $27,900) and a net capital loss in the amount of $1,600 ($24,700 - $26,300).

SSP 1-14 Solution
Case 1

Income under ITA 3(a):		
Net employment income	$123,480	
Interest income	4,622	$128,102
Income under ITA 3(b):		
Taxable capital gains	$ 24,246	
Allowable capital losses	(4,835)	19,411
Balance from ITA 3(a) and (b)		$147,513
Subdivision e deductions		(9,372)
Balance from ITA 3(c)	$ 138,141	
Deductions under ITA 3(d):	Nil	
Net income (Division B income)		$138,141

In this case, Mr. Comfort has no loss carry overs at the end of the year.

Case 2

Income under ITA 3(a):		
Business income		$ 72,438
Income under ITA 3(b):		
Taxable capital gains	$4,233	
Allowable capital loss	(7,489)	Nil
Balance from ITA 3(a) and (b)		$ 72,438
Subdivision e deductions		(22,000)
Balance from ITA 3(c)		$ 50,438
Deduction under ITA 3(d):		
Rental loss		(9,846)
Net income (Division B income)		$ 40,592

In this case, Mr. Comfort has a net capital loss carry over of $3,256 ($7,489 - $4,233)

Case 3

Income under ITA 3(a):		
Employment income		$47,234
Income under ITA 3(b):		
Taxable capital gains [(1/2)($12,472)]	$6,236	
Allowable capital losses [(1/2)($9,332)]	(4,666)	1,570
Balance from ITA 3(a) and (b)		$48,804
Subdivision e deductions		(3,922)
Balance from ITA 3(c)		$44,882
Deduction under ITA 3(d):		
Business loss		(68,672)
Net income (Division B income)		$ Nil

In this case, Mr. Comfort would have a non-capital loss carry over of $23,790 ($68,672 - $44,882).

Case 4

Income under ITA 3(a):		
Property income (e.g., interest)	$ 6,250	
Business income	43,962	$50,212
Income under ITA 3(b):		
Taxable capital gains [(1/2)($12,376)]	$ 6,188	
Allowable capital losses		
[(1/2)($23,874)]	(11,937)	Nil
Balance from ITA 3(a) and (b)		$50,212
Subdivision e deductions		(7,387)
Balance from ITA 3(c)		$42,825
Deduction under ITA 3(d):		
Rental loss		(72,460)
Net income (Division B income)		$ Nil

In this case, Mr. Comfort would have a net capital loss carry over of $5,749 ($11,937 - $6,188) and a non-capital loss carry over of $29,635 ($72,480 - $42,825).

SSP 1-15 solution
Part 1 Solution

ITA 3(a)

Employment income ($82,000 – 7,100)	$74,900	
Business income ($105,000 – 49,000)	56,000	$130,900

ITA 3(b)

Taxable capital gains		$58,000	
Less:			
Allowable capital losses	$104,000		
Less: ABIL	37,000	67,000	Nil
Total of ITA 3(a) and 3(b)			$130,900
Subdivision e deduction			
Deductible RRSP contributions		$22,000	
Deductible moving expenses		9,200	31,200

ITA 3(c) | | | | $ 99,700 |

Rental loss ($37,000 – 12,000)		$25,000	
Investment loss ($19,000 – 10,000)		9,000	
Allowable business investment loss		37,000	71,000

ITA 3(d) – Income for the year | | | | $ 28,700 |

Net capital loss carry over = $ 11,000 ($67,000 - $58,000)

There are no other loss carry overs.

Part 2 Solution

ITA 3(a)

Employment income ($82,000 – 7,100)	$74,900	
Business income ($105,000 – 49,000)	56,000	$130,900

ITA 3(b)

Taxable capital gains		$58,000	
Less:			
Allowable capital losses	$104,000		
Less: ABIL	Nil	104,000	Nil

Total of ITA 3(a) and 3(b)		$130,900
Subdivision e deduction		
Deductible RRSP contributions	$22,000	
Deductible moving expenses	9,200	31,200

ITA 3(c) — $ 99,700

Rental loss ($37,000 – 12,000)	$25,000	
Investment loss ($19,000 – 10,000)	9,000	
Allowable business investment loss	Nil	34,000

ITA 3(d) – Net income for the year — $ 65,700

Net capital loss carry over = $ 46,000 ($104,000 - $58,000)

There are no other loss carry overs.

You can see that the reclassification of the ABIL to a regular capital loss results in $37,000 of additional net income and an increase in the net capital loss of $37,000.

Part 3 Solution

ITA 3(a)

Employment income ($82,000 – 7,100)	$74,900

ITA 3(b)

Taxable capital gains		$41,000	
Less:			
Allowable capital losses	$104,000		
Less: ABIL	37,000	67,000	Nil

Total of ITA 3(a) and 3(b)		$74,900
Subdivision e deduction		
Deductible RRSP contributions	$22,000	
Deductible spousal support	24,000	
Deductible moving expenses	9,200	55,200

ITA 3(c) — $19,700

Rental loss ($37,000 – 12,000)	$25,000	
Business loss ($149,000 – 105,000)	44,000	
Investment loss ($19,000 – 10,000)	9,000	
Allowable business investment loss	37,000	115,000

ITA 3(d) – Income for the year — $ Nil

Net capital loss carry over = $ 26,000 ($67,000 - $41,000)

Non-capital loss carry over = $ 95,300 ($115,000 - $19,700)

CHAPTER 2

Learning Objectives

After completing Chapter 2, you should be able to:

1. Describe the role of the CRA and its basic organization (Paragraph [P hereafter] 2-1 to 2-9)
2. Explain the circumstances under which an individual is required to file an income tax return and the filing methods available (P 2-10 to 2-18).
3. Determine the dates on which income tax returns must be filed by living individuals who either carry on a business or not and the filing rules when individuals die (P 2-19 to 2-25).
4. Explain the basic withholding rules, including their purpose (P 2-26 to 2-33).
5. Explain the circumstances that result in an individual having to make income tax instalment payments (P 2-34 to 2-40).
6. Calculate the amount of any income tax instalment payments required of individuals and determine when they are due (P 2-41 to 2-50).
7. Explain the circumstances in which interest is charged under the ITA, particularly to amounts owing for a year, instalments, and penalties and the importance of the prescribed interest rate (P 2-51 to 2-58).
8. Calculate the penalties that will be assessed for the late filing of income tax returns and large late and deficient instalments (P 2-59 to 2-63).
9. Identify the dates on which the final balances owing for a year by living and deceased individuals are due (P 2-64 to 2-68).
10. Identify the dates on which income tax returns must be filed by corporations and the filing methods available (P 2-69 to 2-74).
11. Calculate the amount of income tax instalment payments required for corporations, including small CCPCs (P 2-75 to 2-80).
12. Identify the dates on which final balances owing for a year by corporations are due (P 2-81 to 2-82).
13. Calculate the interest and penalties that may be assessed on late income tax payments and for the late filing of corporate income tax returns (P 2-83 to 2-86).
14. Explain the general filing and payment requirements for trusts, including the new 2021 reporting rules, including what is required and how these rules change general filing requirements (P 2-87 to 2-97).
15. Explain the circumstances in which a taxpayer is required to file an information return (P 2-98).
16. Describe the record-keeping requirements for books and records and the CRA's role (P 2-99 to 2-104).
17. Briefly describe the My Account and My Business Account services available on the CRA website (P 2-105 to 2-106).
18. Describe the notice of assessment and notice of reassessment, and explain the normal reassessment period and the circumstances where it can be extended (P 2-107 to 2-111).
19. Explain when interest is paid on refunds and how it is calculated for both individuals and corporations (P 2-112 to 2-118).
20. Explain how to make adjustments to previously filed income tax returns (P 2-119 to 2-122).

21. Explain the initial procedures for disputing an assessment, including authorizing a representative, and the procedures for filing a notice of objection, including special rules that apply to large corporations (P 2-123 to 2-137).
22. Describe the procedures for continuing a dispute when a satisfactory settlement has not been reached with the CRA. Describe the steps in this process, particularly the difference between the informal and general procedures (P 2-138 to 2-147).
23. Explain the difference between tax evasion, tax avoidance, and tax planning, including the basic GAAR analysis (P 2-148 to 2-152).
24. Describe the collection and enforcement procedures available to the CRA, the restrictions imposed on collection action, and situations where the restrictions do not apply (P 2-153 to 2-155).
25. Describe some of the common penalties that can be assessed, including those applicable to tax advisors and tax return preparers (P 2-156 to 2-162).
26. Briefly describe the taxpayer relief provisions, particularly those relating to the waiving of interest and penalties. Describe the circumstances that would be required to consider a request for taxpayer relief (P 2-163 to 2-168).
27. Briefly describe the circumstances under which a voluntary disclosure would be permitted and the difference between the limited and general program (P 2-169 to 2-175).

How to Work through Chapter 2

Visit pearsonmylabandmastering.com to access MyLab Accounting for this text. Once there, you can access student resources such as Self-Study Problems, Practice Exams, Flashcards, updates and more.

We recommend the following approach in dealing with the material in this chapter:

Introduction and the CRA—Mandate, Structure, Administration, and Enforcement
- Read paragraphs 2-1 to 2-9 (in the textbook).

Filing Requirements for Living and Deceased Individuals
- Read paragraph 2-10 to 2-22.
- Do Exercise 2-1 (in the textbook) and check the solution in this Study Guide.
- Read paragraph 2-23 to 2-25.
- Do Exercise 2-2 and check the solution in this Study Guide.

Income Tax Withholdings
- Read paragraph 2-26 to 2-33.

Instalment Payments for Individuals
- Read paragraph 2-34 to 2-50.
- Do Exercises 2-3 to 2-5 and check the solutions in this Study Guide.
- Do Self-Study Problem 2-1, which is available on MyLab, and check the solution in this Study Guide.

Interest, Penalties, and Balance Due Dates for Living and Deceased Individuals
- Read paragraph 2-51 to 2-63.
- Do Exercise 2-6 and check the solution in this Study Guide.
- Read paragraph 2-64 to 2-68.

Returns and Payments, Including Instalments, for Corporations
- Read paragraph 2-69 to 2-80.
- Do Exercises 2-7 and 2-8 and check the solutions in this Study Guide.

Balance Due Dates for Corporations
- Read paragraph 2-81 and 2-82.
- Do Exercise 2-9 and check the solution in this Study Guide.

Interest and Penalties for Corporations
- Read paragraph 2-83 to 2-86.
- Do Self-Study Problems 2-2 to 2-4 and check the solutions in this Study Guide.

Returns and Payments for Trusts
- Read paragraph 2-87 to 2-97.
- Do Exercise 2-10 and check the solution in this Study Guide.
- Do Self-Study Problem Two-5 and check the solution in this Study Guide

General Administrative Issues, Including the My Account Service, Books and Records, Assessments, Refunds, and Adjustments to Returns
- Read paragraph 2-98 to 2-122.

Appeals and Notices of Objection
- Read paragraph 2-123 to 2-137.
- Do Exercise 2-11 and check the solution in this Study Guide.
- Read paragraph 2-138 to 2-147.
- Do Self-Study Problem 2-6 and check the solution in this Study Guide.

Tax Evasion, Avoidance, and Planning
- Read paragraph 2-148 to 2-152.

Collection and Enforcement
- Read paragraph 2-153 to 2-160.
- Do Self-Study Problem 2-7 and check the solution in this Study Guide.
- Read paragraph 2-161 to 2-162.

Taxpayer Relief Provisions
- Read paragraph 2-163 to 2-175.

To Complete This Chapter
- Visit MyLab Accounting for more practice problem material, and test yourself with the glossary flashcards.
- Review the Key Terms at the end of the chapter, and consult the glossary for definitions.
- Ensure you have achieved the Chapter 2 Learning Objectives listed in this Study Guide.
- As a review, view the PowerPoint presentations available on MyLab

Practice Examination
- Available on MyLab, write the Practice Examination for this chapter, and mark it using the solutions provided.

Exercise Solutions

Exercise 2-1 Solution
While Mr. Katarski's 2021 tax return does not have to be filed until June 15, 2022, any income tax liability must be paid by April 30, 2022, in order to avoid the assessment of interest

Exercise 2-2 Solution
Sally would have been required to file her 2021 income tax return by June 15, 2022, and her 2022 income tax return by June 15, 2023, because her cohabiting spouse carried on a business as a sole proprietor in both 2021 and 2022.

The 2021 Tax Return   Since Sally died between November 1, 2021, and her 2021 filing due date of June 15, 2022, her 2021 income tax return can be filed the later of (i) June 15, 2022, or (ii) six months from the date of death, or August 15, 2022. Her 2021 tax return therefore does not have to be filed until August 15, 2022. Sally's surviving spouse can also file his 2021 income tax return using August 15, 2022.

The 2022 Tax Return   The six-month extension would only apply for the 2022 year if death occurred between November 1, 2022, and June 15, 2023. As this is not the case the normal filing due date of June 15, 2023, applies to the 2022 income tax return.

Exercise 2-3 Solution
She is not required to make instalment payments since her estimated current-year (2021) net tax owing is less than $3,000. If the estimate is subsequently determined to be incorrect and the actual net tax owing for 2021 exceeds $3,000, then instalments would have been required. Interest will then be charged based on quarterly instalment payments that would have been made had Marlene used the alternative that produced the least total instalments.

Exercise 2-4 Solution
As his net tax owing in the current year and one of the two preceding years (2019) is in excess of $3,000, he is required to make instalment payments. The minimum amount should be based on the year with the smallest net tax owing, which is the 2020 year. The minimum required quarterly payments would be $375 ($1,500/4). Payments would be due on March 15, June 15, September 15, and December 15 of 2021.

Exercise 2-5 Solution
The net tax owing amounts can be calculated as follows:

2019 $1,000 ($53,000 - $52,000)
2020 $7,000 ($59,000 - $52,000)
2021 $4,000 ($64,000 - $60,000)

As the net tax owing exceeds $3,000 in the current year (2021) and the first preceding year (2020), instalments are required.

The three alternatives for calculating instalment payments are as follows:

Alternative 1 • Based on the estimate for the current year, the instalments would be $1,000 ($4,000/4).

Alternative 2 • Based on the estimate for the preceding year, the instalments would be $1,750 ($7,000/4).

Alternative 3 • Based on the second preceding year (2019), the first and second instalments would each be $250 ($1,000/4). The third and fourth instalments would each be $3,250 {[1/2][$7,000 - ($250)(2)]}.

The four instalment payments would total $7,000, the same amount as under alternative 2.

While the first two instalments are lower under alternative 3, the total for all of the instalments under this alternative is the same as alternative 2. The current-year alternative (alternative 1) would be the best option. Payments are due on March 15, June 15, September 15, and December 15 of 2021. Note, however, that if the actual taxes payable for 2021 exceed the estimated taxes payable, then instalment interest would be charged.

Exercise 2-6 Solution
Given the size of her net tax owing, ITA 163.1 will not be applicable and there will be no penalties for late instalments. The penalty for late filing will be based on the number of **complete** months of non-payment, which is two. It will be equal to 7% of taxes payable (5%, plus 1% per month). If in one of the three preceding taxation years she has also late filed, been assessed a late filing penalty, and the CRA has sent her a demand to file her 2021 income tax return, then the penalty could be 14% (10%, plus 2% per month).

Interest will be assessed on the deficient instalments, calculated from the date on which the instalment was due and continuing until the balance due date of April 30, 2022. Interest will also be assessed on the balance owing on her filing date, along with the penalty for late filing. This interest will be assessed for the period May 1 through July 20, 2022. All of the interest will be calculated at the prescribed rate plus 4%.

Exercise 2-7 Solution
Not Small CCPC   If we assume that Madco Ltd. is not a small CCPC, we would choose the third alternative as the second preceding year of 2019 is the lowest tax payable with the first preceding year being less than the current 2021 taxation year. The first two instalments would be due on the last day of January and February 2021. They would be based on the second preceding year and would be $2,667 each ($32,000 ÷ 12). The remaining 10 instalments would be based on the preceding year, less the $5,334 paid in the first two instalments. The amount would be $5,367 [($59,000 - $5,334) ÷ 10] and the instalments would be due on the last day of each month for March to December 2021.

Small CCPC   If we assume that Madco Ltd. is a small CCPC, we would again choose the third alternative for the same reasons. The first instalment would be due on March 31, 2021. The amount would be based on the second preceding year and would equal $8,000 ($32,000 ÷ 4). The remaining three instalments would be based on the preceding year, less the amount paid in the first instalment. These payments would be equal to $17,000 [($59,000 - $8,000) ÷ 3]. These payments would be due on the last days of June, September, and December 2021.

Note that when the initial instalment(s) are based on the second preceding year, the total amount of instalments will generally be the same as when all of the instalments are based on the first preceding year. However, using the second preceding year is preferable where the first preceding year tax payable exceeds that of the second preceding year in that it provides some deferral of taxes.

Exercise 2-8 Solution
Not Small CCPC   If we assume that Fadco is not a small CCPC, the minimum instalments would be based on the estimated taxes payable for the taxation year ending November 30, 2021. The amount would be $1,417 ($17,000/12) and the instalments would be due on the last day of each month beginning December 31, 2020, and continuing to and including November 30, 2021. Note that if the estimate of tax payable for 2021 is too low, interest may be assessed on the deficiency.

Small CCPC   If we assume that Fadco is a small CCPC, the instalments would be based on the estimated taxes payable for the taxation year ending November 30, 2021. The amount would be $4,250 ($17,000/4). These amounts would be due on the last days of February, May, August, and November 2021.

Exercise 2-9 Solution
Radco Inc.'s tax return is due six months after the fiscal year end, on July 31, 2021. Unless Radco is able to claim the small business deduction, the final payment on their taxes is due two months after the year end, on March 31, 2021. If Radco is eligible for the small business deduction, the final payment can be deferred for an additional month, to April 30, 2021, provided the CCPC claimed the small business deduction for either of the 2020 or 2021 taxation year and that taxable income for the preceding taxation year of the CCPC and associated corporations did not exceed $500,000.

Exercise 2-10 Solution
ITA 150(1)(c) would normally require the Sammira Trust to file its 2021 income tax return by March 31, 2022. Since there is no tax payable, ITA 150(1.1)(b) would normally exempt the trust from having to file the return. Beginning in 2021, however, the trust cannot rely on the exemption unless the trust meets one of the exceptions, such as being in existence for less than three months and owning assets valued at $50,000 or less. Since neither of these exceptions apply, the trust therefore has to file an income tax return plus the additional information requested. Failure to file on time could result in penalties (and related interest) between $100 and $2,500, or between $2,500 and $42,000 [(5%)($840,000)] if there is gross negligence.

Exercise 2-11 Solution

The notice of objection must be filed by the later of:

- 90 days after the date on the notice of reassessment (August 13, 2023); or
- one year after the filing due date of April 30, 2022, for the 2021 return that is being reassessed (April 30, 2023).

The later of these two dates is August 13, 2023.

CRA Case Solution

1. It is always important to first assess the facts and determine Amber's rights with respect to her 2019 and 2020 income tax returns. The assessment notice of October 21, 2021, for both Amber's 2019 and 2020 taxation years means that the normal reassessment period of three years expires October 21, 2024. This gives the CRA the opportunity to audit her business for those years until that time.

   Since Amber carried on a business, her filing due date for 2019 would have been June 15, 2020, and the due date for 2020 would have been June 15, 2021.

   The double late filing penalty is technically justified since Amber experienced a late filing penalty in the three immediately preceding taxation years (e.g., 2018) and the CRA issued her demands to file both the 2019 and 2020 income tax returns.

   All of the assessed interest and penalty provisions are within the law with the exception of the gross negligence penalties, which is arguable given the facts. In addition, the amount of income taxes assessed for both years is based on an estimate by the CRA that appears to be too high. Nevertheless, if Amber does nothing then the CRA can and will assume that what they have done is correct. CRA Collections, however, cannot begin any action to collect the amounts owing until 90 days have passed measured from October 21, 2021. This means that collection action can begin January 19, 2022. Amber's only recourse, should she choose not to do anything, is to negotiate a payment arrangement with CRA Collections.

2. The ITA gives Amber a grace period of 90 days before collection action can be taken. This is because the ITA recognizes that she has an opportunity to object to the assessment of taxes within that same 90-day window. Technically the objection deadline for each year is as follows:

   2019 = later of 90 days from the notice of assessment of January 18, 2022, or one year from the filing due date, which would be June 15, 2021. The later date is therefore January 18, 2022.

   2020 = later of 90 days from the notice of assessment of January 18, 2022, or one year from the filing due date, which would be June 15, 2022. The later date is therefore June 15, 2022.

   Since the issues are identical for each of the two years it would be prudent to prepare objections for both years by January 18, 2022.

   We would add that it is sometimes preferable to contact the CRA to discuss the issues where the prospect of immediate resolution is high, such as where an expense (e.g., child care or moving) or credit (e.g., donations or medical) has been disallowed because of lack of supporting receipts or other documentation or explanations.

   In Amber's case, this would not be recommended and could only serve to delay the filing of objections. The facts state that by the time she had met with an expert, more than half of her 90-day objection period had passed (for 2019 only) with no indication that the income tax returns had yet been prepared. If Amber fails to meet the deadline, she could request an extension of time, but this adds more time and cost and further delays the process while her tax bill would continue to grow because of interest charges. Avoiding interest charges means paying existing balances in advance to avoid non-deductible interest, but again the facts indicate that Amber does not have the resources to pay all the debt. In summary, time is quickly running out and Amber needs to immediately authorize the expert she has met with and have them complete and submit the notices of objection for both years.

3.   Amber's best defence is to file the objections by January 18, 2022, and include the income tax returns for both 2019 and 2020 showing that the actual amounts are less than what was indicated on the assessment notices dated October 21, 2021. If the income tax returns cannot be prepared by January 18, 2022, then the objections should indicate that the returns will be provided to the CRA as soon as the objection is assigned to a CRA officer or at an earlier date to regular processing where the income tax returns are completed prior to contact by CRA Appeals. In any case the income tax returns will have to go through regular processing before an appeals officer can rely on them to decide in favour of Amber. The appeals process can take between six and twelve months once the objection has been assigned to an appeals officer.

In general the income tax returns should be accepted as filed, although the CRA could subsequently audit the business before the normal reassessment period of October 21, 2024. If the returns are filed and processed indicating reduced amounts of income tax owing and therefore reduced interest and penalties, then Amber will have achieved partial success. At this point, however, the interest and penalty charges will likely represent a significant amount of her income tax balance owing.

4.   The final step is for Amber to file a taxpayer relief request to have the CRA waive all penalties and interest. Form RC4288 would have to be completed. Amber would have to demonstrate, based on the facts, that she meets at least one of the main criteria: (1) extraordinary circumstances, (2) actions of the CRA, or (3) financial hardship or inability to pay. Paragraph 25(c) of the CRA publication IC07-1R1 titled "Taxpayer Relief Provisions" describes circumstances that fall within the "extraordinary circumstances" condition as a "serious illness or accident." Amber must show that were it not for the accident the interest and penalties assessed for non-compliance would not have occurred. In other words, she must clearly link the accident to her income tax issues, including explaining why there was no one who could have stepped in to comply on her behalf. The chances of success in waiving all interest and penalties are high. The CRA service standards are currently within six months of the file being assigned to a CRA officer.

There are two additional points worthy of mention. The first is that Amber could have challenged the gross negligence penalties as part of her objection with CRA Appeals rather than rely entirely on taxpayer relief. The gross negligence penalties were based on the previous audit results that warned of their application in a subsequent year if compliance (e.g., the deduction of personal expenses) became an issue. As long as Amber ensures that no personal expenses were claimed as business expenses in her 2019 and 2020 income tax returns, the recommendation would be to challenge the gross negligence penalties in the objections. If unsuccessful, they could still be waived under taxpayer relief.

Finally, some might suggest that Amber's taxpayer relief request should have also included financial hardship or inability to pay. This condition, however, requires the submission of additional detailed personal financial information that is time consuming to compile and highly unlikely, by itself, to contribute to a successful taxpayer relief application. The reason is because her business was experiencing increased revenues. The CRA does not simply look to financial hardship at a point in time but considers sustained and ongoing hardship with a high probability that it will continue for the foreseeable future. The facts in this case suggest otherwise.

5.   The lessons to be learned are the following non-exhaustive list in no particular order:

(1) Have a back-up plan when it comes to tax matters in terms of others whom you can rely upon to fulfill any ongoing tax obligations.

(2) Do not ignore communications from the CRA where information and income tax returns are requested.

(3) If something goes wrong, contact the CRA by phone immediately advising them to reference the call and the issues in your file with the CRA. Ask for the CRA agent's name and ID number, noting the date and time and details of the communication.

(4) Know your rights.

(5) Have an awareness of taxpayer relief provisions, including the availability of the Voluntary Disclosure Program.

Self-Study Problem Solutions

Self-Study Problems are available to download from MyLab Accounting.

SSP 2-1 Solution
Instalments are required when an individual's "net tax owing" exceeds $3,000 in the current year and in either of the two preceding years. In somewhat simplified terms, "net tax owing" is defined as the combined federal and provincial taxes payable, less amounts withheld by an employer under ITA 153.

Mr. Grafton's net tax owing figures are as follows:

2019 = $1,700 ($31,500 - $29,800)
2020 = $8,400 ($14,600 - $6,200)
2021 = $3,100 ($27,400 - $24,300) Estimated

As Mr. Grafton's net tax owing in 2021 (the current year) and his net tax owing in 2020 (one of the two preceding years) is greater than $3,000, he is required to make instalment payments.

Amounts
If Mr. Grafton bases the first two quarterly payments on the 2019 net tax owing, they would only be $425 each ($1,700/4). However, the payments for the last two quarters would be $3,775 each {[$8,400 - (2)($425)] ÷ 2}, resulting in total instalment payments of $8,400.

A preferable alternative would be to base the payments on the net tax owing for 2021. These payments would be $775 each ($3,100/4), for a total of $3,100.

Payment Dates
The quarterly payments would be due on March 15, June 15, September 15, and December 15, 2021.

SSP 2-2 Solution
Case One
1. As the corporation's tax payable for both the current and the preceding year exceeds $3,000, instalments are required. As the corporation is a small CCPC, instalments will be quarterly.

2. The three acceptable alternatives would be as follows:

    - Quarterly instalments of $27,405 ($109,620 ÷ 4) based on the current-year estimate
    - Quarterly instalments of $31,290 ($125,160 ÷ 4) based on the first preceding year
    - One instalment of $25,305 ($101,220 ÷ 4) based on the second preceding year, followed by three instalments of $33,285 [($125,160 - $25,305) ÷ 3] for a total of $125,160

3. The best alternative in terms of minimum instalments would be four instalments of $27,405, for total payments of $109,620.

    The instalments are due on March 31, June 30, September 30, and December 31, 2021.

Case Two
1. As the corporation's tax payable for both the current and the preceding year exceeds $3,000, instalments are required. As the corporation is a small CCPC, instalments will be quarterly.

2. The three acceptable alternatives would be as follows:

- Quarterly instalments of $27,405 ($109,620 ÷ 4) based on the current-year estimate
- Quarterly instalments of $26,075 ($104,300 ÷ 4) based on the first preceding year
- One instalment of $25,305 ($101,220 ÷ 4) based on the second preceding year, followed by three instalments of $26,331.67 [($104,300 - $25,305) ÷ 3] for a total of $104,300

3. The best alternative would be one payment of $25,305, followed by three payments of $26,331.67. While the total instalments are the same, $104,300, in both the second and third alternatives, the third alternative is preferable because the first payment is lower. This provides a small amount of tax deferral.

The instalments are due on March 31, June 30, September 30, and December 31, 2021.

Case Three

1. As the corporation's tax payable for both the current and the preceding year exceeds $3,000, instalments are required. As the corporation is not a small CCPC, monthly instalments are required.

2. The three acceptable alternatives would be as follows:

- Monthly instalments of $9,135 ($109,620 ÷ 12) based on the current-year estimate
- Monthly instalments of $10,430 ($125,160 ÷ 12) based on the first preceding year
- Two monthly instalments of $8,435 ($101,220 ÷ 12) based on the second preceding year, followed by 10 monthly instalments of $10,829 {[$125,160 - (2)($8,435)] ÷ 10} for a total of $125,160

3. The best alternative in terms of minimum instalments would be 12 instalments of $9,135 based on the current-year estimate, resulting in a total of $109,620 in instalment payments.

The instalments would be due on the last day of each month, beginning in January 2021.

Case Four

1. As the corporation's tax payable for both the current and the preceding year exceeds $3,000, instalments are required. As the corporation is not a small CCPC, monthly instalments are required.

2. The three acceptable alternatives would be as follows:

- Monthly instalments of $9,135 ($109,620 ÷ 2) based on the current-year estimate
- Monthly instalments of $8,691.67 ($104,300 ÷ 12) based on the first preceding year
- Two monthly instalments of $8,435 ($101,220 ÷ 12) based on the second preceding year, followed by 10 monthly instalments of $8,743 {[$104,300 - (2)($8,435)] ÷ 10} for a total of $104,300

3. The best alternative would be 2 payments of $8,435, followed by 10 payments of $8,743. While the total instalments are the same, $104,300, in both the second and third alternatives, the third alternative is preferable because the first two payments are lower. As indicated in Case Two, this provides a small amount of tax deferral.

The instalments would be due on the last day of each month, beginning in January 2021.

SSP 2-3 Solution
Case One

1. The individual's net tax owing in each of the three years is as follows:

2019 = Nil ($72,300 - $73,700)
2020 = $6,200 ($89,400 - $83,200)
2021 = $3,300 ($78,300 - $75,000)

As the net tax owing exceeds $3,000 in the current year and one of the two preceding years, instalments are required.

2. The three alternatives would be:

   - Quarterly instalments of $825 ($3,300 ÷ 4) based on the current-year estimate
   - Quarterly instalments of $1,550 ($6,200 ÷ 4) based on the first preceding year
   - Based on the second preceding year, the first two instalments would be nil. The remaining two instalments would be $3,100 each [($6,200 - Nil) ÷ 2] for a total of $6,200

3. The best alternative to minimize instalments would be four quarterly instalments of $825 for a total of $3,300.

   The instalments are due on March 15, June 15, September 15, and December 15, 2021.

Case Two

1. The individual's net tax owing in each of the three years is as follows:

   2019 = $7,200 ($72,300 - $65,100)
   2020 = Nil ($89,400 - $90,100)
   2021 = $6,400 ($78,300 - $71,900)

   As the net tax owing exceeds $3,000 in the current year and one of the two preceding years, instalments are required.

2. The three alternatives would be:

   - Quarterly instalments of $1,600 ($6,400 ÷ 4) based on the current-year estimate
   - Quarterly instalments of nil based on the first preceding year
   - Two quarterly instalments of $1,800 ($7,200 ÷ 4) based on the second preceding year. No further instalments would be required

3. The best alternative would be quarterly instalments of nil based on the first preceding year.

Case Three

1. As the corporation's tax payable for both the current and the preceding year exceeds $3,000, instalments are required. As the corporation is a small CCPC, instalments will be quarterly.

2. The three acceptable alternatives would be as follows:

   - Quarterly instalments of $19,575 ($78,300 ÷ 4) based on the current-year estimate
   - Quarterly instalments of $22,350 ($89,400 ÷ 4) based on the first preceding year
   - One instalment of $18,075 ($72,300 ÷ 4) based on the second preceding year, followed by three instalments of $23,775 [($89,400 - $18,075) ÷ 3] for a total of $89,400

3. The best alternative would be four instalments of $19,575 under the current-year estimate for total payments of $78,300. Even though the first payment under alternative three is only $18,075, when you add the remaining three payments the total is $89,400, which is much higher than the total instalments of $78,300 under the current-year alternative.

   The instalments are due on March 31, June 30, September 30, and December 31, 2021.

Case Four

1. As the corporation's tax payable for both the current and the preceding year exceeds $3,000, instalments are required. As the corporation is not a CCPC and is not eligible for the small business deduction, monthly instalments are required.

2. The three acceptable alternatives would be as follows:

   - Monthly instalments of $6,525 ($78,300 ÷ 12) based on the current-year estimate
   - Monthly instalments of $6,208.33 ($74,500 ÷ 12) based on the first preceding year
   - Two monthly instalments of $6,025 ($72,300 ÷ 12) based on the second preceding year, followed by 10 monthly instalments of $6,245 {[($74,500 - (2)($6,025)] ÷ 10} for a total of $74,500

3. In terms of minimizing instalment payments, both the second and third alternatives involve paying $74,500, which is less than the payment of $78,300 under the first alternative. While the problem does not ask you to take into consideration deferral, the third alternative would be the best in that the first two payments are lower.

    The instalments would be due on the last day of each month, beginning in January 2021.

SSP 2-4 Solution
Case A

The individual's actual and estimated net tax owing is equal to the tax payable in each of the three years as follows:

2019 = $18,000
2020 = $14,400
2021 = $13,500 (Estimated)

As the estimated tax payable for the current year and the actual tax payable for the preceding year exceeds $3,000, instalments are required.

Using the estimated tax payable for the current year would result in the minimum instalment payments. Based on this year, the required quarterly instalments would be $3,375 ($13,500 ÷ 4).

They would be due on March 15, June 15, September 15, and December 15, 2021, and would total $13,500.

Since the actual federal and provincial taxes payable for 2021 of $16,000 is higher than the tax payable of $14,400 of the preceding year, the instalments should have been based on $14,400. The instalments should have been $3,600 ($14,400 ÷ 4) for each quarter.

Interest at the prescribed base rate plus 4% is charged on any portion of a required instalment payment that is not remitted on the required instalment due date. The interest is charged from the date the instalment is due until an offset occurs, or until the due date for the balance owing.

Case B

The individual's net tax owing in each of the three years is as follows:

2019 = $11,000 ($18,000 - $7,000)
2020 = Nil (withholdings exceed tax payable. Note this is nil, not a negative amount.)
2021 = $4,500 ($13,500 - $9,000) (Estimated)

As the individual's net tax owing is expected to exceed $3,000 in 2021 and was more than $3,000 in 2019, the payment of instalments is technically required.

Using the 2020 net tax owing would result in minimum instalment payments. Based on this year, no instalment payments would be required.

The fact that the actual federal and provincial taxes payable for 2021 are higher than were estimated is not relevant in this case.

Case C

The corporation's tax payable for the three years is as follows:

2019 = $18,000
2020 = $14,400
2021 = $13,500 (Estimated)

As the corporation's tax payable for both the current and the preceding year exceeds $3,000, instalments are required.

Using the estimated tax payable for the current year would result in the minimum instalment payments. As the corporation is a small CCPC, the required instalments would be quarterly. The amount would be $3,375 ($13,500 ÷ 4).

They would be due on the last days of March, June, September, and December 2021.

Like Case A, since the actual federal and provincial taxes payable for 2021 of $16,000 is higher than the tax payable of $14,400 of the preceding year, the instalments should have been based on $14,400. The instalments should have been $3,600 ($14,400 ÷ 4) for each quarter.

Interest at the prescribed base rate plus 4% is charged on any portion of a required instalment payment that is not remitted on the required instalment due date. The interest is charged from the date the instalment is due until an offset occurs or until the due date for the balance owing.

Case D

The corporation's tax payable for the three years is as follows:

2019 = $18,000
2020 = $14,400
2021 = $16,000 (Estimated and actual)

As the corporation's tax payable for both the current and the preceding year exceeds $3,000, instalments are required.

Using the actual tax payable for 2020 would result in minimum instalment payments. Because the corporation is not a CCPC and is not eligible for the small business deduction, the required instalments would be monthly. The amount would be $1,200 ($14,400 ÷ 2). They would be due on the last day of each month, beginning in January 2021

SSP 2-5 Solution

The three taxable entities are individuals, corporations, and trusts. The required information for each is as follows:

Individuals   For individuals, the taxation year is the calendar year. For individuals without business income, the filing deadline is April 30 of the following year. Individuals with business income, and their spouse or common-law partner, have an extended filing deadline of June 15.

If an individual dies after October of the year and before the filing due date (April 30 or June 15), the due date of the return for the year of death is extended to the later of six months after the date of death and the filing due date.

Instalment payments for all individuals, if required, are to be made quarterly on March 15, June 15, September 15, and December 15.

Corporations   Corporations can choose any fiscal year that does not exceed 53 weeks. The filing deadline is six months after the fiscal year end. In general, corporations must make instalments on the last day of each month. However, if the corporation qualifies as a small CCPC, quarterly instalments are required on the last day of the last month of each three-month period in the corporation's taxation year.

Trusts   Most trusts must use the calendar year as their taxation year. As the required tax return must be filed within 90 days of the taxation year end, returns for trusts will be due March 31 (March 30 in leap years). Legislation requires that quarterly instalments be made on March 15, June 15, September 15, and December 15. Note, however, that the CRA has a general administrative policy not to apply penalties and interest for deficient or no instalment payments.

Trusts—Graduated Rate Estates (GRE)   Trusts that are designated as a GRE are the exception. GREs can use a non-calendar fiscal year for up to three years subsequent to the death of the settlor. GRE returns are due 90 days after the date that has been selected as the taxation year end. GREs are legislatively exempted from making instalment payments as opposed to other trusts that are administratively exempted by the CRA.

SSP 2-6 Solution

Since Mr. Coffee has been your client for many years, there should be an authorization filed with the CRA that allows you to represent him in his affairs. If you have not already been authorized to represent him online, it would be advantageous for you to request that Mr. Coffee take the steps needed to authorize you to access his file through the online Represent a Client service. This will enable you to deal with this dispute and any future disputes more quickly.

With respect to resolving this dispute, the first step would be a call to the CRA to discuss the matter. If there has been a misunderstanding of the facts, an error on your or the CRA's part, or missing information, this may be the only step required and the matter can be resolved.

However, if more formal steps are necessary, they can be outlined as follows:

Notice of Objection As the reassessment relates to the previous year's tax return, it is within the normal reassessment period of three years. This means that a notice of objection can be filed on the later of 90 days of the date on the notice of reassessment or (as Mr. Coffee is an individual) one year from the due date for the return under reassessment. This can be done by accessing My Account or My Business Account from the CRA website and selecting the option "Register My Formal Dispute" (also available through Represent a Client by your representative). It should explain the facts and reasons why the reassessment is not justified.

Tax Court of Canada If there is an adverse decision on the notice of objection, Mr. Coffee has up to 90 days after the mailing date of the response to the notice of objection to appeal to the Tax Court of Canada. Alternatively, if he does not receive a response to his notice of objection within 90 days, he will then be able to appeal to the Tax Court of Canada. As the amount involved is only $5,000, it would probably be advisable for Mr. Coffee to choose the informal procedure. You can then choose to represent him under that procedure.

Federal Courts If Mr. Coffee has elected the informal Tax Court of Canada procedures, no appeal of an adverse decision is possible. An appeal to the Federal Court—Appeals Division would, however, be possible if an adverse decision was rendered under the general procedures. In theory, an adverse decision by the Federal Court could be appealed to the Supreme Court of Canada. However, this can only happen if the Federal Court recommends it or the Supreme Court authorizes such an action. This would be extremely unlikely given the amount involved.

SSP 2-7 Solution

Note to Instructor These cases have been based on examples found in Information Circular 01-1 titled "Third-Party Civil Penalties."

Case A

In view of the business that the taxpayer is in, there was nothing in the income statement that would have made the accountant question the validity of the information provided. Therefore, the accountant could rely on the good faith reliance exception and would not be subject to the preparer penalty.

Case B

The prospectus prepared by the company contains a false statement (overstated fair market value of the software) that could be used for tax purposes. The company knew or would reasonably be expected to know, but for culpable conduct, that the fair market value of the software was a false statement. Since the company is engaged in an excluded activity, it cannot rely on the good faith reliance exception with respect to the valuation. The CRA would consider assessing the company with third-party civil penalties in the amount of $2,000,000 (i.e., the gross entitlements). The CRA would also consider assessing the appraiser with third-party civil penalties. The amount of the penalty would be his gross entitlements from the valuation activity, which is $75,000.

Case C

Although the tax return contains one or more false statements, the tax return preparer would be entitled to the good faith defence since she relied, in good faith, on information (the financial statements that were not obviously unreasonable) provided by another professional on behalf of the client. Therefore, she would not be subject to the preparer penalty.

The third-party penalties may be applied to the other accountant if he knew or would be expected to know, but for circumstances amounting to culpable conduct, that the financial statements contained false statements.

Case D

The accountant would not be subject to the penalties for participating or acquiescing in the understatement of a tax liability. The facts were highly suspect until the accountant asked questions to clear up the doubt in her mind that the client was not presenting her with implausible information. The response addressed the concern and was not inconsistent with the knowledge she possessed.

Case E

Since the tax return preparer efiled the taxpayer's return without obtaining the charitable donation receipt, the CRA would consider assessing the tax return preparer with the preparer penalty. Given that the size of the donation is so disproportionate to the taxpayer's apparent resources as to defy credibility, to proceed unquestioningly in this situation would show wilful blindness and thus an indifference as to whether the ITA is complied with.

Case F

The issue here is whether the accountant is expected to know that GST is not payable on wages, interest expense, and zero-rated purchases. It is clear that the accountant should have known that no GST could be claimed on these items. Given this, in filing a claim that includes a GST refund on the preceding items, the accountant made a false statement, either knowingly or in circumstances amounting to culpable conduct. Consequently, the CRA would consider assessing the accountant with the third-party civil penalty, specifically, the preparer penalty.

CHAPTER 3

Learning Objectives

After completing Chapter 3, you should be able to:

1. Explain the basic rules and concepts of employment income (Paragraph [P hereafter] 3-1 to 3-4).
2. Explain the reasons for using, and the rules associated with, bonus arrangements for employees (P 3-5 to 3-9).
3. Describe the consequences of an employment loss on net income (P 3-10 to 3-11).
4. Distinguish between an employee and a self-employed individual earning business income and list the advantages and disadvantages of both classifications. In addition, explain the concept of a personal service business and the impact of such a classification (P 3-12 to 3-49).
5. Describe how non-salary benefits are taxed and the analysis to determine whether a benefit is required to be included in employment income (P 3-50 to 3-57).
6. List the different amounts that can be included in employment income under ITA 6(1) and the type of benefits that are legislatively excluded under ITA 6(1)(a) (P 3-58 to 3-61).
7. Apply the employee benefit analysis to common benefits, and determine how they are taxed and whether there are any administrative concessions made by the CRA (P 3-62 to 3-63).
8. Explain the basic elements of tax planning for employee benefits, including tax deferral opportunities and what the tax treatment to the employer is (P 3-64 to 3-76).
9. Describe the effects of the GST/HST/PST on taxable benefits (P 3-77 to 3-79).
10. Describe the three different ITA references to cars and trucks and the implications for income tax purposes (P 3-80 to 3-88).
11. Describe the three tax concerns to employees in terms of the use of an automobile in one's employment (P 3-89 to 3-90).
12. Explain the concept of personal travel, its importance, and how it is determined (P 3-91 to 3-94).
13. Calculate the standby charge and operating cost benefits that apply to employees who are provided with an automobile that is leased or owned by their employer (P 3-95 to 3-136).
14. Explain basic tax planning for company cars (P 3-137 to 3-138).
15. Explain the tax treatment of allowances that are provided by employers to their employees for travel costs (P 3-139 to 3-156).
16. Describe the taxation of various types of insurance benefits that are provided by employers to their employees (P 3-157 to 3-162).
17. Explain and calculate the income tax consequences when low-interest-rate or interest-free loans are made to employees as a result of their employment (P 3-163 to 3-172).
18. Calculate the income tax consequences that result from employees receiving and exercising stock options and from the subsequent sale of the acquired shares (P 3-173 to 3-194).
19. List and describe other inclusions in employment income (P 3-195 to 3-204).
20. List and describe specific deductions against employment income that are listed in ITA 8 (P 3-205 to 3-228).
21. Explain how deductible work space in the home costs for employees are calculated and how the employment usage is determined (P 3-229 to 3-235).

How to Work through Chapter 3

Visit pearsonmylabandmastering.com to access MyLab Accounting for this text. Once there, you can access student resources such as Self-Study Problems, Practice Exams, Flashcards, updates and more.

We recommend the following approach in dealing with the material in this chapter:

Employment Income Defined
- Read paragraph 3-1 to 3-9 (in the textbook).
- Do Exercise 3-1 (in the textbook) and check the solution in this Study Guide.
- Do Self-Study Problem 3-1, which is available on MyLab, and check the solution in this Study Guide.
- Read paragraph 3-10 to 3-11.

Employee versus Self-Employed
- Read paragraph 3-12 to 3-49.
- Do Self-Study Problem 3-2 and check the solution in this Study Guide.

Salaries and Fringe Benefits
- Read paragraph 3-50 to 3-51.
- Do Exercise 3-2 and check the solution in this Study Guide.
- Read paragraph 3-52 to 3-63.
- Do Exercises 3-3 to 3-4 and check the solutions in this Study Guide.
- Read paragraph 3-64 to 3-76.
- Do Exercise 3-5 and check the solution in this Study Guide.

GST/HST & PST on Taxable Benefits
- Read paragraph 3-77 to 3-79.
- Do Exercise 3-6 and check the solution in this Study Guide.

Automobile Benefits (Standby Charge and Operating Cost Benefit)
- Read paragraph 3-80 to 3-85.
- Do Exercise 3-7 and check the solution in this Study Guide.
- Read paragraph 3-86 to 3-130.
- Do Exercise 3-8 and check the solution in this Study Guide.
- Read paragraph 3-131 to 3-136.
- Do Exercise 3-9 and check the solution in this Study Guide.
- Read paragraph 3-137 to 3-138.
- Do Self-Study Problems 3-3 to 3-5 and check the solutions in this Study Guide.

Allowances
- Read paragraph 3-139 to 3-153.
- Do Exercises 3-10 and 3-11 and check the solutions in this Study Guide.
- Read paragraph 3-154 to 3-155.
- Do Exercise 3-12 and check the solution in this Study Guide.
- Read paragraph 3-156.

Employee Insurance Benefits
- Read paragraph 3-157 to 3-162.
- Do Exercise 3-13 and check the solution in this Study Guide.

Loans to Employees
- Read paragraph 3-163 to 3-167.
- Do Exercise 3-14 and check the solution in this Study Guide.
- Read paragraph 3-168 to 3-172.
- Do Exercise 3-15 and check the solution in this Study Guide.
- Do Self-Study Problem 3-6 and check the solution in this Study Guide.

Stock Option Benefits
- Read paragraph 3-173 to 3-189.
- Do Exercise 3-16 and check the solution in this Study Guide.
- Read paragraph 3-190 to 3-194.
- Do Exercise 3-17 and check the solution in this Study Guide.
- Do Self-Study Problems 3-7 to 3-9 and check the solutions in this Study Guide.

Other Inclusions
- Read paragraph 3-195 to 3-204.

Specific Deductions, Including Salesperson's Expenses and Work Space in the Home Costs
- Read paragraph 3-205 to 3-219.
- Do Exercise 3-18 and check the solution in this Study Guide.
- Read paragraph 3-220 to 3-235.
- Do Self-Study Problems 3-10 to 3-15 and check the solutions in this Study Guide.

To Complete This Chapter
- Visit MyLab Accounting for more practice problem material, and test yourself with the glossary flashcards.
- Review the Key Terms at the end of the chapter, and consult the glossary for definitions.
- Ensure you have achieved the Chapter 3 Learning Objectives listed in this Study Guide.
- As a review, view the PowerPoint presentations available on MyLab

Practice Examination
- Available on MyLab, write the Practice Examination for this chapter, and mark it using the solutions provided.

Exercise Solutions

Exercise 3-1 Solution
The bonus will be included in Mr. Neelson's employment income of 2021—the year of receipt. With respect to Neelson Inc., the bonus is payable more than 179 days after its September 30 year end, which would be March 28, 2021. Note that the limit is 179 days from the year end, not the date on which the bonus was declared. As a consequence, the company will not be able to deduct the bonus in the year ending September 30, 2020, the year of declaration. It will be deducted in the year ending September 30, 2021, the year in which payment was made.

If the payment was made in October 2021, Mr. Neelson would still be required to include the bonus in employment income for 2021. The expense to the company, however, would be based on the taxation year in which the payment was made. Since October 2021 falls in the taxation year ending September 30, 2022, the company's expense would be delayed to 2022.

Exercise 3-2 Solution
Case 1 There is an economic advantage and therefore a benefit received because of the employment; however, the employer is the primary beneficiary since the phone is principally used for employment purposes. As a result, there is no taxable benefit.

Case 2 The employee receives an economic advantage of $2,000, representing the savings on purchasing the painting. The benefit was received because of the individual's employment—the employer only sold to employees. The primary beneficiary is the employee. Finally, since the benefit is not excluded the employee will be required to include $2,000 in employment income for the year of the purchase.

Case 3 The $200 is definitely a benefit (an economic advantage), but since it has nothing to do with employment, it is not a taxable employment benefit.

Case 4 The employee has (1) received a benefit (an economic advantage), (2) as a result of employment, and (3) the employee is the primary beneficiary. There is no exclusion for this type of benefit. The difficulty in this case is valuing the benefit. Technically there is an argument to be made that the value of the guarantee by the employer would be the benefit, but there would likely be considerable difficulty determining a dollar value for the benefit.

Exercise 3-3 Solution
The tax consequences associated with each of the listed items are as follows:

Gift	Tax Consequence
$15 T-shirt	No consequences as value is immaterial
$75 birthday gift	Taxable as it is a near-cash gift
$400 performance reward	Taxable as it is performance related
$275 10-year award	Non-taxable as it is under $500
$300 wedding gift	These remaining three gifts quality as non-taxable. However, their total value is $700 ($300 + $250 + $150). The $200 excess over $500 will be taxable.
$250 weight loss award	
$150 holiday season gift	

Exercise 3-4 Solution
The tax consequences of the various items would be as follows:

- Technically this would be an economic advantage to the employee and therefore a taxable employment benefit. However, the CRA provides an administrative concession where the discounts are on merchandise, the discounts are available to all employees, the price paid is not below the employer's cost, and the items are not high-priced items.
- Depending on the facts it could be argued that the employer is the primary beneficiary and therefore that the benefit is not taxable. If unsuccessful the $2,000 would be a benefit included in the employment income of the employee when received.
- Special clothing is not a taxable benefit if it is distinctive and the employee is required to wear it at work, or if it is required to protect the employee from some type of employment-related hazard. Business clothing that could be used outside of the employment duties would not qualify as it could be used for personal purposes. The $1,500 should be included in John's employment income as a taxable benefit when received.
- This amount would represent an economic advantage received as a result of the employment where the employee is the primary beneficiary with the result that $450 would normally be a taxable benefit. The CRA, however, applies an administrative concession to allow up to a $500 value to be received without being added to employment income. As a result, there is no taxable benefit to John.
- John receives an economic advantage as a result of employment where he is the primary beneficiary, however contributions to a private health care plan by an employer are a legislative exception to ITA 6(1)(a) and, as a result, there is no taxable benefit.

Exercise 3-5 Solution
From Jill's point of view, the best alternative is the dental plan. Its value is significantly enhanced by the fact that it can be received tax free given that it is a legislative exception to ITA 6(1)(a). The annual vacation trip is clearly a taxable benefit that will become taxable when the trip is taken. With respect to the $4,000 birthday gift, the CRA administrative concession comes into play, exempting the first $500, so only $3,500 will be a taxable employment benefit. Note that the desirability of the dental plan would be affected by whether her spouse has a dental plan.

Exercise 3-6 Solution

Ms. Corelli's taxable benefit would be $4,725—the $4,500 cost of the trip plus the additional $225 in GST.

Exercise 3-7 Solution

1. The shuttle bus in not an automobile because it is a motor vehicle acquired to be used as a bus more than half the time in a business of transporting passengers. It would also be excluded on the basis it was used more than 90% of the time in the year acquired as part of a business of transporting passengers.
2. The two cars are "automobiles." Cars are only excluded from the definition if they are used as a taxi or for other restrictive uses (e.g., emergency vehicles). The vehicles would not be considered "automobiles" if they were vans or pick-up trucks used to deliver goods.
3. The vans would qualify in terms of seating capacity, but since the charity is not carrying on a business none of the exceptions would exclude them. The vans are considered "automobiles."
4. The only car that would be excluded would be one used as a taxi or bus in a transportation business. Since this is not the case here, the car is an "automobile." It would also be a passenger vehicle and therefore the limitations on CCA deductions and leasing costs would be applied. This is discussed in Chapters 5 and 6.
5. Since the seating capacity is more than three people it will only be excluded if it is used more than 90% of the time for transporting passengers in the year acquired. If the first year use is only 70%, none of the exclusions apply and the pick-up truck is an "automobile." If the first year use is 95%, then the exclusion applies and the pick-up truck is not an "automobile."

Exercise 3-8 Solution

As Ms. Lee's employment-related use is more than half of the total (16,000 out of 28,000), she is therefore eligible for a reduced standby charge. She is also eligible for the optional one-half of the standby charge calculation for the operating cost benefit. Given these factors, the taxable benefit would be calculated as follows:

Standby charge	
$[(2\%)(12)(\$25,000 + \$1,250 + \$2,000)(12,000 \div 20,004^*)]$	$4,067
Operating cost benefit—lesser of:	
• $[(\$0.27)(12,000)] = \$3,240$ and	
• $[(1/2)(\$4,067)] = \$2,034$	2,034
Total benefit	$ 6,101

$^*[(12 \text{ Months})(1,667)]$

Exercise 3-9 Solution

The actual operating costs paid by the employer do not affect these calculations as long as the vehicle is an "automobile." Rounded to the nearest whole number, 325 days results in 11 months of availability. As Mr. Forthwith's employment-related use is more than half, he is eligible for a reduced standby charge. He is also eligible for the elective alternative one-half of the standby charge calculation for the operating cost benefit. Given these factors, the taxable benefit would be calculated as follows:

Standby charge $[(2/3)(\$525 + \$68)(11)(3,000 \div 18,337^*)]$	$ 711
Operating cost benefit—lesser of:	
• $[(\$0.27)(3,000)] = \$810$ and	
• $[(1/2)(\$711)] = \$356$	356
Total benefit	$1,067

$^*[(11)(1,667)]$

Exercise 3-10 Solution

Because the allowance is not based solely on kilometres driven for employment use it is deemed to be unreasonable, and she will have to include the $3,600 allowance in her income. Because the allowance has been included in income, she can deduct the employment-related portion of her actual automobile costs as long as any remaining conditions for the specific expense have been met. If all the conditions apply, she would be able to deduct $1,936 [($7,150)(6,500 ÷ 24,000)]. The net inclusion would be $1,664 ($3,600 - $1,936).

Exercise 3-11 Solution

Since the allowance was based solely on a per-kilometre allowance, the rule in ITA 6(1)(b)(x) would not apply to deem a reasonable allowance to be unreasonable. If this were the end of the story, then the employee would be unable to claim any employment expenses on the grounds that he was in receipt of a non-taxable, or tax-free, allowance.

The important part of the analysis first requires determining whether the allowance paid to the employee is reasonable by applying objective standards. Given the cost of an automobile, insurance, fuel, and other operating costs, most would agree that $0.10 per kilometre is unreasonably low. All provinces indicate costs of using an automobile to be approximately $0.35 per kilometre or higher. As a result, the facts suggest that since the allowance is unreasonable, $3,500 [(35,000 km)($0.10)] will be required to be included in employment income. The employee would then be entitled to claim an employment expense of $11,900 [($5,400 + $15,000)(35,000/60,000)].

Exercise 3-12 Solution

The hotel allowance is reasonable and would therefore not be included in Ms. Ohm's employment income. In addition, the per-kilometre allowance is reasonable based on published provincial amounts. As a result, the allowance would be considered reasonable based on the specific facts. The two rules that apply to deem a motor vehicle allowance to be unreasonable do not apply since the allowance is based solely on a per-kilometre rate and Ms. Ohm is not in receipt of an allowance for use plus a reimbursement of operating expenses for the same use.

Based on the facts she will not include any amount received from her employer in employment income, and as a result she will not be entitled to an expense for the use of her automobile. She does not have a choice to decide to include the amounts received in income and then to deduct automobile expenses.

Exercise 3-13 Solution

As his employer contributes to the plan, and the contributions do not create a taxable benefit because the plan provides for periodic benefits to replace the loss of employment income, the $5,250 in benefits received during the year will be included in his employment income. This will be reduced by the $525 ($300 + $225) in contributions that he made during 2020 and 2021, leaving a net inclusion of $4,725 ($5,250 - $525).

Exercise 3-14 Solution

The ITA 80.4(1) benefit is calculated as follows:

The lesser of:	
• [($100,000)(2%)(1/4) + ($100,000)(3%)(1/4) + ($100,000)(1%)(2/4)] = $1,750	
• [($100,000)(2%)] = $2,000	$ 1,750
Less interest payment [($100,000)(1%)]	(1,000)
Net benefit	$ 750

As this is a home purchase loan, the annual benefit cannot exceed the benefit that would result from applying the 2% rate that was in effect when the loan was made. Note that the 2% rate is not compared to the prescribed rate on a quarter-by-quarter basis, but on an annual basis. The lower figure of $1,750 would then be reduced by the $1,000 in interest paid.

Exercise 3-15 Solution

In the absence of the interest-free loan, the employee would borrow $125,000 at 5%, requiring an annual interest payment of $6,250. The after-tax cash outflow associated with the employer providing sufficient additional salary to carry this loan would be calculated as follows:

Required salary [$6,250 ÷ (1 - 0.42)]	$10,776
Corporate tax savings from deducting salary [($10,776)(26%)]	(2,802)
Employer's after-tax cash flow—Additional salary	$ 7,974

Alternatively, if the loan is provided, the employee will have a taxable benefit of $2,500 [(2%) ($125,000)], resulting in income taxes of $1,050 [(42%)($2,500)]. To make this situation comparable to the straight salary alternative, the employer will have to provide the employee with both the loan amount and sufficient additional salary to pay the taxes on the employment interest benefit. The amount of this additional salary would be $1,810 [$1,050 ÷ (1- 0.42)]. The employer's after-tax cash flow associated with providing the additional salary and the loan amount would be calculated as follows:

Required salary [$1,050 ÷ (1- 0.42)]	$1,810
Corporate tax savings from deducting salary [($1,810)(26%)]	(471)
After-tax cost of salary to cover taxes on benefit	$1,339
Employer's lost earnings [(7%)(1- 0.26)($125,000)]	6,475
Employer's after-tax cash flow—Loan	$7,814

Given these results, providing the loan appears to be the better alternative

Exercise 3-16 Solution

At time of exercise, Mr. Guise will have an employment income benefit of $21,250 [($31.50 - $23.00) (2,500 shares)]. As the option price at issue exceeded the fair market value at issue, Mr. Guise will be able to deduct $10,625 [(1/2)($21,250)] in the determination of taxable income.

These results are summarized in the following table:

Fair market value of shares acquired [(2,500)($31.50)]	$78,750
Cost of shares [(2,500)($23)]	(57,500)
ITA 7(1)(a) employment income inclusion =	
Increase in net income	**$ 21,250**
ITA 110(1)(d) deduction [(1/2)($21,250)]	(10,625)
Increase in taxable income	**$ 10,625**

When the shares are sold, there will be an allowable capital loss, calculated as follows:

Proceeds of disposition [($28.00)(2,500)]	$ 70,000
Adjusted cost base [($31.50)(2,500)]	(78,750)
Capital loss	($ 8,750)
Inclusion rate	1/2
Allowable capital loss	($ 4,375)

Mr. Guise will only be able to deduct this loss in 2021 to the extent that he has taxable capital gains on other dispositions. It cannot be deducted against the employment income inclusion.

Exercise 3-17 Solution

There will be no tax consequences in either 2019, when the options are granted, or in 2020, when the options are exercised. This latter result reflects the fact that the acquired shares are those of a CCPC.

When the shares are sold in 2021, there will be a benefit amount of $58,500 [($75.00 - $42.50) (1,800 shares)] that will be included in employment income. As the option price of $42.50 was below the fair market value of $45 at the time the options were granted, no deduction is allowed under ITA 110(1)(d). She is not eligible for the deduction under ITA 110(1)(d.1) because she did not hold the shares for the required two years. These results are summarized in the following table:

Deferred employment income:	
Fair market value of shares acquired [(1,800)($75)]	$135,000
Cost of shares [(1,800)($42.50)]	(76,500)
ITA 7(1)(a) employment income inclusion =	
Increase in net income	**$ 58,500**
ITA 110(1)(d) deduction (option price < FMV)	N/A
ITA 110(1)(d.1) deduction (held less than 2 years)	N/A
Increase in taxable income	**$ 58,500**

When she sells the shares in 2021, Ms. Van will have an allowable capital loss calculated as follows:

Proceeds of disposition [($49)(1,800)]	$ 88,200
Adjusted cost base [($75)(1,800)]	(135,000)
Capital loss	($ 46,800)
Inclusion rate	1/2
Allowable capital loss	($ 23,400)

Ms. Van will only be able to deduct this loss in 2021 to the extent that she has taxable capital gains. Allowable capital losses cannot be deducted against the benefit amount added to employment income.

Exercise 3-18 Solution

The potential deduction is $27,100 [$8,000 + (1/2)($12,000) + $13,100]. However, this total exceeds his commissions and, if these amounts are deducted under ITA 8(1)(f), his deduction will be limited to the commissions of $12,200.

Alternatively, if he uses ITA 8(1)(h), he cannot deduct the advertising or the entertainment expenses, limiting the amount of his deduction to $13,100.

As the two provisions cannot be used simultaneously, Mr. McMaster would use the larger figure of $13,100 that is available under ITA 8(1)(h).

Self-Study Problem Solutions

Self-Study Problems are available to download from MyLab Accounting.

SSP 3-1 Solution

The required information for the four cases included in this problem is shown in the following table:

	Deduction—Empire Inc. Year Ending October 31	Inclusion—Ms. Betz Calendar Year
Case A	2021	2021
Case B	2021	2022
Case C	2022	2022
Case D	2021	2021

In Case A, the bonus is deducted by the employer when accrued because it is paid by the 179th day of its 2021 fiscal year end. It is included in employment income in the year it is received.

In Case B, the bonus is deducted by the employer when accrued because it is paid by the 179th day of its 2021 fiscal year end. It is included in employment income in the year it is received.

In Case C, the bonus is not paid by the 179th day of the employer's fiscal year end. As a consequence, it cannot be deducted until the year ending October 31, 2022. However, as it is paid within three years of Empire's 2021 year end, it is not a salary deferral arrangement. This means it does not have to be included in Ms. Betz's employment income until 2022.

In Case D, the bonus is not paid until more than three years after the end of the calendar year in which Ms. Betz rendered the services. This makes it a salary deferral arrangement, resulting in Ms. Betz having to include it in her 2021 employment income. The employer will deduct the bonus for its fiscal year ending October 31, 2021.

SSP 3-2 Solution

If the individual's services are acquired as an employee, the 2021 costs would be as follows:

Basic salary	$250,000
Company benefits [($250,000)(8%)]	20,000
CPP (maximum)	3,166
Employer's share of EI [(1.4)(1.58%)($56,300)]	1,245
Payroll tax [(2%)($250,000)]	5,000
Total cost	$279,411

This is very close to the $280,000 that would have to be paid if the individual is classified as an independent contractor.

Other Considerations

While the quantitative factors slightly favour employee classification, this is probably not the best choice. Other factors that should be considered include the following:

- Self-employed status relieves the company from any ongoing commitment beyond the period specified in the contract.
- Farnham Ltd. would not be legally responsible for any errors in the work of the engineer if he is self-employed.
- Employment contracts usually require that salary and related benefits grow over time.
- There are added administrative costs of withholding amounts from the salary if the individual is an employee.

  It would appear to be more advantageous to structure the arrangement so that this individual qualifies as an independent contractor. This intent would have to be acceptable to both parties and consistent with the nature of their relationship.

SSP 3-3 Solution

Ms. Marianne Dorsey   The taxable benefit to be included in employment income for the president of the company would be calculated as follows:

Standby charge [(2%)(11)($185,000)]	$40,700
Operating cost benefit [(35,000)($0.27)]	9,450
Total benefit	$50,150

Since Marianne's employment use is less than half of the total kilometres driven, the reduced standby charge is not available nor is the elective option with respect to the operating cost benefit.

Mr. John Dorsey The taxable benefit to be included in employment income would be calculated as follows:

Standby charge [(2%)($71,500)(10)(16,670/16,670*)]	$14,300
Operating cost benefit—Lesser of:	
• [(22,000)($0.27)] = $5,940	
• [(1/2)($14,300)] = $7,150	6,160
Total benefit	$20,460

*The numerator cannot exceed the denominator, which is equal to [(10)(1,667)].

While John is eligible for the reduced standby charge calculation, his personal use is more than 1,667 kilometres per month of availability. This means that the reduction formula leaves the standby charge unchanged. While he is eligible for the alternative calculation of the operating cost benefit, it would produce a larger taxable benefit in this situation.

Ms. Misty Dorsey The taxable benefit to be included in employment income would be calculated as follows:

Standby charge [(2/3)(12)($620 - $100)]	$ 4,160
Operating cost benefit [(37,000)($0.27)]	9,990
Reimbursement [(12)($200)]	(2,400)
Total benefit	$ 11,750

The reduced standby charge and the elective option for the operating cost benefit are both not available since the employment use is less than half of the total use.

Mr. Saul Dorsey The taxable benefit that would be included in employment income would be calculated as follows:

Standby charge [(2/3)(8)($1,200)(1,700/13,336*)]	$ 816
Operating cost benefit—Lesser of:	
• [(1,700)($0.27)] = $459	
• [(1/2)($816)] = $408	408
Total benefit	$1,224

*[(8)(1,667)]

As more than 50% of the use was for employment purposes and the average personal use was less than 1,667 kilometres per month, there is a reduction in the normal standby charge. Saul can elect to use the alternative operating cost benefit since the employment use represents more than half of the kilometres driven.

SSP 3-4 Solution
Mr. Sam Stern
The taxable benefit for the president of the company would be calculated as follows:

Standby charge [(2%)($78,000)(8)]	$12,480
Operating cost benefit [(32,000)($0.27)]	8,640
Taxable benefit	$21,120

As Mr. Stern did not drive the car more than half of the total kilometres for employment purposes, no reduction in the standby charge is available. Since his employment use was not more than half the kilometres, he cannot use the alternative calculation for the operating cost benefit.

Ms. Sarah Blue

The taxable benefit for the marketing vice-president would be calculated as follows:

Standby charge [(2/3)(12)($900)(5,000/20,004)]	$1,800
Operating cost benefit—Lesser of:	
• [(5,000)($0.27)] = $1,350	
• [(1/2)($1,800)] = $900	900
Taxable benefit	$2,700

Since the employment use was more than half of the total kilometres driven, Ms. Blue is eligible for a reduced standby charge. In addition, the fact that it was driven more than half the time for employment purposes entitles her to use the election option to further reduce the overall automobile benefit.

Mr. John Stack

The taxable benefit for the finance vice-president would be calculated as follows:

Standby charge [(2%)($48,000)(12)(10,000/20,004)]	$5,759
Operating cost benefit—Lesser of:	
• [(10,000)($0.27)] = $2,700	
• [(1/2)($5,759)] = $2,880	2,700
Payment for use of company car	(7,000)
Taxable benefit	$ 1,459

Mr. Stack's employment-related driving was more than half of the total kilometres and, as a consequence, he can reduce his standby charge on the basis of actual personal kilometres. Mr. Stack could have calculated the operating cost benefit as one-half of the standby charge, but this would have resulted in a higher benefit.

Mr. Alex Decker

The taxable benefit for the industrial relations vice-president would be calculated as follows:

Standby charge [(2/3)(10)($500)(8,500/16,670)]	$1,700
Operating cost benefit—Lesser of:	
• [(8,500)($0.27)] = $2,295	
• [(1/2)($1,700)] = $850	850
Taxable benefit	$2,550

As Mr. Decker's employment use is more than half of the total kilometres, he can reduce his standby charge on the basis of actual personal kilometres. While the $10,000 deposit will affect the deductibility of the lease payments to the employer, it does not influence the calculation of the employment benefit to Mr. Decker. As the car was driven more than half the time for employment purposes, Mr. Decker can calculate the operating cost benefit as one-half of the standby charge, which results in a lower benefit.

Tax Planning

With respect to the tax planning of management compensation, two points can be made. First, the question of providing company cars as a method of compensation should be examined on a case-by-case basis.

In situations where an automobile is owned by the company and provided to an executive for a fairly long period of time, the employment benefit may exceed the actual value of the benefit. For example, over five years, the taxable benefit without regard for operating costs on Mr. Stern's Mercedes could total $93,600 [(2%)(60)($78,000)]. This is more than $15,000 in excess of the cost of the automobile.

With the limitations on the deductibility of CCA and leasing costs on passenger vehicles, the after-tax cost to the company of owning and leasing luxury cars can be very high. While a complete analysis of this issue will depend on a number of variables, it is possible that some of these executives would be better off receiving additional amounts of salary and billing the company for kilometres driven for employment purposes with their own cars.

The second point is that, except in situations where the car is kept for very short periods of time, the employee will be allocated a smaller employment benefit if the company were to lease the car rather than buy it. In general, monthly lease payments on a three-year lease will tend to be between 2% and 2.5% of the cost of the car.

As the leasing standby charge is based on two-thirds of the monthly lease payment, it is clear that the standby charge under a leasing arrangement will be less than the 2% per month that is determined when the company owns the car. However, for shorter lease terms, the lease payment will be a greater percentage of the car's cost, and this relationship may reverse.

Since the standby charges are either based on the purchase cost of an automobile or the leasing cost, steps taken to minimize both would result in reduced employment benefits.

This could be done by establishing high residual values on leases or by purchasing new automobiles through fleet discounts. In addition, it might be possible to reduce an employment benefit, such as the one determined for Mr. Stern, by selling his car to a leasing company with an immediate leaseback arrangement. Although large refundable deposits on leasing arrangements would reduce the lease payment and therefore the standby charge, there would be a tax cost to the employer, which is discussed further in Chapter 6.

SSP 3-5 Solution

If the employer continues to provide the car, John's only cash outflow will be the taxes assessed on the taxable benefit that results from having the car available. This outflow under the two cases would be calculated as follows:

	Case A $35,000 Cost	Case B $70,000 Cost
Standby charge		
[(2%)($35,000)(12)]	$ 8,400	
[(2%)($70,000)(12)]		$16,800
Operating cost benefit [(40,000 kilometres)($0.27)]	10,800	10,800
Total annual benefit	$19,200	$27,600
Number of years	2	2
Total benefit	$38,400	$55,200
John's marginal tax rate	48%	48%
Total taxes on taxable benefit	$18,432	$26,496

Note that, because John's use of the car is not primarily (more than half) for employment purposes, he cannot use the alternative one-half standby charge calculation of the operating cost benefit.

John Purchases the Automobile

If John purchases the car and pays his own operating costs, the total cash outflow in both cases would be calculated as follows:

Purchase price	$ 20,000
Estimated resale value	(12,000)
Operating costs [(2)(40,000 kilometres)($0.20)]	16,000
Total cash outflow	$24,000

Conclusion—Case A ($35,000)

On the basis of non-discounted cash flows, the best alternative would be to have John's employer continue to provide him with the car. If the cash flows were discounted, the results would be even more favourable for this alternative.

Conclusion—Case B ($70,000)

Since the original cost of the car was $70,000, on the basis of non-discounted cash flows, the best alternative would be to have John purchase the car since the taxable benefit is so high.

Although the requirements of the problem asks that only the cash flows be considered, we would note that the alternative of purchasing the car carries more uncertainty. Both the resale value and the actual operating costs are estimates. If there were a large variation from the estimate for either or both of these amounts, it could substantially affect the total cash outflow of the purchase alternative.

SSP 3-6 Solution

Alternative 1—Provide Additional Salary

In the absence of the interest-free loan, Ms. Monson would borrow $300,000 at 4.5%, requiring an annual interest payment of $13,500. In determining the amount of salary needed to carry this loan, consideration has to be given to the fact that additional salary will be taxed at 46%.

As the interest is not deductible, additional salary of $25,000 [$13,500 ÷ (1 - 0.46)] is needed.

Using this figure, the employer's after-tax cash flow required to provide sufficient additional salary for Ms. Monson to carry a conventional $300,000 mortgage would be calculated as follows:

Required salary [$13,500 ÷ (1 - 0.46)]	$25,000
Tax savings from deducting salary [($25,000)(27%)]	(6,750)
Employer's after-tax cash flow—Additional salary	$18,250

Alternative 2—Provide the Loan

If the loan is provided, Ms. Monson will have a taxable benefit of $6,000 [(2% - nil)($300,000)], resulting in additional taxes payable of $2,760 [(46%)($6,000)]. To make this situation comparable to the straight salary alternative, Elmwood Inc. will have to provide Ms. Monson with both the loan amount and sufficient additional salary to pay the $2,760 in taxes on the employment benefit that will be calculated.

The required amount would be $5,111 [$2,760 ÷ (1 - 0.46)].

Elmwood Inc.'s cash flow associated with the after-tax cost of providing the additional salary as well as the after-tax lost earnings on the $300,000 loan would be calculated as follows:

Required salary [$2,760 ÷ (1 - 0.46)]	$ 5,111
Tax savings from deducting salary [($5,111)(28%)]	(1,431)
After-tax cost of salary to cover taxes on benefit	$ 3,680
Employer's lost earnings [(7%)(1 - 0.28)($300,000)]	15,120
Employer's after-tax cash flow—Loan	$18,800

Conclusion

Given these results, on the basis of cash flows only, payment of additional salary appears to be the better alternative. However, the difference between the alternatives is relatively small. As Ms. Monson is a highly valued employee, there could be non-financial advantages to providing the loan, such as employee loyalty and the retention of her services, especially if the loan is for a longer period of time.

SSP 3-7 Solution

Case A

2019 In 2019, the year in which the options are issued, there would be no income tax consequences for Ms. Wu.

2020 The income tax consequences in 2020 would be as follows:

Fair market value at exercise [(12,000)($31)]	$372,000
Cost of shares [(12,000)($22)]	(264,000)
Employment income inclusion = Increase in **net income**	$108,000
Deduction under ITA 110(1)(d) [(1/2)($108,000)]	(54,000)
Increase in **taxable income**	$ 54,000

2021 When the shares are sold in 2021, the tax consequences would be as follows:

Proceeds of disposition [(12,000)($28)]	$336,000
Adjusted cost base [(12,000)($31)]	(372,000)
Capital loss	($ 36,000)
Inclusion rate	1/2
Allowable capital loss	($ 18,000)

Ms. Wu will only be able to deduct this loss in 2021 to the extent that she has taxable capital gains.

Case B

2019 There are no income tax consequences in 2019.

2020 There are no income tax consequences in 2020.

2021 In 2021, the employment income inclusion would be as follows:

Fair market value at exercise [(12,000)($31)]	$372,000
Cost of shares [(12,000)($22)]	(264,000)
Employment income inclusion = Increase in **net income**	$108,000
Deduction under ITA 110(1)(d) [(1/2)($108,000)]	(54,000)
Increase in **taxable income**	$ 54,000

In addition, there would be an allowable capital loss calculated as follows:

Proceeds of disposition [(12,000)($28)]	$336,000
Adjusted cost base [(12,000)($31)]	(372,000)
Capital loss	($ 36,000)
Inclusion rate	1/2
Allowable capital loss	($ 18,000)

Ms. Wu will only be able to deduct this loss in 2021 to the extent that she has taxable capital gains

SSP 3-8 Solution
Part A

There would be no income tax consequences resulting from the granting of the options in 2019.

Since the option price was below the fair market value at the time the shares were issued, there is no deduction available under ITA 110(1)(d) in the calculation of taxable income. As Patricia's employer is a public company, the exercise of the options in 2020 will result in the following addition to net income and taxable income:

Fair market value at exercise [(1,500)($50)]	$75,000
Option price [(1,500)($45)]	(67,500)
Employment income (increase in net income and taxable income)	$ 7,500

In 2021, when the shares are sold, there is the following addition **to** net income and taxable income:

Proceeds of disposition [(1,500)($55)]	$82,500
Adjusted cost base [(1,500)($50)]	(75,000)
Capital gain	$ 7,500
Inclusion rate	1/2
Taxable capital gain	$ 3,750

Part B

There would be no income tax consequences resulting from the granting of the options in 2019.

If the 2019 trading value for the shares had been $44, the option price would have been above fair market value and the ITA 110(1)(d) deduction would be available. On this basis, the 2020 results would be as follows:

Fair market value at exercise [(1,500)($50)]	$75,000
Option price [(1,500)($45)]	(67,500)
Employment income inclusion	
= Increase in net income	$ 7,500
ITA 110(1)(d) deduction [(1/2)($7,500)]	(3,750)
Increase in taxable income	$ 3,750

The results for 2021 would be unchanged from Part A.

Part C

If Patricia's employer had been a Canadian controlled private corporation, there would be no income tax consequences in either 2019 or 2020.

There is no deduction available under either ITA 110(1)(d) or ITA 110(1)(d.1) when the shares are sold. The option price was below the fair market value when the options were issued. Further, Patricia did not hold the shares for the two years required for the ITA 110(1)(d.1) deduction. When the shares are sold in 2021, there is the following addition to net income and taxable income:

Fair market value at exercise [(1,500)($50)]	$75,000
Option price [(1,500)($45)]	(67,500)
Employment income	7,500
Taxable capital gain [(1/2)(1,500)($55 - $50)]	3,750
Increase in net income and taxable income	$ 11,250

SSP 3-9 Solution

Salary from Maritime Trust [(6/12)($105,000)]		$ 52,500
Salary from Bolten [(6/12)($90,000)]		45,000
Total salaries		$ 97,500
Maritime Trust stock options (Note 1):		
Market price of shares [(5,000)($16)]	$80,000	
Option price [(5,000)($15)]	(75,000)	5,000
Bolten Financial Services stock options (Note 1)		Nil
Automobile benefit (Note 2):		
Standby charge [(2%)($40,000)(4)(6,668/6,668)]	$ 3,200	
Operating cost benefit—Lesser of:		
• [(10,000)($0.27)] = $2,700		
• [(1/2)($3,200)] = $1,600	1,600	4,800
Loan benefit (Note 3)		2,000
Employment income		$109,300

Notes:

1. As Bolten Financial Services is a Canadian controlled private corporation, the exercise of the option to purchase its common stock does not result in a taxable benefit at the time of exercise. Since Maritime Trust Inc. is a public company, the exercise of the option to purchase its common stock does result in a taxable benefit at the time of exercise. Mr. Jurgens has a stock option deduction equal to $2,500 [(1/2)($5,000)] under ITA 110(1) (d) created by the exercise of the Maritime Trust stock option. However, the stock option deduction would reduce taxable income and would not affect employment income. The Bolten stock option income inclusion of $2,000 [(1,000)($22 - $20)] and deduction of $1,000 [(1/2)($2,000)] are both deferred until the shares are sold.

2. As Mr. Jurgens' employment-related kilometres are more than half of the total kilometres, he can make use of the reduced standby charge formula. In this case, however, his personal usage exceeded the 6,668 [(4)(1,667)] kilometre maximum usage allowed by the reduction, so the reduction is nil. His employment usage is more than half of the total and, as a consequence, he can elect to calculate the operating cost benefit as one-half of the standby charge. Since this is less than the amount determined through the usual calculation, it would be the operating cost benefit.

3. The imputed interest on the interest-free loan must be included in employment income as a result of ITA 6(9), a benefit that is determined in ITA 80.4(1). The amount of the benefit is $2,000 [(2%)($200,000)(6/12)].

4. Interest and dividend income is not employment income and is therefore not included.

SSP 3-10 Solution

Ms. Kline's employment income for the year would be calculated as follows:

Gross salary	$73,500
Registered pension plan contributions	(2,400)
Automobile benefit (Note 1)	270
Contributions to group disability plan (Note 2)	Nil
Disability insurance benefit (Note 2)	1,450
Professional dues	(1,650)
Stock option benefit [(200)($70 - $50)] (Note 3)	4,000
Employment income	$75,170

Note 1 Based on the fact that Ms. Kline's employment-related usage is more than 50% of total usage, the automobile benefit is calculated as follows:

Standby charge [(2/3)(11)($700 - $50)(3,000/18,337*)]	$ 780
Operating cost benefit—Lesser of:	
• [(3,000)($0.27)] = $810	
• [(1/2)($780)] = $390	390
Total before payments	$1,170
Reimsement to employer for personal use [(3,000)($0.30)]	(900)
Taxable benefit	$ 270

*[(11)(1,667)]

As Ms. Kline's employment-related usage is more than half, she can elect to use one-half of the standby charge as the operating cost benefit.

Note 2 The contributions to the group disability plan are not deductible but can be applied against the $1,800 received under the plan during the year. Since the employer's contributions to this plan are not a taxable benefit, the $1,800 in benefits received must be included in employment income. However, this benefit can be reduced by the $350 ($175 + $175) in total contributions she has made in 2020 and 2021.

Note 3 Although Ms. Kline would qualify for the deduction of one-half of the stock option benefit under ITA 110(1)(d), it is a deduction from taxable income and would not affect the calculation of employment income.

SSP 3-11 Solution

An operating cost benefit is only determined if there is an employer-provided automobile and the employer pays for some part of the operating costs for the personal use. Since all operating costs are paid by Ms. Firth, there is no operating cost benefit.

In addition, the $7,200 motor vehicle allowance is required to be included in employment income (see Note 1). Given this, Ms. Firth can deduct a portion of her actual expenses based on the percentage of employment use for the vehicle. The deduction would be $5,728 [($6,200) (85,000 km ÷ 92,000 km)].

Ms. Firth's total entertainment, meal, and travel expenses that would be deductible under ITA 8(1)(f) are as follows:

Entertainment expenses [(1/2)($6,500)]	$ 3,250
Travel meals [(1/2)($1,300)]	650
Lodging	3,500
Automobile operating costs [($6,200)(85,000 ÷ 92,000)]	5,728
Total salesperson expenses	$13,128

As this total is less than her commission income of $14,000, all of these expenses can be deducted under ITA 8(1)(f).

Ms. Firth's employment income for the year would be calculated as follows:

Gross salary		$72,000
Commission income		14,000
Additions:		
Disability insurance receipts,		
less employee's premium ($2,000 - $250)	$ 1,750	
Car allowance (Note 1)	7,200	
Automobile benefit (Note 2)	2,471	
Term life insurance benefit [($1,350)(2/3)]	900	
Low-interest loan benefit [($400,000)(2%) - $3,000]	5,000	
Gift (Note 3)	Nil	
Stock option benefit [(1,000)($7- $5)] (Note 4)	2,000	
Tennis club membership (Note 5)	Nil	
Travel allowance	3,600	22,921
Deductions:		
Registered pension plan contributions (Note 6)	($ 3,200)	
Salesperson expenses (preceding calculation)	(13,128)	(16,328)
Employment income		$92,593

Note 1 Since the motor vehicle allowance is not solely based on kilometres, it is considered unreasonable and must be included in employment income under ITA 6(1)(b).

Note 2 The personal benefit on the company car would be calculated as follows:

Reduced standby charge [(2%)($58,000)(11)(7,000/18,337*)]	$4,871
Operating costs benefit	Nil
Total benefit	$4,871
Less: Payments withheld by employer	(2,400)
Taxable benefit	$2,471

*[(1,667)(11)]

Note 3 Employers can provide their employees with a non-cash gift with a value of less than $500 without creating a taxable benefit. The mini iPad costs less than $500.

Note 4 Although Ms. Firth would qualify for the deduction of one-half of the stock option benefit under ITA 110(1)(d), it is a deduction from taxable income and would not affect the calculation of employment income.

Note 5 The $2,500 membership to the Mountain Tennis Club paid by the company for Ms. Firth is not a taxable benefit since the primary beneficiary is the employer.

Note 6 Contributions made to a registered pension plan under the terms of the plan are deductible. The matching contributions made by the employer are not a taxable benefit.

Other Excluded Items Other items not included and the reason for their exclusion:

- Federal and provincial income taxes withheld are not an allowable expense under ITA 8(2).

SSP 3-12 Solution

Mr. Jones' employment income would be calculated as follows:

Salary			$25,800
Taxable benefit from fishing trip			2,450
Commission income			
Sales commissions		$47,700	
Deductions:			
Airline tickets	($2,350)		
Office supplies	(415)		
Client entertainment			
[(50%)($1,750)]	(875)		
CCA (Note 1)	(7,560)		
Operating costs (Note 2)	(5,040)	(16,240)	31,460
Employment income			$59,710

Note 1 The deductible capital cost allowance on the car would be calculated as follows:

Full capital cost allowance*	$10,800
Employment-related usage proportion (35,000/50,000)	70%
Deductible amount	$ 7,560

*While this subject is not covered until Chapter 5, the maximum capital cost allowance would be calculated as follows:

$$\$10,800 = [(\$24,000)(30\%)(150\%)]$$

Note 2 Operating costs are deductible as an employment expense to the extent of the proportion of employment use. The expense is therefore $5,040 [(70%)($7,200)].

Other Notes

- The laptop computer is a capital expenditure and is not an allowable expense. Since an employee cannot deduct CCA other than for an automobile, musical instrument, or aircraft, the purchase cost of the laptop computer would not have any effect on employment income.
- ITA 8(2) prevents claiming an amount as an employment expense unless the expense is specifically allowed. Blue Cross and life insurance premiums are not among the eligible employment expenses and therefore no expense can be claimed for either amount. The payment of premiums for Blue Cross coverage would, however, be eligible for the medical expenses tax credit, which will be discussed in Chapter 4.
- Discounts for employees on merchandise normally sold by an employer are not generally considered to be a taxable benefit.

SSP 3-13 Solution

Part A

As Mr. Worthy's income includes commissions, he has a choice of deducting his expenses under a combination of ITA 8(1)(f), (i), and (j) or, alternatively, under a combination of ITA 8(1)(h), (h.1), (i), and (j).

Deductions under ITA 8(1)(f) are limited to the amount of commissions earned. Alternatively, travelling costs and motor vehicle costs other than capital costs can be deducted under ITA 8(1)(h) and ITA 8(1)(h.1). Deductions under these provisions are not limited to commission income. As discussed in the text, he cannot use both ITA 8(1)(f) and the combination of ITA 8(1)(h) and (h.1).

As the deduction under ITA 8(1)(f) is limited by commission income, alternative calculations are required to determine the maximum deduction. In the calculations that follow, we have minimized the effect of the commission income limit by listing any item that can be deducted under either ITA 8(1)(f) or ITA 8(1)(i) or (j) under the ITA 8(1)(i) and (j) column.

For example, house utilities and maintenance could be deducted under either ITA 8(1)(f) or 8(1)(i). We have included them under ITA 8(1)(i) to maximize the deductions that are not limited by commission income.

The required calculations are as follows:

	ITA 8(1)(f) (limited to $11,000)	ITA 8(1) (h) and (h.1)	ITA 8(1) (i) and (j)
Work space in the home costs			
Monthly charge for residential phone line	-	-	-
Long distance telephone charges	-	-	$ 400
Cell phone airtime	-	-	800
Office supplies	-	-	295
House utilities	-	-	485
House maintenance	-	-	255
House insurance	$ 70	-	-
Property taxes	265	-	-
Capital cost allowance—House	-	-	-
Mortgage interest	-	-	-
Automobile costs:			
Operating costs [(80%)($2,700)]	2,160	2,160	-
Car interest [(80%)($2,300)]	-	-	1,840
Car CCA [(80%)($2,450)]	-	-	1,960
Entertainment			
Deductible portion [(50%)($2,550)]	1,275	-	-
Travel costs			
Hotels	2,850	$2,850	-
Deductible portion of meals [(50%)($900)]	450	450	-
Office furniture			
Interest	-	-	-
Capital cost allowance	-	-	-
Total	$7,070	$5,460	$6,035

Using the preceding calculations, Mr. Worthy's minimum employment income can be calculated as follows:

Salary		$65,000
Commissions	$11,000	
Expenses under ITA 8(1)(f)—Limited to commissions	(7,070)	3,930
Total		$68,930
Expenses under ITA 8(1)(i) and (j)		(6,035)
Employment income		$62,895

Expenses in excess of commission income cannot be deducted under ITA 8(1)(f). Since the total of the expenses is less than the commissions of $11,000, they can all be deducted. The deduction of automobile capital costs (CCA and financing costs) under ITA 8(1)(j) is permitted without regard to other provisions used

Notes:

1. The monthly telephone charge is not deductible. The long distance charges and cell phone airtime to clients can be deducted. The deduction for supplies can be deducted under ITA 8(1)(f) or (i). They have been deducted under ITA 8(1)(i), which is not limited by the commission income.

2. Only 50% of entertainment and meals when travelling is deductible.

3. ITA 8(1)(f) prohibits the deduction of capital expenditures unless they are permitted under ITA 8(1)(j) and ITA 8(1)(p). These latter paragraphs only permit interest or capital cost allowance to be deducted when it is related to automobiles, aircraft, or musical instruments. Therefore, the interest and the capital cost allowance on the house and the office furniture would not be deductible against employment income. This is a good illustration of the importance of distinguishing between employment income and business income. While these amounts cannot be deducted against employment income, they would be deductible against business income.

4. As the car is used 20% for personal purposes, only 80% of the operating costs, capital cost allowance, and interest costs will be deductible.

5. The deduction for home office expenses has been split between ITA 8(1)(i) and (f). Since the maintenance portion can be deducted under ITA 8(1)(i) by any employee, it is not limited by the commission income. The insurance and property tax components are limited as they can only be deducted under ITA 8(1)(f). A limitation, which is not illustrated in this problem, prevents the deduction of home office expenses from creating or increasing an employment loss. If any of these costs had not been deductible during the current year, they could be deducted against employment income in any subsequent year as long as a loss is not created or increased by their deduction in the subsequent year.

6. Mr. Worthy's employer must sign Form T2200 certifying that Mr. Worthy is required to incur travel expenses and maintain his own work space. Mr. Worthy must retain this signed form with his records to deduct car and home office expenses.

Part B
If Mr. Worthy deducted the ITA 8(1)(f) expenses, they would be limited to his commission income of $4,000. Alternatively, he can use the combination of ITA 8(1)(h) and (h.1). His minimum employment income under both alternatives can be calculated as follows:

	ITA 8(1)(f)	ITA 8(1)(h)(h.1)
Salary	$65,000	$65,000
Commissions	4,000	4,000
Expenses under ITA 8(1)(f)—Limited to commissions	(4,000)	N/A
Subtotal	$65,000	$69,000
Expenses under ITA 8(1)(h) and (h.1)	N/A	(5,460)
Expenses under ITA 8(1)(i) and (j)	(6,035)	(6,035)
Employment income	$58,965	$57,505

Using the combination of ITA 8(1)(h), (h.1), (i), and (j) produces a lower employment income figure. Note that when this approach is used, home office expenses are limited to utilities and maintenance. Further, there is no deduction for entertainment costs. However, this approach results in deductions totalling $1,460 ($5,460 - $4,000) more than the amount available using ITA 8(1)(f), (i), and (j) due to the effect of the commission income limit

SSP 3-14 Solution

Mitch Lesner's employment income would be calculated as follows;

Item 1 - Signing bonus (Note 1)	$10,000
Item 1 - Salary received (Note 1)	62,550
Item 1 - RPP contributions withheld	(1,200)
Item 1 - Other items (Note 1)	Nil
Item 2 - Bonus received (Note 2)	2,000
Item 3 - Counselling services (Note 3)	Nil
Item 4 - Group medical coverage (Note 4)	Nil
Item 5 - Employer contribution to RPP (Note 5)	Nil
Item 6 - Professional dues paid (Note 6)	(157)
Item 7 - Wedding gifts (Note 7)	Nil
Item 8 - Squash club membership (Note 8)	Nil
Item 9 - Housing loss reimbursement (Note 9)	1,300
Item 10 - Imputed interest on housing loan (Note 10)	170
Item 11 - Stock option benefit (Note 11)	1,280
Item 12 - Automobile benefit (Note 12)	741
Item 13 - Stationery and supplies	(129)
Item 13 - Long distance calls	(74)
Item 13 - Home office (Note 13)	(563)
Item 14 - Home office allowance (Note 14)	1,500
Employment income	$77,418

Note 1 Amounts received prior to, during, or after employment are required to be included in employment income when received. ITA 6(3)

Salary and other forms of remuneration such as bonuses are included in income when received regardless of when earned.

Income taxes, CPP, and EI withheld are not deductible. Note, however, that the CPP and EI are eligible for a non-refundable tax credit that will reduce tax payable, and part of the EI may be deductible as an "other expense," not an employment expense.

Note 2 Only the $2,000 amount of the bonus that was received in 2021 will be included in that year's employment income. The remaining $5,450 will not be included until it is received in 2022.

Note 3   Employer-provided mental health counselling services are not considered to be a taxable benefit.

Note 4   Group medical plans are generally referred to as private health services plans. Employer-paid premiums for such plans are not considered to be a taxable benefit.

Note 5   Employer contributions to RPPs are not considered to be a taxable benefit.

Note 6   The reimbursement of employee professional dues is considered an employment benefit if the employer is not the primary beneficiary. The employer is not the primary beneficiary where the professional dues are connected to the individual's employment. Such a connection is required to be entitled to claim the amount as an employment expense under ITA 8(1)(i). Therefore, if the professional dues are required as a condition of employment then the $628 reimbursement would not be a taxable benefit. The employment expense of ITA 8(1)(i), however, is only allowed to the extent not reimbursed. As a result there is no taxable benefit and an employment expense of $157 ($785 – $628).

Note 7   Non-cash gifts from employers that total less than $500 per year are not considered taxable benefits. The employer's share of the wedding gifts was $425.

Note 8   Fees for club memberships where the primary beneficiary is the employer are not considered to be a taxable benefit.

Note 9   Employer-reimbursed housing losses fall into two categories—regular housing losses and eligible housing losses. Eligible housing losses occur when there is an eligible relocation, which generally means a relocation or move the expenses of which would qualify for a moving expense deduction had they been paid by the employee. In this case the move is an eligible relocation, meaning that the reimbursement qualifies as an eligible housing loss. The employer reimbursed $17,600 [(80%)($22,000)]. The taxable portion of the loss reimbursement is $1,300 [(1/2)($17,600 - $15,000)].

Note 10   When an employee receives an interest-free or low-interest loan an imputed interest benefit is calculated. The interest benefit is $170 [(1%)($200,000)(31/365)]. Note that the alternative calculation, based on months outstanding, would result in a value of $167 [(1%)($200,000) ÷ 12]. It appears that this value would be accepted by the CRA. There is no reduction in that amount since Mitch is not required to repay any of the interest.

Note 11   Despite the fact that the option price was 20% below fair market value, the granting of the stock options does not create any income tax consequences. However, when he exercises the option by purchasing shares, there is a benefit as follows:

Market value at exercise date ($12,800 ÷ 80%)	$16,000
Option price	(12,800)
Value of benefit (200 shares)	$ 3,200
Per share benefit ($3,200 ÷ 200)	$16 per share

As Oxford Associates is a CCPC, this benefit can be deferred until the shares are sold. As 80 shares are sold, there will be a 2021 employment stock option benefit of $1,280 [(80) ($16)]. Note that, while this is not relevant to the determination of employment income, no deduction would be available under either ITA 110(1)(d) or 110(1)(d.1) as the option price was less than the fair market value at the time the option was granted.

In addition to the employment income inclusion, there is a taxable capital gain of $1,280 {[1/2] [$8,960 - (80/200)($16,000)]}. However, capital gains are not a component of employment income.

Note 12 The kilometres driven in the year total 19,252 (19,414 – 162), of which 5,198 are personal and 14,054 (19,252 - 5,198) are employment related. Since the employment-related driving accounts for more than half of the total kilometres (14,054 ÷ 19,252 = 73%), a reduced standby charge is available. The automobile benefit would be calculated as follows:

Standby charge [(2/3)(8)($430)(5,198 ÷ 13,336*)]	$ 894
Operating cost benefit—Lesser of:	
• [($0. 27)(5,198)] = $1,403	
• [(1/2)($894) = $447	447
Total benefit	$1,341
Reimbursement to employer [(8)($75)]	(600)
Net benefit	$ 741

*[(8)(1,667)]

Note 13 Based on floor space, the home office occupies 8.5% of the apartment [100 ÷ 1,176]. The work space in the home expenses that may be claimed for the period June 1 to November 30 are the following:

Rent paid [(6)($960)]	$5,760
Electricity paid [($870)(6 ÷ 8.5 months)]	614
Paint	253
Total eligible expenses	$6,627
Home office use	8.5%
Deductible expense	$ 563

Note 14 Allowances received are included in employment income unless the allowance is specifically excluded by ITA 6(1)(b). There is no exclusion for this allowance. The amount is $1,500 [(6)($250)].

SSP 3-15 Solution

There are two immediate restrictions. The first is ITA 8(4), which limits Lily's meal expenses to a period of time she was away from her employers' establishment where she ordinarily reported for work. The deductible meal expense is therefore reduced to $1,000. Second, this deductible amount is further reduced by 50% to $500 as a result of ITA 67.1.

Lily can claim $3,100 in rent and $4,000 of motor vehicle expenses under ITA 8(1)(j), whether she decides to claim other expenses under ITA 8(1)(f) or a combination of ITA 8(1)(h) and (h.1).

The ITA 8(1)(f) expenses would equal $7,100 [$3,900 + $2,000 + $700 + $500].

The ITA 8(1)(h) and (h.1) expenses would be the same except for the $3,900 of advertising and promotion (which are not deductible). This equals $3,200 [$7,100 – $3,900].

Lily now has a choice to make. She can either use ITA 8(1)(f), which is limited to her commissions of $2,200, or use ITA 8(1)(h) and (h.1) to claim $3,200. As a result she will claim $3,200.

Lily's maximum deductible employment expenses are as follows:

[Hotel $2,000 + ,otor vehicle operating costs $700 +	
deductible meals $500] ITA 8(1)(h) and (h.1)	$ 3,200
Rent and other work space deductible amounts ITA 8(1)(i)	3,100
CCA and interest on motor vehicle ITA 8(1)(j)	4,000
Total	$10,300

ITA 8(13) prevents an employee from using work space expenses to increase or to create an employment loss. Therefore the amount of work space expenses that are deductible are determined as the least of the following two amounts:

(a) The work space expenses of $3,100, or

(b) Lily's employment income after all expenses other than the work space expenses, which equals $1,200 [$8,700 (salary + commissions) − $300 (RPP ITA 8(1)(m)) − $3,200 − $4,000].

Conclusion: Lily can only deduct $1,200 of her home office expenses. The remaining $1,900 [$3,100 − $1,200] can be carried forward to be deducted in 2022 or subsequent years.

Lily's employment income would be nil, determined as follows:

Employment income		
Salary	$6,500	
Commissions	2,200	$8,700
Employment expenses		
RPP contribution	$ 300	
Hotel and vehicle operating costs	3,200	
CCA and interest	4,000	
Home office expenses	1,200	8,700
Employment income for 2021		$ Nil

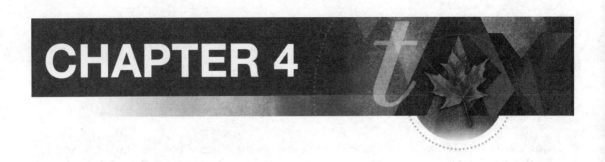

CHAPTER 4

Learning Objectives

Note Regarding Rates and Credits

A schedule of rates, brackets, credit amounts, and other data is available at the beginning of both volumes of this text (but not this Study Guide) and on MyLab. We expect you to refer to this information when calculating the credits covered in this chapter (i.e., you are not expected to memorize the rates, brackets, and credit bases).

After completing Chapter 4, you should be able to:

1. Calculate taxable income when an individual has basic deductions against net income (Paragraph [P hereafter] 4-1 to 4-9).
2. Calculate federal and provincial tax payable before the consideration of any tax credits (P 4-10 to 4-27).
3. Calculate the personal tax credits described in ITA 118(1), which include the:
   - spousal,
   - eligible dependant,
   - Canada caregiver for a child,
   - basic, and
   - Canada caregiver credits (P 4-28 to 4-73).
4. Calculate the age tax credit (P 4-74 to 4-75).
5. Calculate the pension income tax credit (P 4-76 to 4-80).
6. Calculate the Canada employment tax credit (P 4-81 to 4-83).
7. Calculate the adoption expenses tax credit (P 4-84 to 4-88).
8. Calculate the digital news subscriptions credit that is effective in 2020 (P 4-89 to 4-90).
9. Calculate the home accessibility tax credit (P 4-91 to 4-101).
10. Calculate the first-time home buyers' tax credit (P 4-102 to 4-104).
11. Calculate the volunteer firefighters and search and rescue workers tax credit (P 4-105 to 4-108).
12. Calculate the charitable donations tax credit when the donation is in the form of cash (P 4-109 to 4-120).
13. Calculate the medical expense tax credit (P 4-121 to 4-132).
14. Calculate the disability tax credit (P 4-133 to 4-142).
15. Calculate the tax credits related to tuition fees, examination fees, ancillary fees, and student loan interest (P 4-143 to 4-154).
16. Calculate the amount of education-related tax credits that can be carried forward or transferred to another individual (P 4-155 to 4-163).
17. Calculate the Employment Insurance and Canada Pension Plan credits (P 4-164 to 4-170).
18. List the types and amounts of tax credits that can be transferred to a spouse or common-law partner (P 4-171 to 4-173).
19. Calculate the political contributions tax credit (P 4-174 to 4-177).
20. Calculate the labour-sponsored venture capital corporation tax credit (P 4-178 to 4-182).

21. Explain the difference between refundable and non-refundable credits (P 4-183 to 4-185)
22. Explain the basic provisions of the refundable GST credit (P 4-186 to 4-190).
23. Calculate the refundable medical expense supplement (P 4-191 to 4-194).
24. Calculate the Canada Workers Benefit (P 4-195 to 4-199).
25. Calculate the refundable teacher and early childhood educator school supply tax credit (P 4-200 to 4-202).
26. Explain the Climate Action Incentive payments (refundable credit) (P 4-203 to 4-210).
27. Calculate the Canada training credit (P 4-211 to P 4-215).
28. Calculate the OAS and EI clawbacks (P 4-216 to 4-225).
29. Walk through the Comprehensive Example (P 4-226)
30. Complete a simple personal tax return using the ProFile T1 tax preparation software program.

How to Work through Chapter 4

Visit pearsonmylabandmastering.com to access MyLab Accounting for this text. Once there, you can access student resources such as Self-Study Problems, Practice Exams, Flashcards, updates and more.

We recommend the following approach in dealing with the material in this chapter:

Taxable Income of Individuals
- Read the beginning of the chapter to paragraph 4-9 (in the text).

Federal and Provincial Tax Payable before Credits
- Read paragraph 4-10 to 4-22.
- Do Exercise 4-1 and check the solution in this Study Guide.
- Read paragraph 4-23 to 4-27.

Federal Tax Credits—General Comments
- Read paragraph 4-28 to 4-29.

Basic Personal Amount (BPA) and Spousal Tax Credits
- Read paragraph 4-30 to 4-50.
- Do Exercise 4-2 and check the solution in this Study Guide.
- Do Self-Study Problem 4-1, which is available on MyLab, and check the solution in this Study Guide.

Eligible Dependant, Canada Caregiver for Child and Caregiver Tax Credits
- Read paragraph 4-51 to 4-71.
- Do Exercises 4-3 to 4-5 and check the solutions in this Study Guide.
- Read paragraph 4-72 to 4-73.
- Do Exercise 4-6 and check the solution in this Study Guide.

Age, Pension, Canada Employment, and Adoption Expenses Tax Credits
- Read paragraph 4-74 to 4-75.
- Do Exercise 4-7 and check the solution in this Study Guide.
- Read paragraph 4-76 to 4-88
- Do Exercise 4-8 and check the solution in this Study Guide.

Digital News Subscriptions Credit
- Read paragraph 4-89 to 4-90.

Home Accessibility Tax Credit
- Read paragraph 4-91 to 4-101.
- Do Exercise 4-9 and check the solution in this Study Guide.

First-Time Home Buyers' and Volunteer Firefighters and Search and Rescue Workers Tax Credits
- Read paragraph 4-102 to 4-108

Charitable Donations Credit
- Read paragraph 4-109 to 4-116.
- Do Exercise 4-10 and check the solution in this Study Guide.
- Read paragraph 4-117 to 4-120.
- Do Exercise 4-11 and check the solution in this Study Guide.

Medical Expense Credit
- Read paragraph 4-121 to 4-132.
- Do Exercise 4-12 and check the solution in this Study Guide.

Disability Credit
- Read paragraph 4-133 to 4-139.
- Do Exercise 4-13 and check the solution in this Study Guide.
- Read paragraph 4-140 to 4-142.

Education-Related Credits Including Carry Forwards and Transfers
- Read paragraph 4-143 to 4-154.
- Do Exercise 4-14 and check the solution in this Study Guide.
- Read paragraph 4-155 to 4-163.
- Do Exercise 4-15 and check the solution in this Study Guide.

Employment Insurance And Canada Pension Plan Tax Credits
- Read paragraph 4-164 to 4-170.

Credit Transfers to a Spouse or Common-Law Partner
- Read paragraph 4-171 to 4-173.
- Do Exercise 4-16 and check the solution in this Study Guide.
- Do Self-Study Problems 4-2 and 4-3 and check the solutions in this Study Guide.

Political Contributions Credit
- Read paragraph 4-174 to 4-177.
- Do Exercise 4-17 and check the solution in this Study Guide.

Labour-Sponsored Venture Capital Corporation (LSVCC) Credit
- Read paragraph 4-178 to 4-182.
- Do Self-Study Problems 4-4 and 4-5 and check the solutions in this Study Guide.

Refundable Credits—GST and Refundable Medical Expense Supplement
- Read paragraph 4-183 to 4-194.
- Do Exercise 4-18 and check the solution in this Study Guide.

Refundable Credits—Canada Workers Benefit and Teacher School Supply
- Read paragraph 4-195 to 4-202.

Refundable Credits—Climate Action Incentive Payments
- Read paragraph 4-203 to 4-210.

Refundable Credits—Canada Training Credit
- Read paragraph 4-211 to 4-215.

EI and OAS Repayment (Clawback)
- Read paragraph 4-216 to 4-225.
- Do Exercise 4-19 and check the solution in this Study Guide.

Comprehensive Example
- Read paragraph 4-226.
- Do Self-Study Problems 4-6 to 4-8 and check the solutions in this Study Guide.

Sample Personal Tax Return for Chapter 4
- Read the Sample Personal Tax Return for Chapter 4 found in this Study Guide. The complete tax returns are available on MyLab in two formats: a T1 ProFile return file and a .PDF file.

Tax Software Self-Study Problem
- Read the Suggestions for Working with ProFile Software found in this Study Guide.
- Do Tax Software Self-Study Problem—Chapter 4 using the ProFile T1 software. The Self-Study Problem is found in this Study Guide. The complete tax return is available on MyLab.

To Complete This Chapter
- Visit MyLab Accounting for more practice problem material, and test yourself with the glossary flashcards.
- Review the Key Terms at the end of the chapter, and consult the glossary for definitions.
- Ensure you have achieved the Chapter 4 Learning Objectives listed in this Study Guide.
- As a review, view the PowerPoint presentations available on MyLab.

Practice Examination
- Available on MyLab, write the Practice Examination for this chapter, and mark it using the solutions provided.

Sample Tax Return for Chapter 4

The following example contains a T1 individual income tax return completed using the ProFile T1 Personal Income Tax Program for 2020 tax returns from Intuit Canada. As software for 2021 is not yet available, this example contains 2020 rates and credits.

The updated 2021 filing version of the ProFile software will be available in January 2022. Non-filing versions will be available prior to that date, but include a number of 2021 draft forms that have not yet been updated. On installation, the program defaults to check for updates, so non-filing versions may be installed automatically. In January 2022, after the first 2021 filing version is released, the updated 2021 version of this sample return will be available on MyLab at:

http://www.pearsonmylabandmastering.com

This example is expanded in Chapter 11 to contain other components of taxable income and tax payable. In the following example, the relevant T1 schedule or ProFile form name is provided in square brackets to make it easier for users to find where the information is input.

A Word on the CRA Redesign of the T1 Individual Income Tax Return for 2019

The CRA has redesigned the T1 individual income tax return beginning with the 2019 year. The new return has doubled in size, increasing to eight pages from four. The most significant changes are (1) the addition of new questions concerning whether any income received is exempt under the *Indian Act*; (2) the change of line numbers from 3 or 4 digits to 5—for example, net income was previously line 236 and is now line 23600; and (3) the elimination of Schedule 1 (tax calculations including tax credits) and the related worksheet, which are now incorporated into the income tax return. The CRA further explains in the introductory pages to the 2019 Federal Income Tax and Benefit Guide that additional changes include the increased use of plain language, increasing the font size, adding white space, and updating worksheets to simplify calculations.

Sample Files on MyLab
To View the Tax Return Files
The complete sample tax returns are available on MyLab in two versions: a T1 ProFile return file and a .PDF file.

To view the ProFile return files (files with a .20T extension), you must have the ProFile program installed. For information on how to obtain the program for free, see MyLab.

Tips to Increase the Benefits from Viewing the ProFile Files

When viewing the sample return ProFile file, we suggest the following:

- Press <F1> on any ProFile form or field to display related information in the help system. In ProFile dialogue boxes, click the [?] symbol in the top right corner, then click any element for help on that item.
- By pressing <F4> you will open the Form Explorer. In the categories of forms appearing in the shaded box on the left, if you choose "A. Used" near the bottom of the column, all the forms that have calculations for the return will be shown. You can then double click on the form itself to view it.
- Right clicking on a number in a field shows a variety of options, including the form or schedule where the amount originated from.
- Clicking on "Show Auditor" under the "Audit" list will display any warnings or potential errors.

For students who would like more assistance in using the software, we have provided "Suggestions for Working with ProFile Software" in this Study Guide following this example.

Sample T1 Tax Return Data

DISCLAIMER: All characters appearing in this example are fictitious. Any resemblance to real persons, living or dead, is purely coincidental.

George Pilot (SIN 527-000-145) is a married, semi-retired air force pilot living in Banff, Alberta. His wife, Deborah (SIN 130-692-544), was mauled by a grizzly bear while hiking three years ago. The attack left her blind and limited her mobility. [Schedule 2 - Yes to disability amount]

They have been your clients for many years. George was born on February 24, 1969, and Deborah was born on April 10, 1973. They are both Canadian residents and citizens.

After some discussion with George and Deborah, you confirm that they have never owned any foreign property. They both authorize the CRA to provide information to Elections Canada and authorize you to e-file their returns. They are currently living at 69 BBB Street in Banff, Alberta, T9Z 0C0. Their home phone number is (403) 111-1111.

George and Deborah have three children who are all in good health:

- Bryan (SIN 527-000-947) was born on March 12, 2013, and had no income during the year.
- Janice (SIN 527-000-269) was born on June 6, 2007, and is in high school. She had income from babysitting totalling $400 during 2020.
- Willa (SIN 527-000-228) was born on January 22, 2001, and is attending university in Edmonton. Willa had net income of $3,300 during 2020.

George has a passion for flying and was hired in February to fly fire bombers from June 1 to September 30 for the provincial forest service fire control squad located in Banff.

George informs you that on February 12, 2020, he received $2 million from his mother's estate. Using some of these funds, George bought a house in Banff. The remainder of the funds were invested with his stockbroker, $$$$ Inc. In this Chapter 4 version of the example, assume there is no investment income from these funds.

Deborah had no income during the year. [Info - Spousal information - Yes to the question "Is spouse's net income zero?"]

George brings you the following receipts and documents:

1. A T4 (included in this example).

2. A T2202 "Tuition and Enrollment Certificate" for himself from Athabasca University. It showed he was a part-time student for six months and paid $591 in tuition for 2020. [T2202]

3. The 2019 notice of assessment indicates that George's Canada training credit limit for 2020 is $250. See Schedule 11.

4. Two charitable donation receipts. One in George's name for $1,000 from the Canadian Wildlife Federation dated April 10, 2020. A second receipt in Deborah's name for $100 from the Canadian National Institute for the Blind (CNIB) dated December 3, 2020. [Donations]

5. A statement from the Banff Dental Clinic that George paid a total of $1,650 during 2020. This consisted of $850 for himself on November 24, and $200 each for Deborah, Bryan, Willa, and Janice on December 15. [Medical]

6. An invoice from the CNIB in Deborah's name for $375 dated December 26, 2020, for computer peripherals designed exclusively for a person who is blind to use a computer. She had obtained a prescription from her doctor specifying her need for this equipment. [Medical]

7. George spent $14,700 during 2020 on various permanent modifications to the house. His goal for these changes was to allow Deborah to be more mobile inside and outside the house (e.g., outside ramps and railings in the halls and stairways) and to reduce the risk of harm to her (a walk-in bathtub). George has detailed invoices for the renovations. Since Deborah's mobility impairment is not severe, these expenditures do not qualify as allowable medical expenses. [Medical Expense form for line 33099]

8. An agreement of purchase and sale for a house at 69 BBB St. in Banff. The purchase price was $800,000 and the invoice for legal fees totalled $1,200. The deal closed March 31, 2020, and George paid the purchase price of the house in cash. George and his family had been living in a rented townhouse for the last five years. Prior to that George had owned a house, but it went to his ex-wife in the divorce settlement. Deborah has never owned a principal residence. [Profile Other Credits form for line 31270 the Home Buyers' Credit.]

9. An instalment statement for 2020 that showed that George had paid the CRA instalments of $1,500 on September 14 and December 14 ($3,000 in total). These were the instalments requested by the CRA for the year due to his self-employed income in the previous year. [Profile Other Credits Form for line 47600 Tax paid by instalments]

Sample T1 Tax Return Notes
General Notes

- Inheritances are not taxable.

- Due to his low net income, George is eligible for the refundable medical expense supplement and the Canada Workers Benefit.

- Although George could consider carrying forward his medical expenses because his non-refundable tax credits are greater than his tax payable, if he did so he would not receive the refundable medical expense supplement.

- Since Willa is over 17 years of age, her medical expenses are reduced by 3% of her net income.

- Due to his nil tax payable, George's charitable donation credit and his tuition credit are both carried forward. George is also entitled to the refundable Canada training credit of $250 (see line 45350), which reduces his tuition carryover to $341 [$591 - $250].

- As a resident of Alberta George qualifies for the refundable Climate Action Incentive payment for 2020. This refundable credit is available to individuals who are residents of Ontario, Manitoba, Saskatchewan, and Alberta in 2020. The maximum credit for a family of four in Alberta is $981 (see line 45110).

- George's 2020 CPP contribution of $813.75 is calculated as 5.25% of insurable earnings, which are equal to his employment income of $19,000 minus a basic exemption of $3,500. There are two components to the CPP contribution rate of 5.25%. The first is a <u>basic</u> contribution rate of 4.95% and the second an additional amount of 0.03% referred to as an <u>enhancement</u>. The enhancement represents an effort by the federal government to provide increased CPP retirement pension benefits. The basic 4.95% or $767.25 [(0.0495)($19,000 - $3,500)] is treated as a non-refundable tax credit and the enhanced portion of $46.50 {(0.0525 - 0.0495)($19,000 - $3,500)] is allowed as a deduction (new line 22215).

- We have carried forward the initial data from 2019, therefore the "Carryforward Summary" for the tuition and education amounts of $341 and the increase in donations of $1,100 from 2019 to 2020 are the only accurate carryforward amounts for 2020.

Item Specific Notes

- (Item 4) For couples, the CRA's administrative practices permit either spouse to claim some or all of the donations made by the couple. This is not relevant in this version as the donations are carried forward. Complete Schedule 9.
- (Item 6) Both ITA 118.2 and Income Tax Folio S1-F1-C1 clearly state that medical expenses can only be deducted by the individual who paid for them. However, the CRA provides an administrative concession that allows either spouse or common-law partner to claim the medical expense tax credit, without regard to who actually paid for the expenses. As a result, George is claiming the amount Deborah paid for the computer peripherals.
- (Item 7) George's receipts for the expenses eligible for the home accessibility credit total more than the $10,000 maximum for the year on "the worksheet for the return." As a result the maximum credit of $1,500 [(15%)($10,000)] is available. However, since George's non-refundable tax credits already exceed his tax payable, he cannot take advantage of this credit and it cannot be carried forward.
- (Item 8) The home buyers' tax credit of $750 [(15%)($5,000)] is available since George had been living in a rented townhouse for five years and neither he nor Deborah had another principal residence. However, since George's non-refundable tax credits already exceed his tax payable, he cannot take advantage of this credit either and it cannot be carried forward.

Tax Planning Points

- Willa should file a return in order to receive the GST credit and transfer unused tuition fees, report income that would increase future RRSP deductions, report income that will increase the Canada training credit limit, and to help her keep track of her tuition credit carry forward.
- (Item 9) George has paid instalments based on the CRA's instalment reminders. Given the amount of his refund, they were unnecessary. George should review his estimated net tax owing periodically in the future to determine whether instalments should be paid.

Completed Tax Returns
The complete sample tax returns are available on MyLab in two versions: a T1 ProFile return file and a .PDF file.

Suggestions for Working with ProFile Software

Before You Start
To get the maximum benefit from using the ProFile tax software program, we strongly advise that you do the tutorial "Getting Started" included within the program under the Training tab. The data in the sample tax returns can be used in the tutorial. Also on the Training tab is access to "Other Training Options," which include online training and many how-to videos.

Creating a New T1 Return
To provide some guidance on how to use ProFile to create a simple new personal tax return, we suggest the following approach:

1. Start the ProFile software. Open a new file. Ensure that you have chosen the new file in the correct software (T1) and year (2020 or 2021 if the updated data are available).

2. By default, ProFile will open on the form "Info." Fill in the highlighted cells and answer all questions that are applicable. If you do not fill in the highlighted areas, ProFile will generate an audit message. At a minimum, you will need the following information:

   - Taxpayer's social insurance number (SIN)
   - Taxpayer's first and last name
   - Address, city, province, and postal code
   - Telephone number
   - Taxpayer's birth date

   If applicable, you will also need to enter any relevant information for the spouse on the "Info" form. At a minimum, the following information will be necessary:

   - Spouse's social insurance number (SIN)
   - Spouse's first and last name
   - Address, city, province, and postal code
   - Telephone number
   - Spouse's birth date

3. Using the Form Explorer (<F4>), go to the Dependant form and enter all relevant information about any dependants. At a minimum, the following information will be necessary:

   - Dependant's social insurance bumber (SIN) if there is one
   - Dependant's first and last name
   - Dependant's relationship to the taxpayer
   - Dependant's birth date
   - Dependant's net income
   - Address, city, province, and postal code

   Note that if there are child care expenses, the information will flow here from Form T778. If the dependant has tuition fee amounts, the tuition fee information should be entered on the Dependant form.

4. Using the Form Explorer (<F4>), open the relevant information slip form. Enter all relevant information in the appropriate forms. Some common information slip forms are:

   - T3—Statement of Trust Income
   - T4—Statement of Remuneration Paid
   - T5—Statement of Investment Income
   - T2202—Tuition Slips
   - T4AOAS—Statement of Old Age Security

5. Enter any other relevant income information on the appropriate forms. These forms may include the following:

   - S3Details—Capital Gains Entry
     (this form, not Schedule 3, must be used to input details on capital dispositions)
   - T2125—Statement of Business or Professional Activities
   - T2125Asset—T2125 Asset Details
   - T2125CCA—T2125 CCA Details
   - T776—Statement of Real Estate Rentals
   - T776Asset—T776 Asset Details
   - T776CCA—T776 CCA Details

6. Enter any relevant deduction information on the appropriate forms. These forms may include the following:

   - RRSP—RRSP Deduction
   - T777—Statement of Employment Expenses (Use the jump link to T777Details in the upper right-hand corner of the form if applicable)
   - T778—Child Care Expense Deduction

- Support—Support Payments
- T777 Auto—Motor Vehicle Expenses
- Investment income such as interest and taxable dividends was formerly included on Schedule 4, which no longer exists. In the 2020 income tax package you will note that there are no Schedules 1 (previously federal tax), 4 (investment income), 10 (previously refundable medical supplement), and 12 (previously home accessibility expense). The information is either no longer relevant or is included elsewhere, such as the deduction of carrying charges, which is now included on the "worksheet for the return."
- LossNetCap—Net Capital Losses (carry forward information)
- LossNonCap—Non-Capital Losses (carry forward information)

7. Enter any relevant tax credit information on the appropriate forms. These forms may include the following:

- Donations—Donations and Gifts Schedule 9
- Medical—Medical Expenses

8. Enter any remaining relevant information in the appropriate schedule. These schedules may include the following:

- S2—Federal Amounts Transferred from Your Spouse or Common-Law Partner (primarily used if spouse or common-law partner is not filing a tax return)
- T1032—Joint Election to Split Pension Income

9. Use the function "Show Auditor" under the "Audit" list to check for warnings or potential errors.

Tips for Using ProFile Software

- Press the <F5> key or choose Spouse from the Form menu to display the return of the spouse.

- If you cannot determine where a specific slip or other information should be input, one way to search for the correct form is to open the Form Explorer (<F4>) and choose the "Key" mode icon in the top right corner of the menu. If you type a key word into the line above the listing of key words, the appropriate form may be found.

- Press the <F4> key to view the Form Explorer. Choose the form "Summary" to see the tax data of both spouses on the same one page summary. (The second column will be blank for a single taxpayer.)

- If you want to print only the form you have on the screen, use the print icon identified with 1 in the tool bar. The other print icon opens the print selection screen for printing complete returns. If you want to print just one copy of the return, deselect the print sets you don't want on the print selection screen. Before you print the return, review the forms that have been selected in the print set to ensure that you will not be printing forms you do not require. If it is a coupled return, the print settings for the spouse should be reviewed before clicking on Print as both returns will be printed.

- Review marks can be used to flag information that should be reviewed. The cell with the review mark will be listed when the Show Auditor feature is turned on.

- A memo and/or a tape can be attached to a cell to provide backup information.

- If you are having problems with a specific issue, go to the Training tab, "Other Training Options," to access the online how-to videos, which may help solve your problems.

Tax Software Self-Study Problem—Chapter 4

Note The following problem contains 2020 (not 2021) information as software for 2021 is not yet available. If you have an updated 2021 version of ProFile installed on your computer, ensure that when you begin you open a file for 2020, not 2021, as these data are for 2020. Shortly after the first filing version of the 2021 Intuit ProFile software is available in January 2022, the updated 2021 version of this problem will be available on MyLab shortly thereafter at:

http://www.pearsonmylabandmastering.com

This Tax Software SSP is expanded in Chapter 11 to contain other components of taxable income and tax payable.

DISCLAIMER: All characters appearing in this problem are fictitious. Any resemblance to real persons, living or dead, is purely coincidental.

Ms. Eleanor Victoria's husband died two years ago. After her husband died, she moved from her house in Prince George, B.C., to a rented house in Victoria, B.C.

Ms. Victoria's widowed mother, Marjorie Vancouver, lives with Ms. Victoria and takes care of the house, Ms. Victoria's younger daughter, Amy, and all of the household cooking. In addition to OAS benefits, Marjorie has a very small income from her deceased husband's life insurance policy. She has never filed an income tax return and she is not infirm.

Diane Victoria, Eleanor's older daughter, is studying psychology at McGill University in Montreal. Her field is addiction research with a special emphasis on gambling. She does volunteer work at a gambling addiction treatment centre in Montreal in the summers. As Eleanor has paid for her tuition and living costs, Diane has agreed that the maximum tuition amount should be transferred to her mother.

Diane has decided not to file a tax return this year as she knows she does not owe any taxes. Her income was earned driving for a client of the addiction treatment centre who had lost his licence after being charged with impaired driving.

Information concerning Ms. Victoria for 2020 is provided on the following pages.

Required: With the objective of minimizing Ms. Victoria's tax payable, prepare the 2020 income tax return of Eleanor Victoria using the ProFile tax software program. List any assumptions you have made and any notes and tax planning issues you feel should be discussed with Ms. Victoria. Ignore GST implications in your solution by assuming that Ms. Victoria does not qualify for the GST/HST rebate.

Personal Information	
Title	Ms.
First Name	Eleanor
Last Name	Victoria
SIN	527-000-087
Date of birth (Y/M/D)	1973-05-15
Marital Status	Widowed
Canadian Citizen?	Yes
Provide Information to Elections Canada?	Yes
Own Foreign Property of More than $100,000 Canadian?	No

Taxpayer's Address
111 VVV Street Victoria, B.C. V4H 3W4
Phone number (250) 111-1111

Dependants	Child 1	Child 2	Mother
First Name	Diane	Amy	Marjorie
Last Name	Victoria	Victoria	Vancouver
SIN	527-000-293	None	527-000-483
Date of birth (Y/M/D)	2000-05-14	2008-10-11	1948-05-21
Net income	$2,300	Nil	$8,000

T4	Box	Amount
Issuer—1750 Canada Inc.		
Employment income	14	60,201.80
Employee's CPP contributions	16	2,898.00
Employee's EI premiums	18	856.36
RPP contributions	20	2,406.16
Pension adjustment	52	7,829.00
Income tax deducted	22	6,408.00
Employment commissions	42	0
Union dues	44	748.59
Charitable donations	46	175.00

Eleanor has a signed T2200 from her employer specifying her work requires her to have an office in the home. She meets the conditions required to deduct work space in the home expenses. Of the 1,800 square feet in the house, her office, waiting area and storage space totals 310 square feet. She doesn't qualify for the GST rebate.

During 2019 she paid the following:

Rent for the year (no GST charged)	$30,000
Utilities (hydro and gas) for the year	2,500
Cleaning services (no GST charged)	1,200
Insurance for household effects (no GST charged)	400
Car insurance (no GST charged)	700

Eleanor and her family had the following medical expenses, all of which Eleanor paid for:

Patient	(Y/M/D)	Medical Expenses	Description	Amount
Eleanor	2020-08-15	Grace Hospital	Ambulance charge	392
Eleanor	2020-08-18	Paramed Home Health	Nursing care	1,350
Marjorie	2020-05-20	Dr. Zhang (Optometrist)	Contact lenses	110
Marjorie	2020-07-06	Pharmacy	Prescription	75
Diane	2020-09-01	Dr. Glassman	Physiotherapist	100
Amy	2020-05-11	Walk Right Foot Clinic	Orthotics	450
Amy	2020-01-23	Dr. Tamo	Dental Fees	1,120

T2202 - (Diane)	Box	Amount
Tuition fees—for Diane Victoria (daughter)	A	7,000
Number of months in school—part time	B	2
Number of months in school—full time	C	8

Donor	Charitable Donation Receipts	Am't
Eleanor	Heart and Stroke Foundation	375
Eleanor	Terry Fox Foundation	50
Diane	Addiction Research Council of Canada	100

Exercise Solutions

Exercise 4-1 Solution

The required tax payable would be calculated as follows:

Tax payable on first $49,020 at 20.05% (15.00% + 5.05%)	$ 9,829
Tax payable on next $7,680 ($56,700 - $49,020)	
at 29.65% (20.5% + 9.15%)	2,277
Total tax payable before credits	$ 12,106

Her average rate of tax is 21.35% ($12,106 ÷ $56,700).

Exercise 4-2 Solution

Assuming Johan's wife does not have a mental or physical infirmity, the required amount would be calculated as follows:

Basic personal amount (Johan)	$13,808
Spousal amount ($13,808 - $2,600)	11,208
Credit base	$ 25,016
Rate	15%
Personal tax credits—No infirmity	$ 3,752

If there were a mental or physical infirmity, the amount would be calculated as follows:

Basic personal amount (Johan)	$13,808
Spousal amount ($13,808 + $2,295 - $2,600)	13,503
Credit base	$ 27,311
Rate	15%
Personal tax credits—With infirmity	$ 4,097

Exercise 4-3 Solution

As her father is not infirm, Joan would not be entitled to a Canada caregiver credit for him. She is entitled to a Canada caregiver credit for her mother, who is infirm. The credit would be:

$$[15\%][\$7,348 - (\$21,400 - \$17,256)] = \$481$$

Exercise 4-4 Solution

Marcia will be entitled to the spousal tax credit, including the additional amount for an infirm spouse. The entitlement to claim the spousal credit for the spouse prevents a claim for the Canada caregiver credit (ITA 118(4)(c). A Canada caregiver credit can be claimed for the adult son since Marcia is not entitled to an eligible dependant claim for him. The total credits would be calculated as follows:

Spousal credit including infirm amount	
($13,808 + $2,295 - $5,600)	$ 10,503
Canada caregiver credit ($7,348 - nil)	7,348
Total base	$ 17,851
Rate	15%
Marcia's tax credits related to spouse and son	$ 2,678

Exercise 4-5 Solution

Darcy would claim the Canada caregiver amount for his child under ITA 118(1)(b.1). He would also claim the eligible dependant credit for Janice. Because he claims the Canada caregiver amount for a child, he cannot claim the additional amount for an infirm eligible dependant since it is separately covered under ITA 118(1)(b.1). He would also not be eligible to claim the Canada caregiver credit under ITA 118(1)(d) because it does not apply to a child under 18 years of age. His total credits would be as follows:

$$[(15\%)(\$2,295) + (15\%)(\$13,808 + Nil)] = \$2,415$$

Exercise 4-6 Solution

The base for Sandy's eligible dependant credit for her mother would be nil ($13,808 + $2,295 - $18,000), resulting in an eligible dependant tax credit of nil. Her calculation of the Canada caregiver amount would have resulted in a tax credit base of $6,604 [$7,348 - ($18,000 - $17,256)] had it been available (ITA 118(4)(c)). As the eligible dependant tax credit was nil, the additional amount is $6,604 ($6,604 - nil), resulting in a credit of $991 [(15%)($6,604)].

Exercise 4-7 Solution

The tax credit base of Mr. Smythe's age credit would be $5,822 [$7,713 - (15%)($51,500 - $38,893)].

The amount of the age credit that can be applied against his gross federal tax payable is $873 [(15%)($5,822)].

Exercise 4-8 Solution

The adoption expenses tax credit would be calculated as follows:

Cost of first foreign trip	$ 4,250
Cost of second foreign trip	6,420
Foreign orphanage fee	1,600
Canadian adoption agency fee	3,200
Legal fees	2,700
Medical costs (qualify for medical expense credit)	Nil
Total eligible expenses	$18,170

Since the $5,000 employer reimbursement is a taxable benefit and included in employment income, it does not reduce the total eligible adoption expenses.

The adoption period begins at the time an application is made for registration with an adoption agency licensed by a provincial government. This means that all of the expenses listed in the preceding table would be eligible expenses made during the adoption period. However, for 2021, there is an overall limit of $16,729 and the maximum credit that can be claimed is $2,509 [(15%)($16,729)].

Exercise 4-9 Solution

The snow removal contract would not be a qualifying expenditure. The base for the home accessibility tax credit would be limited to the lesser of $10,000 and the qualifying expenditures of $8,500.

This will result in a tax credit base of $8,500 and an amount of $1,275 [(15%)($8,500)] that will be applied to reduce gross taxes payable.

Either spouse can claim the credit, and it will be worth the same amount to either spouse. Since it is non-refundable, whoever claims the credit should have at least $1,275 in gross federal tax payable. Alternatively, the $8,500 base amount can be split between the two spouses at their discretion.

Exercise 4-10 Solution

With net income of $350,000, the maximum base for Mr. Hoffman's credit is $262,500 [(75%)($350,000)]. As his eligible charitable donations are less than this, he can use the full amount as the base for his credit. Given this, the calculation of the credit is as follows:

$$[(15\%)(A)] + [(33\%)(B)] + [(29\%)(C)], \text{ where}$$

A = $200
B = The lesser of:
  • $225,000 - $200 = $224,800
  • $325,000 - $216,511 = $108,489 (note that taxable income is used here)
C = $116,311 [$225,000 - ($200 + $108,489)]

The charitable donation credit would be equal to $69,561, calculated as [(15%)($200)] + [(33%)($108,489)] + [(29%)($116,311)].

Exercise 4-11 Solution

With net income of $350,000, the maximum base for Ms. Hoffman's credit is $262,500 [(75%)($350,000)]. As her donation credit carry forward is less than this, she can use the full amount as the base for her credit. Given this, the calculation of the credit is as follows:

$$[(15\%)(A)] + [(33\%)(B)] + [(29\%)(C)], \text{ where}$$

A = $200
B = The lesser of:
  • $225,000 - $200 = $224,800
  • $250,000 - $216,511 = $33,489 (note that taxable income is used here)
C = $191,311 [$225,000 - ($200 + $33,489)]

The charitable donation credit would be equal to $66,561, calculated as [(15%)($200)] + [(33%)($33,489)] + [(29%)($191,311)]. If she had any unused portions of her 2021 donation, the last year it would be available to be claimed would be 2025.

Exercise 4-12 Solution

Amount B	Qualifying expenses ($4,330 + $4,600)		$ 8,930
Amount C	Lesser of:		
	• [(3%)($150,000)] = $4,500		
	• 2021 threshold amount = $2,421		(2,421)
	Subtotal		$ 6,509
Amount D			
	Max's medical expenses	$ 8,425	
	Reduced by the lesser of:		
	• $2,421		
	• [(3%)($8,250)] = $248	(248)	8,177
	Matt's medical expenses	$ 120	
	Reduced by the lesser of:		
	• $2,421		
	• [(3%)($6,000)] = $180	(180)	Nil*
	Allowable amount of medical expenses		$14,686
Amount A	The appropriate rate (minimum rate)		15%
	Medical expense tax credit		$ 2,203

*As medical expenses can only be reduced to nil, the net result cannot be negative in this calculation.

Exercise 4-13 Solution

As Keith has no income, his disability credit can be transferred to John. As Keith is over 17, the disability child supplement is not available. In addition to the disability credit, John will be able to take the Canada caregiver credit as well as a credit for Keith's medical expenses.

The total credits related to Keith would be as follows:

Transfer of Keith's disability amount		$ 8,662
Canada caregiver credit		7,348
Keith's medical expenses	$16,240	
Reduced by the lesser of:		
• 2021 threshold amount = $2,421		
• [(3%)(nil)] = nil	Nil	16,240
Total credit base		$32,250
Rate		15%
Total credits related to Keith		$ 4,838

Exercise 4-14 Solution

Ms. Bright's education-related tax credits would be calculated as follows:

Tuition amount:		
Total (including $1,000 prepayment)	$3,200	
Ineligible ancillary fees ($400 - $250)	(150)	$3,050
Interest on student loan		325
Total credit base		$3,375
Rate		15%
Total available credits		$ 506

Another way of looking at the eligible tuition is that $2,800 was paid for tuition plus an additional amount of $400 for ancillary fees. Since the ancillary fees were not charged to all part- or full-time students, only $250 of the $400 is allowed. As a result, the qualifying tuition would be $3,050 [$2,800 + $250].

Exercise 4-15 Solution

The available tuition credit would be calculated as follows:

Tuition amount (maximum transfer = $5,000)	$23,500
Rate	15%
Tuition credit (maximum transfer = $750)	$ 3,525

Note that the transfer and carry forward amounts calculated in the following alternative approaches ignore the medical expense credit.

ITA Approach The $750 maximum transfer of the tuition credit must be reduced by Jerry's tax payable, before deducting his medical expense credit of $179 [(15%)($15,000 - $13,808)]. This will leave a maximum transfer of $571 ($750 - $179) and a carry forward credit of $2,775 ($3,525 - $179 - $571).

Tax Return Approach The $5,000 maximum transfer of the tuition credit must be reduced by $1,192 ($15,000 - $13,808)], the excess of Jerry's taxable income over his basic personal amount. This results in a maximum transfer of $3,808 ($5,000 - $1,192) and a carry forward amount of $18,500 ($23,500 - $1,192 - $3,808). Multiplying this by 15% gives the same $2,775 that we calculated under the alternative approach.

Note on the medical expense credit: It is doubtful that Jerry would lose the medical expense credit. He could claim some of his current-year medical expenses in the following year based on the 12-month period discussed in the chapter. Alternatively, Jerry would likely qualify as a dependant of his parents, who would then be able to claim his medical expenses.

Exercise 4-16 Solution

His tax credits would be calculated as follows:

Basic personal amount	$13,808
Spousal including infirm amount ($13,808 + $2,295 - nil)	16,103
Age [$7,713 - (15%)($42,000 - $38,893)]	7,247
Pension income*	2,000
Transfer of spouse's age credit	7,713
Transfer of spouse's disability credit	8,662
Transfer of spouse's tuition credit—Lesser of:	
• Actual tuition = $2,200	
• Maximum transfer = $5,000	2,200
Credit base	$57,733
Rate	15%
Total credits	$ 8,660

*A payment from a life annuity purchased with funds in an RRSP is eligible pension income.

Exercise 4-17 Solution

Ms. Unger's $487 credit would be calculated as follows:

	Contributions	Credit Rate	Tax Credit
First	$400	3/4	$300
Next	350	1/2	175
Remaining	35	1/3	12
Maximum credit	$785		$487

Exercise 4-18 Solution

The regular medical expense credit would be calculated as follows:

Medical expenses	$6,250
Lesser of:	
• [(3%)($28,400)] = $852	
• 2021 threshold amount = $2,421	(852)
Allowable amount of medical expenses	$5,398
Rate	15%
Medical expense credit	$ 810

The refundable supplement would be calculated as follows:

Lesser of:	
• $1,285 (2021 maximum)	
• [(25/15)($810)] = $1,350	$1,285
Reduction [(5%)($28,400 - $28,446)]	Nil
Refundable medical expense supplement	$1,285

Ms. Brunt's total tax payable (refund) would be calculated as follows:

Tax payable before credits [(15%)($28,400)]		$4,260
Non-refundable credits:		
Basic	$ 13,808	
Common-law partner	13,808	
Allowable medical expenses	5,398	
Total	$ 33,014	
Rate	15%	(4,952)
Tax before refundable supplement		$ Nil*
Refundable medical expense xupplement		(1,285)
Tax payable (refund)		($1,285)

*Negatives are rarely recognized in income tax. When you see a potential for a negative put "Nil" in its place.

Exercise 4-19 Solution

Ms. Jacobi's income before deducting either the EI or OAS repayments would be as follows:

Employment income	$75,000
EI benefits	10,000
OAS benefits	7,400
Income before deductions	$92,400

Dealing first with the EI repayment, Ms. Jacobi would have to repay $3,000, the lesser of:

- $3,000 [(30%)($10,000)]
- $6,608 [(30%)($92,400 - $70,375)]

Using this deduction, the clawback of her OAS payments would be the lesser of:

- $7,400, the OAS payments included in income, and
- $1,433 [(15%)($92,400 - $3,000 - $79,845)].

As a result, her 2021 net income would be as follows:

Income before deductions	$92,400
ITA 60(v.1) deduction (EI)	(3,000)
ITA 60(w) deduction (OAS)	(1,433)
2021 net income	$ 87,967

Self-Study Problem Solutions

Self-Study Problems are available to download from MyLab Accounting.

SSP 4-1 Solution
Case One

In Case One, the combined tax payable would be calculated as follows:

Barbra's tax payable

Federal tax before credits [(15%)($42,000)]	$ 6,300	
Basic personal credit [($13,808)(15%)]	(2,071)	$ 4,229

Sally's tax payable

Tax on first $151,978	$ 31,426	
Tax on next $28,022 ($180,000 - $151,978) at 29%	8,126	
Federal tax before credits	$ 39,552	
Basic personal credit [($13,206*)(15%)]	(1,981)	37,571
Combined tax payable		$ 41,800

*The base for Sally's basic personal amount is calculated as follows:

$13,808 - [($1,387)($180,000 - $151,978) ÷ $64,533]

Case Two

In Case Two, the income tax payable for each individual would be the same and the combined tax payable would be calculated as follows:

Barbra's tax payable

Tax on first $98,040	$ 17,402	
Tax on next $12,960 ($111,000 - $98,040) at 26%	3,370	
Federal tax before credits	$ 20,772	
Basic personal credit [($13,808)(15%)]	(2,071)	$ 18,701

Sally's tax payable

Tax on first $98,040	$ 17,402	
Tax on next $12,960 ($111,000 - $98,040) at 26%	3,370	
Federal tax before credits	$ 20,772	
Basic personal credit [($13,808)(15%)]	(2,071)	18,701
Combined income tax payable		$ 37,402

Case Three

In Case Three, only Barbra would have income tax payable, which would be calculated as follows:

Tax on first $216,511	$ 50,141
Tax on next $5,489 ($222,000 - $216,511) at 33%	1,811
Federal tax before credits	$ 51,952
Basic personal credit [($12,421*)(15%)]	(1,863)
Common-law partner credit [($12,421)(15%)]	(1,863)
Barbra's tax payable	$ 48,226

*Since Barbra's taxable income exceeds the top marginal income tax bracket of $216,511, her BPA is automatically $12,421.

SSP 4-2 Solution
Case 1

Leonard Wilkins will qualify for the following credits:

Basic personal amount	$ 13,808
Spousal ($13,808 - $8,720)	5,088
Canada caregiver—24-year-old son	7,348
Total credit base	$ 26,244
Rate	15%
Total credits	$ 3,937

Note: Although their daughter is under 18 years of age, she is not infirm and therefore no tax credit can be claimed.

Case 2

Pete Webb will qualify for the following credits:

Basic personal amount	$13,808
Spousal ($13,808 - $3,920)	9,888
EI (maximum)	890
CPP (maximum)	2,876
Canada employment	1,257
Total credit base	$28,719
Rate	15%
Total credits	$ 4,308

Case 3

Candace Hall will qualify for the following tax credits:

Basic personal amount	$13,808
Spousal ($13,808 - $5,130)	8,678
Age [$7,713 - (15%)($69,420 - $38,893)]	3,134
Pension income	2,000
Total credit base	$27,620
Rate	15%
Total credits	$ 4,143

Note that, because her income is below the $79,845 income threshold, there will be no clawback of Ms. Hall's OAS receipts.

Case 4

Gladys Crawford will qualify for the following tax credits:

Basic personal amount	$13,808
Spousal ($13,808 - $2,600)	11,208
Medical expenses (see note)	20,795
Total credit base	$45,811
Rate	15%
Total credits	$ 6,872

Note The claim for medical expenses is determined as follows:

Expenses for Gladys, her spouse, and under-18 children		
($5,150 + $4,240 + $2,040 + $3,220)		$14,650
Reduced by the lesser of:		
• [(3%)($126,470)] = $3,794		
• 2021 threshold amount = $2,421		(2,421)
20-year-old's medical expenses	$8,840	
Reduced by the lesser of:		
• [(3%)($9,130)] = $274		
• $2,421	(274)	8,566
Allowable medical expenses		$20,795

Case 5
Austin Schneider will qualify for the following credits:

Basic personal amount	$13,808
Eligible dependant (see note)	13,808
Total credit base	$27,616
Rate	15%
Total credits	$ 4,142

Note The eligible dependant credit can be taken for any child. It should not be claimed for the 14 year old, as the amount of the credit would be reduced because of his net income.

SSP 4-3 Solution
The amount of the personal tax credits would be as follows:

1. **Ms. Jones** will qualify for the following credits:

Basic personal amount	$13,808
Spousal ($13,808 - $3,750)	10,058
Total credit base	$23,866
Rate	15%
Total credits	$ 3,580

There is no tax credit available for her son.

2. **Ms. Martin** will qualify for the following credits:

Basic personal amount	$13,808
Spousal including infirm amount	
($13,808 + $2,295)	16,103
Age	7,713
Pension	2,000
Spouse's disability	8,662
Total credit base	$48,286
Rate	15%
Total credits	$ 7,243

As Ms. Martin's net income is less than the relevant income thresholds, there will be no reduction in her age credit or clawback of her OAS benefits.

3. **Mr. Sharp** will qualify for the following credits:

Basic personal amount	$13,808
Spousal	13,808
Canada caregiver amount (20-year-old child)	7,348
Total credit base	$34,964
Rate	15%
Total credits	$ 5,245

4. **Mr. Barton** will qualify for the following credits:

Basic personal amount	$13,808
Eligible dependant (any child)	13,808
Total credit base	$27,616
Rate	15%
Total credits	$ 4,142

5. **Ms. Cole** will qualify for the following credits:

Basic personal amount	
$13,808 - [$1,387][($175,000 - $151,978) ÷ $64,533]	$ 13,313
Spousal ($13,313 - $36,000)	Nil
EI (maximum)	890
CPP (maximum)	2,876
Canada employment	1,257
Total credit base	$ 18,336
Rate	15%
Total credits	$ 2,750

Her spouse's net income will have to be considered for the entire year even though they were not married for the full year.

6. **Mr. Smead** will qualify for the following credits:

Basic personal amount	$ 13,808
Eligible dependant—Son	13,808
Canada caregiver—Mother	
[$7,348 - ($18,500 - $17,256)]	6,104
Total credit base	$ 33,720
Rate	15%
Total credits	$ 5,058

While Mr. Snead could have claimed his mother for the eligible dependant credit, her level of net income would have reduced the credit base amount to nil. Choosing his son for the eligible dependant credit and his mother for the Canada caregiver credit maximizes his total tax credits for the year.

SSP 4-4 Solution

Mr. Lane's federal income tax payable (refund) would be calculated as follows:

Net income and taxable income		$70,000
Tax on first $49,020		$ 7,353
Tax on next $20,980 ($70,000 - $49,020) at 20.5%		4,301
Federal tax before credits		$11,654
Basic personal amount	($ 13,808)	
Eligible dependant (Note 1)	(13,808)	
EI (maximum)	(890)	
CPP (maximum)	(2,876)	
Canada employment	(1,257)	
Medical expenses (Note 2)	(2,300)	
Credit base	($34,939)	
Rate	15%	(5,241)
Federal political tax credit [(3/4)($400) + (1/2)($50)]		(325)
Federal tax payable		6,088
CPP overpayment ($3,201 - $3,166)		(35)
Federal tax withheld (given)		(10,100)
Federal income tax refund		($ 4,047)

Note 1 The eligible dependant amount can be claimed for any of the three children. However, since any net income reduces the credit it would not be adviusable to claim the 15-year-old as he is the only child with net income.

Note 2 Allowable medical expenses are as follows:

Minor child's medical expenses	$4,400
Reduced by the lesser of:	
• [(3%)($70,000)] = $2,100	
• 2021 threshold amount = $2,421	(2,100)
Allowable medical expenses	$2,300

Since his 15-year-old son is under 18 years of age, his allowable medical expenses are not affected by his net income. If he was 18 or older, they would be.

SSP 4-5 Solution
Part A
The income tax payable calculation for Marg is as follows:

Taxable income		$15,300
Basic personal amount		(13,808)
EI		(242)
CPP [(4.95%)($15,300 - $3,500)]		(584)
Canada employment		(1,257)
Subtotal	$	Nil

Note 1 Marg has a tuition amount available of $6,300. Because her tax payable is nil, she does not need to use any of this credit. This means the maximum of $5,000 can be transferred to her father. This will leave her with a carry forward amount of $1,300 ($6,300 - $5,000).

Since Marg's medical expenses were paid for by her father, she cannot claim them herself and they must be claimed by her father. Even if she had paid for them herself and claimed them, she would not increase the transfer to her father as the medical expense tax credit is not taken into consideration in determining the tuition amount that can be transferred.

Note: We have shown that Marg's tax payable would have been nil with the tax credits she had available to her, but we would add that the correct approach is to first determine gross taxes payable, which would have been $2,295 [(15%)($15,300)]. From that amount you would have totalled the non-refundable credits, which totals $15,891. The tax credit amount would then be 15% of that total tax credit base, which would generate $2,384, which when applied against the gross taxes payable would have resulted in a nil balance of income tax owing.

Part B
Mr. Barth's minimum employment income for the year would be calculated as follows:

Gross salary	$ 82,500
Additions:	
Bonus (Note 2)	20,000
Automobile benefit (Note 3)	7,520
Counselling benefit (Note 4)	1,500
Imputed interest benefit (Note 5)	375
Stock option benefit [($18 - $15)(1,000)] (Note 6)	3,000
Deductions:	
RPP contributions	(3,200)
Professional dues	(1,800)
Employment encome	$109,895

Note 2 As the bonus is not payable until more than three years after the end of the employer's taxation year, it is a salary deferral arrangement and must be included in income under ITA 6(11) for the year in which the services were rendered.

Note 3 Since Mr. Barth's employment-related usage is not more than 50%, there is no reduction of the full standby charge. In addition, he cannot use the alternative calculation of the operating cost benefit. Given this, the automobile benefit is calculated as follows:

Standby charge [(2%)($47,500)(10)]	$9,500
Operating cost benefit [(6,000)($0.27)]	1,620
Payments withheld	(3,600)
Taxable benefit	$7,520

Note 4 Counselling services, with the exception of those items specified under ITA 6(1), are considered taxable benefits. The items specified under ITA 6(1)(a)(iv) are counselling with respect to mental or physical health or with respect to re-employment or retirement. As a consequence, the counselling on personal finances is a taxable benefit.

Note 5 The imputed interest benefit is calculated as follows:

Taxable benefit [($150,000)(2%)(3/12)]	$750
Reduction for interest paid within 30 days of the year end	(375)
Addition to employment income	$375

Note 6 As the option price was greater than the market price at the time the options were issued, one-half of this amount can be deducted in the determination of taxable income (ITA 110(1)(d)). The tax cost (e.g., adjusted cost base) of the stock option shares becomes their fair market value at the exercise date ($18 per share). Since they were sold for $18 per share, there is no capital gain or loss.

Taxable Income

Mr. Barth's taxable income would be calculated as follows:

Employment income	$109,895
Deductible CPP ($3,166 - $2,876)	(290)
Net income	109,605
Stock option deduction [(1/2)($3,000)] (Note 6)	(1,500)
Taxable income	$108,105

Tax Payable

Mr. Barth's tax payable would be calculated as follows:

Tax on first $98,040		$17,402
Tax on next $10,065 ($108,105 - $98,040) at 26%		2,617
Federal tax before credits		$20,019
Basic personal amount	($13,808)	
Spousal including infirm amount		
($13,808 + $2,295 - $1,250)	(14,853)	
Spouse's disability	(8,662)	
EI	(890)	
CPP	(2,876)	
Canada employment	(1,257)	
Medical expenses (Note 7)	(1,590)	
Marg's tuition transfer (see Part A)	(5,000)	
Credit base	($48,936)	
Rate	15%	(7,340)
Charitable donations (Note 8)		
[(15%)($200) + (29%)($2,000 - $200)]		(552)
Net federal tax		$12,127
Federal income tax withheld during year		(16,000)
Federal income tax refund		($ 3,873)

Note 7 Allowable medical expenses are as follows:

John and spouse medical expenses ($200 + $3,550)		$3,750
Reduced by the lesser of:		
• [(3%)($109,605)] = $3,288		
• 2021 threshold amount = $2,421		(2,421)
Marg's medical expenses	$720	
Reduced by the lesser of:		
• [(3%)($15,300)] = $459		
• $2,421	(459)	261
Allowable medical expense		$1,590

Note 8 As none of his income is taxed at 33%, this rate will not be applicable to the calculation of the charitable donations tax credit.

SSP 4-6 Solution

Mr. Kern's minimum employment income for the year would be calculated as follows:

Gross salary	$67,600
Additions:	
Automobile benefit (Note 1)	857
Disability insurance benefit (Note 2)	1,300
Stock option benefit [($83 - $75)(200)]	1,600
Deductions:	
RPP contributions	(1,800)
Contributions to group disability plan	Nil
Professional dues	(1,233)
Employment income	$68,324

Note 1 Based on the fact that Mr. Kern's employment-related usage is more than 50% of total usage, the automobile benefit is calculated as follows:

Standby charge [(2/3)(9)($815 - $89)(3,000/15,003*)]	$ 871
Operating cost benefit—Lesser of:	
• [(3,000)($0.27)] = $810	
• [(1/2)($871)] = $436	436
Total before payments	$1,307
Payments for personal use [($50)(9)]	(450)
Taxable benefit	$ 857

*[(9)(1,667)]

As Mr. Kern's employment-related usage is more than 50%, he can elect to use one-half the standby charge as the operating cost benefit.

Note 2 As his employer contributed to the plan and the contributions did not create a taxable benefit, the $1,650 in benefits received during the year must be included in employment income. However, this benefit is reduced by the $350 ($200 + $150) in total contributions he has made in 2020 and 2021.

Net and Taxable Income

Taxable income would be calculated as follows:

Employment income	$68,324
Deductible CPP	(290)
Net income	68,034
Stock option deduction [(1/2)($1,600)]	(800)
Taxable income	$67,234

Tax Payable

Tax payable would be calculated as follows:

Tax on first $49,020		$ 7,353
Tax on next $18,214 ($67,234 - $49,020) at 20.5%		3,734
Federal tax before credits		$11,087
Basic personal amount	($13,808)	
Spousal ($13,808 - $3,660)	(10,148)	
EI	(890)	
CPP	(2,876)	
Canada employment	(1,257)	
Medical expenses (Note 3)	(3,916)	
David's transfer of tuition (Note 4)	(5,000)	
Credit base	($ 37,895)	
Rate	15%	(5,684)
Charitable donations carried forward (Note 5)		
[(15%)($200) + (29%)($500 - $200)]		(117)
Net federal tax		$ 5,286
Federal amounts withheld during year (given)		(7,200)
Federal income tax refund		($ 1,914)

Note 3   The allowable medical expenses would be calculated as follows:

Samuel and spouse medical expenses ($2,100 + $770)		$ 2,870
Reduced by the lesser of:		
• [(3%)($68,034)] = $2,041		
• 2021 threshold amount = $2,421		(2,041)
David's medical expenses	$3,260	
Reduced by the lesser of:		
• $2,421		
• [(3%)($5,780)] = $173	(173)	3,087
Allowable medical expenses		$ 3,916

Note 4   The transfer from David is as follows:

Tuition fees	$6,700
Maximum transfer	(5,000)
Carry forward (for David's use only)	$1,700

David's tax payable is nil because the income taxes on his net income of $5,780 completely eliminated by his basic personal credit of $13,808. He can therefore transfer the maximum amount of $5,000 of his tuition to his father. The remaining $1,700 can be carried forward indefinitely, but must be used by David.

Note 5   As none of his income is taxed at 33%, this rate will not be applicable to the calculation of the charitable donations tax credit.

SSP 4-7 Solution
Part A
Ms. Van Horne's minimum employment income would be calculated as follows:

Salary		$126,000
Add:		
Commissions		32,000
Bonus [(1/2)($25,000)]		12,500
Employer's life insurance contribution		550
Automobile benefit (Note 1)		2,237
Stock option benefit (Note 2)		30,000
Deduct:		
RPP contributions		(7,400)
Employment-related expenses (Note 3)		(17,700)
Employment income		$178,187

Note 1   The automobile benefit would be calculated as follows:

Standby charge [(2/3)(11)($728 - $50)(5,500 ÷ 18,337*)]	$1,491
Operating cost benefit—Lesser of:	
• [(1/2)($1,491)] = $746	
• [($0.27)(5,500)] = $1,485	746
Total benefits	$2,237

*[(11)(1,667)]

As Ms. Van Horne's employment-related use was more than 50%, there is a reduction in the standby charge and she can use the alternative calculation of the operating cost benefit.

Note 2 The employment income inclusion resulting from the exercise of the stock option is $30,000 [(5,000)($31 - $25)]. As the option price was equal to the market price at the time the options were issued, one-half of this amount can be deducted in the determination of taxable income (ITA 110(1)(d)).

Note 3 As Ms. Van Horne's commission income of $32,000 exceeds her deductible employment expenses, they are fully deductible through ITA 8(1)(f). They are calculated as follows:

Advertising	$ 5,600
Entertainment [(1/2)($9,000)]	4,500
Meals (reimbursed)	Nil
Hotels [(1/2)($8,400)]	4,200
Airline tickets	3,400
Deductible expenses	$17,700

Part B

Ms. Van Horne's minimum taxable income would be calculated as follows:

Employment income	$178,187
Deductible CPP ($3,166 - $2,876)	(290)
Net income	177,897
Stock option deduction [(1/2)($30,000)]	(15,000)
Taxable income	$162,897

Part C

Based on the taxable income calculated in Part B, Ms. Van Horne's tax payable would be calculated as follows:

Tax on first $151,978		$31,426
Tax on next $10,919 ($162,897 - $151,978) at 29%		3,167
Tax before credits		$34,593
Basic personal amount (Note 4)	($13,573)	
Eligible dependant—Son		
[($13,573 - $2,500)]	(11,073)	
Caregiver (Note 5)	(7,348)	
EI premiums	(890)	
CPP contributions	(2,876)	
Canada employment	(1,257)	
Transfer of tuition (Note 6)	(5,000)	
Medical expenses (Note 7)	(3,700)	
Credit base	(45,717)	
Rate	15%	(6,858)
Charitable donations		
[(15%)($200) + (29%)($1,800 - $200)]		(494)
Federal political contributions		
[(3/4)($400) + (1/2)($350) + (1/3)($900 - $400 - $350)]		(525)
Federal income tax payable		$26,716

Note 4 The basic personal amount would be calculated as follows:

$$\$13,808 - [\$1,387][(\$162,897 - \$151,978 \div \$64,533)] = \$13,573$$

Note 5 The father's $8,000 income is below the threshold for the caregiver credit of $17,085 (his casino winnings are not included in his net income since they are not considered a source of income). This means that Ms. Van Horne can claim the full amount of the caregiver credit.

Note 6 The transfer from her daughter is as follows:

Tuition fees	$7,000
Total amount available	$7,000
Maximum transfer	(5,000)
Carry forward (for daughter's use only)	$2,000

Her daughter's available tax credits exceed her net income, therefore she does not require any part of her tuition fees to reduce her taxes payable to nil. She can therefore transfer the maximum amount of $5,000 to her mother. The remaining $2,000 can be carried forward indefinitely, but must be used by her daughter.

Note 7 The base for Ms. Van Horne's medical expense credit can be calculated as follows:

Ms. Van Horne and her children ($850 + $1,480)	$2,330	
Reduced by the lesser of:		
[(3%)($177,897)] = $5,337		
2021 threshold amount = $2,421	(2,421)	Nil
Father's medical expenses	$3,940	
Reduced by the lesser of:		
$2,421		
[(3%)($8,000)] = $240	(240)	3,700
Allowable medical costs		$3,700

SSP 4-8 Solution
Part A
Lydia's minimum employment income would be calculated as follows:

Salary	$73,500
Additions:	
Bonus (Note 1)	6,000
Stock options (Note 2)	Nil
Automobile benefit (Note 3)	1,176
Gifts (Note 5)	650
Interest-free loan benefit (Note 6)	1,333
Deductions:	
RPP contributions	(2,600)
Professional dues	(350)
Client meals and entertainment (Note 4)	Nil
Employment income	$79,709

Note 1 The $4,000 that will be paid in 2022 is not included in net income until it is received. However, the amount that will be paid in 2025 is a salary deferral arrangement and, given this, it will have to be included in 2021 employment income, which is the year in which the services were provided.

Note 2 The stock option benefit would be calculated as follows:

$$[(200)(\$90 - \$72)] = \$3,600$$

Since the employer is a CCPC, the taxation of this benefit is deferred until the shares are sold. Note that, because the option price was less than the fair market value of the shares at the time the options were granted, no ITA 110(1)(d) deduction will be available in the determination of taxable income when they are sold. However, if she holds the shares for more than two years before selling, she will be eligible for the ITA 110(1)(d.1) deduction.

Note 3 The automobile benefit would be calculated as follows:

Standby charge [(2/3)(11)($565 - $75)(4,000 ÷ 18,337*)]	$ 784
Operating cost benefit—Lesser of:	
• [(1/2)($784)] = $392	
• [($0.27)(4,000)] = $1,080	392
Total benefits	$1,176

*[(11)(1,667)]

As Lydia's employment-related use was more than 50%, the reduced standby charge is available. In addition, she can use the alternative calculation of the operating cost benefit.

Note 4 Lydia's meal and entertainment costs exceed her employer's reimbursement by $2,400 ($5,600 - $3,200), which relates to her personal consumption of meals. The unreimbursed expenses would potentially be deductible under either ITA 8(1)(f) or (h), however neither of these deductions apply. Both of the ITA provisions first require a contract of employment that requires her to pay for her own expenses. Technically she could argue that there is an understanding between herself and the employer, particularly given that not all of the expenses were reimbursed. That argument, however, would not assist her since ITA 8(4) would prevent her claiming any part of the meal expenses that were for personal consumption.

Note 5 The gift certificate for $150 is taxable because it is a near-cash gift. The first $500 of the long-service award will not be a taxable benefit. However, the excess of $500 ($1,000 - $500) will be a taxable benefit. As the value of the Christmas gift basket is under $500, it will not create a taxable benefit. The total taxable benefit for gifts is $650 ($150 + $500).

Note 6 The taxable benefit on the loan is calculated as follows:

$$[(2\%)(\$100,000)(8/12)] = \$1,333$$

Part B

Net and taxable income would be calculated as follows:

Employment income	$79,709
Deductible CPP contributions ($3,166 - $2,876)	(290)
Net income and taxable income	$79,419

As there are no Division C deductions, Lydia's taxable income would be equal to her net income of $79,419. There would be no stock option deduction as the stock option benefit is deferred to the year in which the stock option shares are sold since the employer is a CCPC.

Part C

Lydia's tax payable would be calculated as follows:

Tax on first $49,020		$ 7,353
Tax on bext $30,399 ($79,419 - $49,020) at 20.5%		6,232
Federal tax before credits		$13,585
Basic personal amount	($13,808)	
Spousal ($13,808 - $8,600)	(5,208)	
Canada caregiver—Mary	(7,348)	
Transfer of Harry's tuition (Note 7)	(4,708)	
First-time home buyers' plan	(5,000)	
EI premiums	(890)	
CPP contributions	(2,876)	
Canada employment	(1,257)	
Medical expenses (Note 8)	(19,001)	
Credit base	($60,096)	
Rate	15%	(9,014)
Charitable donations [(15%)($200) + (29%)($2,000 - $200)] (Note 9)		(552)
Federal income tax payable		$ 4,019

Note 7   Harry will have to reduce his own tax payable to nil before transferring any part of his tuition amount. He will require $292 ($14,100 - $13,808) of this amount, and his transfer will be limited to $4,708 ($5,000 - $292). This will leave Harry with a carry forward of $6,300 ($11,300 - $292 - $4,708). The residence and textbook costs are not eligible for a credit.

Note 8   There are three medical expenses in the problem that do not qualify for the medical expenses tax credit: Botox treatment, hair replacement procedures, and liposuction. (These exclusions are listed in the text.) All of the allowable medical expenses of Lydia, Mark, and Barry are eligible for reimbursement from the health care plan and the reimbursement is deducted. As both Mary and Harry are older than 17, their expenses are not eligible for reimbursement.

The base for Lydia's medical expense credit can be calculated as follows:

Lydia - Prescriptions	$ 2,500
Lydia - Botox treatments	Nil
Mark - Dentist fees for root canals (3)	7,200
Mark - Hair replacement procedures	Nil
Barry - Dentist fees, including $1,000 for a tooth replacement	2,100
Allowable medical expenses	$11,800
Reimbursement [(50%)(11,800)]	(5,900)
Reduced by the lesser of:	
• [(3%)($79,419)] = $2,383	
• 2021 threshold amount = $2,421	(2,383)

Mary's allowable medical expenses		
($8,400 + $3,900 + Nil)	$12,300	
Reduced by the lesser of:		
• $2,421		
• [(3%)($3,100)] = $93	(93)	12,207
Harry's allowable medical expenses		
($1,500 + $2,200)	$ 3,700	
Reduced by the lesser of:		
• $2,421		
• [(3%)($14,100)] = $423	(423)	3,277
Allowable medical costs		$19,001

Note 9   As none of her income is taxed at 33%, this rate will not be applicable to the calculation of the charitable donations tax credit.

Solution to Tax Software Self-Study Problem—Chapter 4

The complete tax return is available on MyLab in two versions: a T1 ProFile return file and a .PDF file. Note that prior to late January 2022, the returns will be for 2020, not 2021, as the 2021 filing version will not yet be available.

For more information on how to use the ProFile tax program, refer to the Chapter 4 sample tax return in this Study Guide.

Notes to Tax Return

- Diane transfers the $5,000 maximum tuition amount to Eleanor and carries forward the remaining $2,000 [$7,000 - $5,000]. The carry forward can only be used by Diane.

- Eleanor cannot claim the charitable donation made by Diane, but Diane can carry it forward for up to five years.

- Since Amy is under 18 and wholly dependent, Eleanor claimed the eligible dependant credit for Amy.

- Because Marjorie is not infirm, Eleanor can claim no credit for her.

- Since Diane and Marjorie are over 17 years of age, their medical expenses are reduced by 3% of their net income. This means that none of Marjorie's medical expenses can be claimed by Eleanor.

- In calculating work space in the home costs, the household insurance would only be deductible as a result of ITA 8(1)(f), which requires commission income. Since there is no commission income indicated on the T4 information return, the insurance cannot be deducted. The car insurance is not relevant as there is no information that Eleanor uses her car for employment purposes.

Tax Planning Points

- Although she is technically not required to file, Marjorie should file an income tax return, otherwise she will not be eligible for the GST credit.

- Although she is also not technically required to file, Diane should file an income tax return, otherwise she will not be eligible for the GST credit and she will not benefit from the RRSP deduction room created during the year. Filing an income tax return will also make her tuition credit and charitable donation tax credit easier to keep track of for carry forward purposes.

CHAPTER 5

Learning Objectives

After completing Chapter 5, you should be able to:

1. Explain the general differences between a capital expenditure and an expenditure on income account (Paragraph [P hereafter] 5-1 to 5-2).
2. Describe the two types of capital property and how the ITA treats them as opposed to the treatment of expenditures on income account (P 5-3 to 5-8).
3. Describe the types of property specifically excluded from depreciable property (P 5-9 to 5-11).
4. Describe the general differences between the accounting for depreciable property and the income tax approach to depreciable property (P 5-12 to 5-24).
5. Determine the types of costs that are included in the amounts that are added to depreciable property classes (P 5-25 to 5-34).
6. Describe how income versus capital determinations are made in deciding whether one has a capital expenditure or not. Is there a checklist approach that can be used? What factors does the CRA usually look at? (P 5-35 to 5-41).
7. In general terms, describe the three types of rules that impact the CCA deduction that may be claimed (P 5-42 to 5-43).
8. Explain the purpose for the available-for-use rules and how these rules to different property (P 5-44 to 5-48).
9. Describe the general rules for including depreciable property in classes and the exceptions that allow separate classes (P 5-49 to 5-54).
10. Describe the basic CCA/UCC rules, including the calculations and interaction among specialty rules such as the AccII and the short fiscal period rule (P 5-55 to 5-58).
11. Be aware of the rates and methods that are applicable to common CCA classes to determine the maximum CCA for the period (P 5-59).
12. Describe the old half-year rule and its impact on the determination of maximum CCA for the period (P 5-60 to 5-63).
13. Explain what "net additions" are and the role they play in determining CCA (P 5-64).
14. Describe the Accelerated Investment Incentive (AccII), when it applies, and when it does not apply (P 5-65 to 5-76).
15. Describe the application of the AccII to classes 12, 13, 14, and 53. Explain how this differs from when the AccII is applied to other classes (P 5-77 to 5-82).
16. Describe the enhanced CCA provisions for zero-emission vehicles and zero-emission passenger vehicles in class 54 (P 5-83 to 5-90).
17. Explain the purpose of the short fiscal period rules and how they apply in the determination of maximum CCA (P 5-91 to 5-93).
18. Describe the additions to class 14.1, the general meaning of goodwill, and the special treatment it receives (P 5-94 to 5-100).

19. Describe situations in which tax planning considerations may be important in relation to depreciable property (P 5-101 to 5-105).
20. Explain how dispositions effect the UCC of a class of depreciable property and the circumstances under which recapture, terminal losses, and capital gains can occur (P 5-106 to 5-120).
21. Explain the application of recapture and terminal losses to employees (P 5-121).
22. Explain the special disposition rule that applies to zero-emission passenger vehicles in class 54 (P 5-122 to 5-123).
23. Explain how the treatment of dispositions in class 14.1 differs from that for other CCA classes (P 5-124 to 5-129).
24. Explain Figure 5-2 in your own words (P 5-130).
25. Re-create the commonly used CCA schedule for a situation using your own numbers (P 5-131 to 5-132).
26. Describe the two separate class elections in your own words and explain why they may be useful (P 5-133 to 5-142).

How to Work through Chapter 5

Visit pearsonmylabandmastering.com to access MyLab Accounting for this text. Once there, you can access student resources such as Self-Study Problems, Practice Exams, Flashcards, updates, and more.

We recommend the following approach in dealing with the material in this chapter:

Capital Expenditures versus Expenditures on Income Account
- Read paragraph 5-1 and 5-2 (in the text).

Two Types of Capital Property and Their Income Tax Treatment
- Read paragraph 5-3 to 5-8.

Depreciable Property Exclusions
- Read paragraph 5-9 to 5-11.
- Do Exercise 5-1 and check the solution in this Study Guide.

Income Tax versus Accounting
- Read paragraph 5-12 to 5-24.

Additions to Capital Cost
- Read paragraphs 5-25 to 5-34.

Expenditures on Depreciable Property—Capital vs. Income
- Read paragraph 5-35 to 5-41.

CCA—General Restrictions
- Read paragraph 5-42 and 5-43.

Available-for-Use Rules
- Read paragraph 5-44 to 5-48.

Classes of Depreciable Property
- Read paragraph 5-49 to 5-54.

Capital Cost Allowance—General Overveiw
- Read paragraph 5-55 to 5-58.

Commonly Used CCA Classes
- Read paragraph 5-59.
- Do Exercises 5-2 and 5-3 and check the solutions in this Study Guide.

The Old Half-Year Rule
- Read paragraph 5-60 to 5-63.

Net Additions
- Read paragraph 5-64.

Accelerated Investment Incentive (AccII)
- Read paragraph 5-65 to 5-72

Application—Declining Balance Classes
- Read paragraph 5-73 to 5-76.
- Do Exercise 5-4 and check the solution in this Study Guide.

AccII Application—Classes 12 and 13
- Read paragraph 5-77 to 5-80.
- Do Exercise 5-5 and check the solution in this Study Guide.

AccII Application—Class 14
- Read paragraph 5-81.
- Do Exercise 5-6 and check the solution in this Study Guide.

AccII Application—Class 53
- Read paragraph 5-82.
- Do Exercise 5-7 and check the solution in this Study Guide.

Zero-Emission Vehicles
- Read paragraph 5-83 to 5-90.

Short Fiscal Periods
- Read paragraph 5-91 to 5-93.
- Do Exercise 5-8 and check the solution in this Study Guide.

Class 14.1
- Read paragraph 5-94 to 5-100.

Tax Planning Considerations for CCA
- Read paragraph 5-101 to 5-105.

Dispositions of Depreciable Property
- Read paragraph 5-106 to 5-120.
- Do Exercises 5-9, 5-10, 5-11, and 5-12 and check the solutions in this Study Guide.
- Read paragraph 5-121.

Dispositions of Class 54 (Zero-Emission Passenger Vehicles)
- Read paragraph 5-122 to 5-123.

Dispositions of Class 14.1—Differences from Other Classes
- Read paragraph 5-124 to 5-127.
- Do Exercise 5-13 and check the solution in this Study Guide.
- Read paragraph 5-128 to 5-129.

Disposition Summary — Income Tax Consequences
- Read paragraph 5-130.

CCA Schedule — Example
- Read paragraph 5-131 to 5-132.
- Do Self-Study Problems 5-1 to 5-7, which are available on MyLab, and check the solutions in this Study Guide.

Separate Class Election
- Read paragraph 5-133 to 5-140.
- Do Exercise 5-14 and check the solution in this Study Guide.
- Read paragraph 5-141 to 5-142.
- Do Self-Study Problem 5-8 and check the solution in this Study Guide.

To Complete This Chapter
- Visit MyLab Accounting for more practice problem material, and test yourself with the glossary flashcards.
- Review the Key Terms at the end of the chapter, and consult the glossary for definitions.
- Ensure you have achieved the Chapter 5 Learning Objectives listed in this Study Guide.
- As a review, view the PowerPoint presentations available on MyLab.

Practice Examination
- Available on MyLab, write the Practice Examination for this chapter, and mark it using the solutions provided.

Exercise Solutions

Exercise 5-1 Solution

1. A pet store acquires six puppies to sell—The puppies are a capital expenditure, however since they are also inventory to the pet store business they are not depreciable property.

2. A warehouse facility purchases two guard dogs—The guard dogs are a capital expenditure but they are not depreciable property since animals are excluded.

3. You purchase 100 shares of a public corporation for $5,000—Shares represent a capital expenditure that is non-depreciable capital property.

4. You purchase an existing business and pay an additional amount for goodwill—Goodwill is intangible property that is a capital expenditure. Goodwill is not excluded from depreciable property and is depreciable property (class 14.1).

5. You purchase a cottage that you rent out on a monthly basis—The cost of the cottage is a capital expenditure that is also depreciable property (class 1).

6. You replace all of the plumbing for the cottage at a cost of $15,000 while it is still being rented—The expenditure is a capital expenditure that attaches to the cottage, increasing the depreciable property base (class 1).

7. At the beginning of 2021 you stop renting the cottage and use it exclusively for personal use—The cost of the cottage remains a capital expenditure, however since it is no longer being used to earn income it is no longer depreciable property.

8. You pay $250,000 to purchase a franchise to operate a coffee shop—The purchase of a franchise is intangible property that is a capital expenditure. The expenditure is depreciable property (generally class 14).

Exercise 5-2 Solution

The correct classes for each of the properties would be as follows:

Property	Class
Taxicab	16
Reference books replaced every five to ten years	8
Periodicals and other books replaced every year	N/A
Manufacturing and processing equipment	53
Franchise with a limited life	14
Passenger vehicle with a cost of $120,000*	10.1
Government licence with an unlimited life	14.1
Water storage tank	6
Photocopy machine*	8
Leasehold improvements	13
Rental building* (not including the land)	1

*The rental building is automatically included in a separate class. In addition, as covered later in the chapter, an election can be made to include the photocopy machine in a separate class as long as its capital cost exceeds $1,000.

Note that books and periodicals replaced each year would not be considered capital expenditures and therefore would be expensed each year (income account).

Exercise 5-3 Solution

Ignoring the AccII, the impact would be calculated as follows:

Correct 2021 CCA [($326,000)(30%)(1.5 AccII)]	$146,700
CCA claimed in 2021 [($326,000)(4%)(1.5) AccII]	(19,560)
Understatement of 2021 CCA	$ 127,140

Exercise 5-4 Solution

The maximum CCA for 2021 and the January 1, 2022, UCC balance are calculated as follows:

January 1, 2021, UCC		$ 950,000
Add: Acquisitions during the year	$300,000	
Deduct: Dispositions during the Year*	(144,000)	156,000
Add: AccII adjustment [(1/2)($156,000)]		78,000
CCA base (December 31, 2020, UCC)		$1,184,000
2020 CCA [(30%)($1,184,000)]		(355,200)
AccII adjustment reversal		(78,000)
January 1, 2022, UCC		$ 750,800

*Detailed coverage on dispositions is covered later in the chapter. We have included dispositions during the year to more fully illustrate the calculation of the AccII adjustment. You can verify the ending UCC balance by taking the opening balance of $950,000, adding the net additions of $156,000, and subtracting CCA of $355,200. This equals $750,800.

Exercise 5-5 Solution

The required CCA calculations for 2021 would be as follows:

On 2016 improvements ($52,000 ÷ 15)	$3,467
On 2021 improvements [(150%)($31,000 ÷ 10)]	4,650
2021 CCA	$8,117

The required CCA calculations for 2022 would be as follows:

On 2016 improvements ($52,000 ÷ 15)	$3,467
On 2021 improvements ($31,000 ÷ 10)	3,100
2022 CCA	$6,567

While this is not required by the exercise, you should note that the 2030 CCA on the 2020 improvements would be limited to $1,550 ($31,000 - $4,650 - (8)($3,100)), the balance in the UCC for these improvements.

Exercise 5-6 Solution
The required calculations are as follows:

Acquisition amount	$375,000
CCA for 2021 [(150%)($375,000 ÷ 10)(275/365)]	(42,380)
January 1, 2022, UCC	$332,620

Exercise 5-7 Solution
The required calculations are as follows:

January 1, 2021, UCC	$500,000
Acquisitions during the year	100,000
AccII adjustment [(100%)($100,000)]	100,000
CCA base	$700,000
2021 CCA [(50%)($700,000)]	(350,000)
AccII adjustment reversal	(100,000)
January 1, 2022, UCC	$250,000

While this is not required, the ending UCC can be verified as follows:

January 1, 2021, UCC	$500,000
Acquisitions during the year	100,000
CCA deductions (ITA 20(1)(a)):	
CCA on opening UCC [(50%)($500,000)]	(250,000)
CCA on additions [(100%)($100,000)]	(100,000)
January 1, 2022, UCC	$250,000

Exercise 5-8 Solution
The required information is calculated as follows:

Capital cost of additions	$115,000
AccII adjustment [(50%)($115,000)]	57,500
CCA base	$172,500
2021 CCA [(20%)($172,500)(153/365)]	(14,462)
AccII adjustment reversal	(57,500)
January 1, 2022, UCC	$100,538

Exercise 5-9 Solution
The only immediate income tax consequence would be a taxable capital gain of $2,500 [(1/2)($23,000 - $18,000)].

Following the basic rule for dispositions, we would subtract from the class 8 UCC the lesser of the proceeds of disposition ($23,000) and the capital cost of the property sold ($18,000). Subtracting the lesser figure of $18,000 would leave a large positive balance in the class. As there are no other dispositions during the year, we can conclude that the balance will be positive at the end of the year, allowing for a CCA claim. Since the UCC would not be negative there would be no recapture, and since there are properties remaining in the class there can be no terminal loss. Maximum CCA for the year would be $51,400 (($275,000 - $18,000)(20%)).

Exercise 5-10 Solution

The required information would be calculated as follows:

UCC balance January 1, 2021	$24,883
Add: Acquisitions during the year	Nil
Deduct: Dispositions during the year—Lesser of:	
• Capital cost = $27,000	
• Proceeds of disposition = $28,500	(27,000)
Deduct: AccII adjustment	N/A*
December 31, 2021, UCC balance	($ 2,117)
Recapture of CCA	2,117
January 1, 2022, UCC balance	Nil

*Since there are no net additions there is no AccII adjustment.

The effect would be an addition to business income of $2,117 in recaptured CCA.
While there would also be a taxable capital gain of $750 [(1/2)($28,500 - $27,000)], this would not be included in business income.

Exercise 5-11 Solution

The required information would be calculated as follows:

UCC balance January 1, 2021	$24,883
Add: Acquisitions during the year	Nil
Deduct: Dispositions during the year—Lesser of:	
• Capital cost = $54,000	
• Proceeds of disposition = $18,000	(18,000)
December 31, 2021, UCC balance	
(no remaining property)	$ 6,883
Terminal loss	(6,883)
January 1, 2022, UCC balance	Nil

As there is a positive balance in the class on the last day of the taxation year, but no remaining property, there would be a terminal loss of $6,883. This loss is deducted in the calculation of business income for 2021. Note: We have combined the dispositions for convenience, but be aware that the ITA requires separate determinations for each property.

Exercise 5-12 Solution

The accounting results would be calculated as follows:

Proceeds of disposition	$126,000
Carrying value	(43,500)
Accounting gain	$ 82,500

For income tax purposes, there would be a taxable capital gain calculated as follows:

Proceeds of disposition	$126,000
ACB (e.g., capital cost)	(97,000)
Capital gain	$ 29,000
Inclusion rate	1/2
Taxable capital gain	$ 14,500

There would be a reduction of $97,000 in the UCC of the class for the disposition, which is equal to the lesser of the POD of $126,000 and the capital cost of $97,000. The UCC on the last day of the taxation year would be $2,365,000 ($2,462,000 - $97,000). CCA could be claimed on that UCC balance.

While this disposition would reduce the maximum CCA for the current and subsequent years, there would be no recapture since the UCC balance is not negative at year end. In addition, there is no terminal loss given that there are still properties remaining in the class.

If the $82,500 accounting gain had been included in accounting-based income it would have to be subtracted in the reconciliation process of converting accounting income to net income. In addition, the taxable capital gain would also have to be included. Reconciliations from accounting-based income to net income are covered in Chapter 6.

Exercise 5-13 Solution

CCA on class 14.1 for 2021 would be calculated as follows:

UCC balance—January 1, 2021,	Nil
2020 additions ($85,000 + $105,000)	$190,000
AccII adjustment [(1/2)($190,000)]	95,000
CCA base	$285,000
2021 CCA [(5%)($285,000)]	(14,250)
AccII adjustment reversal	(95,000)
UCC balance—January 1, 2022	$175,750
Deduct: Dispositions during the year—Lesser of:	
Capital cost = $190,000 (see Note)	
Proceeds of disposition =	
($65,000 + $105,000) = $170,000	(170,000)
UCC balance—December 31, 2022, subsequent to the sales	$ 5,750

Note   The capital cost of the single goodwill property is $190,000 ($85,000 + $105,000).

There would be no immediate tax consequences resulting from the dispositions. Subsequent to the sales, Dextrin Inc. has a class 14.1 UCC of $5,750 consisting of goodwill with a capital cost of $20,000 ($190,000 - $170,000). The company would be able to claim CCA of $288 [(5%)($5,750)], which would result in a UCC balance of $5,462 at January 1, 2023 [$5,750 - $288].

Exercise 5-14 Solution

Photocopiers would be included in class 8, a 20% declining balance class. The following table compares the CCA if no election is made with the results if the separate class election is made.

	No Election 10 Copiers	With Election 2 Copiers	With Election 8 Copiers
January acquisitions @ $20,000	$200,000	$40,000	$160,000
Dispositions	(6,000)	(6,000)	N/A
Terminal loss		$34,000	
December acquisitions @ $22,000	44,000	$44,000	
AccII adjustments	119,000	22,000	80,000
CCA base	$357,000	$66,000	$240,000
CCA rate	20%	20%	20%
CCA	$ 71,400	$13,200	$ 48,000

If no election is made, there will be a deduction for CCA of $71,400. Alternatively, if each machine is allocated to a separate class, there will be a combined deduction for CCA of $61,200 ($13,200 + $48,000). In addition, there will be a terminal loss of $34,000. The use of the election increases the total deductible amount by $23,800 [($13,200 + $48,000) + $34,000 terminal loss - $71,400].

Self-Study Problem Solutions

Self-Study Problems are available to download from MyLab Accounting.

SSP 5-1 Solution

The required calculation of the maximum CCA is as follows:

	Class 1	Class 8	Class 10
Opening balance	$2,597,000	$718,000	$ 524,000
Additions	Nil	Nil	374,000
Dispositions			
Proceeds of disposition	Nil	Nil	(234,000)
AccII adjustment			
[(1/2)($374,000 - $234,000)]	Nil	Nil	70,000
CCA base	$2,597,000	$718,000	$ 734,000
CCA rate	4%	20%	30%
Maximum CCA	$ 103,880	$143,600	$ 220,200

Since the building was not acquired after March 18, 2007, the CCA rate is only 4%.

This gives a maximum amount for CCA of $467,680 for the taxation year ($103,880 + $143,600 + $220,200).

Part B

Since the company only has net and taxable income before CCA of $328,000 and the problem states that loss carry overs should not be considered, maximum CCA would not be deducted as this would produce a loss. Only $328,000 in CCA should be taken to reduce the taxable income to nil.

Given that the CCA deduction is limited to $328,000, it would normally be deducted from the class with the lowest rates. This would leave the unclaimed amounts in classes with higher rates, which, in turn, would maximize the amount that could be deducted in subsequent years. Taking this approach, the recommendation would be to claim the CCA as follows:

Class 1 (maximum available)	$103,880
Class 8 (maximum available)	143,600
Class 10 (required balance)	80,520
Total CCA	$328,000

This CCA claim would reduce taxable income to nil.

Note that if there were plans to sell the building for more than its opening UCC, this could affect the choice of classes from which to deduct CCA as any CCA claimed from class 1 would have to be added to income as recaptured CCA when the building is sold.

SSP 5-2 Solution
Class 1

The required information is calculated as follows:

January 1, 2021 UCC balance		$115,000
Additions		Nil
Dispositions—Lesser of:		
• Capital cost = $190,000		
• Proceeds of disposition = $110,000		(110,000)
December 31, 2021, balance with no property remaining		$ 5,000
Terminal loss		(5,000)
January 1, 2022, UCC balance		Nil

Since the building sold is the last property in the class, there is a terminal loss of $5,000, which is deducted in the determination of 2021 business income. The proceeds of disposition for the building total $110,000, which is below its capital cost of $190,000. Therefore there is no capital gain. As the adjusted cost base of the land is equal to the proceeds of disposition, there is no gain on the disposition of the land. Since land is non-depreciable capital property, a disposition can result in a capital gain or capital loss. Only capital gains are possible for depreciable property, however.

Class 8

The required information is calculated as follows:

January 1, 2021, UCC balance		$ 96,000
Additions	$52,000	
Dispositions—Lesser of:		
• Capital cost = $75,000		
• Proceeds of disposition = $35,000	(35,000)	17,000
AccII adjustment [(1/2)($17,000)]		8,500
CCA base		$121,500
CCA at 20%		(24,300)
AccII adjustment reversal		(8,500)
January 1, 2022, UCC balance		$ 88,700

Class 10

The required information is calculated as follows:

January 1, 2021, UCC balance		$ 6,700
Additions	$ 8,000	
Dispositions—Lesser of:		
• Cost = $20,000		
• Proceeds = $25,000	(20,000)	(12,000)
AccII adjustment (only if net additions are positive)		N/A
Negative ending balance		($ 5,300)
Recapture		5,300
January 1, 2022, UCC balance		Nil

The used automobile is a passenger vehicle that would not be included in class 10.1 since its capital cost does not exceed $30,000.

There is no AccII adjustment since there are no "net additions."

The excess of the $25,000 proceeds over the capital cost of $20,000 is a $5,000 capital gain, one-half of which would be a taxable capital gain of $2,500.

CCA can only be claimed if on the last day of the taxation year (December 31, 2021) there is a positive balance in the UCC and property remains in the class at that time. The negative balance of $5,300 is recapture, which will be fully included in 2021 business income.

Class 53

The required information is as follows:

January 1, 2021, UCC balance	$75,000
CCA at 50%	(37,500)
January 1, 2022, UCC balance	$ 37,500

Summary of results (required)

The preceding results can be summarized as follows:

Terminal loss—Class 1	($ 5,000)
CCA—Class 8	(24,300)
Recapture—Class 10	5,300
CCA—Class 53	(37,500)
Decrease in business income	($61,500)
Taxable capital gain—Class 10 [(1/2)($25,000 - $20,000)]	2,500
Impact on 2021 net income	($59,000)

Note that detailed coverage of capital gains is available in Chapter 8 of the text.

SSP 5-3 Solution
2018 Solution

The required calculations are as follows:

September 1, 2018, UCC balance	Nil
Additions to class 10 [(20 Cars)($21,500)]	$430,000
One-half net additions [(1/2)($430,000)]	(215,000)
CCA base	$215,000
CCA [(30%)($215,000)(122/365)]	(21,559)
One-half net additions	215,000
Class 10 UCC balance January 1, 2019	$408,441

The first-year fiscal period is only 122 days, between September 1 and December 31, 2018, therefore the short fiscal period rule applies to reduce CCA that can be claimed. In addition since the purchase of the compact cars was prior to November 21, 2018, the AccII does not apply, instead the old half-year rule applies, as illustrated.

2019 Solution

The required calculations are as follows:

January 1, 2019, UCC balance	$408,441
Additions [(6 cars)($22,800)]	136,800
Dispositions—Lesser of:	
• Capital cost = 6 @ $21,500 = $129,000	
• Proceeds of disposition = 6 @ $11,400 = $68,400	(68,400)
AccII adjustment net additions [(1/2)($136,800 - $68,400)]	34,200
CCA base	$ 511,041
CCA [(30%)($511,041)]	(153,312)
AccII reversal	(34,200)
January 1, 2020, UCC balance	$323,529

2020 Solution

With respect to class 10 cars, the required calculations are as follows:

January 1, 2020, UCC balance	$323,529
Additions [(18 cars)($24,300)]	437,400
Dispositions—Lesser of:	
• Capital cost = 14 @ $21,500 = $301,000	
• Proceeds of disposition = $137,200	(137,200)
AccII adjustment [(1/2)($437,400 - $137,200)]	150,100
CCA base	$773,829
CCA [(30%)($773,829)]	(232,149)
AccII adjustment reversal	(150,100)
January 1, 2021, UCC balance	$391,580

With respect to the BMW convertibles, each would have to be allocated to a separate class 10.1. Further, the addition to each class 10.1 would be limited to $30,000. The required calculations would be as follows:

	BMW 1 Class 10.1	BMW 2 Class 10.1
2020 purchases	$30,000	$30,000
AccII adjustment	15,000	15,000
CCA base	$45,000	$45,000
CCA [(30%)($45,000)]	(13,500)	(13,500)
AccII adjustment reversal	(15,000)	(15,000)
UCC for January 1, 2021	$16,500	$ 16,500

2021 Solution
The required calculations for the class 10 vehicles are as follows:

January 1, 2021, UCC balance	$391,580
Dispositions—Lesser of:	
• Capital cost = 18 @ $24,300 + 6 @ $22,800 = $574,200	
• Proceeds of disposition = 24 @ $8,300 = $199,200	(199,200)
Balance before terminal loss	$ 192,380
Terminal loss	(192,380)
October 1, 2021, UCC balance	Nil

After all of the property in class 10 has been sold there is a positive UCC balance of $192,380. This results in a terminal loss that will be fully deducted in the calculation of the partnership's business income. A subsequent adjustment will be made to the UCC balance to reset it to nil. Since the business ceased operations on September 30, 2021, the next day would be October 1, 2021.

There is no recapture or terminal loss recognition in the ITA for class 10.1 property. The ITA allows 50% of the maximum CCA that would have been available had the properties not been sold in the year of the sale. As a result the partnership would be entitled to a 2021 CCA claim of $3,702 [(1/2)(2 vehicles)(30%)($16,500)(273/365)].

SSP 5-4 Solution
Part A
The maximum CCA for the three years would be calculated as follows:

2019	Class 1	Class 10	Class 8
April 1, 2019, UCC balance	Nil	Nil	Nil
Additions	$180,000	$150,000	$48,000
AccII adjustment [(50%)(additions)]	90,000	75,000	24,000
CCA base	$270,000	$225,000	$72,000
Maximum CCA			
Class 1 [(6%)($270,000)(275 ÷ 365)]*	(12,206)		
Class 10 [(30%)($225,000)(275 ÷ 365)]		(50,856)	
Class 8 [(20%)($72,000)((275 ÷ 365)]			(10,849)
AccII reversal	(90,000)	(75,000)	(24,000)
January 1, 2020, UCC balance	$ 167,794	$ 99,144	$ 37,151

*As the class 1 building is being used 100% for non-residential purposes that is not manufacturing and processing, it would qualify for the 6% CCA rate.

The total maximum CCA for 2019 would be $73,911 ($12,206 + $50,856 + $10,849).

2020	Class 1	Class 10	Class 8
January 1, 2020, UCC balance	$167,794	$ 99,144	$ 37,151
Additions	Nil	72,000	Nil
Disposition—Lesser of:			
Capital cost = $75,000			
Proceeds = [(3)($14,000)] = $42,000	Nil	(42,000)	Nil
AccII adjustment			
[(1/2)($72,000 - $42,000)]	Nil	15,000	Nil
CCA base	$167,794	$144,144	$ 37,151
Maximum CCA			
Class 1 [(6%)($167,794)	(10,068)		
Class 10 [(30%)($144,144)]		(43,243)	
Class 8 [(20%)($37,151)]			(7,430)
AccII reversal	Nil	(15,000)	Nil
January 1, 2021, UCC balance	$157,726	$ 85,901	$29,721

The total maximum CCA for 2020 would be $60,741 ($10,068 + $43,243 + $7,430).

2021	Class 1	Class 10	Class 10.1	Class 8
January 1, 2021, UCC balance	$ 157,726	$ 85,901	Nil	$29,721
Additions (class maximum)*	Nil	Nil	$30,000	Nil
Class 10 disposition—Lesser of:				
Capital cost = $25,000				
Proceeds = $27,000	N/A	(25,000)	N/A	N/A
Class 8 dispositions—Lesser of:				
Capital cost = $12,000				
Proceeds = Nil	N/A	N/A	N/A	Nil
AccII adjustment				
[(50%)($30,000)]	N/A	N/A	15,000	N/A
Balance	$ 157,726	$60,901	$45,000	$29,721
Maximum CCA				
Class 1 [(6%)($157,726)]	(9,464)			
Class 10 [(30%)($60,901)]		(18,270)		
Class 10.1 [(30%)($45,000)]			(13,500)	
Class 8 [(20%)($29,721)]				(5,944)
AccII adjustment reversal	N/A	N/A	(15,000)	N/A
January 1, 2022, UCC balance	$148,262	$42,631	$16,500	$23,777

*Additions to class 10.1 are limited to $30,000.

The total maximum CCA for 2021 would be $47,178 ($9,464 + $18,270 + $13,500 + $5,944).

Part B

The income tax consequences of the unusual events would be as follows:

Theft of Equipment This is a disposition with nil proceeds. There will be no immediate income tax effect as the equipment was not the last property in the class on December 31, 2020 (the last day of the taxation year).

Car Sale As the car was sold for $2,000 more than its capital cost, there would be a capital gain of $2,000, resulting in a taxable capital gain of $1,000 [(1/2)($2,000)]. However, as there is still a positive balance in the class at the end of the year (December 31, 2021) with properties remaining in the class, no terminal loss could be claimed.

SSP 5-5 Solution
Case One
For the year ending December 31, 2021, the maximum CCA, as well as the UCC balance for January 1, 2022, for Traxit's class 14.1 would be as calculated as follows:

January 1, 2021, UCC balance	Nil
2021 additions ($56,000 + $124,000)	$180,000
AccII adjustment [(50%)($180,000)]	90,000
CCA base	$270,000
2021 CCA [(5%)($270,000)]	(13,500)
AccII adjustment reversal	(90,000)
January 1, 2022, UCC balance	$166,500

The results for 2022 would be calculated as follows:

January 1, 2022, UCC balance	$166,500
Disposition—Lesser of:	
Capital cost = $180,000	
Proceeds of disposition = $97,000	(97,000)
CCA base	$ 69,500
2021 CCA [(5%)($69,500)]	(3,475)
January 1, 2023, UCC	$ 66,025

There would be no immediate income tax consequences resulting from the sale of goodwill, other than a reduction in the UCC and in the capital cost of the single goodwill property, which is now $83,000 [$180,000 - $97,000].

Case Two
For the year ending December 31, 2021, the maximum CCA, as well as the UCC balance for January 1, 2022, for Traxit's class 14.1 would be as calculated as follows:

January 1, 2021, UCC balance	Nil
2021 additions ($34,000 + $47,000)	$ 81,000
AccII adjustment [(50%)($81,000)]	40,500
CCA base	$121,500
2021 CCA [(5%)($121,500)]	(6,075)
AccII adjustment reversal	(40,500)
January 1, 2022, UCC	$ 74,925

The results for 2022 would be calculated as follows:

January 1, 2022, UCC balance	$74,925
Disposition—Lesser of:	
Capital cost = $81,000	
Proceeds of disposition = $85,000	(81,000)
Negative ending balance (December 31, 2022)	($ 6,075)
Recapture of CCA	6,075
January 1, 2023, UCC	Nil
Proceeds of disposition	$85,000
ACB (i.e., capital cost)	(81,000)
Capital gain	$ 4,000
Inclusion rate	1/2
Taxable capital gain	$ 2,000

There would be an increase in net income of $8,075 ($6,075 + $2,000).

SSP 5-6 Solution
Class 1—Buildings (Existing and Separate Class)

As the new building has been included in a separate class 1 as the result of an election, two calculations are required here. The CCA on the existing class 1 would be as follows:

January 1, 2021, UCC balance	$590,000
Disposition—Lesser of:	
Proceeds = $290,000	
Capital cost = $300,000	(290,000)
CCA base	$300,000
CCA rate	4%
Maximum CCA for 2021	$ 12,000

Since the buildings in this class were not acquired after March 18, 2007, they are not eligible for the enhanced CCA rates of 6% or 10%.

Since the replacement building is new, used 100% for non-residential purposes, and included in a separate class 1, it qualifies for an enhanced CCA rate. Since it is not used for manufacturing and processing, the enhanced rate is 6%. Using this rate, the CCA on the new building would be as follows:

January 1, 2021, UCC balance	Nil
Additions ($500,000 - $125,000)	$375,000
AccII adjustment [(50%)($375,000)]	187,500
CCA base	$562,500
CCA rate	6%
Maximum CCA for 2021	$ 33,750

Class 8—Furniture

The required calculation here would be as follows:

January 1, 2021, UCC balance	$570,000
Additions	14,000
AccII adjustment [(50%)($14,000)]	7,000
CCA base	$591,000
CCA rate	20%
Maximum CCA for 2021	$ 118,200

Class 10—Vehicles

The required calculations here would be as follows:

January 1, 2021, UCC balance	$61,000
Additions	22,000
AccII adjustment*	N/A
Old half-year rule**	N/A
CCA base	$83,000
CCA rate	30%
Maximum CCA for 2021	$24,900

*Depreciable property is not eligible for the AccII if (1) CCA or terminal loss deductions had been made previously by anyone whether or not they were non-arm's length with the purchaser, (2) the property was owned or acquired by someone non-arm's length with the purchaser, or (3) a rollover rule applied to the purchase of the property. Meeting any one of these conditions would prevent the AccII from being available to the purchaser. In this case both of the first two conditions are met, excluding the property from the AccII. At this point a shareholder who has a controlling interest in a corporation is considered to be non-arm's length with that corporation. Non-arm's-length concepts are discussed in Chapters 9 and 14.

**If the AccII does not apply then the old half-year rules could apply (see Paragraph 5-71). In this case the old half-year rule does not apply because of an exception to that rule that prevents its application if the transaction is between non-arm's-length persons, the property was depreciable property to the non-arm's-length seller, and that seller owned the property for more than one year (ITR 1100(2.2)). The rule is designed to avoid the old half-year rule where, in general, the non-arm's-length seller had been subject to the old half-year rule on that property. If the property had not been depreciable property to the shareholder (meaning that it was not used in any manner to earn income), then the AccII would not have applied but the old half-year rule would have applied.

The shareholder would be able to deduct a terminal loss of $4,000 [$26,000 UCC - $22,000 disposition] since there would have been no property remaining in the class and a positive UCC balance on the last day of the taxation year.

Summary (not required)
The maximum CCA is as follows:

Class 1	$ 12,000
Class 1	33,750
Class 8	118,200
Class 10	24,900
Maximum CCA	$188,850

SSP 5-7 Solution
Class 1—Building
There were no additions or dispositions in this class. As a consequence, the maximum 2021 CCA would be $25,000 [(4%)($625,000)]. The January 1, 2022, UCC of class 1 would be $600,000 ($625,000 - $25,000). Even though the building was acquired after March 18, 2007, it would not have been eligible for an enhanced CCA rate since it was not purchased new.

Class 8—Office Furniture and Equipment
The required calculations for this class would be as follows:

January 1, 2021, UCC balance		$155,000
Additions	$27,000	
Dispositions—Lesser of:		
• Capital cost = $22,000		
• Proceeds of disposition = $35,000	(22,000)	5,000
AccII adjustment [(50%)($5,000)]		2,500
CCA base		$162,500
2021 CCA [(20%)($162,500)]		(32,500)
AccII adjustment reversal		(2,500)
January 1, 2022, UCC balance		$ 127,500

The sale of the furniture and equipment would result in a taxable capital gain that would be calculated as follows:

Proceeds of disposition	$35,000
ACB (i.e., capital cost)	(22,000)
Capital gain	$13,000
Inclusion rate	1/2
Taxable capital gain for 2021	$ 6,500

Class 10—Vehicles
The required calculations for this class would be as follows:

January 1, 2021, UCC balance		$118,000
Additions	$33,000	
Disposition of Truck—Lesser of:		
• Capital cost = $23,000		
• Proceeds of disposition = $8,500	(8,500)	
Disposition of car—Lesser of:		
• Capital cost = $17,000		
• Proceeds of disposition = $8,000	(8,000)	16,500
AccII adjustment [(50%)($16,500)]		8,250
CCA base		$142,750
2021 CCA [(30%)($142,750)]		(42,825)
AccII adjustment reversal		(8,250)
January 1, 2022, UCC balance		$ 91,675

Note that the amount received from the insurance company on the destroyed vehicle is treated as proceeds of disposition.

Class 12—Tools
Tools that cost $500 or less are allocated to class 12 where they are not subject to the half-year rule or the AccII provisions. This means that they are eligible for a CCA rate of 100% in the year of purchase. As a consequence, the entire $34,000 can be deducted as CCA for 2021, leaving a nil UCC balance at January 1, 2022.

Class 13—Leasehold Improvements
In general, leasehold improvements will be amortized over the term of the lease on a straight-line basis. For purposes of applying this calculation, the term of the lease would include the first renewal option, beginning in a period after the improvements were made. In the case of the original improvements, the period to be used is 12 years. With respect to the improvements during the current year, the amortization period will be 9 years. Also note that class 13 property is eligible for the AccII to the extent of net additions. The required calculations are as follows:

Opening UCC balance		$ 61,750
Additions		45,000
CCA base		$106,750
CCA for 2021:		
• 2017 improvements ($78,000 ÷ 12)	($6,500)	
• 2020 improvements including AccII		
Adjustment [($45,000 ÷ 9)(150%)]	(7,500)	(14,000)
January 1, 2022, UCC balance		$ 92,750

Class 14—Intangible Property

The required calculations for this class are as follows:

January 1, 2021, UCC balance	Nil
Disposition—Lesser of:	
• Capital cost = Nil	
• Proceeds of disposition = $87,000	Nil
January 1, 2022, UCC balance	Nil

Proceeds of disposition	$ 87,000
ACB (i.e., capital cost)	Nil
Capital gain	$ 87,000
Inclusion rate	1/2
Taxable capital gain for 2021	$43,500

Class 50—Computer Hardware

The required calculations are as follows:

January 1, 2021, UCC balance	$ Nil
Additions	28,000
AccII adjustment [(50%)($28,000)]	14,000
CCA base	$42,000
2021 CCA [(55%)($42,000)]	(23,100)
AccII adjustment reversal	(14,000)
January 1, 2022, UCC balance	$ 4,900

Class 53—Manufacturing Equipment

The required calculations are as follows:

January 1, 2021, UCC balance	$217,000
Dispositions—Lesser of:	
• Capital cost = $752,000	
• Proceeds of disposition = $188,000	(188,000)
UCC balance December 31, 2021, no property remaining	$ 29,000
Terminal loss for 2021	(29,000)
January 1, 2022, UCC balance	Nil

After all of the remaining property in class 53 has been sold, there is still a positive $29,000 UCC balance. This results in a terminal loss that will be deducted in full from the 2021 net income of the Atlantic Manufacturing Company.

Other Income Effects

In addition, the following income tax consequences resulted from the information provided in the problem:

Taxable capital gain on class 8 properties	$ 6,500
Taxable capital gain on class 14.1 properties	43,500
Terminal loss on class 53 properties	(29,000)
Total net impact on 2021 net income	$21,000

Summary of CCA and UCC results (not required)

The maximum 2021 CCA and the January 1, 2022, UCC balances can be summarized as follows:

	Maximum CCA	UCC
Class 1	$25,000	$600,000
Class 8	32,500	127,500
Class 10	42,825	91,675
Class 12	34,000	Nil
Class 13	14,000	92,750
Class 14.1	Nil	Nil
Class 50	23,100	4,900
Class 53	Nil	Nil

SSP 5-8 Solution
Part A

The required calculation of the maximum CCA is as follows:

Class 8 [(20%)($163,000)]	$ 32,600
Class 10 (Note 1)	43,950
Class 12 (Note 2)	42,000
Class 13 (Note 3)	24,000
Class 14.1 [(5%)($132,330)]	6,617
Maximum total CCA	$149,167

Note 1 The class 10 CCA would be calculated as follows:

Opening balance	$ 112,000
Additions	52,000
Proceeds of disposition (less than cost)	(29,000)
AccII adjustment [(1/2)($52,000 - $29,000)]	11,500
CCA base	$146,500
CCA rate	30%
Maximum CCA	$ 43,950

Note 2 The rate for class 12 is 100%. However, some additions to this class are subject to the old half-year rules. The existence of an opening balance of $42,000 and the statement that maximum CCA has always been taken indicates that there must have been $84,000 of capital costs in 2020 that were subject to this rule. Given this, the remaining balance can be deducted in 2021.

Note 3 The $180,000 UCC balance in class 13 is equal to 75% of $240,000. This means that during the two years 2019 and 2020, 25% of the capital cost was claimed as CCA. As the AccII rules are applicable to this class, this represents a 150% claim for 2019 and a full year for 2020. Since class 13 is a straight-line class, this indicates that the CCA rate is 10% ($24,000 CCA claim for 2020 ÷ $240,000). Based on this analysis, maximum CCA for 2021 would be $24,000 [(10%)($240,000)].

Part B

Since the company only has net and taxable income before CCA of $43,000, and the problem states that loss carry overs should be ignored, maximum CCA would not be deducted. Only $43,000 in CCA should be taken to reduce the taxable income to nil.

As to which CCA classes should be reduced, the general rule is to deduct the required amount from the balances with the lowest rates. By leaving the balances with higher rates untouched, larger amounts of CCA can be deducted in later periods as required.

Following this general rule, the recommended CCA would be as follows:

Class 14.1 (maximum available)	$ 6,617
Class 13 (maximum available)	24,000
Class 8 ($43,000 - $6,617 - $24,000)	12,383
Total CCA	$43,000

The deduction of this amount of CCA would reduce both taxable income and taxes payable to nil.

CHAPTER 6

Learning Objectives

After completing Chapter 6, you should be able to:

1. Apply the source of income concept to a business [Paragraphs (P hereafter)] 6-1 to 6-5).
2. Explain why the concept of a business is so important to the ITA (P 6-6 to 6-10).
3. Define a business (P 6-11 to 6-15).
4. Differentiate in general terms between a source of income that is a business versus a property (P6-16).
5. Describe the general circumstances that determine when a business commences (P 6-17 to 6-19).
6. Explain the importance of a personal element to a business (P 6-20 to 6-24).
7. Apply a basic source of income analysis (P 6-25 and 6-26).
8. Explain the concept of an adventure or concern in the nature of trade (P 6-27 to 6-32).
9. Describe the three general types of business property recognized by the ITA (P 6-33 and 6-34).
10. Describe the general principles as to what is required to be included in business income (P 6-35 to 6-39).
11. Explain the meaning of "profit" and the relevance of accounting (P 6-40 to 6-44).
12. Describe and explain the importance of the 9-12-18-20 rule (P 6-45 to 6-49).
13. Explain the purpose and function of ITA 12(1)(a) and (b) (P 6-50 to 6-57).
14. Describe what is meant by the "quality of income" and its importance (P 6-58 and 6-59).
15. Apply the system of reserves that can be used in determining business income (P 6-60 to 6-75).
16. Describe the general limitations on business expenses (P 6-76 to 6-83).
17. Explain the capital expenditure limitation and how to identify capital versus income expenditures (P 6-84 to 6-92).
18. Explain and apply some of the more common business expense limitations (P 6-93 to 6-111).
19. Apply an expenditure analysis using the Figure 6-1 flowchart (P 6-112).
20. Apply the work space at home expense limitation (P 6-113 to 6-122).
21. Understand the basic limitation on foreign media advertising (P 6-123 to 6-125).
22. Describe the basic inventory concepts used in the ITA (P 6-126 to 6-133).
23. Familiarize yourself with the more common expenses allowed by ITA 20 (P 6-134).
24. Apply the various Subdivision f limitations (P 6-135 to 6-164).
25. Understand and apply the reconciliation process (P 6-165 to 6-170).
26. Describe the rules for determining fiscal periods, taxation years, and the elective treatment available in ITA 249.1(4), including the additional business income adjustments (P 6-171 to 6-180).
27. Explain and apply the restricted farming concept, including the three different types of activity (P 6-181 to 6-185).
28. Explain how the ITA handles work-in-process (WIP) (P 6-186 to 6-188).
29. Explain how the ITA treats inventories and accounts receivable on the sale of a business (P 6-189 to 6-193).

How to Work through Chapter 6

Visit pearsonmylabandmastering.com to access MyLab Accounting for this text. Once there, you can access student resources such as Self-Study Problems, Practice Exams, Flashcards, updates, and more.

We recommend the following approach in dealing with the material in this chapter:

Introduction
- Read paragraph 6-1 to 6-5 (in the text).
- Do Exercise 6-1 (in the text) and check the solution in this Study Guide.

The Importance of a Business and Defining a Business
- Read paragraph 6-6 to 6-16.
- Do Exercise 6-2 and check the solution in this Study Guide.

The Concept of a Business, the Personal Element, an Adventure, Types of Business Property, and the Source Analysis
- Read paragraph 6-16 to 6-34.
- Do Self-Study Problem 6-1, which is available on MyLab, and check the solution in this Study Guide.

Business Profit, the Quality of Income, and the 9-12-18-20 Rule
- Read paragraph 6-35 to 6-53.
- Do Exercise 6-3 and check the solution in this Study Guide.
- Read paragraph 6-54 to 6-59.
- Do Exercise 6-4 and check the solution in the Study Guide.

Reserves for Doubtful Debts, Undelivered Goods, and Unpaid Amounts
- Read paragraph 6-60 to 6-72.
- Do Exercise 6-5 and check the solution in this Study Guide.
- Read paragraph 6-73.
- Do Exercise 6-6 and check the solution in this Study Guide.
- Read paragraphs 6-74 to 6-75.
- Do Exercise 6-7 and check the solution in this Study Guide.
- Do Self-Study Problems 6-2 and 6-3 and check the solutions in this Study Guide.

Limitations on Deductions from Business and Property Income, Including Work Space in the Home Costs
- Read paragraph 6-76 to 6-122.
- Do Exercise 6-8 and check the solution in this Study Guide.
- Do Self-Study Problem 6-4 and check the solution in this Study Guide.
- Read paragraph 6-123 to 6-125.

Specific Deductions from Business Income, Including Cost of Sales
- Read paragraph 6-126 to 6-133.
- Do Exercise 6-9 and check the solution in this Study Guide.
- Do Self-Study Problem 6-5 and check the solution in this Study Guide.
- Read paragraph 6-134.

Limitations on Deductions from Business Income
- Read paragraph 6-135 to 6-149.
- Do Exercise 6-10 and check the solution in this Study Guide.

Restrictions on Automobile Costs
- Read paragraph 6-150 to 6-157.
- Do Exercise 6-11 and check the solution in this Study Guide.
- Do Self-Study Problems 6-6 to 6-8 and check the solutions in this Study Guide.

Leasing Property
- Read paragraph 6-158 to 6-160.
- Do Exercise 6-12 and check the solution in this Study Guide.

Illegal Payments, Fines, and Penalties
- Read paragraph 6-161 and 6-164.

Reconciliation of Accounting Net Income and Net Income
- Read paragraph 6-165 to 6-170.
- Do Self-Study Problems 6-9 to 6-11 and check the solutions in this Study Guide.

Taxation Year and Additional Business Income
- Read paragraph 6-171 to 6-180.
- Do Exercise 6-13 and check the solution in this Study Guide.
- Do Self-Study Problem 6-12 and check the solution in this Study Guide.

Farming Income and Losses, Including Restricted Farm Losses
- Read paragraph 6-181 to 6-185.
- Do Exercise 6-14 and check the solution in this Study Guide.
- Read paragraph 6-186 to 6-188.
- Do Self-Study Problem 6-13 and 6-14 and check the solutions in this Study Guide.

Sale of a Business, Including ITA 22 Election on Accounts Receivable
- Read paragraph 6-189 to 6-193.
- Do Exercise 6-15 and check the solution in this Study Guide.
- Do Self-Study Problems 6-15 to 6-17 and check the solutions in this Study Guide.

To Complete This Chapter
- Visit MyLab Accounting for more practice problem material, and test yourself with the glossary flashcards.
- Review the Key Terms at the end of the chapter, and consult the glossary for definitions.
- Ensure you have achieved the Chapter 6 Learning Objectives listed in this Study Guide.
- As a review, view the PowerPoint presentations available on MyLab.

Practice Examination
- Available on MyLab, write the Practice Examination for this chapter, and mark it using the solutions provided.

Exercise Solutions

Exercise 6-1 Solution
A starting point would be a change of intention to one where the primary motive would be to make a profit. Converting the activity to a source of income, however, would require more than a simple change of intention. An evaluation of the potential to earn a positive return would have to be undertaken, including whether the existing property is sufficient to generate a profit or whether additional property would have to be purchased. Evaluating the market potential for increased sales and other factors would need to be considered. In effect there should be some plan in place to take the personal activity to the next level. The plan itself would be the starting point, but actual implementation would be necessary to establish a source of income. There is no requirement to actually earn a profit, however, as long as the motive is well-established and the business structure has been put in place.

If you suggested purchasing additional land, advertising, connecting with retailers, purchasing equipment to increase production, and perhaps hiring an individual or two, you are on the right track.

Exercise 6-2 Solution
(1) You are considered to be carrying on a business if you devoted your time, attention, and labour to an activity that had a potential to be profitable. You can meet these conditions by employing

individuals to do the work for you or contract with individuals to perform the work on contract. In this case you would be considered to be carrying on a farming business.

(2) You have two sources of income—one from the farming business and a second being the farmhouse, which is being used as a rental property. Income from the rental property would be considered income from property because of its passive nature.

(3) ITA 20(1)(aa) allows an expense for landscaping costs around a building used to carry on a business. Since the rental property is not a business, the landscaping costs would not be deductible.

Exercise 6-3 Solution
ITA 12(1)(b) requires you to include an amount receivable for services rendered or products sold in the year in the course of a business. Receivable means a legally enforceable claim without any conditions attached to the amount or part of the amount. In this case, since $30,000 of the contract price is conditional on approval of an architect, it is not considered receivable. Therefore only $270,000 will be shown as business income in 2021 from this contract. The remaining $30,000 will be included in business income for 2022, assuming the work meets the approval of the architect.

Exercise 6-4 Solution
The non-refundable deposit of $400 per person has the "quality of income" since it is not required to be refunded and you are entitled to do whatever you want with the amounts. The non-refundable deposit is therefore required to be included in your business income through ITA 9. ITA 12(1)(a) would not apply to the non-refundable deposit because it is not contingent on you having to provide any services.

Part of the annual advance payment of $75 for each of the months September 1 to December 31, 2021, represents business income earned that has the quality of income and is therefore required to be included in your business income for 2021 as a result of ITA 9. The remaining eight months of advance payments are required to be included in your business income as a result of ITA 12(1)(a), but you are entitled to deduct the same amount as a reserve for 2021 (ITA 20(1)(m)).

Summary:

Non-refundable deposit—ITA 9	$ 80,000	[($400)(200 people)]
Fees earned—ITA 9	60,000	[($75)(4 months)(200 people)]
Unearned advance—ITA 12(1)(a)	120,000	[($75)(8 months)(200 people)]
Less: Reserve—ITA 20(1)(m)	(120,000)	
Business income for 2021	$140,000	

Exercise 6-5 Solution
The net bad/doubtful debt expense for accounting purposes would be as follows:

2021 estimate of future doubtful debts (credit allowance)	($18,400)
Increase in expense to eliminate debit balance in allowance ($17,200 actual bad debts - $16,000 allowance)	(1,200)
2021 expense for accounting purposes	($ 19,600)

For income tax purposes, the net expense will be the same $19,600 calculated as follows:

Add: 2020 reserve for income tax—ITA 12(1)(d)		$16,000
Deduct:		
2021 Bad debt expense—ITA 20(1)(p)	($ 17,200)	
2021 Reserve for doubtful debts—ITA 20(1)(l)	(18,400)	(35,600)
2021 Net expense for income tax		($ 19,600)

Exercise 6-6 Solution

The amount to be included in business income would be calculated as follows:

Cash sales	$53,400—ITA 12(1)(a)
Accounts receivable	26,300—ITA 12(1)(b)
Reserve for undelivered services	(5,600)—ITA 20(1)(m)
Reserve for doubtful accounts	(425)—ITA 20(1)(l)
Total increase	$73,675

Exercise 6-7 Solution

As some of the proceeds are not receivable for more than two years after the date of sale, a reserve can be deducted under ITA 20(1)(n) for the years 2021, 2022, and 2023. As December 31, 2024, is more than 36 months after the sale was made, no reserve can be deducted for 2024 or 2025. Note that the previous year's reserve is added to income before deducting the new reserve. The maximum reserve is based on the gross profit of $65,000. None of this profit will be recognized in 2021 as no proceeds are received. In 2022 and 2023, 25% of the profit will be recognized, with the remainder being in 2024, when no reserve can be deducted. The gross profit percentage on which the reserve is based is 45% [$54,000/$120,000].

The maximum reserve that can be deducted in each year, as well as the minimum income to be recognized in each year, is shown in the following schedule:

	Income	Proceeds Received
2021 reserve = [(45%)($120,000)] = $54,000	Nil	Nil
2022 reserve = [(45%)($90,000)] = $40,500	$ 13,500	$ 30,000
2023 reserve = [(45%)($60,000)] = $27,000	13,500	30,000
2024 reserve = Nil (> 36 months from sale)	27,000	30,000
2025 reserve = Nil (all proceeds received)	Nil	30,000
Totals	$54,000	$120,000

Note that the technically correct calculation of income involves adding back the previous year's reserve and deducting the new reserve. For example, the calculation for 2023 involves adding back the 2022 reserve of $40,500 and deducting the new 2023 reserve of $27,000 to calculate the business income addition of $13,500 ($48,500 - $27,000).

Exercise 6-8 Solution

The following work space in the home expenses would be deductible in each of the three scenarios:

	Part A	Part B	Part C
Utilities	$2,400	$ 2,400	$ 2,400
Maintenance and repairs	4,600	4,600	4,600
Property taxes	Nil	5,200	5,200
House insurance	Nil	2,300	2,300
Interest on mortgage	Nil	Nil	7,800
House CCA	Nil	Nil	12,000
Subtotal	$ 7,000	$14,500	$34,300
Percentage	25%	25%	25%
Subtotal	$1,750	$ 3,625	$ 8,575
Repainting and rewiring (100%)	1,000	1,000	1,000
Internet service fees [(95%)($960)]	Nil	Nil	912
Monthly phone [(95%)($600)]	Nil	Nil	570
Long distance charges (100%)	390	390	390
Maximum deduction	$3,140	$ 5,015	$11,447

Exercise 6-9 Solution

The average per-unit cost of $2.87 ($663,850 ÷ 231,000) is calculated as follows:

Price	Units	Total
$2.50	50,000	$ 125,000
$2.85	35,000	99,750
$2.95	62,000	182,900
$3.05	84,000	256,200
Totals	231,000	$ 663,850

The following calculations will be used in this solution.

Fair market value (using replacement cost) [($3.10)(102,000)]	$316,200
Fair market value (using net realizable value) [(90%)($4.50)(102,000)]	413,100
FIFO cost [(84,000)($3.05) + (102,000 - 84,000)($2.95)]	309,300
Average cost [($2.87)(102,000)]	292,740

For tax purposes, the inventory value can be determined by any of the following methods.

Fair market value = Replacement cost	$316,200
Fair market value = Net realizable value	413,100
Lower of FIFO cost ($309,300) or replacement cost ($316,200)	309,300
Lower of FIFO cost ($309,300) or net realizable value ($413,100)	309,300
Lower of average cost ($292,740) or replacement cost ($316,200)	292,740
Lower of average cost ($292,740) or net realizable value ($413,100)	292,740

Exercise 6-10 Solution

Since the fiscal period of the business runs from September 15, 2021, to December 31, 2021, there is a short fiscal period of 108 days [16 days in September + 31 for October + 30 for November and 31 for December]. The short fiscal period will affect the CCA that can be claimed. The base amount for the CCA calculation is limited to the class 10.1 maximum of $30,000. With respect to the interest, ITA 20(1)(c) would have allowed an expense of $1,200, but ITA 67.2 limits what can be claimed based on the number of days in the year in which the interest accrues. Since the financing occurred October 1, 2021, there would be 92 days between October 1 and December 31, 2021. The limitation allows only $10 per day.

As a result, the amounts that can be deducted are as follows:

CCA [(150%)(108/365)(30%)($30,000)]	$3,995
Interest costs—Lesser of:	
• Amount incurred = $1,200 (ITA 20(1)(c))	
• [($10)(92 days)] = $920 (ITA 67.2)	920
Total deduction	$4,915

Exercise 6-11 Solution

The amount he can deduct is limited to $2,229, the least of:

- $4,925 [($985)(5)];
- $4,080 [($800)(153/30)]; and
- $2,229 {[$4,925][$30,000 ÷ (85%)($78,000)]}.

Exercise 6-12 Solution

For income tax purposes, the lease would be treated as an operating lease, with the deduction being based only on the lease payments. The lessor, as the property owner, would be entitled to claim CCA and other expenses related to the ownership. Under accounting standards, the lease would have to be treated as a purchase and capitalized. This is because during the lease term the lease transfers "substantially all of the benefits and risks of ownership related to the leased

---

property from the lessor to the lessee." This means that the accounting deductions would be for amortization on the capitalized property and interest costs on the associated liability.

Exercise 6-13 Solution

Mr. Gelato has an option to include the $102,000 of busines income in his 2022 income tax return. He can, however, elect under ITA 34.1(2) to include $92,617 [($102,000)(306/337)] for the 2021 taxation year and the remaining $9,383 in the 2022 taxation year. In the calculation, 306 represents the number of days between March 1, 2021, and December 31, 2021, and 337 represents the number of days in that first fiscal period from March 1, 2021, to January 31, 2022.

Regardless of the option he chooses he will be required to include $101,092 [($102,300)(334/337)] as additional business income (ITA 34.1(1)) for the 2022 taxation year. In the calculation, 334 represents the number of days between March 1, 2022, and December 31, 2022, and 337 represents the number of days in that first fiscal period from March 1, 2021, to January 31, 2022.

Summary: If he chooses to elect to include part of the 2022 business income in 2021, the result would be that 2021 business income would be $92,617 and 2022 business income would be $110,475 [$9,383 + $101,092] for a total for both years of $203,092. Without choosing the first-year option, no business income would be included in 2021 and $203,092 [$102,000 + $101,092] would be included in 2022.

Exercise 6-14 Solution

For Ms. Morph, farming is not a primary source of income and it is debatable whether the activity would be considered a business and therefore a source of income. However, on the assumption that the farming is a business, the farm losses would be restricted by ITA 31. The unrestricted part of the farm loss would be $10,600 [$2,500 + (50%)($18,700 - $2,500)]. The remaining $8,100 ($18,700 - $10,600) would be a restricted farm loss (RFL) available for carry over to future years to be applied against profits from the same farming business.

The facts suggest that there is a personal element, meaning that the activity can be evaluated based on whether it is sufficiently commercial-like in nature. The small investment together with the limited market suggest it is not a source of income and therefore more of a hobby than a business. If this were the case, then none of the losses would be deductible since there would be no business and therefore no source of income.

Exercise 6-15 Solution

Mr. Nero would include in his 2021 business income the 2020 reserve of $3,800. He could then deduct the $5,250 ($53,450 - $48,200) loss on the receivables. The net income tax effect for Mr. Nero of the ITA 22 election would be a net reduction in business income of $1,450 ($5,250 - $3,800).

Mr. Labelle would have to include the $5,250 difference between the face value and the price paid in his business income. Subsequent to the sale, 100% of any difference between the $53,450 face value of the receivables and amounts actually collected will be deductible when calculating Mr. Labelle's business income.

In addition, Mr. Labelle could establish a reserve for doubtful debts related to any uncollected receivables that are outstanding at the end of the year.

Self-Study Problem Solutions

Self-Study Problems are available to download from MyLab Accounting.

SSP 6-1 Solution
Case 1

The purchase of the property together with the actions of the individual substantiate a profit motive and therefore a source of income. The activity, however, would not normally qualify as a business considering that it was a single property transaction. However, the concept of an adventure or

concern in the nature of trade would apply to characterize the source as business income. As a result the residence would be considered inventory. There would be a fully taxable business profit of $155,000 [$380,000 – $225,000]. Answers to each of the four questions are as follows:
(1) Yes
(2) Business income
(3) Inventory
(4) Business profits of $155,000

Case 2

The answer is identical to Case 1 and for the same reasons. Answers to each of the four questions are as follows:
(1) Yes
(2) Business income
(3) Inventory
(4) Business profits of $210,000 [$500,000 – ($140,000 cost + $150,000 capital expenditures)]

Case 3

The purchase of the old residence was not a source of income until it was rented out in January 2020. While it was used personally it was a non-depreciable capital property. When the home began to be used as a rental property it became a depreciable property eligible for CCA and other operating expenses. Answers to each of the four questions are as follows:
(1) Yes
(2) Property income
(3) Depreciable property
(4) Capital gain of $150,000 [$315,000 – $165,000 cost]. Only 50%, or $75,000, would be included in income as a taxable capital gain. Note: There are many other issues surrounding this topic that will be discussed in Chapter 7.

Case 4

Technically when the owner established an intention to rent out the property and took measures to rent it, including advertising or consulting with a real estate company, the source of income would be established regardless of the one-year delay. The answers shown in Case 3 are unchanged. Because of the lack of rental income the individual would have a rental loss representing the expenses related to the ownership of the property.

Case 5

In this instance there would be no source of income since there is no profit motive and the activity is overshadowed by a personal element. Answers to each of the four questions are as follows:
(1) No
(2) Personal only—no business or property income
(3) Non-depreciable capital property
(4) None of the amounts received as rent would be included in income and none of the expenses could be deducted. Since there is no source of income the income/expenses are ignored. The sale of the property, however, is a different matter. Capital gain of $150,000 [$315,000 – $165,000 cost]. Only 50% of $75,000 would be potentially included in income as a taxable capital gain. Note: Even though the home was only sold for $165,000, there is a rule in ITA 69 that deems transactions between related persons to take place at fair market value. This will be discussed in Chapter 9.

Case 6

In this case Tasha had a source of income that was income from a business. She had inventory, depreciable property (the building and goodwill), and non-depreciable capital property (the land). A source that is business income can have inventory, depreciable property, and non-depreciable capital property. The answers to each of the four questions are as follows:
(1) Yes
(2) Business income

(3) Inventory, depreciable, and non-depreciable capital property

(4) The sale of the inventory would have resulted in business income of $22,000 [$85,000 − $63,000]; the sale of the land would result in a taxable capital gain of $22,500 [(50%)($145,000 - $100,000)]; the sale of the goodwill would result in a taxable capital gain of $50,000 [(50%)($100,000 − Nil cost)]; and the sale of the building would result in a taxable capital gain of $15,000 [(50%)($270,000 − $240,000)] and a recapture of $50,000 [UCC of $190,000 − the lesser of (i) capital cost of $240,000 and (ii) sale price (proceeds of disposition) $270,000)].

SSP 6-2 Solution

The net deduction for bad debts in the calculation of 2021 business income would be calculated as follows:

Add:	
2020 reserve for doubtful debts—ITA 12(1)(d)	$ 11,500
Recoveries of 2020 bad debts during 2021—ITA 12(1)(i)	1,500
Deduct:	
Actual bad debts during 2020 ($8,800 - $700)—ITA 20(1)(p)	(8,100)
2020 reserve for doubtful debts ($15,900 + $700)—ITA 20(1)(l)	(16,600)
2021 Net deduction from business income	($ 11,700)

Note that the facts indicate that the $700 that was due from Dr. Allworth's personal friend should have been claimed as a doubtful debt rather than a bad debt. The effect of the deduction calculations is to shift that amount from the bad debt deduction to a doubtful debt reserve. The $190 recovery in 2020 would have been included in business income for 2020 and therefore would have no effect on 2021 business income.

SSP 6-3 Solution

The results for the two years would be as follows:

	2021	2022
Cash collections ($259,000 - $88,000)	$171,000	
Cash collections ($360,000 - $72,000)		$288,000
Ending receivables	88,000	72,000
Reserve for doubtful cebts:		
Add prior-year reserve	Nil	7,000
Deduct current-year reserve	(7,000)	(9,500)
Deduct actual write-offs	Nil	(6,500)
Advances from customers	27,000	21,000
Reserve for undelivered merchandise:		
Add prior-year reserve	Nil	27,000
Deduct current-year reserve	(27,000)	(21,000)
Gross profit on sale of unused materials	15,000	Nil
Reserve for unpaid amounts:		
Add prior-year reserve		9,677
Deduct current-year reserve*		
{[$15,000][($62,000 - $22,000) ÷ $62,000]}	(9,677)	
{[$15,000][($62,000 - $42,000) ÷ $62,000]}		(4,839)
Net effect	$257,323	$382,838

*As some of the proceeds on the sale of unused materials are not due until two years after the date of the sale, a reserve for unpaid amounts can be deducted. The three-year time limit is not relevant as the full balance is to be paid off prior to the end of that period.

SSP 6-4 Solution
Part A

Under ITA 18(12), the following conditions must be satisfied for expenses related to a work space in a self-contained domestic establishment to be deductible:

- The work space is either the individual's principal place of business; or
- The work space is used exclusively for the purpose of earning income from business and is used on a regular and continuous basis for meeting clients, customers, or patients of the individual in respect of the business.

With respect to Ms. Hart's mail-order business, the use of the livable space in her home appears to be her principal place of business. This means that she would be able to deduct costs for the work space in her home when determining her business income.

Part B

The calculation of the minimum business income to be reported in Ms. Hart`s personal tax return is as follows:

Revenues		$89,000
Less: Expenses other than home work space costs:		
Cost of merchandise sold	($46,000)	
Packaging materials	(1,547)	
Shipping costs	(3,216)	
Miscellaneous office supplies	(825)	
Telephone	(210)	
Advertising brochures	(156)	
CCA (Note 1)	(5,414)	(57,368)
Income before home work space costs		$31,632
Less: Home work space costs (Note 2)		(2,174)
Business income		$29,458

Note 1 Maximum CCA amounts on the depreciable property of the business (not including CCA on the house) for the short fiscal year would be calculated as follows (alternative calculations shown in the two columns):

	100%	Short Fiscal Year (346/365)
Class 8 [($14,000)(150%)(20%)]	$4,200	$3,981
Class 50 [($1,350)(150%)(55%)]	1,114	1,056
Class 12 [($795)(1/2)(100%)]*	398	377
Total	$5,712	
Short fiscal year factor	346/365	
Maximum CCA	$5,414	$5,414

*The AccII provisions do not apply to class 12. Instead the half-year rule would apply.

Note 2   The home work space costs would be calculated as follows:

Utilities for home (heat, light, and water)	$	2,850
Mortgage interest paid		4,183
House insurance		400
Property taxes		1,230
Repairs and maintenance for home		1,125
Total operating costs	$	9,788
Class 1 CCA [($355,000 - $80,000)(1/2)(4%)]*		5,500
Total costs for the home	$	15,288
Percentage of floor space		15%
Subtotal	$	2,293
Short fiscal year factor		346/365
Deductible home work space costs	$	2,174

*As the residence was owned by Veronica prior to a portion being converted to business use, the AccII provisions would not be available. When a home that is used exclusively for personal use begins to be used for income earning purposes there are special rules in the ITA that determine the amount upon which CCA can be claimed. Since this topic (change-of-use rules) is only covered in Chapter 8, we have not attempted to apply these rules or provided information necessary to determine the appropriate amount of CCA that could be claimed. For those familiar with the change-of-use rules, we would be required to make an assumption that the value of the home at the time it begins to be used in part for income earning purposes has not changed.

Part C

There are two issues that should be discussed with Ms. Hart.

- The problem asks to determine the "minimum" business income, meaning that expenses must be maximized. This means that CCA must be deducted on Ms. Hart's home. The problem with this is that, if she takes CCA, it could jeopardize the principal residence exemption on this property, resulting in the payment of taxes on a portion of the taxable capital gain that might arise on any future sale of the property, assuming real estate prices are increasing. This is discussed in more detail in Chapter 8.

- Although it is not relevant for this year, Ms. Hart should be aware in the future that the deduction of work space in home costs cannot be used to create or increase a loss. However, any amount not deductible because it is greater than her income in a particular year (after deducting all expenses other than work space expenses) can be deducted in any subsequent year provided there is sufficient income from the same business in that subsequent year. This provides for an unlimited carry forward of unused work space in home costs (see S4-F2-C2, "*Business Use of Home Expenses*").

SSP 6-5 Solution
Market Determination—Two Possible Values

For income tax purposes, the business can measure market (FMV) using either replacement cost or net realizable value. These values would be as follows:

Replacement cost [($16.75)(5,000)]	$ 83,750
Net realizable value [($18.30)(5,000)]	$ 91,500

Cost Determination—Two Possible Values

In the determination of cost, taxpayers are permitted to use specific identification (this would not appear to be practical here), a first in, first out (FIFO) assumption, or average cost.

Using the FIFO method, the appropriate value for the ending inventory would be determined as follows:

1,500 units at $16.50	$24,750
3,200 units at $21.42	68,544
300 units at $20.25	6,075
5,000 units at FIFO cost	$99,369

Based on average cost, the ending inventory value would be calculated as follows:

Number of units	5,000
Average cost [($297,644 ÷ 15,300)]	19.45
5,000 units at average cost	$97,250

Lower of Cost and Market—Four Possible Values

For income tax purposes, the possible values here would be as follows:

Lower of replacement cost and FIFO cost	$83,750
Lower of replacement cost and average cost	83,750
Lower of net realizable value and FIFO cost	91,500
Lower of net realizable value and average cost	91,500

For accounting purposes, only the last two values would be acceptable.

SSP 6-6 Solution
Part A

In Part A (i), Ms. Wise is an employee and, because her income includes commissions, she can deduct expenses related to her employment income under ITA 8(1)(f), provided no deduction is made under ITA 8(1)(h) or ITA 8(1)(h.1).

Deductions under ITA 8(1)(f) are limited to the amount of commissions earned. Alternatively, travelling costs and motor vehicle costs other than capital costs can be deducted under ITA 8(1)(h) and ITA 8(1)(h.1). Deductions under these provisions are not limited by commission income.

The deduction of dues and other expenses under ITA 8(1)(i) and automobile capital costs (CCA and interest costs) under ITA 8(1)(j) is permitted without regard to other provisions used.

	ITA 8(1)(f) (Limited to $15,000)	ITA 8(1) (h) and (h.1)	ITA 8(1) (i) and (j)	Part A(ii)
Professional dues	-	-	$ 600	$ 600
Automobile costs:				
Operating costs [(35,000/50,000)($6,000)]	$ 4,200	$ 4,200	-	4,200
Financing costs [(35,000/50,000)($2,500)]	-	-	1,750	1,750
CCA (see Note)	-	-	3,465	3,465
Home office costs:				
Utilities [(40%)($3,550)]	-	-	1,420	1,420
Maintenance [(40%)($1,500)]	-	-	600	600
Insurance [(40%)($950)]	380	-	-	380
Property taxes [(40%)($4,700)]	1,880	-	-	1,880
Interest [(40%)($13,500)]	-	-	-	5,400
CCA [($140,000)(4%)]	-	-	-	5,600
Deductible travel costs	19,000	19,000	-	19.000
Country club charges	4,750	-	-	4,750
Total	$30,210	$23,200	$7,835	$ 49,045

Note The passenger vehicle car will be included in a separate class 10.1 capped at $30,000. The excess of $23,000 will not be deductible. Maximum CCA for 2020 would have been $13,500 [(30%)(1.5)($30,000)]. The deductible amount for 2020 would have been this amount multiplied by the employment portion of the total use.

The January 1, 2021, UCC would be $16,500 ($30,000 - $13,500) and maximum CCA for 2021 would have been $4,950 [(30%)($16,500)]. Note that, in determining the relevant UCC value, the full amount of maximum 2020 CCA was deducted, not just the portion that was actually deducted in that year. The deductible amount for 2021 equals $3,465 [(35,000/50,000)($4,950)].

The deduction for home office costs has been split between ITA 8(1)(i) and (f). Since the utilities and maintenance portion can be deducted under ITA 8(1)(i), it is not limited by the commission income. The insurance and property tax components are limited as they can only be deducted under ITA 8(1)(f). A limitation, which is not illustrated in this problem, prevents the deduction of home office costs from creating or increasing an employment loss.

Of the $23,000 of travel expenses, 50% of the $8,000 for business meals is not deductible. The remaining $19,000 is deductible [$23,000 - (1/2)($8,000)] under either ITA 8(1)(f) or 8(1)(h).

The country club charges of $12,000 includes non-deductible membership fees of $2,500 and non-deductible meal expenses of $4,750 [(50%)($9,500)]. The remaining $4,750 is deductible under ITA 8(1)(f).

As the ITA 8(1)(f) amount is limited to the $15,000 in commission income, the total deduction using ITA 8(1)(f), (i), and (j) is $22,835 ($15,000 + $7,835).

The total deduction using ITA 8(1)(h), (h.1), (i), and (j) is $31,035 ($23,200 + $7,835). Note that when this approach is used, home office costs are limited to utilities and maintenance. Further, there is no deduction for entertainment costs. However, this approach results in deductions totalling $8,200 ($31,035 - $22,835) more than the amount available using ITA 8(1)(f), (i), and (j) due to the effect of the commission income limit.

Comparing Parts A (i) and A (ii), there is a difference of $18,010 ($49,045 - $31,035) between the maximum employee and business calculations, illustrating the importance of the difference between being an employee and being in business (i.e., self-employed). This problem is, of course, somewhat unrealistic in that, if Ms. Wise were an employee, it is likely that she would be compensated or reimbursed for at least part of her employment-related expenses.

Part B

As will be discussed in Chapter 8, capital gains on an individual's principal residence are, in general, not subject to income taxes. When a part of a home begins to be used for income earning purposes there are rules in the ITA that treat that change of use as if part of the property had been sold with its status no longer being part of a principal residence. Elective options apply to neutralize the income tax implications by deeming the change never to have occurred. Unfortunately, these elective options for the change-of-use rules have technically never applied to partial changes of use until recently (after March 18, 2019). Prior to that time the CRA used an administrative practice (see Paragraph 2.59 of Folio S1-F3-C2, "Principal Residences"). One of the conditions was that no CCA claim could be made for that portion of the home. ITA 45(2) now appears to allow an elective option for a partial change of use with the result that all of the home remains a principal residence. In that situation no CCA could be claimed since no part of the home would be considered to be used to earn income. If we follow the administrative practice until the legislation becomes law it would not be wise for Ms. Wise to claim CCA on her office space.

SSP 6-7 Solution
Part A
Ford Focus The tax consequences resulting from the sale of the Ford Focus can be calculated as follows:

January 1, 2021, UCC	$12,980
Disposition—Lesser of:	
Capital cost = $23,600	
Proceeds of disposition = $18,200	(18,200)
UCC—December 31, 2021	($ 5,220)
Recapture of CCA	(5,220)
UCC—January 1, 2022	Nil

Because of its price, the new Mercedes will have to be allocated to a separate class 10.1. This means that the Ford Focus was the last property in class 10. Given this, the negative balance of $5,220 will be added to business income as recapture of CCA.

As there is no positive balance in this class at December 31, 2021, no CCA can be claimed.

Mercedes E-Class Sedan The maximum CCA that can be claimed for the Mercedes would be calculated as follows:

Capital cost (limited to $30,000)	$30,000
AccII adjustment [(50%)($30,000)]	15,000
CCA base	$45,000
Rate	30%
Maximum CCA	$13,500

The net effect on income due to the two automobiles would be as follows:

Recapture of CCA	$ 5,220
CCA	(13,500)
Operating costs (fully deductible)	(17,460)
Total deductible costs	($25,740)

Part B
Because the Ford Focus was used primarily (more than 50%) for employment purposes, it is eligible for the reduced standby charge and the alternative operating cost benefit calculation. The minimum benefit on this vehicle would be calculated as follows:

Standby charge:	
[(2%)($23,600)(4)(6,668 ÷ 6,668*)]	$1,888
Operating cost benefit—Lesser of:	
• [($1,888)(1/2)] = $944	
• [(13,000)($0.27)] = $3,510	944
Ford Focus—Minimum employment benefit	$2,832

*[(4)(1,667)] Also note that, as the personal use was greater than 1,667 kilometres per month, the numerator is equal to the denominator. Remember that the reduced standby charge will only apply where (1) the automobile use is primarily for employment purposes and (2) the average monthly personal kilometres do not exceed 1,667.

Less than 50% of the Mercedes' mileage was for employment purposes. Given this, there is no reduction of the standby charge and no alternative calculation of the operating cost benefit available. The minimum total benefit is calculated as follows:

Standby charge [(2%)($52,000)(8)]	$ 8,320
Operating cost benefit [(23,000)($0.27)]	6,210
Mercedes Sedan—Minimum employment benefit	$14,530

The total benefit on the two automobiles would be calculated as follows:

Ford Focus	$ 2,832
Mercedes Sedan	14,530
Total taxable employment benefit	$17,362

SSP 6-8 Solution

Analysis

The choice between the two alternatives will be based on the comparative tax flows of the two alternatives. The relevant calculations are provided in the sections that follow.

Employer Provides Automobile

If Jordan elects to have the employer provide the BMW, he will have a taxable employment benefit in each year. Since his employment-related mileage is greater than 50%, he is eligible for the reduced standby charge and the alternative operating cost benefit calculation. The after-tax consequence of this choice would be as follows:

Standby charge (reduced) [(2%)(12)($125,000)(18,000 ÷ 20,004*)]	$26,995
Operating cost benefit—Lesser of:	
• [(1/2)($26,995)] = $13,498	
• [($0.27)(18,000)] = $4,860	4,860
Total automobile benefit	$31,885
Marginal tax rate	50%
Annual increase in income tax	$15,928

*[(12)(1,667)]

Jordan Buys the Automobile

The pre-tax cash inflows (outflows) associated with this alternative are as follows:

	2021	2022	2023
Loan proceeds	$125,000	N/A	N/A
Automobile purchase	(125,000)	N/A	N/A
Allowance received [(12)($2,000)]	24,000	$24,000	$ 24,000
Loan repayment	N/A	N/A	(125,000)
Proceeds from sale of car	N/A	N/A	52,000
Operating costs [($0.32)(65,000)]	(20,800)	(20,800)	(20,800)
Pre-tax cash inflows (outflows)	$ 3,200	$ 3,200	($ 69,800)

The income tax savings (costs) associated with this alternative are as follows:

	2021	**2022**	**2023**
Operating costs [($0.32)(65,000)]	($20,800)	($20,800)	($20,800)
CCA (Note 1)			
[(150%)(30%)($30,000)]	(13,500)		
[(30%)($16,500)]		(4,950)	
[(1/2)(30%)($11,550)]			(1,733)
Automobile costs before			
imputed interest	($ 34,300)	($ 25,750)	($ 22,533)
Employment usage			
(47,000 ÷ 65,000)	72.3%	72.3%	72.3%
Deductible amount	($ 24,799)	($ 18,617)	($ 16,291)
Allowance	24,000	24,000	24,000
Net taxable benefit on loan (Note 2)	692	692	692
Inclusion in taxable income	($ 107)	$ 6,075	$ 8,401
Marginal tax rate	50%	50%	50%
Increase (decrease) in tax	($ 54)	$ 3,038	$ 4,201

Note 1 CCA claims on class 10.1 property is limited to $30,000. When the property is sold, no recapture or terminal loss can be recognized on class 10.1. However, 50% of the normal CCA can be claimed in the year of disposal.

Note 2 There will be a taxable employment benefit on the loan of $2,500 in interest per year [(2%)($125,000)]. However, ITA 80.5 deems such interest to be interest paid pursuant to a legal obligation, which then allows an employment expense for the imputed interest for the automobile purchase (ITA 8(1)(j)(i)). Since the automobile is a class 10.1 passenger vehicle, the interest expenses are subject to the limitation in ITA 67.2. However, since the daily limit does not exceed the limit of $10 a day, there is no reduction to what would have been allowed. The interest deduction is $1,808 [($2,500)(47,000 ÷ 65,000)], based on the portion of the automobile mileage that is used for employment purposes. As a result, the net benefit to be included in employment income would be $692 ($2,500 - $1,808).

The net after-tax cash outflow would be calculated as follows:

	2021	**2022**	**2023**
Pre-tax cash inflow (outflow)	$3,200	$ 3,200)	($69,800)
Tax inflow (outflow)	54	(3,038)	(4,201)
Net cash inflow (outflow)	$3,254	$ 162	($ 74,001)

Best Alternative
A comparison of the two alternatives is as follows:

Net cash inflows (outflows)	**2021**	**2022**	**2023**	**Total**
Employer provided	($15,928)	($15,928)	($15,928)	($ 47,784)
Employee purchase	3,254	162	(74,001)	(70,585)

Without consideration of the time value of money, the employer-provided alternative is clearly preferable. The total cash outflow under this approach is $47,784, as compared to $70,585 under the employee purchase alternative, a difference of $22,801.

Other Considerations

The preceding calculations could be quite different if any of the required estimates prove not to be accurate, such as if the actual number of kilometres driven or personal kilometres driven were different from the estimate, or if the resale value were not actually $52,000. However, given the much lower cash outflow under the employer-provided alternative, it is unlikely that the conclusion would change.

SSP 6-9 Solution

The appropriate reconciliation treatment for each of the listed items would be as follows:

1. Neither current nor future income taxes can be deducted in the calculation of net income. As a consequence, $123,000 would be added back to the accounting income to neutralize the expense.

2. Interest on late tax instalments is not deductible in the calculation of net income as a result of ITA 18(1)(t). As a consequence, $400 would be added back in the reconciliation to net income.

3. In the calculation of net income, amortization expense of $83,000 must be added back to accounting income and CCA of $97,000 is deducted.

4. The club membership dues of $2,500 are not deductible for tax purposes (ITA 18(1)(l)) and must be added back in the reconciliation process. In addition, 50% of the cost of meals and entertaining clients would not be deductible (ITA 67.1). This means that the non-deductible portion of the $9,600 total would be $4,800. This amount would also be added back to offset the $9,600 expense claimed in the accounting income.

5. The accounting expense of $5,200 for the bad debt is equivalent to the income tax treatment (ITA 20(1)(p)) and therefore no adjustment is required to reconcile that amount. The doubtful debt reserve claimed for 2020 of $3,400 will have to be added to business income in 2021 (ITA 12(1)(d)), and the 2021 doubtful debt reserve of $4,200 can be claimed as a business expense in 2021 (ITA 20(1)(l)).

6. As this life insurance policy was required to obtain financing, the premiums would be deductible (ITA 20(1)(e.2)). No adjustment is required in the reconciliation process.

7. Provided that they are paid within 180 days of year end, bonuses are deductible when declared by a business. This means that the full amount would be deductible and no adjustment is required in the reconciliation process.

8. Since bond discount amortization results in an increase of interest expense and the ITA only allows interest required as a result of a legal obligation to pay interest (ITA 20(1)(c)), the bond amortization impact must be removed by adding it back in the reconciliation process.

9. ITA 20(1)(aa) specifically permits such costs to be deducted in the year in which they are paid. Therefore, a deduction of $27,000 will be required in the reconciliation process.

SSP 6-10 Solution

The minimum business income of Fairway Distribution would be calculated as follows:

Accounting income as reported	$273,000
Additions:	
Item 2—Amortization	78,500
Item 3—Cost of advertising in foreign newspaper (Note 1)	3,500
Item 3—Donations to charities (Note 2)	1,260
Item 3—Cost of real estate appraisal (Note 3)	1,470
Item 3—Cost of landscaping (Note 4)	5,260
Item 3—Mrs. Fairway's management fee (Note 5)	123,000
Subtotal	$485,990
Deductions:	
Item 1—Bad debt expense adjustment (Note 6)	(4,200)
Item 2—CCA (given)	(123,600)
Business income	$358,190

Note 1 In general, the cost of advertising in foreign media that is directed toward Canadian markets cannot be deducted for income tax purposes. While there is an exception for foreign periodicals, it does not apply to foreign newspapers.

Note 2 Donations to charities cannot be deducted in the calculation of business income. They will instead be the basis for an income tax credit in the calculation of tax payable for Mr. Fairway.

Note 3 The cost of appraising capital property for purposes of sale is a capital expenditure not deductible as a result of ITA 18(1)(b). Rather, it is an addition to the capital cost of the appraised property.

Note 4 While landscaping costs related to business properties and paid are deductible, the cost of landscaping around one's principal residence would have nothing to do with the business and therefore would be disallowed as a business expense by ITA 18(1)(a) and (h).

Note 5 If Mrs. Fairway is in fact an employee of her spouse, the management fee could be challenged on the basis that it is unreasonable in the circumstances (ITA 67). The facts, however, suggest that she is not an employee and therefore the amount paid to her is not a business expense and as a result the expense would be disallowed by ITA 18(1)(a).

Note 6 For income tax purposes, the doubtful debt adjustment would be calculated as follows:

Last year's reserve	$15,000
This year's reserve	(19,200)
Bad bebt expense adjustment	($ 4,200)

The bad debt accounting write-off of $17,500 is the same adjustment as would have been allowed for income tax purposes (ITA 20(1)(p)), so it can be ignored in the reconciliation process. This leaves the add back of the previous year's doubtful debt reserve and the claim of the current doubtful debt reserve as the only necessary accounts receivable adjustments.

SSP 6-11 Solution

The net income of Darlington Inc. would be calculated as follows:

Accounting income	$ 596,000
Additions:	
Item 1—Income tax expense	55,000
Item 3—Foreign advertising (Note 1)	Nil
Item 4—Amortization expense	623,000
Item 4—Taxable capital gain on class 8 disposition	
[($550,000 - $400,000)(1/2)]	75,000
Item 5—Non-deductible meals and entertainment	
[(50%)($41,400)]	20,700
Item 6—Club fees	2,500
Item 7—Property taxes on vacant land (Note 4)	15,000
Subtotal	$ 1,387,200
Deductions:	
Item 2—Landscaping costs (Note 2)	(95,000)
Item 4—Accounting gain on class 8 disposition	(225,000)
Item 4—CCA (Note 3)	(1,017,250)
Terminal loss (see class 10 CCA calculation)	(113,000)
Net loss	($ 63,050)

Note 1 ITA 19.01 provides for the full deduction of advertising costs in foreign periodicals directed at the Canadian market, provided 80% or more of their non-advertising content is original editorial content. If the original editorial content is less than 80%, the deduction is equal to 50% of the costs. Note that this applies only to periodicals and not other print or broadcast media.

Note 2 Landscaping costs are fully deductible in the year the expenses are paid.

Note 3 The calculations for determining CCA are as follows:

Class 1—Buildings The required calculations for this class would be as follows:

Headquarters Building

January 1, 2021, UCC balance	$1,000,000
2021 CCA at 4%	(40,000)
January 1, 2022, UCC balance	$ 960,000

New Building (Separate Class)

Addition	$ 525,000
AccII adjustment [(50%)($525,000)]	262,500
CCA base	$ 787,500
2021 CCA at 6%	(47,250)
AccII adjustment reversal	(262,500)
January 1, 2022, UCC balance	$ 477,750

Class 8—Office Furniture and Equipment The required calculations for this class would be as follows:

January 1, 2021, UCC balance		$4,200,000
Additions	$700,000	
Dispositions—Lesser of:		
• Proceeds = $550,000		
• Cost = $400,000	(400,000)	300,000
AccII adjustment [(50%)($300,000)]		150,000
CCA base		$4,650,000
2021 CCA at 20%		(930,000)
AccII adjustment reversal		(150,000)
January 1, 2022 UCC balance		$3,570,000

With respect to the sale that occurred during the year, there would be a capital gain of $150,000 ($550,000 - $400,000). One-half, or $75,000, is included in the company's net income, and the accounting gain of $225,000 is deducted.

Class 10—Vehicles The calculations for this class are as follows:

January 1, 2021, UCC balance	$800,000
Disposition—Lesser of:	
Capital cost = $1,200,000	
Proceeds of disposition = $687,000	(687,000)
December 31, 2021 UCC balance (no remaining property)	$ 113,000
Terminal loss	(113,000)
January 1, 2022, UCC balance	Nil

Note 4 The property taxes on the vacant land are not deductible (ITA 18(2)). They can be added to the cost of the land (if the land were acquired for the purpose of earning either business or property income) and may be deducted to the extent of any income earned on the land net of all other expenses except interest and property taxes.

Summary of the Results (not required)

The maximum 2021 CCA and January 1, 2022, UCC balances can be summarized as follows:

Class	Maximum CCA	UCC
Class 1—Main class	$ 40,000	$ 960,000
Class 1—Separate class	47,250	477,750
Class 8	930,000	3,570,000
Class 10	Nil	Nil
Total	$1,017,250	

In addition, there was a taxable capital gain on the sale of the class 8 property of $75,000 and a terminal loss in class 10 of $113,000.

SSP 6-12 Solution
Part I

A. ITA 12(1)(l) requires partners to include their respective allocations of business income from the partnership. As explained in more detail in Chapter 18, partners are considered at law to be carrying on the business of the partnership with other partners, and therefore they are required to include in their income their share of partnership profits.

B. The basic rules of ITA 96(1)(b), 249(1)(a), and 249.1(1) together require that, in general, a partnership with members who are resident individuals use a December 31 fiscal year end. While ITA 249.1(4) allows a partnership to elect a fiscal year end other than December 31, this election requires complex adjustments for "additional business income" that may or may not be worthwhile.

C. This question requires an analysis of whether the arrangement with the seamstresses is one of employment. This material is discussed in Chapter 3, which covers employment income. Detailed guidance can be found in the CRA Guide titled "Employee or Self-Employed?" (RC4110).

The general approach to the employee versus self-employed question is to determine the intent of the parties to the arrangement. While not conclusive, the first question that will be examined in making this determination is whether the business and the workers intended to have an employee/employer relationship or, alternatively, have the work done by the individuals as self-employed contractors. While there is not sufficient information to make this determination given the information in the problem, the partners should be advised that intent should be determined and supported by the appropriate actions (e.g., have the workers register for GST if they wish to treat them as self-employed contractors).

In the absence of information on intent, other factors can be considered as follows:

Control It appears that Montpetit does not exercise a large degree of control over the seamstresses. They are free to work when they choose and may provide their services to different payers at the same time. The seamstresses can choose to accept or refuse work from Montpetit.

Ownership of Tools and Equipment The seamstresses provide the tools and equipment required for the work and the work is done in their homes, not in space provided by Montpetit.

Ability to Subcontract or Hire Assistants It appears that Montpetit does not exercise control over who does the work as long as the quality is satisfactory.

Financial Risk Since the work is done for a set fee and the fabric and accessories are provided, there may be little financial risk for seamstresses.

Responsibility for Investment and Management There is not enough information for this factor to be considered.

Opportunity for Profit Since the work is done for a set fee, a seamstress cannot increase her proceeds and hence the profit from a gown. Since the fabric and accessories are supplied and there would appear to be no other material expenditures needed for a gown, there is no opportunity to decrease expenses and increase profit on a gown. As a result, it does not appear that a profit could arise. Note that the main factor is that the business of the individuals allows them to make a profit based on volume and expenses that are within their control.

In addition to these factors, the work is for a specific gown, not general sewing as part of an ongoing relationship.

On balance, the seamstress contracts for the creation of designer gowns are likely contracts for service (self-employment contracts). Given this, source deductions would not be required.

Part II

A. The $2,400 legal fees would represent capital expenditures and would be initially disallowed as a result of ITA 18(1)(b). These capital expenditures, however, would fall within class 14.1. The rate for this class is 5% and it is eligible for the AccII provisions. For the current year, the partnership could claim CCA of $180 [(5%)(1.5)($2,400)].

B. The sewing machines are capital expenditures and cannot be deducted in the current year as a result of ITA 18(1)(b). However, a deduction will be available for CCA for class 8 in the amount of $3,750 [(20%)(1.5)($2,500)(5)]. The sewing accessories of $8,500 can be deducted in the first year as they will be used and replaced in the same year.

C. Interest paid to partners on partnership loans are allowed as an expense to the extent reasonable. An interest component on capital contributions that influences the allocations of income from the partnership would not be allowed, however. In this case the interest expense on genuine partner loans represents a valid business expense. Partners would be required to include the interest earned in their income. The $10,000 partner capital contributions are not deductible to the partners.

D. The designer clothes held on consignment at year end are inventory of the partnership and are not deductible as cost of sales. The inventory will be valued either at lower of cost and market or, alternatively, market. The cost is given as $95,000 ($50,000 + $45,000) and the retail price is given as $260,000. It is likely that the net realizable value will be less than the full retail value, but the value cannot be determined with the information given.

E. The $15,000 payment for a limited-term distribution right is a capital cost that cannot be currently deducted (ITA 18(1)(b)). However, the expenditure would be added to class 14 (limited life intangibles) where it will be available for the deduction of CCA. If the cost were incurred at the beginning of the current year, the CCA claim would be $4,500 [(1/5 years)(1.5)($15,000)].

F. The payment of the annual membership is not deductible (ITA 18(1)(l). The Crepe Suzette Diner expenses for entertainment of clients would be deductible, but they are subject to a 50% limitation (ITA 67.1), which means $750 [(50%)($1,500)] of these costs would be allowed as a business expense. The amount paid for the personal consumption of the three partners would not be a business expense.

SSP 6-13 Solution

Christine's minimum business income for 2021 can be calculated as follows:

Design Power
Statement of Income and Expenses
For the Seven-Month Period Ended December 31, 2021

Revenues		
Revenue collected	$22,000	
Revenue billed	4,000	
Work-in-progress (Note 1)	1,500	$27,500
Expenses		
Capital cost allowance (Note 2)	($ 6,446)	
Work space in home expenses [(20%)($6,400)]	(1,280)	
Legal and business licence fees	(1,000)	
Meals and entertainment [(50%)($500)]	(250)	
Automobile expenses (Note 3)	(1,960)	
Office and computer supplies	(650)	
Printing subcontract fees	(1,800)	(13,386)
2021 business income		$14,114

Note 1 ITA 12(1)(b) would require the unbilled amount to be included in income. ITA 9 would also apply since the amount appears to have the quality of income. ITA 10(4)(a) considers WIP to be inventory with a value equal to the amount that is reasonably expected to become receivable after the end of the year.

Note 2 CCA amounts are calculated as follows:

	Class 8 Furniture	Class 10 Car	Class 50 Computer
Additions	$2,000	$18,000	$5,000
AccII adjustment (50% of additions)	1,000	9,000	2,500
CCA base	$3,000	$27,000	$7,500
CCA rate	20%	30%	55%
CCA for full year	$600	$8,100	$4,125
Non-business car usage (30%)	N/A	(2,430)	N/A
Balance	$600	$5,670	$4,125
Short fiscal period factor	214/365	214/365	214/365
Deductible amount	$352	$3,324	$2,418

Class 12 (Software) rate is 100%, but class 12 applies the former half-year rule and not the AccII. As a result, the CCA for class 12 is:

Class 12 CCA = ($1,200)(1/2)(100%)(214/365) = $352

The non-business usage of the car is 30%. CCA is also restricted by the fact that Christine's taxation year only contains 214 days. Given these factors, the total maximum CCA is $6,446 ($352 + $3,324 + $2,418 + $352). Note that the CCA calculation is based on the number of days in the fiscal period (ITR 1100(3)) and not the number of days in which the property is owned in the year.

Note 3 As the interest amount is well below the prescribed limit, the amount is eligible for deduction, limited only by the amount of business usage. Also note that no portion of the down payment is deductible.

The deduction for automobile costs can be calculated as follows:

Gasoline and oil	1,100
Licence and registration	200
Insurance	800
Interest on car loan	700
Potential automobile cost deduction	$2,800
Business usage	70%
Deductible amount	$1,960

SSP 6-14 Solution

Carla's minimum business income can be calculated as follows:

Carla Jensen
Statement of Business Income
For the Year Ending December 31, 2021

Revenues		
Billable hours (billed)	$81,000	
December 31, 2021		
unbilled work-in-process	35,000	$116,000
Expenses		
Building operating costs	($24,500)	
Vehicle operating costs (Note 1)	(7,200)	
Payments to assistants	(13,500)	
Miscellaneous office costs	(3,750)	
Business meals [(50%)($4,200)]	(2,100)	
CCA (Note 2)	(36,633)	
Terminal loss for class 10 (Note 3)	(4,955)	(92,638)
2021 business income		$ 23,362

Note 1 The car leasing costs would be wholly deductible as the monthly lease charge and the manufacturer's list price are within the prescribed limits of $800 and $35,294.

Note 2 The total CCA deductible would be as follows (calculations shown separately):

Class 1	$13,560
Class 8	17,700
Class 12	363
Class 14.1	3,525
Class 50	1,485
Total CCA	$36,633

Class 1 As the building is used 100% for non-residential purposes, it is eligible for the enhanced rate of 6%. This means that the maximum CCA would be:

Class 1 [($226,000)(6%)]	$ 13,560

Class 8 The required calculations are as follows:

Opening balance		$ 46,500
Additions	$34,000	
Disposal—Lesser of:		
• Proceeds = $6,000		
• Cost = $18,000	(6,000)	28,000
AccII adjustment		14,000
CCA base		$88,500
Rate		20%
Class 8 CCA		$ 17,700

Class 12   The former half-year rules apply to class 12 and not the AccII. The CCA on the applications software would be calculated as follows:

Class 12 [(1/2)($725)(100%)]	$363

Class 14.1   The CCA on the client list would be calculated as follows:

Class 14.1 [(150%)($47,000)(5%)]	$3,525

Class 50   The CCA on the new computer would be calculated as follows:

Class 50 [(150%)($1,800)(55%)]	$1,485

Note 3   As the only vehicle used by the business was disposed of during the year, there is no CCA for class 10. However, as there is a balance left in the class, there would be a terminal loss calculated as follows:

UCC of the class at the beginning of the year	$17,255
Deduct: Dispositions during the year—Lesser of:	
• Capital cost = $20,300	
• Proceeds of disposition = $12,300	(12,300)
Ending balance with no remaining property = Terminal loss	$ 4,955

SSP 6-15 Solution
Part A—No Election

If the ITA 22 election is not made, the tax consequences for Gail Gates would be as follows:

Add: 2020 reserve for doubtful debts	$15,000
2021 business income addition	$15,000

While Gail has an allowable capital loss of $7,000 [(1/2)($249,000 - $263,000)], she will not be able to deduct this amount as she has had no capital gains in the previous three years and does not expect to have any in the current or subsequent years.

If the ITA 22 election is not made, the income tax consequences to Mandy Portals would be as follows:

Proceeds of disposition (amount collected)	$ 251,000
Adjusted cost base	(249,000)
Capital gain	$ 2,000
Inclusion rate	1/2
2021 addition to net income (not business income)	$ 1,000

Part A—Election

If the ITA 22 election is made, the income tax consequences for Gail would be as follows:

Add: 2020 reserve for doubtful debts	$15,000
Deduct: Business deduction ($263,000 - $249,000)	(14,000)
2021 addition to business income	$ 1,000

If the ITA 22 election is made, the tax consequences to Mandy would be as follows:

Add: Face value —Price paid ($263,000 - $249,000)	$14,000
Deduct: Actual write-offs ($263,000 - $251,000)	(12,000)
2021 addition to business income	$ 2,000

Part B

For Gail Gates, the ITA 22 election is advantageous, converting $15,000 of business income into $1,000 of business income.

For Mandy Portals, the fact that actual collections ($251,000) exceed the estimated value of the accounts receivable on the date of the sale ($249,000) means that the ITA 22 election would not be desirable as it would double her business income from $1,000 to $2,000, although the materiality should not interfere with agreeing to the joint election for Gail's sake.

SSP 6-16 Solution
Employment Income

The required calculations here are as follows:

Salary	$123,000
Additions	
Commissions	11,500
Car allowance [($800)(12)]	9,600
Stock option benefit [($28 - $23)(500)]	2,500
Deductions	
RPP contributions	(6,300)
Car operating costs [($9,300)(31,000 ÷ 46,000)]	(6,267)
Class 10.1 CCA [($30,000)(30%)(150%)(31,000 ÷ 46,000)]	(9,098)
Travel [($8,500 + $4,500 + (1/2)($2,000)]	(14,000)
Client meals and entertainment (see Notes)	Nil
Parking	Nil
Employment income	$ 110,935

Notes:

- The fact the initial option price is below market value does not change the calculation of the employment income inclusion. However, there will be no deduction under ITA 110(1)(d) in the determination of taxable income.

- The car allowance must be included in income as it is not based solely on kilometres.

- The base for the CCA on the car is limited to $30,000 by class 10.1.

- Travel and client promotion costs of $18,300 [($8,500 + $4,500 + (1/2)($2,000 + $8,600)] could be deducted under ITA 8(1)(f). However, this deduction is limited to his commission income of $11,500. He is better off deducting the travel costs of $14,000 [$8,500 + $4,500 + (1/2)($2,000)] using ITA 8(1)(h). As discussed in the text, he cannot use both of the provisions in the same year. Client meals and entertainment are not deductible under ITA 8(1)(h) and would require the use of ITA 8(1)(f).

Business Income

The required calculations for business income are as follows:

Business income before CCA (given)	$189,000
Class 1 CCA [(4%)($472,200)]	(18,888)
Class 8 CCA [(20%)($143,300)]	(28,660)
Class 50 CCA [(55%)($12,500)]	(6,875)
Business income	$ 134,577

Net Income and Taxable Income

Since there is no stock option benefit deduction, the required calculation here is as follows:

Employment income	$110,935
Business income	134,577
Deductible CPP ($3,166 - $2,876)	(290)
Net income and taxable income	$245,222

Tax Payable

The required calculations are as follows:

Tax on first $216,511		$ 50,141
Tax on next $28,711 ($245,222 - $216,511) At 33%		9,475
Tax before credits		$ 59,616
Tax credits:		
Basic personal amount (Andrew)	($12,421)	
Common-law partner including infirm amount		
($12,421 + $2,295 - $4,500)	(10,216)	
Canada caregiver—Bart	(7,348)	
Transfer of John's disability credit	(8,662)	
EI premiums	(890)	
CPP contributions	(2,876)	
Canada employment	(1,257)	
Transfer of tuition—Lesser of:		
• Absolute limit of $5,000		
• Actual tuition of $17,000	(5,000)	
Medical expenses (see Note)	(17,395)	
Total credit base	($66,065)	
Rate	15%	(9,910)
Federal tax payable		$ 49,706

Note The medical expense credit base would be calculated as follows:

Medical expenses for Andrew, John, and Carl		
($2,300 + $12,600 + $400)		$15,300
Reduced by the lesser of:		
• [(3%)($245,222)] = $7,357		
• 2021 threshold amount = $2,421		(2,421)
Balance before dependants 18 and over		$12,879
Bart's medical expenses	$4,600	
Reduced by the lesser of:		
• $2,421		
• [(3%)($2,800)] = $84	(84)	4,516
Total medical expense claim		$ 17,395

SSP 6-17 Solution
Employment Income

The employment income component of net income would be calculated as follows:

Salary		$ 89,000
Additions		
Commissions		12,000
Automobile benefit (Note 1)		1,140
Travel allowance (Note 2)		Nil
Art course tuition benefit (Note 3)		600
Near-cash gift (Note 4)		400
Stock option benefit [(1,500)($61 - $52)]		13,500
Deductions		
RPP contributions		(3,750)
Union dues		(430)
Employment income		$112,460

Note 1 The automobile benefit would be calculated as follows:

Standby charge [(2/3)($459)(11)(8,500 ÷ 18,337)]	$ 1,560
Operating cost benefit—Lesser of:	
• [($0.27)(8,500)] = $2,295	
• ($1,560 ÷ 2) = $780	780
Total benefit before repayment	$ 2,340
Repayment	(1,200)
Automobile benefit	$ 1,140

Note 2 It is always a question of fact as to whether allowances received are reasonable in the circumstances. A strict comparison of actual costs to the allowance is not determinative but is a guide in assessing reasonableness. Based on such a comparison, travel costs incurred were $4,725 [$2,850 + $1,875] versus a monthly allowance of $400 or $4,800 for the year. Based on this fact alone the allowance appears reasonable and would therefore not be included in income; however, unless the allowance was included in income no employment expenses could be claimed.

Note 3 Tuition for the marketing course would appear to be employment related and, as a consequence, would not be included in Mr. Bowles' employment income given that the primary beneficiary of the course would be the employer.

Note 4 While the non-cash gift for years of service does not have to be included in income since it is under $500, the $400 gift certificate (i.e., a near-cash gift), must be included.

Business Income

The business income component of net income would be calculated as follows:

Amounts billed		$ 50,250
Deductions:		
Office rent (12 months at $500)	($ 6,000)	
CCA (Note 5)	(7,967)	
Part-time assistant	(5,725)	
Office supplies	(347)	
Monthly telephone service	(312)	
Cell phone charges	(211)	
Meals and entertainment [(1/2)($3,150)]	(1,575)	(22,137)
Business income		$ 28,113

Note 5 Maximum CCA would be calculated as follows:

Class 13 [(150%)($12,000 ÷ 5*)]	$3,600
Class 8 [(150%)(20%)($10,000)]	3,000
Class 50 [(150%)(55%)($1,150)]	949
Class 12 [(1/2)(100%)($836)] (no AccII adjustment)	418
Total	$7,967

*With respect to the class 13 amount, this is a straight-line class and it is subject to the half-year rules. While the term of the lease is only three years, the deductible amount is the lesser of the capital cost divided by the term of the lease and one-fifth of the capital cost. In this case, the deduction is limited to one-half of one-fifth of the capital cost.

Net Income and Taxable Income

Mr. Bowles has net income and taxable income as follows:

Employment income	$ 112,460
Business income	28,113
Deductible CPP contribution ($3,166 - $2,876)	(290)
Net income	$ 140,283
Stock option deduction [($13,500)(1/2)]	(6,750)
Taxable income	$ 133,533

Federal Tax Payable

The required calculations are as follows:

Tax on first $98,040		$ 17,402
Tax on next $35,493 ($133,533 - $98,040) at 26%		9,228
Tax before credits		$ 26,630
Tax credits:		
Basic personal amount	($ 13,808)	
Spouse ($13,808 - $3,450)	(10,358)	
EI premiums	(890)	
CPP contributions	(2,876)	
Canada employment	(1,257)	
Tuition credit—Mr. Bowles (Note 6)	(600)	
Transfer of tuition—Lesser of:		
• $5,000		
• $9,800	(5,000)	
Medical expenses (Note 7)	(10,069)	
Total credit base	($ 44,858)	
Rate	15%	(6,729)
Charitable donations		
[(15%)($200) + (29%)($1,425 - $200)]		(385)
Political contributions [(3/4)($275)]		(206)
Federal tax payable before refundable credits		$ 19,310

Note 6   As Mr. Bowles included the reimbursement of the art course in his employment income as a taxable benefit, he can claim the tuition fee credit.

Note 7   The amount of medical expenses that can be included is calculated as follows:

Medical expenses for Martin, Sally, and Marie ($2,500 + $1,850 + $1,600)		$ 5,950
Lesser of:		
• [(3%)($133,533)] = $4,006		
• 2021 threshold amount = $2,421		(2,421)
Balance before dependants 18 and over		$ 3,529
Ellen's medical expenses	$ 6,540	
Reduced by the lesser of:		
• $2,421		
• [(3%)(nil)] = Nil	Nil	6,540
Total medical expense claim		$ 10,069

CHAPTER 7

Learning Objectives

After completing Chapter 7, you should be able to:

1. Link the previous chapter discussions on sources of employment and business income to the last source of income that is property income (Paragraph [P hereafter] 7-1 to 7-5).
2. Explain the difference between a business and property source of income (P 7-6 to 7-11).
3. Explain and apply the source analysis to be able to identify a property source of income (P 7-12 to 7-13).
4. Provide some examples of how the ITA treats business and property income differently (P 7-14 to 7-15).
5. Describe how interest expense deductibility fits into the 9-12-18-20 rule (P 7-16 to 7-19).
6. Explain what is required by ITA 20(1)(c) to be entitled to an interest expense deduction (P 7-20 to 7-24).
7. Describe the meaning of "interest" for income tax purposes (P 7-25 to 7-27).
8. Describe the income tax principles of interest expense deductibility that relate to the purpose test, direct and indirect use, and tracing. Explain how these principles can be used in income tax planning to obtain an interest expense deduction (P 7-28 to 7-40).
9. Explain how interest expense is treated in other common situations (P 7-41 to 7-51).
10. Explain the tax treatment of discounts and premiums on long-term debt and how it differs from the accounting treatment (P 7-52 to 7-61).
11. Explain and apply the methods used to calculate interest income for both individuals and corporations (P 7-62 to 7-68).
12. Explain how investors in debt obligations are treated for income tax purposes with respect to premiums and discounts and the basis for that treatment. (P 7-69 to 7-73).
13. Explain and apply the rules related to accrued interest at the time debt obligations are sold (P 7-74 to 7-77).
14. Explain the purpose of ITA 12(1)(g) and its role in the 9-12-18-20 rule (P 7-78 to 7-81).
15. Explain how rental income is treated in the ITA, with emphasis on special CCA rules (P 7-82 to 7-92).
16. Explain the concept of integration and why there are two taxable dividends (eligible and non-eligible). In addition, describe and apply the mechanism used in the ITA for individuals who receive taxable dividends (P 7-93 to 7-123).
17. Compare the after-tax returns from various types of investments (P 7-124 to 7-125).
18. Describe the two types of mutual fund entities, the difference in income tax treatment, the flow through of investment income from a mutual fund trust, and the ACB concept as it applies to mutual fund trusts (P 7-126 to 7-137).
19. Describe, in your own words, the meaning of stock dividends and capital dividends and their income tax treatment (P 7-138 to 7-144).
20. Explain the general income tax treatment of foreign source business and non-business income where foreign income taxes are charged (P 7-145 to 7-150).
21. Describe the three general categories of shareholder benefits (P 7-151 to 7-153).

How to Work through Chapter 7

Visit pearsonmylabandmastering.com to access MyLab Accounting for this text. Once there, you can access student resources such as Self-Study Problems, Practice Exams, Flashcards, updates, and more.

We recommend the following approach in dealing with the material in this chapter:

Introduction
- Read paragraph 7-1 to 7-5 (in the text).

Income from Property–General Concepts
- Read paragraph 7-6 to 7-11.

The Source of Income Analysis
- Read paragraph 7-12 to 7-13.
- Do Exercise 7-1 (in the text) and check the solution in this Study Guide.

Income from Property vs. Business–The Importance
- Read paragraph 7-14 to 7-15.

Interest as a Deduction–The Problem with Interest Expense
- Read paragraph 7-16 to 7-19.

ITA 20(1)(c) Revisted and What Is Interest?
- Read paragraph 7-20 to 7-27.

Direct or Indirect Use
- Read paragraph 7-28 to 7-33.
- Do Exercise 7-2 and check the solution in this Study Guide.

The Purpose Test and Tracing
- Read paragraph 7-34 to 7-40.

The Disappearing Source, Other Exceptions, and the Treatment of Common and Preferred Shares
- Read paragraph 7-41 to 7-51.
- Do Self-Study Problem 7-1 and check the solution in this Study Guide.

Discount and Premium on Debt Obligations
- Read paragraph 7-52 to 7-58.
- Do Exercise 7-3 and check the solution in this Study Guide.
- Read paragraph 7-59 to 7-61.

Interest Income–General Provisions for Individuals and Corporations
- Read paragraph 7-62 to 7-68.
- Do Exercise 7-4 and check the solution in this Study Guide.

The Impact of Discount and Premium to Investment Contract Holders
- Read paragraph 7-69 to 7-73.

Accrued Interest on Disposition–ITA 20(14)
- Read paragraph 7-74 to 7-77.
- Do Exercise 7-5 and check the solution in this Study Guide.

Payments Based on Production or Use–ITA 12(1)(g)
- Read paragraph 7-78 to 7-81.

Rental Income–CCA Limitations
- Read paragraph 7-82 to 7-92.
- Do Exercise 7-6 and check the solution in this Study Guide.
- Do Self-Study Problem 7-2 and check the solution in this Study Guide.

Cash Dividends from Taxable Canaadian Corporations–Eligible and Non-Eligible
- Read paragraph 7-93 to 7-115.
- Do Exercise 7-7 and check the solution in this Study Guide.
- Read paragraph 7-116 to 7-123.
- Do Exercise 7-8 and check the solution in this Study Guide.

Comparison of Investment Returns
- Read paragraph 7-124 to 7-125.
- Do Self-Study Problems 7-3 to 7-6 and check the solutions in this Study Guide.

Mutual Funds
- Read paragraph 7-126 to 7-137.
- Do Exercise 7-9 and check the solution in this Study Guide.
- Do Self-Study Problem 7-7 and check the solution in this Study Guide.

Stock Dividends and Capital Dividends
- Read paragraph 7-138 to 7-144.
- Do Exercise 7-10 and check the solution in this Study Guide.

Foreign Source Income
- Read paragraph 7-145 to 7-150.
- Do Exercise 7-11 and check the solution in this Study Guide.

Shareholder Benefits
- Read paragraph 7-151 to 7-153.
- Do Self-Study Problems 7-8 and 7-9 and check the solutions in this Study Guide.

To Complete This Chapter
- Visit MyLab Accounting for more practice problem material, and test yourself with the glossary flashcards.
- Review the Key Terms at the end of the chapter, and consult the glossary for definitions.
- Ensure you have achieved the Chapter 7 Learning Objectives listed in this Study Guide.
- As a review, view the PowerPoint presentations available on MyLab.

Practice Examination
- Available on MyLab, write the Practice Examination for this chapter, and mark it using the solutions provided.

Exercise Solutions

Exercise 7-1 Solution
Case 1 Analysis   (1) You acquired property to be used in an activity to earn income. (2) There is no personal element to the activity. (3) The level of the activity does not reach the level of a business and is passive in nature.

Case 1 Conclusion   The activity is a source of income that is income from property.

Case 2 Analysis   (1) You acquired property to be used in an activity to earn income. (2) There is no personal element to the activity. (3) The level of the activity has reached the level of a business based on the time, attention, and labour required to be devoted to the activity as a result of the additional services provided, including the necessity of hiring additional staff.

Case 2 Conclusion   The activity is a source of income that is income from a business.

Case 3 Analysis   (1) You acquired property to be used in an activity to earn income. Remember that all that is necessary at this first stage is to determine whether any gross income will be earned, irrespective of the amount. (2) There is a personal element to the activity given the nature of your relationship with the tenants. This requires determining whether the activity is conducted in a manner similar to that of another person providing similar services. Clearly this second part of the analysis fails, given that no owner would offer such rates to tenants unless the rates are reflective of what could be obtained in an arm's-length relationship–for example, the rental of an apartment in a noisy neighbourhood or where the building is below a certain standard. In these cases the profit motive is overshadowed by the owner's motivation to help friends and family. (3) The level of activity would suggest a passive nature.

Case 3 Conclusion   Since there is no profit motive due to the personal element, there is no source of income. As a result the third stage that looks to the level of activity is not necessary.

Exercise 7-2 Solution

Using the direct-use approach in this case requires borrowing money and investing that money in either a business or investment property. The four recommended transactions would be as follows:

- #1   Sell the investments for $200,000.
- #2   Use the funds to pay off your mortgage.
- #3   Borrow $200,000 from the bank using your home as collateral security.
- #4   Use the borrowed funds to repurchase the investments you sold.

The result is that your mortgage interest is now deductible against the income from your investments (e.g., interest or dividends but not capital gains or capital losses). We would caution that the four transactions must be legally completed in all aspects and in the exact order specified to achieve this result. See also the example at paragraph 1.33 of Folio S3-F6-C1. The one downside to selling the investments is that there may be some income tax implications as a result. These implications will be discussed in Chapter 8.

Exercise 7-3 Solution

Income tax consequences   The tax consequences would be as follows:

Annual deduction–2021 through 2023 [($1,000,000)(4%)]	$ 40,000

Maturity amount	$1,000,000
Bond proceeds initially received	(985,000)
2023 loss	$ 15,000

The bonds are not issued for less than 97% of the maturity amount. In addition, the 4/3 test is met since the effective interest rate of 4.57% does not exceed 4/3 of the coupon rate, or 5.33% [(4%)(4/3)]. As a result, the discount amount would be fully deductible. This gives a total deduction of $135,000 over the three-year period [(3)($40,000) + $15,000].

Accounting Treatment   The accounting consequences would be as follows:

Annual interest payment [($1,000,000)(4%)]	$40,000
Discount amortization [($1,000,000 - $985,000) ÷ 3]	5,000
Annual interest expense–2021 through 2023	$45,000

Payment of the maturity amount in 2023 would have no income tax consequences. Note that the total for the three-year period would be the same $135,000 [(3)($45,000)] that was deducted for income tax purposes. In the reconciliation process in the first two years, the accounting expense would be $45,000 when the income tax treatment only allows $40,000, requiring an adjustment to add back $5,000 for each of those two years. In the third year the income tax expense would be $55,000 [$40,000 (ITA 20(1)(c)) + $15,000 (ITA 20(1)(f))] when the accounting expense would only have been $45,000. An additional adjustment to deduct the $10,000 difference would be required to reconcile that third year.

Exercise 7-4 Solution

The total interest earned over the six-year period is $28,800 [($60,000)(8%)(6 years)]. It will be included in income as follows:

Year	Interest Paid	Interest Reported
2021	Nil	Nil
2022	Nil	$ 4,800
2023	Nil	4,800
2024	$15,600	6,000
2025	Nil	3,600
2026	Nil	4,800
2027	13,200	4,800
Total	$28,800	$28,800

2021 As there was no anniversary date in 2021 and no amount received or receivable, no interest will have to be included in Ms. Dumont's 2021 income.

2022 The first anniversary date occurs on September 30, 2022, and this requires that $4,800 [(8%)($60,000)] of interest be included in her income for the year.

2023 The second anniversary date occurs on September 30, 2023, and this requires that an additional $4,800 of interest be included in her income for the year.

2024 An additional $4,800 will have to be included in her income because of the third anniversary date of September 30, 2024. Also during this year, a payment of $15,600 [($4,800)(3.25)] is received. Of this total, $14,400 [(3)($4,800)] has been inlcuded in her income for the preceding years 2022 and 2023 and in the current year because of the three anniversary dates. As a result the additional $1,200 ($15,600 - $14,400) will be required to be added to her income for 2024, bringing the total for the year to $6,000 ($4,800 + $1,200).

2025 The anniversary date of September 30, 2025, would require adding $4,800 of interest to her income, but since $1,200 of that amount was included in 2024 (for the period October 1, 2024, to December 31, 2024) she is only required to include $3,600 of this amount for the 2025 year (covers the period January 1, 2025, to September 30, 2025).

2026 $4,800 will be included for the year based on the anniversary date of September 30, 2026.

2027 Payment of $13,200 [(2.75 years)($4,800)] will be received. As $8,400 ($3,600 + $4,800) of the amount received has been recorded on the previous two anniversary dates (September 30, 2026, and September 30, 2027), the total for 2027 will be $4,800 ($13,200 - $8,400).

Exercise 7-5 Solution

Mr. Lay will include the full $6,000 received in his net income as interest income. However, he can deduct the interest that was accrued on the bonds at the time of purchase of $1,989 [($3,000)(120/181)]. The net amount that will be included in his 2021 income is $4,011 ($6,000 - $1,989). The tax cost or ACB of the bonds purchased will be $50,000 [original cost of $51,989 minus the accrued interest of $1,989] as a result of ITA 53(2)(l).

Exercise 7-6 Solution

The maximum CCA for class 1 would be calculated as follows:

Initial cost of the building	$ 143,000
Capital expenditures	35,000
Capital cost	$ 178,000
AccII	150%
Adjusted CCA base	$ 267,000
Rate	4%
Maximum CCA	$ 10,680

The required rental income calculation would be as follows:

Gross rents	$ 7,200
Rental expenses other than CCA	(5,100)
Rental income before CCA	$2,100
CCA (maximum)	(2,100)
Rental income	Nil

As CCA cannot be used to create or increase a rental loss, the actual CCA claim is limited to $2,100, the rental income before CCA. The facts indicate that the rental activity is not a business but rather a source of property income. If the activity had been a business the short fiscal period rules (ITR 1100(3)) would have applied to prorate the maximum CCA of $10,680 based on the number of days in the fiscal period. However, since the activity is property income the short fiscal period rules do not apply and CCA is calculated for the whole year.

Exercise 7-7 Solution

The income tax payable by Ms. Holt would be calculated as follows:

Eligible dividends received	$15,000
Gross up at 38%	5,700
Taxable dividends	$20,700
Combined federal/provincial tax rate (29% + 14.5%)	43.5%
Income tax before dividend tax credit	$ 9,005
Dividend tax credit [(6/11 + 30%)($5,700)]	(4,819)
Federal and provincial tax payable	$ 4,186

The after-tax retention is equal to the dividends received of $15,000 less the tax payable of $4,186 or $10,814.

Exercise 7-8 Solution

The income tax payable by Mr. Johns would be calculated as follows:

Non-eligible dividends received	$ 17,000
Gross up at 15%	2,550
Taxable non-eligible dividends	$19,550
Combined federal/provincial income tax rate (29% + 12%)	41%
Income tax before the dividend tax credit	$ 8,016
Dividend tax credit [(9/13 + 30%)($2,550)]	(2,530)
Net federal and provincial tax payable	$ 5,486

The after-tax retention is $11,514 ($17,000 of actual dividends received - $5,486 of income taxes on the non-eligible dividends).

Exercise 7-9 Solution

Given the purchase price per unit is $13, the reinvestment will result in Ms. Tompkins receiving 80.77 ($1,050 ÷ $13) additional units. This will leave her holding 3,580.77 units with an ACB of $40,425 ($39,375 + $1,050). The ACB per unit after the reinvestment would be $11.29 ($40,425 ÷ 3,580.77).

Exercise 7-10 Solution

The required calculations would be as follows:

Original shares held	200,000
Stock dividend percentage	10%
New shares acquired	20,000
Per share addition to PUC	$ 15
Eligible stock dividend received	$300,000
Gross up at 38%	114,000
Taxable eligible dividend	$414,000

There would be a federal dividend tax credit of $62,182 [(6/11)($114,000)]. The $300,000 stock dividend would be added to the $2,400,000 [($12)(10%)(2,000,000)] original cost of his shares, and the ACB per share would be calculated as follows:

$$[(\$2,400,000 + \$300,000) ÷ (200,000 + 20,000)] = \$12.27$$

Note that his percentage of the shares remains constant at 10% (220,000 ÷ 2,200,000).

Exercise 7-11 Solution

The federal tax payable on the foreign income would be calculated as follows:

	Non-Business Income	Business Income
Foreign income	$30,000	$30,000
Deduction of excess withholding [$7,500 - (15%)($30,000)]–ITA 20(11)	(3,000)	N/A
Increase in net and taxable income	$ 27,000	$30,000
Rate	29%	29%
Tax tayable before credit	$ 7,830	$ 8,700
Foreign tax credit [(15%)($30,000)]–ITA 126(1)	(4,500)	
Foreign tax credit–ITA 126(2)		(7,500)
Net federal tax payable	$ 3,330	$ 1,200

Note that the total tax cost if the foreign income is business income is $8,700 ($7,500 + $1,200). This is the same amount that would have been paid by Norah had the income been earned in Canada [(29%)($30,000) = $8,700]. This compares to income tax of $10,830 ($7,500 + $3,330) in the non-business income case. This reflects the fact that the $3,000 deduction of the excess foreign tax only saves $870 [(29%)($3,000)]. The shortfall of $2,130 [$3,000 - $870} accounts for the same difference of $2,130 [$10,830 - $8,700].

Self-Study Problem Solutions

Self-Study Problems are available to download from MyLab Accounting.

SSP 7-1 Solution
Case A

The interest would be deductible as the borrowed money was directly used to acquire the Bee Ltd. shares.

Case B

Since the value of one of the properties is equivalent to the borrowed money outstanding, she could allocate all of the $225,000 to property B or alternatively, $50,000 to property A with the other $175,000 going to property B. Any other allocation totalling $225,000 would be acceptable.

Case C

When the value of the replacement property is less than the amount borrowed, the taxpayer must use a pro rata allocation of the borrowed money. In this case, the result would be an allocation of $71,053 [($60,000 ÷ $190,000)($225,000)] to property A and an allocation of $153,947 [($130,000 ÷ $190,000)($225,000)] to property B.

Case D

Expenses are only deductible when there is an existing source of income to apply the expenses against. When that source ceases to exist because it has been sold, then the source of income concepts would not allow any expenses to be claimed. ITA 20.1, however, (the disappearing source rules) deems the source to exist for the purpose of allowing interest expenses to continue to be claimed. Interest expense on the $145,000 loan balance will therefore continue to be deductible. The result is that the interest expenses will create a property loss until the loan is paid in full.

SSP 7-2 Solution

2020

The maximum CCA for 2020 would be calculated as follows:

	Class 1	Class 8
Addition	$ 690,000	$43,000
AccII adjustment	345,000	21,500
CCA base	$1,035,000	$64,500
Maximum CCA:		
[(4%)($1,035,000)]	(41,400)	
[(20%)($64,500)]		(12,900)
AccII adjustment reversal	(345,000)	(21,500)
January 1, 2021, UCC	$ 648,600	$30,100

Rental income for 2020 would be calculated as follows:

Rental revenue	$81,000
Expenses other than CCA	(23,400)
Income before CCA	$ 57,600
Class 1 CCA	(41,400)
Class 8 CCA	(12,900)
Rental income	$ 3,300

Note that there is no proration of CCA for a short fiscal period since a fiscal period is only possible for an individual if they carry on a business. Since the rental activity is not a business, the taxation year is the calendar year.

2021

The results of the class 8 disposition would be calculated as follows:

January 1, 2021, UCC	$30,100
Disposition–Lesser of:	
• Cost = $43,000	
• Proceeds of disposition = $31,000	(31,000)
Negative balance at year end	($ 900)
Recapture of CCA	900
January 1, 2022, UCC–Class 8	Nil

The recapture of CCA will be added to the class 8 UCC after the end of 2021, leaving a January 1, 2022, balance of nil.

The maximum CCA for 2021 would be $25,944 [(4%)($648,600)]. As this is less than rental income before the deduction of CCA, this full amount can be deducted. Rental income for 2021 would be calculated as follows:

Rental revenue	$54,500
Recapture of CCA	900
Expenses other than CCA	(29,400)
Income before CCA	$26,000
CCA	(25,944)
Rental income	$ 56

The January 1, 2022, UCC of the class 1 building would be calculated as follows:

January 1, 2021, UCC	$648,600
2021 CCA	(25,944)
January 1, 2022, UCC–Class 1	$622,656

SSP 7-3 Solution
Part A–Bonds (Interest)
The after-tax returns on the bonds would be calculated as follows:

	Sarah	Sally	Suzanne
Interest [(4.5%)($15,000)]	$675	$675	$675
Federal/provincial tax payable			
Sarah (15% + 5% = 20%)	(135)		
Sally (26% + 11% = 37%)		(250)	
Suzanne (33% + 16% = 49%)			(331)
After-tax return–Interest	$540	$425	$344

Part B–Preferred Shares (Dividends)
The after-tax returns resulting from an investment in preferred shares begins with the calculation of the federal and provincial income tax payable:

	Sarah (20%)	Sally (37%)	Suzanne (49%)
Dividends [(5.6%)($15,000)]	$ 840	$ 840	$ 840
Gross up of 38%	319	319	319
Taxable dividend	$1,159	$1,159	$1,159
Combined rate (see Part A)	20%	37%	49%
Tax before dividend tax credit	$ 232	$ 429	$ 568
Dividend tax credit			
[(6/11 + 27%)($319)]	(260)	(260)	(260)
Tax payable (tax savings)	($ 28)	$ 169	$ 308

Based on the preceding calculations of federal and provincial tax payable, the after-tax returns on the preferred shares are calculated as follows:

	Sarah (20%)	Sally (37%)	Suzanne (49%)
Dividends [(5.6%)($15,000)]	$840	$840	$840
Tax savings (tax payable)	28	(169)	(308)
After-tax return–Dividends	$868	$671	$532

Comparison
A comparison of the after-tax rates of return can be made as follows:

	Sarah (20%)	Sally (37%)	Suzanne (49%)
After-tax dividends	$868	$671	$532
After-tax interest	(540)	(425)	(344)
Advantage of preferred shares	$328	$246	$188

Recommendation
For each of the sisters, the preferred shares offer a greater after-tax return. Note, however, that the advantage of the dividends declines as the taxpayer's tax rate increases. In addition, there is a somewhat higher level of risk associated with preferred shares.

SSP 7-4 Solution
In the following solution, note that the after tax return amount should not include the original $600,000 investment.

Guaranteed Investment Certificate
The required calculations for this investment are as follows:

Interest received [($600,000)(4.5%)]	$27,000
Combined federal/provincial tax rate (29% + 12%)	41%
Income tax payable	$11,070

Interest received	$27,000
Income tax payable	(11,070)
After-tax return–Guaranteed investment certificate	$15,930

Preferred Shares
The required calculations for this investment are as follows:

Dividends received [($600,000)(5.25%)]	$31,500
Gross up of 38%	11,970
Taxable income	$43,470
Combined federal/provincial tax rate (29% + 12%)	41%
Tax payable before dividend tax credit	$17,823
Federal/provincial dividend tax credit [($11,970)(6/11 + 28%)]	(9,881)
Total tax payable	$ 7,942

Dividends received (before gross up)	$31,500
Tax payable	(7,942)
After-tax return–Preferred shares	$23,558

Common Shares

The required calculations for this investment are as follows:

Proceeds of disposition	$675,000
Adjusted cost base	(600,000)
Capital gain	$ 75,000
Inclusion rate	1/2
Taxable capital gain	$ 37,500
Combined federal/provincial tax rate (29% + 12%)	41%
Tax payable	$ 15,375
Capital gain realized (100%)	$ 75,000
Tax payable	(15,375)
After-tax return–High-tech shares	$ 59,625

SSP 7-5 Solution

The major considerations in deciding between the three alternative investment strategies are the after-tax return and the certainty of the related cash flows.

Guaranteed Investment Certificate (GIC)   As long as the certificate is purchased from a financial institution that is guaranteed by the federal government, there is virtually no risk that the principal or interest would be lost. Your combined federal and provincial tax rate for interest is 51% (33% + 18%). This means that the $100,000 investment would provide an after-tax amount calculated as follows:

Interest [($100,000)(5.5%)]	$5,500
Federal/provincial tax payable [($5,500)(33% + 18%)]	(2,805)
After-tax cash flow–GIC	$2,695

Common Share Purchase   If you invest the $100,000 in common shares, you will be exposing yourself to a greater risk and uncertainty of cash flows than the GIC alternative. There is no guarantee that the shares will pay a dividend of $5,000 during the year. There is the possibility that more or less than $5,000 will be paid. In addition, the estimated market price of at least $106,000 on December 31, 2021, is not certain. The price on that date could be higher or lower.

Assuming that the shares do pay $5,000 in dividends and you sell the shares for $106,000 on December 31, 2021, your after-tax return on the investment would be as follows:

Dividends received	$5,000
Gross up [(38%)($5,000)]	1,900
Taxable dividends	$6,900
Taxable capital gain [(1/2)($106,000 - $100,000)]	3,000
Taxable income	$9,900
Combined tax rate (33% + 18%)	51%
Income tax payable before dividend tax credit	$5,049
Dividend tax credit [($1,900)(6/11 + 27%)]	(1,549)
Income tax payable	$3,500
Dividends received	$5,000
Capital gain (100%)	6,000
Tax payable	(3,500)
After-tax cash flow–Common shares	$7,500

Rental Property   If you invest the $100,000 in real estate, you will be choosing the highest-risk alternative. Rental properties can require significant personal involvement if there are problems with the tenant or repairs become necessary. The transaction costs (e.g., real estate commissions and legal fees) would be much higher on this investment than on either of the other two. In addition, the real estate investment is the least liquid of the three alternatives and you might encounter difficulties in the disposition of this investment. The estimated net proceeds of $175,000 on December 31, 2021, is not certain. The net proceeds could be higher or lower.

Assuming that the property has the anticipated revenues and expenses and you net $175,000 when you sell the property on December 31, 2021, your after-tax return on the investment would be as follows:

Gross rents	$13,200
Expenses	(9,600)
CCA (property sold prior to year end)	N/A
Rental income	$ 3,600

In addition to this rental income, you anticipate a capital gain of $10,000 ($175,000 - $165,000), of which one-half, or $5,000, would be included in your income. Based on these figures, the income tax payable would be calculated as follows:

Rental income	$3,600
Taxable capital gain	5,000
Taxable income	$8,600
Tax rate (33% + 18%)	51%
Tax payable	$4,386

The total after-tax cash flow would be as follows:

Rental income	$ 3,600
Capital gain (cash flow is 100% of gain)	10,000
Tax tayable	(4,386)
After-tax cash flow–Rental property	$ 9,214

Conclusion   Based purely on after-tax returns, it would appear that you should acquire the rental property. However, as previously indicated, this alternative involves the most risk and uncertainty.

In choosing between the GIC and the shares of Norton Ltd., the after-tax cash flows from the shares are considerably higher. However, the return on the shares is made up of dividends and a potential capital gain, both of which are more uncertain than the interest on the GIC. Given this, the possibility of greater than anticipated dividends and/or capital gains must be weighed against the additional risk of lower than anticipated returns.

Other factors that may influence your decision are as follows:

- The funds are locked into the investment certificate and can only be withdrawn prior to maturity at a severe interest penalty, if at all.

- The investment in common shares would give you more flexibility if you should require some of the funds before the end of the year. All or some portion of the shares could be sold during the year.

- Any dividends or rent that is paid will be available for your use as at the payment date. The interest will not be available to you until maturity.

SSP 7-6 Solution

Ms. Smursch's minimum 2021 net income would be calculated as follows:

Income from a business or profession:		
Billed hours (given)	$345,000	
December 31, 2021, unbilled		
Work-in-progress	14,000	
Office supplies and office expenses	(23,000)	
Rent	(60,000)	
Meals and entertainment [(1/2)($18,000)]	(9,000)	
Convention dxpenses (Note 1)	(2,400)	$264,600
Property income:		
Income from income trust [($2.00)(2,500)]		5,000
Taxable capital gain (Note 2)		8,417
Minimum 2021 net income		$ 278,017

Note 1 While convention expenses are usually considered capital expenditures, the initial expenses are denied by ITA 18(1)(b) but allowed if ITA 20(10) applies. The costs of the Paris convention, however, are not subject to these limitations since they are disallowed on the basis that they are personal in nature (ITA 18(1)(h)).

Note 2 The adjusted cost base (ACB) of the Mutual Fund Trust units would be calculated as follows:

Original cost [(2,500)($43.00)]	$ 107,500
Reinvestment of distribution [(2,500)($3.50)]	8,750
Tax-free return of capital [(2,500)($1.50)]	(3,750)
ACB	$112,500

The taxable capital gain on the disposition of all the units would be calculated as follows:

Proceeds of disposition	$129,333
ACB	(112,500)
Capital gain	$ 16,833
Inclusion rate	1/2
Taxable capital gain	$ 8,417

The distribution reinvestment resulted in 194.44 additional units ($8,750 ÷ $45). However, this number is irrelevant as all of the units were sold.

SSP 7-7 Solution
Taxable income and income tax payable

The amount of taxable income and income tax payable resulting from the investments would be calculated as follows:

Interest on term deposit [(7%)(£200,000)($1.70)]	$ 23,800	
Excess withholding (see Note)–ITA 20(11)	(2,380)	$21,420
B&B Trust distribution [($1.50)(8,000)]	$ 12,000	
Return of capital [($0.50)(8,000)]	(4,000)	8,000
Liberty Inc. dividends [($1.60)(2,000)]	$ 3,200	
Dividend gross up [(38%)(3,200)]	1,216	4,416
Temple taxable capital gain [(1/2)($0.40)(2,500)]		500
Temple eligible dividends [($1.00)(2,500)]	$ 2,500	
Dividend gross up [(38%)($2,500)]	950	3,450
Temple interest [($1.00)(2,500)]		2,500
Additional taxable income		$40,286
Tax rate (29% + 16%)		45%
Tax before credits		$ 18,129
Dividend tax credit [($1,216 + $950)(6/11 + 30%)]		(1,831)
Foreign tax credit–Note [(15%)($23,800)]		(3,570)
Additional income tax payable		$ 12,728

Note–Foreign Source Property Income The foreign tax credit provided under ITA 126(1) is limited to a maximum of 15% of the foreign source non-business income. Any amount in excess of that amount is claimed as an expense against the source of income. With a foreign income tax rate at 25%, this deduction would be equal to $2,380 [(25% - 15%)(7%)(£200,000)($1.70)].

ACB–B&B Trust
The reinvestment of the $12,000 [($1.50)(8,000)] distribution at $52 per unit would acquire an additional 230.77 units. After recognizing these changes, the ACB per unit would be as follows:

$$\$30.13 \ [(\$240,000 + \$12,000 - \$4,000) \div (8,000 + 230.77)]$$

ACB–Temple
The reinvestment of the $6,000 [($2.40)(2,500)] distribution at $38 per unit would acquire an additional 157.89 units. After recognizing these changes, the ACB per unit would be as follows:

$$\$39.88 \ [(\$100,000 + \$6,000) \div (2,500 + 157.89)]$$

SSP 7-8 Solution
Employment Income

Jeremy's employment income would be calculated as follows:

Gross wages	$74,000
RPP contributions	(5,600)
Union dues	(896)
Employment income	$ 67,504

Property Income

Jeremy's property income would be calculated as follows:

Eligible dividends	$ 8,600
Gross up of eligible dividends (38%)	3,268
Non-eligible dividends received	6,400
Gross up of non-eligible dividends (15%)	960
Foreign dividends	16,000
Interest	3,420
Property income	$38,648

Business Income

Jeremy's business income would be calculated as follows:

Net cash flow	$ 187,000
Principal payments on car loan ($14,400 - $5,100)	9,300
Non-deductible interest [$5,100 - (365)($10 daily maximum)]	1,450
December 31 billed receivables	26,700
January 1 billed receivables	(23,200)
December 31 work-in-process	31,300
January 1 work-in-process	(28,900)
December 31 accounts payable	(14,200)
January 1 accounts payable	15,600
Subtotal	$205,050
CCA ($22,430 + $9,253 + $13,500) (Note 1)	(45,183)
Car operating costs (already deducted)	Nil
Business income	$ 159,867

Note 1 The CCA would be calculated as follows:

Class 1 CCA

January 1, 2021, UCC	$342,837
Additions (improvements)	62,000
Half-year adjustment [(50%)($62,000)]	(31,000)
Base for CCA	$373,837
Rate	6%
CCA	$ 22,430

As the building was acquired new and is used 100% for non-residential purposes, it is eligible for the 6% CCA rate. The fact that it was the only building owned by the business would result in it automatically being allocated to a separate class, but it must be elected upon to place it in a separate class 1 to qualify for the 6% rate.

In addition, the capital improvements do not qualify for the AccII because the property was owned by the same person before the expenditures were made.

Class 8 CCA

January 1, 2021, UCC	$10,564
Additions	47,000
Disposals–Lesser of:	
• Proceeds of disposition = $23,200	
• Capital cost = $25,000	(23,200)
AccII adjustments [(50%)($47,000 - $23,200)]	11,900
Base for CCA	$46,264
Rate	20%
CCA	$ 9,253

Class 10.1 CCA

As the cost of the automobile exceeds $30,000, the addition to Class 10.1 is limited to $30,000. The maximum deduction for 2021 would be $13,500 [(150%)(30%)($30,000)].

Net and Taxable Income

There are no taxable income deductions available. As a consequence, taxable income is equal to net income.

Employment income	$ 67,504
Property income	38,648
Business income	159,867
Pension income	32,500
Deductible CPP ($3,166 - $2,876)	(290)
Net and taxable income	$298,229

Tax Payable

Tax payable would be calculated as follows:

Tax on first $216,511		$50,141
Tax on next $81,718 ($298,229 - $216,511) at 33%		26,967
Tax before credits		$ 77,108
Tax credits:		
Basic personal amount (Jeremy)	($12,421)	
Spouse ($12,421 - $8,400)	(4,021)	
Canada Caregiver–Sarah	(7,348)	
Jeremy's age credit [$7,713 - (15%)($298,229 - $38,893)]	Nil	
Jeremy's pension credit	(2,000)	
EI	(890)	
CPP	(2,876)	
Canada employment	(1,257)	
Transfer of spouse's age credit [$7,713 - (15%)($8,400 - $38,893)]	(7,713)	
Transfer of spouse's pension credit	(2,000)	
Transfer of Sarah's disability credit	(8,662)	
Transfer of Samantha's tuition credit (Note 2)	(5,000)	
Medical expenses (Note 3)	(14,479)	
Total credit base	($68,667)	
Rate	15%	(10,300)
Charitable donations (Note 4)		(756)
Dividend tax credit on:		
Eligible dividends [(6/11)($3,268)]		(1,783)
Non-eligible dividends [(9/13)($960)]		(665)
Foreign tax credit–Amount withheld [(15%)($16,000)]		(2,400)
Federal tax payable		$61,204

Note 2 Samantha's child support received is not included in her net income. Given this, Samantha has no net income and would qualify as a dependant of Jeremy's. Even though she lives with Jeremy, he cannot claim the Canada caregiver tax credit for her or her children as they are not mentally or physically infirm.

The maximum transfer of the tuition credit would be the lesser of:

- The actual tuition of $16,400.
- The absolute maximum of $5,000.

- The unused tuition of $11,400 is available to be carried forward and used in future years by Samantha only.

Note 3   The claim for medical expenses is determined as follows:

Medical expenses of Jeremy and Sandra ($4,000 + $1,700)		$ 5,700
Reduced by the lesser of:		
• [(3%)($298,229)] = $8,950		
• 2021 threshold amount = $2,421		(2,421)
Balance before dependants 18 and over		$ 3,279
Sarah's medical expenses	$9,400	
Reduced by the lesser of:		
• $2,421		
• [(3%)(nil)] = Nil	Nil	9,400
Samantha's medical expenses	$1,800	
Reduced by the lesser of:		
• $2,421		
• [(3%)(nil)] = Nil	Nil	1,800
Total medical expense claim		$14,479

Note 4   Jeremy's charitable donations tax credit would be calculated as follows:

15% of $200	$ 30
33% of the lesser of:	
($2,400 - $200) = $2,200	
$298,229 - $216,511 = $81,718	726
29% of [$2,400 - ($200 + $2,200)]	Nil
Total credit	$756

SSP 7-9 Solution
Business Income
Derek's business income is calculated as follows:

Accounting income		$211,000
Additions:		
Amortization expense	$18,000	
Meals and entertainment (Note 1)	5,750	
Automobile operating costs–Personal (Note 2)	1,350	25,100
		$236,100
Deductions:		
Capital cost allowance		
Automobile (Note 3)	($ 9,703)	
Furniture and fixtures (Note 4)	(11,100)	
Building [(6%)($450,000)] (Note 5)	(27,000)	(47,803)
Business income		$188,297

Note 1   As the business deducted 100% of the meals and entertainment costs, the non-deductible one-half of this amount needs to be added back to arrive at business income.

Note 2   As the business deducted 100% of the automobile operating costs, the portion related to Derek's personal use must be added back. This amount would be $1,350 [($4,800)(9,000 ÷ 32,000)].

Note 3 The addition to UCC for the car would be limited to $30,000, and it would be allocated to a separate class 10.1. Maximum CCA for 2021 would be $13,500 [(150%)(30%)($30,000)]. However, the business can only deduct $9,703 [($13,500) (23,000 ÷ 32,000)].

Note 4 CCA for class 8 would be calculated as follows:

UCC January 1, 2021	$42,000
Additions	12,000
Disposals–Lesser of:	
Proceeds of disposition = $3,000	
Capital cost = $10,000	(3,000)
AccII adjustment [(50%)($12,000 - $3,000)]	4,500
Base for CCA	$55,500
Rate	20%
Class 8 CCA	$11,100

Note 5 As the building was acquired new, was used 100% for non-residential purposes, and was elected to be maintained in a separate class, the 6% CCA rate applies.

Property Income

Derek's property income is calculated as follows:

Eligible dividends on Breax	$ 8,000
Gross up on eligible dividends [(38%)($8,000)]	3,040
Realco Mutual Fund Trust units [(5,000)($1.50)]	7,500
Debt securities (Note 6)	12,000
Foreign term deposit (Note 7)	15,000
Total property income	$45,540

Note 6 Derek would have to recognize $8,000 [(8%)($100,000)] in interest on the July 1, 2021, anniversary date of the debt security. In addition, because a $12,000 payment is received on December 31, 2021, he would have to recognize an additional $4,000 ($12,000 less the $8,000 recognized on the anniversary date).

Note 7 As non-business income is involved, the foreign tax credit will be limited to $3,000 [(15%)($20,000)]. The remaining $5,000 ($8,000- $3,000) can be deducted against the interest. This leaves an inclusion of $15,000 ($20,000- $5,000).

Capital Gain

The ACB of the Breax shares that were sold was $52 ($130,000 ÷ 2,500). Given this, the capital gain on the Breax common shares would be calculated as follows:

Proceeds [($65)(1,000)]	$65,000
ACB [($52)(1,000)]	(52,000)
Capital gain	$13,000
Inclusion rate	1/2
Taxable capital gain	$ 6,500

Net and Taxable Income

There are no taxable income deductions available. As a consequence, taxable income is equal to net income.

Business income	$188,297
Total property income	45,540
Taxable capital gain	6,500
Net and taxable income	$240,337

Income Tax Payable

Income tax payable would be calculated as follows:

Tax on first $216,511		$50,141
Tax on next $23,826 ($240,337 - $216,511) at 33%		7,863
Tax before credits		$58,004
Tax credits:		
Basic personal amount (Derek)	($12,421)	
Spouse ($12,421 - $9,500)	(2,921)	
Canada caregiver for a child	(2,295)	
Disability transferred from Brad	(8,662)	
Disability supplement for Brad (Note 8)	Nil	
First-time home buyers'	(5,000)	
Transfer of Bill's tuition credit (Note 9)	(5,000)	
Medical expenses (Note 10)	(18,579)	
Total credit base	($54,878)	
Rate	15%	(8,232)
Dividend tax credit on eligible dividends		
[(6/11)($3,040)]		(1,658)
Foreign tax credit [(15%)($20,000)]		(3,000)
Federal income tax payable		$ 45,114

Note 8 Since Brad's medical expenses claimed for the medical expense tax credit total more than $8,012 ($5,053 + $2,959), Derek cannot claim the disability supplement for him.

Note 9 As Bill's income is below the basic credit amount of $13,808, he cannot use any of his available tuition credit. Given this, the maximum transfer is the lesser of

- the actual tuition of $8,500, or
- the absolute maximum of $5,000.

Note 10 The base for the medical expense tax credit is calculated as follows:

Medical expenses of Derek, Emily, Brad, and Barbara		
($1,400 + $1,600 + $11,400 + $2,300)		$16,700
Lesser of:		
• [(3%)($240,337)] = $7,210		
• 2021 threshold amount = $2,421		(2,421)
Balance before dependants 18 and over		$14,279
Bill's medical expenses	$ 4,600	
Reduced by the lesser of:		
• $2,421		
• [(3%)($10,000)] = $300	(300)	4,300
Medical expense tax credit base		$18,579

CHAPTER 8

Learning Objectives

After completing Chapter 8, you should be able to:

1. Describe the four types of property, their connection to a source of income, and whether a disposition could result in a capital gain or a capital loss (Paragraph [P hereafter] 8-1 to 8-4).
2. Briefly explain the history of capital gains and how they are taxed differently than other income (P 8-5).
3. Describe the two different types of property ownership, what makes them different, and which applies for income tax purposes (P 8-6 to 8-10).
4. Explain the basic capital gain and capital loss calculations along with a description, in your own words, of the key concepts that are essential to an understanding of this topic (P 8-11 to 8-13).
5. Describe the legislative scheme of how the ITA handles capital gains and capital losses with respect to the 40-39-38 rule (P 8-14 to 8-16).
6. Explain the reasoning for the superficial loss rules and their application (P 8-17 to 8-26).
7. Describe a "negative ACB" and the typical circumstances where it would apply and the result (P 8-27 to 8-30).
8. Explain how the ITA handles GST and HST when it comes to the ACB of capital property (P 8-31 to 8-32).
9. Calculate capital gains and losses on dispositions of identical properties (P 8-33 to 8-36).
10. Determine the tax consequences associated with partial dispositions of capital property (P 8-37).
11. Describe and calculate the impact of warranties on capital gains and capital losses (P 8-38).
12. Apply the rules related to capital gains reserves (P 8-39 to 8-60).
13. Determine the income tax consequences of a bad debt arising on a debt from the sale of capital property (P 8-61 to 8-67).
14. Explain the reasoning behind the terminal loss reallocation rule and apply it to sales of land and buildings (P 8-68 to 8-74).
15. Describe the basic rules of the principal residence exemption and how to apply the basic rules on the sale of a principal residence (P 8-75 to 8-84).
16. Describe personal-use property and listed personal property, including how they are different. Determine the income tax consequences that result when they are sold for a gain or a loss (P 8-85 to 8-92).
17. Explain the basic concepts of how foreign currency affects income tax, including how conversions of foreign currency can create Canadian income tax consequences. Be able to calculate the foreign currency impact on capital gains and capital losses (P 8-93 to 8-98).
18. Describe in your own words the change-in-use concept and its purpose. Determine the amount of capital gain or loss resulting from a change in the use of capital property (P 8-99 to 8-111).
19. Explain the CRAs administrative concession when there are certain changes of use in a principal residence (P 8-112 to 8-113).
20. Describe and apply the ITA 45(2) election and its effect on the change-in-use rules (P 8-114 to 8-120).
21. Describe and apply the ITA 45(3) election and its effect on the change-in-use rules (P 8-121 to 8-125).

22. Describe how the change-in-use rules apply to the use of automobiles where the income earning use changes each year (P 8-126 to 8-129).
23. Explain the reasoning for the rules that deemed there to be dispositions of certain property when a Canadian resident individual becomes a non-resident. Explain the income tax treatment (P 8-130 to 8-133).
24. Describe and apply the provisions that allow capital gains arising on the disposition of eligible small business corporations (ESBCs) to be reduced (P 8-134 to 8-137).
25. Explain the purpose of the replacement property rules and apply the ITA 44(1) deferral provisions to determine the impact of the election on both the disposition of replaced property and the purchase of replacement property (P 8-138 to 8-150).
26. Explain the purpose of the replacement property rules and apply the ITA 13(4) deferral provisions to determine the impact of the election on both the disposition of replaced property and the purchase of replacement property (P 8-151 to 8-154).
27. Apply the deferral provisions for both capital gains and recapture arising on voluntary and involuntary dispositions of capital property that is subsequently replaced (P 8-155 to 8-162).
28. Explain the rationale for the ITA 44(6) reallocation election and how it applies (P 8-163 to 8-167).
29. Explain how knowledge of capital gains and capital losses can be of benefit in tax planning (P 8-168 to 8-170).

How to Work through Chapter 8

Visit pearsonmylabandmastering.com to access MyLab Accounting for this text. Once there, you can access student resources such as Self-Study Problems, Practice Exams, Flashcards, updates, and more.

We recommend the following approach in working through this chapter:

Capital Gains and Capital Losses–Introduction and Overview
- Read paragraph 8-1 to 8-16 (in the text).
- Do Exercise 8-1 (in the text) and check the solution in this Study Guide.

Superficial Losses
- Read paragraph 8-17 to 8-26.
- Do Exercise 8-2 and check the solution in this Study Guide.

Select ACB Considerations (Negative ACB and GST/HST)
- Read paragraph 8-27 to 8-32.
- Do Exercise 8-3 and check the solution in this Study Guide.

Identical Properties
- Read paragraph 8-33 to 8-36.
- Do Exercise 8-4 and check the solution in this Study Guide.
- Do Self-Study Problem 8-1, which is available on MyLab, and check the solution in this Study Guide.

Partial Dispositions and Warranties on Capital Property
- Read paragraph 8-37 to 8-38.
- Do Exercise 8-5 and check the solution in this Study Guide.
- Do Self-Study Problem 8-2 and check the solution in this Study Guide.

Capital Gains Reserves
- Read paragraph 8-39 to 8-60.
- Do Exercise 8-6 and check the solution in this Study Guide.
- Do Self-Study Problems 8-3 and 8-4 and check the solutions in this Study Guide.

Bad Debts on Sales of Capital Property
- Read paragraph 8-61 to 8-67.
- Do Exercise 8-7 and check the solution in this Study Guide.
- Do Self-Study Problems 8-5 and 8-6 and check the solutions in this Study Guide.

Loss Restrictions on the Sale of Land and Buildings
- Read paragraph 8-68 to 8-74.
- Do Exercise 8-8 and check the solution in this Study Guide.

Principal Residence
- Read paragraph 8-75 to 8-84.
- Do Exercises 8-9 and 8-10 and check the solutions in this Study Guide.
- Do Self-Study Problem 8-7 and check the solution in this Study Guide.

Personal-Use and Listed Personal Property
- Read paragraph 8-85 to 8-92.
- Do Exercise 8-11 and check the solution in this Study Guide.
- Do Self-Study Problem 8-8 and check the solution in this Study Guide.

Gains and Losses on Foreign Currency
- Read paragraph 8-93 to 8-98.
- Do Exercise 8-12 and check the solution in this Study Guide.
- Do Self-Study Problem 8-9 and check the solution in this Study Guide.

Deemed Dispositions–Change in Use, Including Principal Residences
- Read paragraph 8-99 to 8-111.
- Do Exercise 8-13 and check the solution in this Study Guide.
- Read paragraph 8-112 to 8-120.
- Do Exercise 8-14 and check the solution in this Study Guide.
- Read paragraph 8-121 to 8-125.
- Do Exercise 8-15 and check the solution in this Study Guide.
- Do Self-Study Problems 8-10 and 8-11 and check the solutions in this Study Guide.
- Read paragraph 8-126 to 8-129.

Deemed Dispositions on Becoming a Non-Resident of Canada
- Read paragraph 8-130 to 8-133.
- Do Exercises 8-16 and 8-17 and check the solutions in this Study Guide.
- Do Self-Study Problem 8-12 and check the solution in this Study Guide.

Deferral Provisions on Small Business Investments
- Read paragraph 8-134 to 8-137.
- Do Exercise 8-18 and check the solution in this Study Guide.
- Do Self-Study Problem 8-13 and check the solution in this Study Guide.

Deferral of Replacement Property
- Read paragraph 8-138 to 8-154.
- Do Exercise 8-19 and check the solution in this Study Guide.

Replacement Property–Combined Use of Deferral Elections
- Read paragraph 8-155 to 8-167.
- Do Exercise 8-20 and check the solution in this Study Guide.

Capital Gains and Tax Planning
- Read paragraph 8-168 to 8-170.
- Do Self-Study Problems 8-14 to 8-18 and check the solutions in this Study Guide.

To Complete This Chapter
- Visit MyLab Accounting for more practice problem material, and test yourself with the glossary flashcards.
- Review the Key Terms at the end of the chapter, and consult the glossary for definitions.
- Ensure you have achieved the Chapter 8 Learning Objectives listed in this Study Guide.
- As a review, view the PowerPoint presentations available on MyLab.

Practice Examination
- Available on MyLab, write the Practice Examination for this chapter, and mark it using the solutions provided.

Exercise Solutions

Exercise 8-1 Solution
We recommend using Figure 8-2 as a guide to assist in answering the cases.

1. The first step is to identify the type of property. In this first case the property is personal property. Since the POD exceeds the cost, there will be a capital gain on the sale of $3,700 [$4,900 POD - $1,200 ACB]. A taxable capital gain of $1,850 will be included in net income at ITA 3(b).

2. Again the first step is to identify the type of property for income tax purposes. In this case paintings are depreciable property if the painting is used in a business, is not inventory, cost more than $200, and the artist is a Canadian citizen or resident. In this case, since the property is depreciable property (class 8), there can be no capital loss. If the artist were not a Canadian, the painting would have been non-depreciable capital property, in which case there would have been a $300 capital loss. An allowable capital loss of $150 would be included in the ITA 3(b) amount to be offset against taxable capital gains. Reference for this example is ITR 1102(1)(e).

3. The land is non-depreciable capital property that is not personal-use property. WIth POD of $23,000 and an ACB of $30,000, the sale results in a $7,000 capital loss. There will also not be a terminal loss because the printing press was replaced in the same year, thus ensuring that the Class has at least one property at the end of the year.

4. Technically there appears to be a loss of $29,000 [cost $40,000 - POD $11,000]. However, since the printing press is depreciable property ITA 39 prevents any capital loss. There will also not be a terminal loss because the printing press was replaced in the same year, thus ensuring that the class has at least one property at the end of the year.

5. In this case the antique desk is inventory of a business, and therefore the $7,000 loss would contribute to the business profit or loss. ITA 39 prevents any inventory loss as qualifying as a capital loss.

6. The building is depreciable property and the land is non-depreciable capital property. The POD of the building is $620,000 and the ACB (i.e., capital cost) is $560,000. The $60,000 difference is a capital gain and a $30,000 taxable capital gain. Since the ACB of the land of $100,000 exceeds the POD of $80,000, there is a capital loss of $20,000 and an allowable capital loss of $10,000 that could be applied to taxable capital gains.

7. Since the shares are non-depreciable capital property, both capital gains and capital losses are possible. In this case the POD and ACB are the same, suggesting there are no capital gains or capital losses. However, the selling costs of $1,000 cause a capital loss of that same amount, which would be calculated as [ACB of $17,000 + selling costs of $1,000] = POD of $17,000. The allowable capital loss would be $500, which could only be applied to taxable capital gains.

Exercise 8-2 Solution
To determine whether there is a superficial loss you must answer yes to each of the following three questions:

Question 1: Was there a disposition of capital property that resulted in a capital loss? YES

Question 2: Was the same property purchased in the period that began 30 days before the disposition and that ended 30 days after the disposition? YES. Period starts July 21, 2021, and ends September 19, 2021.

Question 3: On the thirtith day after the disposition, did the individual still own the property? YES. September 19, 2021

Since only 60% of the shares were replaced, then only 60% of the loss is a superficial loss.

Proceeds of disposition [(1,000)($14.50)]	$14,500
Adjusted cost base [(1,000)($23.00)]	(23,000)
Loss–ITA 40	($ 8,500)
Superficial loss [(60%)($8,500)]–ITA 40(2)(g)	5,100
Capital loss–ITA 39	($ 3,400)
Inclusion rate	1/2
Allowable capital loss–ITA 38	($ 1,700)

The ACB of the acquired shares would be calculated as follows:

Cost [(600)($13.75)]	$ 8,250
Add: Superficial loss–ITA 53(1)(f)	5,100
Adjusted cost base	$13,350

Exercise 8-3 Solution

Government assistance reduces the capital cost (ITA 13(7.1)) of depreciable property and the ACB of non-depreciable capital property (ITA 53(2)(k)). The initial cost of the building is $5,000,000 and the initial cost of the land $600,000. The government assistance on the building is $1,400,000 and $100,000 on the land.

1. ACB of the land: The ACB of the land is its cost of $600,000 less the government assistance of $100,000 (ITA 53(2)(k)), or $500,000.
2. Capital cost of the building: The capital cost of the building is its initial cost of $5,000,000 minus the government assistance of $1,400,000 (ITA 13(7.1)), or $3,600.000. Since the ACB of depreciable property is capital cost, the ACB is the same amount.
3. The maximum CCA claim for 2021 would be $324,000 [(150%)($3,600,000)(6% CCA rate)]. The "150%" relates to the additional 50% of CCA that is allowed as a result of the AccII (see Chapter 5).

Exercise 8-4 Solution

The weighted average cost calculations are as follows:

Purchase Date or Sale Date	Shares Purchased (Sold)	Cost per Share	Total Cost	Average Cost/Share
January 15, 2020	650	$23.50	$15,275	
March 12, 2020	345	24.25	8,366	
Subtotal	995		$23,641	$23.76
September 15, 2020	(210)	$23.76	(4,990)	
Subtotal	785		$18,651	$23.76
February 14, 2021	875	$26.75	23,406	
Subtotal	1,660		$42,057	$25.34
October 1, 2021	(340)	$25.34	(8,616)	
End of year balances	1,320		$33,441	$25.33

Ms. Montrose's taxable capital gain for 2020 is calculated as follows:

Proceeds of disposition [($25.50)(210)]	$5,355
Adjusted cost base [($23.76)(210)]	(4,990)
Capital gain	$ 365
Inclusion rate	1/2
Taxable capital gain	$ 183

Ms. Montrose's taxable capital gain for 2021 is calculated as follows:

Proceeds of disposition [($29.50)(340)]	$10,030
Adjusted cost base [($25.34)(340)]	(8,616)
Capital gain	$ 1,414
Inclusion rate	1/2
Taxable capital gain	$ 707

Exercise 8-5 Solution

The sale occurred in the 2020 taxation year ending December 31. This means that the filing due date for that year is six months later on June 30, 2021. Since the consideration for the warranty of $4,000 was received on or before June 30, 2021, it is included in the POD when the property was sold in 2020. In addition, since the first expenditure of $2,000 occurred on or before the same date it reduces the POD. The second expenditure of $2,800 occurred after June 30, 2021, therefore it is considered a separate capital loss for the 2021 year.

For 2020, there will be a taxable capital gain of $26,500 [1/2][((POD of $288,000 + $4,000 - $2,000) - ACB $237,000)]. For 2021, there will be an allowable capital loss of $1,400 [(1/2)($2,800)]. This allowable capital loss will only be deductible in the determination of 2021 net income to the extent that there are 2021 net taxable capital gains (an ITA 3(b) amount). Any undeductible allowable capital loss will be treated as a net capital loss for 2021 subject to the carry over provisions described in Chapter 11.

Exercise 8-6 Solution

Mr. Goodson's capital gain on the sale is $71,800 ($382,000 - $293,000 - $17,200) and the uncollected proceeds are $300,000. Given this, the maximum reserve for 2021 is $56,387, the lesser of:

- [($71,800)($300,000 ÷ $382,000)] $56,387 (Reserve)
- [($71,800)(20%)(4 - 0)] $57,440 (Reserve)

His taxable capital gain for 2021 is $7,707 [(1/2)($71,800 - $56,387)].

At the end of 2021, the uncollected proceeds are $240,000 ($300,000 - $60,000). Based on this, the capital gain to be recognized for 2021 would be as follows:

2021 reserve added to net income	$56,387
2022 reserve–Lesser of:	
• [($71,800)($240,000 ÷ $382,000)] = $45,110	
• [($71,800)(20%)(4 - 1)] = $43,080	(43,080)
2022 capital gain	$13,307

The taxable capital gain for 2022 is $6,654 [(1/2)($13,307)].

Exercise 8-7 Solution

For 2020, there will be an allowable capital loss of $7,500 [(1/2)($110,000 - $125,000)]. In 2021 an election can be filed under ITA 50(1) since the debt has been established to be a bad debt in that year. The effect of the election is to deem there to be a disposition of the note receivable for nil proceeds at the end of the year and a reacquisition for a nil cost at the beginning of 2022. As a result there will be an allowable capital loss of $17,500 [(1/2)(nil POD - ACB of $35,000)]. In 2022 the receipt of $3,000, on the final settlement of the debt receivable, results in a taxable capital gain of $1,500 [(1/2)($3,000 POD - ACB of $ nil)].

Exercise 8-8 Solution

Since the proceeds of the building of $500,000 is less than the UCC of $615,000, creating a terminal loss situation, ITA 13(21.1) applies.

A comparison of the income tax effects for Part 1 (without ITA 13(21.1)) and Part 2 (with ITA 13(21.1)) is as follows:

(See following explanations)	**Part 1**	**Part 2**
Building–FMV	$500,000	
Building–Deemed proceeds		$615,000
UCC	(615,000)	(615,000)
Terminal loss	($115,000)	Nil

(See following explanations)	**Part 1**	**Part 2**
Land–FMV	$750,000	
Land–Deemed proceeds		
($1,250,000 - $615,000)		$635,000
ACB	(425,000)	(425,000)
Capital gain	$325,000	$210,000
Inclusion rate	1/2	1/2
Taxable capital gain	$162,500	$105,000
Terminal loss	(115,000)	Nil
Net income result	$ 47,500	$105,000

Part 1 Explanation   In the absence of ITA 13(21.1), there would be a taxable capital gain of $162,500 on the land. There would also be a deduction of $115,000 ($615,000 - $500,000) for the terminal loss on the building. The net income result is $47,500.

Part 2 Explanation   ITA 13(21.1)(a) modifies the results in such situations by deeming the POD for the building to be:

The lesser of:

- The FMV of the land and building $1,250,000
  Reduced by the lesser of:
  - The ACB of the land = $425,000
  - The FMV of the land = $750,000   (425,000) $825,000

- The greater of:
  - The FMV of the building = $500,000
  - The lesser of:
    The cost of the building = $930,000
    The UCC of the building = $615,000 $615,000

With the building proceeds at $615,000, the terminal loss is eliminated. The $635,000 deemed proceeds for the land result in a capital gain of $210,000. In effect, this eliminates the terminal loss of $115,000 by reducing the capital gain by the same amount (from $325,000 to $210,000) and increases the net income inclusion by one-half of this amount, or $57,500 ($105,000 - $47,500).

Exercise 8-9 Solution
There would be no income tax consequences due to either of the sales. There would be a capital gain on the first sale of $20,500 ($109,500 - $89,000). This gain could be eliminated by designating the first property as his principal residence for the six years 2012 through 2017. The gain would be calculated as follows:

$$\left(\$20,500 \times \frac{(5 + 1)}{6}\right) = \underline{\$20,500} \quad \text{(Gain)}$$

The $26,000 ($178,000 - $152,000) capital gain on the second home could be eliminated by designating the second property as his principal residence for the years 2017 through 2021 and adding the plus one in the numerator. Since the result of six would exceed the five years of ownership in "C," the "B" amount is reduced to five. The gain would be calculated as follows:

$$\left(\$26,000 \times \frac{5}{5}\right) = \underline{\$26,000} \quad \text{(Gain)}$$

Exercise 8-10 Solution
The total gain on the two properties can be calculated as follows:

	City Home (12 Years)	**Cottage (9 Years)**
Sales price	$198,000	$143,500
Adjusted cost base	(126,000)	(85,000)
Total capital gain	$ 72,000	$ 58,500

In this example, the years 2013 through 2021 could be allocated to either property. This raises the question of which property should be designated as the principal residence during these years. If both properties had been owned for the same length of time, you would simply allocate the number of years owned, less one year, to the property with the larger gain. However, that is not the case here. Given the different ownership periods, the optimum solution requires the calculation of an average annual increase in value for each property.

The annual calculations are as follows:

Average annual gain–City home ($72,000 ÷ 12)	$6,000
Average annual gain–Cottage ($58,500 ÷ 9)	$6,500

Given these values, the cottage should be designated for the years 2014 through 2021 (one year less than owned). When these eight years are combined with the plus one in the numerator of the reduction formula, the $58,500 gain on the cottage will be completely eliminated. This leaves the years 2010 through 2013 for the Ottawa house, resulting in the following gain reduction:

$$\left(\$72,000 \times \frac{(4 + 1)}{12}\right) = \underline{\$30,000} \quad \text{(Reduction, Not Gain)}$$

This will leave a total capital gain on the sale of the two properties of $42,000 ($58,500 - $58,500 + $72,000 - $30,000).

Exercise 8-11 Solution
The results would be as follows:

	Personal-Use Property	**Listed Personal Property**
Gain on sailboat ($68,000 - $43,000)	$25,000	
Gain on oil painting ($25,000 - $1,000)		$24,000
Loss on personal automobile	Nil	
Loss on necklace ($18,000 - $46,000)		(28,000)
Capital gain	$25,000	Nil
Inclusion rate	1/2	N/A
Net taxable capital gain–ITA 3(b)	$12,500	Nil

The only income tax consequence of these dispositions for the current year is a taxable capital gain of $12,500 [(1/2)($25,000)]. The capital gain on the oil painting is completely eliminated by the capital loss on the necklace. As the loss on the necklace is greater than the gain on the painting, there is an LPP loss carry over of $4,000 [($28,000 - $24,000)]. In the year that the loss is applied, half of the loss, or $2,000, will reduce the "taxpayer's net gain" on LPP, which is the amount required to be included in net income under ITA 3(b).

Exercise 8-12 Solution

On January 5, 2020, Mr. Pratt purchased foreign currency for $7,350 [(TT$35,000)($0.21)]. The ACB of the foreign curency is therefore $7,350. On June 5, 2020, he disposes of $30,600 of the $35,000 foreign currency dollars at an exchange rate of $0.23. The result is a capital gain of $612 [(TT$30,600)(C$0.23 - C$0.21)]. Since the capital gain involves a disposition of foreign currency by an individual, ITA 39(1.1) applies and the gain is reduced to $412 [$612 - $200]. The taxable capital gain will be half of that amount, or $206, which will be included in his 2020 net income. The use of the foreign currency to purchase shares establishes the ACB of those shares at $7,038 [(TT$30,600)(C$0.23)].

In 2021, the shares are sold for POD of $8,208 [(450)(TT$96)($0.19)]. As a result, the capital gain will be equal to $1,170 {[POD $8,208 - ACB $7,038]}. The capital gain is determined under ITA 39(1), not (1.1), therefore the capital gain does not qualify for the $200 exclusion. The immediate conversion of the foreign currency to Canadian dollars results in equal POD and ACB, therefore there is no capital gain or capital loss on that conversion.

Mr. Pratt will add a taxable capital gain of $206 to his 2020 net income and a taxable capital gain of $585 [(1/2)($1,170)] to his 2021 net income.

Exercise 8-13 Solution

The change in use will result in the following capital gains on the land and building:

	Land	Building
Proceeds of disposition	$120,000	$111,000
Adjusted cost base	(20,000)	(23,000)
Capital gain	$100,000	$ 88,000
Inclusion rate	1/2	1/2
Taxable capital gain	$ 50,000	$ 44,000

For capital gains purposes, the ACB for the building will be $111,000 and the ACB of the land will be $120,000.

As the change is from personal use to an income earning use and the FMV is greater than the cost, the capital cost and therefore the UCC for the building will be its original cost plus one-half of the difference between the FMV and the cost, which is equal to the taxable capital gain of $44,000. The CCA calculation would be as follows:

Original cost	$23,000
[(1/2)($111,000 - $23,000)]	44,000
Capital cost for CCA purposes = UCC	$67,000
One-half net additions	(33,500)
CCA base	$33,500
Rate	4%
Maximum CCA for 2021	$ 1,340

Note that the short fiscal period rule only applies where a "taxation year" is less than 365 days. A taxation year for an individual is the calendar year (ITA 249(1)). An individual is only permitted a fiscal period for business carried on as a sole proprietor or as a member of a partnership. As a result, it is the calendar year that is used for determining property income. Since a calendar year cannot be less than 365 days, the short fiscal period rules do not apply. Also note that the half-year rule is generally not applicable to non-arm's-length transfers if the transferor used the property as a depreciable property prior to the transfer. For this purpose a deemed disposition and deemed reacquisition are considered a non-arm's-length transaction (ITR 1100(2.21)) ensuring that, in general, the half-year rule will apply in change-of-use situations.

Exercise 8-14 Solution

When Ms. Wheatley moved out of the home on December 31, 2019, it was no longer ordinarily inhabited by her from 2020 onward. The home, however, would have qualified as a principal residence for the four years of 2016, 2017, 2018, and 2019. When the home begins to be used as a rental property in 2020 there is a change in use. There would be deemed POD of $210,000 (the FMV at the time the property becomes a rental property) less an ACB of $220,000. The result is a capital loss of $10,000, which is deemed to be nil because it is a loss from the disposition of personal-use property that is not listed personal property (ITA 40(2)(g)). The deemed reacquisition cost would be $210,000.

The maximum CCA for 2020 would be $4,200 [($210,000)(4%)(1/2)]. This would result in rental income for 2020 of $4,800 ($21,600 - $12,600 - $4,200). The UCC on January 1, 2021, would be $205,800 [$210,000 - CCA $4,200].

When the home is sold in 2021 the capital gain is $135,000 [POD $345,000 - ACB $210,000]. The principal residence exemption would be $112,500 [(capital gain $135,000)(4 + 1)/6)]. The taxable capital gain required to be included in net income for 2021 would be $11,250 [(50%)($135,000 capital gain - $112,500 principal residence exemption)].

In addition, there would be recapture of CCA of $4,200 in 2021, equal to the amount of CCA taken in 2020, for a total income inclusion of $15,450 ($11,250 + $4,200).

ITA 45(2) Election   If she did not take CCA in 2020, her rental income would have been $9,000 ($21,600 - $12,600), $4,200 higher than when no ITA 45(2) election is made. However, she could then elect under ITA 45(2), and this means that the property could continue to be designated as her principal residence in 2020 and 2021. By designating the property as her principal residence for each of the 2016 to 2020 years, all of the capital gain would be exempt. The gain would be nil [(capital gain $135,000)(5 + 1)/6)]. This is a slightly better alternative, as shown in the following table. We would add that if the property had been sold before January 1, 2020, the result would have been the same since all of the capital gain on the principal residence would have been exempt.

	No Election	**ITA 45(2) Election**
2020 income	$ 4,800	$9,000
2021 income	15,450	Nil
Total	$20,250	$9,000

Exercise 8-15 Solution

No ITA 45(3) Election   The maximum CCA for 2020 would be $22,500 [($375,000)(4%)(1.5 AccII)]. However, as the deduction of CCA cannot be used to create a rental loss, the deduction is limited to $9,800, the net rental income before deducting CCA. This would result in a 2020 net rental income of nil ($9,800 - $9,800). UCC at January 1, 2021 would be $365,200 [capital cost $375,000 - 2020 CCA of $9,800].

Because he has deducted CCA for 2020, the property would not qualify for the ITA 45(3) election as his principal residence and, when he moves in on January 1, 2021, the change in use will result in a deemed disposition and reacquisition at the FMV of $450,000. This will result in a taxable capital gain of $37,500 [($450,000 - $375,000)(1/2)]. There would also be recapture of the $9,800 of CCA taken in 2020 [UCC $365,200 - $375,000 (the lesser of POD $450,000 and cost of $375,000)].

When he sells the property at the end of the year for $510,000, there will be an additional taxable capital gain of $30,000 [($510,000 - $450,000)(1/2)]. However, as he lived in the condominium during 2020, this gain would be eliminated through the use of the principal residence exemption. This would leave a 2021 income inclusion of $47,300 ($37,500 + $9,800 + nil capital gain on the principal residence).

ITA 45(3) Election If he does not take CCA in 2020, his rental income will be $9,800. However, if he makes the ITA 45(3) election, the unit can be designated as his principal residence for both 2020 and 2021. This means that there will be no additional income in 2021. This is clearly a better alternative, as shown in the following table:

	No Election	ITA 45(3) Election
2020 income	$ Nil	$9,800
2021 income	47,300	Nil
Total	$ 47,300	$9,800

Exercise 8-16 Solution
John would be considered to have disposed of the shares on severing his Canadian residency. He will be considered to have dispoesed of the shares prior to April 21, 2021, resulting in a taxable capital gain of $55,000 [(1/2)($1,030,000 - $920,000)]. John will be a part-year resident and will have to file an income tax return for 2021 that covers the period January 1, 2021, to April 20, 2021.

Exercise 8-17 Solution
As real property is exempt from the deemed disposition rules, there would be no income tax consequences with respect to the rental property at the time she became a non-resident of Canada. However, real property situated in Canada is "taxable Canadian property" and, as mentioned in Chapter 1, she would be liable for Canadian income taxes on both recapture and capital gains resulting from a subsequent disposition of the rental property, even after she becomes a non-resident. This topic is discussed further in Chapter 20.

Exercise 8-18 Solution
The capital gain on the Hamilton Ltd. shares would be calculated as follows:

POD	$1,350,000
ACB	(750,000)
Capital gain	$ 600,000

Since only 88.9% [$1.2M ÷ $1.35M)] of the proceeds were used to acquire replacement ESBC common shares, then only 88.9% of the capital gain of $600,000, or $533,400, can be deferred.

The ACB of the JH Inc. ESBC shares would be determined as follows:

Initial cost	$1,200,000
Deferred capital gain–ITA 53(2)(a)	(533,400)
ACB	$ 666,600

Exercise 8-19 Solution
The company would have to recognize recapture of $750,000 ($650,000 UCC - $1,400,000 POD) for 2020. The opening UCC balance for 2021 would be nil. The ITA 13(4) election reduces the POD of $1,400,000 that resulted in the recapture by $750,000 [the lesser of the actual recapture of $750,000 and the capital cost of the replacement of $2,350,000]. As a result, there would be no recapture for 2020 as the UCC would be nil [2020 UCC of $650,000 - revised POD of $650,000]. When the replacement is purchased for $2,350,000 in 2021, it is added to the UCC and a deemed disposition is subtracted equal to the $750,000 reduction in the 2020 recapture. The result is that the UCC at the end of 2021 is $1,700,000 [nil opening UCC for 2021 + $2,350,000 addition - $750,000 deemed disposition]. Using the ITA 13(4) formula, the amended 2020 recapture of CCA would be calculated as follows:

Opening 2020 UCC balance		$650,000
Deduction:		
Lesser of:		
• Proceeds of disposition = $1,400,000		
• Capital cost = $1,500,000	$1,400,000	
Reduced by the lesser of:		
• Actual recapture = $750,000		
• Replacement cost = $2,350,000	(750,000)	(650,000)
Recapture of CCA (reassessed)–2020 closing UCC		Nil

The result is that the UCC of the replacement building would be limited to $1,600,000 ($2,350,000 - $750,000). This also reflects the economic substance of the replacement transaction ($650,000 + $2,350,000 - $1,400,000 = $1,600,000).

Exercise 8-20 Solution

As the replacement did not occur until 2021, Hadfeld's 2020 net income will include a capital gain of $225,000 ($950,000 POD - $725,000 ACB), of which one-half, or $112,500, is taxable, and recapture of $101,850 ($725,000 capital cost - $623,150 UCC).

Since the cost of the replacement property of $980,000 exceeded the POD for the old property of $950,000, both the capital gains and the recapture can be eliminated with an election under ITA 13(1) and 44(1) together with a request to reassess the 2020 income tax return to exclude these amounts from net income. The deemed capital cost and UCC of the new building are as follows:

Actual capital cost	$980,000
Capital gain deferred by ITA 44(1) ($950,000 - $725,000)	(225,000)
Deemed capital cost	$755,000
Recapture deferred by ITA 13(4) ($725,000 - $623,150)	(101,850)
2020 UCC	$653,150

Each of these amounts are $30,000 more than the old capital cost and UCC. This reflects the $30,000 ($980,000 - $950,000) over and above the insurance proceeds that the company spent on replacing the building.

Self-Study Problem Solutions

Self-Study Problems are available to download from MyLab Accounting.

SSP 8-1 Solution
Part A

The total cost of the 1,222 shares remaining on December 31, 2021, would be $17,077. This is calculated in the following table:

Acquisition or Sale Date	Shares Purchased (Sold)	Cost per Share	Total Cost	Average Cost/Share
March 2015	650	$11.00	$ 7,150	
September 2016	922	13.00	11,986	
May 2018	480	17.00	8,160	
Subtotal	2,052		$27,296	$13.30
November 2018	(610)	$13.30	(8,113)	
July 2021	240	18.00	4,320	
Subtotal	1,682		$23,503	$13.97
October 2021	(460)	$13.97	(6,426)	
December 31, 2021, balances	1,222		$17,077	

Part B

The weighted average cost of the shares sold during July, 2021 would be calculated as follows:

April 2020 purchase [(2,200)($12)]	$26,400
December 2020 purchase [(1,450)($17)]	24,650
Total cost	$51,050
Average cost ($51,050 ÷ 3,650)	$ 13.99

Given this weighted average cost, the taxable capital gain on the July 2021 sale of shares would be calculated as follows:

Proceeds [(2,840)($22)]	$62,480.00
Cost [(2,840)($13.99)]	(39,731.60)
Capital gain	$22,748.40
Inclusion rate	1/2
Taxable capital gain	$11,374.20

SSP 8-2 Solution

ITA 42 requires that amounts received or receivable for warranties, covenants, or other conditional or contingent obligations provided in respect of the disposition of capital property be treated as proceeds of disposition if received or receivable before the filing date for the income tax return of the person for that year. Any outlays or expenses on fulfilling those obligations or commitments reduce the POD if made on or before the same income tax filing date. Outlays or expenses made after that filing date are deemed to be capital losses. Since the income tax return for Mr. Rowe for 2020 must be filed by April 30, 2021, that is the date that establishes the income tax treatment for outlays or expenses.

In this case the outlay of $1,040,000 is required to be paid in December 2021, which is after the filing date for Mr. Rowe's 2020 taxation year. Therefore, the outlay will be deemed to be a capital loss of the same amount, which represents an allowable capital loss of $520,000 [(50%)($1,040,000)] for the 2021 taxation year. As a result, the 2020 impact is that Mr. Rowe will include a taxable capital gain of $600,000 [(1/2)($2,600,000 - $1,400,000)] in his 2020 net income.

The 2021 allowable capital loss must first be deducted against taxable capital gains that occur in 2021. If there are no taxable capital gains in 2021, then Mr. Rowe will recognize a 2021 net capital loss of $520,000, which can be carried back to 2020 to effectively reduce the net taxable capital gains and therefore the taxable income for that year. This would allow him to recover much of the income tax paid on that 2020 taxable capital gain. Net capital loss applications are discussed in Chapter 11.

Note: The facts presented in this problem are not consistent with the standard warranty obligation situation to which ITA 42 typically applies. In practice, the terms of the agreement would need to be carefully reviewed to determine the true nature of the transaction. An unfulfilled promise to be able to sell property at a predetermined amount has the characteristics of what are called earnout agreements. In addition, there may be characteristics of a consignment arrangement or repurchase agreement, both of which may suggest that no true disposition has taken place until the December 2021 date has passed. This emphasizes that income tax is sometimes not straightforward. The goal in this problem is to describe the mechanical aspects of ITA 42 on the presumption that it applies to the facts.

SSP 8-3 Solution

The capital gain on the two tracts of land would be calculated as follows:

	Tract A	Tract B
POD	$127,000	$106,000
ACB	(71,000)	(87,000)
Capital gain	$ 56,000	$ 19,000

2021 Solution

At the end of 2021, the proceeds not due until after the end of the year for Tract A are $110,000 ($127,000 - $17,000). The corresponding amount for Tract B is $74,000 ($106,000 - $32,000).

The minimum taxable capital gain to be included in Ms. Helm's net income for 2021 would be calculated as follows:

	Tract A	Tract B
Total capital gain	$56,000	$19,000
Maximum reserve for 2020:		
Tract A–Lesser of:		
[($56,000)($110,000 ÷ $127,000)] = $48,504		
[($56,000)(20%)(4)] = $44,800	(44,800)	
Tract B–Lesser of:		
[($19,000)($74,000 ÷ $106,000)] = $13,264		
[($19,000)(20%)(4)] = $15,200		(13,264)
Subtotal	$11,200	$ 5,736
Inclusion rate	1/2	1/2
2021 inclusion	$ 5,600	$ 2,868

2022 Solution

At the end of 2022, the proceeds not due until after the end of the year for Tract A are $85,000 ($110,000 - $25,000). The proceeds not due until after the end of the year for Tract B remain unchanged at $74,000.

The minimum taxable capital gain to be included in Ms. Helm's net income for 2022 would be calculated as follows:

	Tract A	Tract B
2021 reserve added back	$44,800	$13,264
2022 reserve:		
Tract A–Lesser of:		
[($56,000)($85,000 ÷ $127,000)] = $37,480		
[($56,000)(20%)(3)] = $33,600	(33,600)	
Tract B–Lesser of:		
[($19,000)($74,000 ÷ $106,000)] = $13,264		
[($19,000)(20%)(3)] = $11,400		(11,400)
Subtotal	$11,200	$ 1,864
Inclusion rate	1/2	1/2
2022 inclusion	$ 5,600	$ 932

SSP 8-4 Solution
Capital Gain and Recapture
The immediate tax consequences of the sale can be calculated as follows:

	Land	Building	Total Gain
POD	$300,000	$1,200,000	
ACB	(250,000)	(950,000)	
Capital gain	$ 50,000	$ 250,000	$300,000

	Building
Opening UCC balance of class 1	$790,742
Lesser of:	
• POD = $1,200,000	
• Capital cost = $950,000	(950,000)
Negative ending balance = Recapture of CCA	($ 159,258)

Part A–Down Payment = 10%

2021 Results
The $159,258 of recapture must be included in business income in the year.

With a down payment of $150,000 [(10%)($1,500,000)], interest must be accrued on the outstanding balance of $1,350,000 ($1,500,000 - $150,000). At 6%, the amount would be $81,000.

With respect to the capital gains, under ITA 40(1)(a)(iii) the amount that can be deducted as a capital gains reserve is equal to the lesser of:

- [(Capital gain)(proceeds due after the end of the year ÷ total proceeds)]
- [(Capital gain)(20%)(4 - number of preceding years ending after disposition)]

While the gains on the land and building must be calculated separately, there is no reason to separate them for the purposes of determining the available reserve. This is based on the fact that, in the absence of some reason to apply it differently, the 10% down payment would apply equally to both properties.

With a down payment of $150,000, the available reserve would be the lesser of:

- [($300,000)($1,350,000 ÷ $1,500,000)] = $270,000
- [($300,000)(20%)(4 - 0)] = $240,000

Using the lesser figure of $240,000, the taxable capital gain to be included in net income would be $30,000 [(1/2)($300,000 - $240,000). The total inclusion in net income for 2021 would be as follows:

Recapture	$ 159,258
Interest	81,000
Taxable capital gain	30,000
Total increase in net income for 2021	$ 270,258

2022 Results
For this year, the reserve would be the lesser of:

- [($300,000)($1,350,000 ÷ $1,500,000)] = $270,000
- [($300,000)(20%)(4 - 1)] = $180,000

Based on this, the total inclusion in net income for 2022 would be as follows:

2021 reserve added to income	$240,000
2022 reserve	(180,000)
Capital gain	$ 60,000
Inclusion rate	1/2
Taxable capital gain	$ 30,000
Interest (same as 2021)	81,000
Total net income increase for 2022	$111,000

2023 Results

For this year, the reserve would be the lesser of:

- [($300,000)(nil ÷ $1,500,000)] = Nil
- [($300,000)(20%)(4 - 2)] = $120,000

Based on this, the total inclusion in net income for 2023 would be as follows:

2022 reserve added to income	$180,000
2023 reserve	N/A
Capital gain	$180,000
Inclusion rate	1/2
Taxable capital gain	$ 90,000
Interest	Nil
Total increase in net income for 2023	$ 90,000

Part B–Down Payment = 30%

2021 Results

While the down payment is changed in this case, the amount of recapture would be the same as in Part A. However, the interest would be reduced to $63,000 [(6%)($1,500,000 - $450,000)].

With the down payment of $450,000 [(30%)($1,500,000)], the available reserve would be the lesser of:

- [($300,000)($1,050,000 ÷ $1,500,000)] = $210,000
- [($300,000)(20%)(4 - 0)] = $240,000

Using the lesser figure of $210,000, the taxable capital gain to be included in net income would be $45,000 [(1/2)($300,000 - $210,000)].

The total inclusion in net income for 2021 would be as follows:

Recapture	$159,258
Interest	63,000
Taxable capital gain	45,000
Total increase in net income for 2021	$267,258

2022 Results

For this year, the reserve would be the lesser of:

- [($300,000)($1,050,000 ÷ $1,500,000)] = $210,000
- [($300,000)(20%)(4 - 1)] = $180,000

Based on this, the total inclusion in net income for 2022 would be as follows:

2021 reserve added to income	$210,000
2022 reserve	(180,000)
Capital gain	$ 30,000
Inclusion rate	1/2
Taxable capital gain	$ 15,000
Interest (same as 2021)	63,000
Total net income increase for 2022	$ 78,000

2023 Results

For this year, the results are the same as in Part A. The reserve would be the lesser of:

- [($300,000)(nil ÷ $1,500,000)] = Nil
- [($300,000)(20%)(4 - 2)] = $120,000

Based on this, the total inclusion in net income for 2023 would be as follows:

2022 reserve added to income	$180,000
2023 reserve	N/A
Capital gain	$180,000
Inclusion rate	1/2
Taxable capital gain	$ 90,000
Interest	Nil
Total increase in net income for 2023	$ 90,000

SSP 8-5 Solution

For 2020, Mrs. Simpkins would realize a capital gain of $10,000 ($25,000 - $15,000), of which one-half is taxable, resulting in a taxable capital gain of $5,000. While this could have been reduced through the use of capital gain reserves, Mrs. Simpkins chose not to do so.

In 2021, the inability to collect on the note would suggest that the debt may not be collectible. She would not be able to claim the balance owing of $10,000 as a write-off since the amount remains owed to her. The ITA requires that the disposition of a debt receivable be evidenced by a legal extinguishment, settlement, or forgiveness which, in many cases, can take a number of years. The ITA, however, offers a solution under ITA 50(1) that requires filing an election for the year in which it is established that the debt has become a bad debt. The debt must relate to a capital property.

The effect of the election is that Mrs. Simpkins will be considered to have disposed of the debt receivable and to have received nothing (e.g., nil POD). Since the ACB of the debt to her is the amount owing of $10,000, she would then recognize a $10,000 capital loss [$nil POD - $10,000 ACB] of which 50% or $5,000 would be an allowable capital loss for 2021. ITA 50(1) also considers her to have reacquired the debt receivable immediately thereafter at a cost and therefore ACB of nil. This means that if she receives any amounts toward that debt they will be treated as a capital gain at that time.

Any part of the 2021 allowable capital loss that cannot be used because taxable capital gains are not sufficient becomes a net capital loss for 2021. Net capital loss carry overs are covered in Chapter 11.

SSP 8-6 Solution
Capital Gains Reserve

With respect to the capital gains, under ITA 40(1)(a)(iii) the amount that can be deducted as a capital gains reserve is equal to the lesser of:

- [(Capital gain)(proceeds due after the end of the year ÷ total proceeds)]
- [(Capital gain)(20%)(4 - number of preceding years ending after disposition)]

2021 Results

The only income tax consequence in this year is the capital gain that occurs on the sale. The gain, along with the maximum deductible reserve, would be calculated as follows:

POD	$6,680,000
ACB	(2,160,000)
Capital gain	$4,520,000
Reserve—Lesser of:	
• [($4,520,000)($4,500,000 ÷ $6,680,000)] = $3,044,910	
• [($4,520,000)(20%)(4 - 0)] = $3,616,000	(3,044,910)
Capital gain	$1,475,090
Inclusion rate	1/2
Taxable capital gain	$ 737,545

As no provision can be made for the estimated cost of the warranty (ITA 18(1)(e)), the total increase in net income for 2021 would be $737,545.

2022 Results

For this year, the reserve would be the lesser of:

- [($4,520,000)($3,000,000 ÷ $6,680,000)] = $2,029,940
- [($4,520,000)(20%)(4 - 1)] = $2,712,000

Based on this, the total increase in net income for 2022 would be as follows:

2021 reserve added to income	$3,044,910
2022 reserve	(2,029,940)
Capital gain	$1,014,970
Inclusion rate	1/2
Taxable capital gain	$ 507,485
Interest [(4%)($4,500,000)]	180,000
Total increase	$ 687,485

2023 Results

For this year, the reserve would be the lesser of:

- [($4,520,000)($1,500,000 ÷ $6,680,000)] = $1,014,970
- [($4,520,000)(20%)(4 - 2)] = $1,808,000

There will be a capital gain consisting of the addition of the 2022 reserve in net income and the deduction of a new reserve for 2023. There will also be a capital loss due to the $1,000,000 payment to the developer as a result of ITA 42. As this payment is required by a warranty on capital property, it is a capital loss.

Based on this, the total increase in net income for 2023 would be as follows:

2021 reserve added to income	$2,029,940
2022 reserve	(1,014,970)
Capital gain	$1,014,970
Capital loss warranty payment [(50)($20,000)]	(1,000,000)
Net capital gain	$ 14,970
Inclusion rate	1/2
Net taxable capital gain	$ 7,485
Interest [(4%)($3,000,000)]	120,000
Total increase	$ 127,485

2024 Results

With the bankruptcy of the developer, no interest will be collected in 2024. Since the debt has been established to have become a bad debt in the year, an election under ITA 50(1) can be filed to be able to claim the amount owing of $1,500,000 [nil - ($4,500,000 - $3,000,000)] as a capital loss. Any subsequent amounts paid by the bankruptcy trustee would be treated as a capital gain at that time of receipt.

In addition the interest receivable of $60,000 for 2024 would have to be included in net income; however, the circumstances would permit the claiming of a bad debt of the same amount through ITA 20(1)(p). Any subsequent payments against this receivable would be treated as income at that time.

Lawrence will include the 2023 reserve of $1,014,970 in 2024 net income. Since the loan was to be paid off in 2024, no further reserves could be claimed because of the requirement that there be an amount owing after the end of the year.

The capital loss can be deducted to the extent of the capital gain of $1,014,970. The remaining allowable capital loss of $242,515 [(1/2)($1,500,000 - $1,014,970)] can only be deducted in 2024 to the extent of taxable capital gains in that year. Any part of that allowable capital loss that cannot be applied against 2024 net taxable capital gains then becomes a 2024 net capital loss that can be applied back three taxation years against net taxable capital gains in 2021, 2022, and 2023.

Note: The facts presented in this problem are not consistent with the standard warranty obligation situation to which ITA 42 typically applies. In practice, the terms of the agreement would need to be carefully reviewed to determine the true nature of the transaction. An unfulfilled promise to be able to sell property at a predetermined amount has the characteristics of what are called earnout agreements. In addition, there may be characteristics of a consignment arrangement or repurchase agreement, both of which may suggest that no true disposition has taken place until the December 2023 date has passed. We add this note of caution since income tax is sometimes not straightforward. Our goal in this problem is to describe the mechanical aspects of ITA 42 on the presumption that it applies to the facts.

Summary (Not Required)

The results can be summarized as follows:

Year	Interest	Net Taxable Gain (Allowable Loss)
2021	Nil	$ 737,545
2022	$ 180,000	507,485
2023	120,000	7,485
2024	Nil	(242,515)
Totals	$ 300,000	$1,010,000

The amount of the taxable capital gain can be verified as follows:

Initial capital gain	$4,520,000
Warranty payment	(1,000,000)
Bad debt	(1,500,000)
Capital gain	$2,020,000
Inclusion rate	1/2
Taxable capital gain	$1,010,000

SSP 8-7 Solution

The gains on the two properties can be calculated as follows:

	Country Home	Condominium
POD	$1,200,000	$900,000
ACB	(850,000)	(625,000)
Real estate commissions		
[(5%)($1,200,000)]	(60,000)	
[(5%)($900,000)]		(45,000)
Total capital gain	$ 290,000	$230,000

The average annual gain was $18,125 ($290,000 ÷ 16) on the country home and $28,750 ($230,000 ÷ 8) on the condominium. This would indicate that the maximum number of years should be allocated to the condominium. However, because of the plus one in the reduction formula, one year can be left off.

Based on this analysis, the seven years 2015 through 2021 should allocated to the condominium, with the nine years 2006 through 2014 being allocated to the country home. The required calculations would be as follows:

	Country Home	Condominium
Total capital gain	$290,000	$230,000
Exemption:		
Country home		
[$290,000][(9 + 1) ÷ 16]	(181,250)	
Condominium		
[$230,000][(7 + 1) ÷ 8]		(230,000)
Capital gain	$108,750	Nil
Inclusion rate	1/2	N/A
Taxable capital gain	$ 54,375	Nil

This gives a total taxable capital gain on the two properties of $54,375.

SSP 8-8 Solution
Classification of Property

All of the items sold are personal-use property. However, if they can be classified as "listed personal property," their income tax treatment will be different. Under ITA 54, listed personal property consists of the following items:

(i)   print, etching, drawing, painting, sculpture, or other similar work of art;
(ii) jewellery;
(iii) rare folio, rare manuscript, or rare book;
(iv) stamp; or
(v)   coin.

The Paul Borduas painting, as well as the Hemingway first edition, clearly fall into the listed personal property classification. The Bentley and the Chris Craft race boat do not.

Effect on Net Income

The overall amount to be included in net income can be calculated as follows:

Personal-use property (Note 1)		
Gain on antique boat ($62,000 - $45,000)	$17,000	
Loss on Bentley automobile	Nil	
Loss on fountain pens	Nil	$ 17,000
Listed personal property		
Gain on first edition ($31,000 - $12,000)	$19,000	
Gain on painting ($132,000 - $128,000)	4,000	
Total listed personal property gains	$23,000	23,000
Net capital gains		$40,000
Inclusion rate		1/2
Increase in net income		$20,000

Note 1 Unless an item of personal-use property can be classified as listed personal property, losses cannot be deducted. However, gains on such property are required to be included in net income without regard to their classification as either personal-use property or listed personal property.

SSP 8-9 Solution

The taxable capital gain on the sale of the shares would be calculated as follows:

POD [(3,500)(€33.50)($1.49)]	$174,703
ACB [(3,500)(€30.00)($1.46)]	(153,300)
Capital gain on share sale	$ 21,403
Inclusion rate	1/2
Taxable capital gain	$ 10,702

The taxable capital gain on the conversion of the foreign exchange would be calculated as follows:

POD [(€117,250)($1.52)]	$178,220
ACB of foreign currency [(€117,250)($1.49)]	(174,703)
Gain–ITA 40	$ 3,517
ITA 39(1.1) exemption	(200)
Capital gain	$ 3,317
Inclusion rate	1/2
Taxable capital gain	$ 1,659

Ms. Laval's net income would increase by a total taxable capital gain of $12,361 ($10,702 + $1,659).

Because Ms. Laval is an individual, the ITA 39(1.1) deduction of $200 reduces the capital gain on the foreign exchange conversion.

SSP 8-10 Solution
2019 Results

During 2019, 100% of the property was used to earn business income. The CCA for the year would be calculated as follows:

Capital cost	$525,000
AccII	262,500
CCA base	$ 787,500
Maximum CCA [(4%)($787,500)]	(31,500)
AccII reversal	(262,500)
UCC–January 1, 2020	$493,500

There are no additional income tax consequences in 2019.

2020 Results

On January 1, 2020, there would be a deemed disposition/acquisition of 25% of the property. The transaction would be measured using the building's FMV of $460,000. Given this, the maximum CCA on the remaining 75% would be calculated as follows:

Opening UCC	$493,500
Deemed disposition–Lesser of:	
• Capital cost [(25%)($525,000)] = $131,250	
• Deemed proceeds [(25%)($460,000)] = $115,000	(115,000)
CCA base	$378,500
Maximum CCA [(4%)($378,500)]	(15,140)
UCC–January 1, 2021	$363,360

While the value of the building has declined from $525,000 to $460,000, no loss can be recognized. There remains property in the class, therefore a terminal loss cannot be recognized. In addition, we would remind you that you cannot have a capital loss on depreciable property.

The allowable capital loss on the land of $2,500 [(25%)(1/2)(POD $100,000 - ACB $120,000)] can be deducted against other taxable capital gains. Since her income from other sources is so high, she will claim maximum CCA regardless of how the business is doing.

The cost to Laci of the 25% of the property that is being used for personal purposes would be $115,000 [(25%)($460,000)] allocated to the building and $25,000 [(25%)($100,000)] allocated to the land.

2021 Results

On January 1, 2021, there would be a deemed acquisition of 25% of the property for business purposes. The capital cost of the building acquisition would be $140,000 [(25%)($560,000)]. However, as the change is from personal use to business use and the FMV of the building is greater than its cost, the UCC will be limited to her cost plus one-half of the difference between FMV and cost, or $127,500 [$115,000 + (1/2)($140,000 - $115,000)].

Maximum CCA for would be calculated as follows:

Opening UCC	$363,360
Deemed acquisition	
[$115,000 + (1/2)($140,000 - $115,000)]	127,500
AccII or one-half net additions*	N/A
CCA base	$490,860
Maximum CCA [(4%)($490,860)]	(19,634)
UCC–January 1, 2022	$471,226

*The AccII is not available on a change in use since the owner of the deemed disposition and the deemed acquisition are the same. The half-year rule would normally apply to a change in use as long as CCA had not been previously claimed on the change in use portion. In this case, since the property was originally used 100% for business use, all of the property was eligible for CCA. This prevents the application of the half-year rule.

As a result of the deemed disposition, Laci would have a taxable capital gain on both the land and the building. They would be calculated as follows:

	Land	Building
Proceeds of disposition		
[(25%)($130,000)]	$32,500	
[(25%)($560,000)]		$140,000
Adjusted cost base [(25%)($100,000)]	(25,000)	
Capital cost [(25%)($460,000)]		(115,000)
Capital gains	$ 7,500	$ 25,000
Inclusion rate	1/2	1/2
Taxable capital gains	$ 3,750	$ 12,500

Even though Laci has a home other than the apartment, she could eliminate these gains by making use of the one-plus year in the principal residence exemption formula.

SSP 8-11 Solution

2020 Results

During 2020, 80% of the property is used for income earning purposes. Based on this the maximum CCA that can be deducted for this year is calculated as follows:

Capital cost [(80%)($500,000)]	$400,000
AccII	200,000
CCA base	$600,000
Maximum CCA [(4%)($600,000)]	(24,000)
AccII reversal	(200,000)
UCC–January 1, 2021	$376,000

There are no additional income tax consequences during this year.

2021 Results–Business to Personal Use

On January 1, 2021, there would be a deemed disposition/acquisition of 20% of the total property. This would result in a taxable capital gain on the land calculated as follows:

POD [(20%)($230,000)]	$46,000
ACB [(20%)($225,000)]	(45,000)
Capital gain	$ 1,000
Inclusion rate	1/2
Taxable capital gain on land	$ 500

There would also be taxable capital gain on the building, calculated as follows:

POD [(20%)($585,000)	$117,000
ACB [(20%)($500,000)]	(100,000)
Capital gain	$ 17,000
Inclusion rate	1/2
Taxable capital gain on the building	$ 8,500

The maximum CCA for 2021 would be calculated as follows:

Opening UCC	$376,000
Disposition–Lesser of:	
Capital cost [(20%)($500,000)] = $100,000	
Proceeds of disposition	
[(20%)($585,000) = $117,000	(100,000)
CCA base	$276,000
Maximum CCA [(4%)($276,000)]	(11,040)
UCC–January 1, 2022	$264,960

2022 Results–Personal to Business Use

On January 1, 2022, there would be a deemed disposition/acquisition of 40% of the total property. This would result in a taxable capital gain on the land, calculated as follows:

POD [(40%)($245,000)]		$98,000
ACB:		
[(20%)($225,000)]	($45,000)	
[(20%)($230,000)]	(46,000)	(91,000)
Capital gain		$ 7,000
Inclusion rate		1/2
Taxable capital gain on land		$ 3,500

There would also be a taxable capital gain on the building, calculated as follows:

POD [(40%)($630,000)]		$252,000
ACB:		
[(20%)($500,000)]	($100,000)	
[(20%)($585,000)]	(117,000)	(217,000)
Capital gain		$ 35,000
Inclusion rate		1/2
Taxable capital gain		$ 17,500

With respect to maximum CCA, this change in use involves a deemed disposition/acquisition from personal use to business use. In addition, the FMV of the building is greater than her cost. Given this, the UCC will be limited to Ms. Darn's cost plus one-half of the difference between FMV and cost. As calculated in the preceding table, the increase in value is $35,000, with one-half of this amount being $17,500.

Maximum CCA for would be calculated as follows:

Opening UCC		$264,960
Deemed acquisition cost		
[(20%)($500,000)]	$100,000	
[(20%)($585,000)]	117,000	
Cost adjustment–ITA 13(7)	17,500	234,500
One-half net additions [(1/2)($234,500 - 121,500)]*		(56,500)
CCA base		$442,960
Maximum CCA [(4%)($442,960)]		(17,718)
One-half net additions		56,500
UCC–January 1, 2023		$481,742

*As previously mentioned, the AccII adjustment does not apply to a change in use since the deemed disposition and deemed acquisition are by the same person. The half-year rule, however, would apply unless property is acquired in a non-arm's-length transaction (i.e., a change in use is deemed a non-arm's-length transaction) and the property was depreciable property and was owned by the non-arm's-length person as depreciable property for at least one year.

In this case, in 2020 20% was used personally and was therefore not depreciable property. The cost of that first 20% personal-use portion was $100,000. In 2021 an additional 20% portion was converted from income earning use to personal use. This second 20% portion was depreciable property before its conversion. The cost of the second 20% portion was $117,000. In 2022 both 20% personal-use portions were converted to income earning use. The FMV of the two portions totalled $252,000 [(40%)($630,000)].

ITA 13(7) limits the capital cost to the business equal to the cost of each portion plus half of the increase in value on each portion, which equals the taxable capital gain for each. The capital cost of the first portion equals cost of $100,000 plus one-half of the gain of $26,000 [(20%)($630,000) - $100,000)] or $13,000 [(50%)($26,000)]. The capital cost of the second portion equals cost of $117,000 plus one-half of the gain of $9,000 [(20%)($630,000) - $117,000)], or $4,500 [(50%)($9,000)]. Therefore, the capital cost of the first portion is $113,000 and $121,500 for the second portion. The total for both portions equals $234,500, as shown in the 2022 calculations above.

Since the second portion meets the exception for the half-year rule it is subtracted, leaving only the first portion of $113,000 to which the half-year rule would apply. Half of that amount is $56,500.

Note to Students
The facts of this problem lead to a complex situation with the half-year rule that requires identifying the part of the property upon which CCA had previously been claimed to be able to apply that half-year rule. To clarify, if all of a property had been used for income earning purposes then converted to personal use then back to income earning purposes, the half-year rule would not have appled to the final conversion since the property was depreciable property previously. The tax policy rationale is that the half-year rule should apply only once to a property or part of a property.

SSP 8-12 Solution
Mr. Lange's net taxable capital gains on deemed dispositions resulting from his ceasing to be a resident of Canada would be calculated as follows:

Vacant land	N/A
Automobile	N/A
Coin collection ($11,000 - $5,000)	$ 6,000
Enbridge shares ($38,000 - $24,000)	14,000
BCE shares ($35,000 - $42,000)	(7,000)
Royal Bank shares ($23,000 - $15,000)	8,000
Nal Enterprises Ltd. shares ($153,000 - $26,000)	127,000
Capital gain	$148,000
Inclusion rate	1/2
Net taxable capital gains	$ 74,000

The vacant land is exempt from the deemed disposition rules. However, as it is taxable Canadian property, a later sale of this land will be required to be included in income in Canada even though Mr. Lange would be a non-resident at that time.

The loss on the automobile is not deductible as it would be a personal property loss (ITA 40(2)(g)(iv)).

SSP 8-13 Solution
First Sale

Since Ms. Tosh has held the Tech Ltd. common shares for more than 185 days, it is a qualifying disposition. Since the Small Oil common shares were purchased immediately, they can be designated as replacement shares.

Preferred shares cannot be designated as replacement shares. As a result, the Small Bank Inc. shares do not qualify as replacement shares.

The capital gain on the Tech Ltd. disposition is $700,000 ($4,200,000 - $3,500,000). As the cost of replacement shares is only $3,800,000, the permitted deferral is limited as per the following calculation:

$$[(\$700,000)(\$3,800,000 \div \$4,200,000)] = \$633,333 \text{ deferral}$$

Given this, the ACB of the Small Oil shares would be calculated as follows:

Unadjusted cost	$3,800,000
Deferral amount	(633,333)
ACB of Small Oil shares	$ 3,166,667

Second Sale

Since Ms. Tosh has held the Future Inc. common shares for more than 185 days, it is a qualifying disposition. Since the ESBC common shares were purchased in the current year, they can be designated as replacement shares.

The capital gain on the disposition of Future Inc. shares is $1,800,000 ($5,600,000 - $3,800,000). Of the $5,600,000 in proceeds, only $5,200,000 ($2,400,000 + $2,800,000) was invested in replacement shares. This means that the permitted deferral will be limited as per the following calculation:

$$[(\$1,800,000)(\$5,200,000 \div \$5,600,000)] = \$1,671,429 \text{ deferral}$$

Using this information, the adjusted cost base of the newly acquired shares would be calculated as follows:

	Sombra Shares	Ziff Shares
Purchase price	$2,400,000	$2,800,000
Deferral:		
[($1,671,429)($2,400,000 ÷ $5,200,000)]	(771,429)	
[($1,671,429)($2,800,000 ÷ $5,200,000)]		(900,000)
ACB	$1,628,571	$1,900,000

Net Taxable Capital Gain

If Ms. Tosh does not purchase any other replacement shares within 120 days of December 31, 2021, the two sales would result in a taxable capital gain, calculated as follows:

	Total Gain	Deferral	Net Gain
Tech Ltd. shares	$ 700,000	$ 633,333	$ 66,667
Future Inc. shares	1,800,000	1,671,429	128,571
Totals	$2,500,000	$2,304,762	$195,238
Inclusion rate			1/2
Net taxable capital gain			$ 97,619

Tax Advice

Less than all of the proceeds from the 2021 sales were invested in ESBCs. The shortfall totalled $800,000, $400,000 ($4,200,000 - $3,800,000) on the first sale and $400,000 ($5,600,000 - $5,200,000) on the second sale. If she invests in her brother's company within 120 days of December 31, 2021, she can designate up to $800,000 of this amount as replacement shares, allowing her to defer all of the capital gains on the two sales of shares.

If she wants to invest in her brother's company after the 120 days have passed, she should review her other investments to determine if she can use the deferral provisions on other small business investments to her advantage to obtain the $1,000,000.

There is the question of whether Ms. Tosh should invest in her brother's new company, but that would involve an analysis that goes beyond the scope of the material in the text.

SSP 8-14 Solution
2021 Results

The insurance settlement are POD and would create recaptured CCA, as follows:

Opening UCC balance	$368,000
Disposition–Lesser of:	
• Cost = $500,000	
• POD = $490,000	(490,000)
Negative closing balance = Recapture	($122,000)
Recapture	122,000
January 1, 2022, UCC	Nil

The $122,000 in recapture would be included in 2021 business income and added back to the UCC to create a nil UCC balance.

2022 Results

Using ITA 13(4), Trail Resources Ltd. would file an election and request a reassessment of the 2021 taxation year. The revised recapture would be calculated as follows:

January 1, 2021, UCC balance		$368,000
Deduction:		
Lesser of:		
• POD = $490,000		
• Capital cost = $500,000	$490,000	
Reduced by the lesser of:		
• Actual recapture = $122,000		
• Replacement cost = $650,000	(122,000)	(368,000)
2021 reassessed recapture		Nil

The revised amount of nil for the recapture on the disposition of the old building will replace the initially reported amount of $122,000 that was included in the original 2021 income tax return.

The UCC of the new building will be adjusted for this change as follows:

Cost of new building	$650,000
Reversal of recapture–ITA 13(4)	(122,000)
2022 UCC	$528,000

Given this, the required maximum CCA for 2022 and the January 1, 2023, UCC balance would be calculated as follows:

Opening UCC–Class 1	Nil
Addition of UCC of new building	$528,000
AccII adjustment	264,000
2022 base for CCA	$792,000
Maximum CCA [($792,000)(6%)]	(47,520)
AccII adjustment reversal	(264,000)
January 1, 2023, UCC	$480,480

The AccII adjustment is based on the "net additions," which represents the addition of $650,000 minus any POD in the same year. The ITA 13(4) reduction of recapture is treated as deemed POD, and therefore it is considered when determining the net additions.

The accuracy of the CCA base calculation can be verified by noting that the $528,000 is equal to the initial UCC of $368,000 plus the cost of the new building of $650,000 less the insurance proceeds of $490,000.

SSP 8-15 Solution
Part A
The 2021 income tax consequences would be as follows:

Land The company would have a taxable capital gain on the land calculated as follows:

POD	$1,100,000
ACB	(350,000)
Capital gain	$ 750,000
Inclusion rate	1/2
Taxable capital gain	$ 375,000

Building The company would have a taxable capital gain and recapture calculated as follows:

POD	$2,300,000
ACB	(2,100,000)
Capital gain	$ 200,000
Inclusion rate	1/2
Taxable capital gain	$ 100,000

Opening UCC	$ 850,000
Deduct disposition–Lesser of:	
Capital cost = $2,100,000	
POD = $2,300,000	(2,100,000)
Negative closing UCC balance = Recapture	($1,250,000)
Recapture	1,250,000
UCC–January 1, 2022	Nil

Equipment The company would have recapture calculated as follows:

Opening UCC	$165,000
Deduct disposition–Lesser of:	
Capital cost = $450,000	
Proceeds of disposition = $320,000	(320,000)
Negative closing UCC balance = Recapture	($155,000)
Recapture	155,000
UCC–January 1, 2022	Nil

Part B

Land With respect to the land, the capital gain resulting from the use of the ITA 44(1) election would be the lesser of:

- $750,000 (actual capital gain); or
- $500,000 (the excess of the $1,100,000 proceeds of disposition for the old land over the $600,000 cost of the replacement land).

The taxable amount would be $250,000 [(1/2)($500,000)] and this would be included in the revised 2021 net income. The original gain of $375,000 would be replaced in the reassessed net income and income tax return.

If the ITA 44(1) election is used in 2022, the deemed ACB of the replacement land would be calculated as follows:

Actual cost	$600,000
Capital gain reduction ($750,000 - $500,000)	(250,000)
ACB of replacement land	$350,000

Note that the deemed cost of the replacement land has been reduced to the ACB of the replaced land.

Building If the ITA 44(1) election is used in 2022, the reassessed 2021 capital gain would be nil, the lesser of:

- $200,000 (actual capital gain); or
- nil (reflecting the fact that there was no excess of the $2,300,000 POD for the old building over the $2,500,000 cost of the replacement building).

Using this election will reduce the deemed capital cost for the building as follows:

Actual cost	$2,500,000
Capital gain reduction	(200,000)
Deemed capital cost of replacement building	$2,300,000

If the ITA 13(4) election is used in 2022, the reassessed 2021 recapture would be calculated as follows:

January 1, 2020, UCC balance		$850,000
Deduction:		
Lesser of:		
• POD = $2,300,000		
• Capital cost = $2,100,000	($2,100,000)	
Reduced by the lesser of:		
• Actual recapture = $1,250,000		
• Replacement cost = $2,500,000	1,250,000	(850,000)
Recapture 2021 (reassessed)		Nil

If both elections are used in 2022, the UCC of the replacement building is calculated as follows:

Deemed capital cost	$2,300,000
Recapture reduction–ITA 13(4) (deemed POD)	(1,250,000)
UCC–Replacement building	$1,050,000

Note that the $1,050,000 UCC for the new building is equal to the UCC of the old building ($850,000) plus the additional $200,000 ($2,500,000 - $2,300,000) in funds required for its replacement.

These nil amounts for the capital gain and the recapture on the disposition of the old building will replace the original amounts determined of $100,000 and $1,250,000, respectively, that were included in the original net income for 2021.

Equipment   As this is a voluntary disposition, the ITA 13(4) and 44(1) elections can only be used on real property (land and buildings). They cannot be used on the equipment and, as a consequence, the $155,000 in recapture is not eligible for the election and will remain unchanged. The capital cost and the UCC of the new equipment will be $520,000.

Part C

The Election   The ITA 44(6) election applies when there is a disposition involving both land and building. If, for either of the land or building, the POD exceed the ACB such that there remains a capital gain that could not be eliminated by the ITA 44(1) election largely because the replacement cost was not high enough, the election allows a reallocation of the POD from the property with the capital gain to the other property to further reduce the remaining capital gain.

As will be demonstrated in this problem, this can provide some relief when ITA 44(1) and ITA 13(4) fail to eliminate all of the capital gains arising on one part of the disposition of the old property. ITA 44(1) fully eliminated the capital gain on the building. However, a $500,000 capital gain remained on the land because the replacement land of $600,000 was less than the $1,100,000 of POD on the replaced land. This would suggest that it could be advantageous to transfer some of the POD from the land to the building.

The excess of the POD of the old land over the cost of the replacement land was $500,000 ($1,100,000 - $600,000). This is the maximum available transfer from the land to the building allowed by ITA 44(6). However, the excess of the cost of the replacement building over the old building's POD is only $200,000 ($2,500,000 - $2,300,000). If a transfer in excess of this amount is made, any reduction in the capital gain on the land will be matched by an increased capital gain on the building.

Applying ITA 44(6) in an optimal manner requires a transfer of POD of $200,000. This results in the following adjusted POD:

	Land	Building
Actual POD	$1,100,000	$2,300,000
Optimal transfer land to building	(200,000)	200,000
Reallocated POD	$ 900,000	$2,500,000

Application to Land   If both ITA 44(1) and ITA 44(6) are applied, the resulting capital gain on the land will be calculated as the lesser of

- $550,000 ($900,000 - $350,000); or
- $300,000 (the excess of the $900,000 reallocated POD for the old land over the $600,000 cost of the replacement land).

This is a reduction of $200,000 ($500,000 - $300,000) from the amount that was calculated when only ITA 44(1) was applied. However, the ACB of the replacement land would be unchanged by the use of ITA 44(6):

Actual cost	$600,000
Capital gain reduction ($550,000 - $300,000)	(250,000)
Deemed cost of replacement land	$350,000

Application to Building   With the POD transfer limited to $200,000, the capital gain on the building is still nil. Specifically, the gain will be the lesser of

- $400,000 ($2,500,000 - $2,100,000); or
- nil (reflecting the fact that there was no excess of the $2,500,000 reallocated POD for the old building over the $2,500,000 cost of the replacement building).

However, the capital cost and UCC of the building will be reduced by the application of ITA 44(6):

Actual cost	$2,500,000
Capital gain reduction by the two elections	(400,000)
Deemed capital cost	$2,100,000
Recapture reduced by election	(1,250,000)
UCC–Replacement building	$ 850,000

Note that the UCC for the new building is equal to the UCC of the old building.

Comparison   The table that follows compares the results of using only ITA 44(1) and ITA 13(4) with the results that arise when the ITA 44(6) election is also used.

	No ITA 44(6)	With ITA 44(6)
Capital gains		
Land	$ 500,000	$ 300,000
Building	Nil	Nil
Replacement property		
Adjusted cost base of land	$ 350,000	$ 350,000
Capital cost of building	2,300,000	2,100,000
UCC	1,050,000	850,000

As you can see in the table, the use of ITA 44(6) has reduced the capital gain on the land by $200,000. However, it has done so at the cost of reducing the capital cost and UCC of the replacement building. There is a tax cost associated with this trade off in that only one-half of the capital gain, or $100,000, would have been included in net income but the cost is giving up $200,000 of future CCA.

SSP 8-16 Solution
Part A
The POD were greater than the relevant capital costs for all the destroyed and expropriated property. As a result, the 2021 effect in net income would be as follows:

	Old Land	Old Building	Old Contents
POD	$723,000	$4,800,000	$1,256,000
ACB	(256,000)	(3,700,000)	(972,000)
Capital gains	$467,000	$1,100,000	$ 284,000
Inclusion rate	1/2	1/2	1/2
Taxable capital gains	$233,500	$ 550,000	$ 142,000

Opening UCC	$1,856,000	$ 72,000
Capital cost (less than POD)	(3,700,000)	(972,000)
Closing UCC	($1,844,000)	($900,000)
Recapture of CCA	1,844,000	900,000
UCC–January 1, 2022	Nil	Nil

The increase in 2021 net income totals $3,669,500 ($233,500 + $550,000 + $142,000 + $1,844,000 + $900,000).

Part B–Land
As the land, building, and class 8 property were replaced before the end of the second taxation year following the involuntary dispositions, Fraser can use both of the elections under ITA 44(1) and ITA 13(4) to reverse some of the increase in 2021 net income. These changes will be implemented through elections followed by a request to reassess the 2021 income tax return.

With respect to the land, the capital gain resulting from the use of the ITA 44(1) election would be the lesser of

- $467,000 (actual capital gain); or
- $223,000 (the excess of the $723,000 POD for the old land over the $500,000 cost of the new land).

The taxable amount of this capital gain will be $111,500 [(1/2)($223,000)]. The original gain of $467,000 would be replaced in the reassessed 2021 income tax return.

Part B–Building
With respect to the building, the capital gain resulting from the use of the ITA 44(1) election would be nil, the lesser of

- $1,100,000 (actual capital gain); or
- nil (reflecting the fact that the $4,800,000 POD did not exceed the replacement cost of $5,700,000. In other words, all of the POD went toward acquiring the replacement, which allows the recapture to be fully reversed).

Under ITA 13(4), the revised recapture would be calculated as follows:

January 1, 2021, UCC balance		$1,856,000
Deduction:		
Lesser of:		
• POD = $4,800,000		
• Capital cost = $3,700,000	($3,700,000)	
Reduced by the lesser of:		
• Actual recapture = $1,844,000		
• Replacement cost = $5,700,000	1,844,000	(1,856,000)
Recapture 2021 CCA (reassessed)		Nil

These new nil figures for the capital gain and recapture on the building disposition will replace the amounts originally with the 2021 income tax return.

Part B–Building Contents
If this were a voluntary disposition, the class 8 property would not have qualified for either of the two elections, which are restricted to "former business property" (e.g., land and buildings). However, as this is an involuntary disposition, both elections are permitted.

Under ITA 44(1), the revised capital gain would be $23,000, the lesser of

- $284,000 (actual capital gain); or
- $23,000 (the excess of the $1,256,000 POD for the old building contents over the $1,233,000 capital cost of the replacement property)

The taxable amount of the gain will be $11,500 [(1/2)($23,000)].

Under ITA 13(4), the revised recapture would be reduced from $900,000 to nil. The calculation is as follows:

January 1, 2021, UCC balance		$72,000
Deduction:		
Lesser of:		
• POD = $1,256,000		
• Capital cost = $972,000	($972,000)	
Reduced by the lesser of:		
• Actual recapture = $900,000		
• Replacement cost = $1,233,000	900,000	(72,000)
Recapture of 2021 CCA (reassessed)		Nil

The revised amounts of capital gains and recapture will replace the amounts of $284,000 and $900,000, respectively, that were included in the original 2021 income tax return.

Comparison–Part A and Part B

As shown in the table that follows, the disposition of the land, building, and class 8 property resulted in an increase in 2021 net income of $3,669,500. When the two elections were used, the reassessed 2021 income tax return will result in a revision in 2021 net income of only $123,000. This represents a reduction in net income of $3,546,500 ($3,669,500 - $123,000).

	Part A as Reported	Part B with Elections
Land–Taxable capital gain	$ 233,500	$111,500
Building–Taxable capital gain	550,000	Nil
Class 8 property–Taxable capital gain	142,000	11,500
Building–Recaptured CCA	1,844,000	Nil
Class 8 property–Recaptured CCA	900,000	Nil
Total increase in net income	$3,669,500	$123,000

Part C

Assuming Fraser decides to use the elections under ITA 44(1) and ITA 13(4), the income tax attributes of the replacement properties, including cost, capital cost, ACB, and UCC, would be as follows:

	Land	Building	Class 8
Actual cost of replacement property	$500,000	$5,700,000	$1,233,000
Capital gain reduction–ITA 44(1)			
Land ($467,000 - $223,000)	(244,000)		
Building ($1,100,000 - nil)		(1,100,000)	
Contents ($284,000 - $23,000)			(261,000)
Deemed cost of replacement property	$256,000	$4,600,000	$ 972,000

	Building	Contents
Deemed capital cost of replacement property	$4,600,000	$972,000
Recapture reduction–ITA 13(4)		
Building ($1,844,000 - nil)	(1,844,000)	
Contents ($900,000 - nil)		(900,000)
UCC–Replacement property	$2,756,000	$ 72,000

The deemed cost of the replacement land has been reduced to the ACB of the old land.

The $4,600,000 deemed capital cost of the replacement building is equal to the $3,700,000 capital cost of the old building plus the additional $900,000 ($5,700,000 - $4,800,000) in funds paid by Fraser above the insurance proceeds.

In a similar fashion, the UCC for the new building is equal to the UCC of the old building ($1,856,000), plus the additional $900,000 ($5,700,000 - $4,800,000) in funds paid by Fraser above the insurance proceeds.

The deemed capital cost of the replacement class 8 property is equal to the $972,000 capital cost of replaced property.

In a similar fashion, the UCC for the replacement class 8 property is equal to the $72,000 UCC of the replaced property. Since the $1,233,000 cost of the replacement property is less than the $1,256,000 in insurance proceeds, there is no increase in the UCC.

Part D–Optimal Transfer

The ITA 44(6) election applies when there is a disposition involving both land and building. If, for either of the land or building, the POD exceed the ACB such that there remains a capital gain that could not be eliminated by the ITA 44(1) election largely because the replacement cost was not high enough, the election allows a reallocation of the POD from the property with the capital gain to the other property to further reduce the remaining capital gain. It is important to note that the ITA 44(6) reallocation election only applies to "former business property" (e.g., land and buildings), and as a result the class 8 property does not qualify.

As will be demonstrated in this problem, this can provide some relief when ITA 44(1) and ITA 13(4) fail to eliminate all of the capital gains arising on one part of the disposition of the old property. ITA 44(1) fully eliminated the capital gain on the building. However, a $223,000 capital gain remained on the land because the replacement land of $500,000 was less than the $723,000 of POD on the replaced land. This would suggest that it could be advantageous to transfer some of the POD from the land to the building.

The excess of the proceeds of disposition of the old land over the cost of the replacement land was $223,000 ($723,000 - $500,000). This is the maximum available transfer from the land to the building allowed by ITA 44(6). However, the excess of the cost of the replacement building over the old building's POD is $900,000 ($5,700,000 - $4,800,000), which is more than enough to eliminate all of the capital gain on the disposition of the replaced land.

Applying ITA 44(6) will result in the following adjusted POD:

	Land	Building
Actual POD	$723,000	$4,800,000
Transfer needed–Land to building	(223,000)	223,000
Adjusted POD	$500,000	$5,023,000

Part D–Application to Land

If both the ITA 44(1) and the ITA 44(6) elections are used, the capital gain on the land will be nil, calculated as the lesser of

- $244,000 ($500,000 - $256,000); or
- nil (the excess of the $500,000 adjusted POD for the old land over the $500,000 cost of the new land).

Given this result, the ACB of the replacement land will be calculated as follows:

Actual cost	$500,000
Capital gain reversed by the two elections	(244,000)
Deemed cost of the replacement land	$256,000

Note that this is equal to the ACB of the replaced land.

Part D–Application to the Building

With the POD transfer limited to $223,000, the capital gain on the building is still nil. Specifically, the gain will be the lesser of

- $1,323,000 ($5,023,000 - $3,700,000); or
- nil (there is still no excess of the $5,023,000 POD over the replacement cost of $5,700,000).

The deemed capital cost and UCC for the building would be calculated as follows:

Actual cost	$5,700,000
Capital gain reduction–ITA 44(1) & (6)	(1,323,000)
Deemed capital cost	$4,377,000
Recapture reduction–ITA 13(4)	(1,844,000)
UCC–Replacement building	$2,533,000

Part D–Comparison

The table that follows compares the results of using only ITA 44(1) and ITA 13(4) with the results that arise when the ITA 44(6) election is also used.

	No ITA 44(6)	With ITA 44(6)	Difference
Capital gains			
Land	$ 223,000	Nil	($223,000)
Building	Nil	Nil	
Replacement property			
Cost of land	$ 256,000	$ 256,000	Nil
Capital cost of building	4,600,000	4,377,000	(223,000)
UCC	2,756,000	2,533,000	(223,000)

As you can see in the table, the use of ITA 44(6) has reduced the capital gain on the land by $223,000. However, it has done so at the cost of reducing the capital cost and UCC of the replacement building by the same amount. There is a tax cost associated with this trade off in that only one-half of the capital gain, or $111,500, would have been included in net income, but the cost is giving up $223,000 of future CCA.

SSP 8-17 Solution
Employment Income

The deduction of many employment expenses are often subject to a limitation found in ITA 8(1)(f) that restricts what can be claimed to the commission income received in that year. Since the commissions received of $62,500 exceed the total of permissible employment expenses, that limitation is not a concern in this case. Paul's 2021 employment income would be calculated as follows:

Salary	$ 85,000
Additions:	
Commissions	62,500
Stock option benefit [(1,500)($19 - $15)]	6,000
Expense allowance [(12)($2,500)]	30,000
Deductions:	
RPP contributions	(4,100)
Professional association dues	(1,500)
Home office expenses (Note 1)	(2,290)
Automobile costs	
CCA (Note 2)	(3,960)
Operating costs [(80%)($6,100)]	(4,880)
Hotel costs	(11,500)
Airline and other transportation	(9,200)
Client meals and entertainment [(1/2)($10,400)]	(5,200)
2021 employment income	$140,870

Note 1 As Paul has commission income, he can deduct 20% of his home office expenses with the exception of the mortgage interest. This will provide a deduction of $2,290 [(20%)($3,400 + $7,200 + $850)].

Note 2 The 2021 CCA would be based on a UCC calculated as though 100% of the available CCA had been taken in 2020. The 100% CCA for 2020 would be $13,500 [(150%)(30%)($30,000)]. Using this amount, the deductible 2021 CCA would be $3,960 [(80%)(30%)($30,000 - $13,500)]. Note that the original base for CCA is limited to the class 10.1 maximum of $30,000.

Property Income

The required calculations here would be as follows:

Non-eligible dividends	$ 5,400
Gross up on non-eligible dividends [(15%)($5,400)]	810
Net rental income (Note 3)	9,500
Property income	$ 15,710

Note 3 As the change in use is from personal to business, the base for calculating CCA would be as follows:

Cost of the building		$175,000
FMV at the time of the change in use		
FMV	$275,000	
Cost	(175,000)	
Increase in value	$100,000	
Inclusion factor	1/2	50,000
Capital cost for UCC & CCA purposes		$225,000
One-half net additions [(1/2)(($225,000)]		(112,500)
CCA base		$112,500
Rate for class 1		4%
CCA		$ 4,500

Using this CCA figure, rental income would be $9,500 ($14,000 - $4,500). The AccII is not available on a change in use since the owner of the deemed disposition and the deemed acquisition are the same. The half-year rule would normally apply to a change in use as long as CCA had not been previously claimed on the change-in-use portion. In this case, since the property was originally used 100% for personal use, no CCA would have been previously claimed on the property and as a result the half-year rule applies.

Net Taxable Capital Gains

The required calculations here would be as follows:

Stock option shares [(1,500)($22 - $19)]		$ 4,500
Sale of paintings (Note 4)		Nil
Land sale		
Total gain ($350,000 - $100,000)	$250,000	
Capital gain reserve (Note 5)	(178,571)	71,429
Change in use:		
Cottage–Land ($100,000 - $75,000)	$ 25,000	
Cottage–Building ($275,000 - $175,000)	100,000	125,000
Capital gains		$200,929
Inclusion rate		1/2
Taxable capital gains		$ 100,465

Note 4 The paintings would be listed personal property (LPP), which means that losses are only deductible to the extent of gains on LPP. While there was a gain on one painting of $5,000 ($15,000 - $10,000), there was a loss on the second painting of $6,000 ($10,000 - $4,000). This loss can be used to eliminate the gain on the first painting. However, the remaining $1,000 ($6,000 - $5,000) cannot be deducted in the current year. It can be carried back three years and forward seven years to be applied against LPP gains in those other years. This carry over will be discussed in Chapter 11.

Note 5 The total POD for the land would be the sale price of $350,000. Given this, the gain on the land would be $250,000 ($350,000 - $100,000). The maximum reserve would be $178,571, the lesser of:

- $178,571 [($250,000)($250,000 ÷ $350,000)]; or
- $200,000 [($250,000)(20%)(4 - 0)].

Net and Taxable Income

The required calculations here would be as follows:

Employment income	$ 140,870
Property income	15,710
Taxable capital gains	100,465
ITA 60(e.1) CPP deduction [$3,166 - $2,876]	(290)
Net income	**$256,755**
Stock option deduction [(1/2)($6,000)]	(3,000)
Taxable income	**$253,755**

Federal Income Tax Payable

The required calculations here would be as follows:

Tax on first $216,511		$50,141
Tax on next $37,244 ($253,755 - $216,511) at 33%		12,291
Tax before credits		$62,432
Tax credits:		
Basic personal amount	($ 12,421)	
Spouse ($12,421 - $8,400)	(4,021)	
Canada caregiver for child–May	(2,295)	
Transfer of May's disability	(8,662)	
Disability supplement	(5,053)	
Transfer of tuition credit (Note 6)	(5,000)	
Medical expenses (Note 7)	(14,379)	
EI	(890)	
CPP	(2,876)	
Canada employment	(1,257)	
Total credit base	($ 56,854)	
Rate	15%	(8,528)
Subtotal		$53,904
Charitable donations credit (Note 8)		(360)
Non-eligible dividend tax credit [(9/13)($810)]		(561)
2021 federal income tax payable		$52,983

Note 6 The transfer of Virginia's tuition credit would be $5,000, the lesser of:

- $5,000 limit
- $9,350 actual

Note 7 The base for the medical expense tax credit would be calculated as follows:

Total medical expenses	$16,800
Lesser of:	
• [(3%)($256,755)] = $7,703	
• 2021 threshold amount = $2,421	(2,421)
Medical expense tax credit base	$14,379

Note 8 The charitable donations tax credit would be calculated as follows:

15% of $200	$ 30
33% of the lesser of:	
$1,200 - $200 = $1,000	
$253,755 - $216,511 = $37,244	330
29% of nil ($1,200 - $1,200)	Nil
Total donation credit	$360

SSP 8-18 Solution
Employment Income

The deduction of many employment expenses are often subject to a limitation found in ITA 8(1)(f) that restricts what can be claimed to the commission income received in that year. Since the commissions received of $43,000 exceed the total of permissible employment expenses, that limitation is not a concern in this case. The required calculations would be as follows:

Salary	$136,000
Additions	
Commissions	43,000
One-half total bonus (Note 1)	11,000
Expense allowance [(12)($2,500)]	30,000
Stock option benefit [(500)($108 - $92)]	8,000
Deductions	
RPP contributions	(4,200)
Professional association dues	(1,500)
Automobile costs	
CCA (Note 2)	(3,960)
Operating costs [(80%)($6,300)]	(5,040)
Hotel costs	(9,700)
Airline and other transportation	(5,400)
Client meals and entertainment [(1/2)($9,300)]	(4,650)
Work space in home expenses (Note 3)	(978)
Employment income	$192,572

Note 1 As the bonus is paid more than 179 days after the employer's year end, the employer will not be able to deduct the full amount of the bonus expense in 2021. This, however, does not change Lorenzo's position, as he is required to include any remuneration received in the year.

Note 2 The 2020 CCA would be based on a UCC calculated as though 100% of the available CCA had been claimed in 2020. The 100% CCA of the class 10.1 vehicle for 2020 would be $13,500 [(150% AccII)(30%)($30,000 maximum)]. Using this figure, the deductible 2021 CCA would be $3,960 [(80%)(30%)($30,000 - $13,500)].

Note 3 As Lorenzo has commission income, he can deduct 12% of all of the home office costs except the mortgage interest. This will provide a deduction of $978 [(12%)($1,250 + $1,300 + $5,600)].

Property Income

The required calculations here would be as follows:

Rental income (Note 4)	$2,610
Income trust distribution [(500)($2.40)]	1,200
Eligible dividends	4,200
Gross up on eligible dividends [(38%)($4,200)]	1,596
Property income	$9,606

Note 4 As the change in use is from personal to business, the base for calculating CCA would be as follows:

Cost of building		$ 63,000
FMV at the time of the change in use		
FMV	$250,000	
Cost	(63,000)	
Increase in value	$187,000	
Inclusion factor	1/2	93,500
Capital cost for UCC and CCA purposes		$156,500
One-half net additions [(1/2)($156,500)]		(78,250)
CCA base		$ 78,250
Rate for class 1		4%
CCA		$ 3,130

Using this CCA amount, rental income would be $2,610 ($5,740 - $3,130). The AccII is not available on a change in use since the owner of the deemed disposition and the deemed acquisition are the same. The half-year rule would normally apply to a change in use as long as CCA had not been previously claimed on the change-in-use portion. In this case, since the property was originally used 100% for personal use, no CCA would have been previously claimed on the property and as a result the half-year rule applies.

Taxable Capital Gains

The required calculations here would be as follows:

Stock option shares [(500)($115 - $108)]		$ 3,500
Sculpture (Note 5)		38,000
Change in use:		
Cottage–Land ($100,000 - $42,000)	$ 58,000	
Cottage–Building ($250,000 - $63,000)	187,000	245,000
Real Property Income Trust (Note 6)		2,161
Land sale ($180,000 - $78,000)	$102,000	
Reserve for land sale (Note 7)	(71,400)	30,600
Capital gains		$319,261
Inclusion rate		1/2
Taxable capital gains		$ 159,631

Note 5 As the actual ACB of this personal-use property is less than $1,000, its deemed ACB is $1,000 (ITA 46). This results in a gain of $38,000 ($39,000 - $1,000).

Note 6 The $1,200 income trust distribution was used to acquired 20.51 additional units ($1,200 ÷ $58.50). Using this figure, the capital gain calculation would be:

Proceeds of disposition [(520.51)($60.25)]	$31,361
Adjusted cost base [(500)($56) + $1,200)]	(29,200)
Capital gain	$ 2,161

Note 7 The gain on the land would be $102,000 ($180,000 - $78,000). The maximum reserve would be $71,400, the lesser of

- $71,400 [($102,000)($126,000 ÷ $180,000)]; or
- $81,600 [($102,000)(20%)(4 - 0)].

Net and Taxable Income

The required calculations here would be as follows:

Employment income	$192,572
Property income	9,606
Net taxable capital gains	159,631
Deductible CPP ($3,166 - $2,876)	(290)
Net income	$361,519
Stock option deduction [(1/2)($8,000)]	(4,000)
Taxable income	$ 357,519

Federal Tax Payable

The required calculations here would be as follows:

Tax on first $216,511		$50,141
Tax on next $141,008 ($357,519 - $216,511) at 33%		46,533
Tax before credits		$96,674
Tax credits:		
Basic personal amount	($12,421)	
Spouse ($12,421 - $6,300)	(6,121)	
Canada caregiver for child–Anita	(2,295)	
Transfer of Anita's disability	(8,662)	
Disability supplement	(5,053)	
Transfer of tuition–Lesser of:		
• Absolute limit of $5,000		
• Actual tuition of $9,300	(5,000)	
Medical expenses (Note 8)	(15,204)	
EI	(890)	
CPP	(2,876)	
Canada employment	(1,257)	
Total credit base	($59,779)	
Rate	15%	(8,967)
Subtotal		$ 87,707
Charitable donations credit (Note 9)		(756)
Dividend tax credit [(6/11)($1,596)]		(871)
Federal income tax payable		$86,080

Note 8   The base for the medical expense tax credit would be calculated as follows:

Total medical expenses	$ 17,625
Lesser of:	
• [(3%)($361,519)] = $10,846	
• 2021 threshold amount = $2,421	(2,421)
Medical expense tax credit base	$15,204

Note 9   The charitable donations tax credit would be calculated as follows:

15% of $200	$ 30
33% of the lesser of:	
$2,200 ($2,400 - $200)	
$141,008 ($357,519 - $216,511)	726
29% of nil ($2,200 - $2,200)	Nil
Total donation credit	$756

CHAPTER 9

Learning Objectives

After completing Chapter 9, you should be able to:

1. Describe the role that Subdivisions d, e, and f play in determining net income (Paragraph [P hereafter] 9-1 to 9-4).
2. Identify the major other sources of income that are listed under Subdivision d of the *ITA* (P 9-5 to 9-18).
3. Identify the income inclusions from deferred income plans (P 9-19 and 9-22).
4. Apply the rules related to education assistance payments, social assistance, and workers' compensation payments (P 9-23 to 9-28).
5. Determine the income tax treatment of CPP contributions for both employees and self-employed individuals, including the new system that allows a partial deduction instead of a non-refundable tax credit (P 9-29 to 9-32).
6. Determine the deductible amount of moving expenses for an individual (P 9-33 to 9-49).
7. Determine the deductible amount of child care expenses (P 9-50 to 9-60).
8. Apply the provisions related to the disability supports deduction (P 9-61 to 9-69).
9. Explain and apply the rules for pension income splitting (P 9-70 to 9-79).
10. Explain the tax treatment of child support and spousal support payments and receipts (P 9-80 to 9-89).
11. Determine the taxable portion of annuity payments received (P 9-90 to 9-96).
12. Describe the potential income-splitting opportunities provided by RESPs, TFSAs, and RDSPs (P 9-97 to 9-100).
13. Describe the major features of Tax-Free Savings Accounts (TFSAs) (P 9-101).
14. Explain the provisions associated with registered education savings plans, Canada Education Savings Grants, and Canada Learning Bonds (P 9-102 to 9-125).
15. Compare the major features of TFSAs, RRSPs, and RESPs (P 9-126 to 9-131).
16. Describe the major features of registered disability savings plans (RDSPs) (P 9-132 to 9-134).
17. Determine the tax consequences of non-arm's-length transfers of property at values other than fair market value (P 9-135 to 9-153).
18. Describe the special rollover provisions applicable to inter vivos transfers of capital property to a spouse (P 9-154 to 9-161).
19. Determine the tax consequences of non-arm's-length transfers of depreciable property (P 9-162 to 9-168).
20. Describe the special rollover provisions applicable to inter vivos transfers of farm or fishing property to a child (P 9-169 to 9-174).
21. Explain the basic requirements for deemed dispositions on death and any rollovers available at that time (P 9-175 to 9-183).
22. Apply the income attribution rules to inter vivos transfers of capital property to a spouse and to related individuals who are under the age of 18 (P 9-184 to 9-202).
23. Describe the income attribution rules applicable to transfers to other related parties (P 9-203 to 9-207).

24. Describe some of the tax planning techniques that are available to mitigate income attribution (P 9-208).

How to Work through Chapter 9

Visit pearsonmylabandmastering.com to access MyLab Accounting for this text. Once there, you can access student resources such as Self-Study Problems, Practice Exams, Flashcards, updates, and more.

We recommend the following approach in dealing with the material in this chapter:

Coverage and Organization of Chapter 9
- Read the overview in paragraph 9-1 to 9-4 (in the text).

Inclusions–Pension Benefits, Retiring Allowances, and Death Benefits.
- Read paragraph 9-5 to 9-18 **(note paragraphs 9-12 and 9-13 on the interaction between ITA 56 and 60)**.

Inclusions–Deferred Income Plans, Scholarships, and Social Assistance Payments
- Read paragraph 9-19 to 9-28.

Deductions–CPP Contributions on Self-Employed Earnings
- Read paragraph 9-29 to 9-32.

Deductions–Moving Expenses
- Read paragraph 9-33 to 9-49.
- Do Exercise 9-1 (in the text) and check the solution in this Study Guide.
- Do Self-Study Problem 9-1, which is available on MyLab, and check the solution in this Study Guide.

Deductions–Child Care Expenses
- Read paragraph 9-50 to 9-60.
- Do Exercise 9-2 and check the solution in this Study Guide.
- Do Self-Study Problems 9-2 and 9-3 and check the solutions in this Study Guide.

Deductions–Disability Supports Deduction
- Read paragraph 9-61 to 9-69.
- Do Exercise 9-3 and check the solution in this Study Guide.

Related Inclusions/Deductions–Pension Income Splitting
- Read paragraph 9-70 to 9-79.
- Do Exercise 9-4 and check the solution in this Study Guide.
- Do Self-Study Problems 9-4 and 9-5 and check the solutions in this Study Guide.

Related Inclusions/Deductions–Spousal and Child Support
- Read paragraph 9-80 to 9-89.
- Do Exercise 9-5 and check the solution in this Study Guide.

Related Inclusions/Deductions–Annuity Payments Received
- Read paragraph 9-90 to 9-96.
- Do Exercise 9-6 and check the solution in this Study Guide.

Registered Savings Plans
- Read paragraph 9-97 to 9-100.

Tax-Free Savings Accounts (TFSAs)
- Read paragraph 9-101.

Registered Education Savings Plans (RESPs), Canada Education Savings Grants
- Read paragraph 9-102 to 9-111.
- Do Exercise 9-7 and check the solution in this Study Guide.
- Read paragraph 9-112 to 9-125.
- Do Self-Study Problem 9-6 and check the solution in this Study Guide.

Comparison of TFSAs, RRSPs, and RESPs
- Read paragraph 9-126 to 9-131.

Registered Disability Savings Plans (RDSPs)
- Read paragraph 9-132 to 9-134.

Non-Arm's-Length Transfers of Property–Inadequate Considerations (ITA 69)
- Read paragraph 9-135 to 9-153.
- Do Exercise 9-8 and check the solution in this Study Guide.
- Do Self-Study Problem 9-7 and check the solution in this Study Guide.

Inter Vivos Transfers to a Spouse
- Read paragraph 9-154 to 9-161.
- Do Exercise 9-9 and check the solution in this Study Guide.

Non-Arm's-Length Transfers of Depreciable Property
- Read paragraph 9-162 to 9-168.
- Do Exercises 9-10 and 9-11 and check the solutions in this Study Guide.
- Do Self-Study Problem 9-8 and check the solution in this Study Guide.

Inter Vivos Transfer of Farm or Fishing Property to a Child
- Read paragraph 9-169 to 9-174.
- Do Exercise 9-12 and check the solution in this Study Guide.

Deemed Dispositions–On Death
- Read paragraph 9-175 to 9-182.
- Do Exercise 9-13 and check the solution in this Study Guide.
- Read paragraph 9-183.
- Do Self-Study Problem 9-9 and check the solution in this Study Guide.

Income Attribution
- Read paragraph 9-184 to 9-202.
- Do Exercises 9-14 to 9-16 and check the solutions in this Study Guide.
- Read paragraph 9-203 to 9-207.
- Do Self-Study Problems 9-10 and 9-11 and check the solutions in this Study Guide.

Tax Planning and Income Attribution
- Read paragraph 9-208.
- Do Self-Study Problems 9-12 and 9-13 and check the solutions in this Study Guide.

To Complete This Chapter
- Visit MyLab Accounting for more practice problem material, and test yourself with the glossary flashcards.
- Review the Key Terms at the end of the chapter, and consult the glossary for definitions.
- Ensure you have achieved the Chapter 9 Learning Objectives listed in this Study Guide.
- As a review, view the PowerPoint presentations available on MyLab.

Practice Examination
- Available on MyLab, write the Practice Examination for this chapter, and mark it using the solutions provided.

Exercise Solutions

Exercise 9-1 Solution

The relocation is an eligible relocation since the purpose of the move is to (1) enable her to be employed at a new work location, (2) she moved from a home (the rented apartment) in which she ordinarily resided to a new home in which she ordinarily resided, and (3) the distance between her old home and new work location and her new home and new work location is more than 40 kilometres.

Ms. Chevlak paid $8,900 for moving expenses that include $1,300 for the house hunting trip, $6,400 for moving expenses, and $1,200 for a lease cancellation penalty. Of this amount, only the $1,300 house hunting trip is not an eligible moving expense because it was incurred prior to the acquisition of the new home, however the remaining $7,600 does qualify. If an allowance of $6,000 was paid it is suggested that this would be added to employment income, with the result that the employment at the new work location would be $8,000 [$2,000 salary + $6,000 allowance]. In that case ITA 62(1) would apply to allow a deduction of $7,600 because the allowance was fully included in her employment income and the amount claimed is less than her employment income at the new work location. As a result, her net income would increase by $400 with respect to the move [$8,000 employment income- $7,600 ITA 62 moving expense deduction].

However, the CRA administers this situation much differently. They first recognize that none of the $6,000 amount would be required to be included in her employment income. The CRA practice is then to allow a claim for moving expenses equal to the amount by which the actual moving expenses ($8,900) exceed the assistance of $6,000 from the employer. As a result, she would be entitled to claim $2,900 of moving expenses to the extent she would have eligible moving expenses. Since income at the new work location is only $2,000, she would only be able to claim $2,000 and would carry forward the remainig $900 to 2022. The effect is that her net income with respect to the move would be nil [$2,000 employment income at the new work location minus the limited ITA 62 moving expense deduction of $2,000]. In addition, she would have $900 of moving expenses to deduct in 2022. The effect of the CRA treatment is that the first part of the assistance is applied against the non-deductible house hunting trip and the remaining $4,700 against the qualifying moving expenses of $7,600. This beneficial treatment is consistent with other administrative concessions provided by CRA.

Exercise 9-2 Solution

The deduction will have to be made by the lower net income spouse, Mr. Sampras, as his net income is only $14,000 while the net income of Mrs. Sampras is $54,000. The deduction will be the least of the following amounts:

- The actual costs of $10,500
- Annual child care expense amount of $18,000 [(1)($8,000) + (2)($5,000)]
- 2/3 of Mr. Sampras' earned income, an amount of $13,000 [(2/3)($14,000 + $5,500)]

The least of these three amounts is $10,500, which Mr. Sampras can claim as a child care expense deduction under ITA 63 for the year.

Exercise 9-3 Solution

As Jose is not eligible for the disability tax credit, he will deduct the cost of full-time attendant care under ITA 64. When combined with the other disability support costs and the reimbursement, the qualifying costs total $36,000 ($23,000 + $18,000 - $5,000). As this is less than his qualifying employment income of $81,000 [$78,000 + $3,000], he will be able to deduct the full amount of these expenditures as his disability supports deduction. His net income for 2021 would be $42,000 [employment income of $78,000 - ITA 64 deduction of $36,000].

Exercise 9-4 Solution

In the absence of pension income splitting, John would not pay any income taxes for 2021 since income tax on $7,400 is offset by income tax credits in excess of that amount. Joanna's 2021 net income before any OAS clawback would be $92,400 ($85,000 + $7,400). There would be an OAS clawback of $1,883 [(15%)($92,400 - $79,845), leaving Joanna with net and taxable inocme of $90,517 ($92,400 - $1,883). Based on this amount, her 2021 income tax payable would be calculated as follows:

Tax on first $49,020		$ 7,353
Tax on next $41,497 ($90,517 - $49,020) at 20.5%		8,507
Total before credits		$15,860
Basic personal	($13,808)	
Credits:		
Spousal ($13,808 - $7,400)	(6,408)	
Age [$7,713 - (15%)($90,517 - $38,893)]	Nil	
Pension	(2,000)	
Spouse's age	(7,713)	
Total	($29,929)	
Rate	15%	(4,489)
Federal tax payable		$ 11,371
OAS clawback		1,883
Federal income tax owing–Joanna only		$ 13,254

If maximum pension splitting is used, the eligible pension income for the split will equal $42,500 [(50%)($85,000)]. Joanna's net and taxable income wil be $49,900 [$85,000 + $7,400– ITA 60(c) of $42,500]. John's net and taxable income will also be $49,900 [$7,400 + $42,500 ITA 56(1)(a.2)]. Since this is below the income threshold of $79,845, there will be no clawback of OAS for Joanna or John. Based on these numbers, the federal income tax payable for both Joanna and John would be the same and is calculated as follows:

Tax on first $49,020		$ 7,353
Tax on next $880 ($49,900 - $49,020) at 20.5%		180
Total before credits		$ 7,533
Credits:		
Basic personal	($13,808)	
Age [$7,713 - (15%)($49,900 - $38,893)]	(6,062)	
Pension	(2,000)	
Total	($21,870)	
Rate	15%	(3,281)
Federal tax payable		$4,252
OAS clawback		Nil
Federal income tax owing for each		$ 4,252

With pension income splitting, the total amount owing by Joanna and John would be $8,504 [(2)($4,252)]. This is an improvement of $4,750 over the $13,254 that Joanna would have paid without income splitting. Further savings would be available after taking into consideration provincial income tax.

Exercise 9-5 Solution
The total required child support is $9,000 [(6 months)($1,500)]. ITA 56 and ITA 60 apply any payments made to child support first and then to spousal support. Since Sandra only paid $12,000, $9,000 will be considered non-deductible child support and the $3,000 difference deductible spousal support. This means that Sandra will be entitled to deduct $3,000 under ITA 60(b) and Jerry will be required to include $3,000 in net income as a result of ITA 56(1)(b).

Exercise 9-6 Solution

A total of $63,492 [(4)($15,873)] in payments will be received during the term of the annuity. The $15,873 annual payment is required to be included in net income as a result of ITA 56(1)(d) because the annuity payment is not made through a deferred income plan where it would be included in income elsewhere. The inclusion under ITA 56(1)(d) entitles the individual to claim a deduction under ITA 60(a) to effectively remove the capital component of the annuity payment, isolating the income part of the payment. The ITA 60(a) deduction would be calculated as follows:

$$\left[\frac{\$55,000}{\$63,492}\right][15,873] = \underline{\$13,750}\ \text{Deduction}$$

As a result, Mr. Hollock's net income will increase by $2,123 ($15,873 - $13,750) each year. Over the four-year term this represents income plus a recovery of the $55,000 investment [(4)($13,750)].

Exercise 9-7 Solution

For 2020, the contributions to Jeanine's RESP total $1,700 ($500 + $1,200). This is within the $2,500 limit for contributions eligible for CESGs and results in unused CESG contribution room of $800 [$2,500 - $1,700]. This means that the 2020 CESG would be calculated as follows:

Additional $500 at 20%	$100
Basic $1,700 at 20%	340
Total CESG for 2020	$440

For 2021, the contributions to Jeanine's RESP total $3,900 ($1,500 + $2,400). The CESG contribution room is limited to $3,300 [$2,500 current year + $800 unused from the previous year]. This means that $600 ($3,900 - $3,300) of the total contributions will not be eligible for CESGs. Given this, the 2021 CESG would be calculated as follows:

Additional $500 at 20%	$100
Basic $3,300 at 20%	660
Total CESG for 2021	$760

There would be no unused CESG room at the end of 2021. If it is expected that annual contributions to Jeanine's RESP will be less than $2,500 in the future, this would suggest that Jeanine's father should limit his 2021 contribution to $900 and defer the extra $600 to the following year. In that year, the additional $600 would be eligible for the CESG in 2022.

Exercise 9-8 Solution

Mr. Lipky's POD will be equal to the FMV of the amount received of $95,000, resulting in a capital loss of $5,000 (POD $95,000 - ACB $100,000). His brother's cost is equal to the FMV of the consideration he gave up to acquire the property of $95,000. Since the brothers are related persons they are deemed not to deal with each other at arm's length, which allows ITA 69 to apply. ITA 69(1)(a) applies were a person has acquired property in a non-arm's-length transaction at an amount greater that its FMV. Since the brother acquired a property worth $75,000 for $95,000 his deemed cost is $75,000, which becomes the ACB. An immediate sale of the property for $75,000 therefore results in no capital gain or capital loss [POD $75,000 - ACB $75,000]. Had the property been sold between the brothers for $75,000, Mr. Lipky would have realized a $25,000 capital loss and an immediate sale by the brother would have resulted in no capital gain or capital loss. In this case Mr. Lipky is penalized because his capital loss is reduced by $20,000. In addition, the brother cannot realize a capital loss based on his cost of $95,000.

Exercise 9-9 Solution

ITA 73(1) applies   If Mr. Schwartz does not elect to avoid ITA 73(1), then the rollover will apply as follows:

- His deemed POD will be equal to the $225,000 ACB of the land. As a result, there will be no income tax consequences to Mr. Schwartz as a result of the transfer.
- The cost and therefore the ACB to his spouse will be deemed to be $225,000.

ITA 73(1) does not apply   If Mr. Schwartz elects to avoid ITA 73(1), then the income tax consequences of the transaction will be determined under ITA 69(1) at FMV for both spouses:

- The ACB of the land to his spouse will be $300,000.
- Mr. Schwartz will have to include a taxable capital gain in his net income calculated as follows:

POD	$300,000
ACB	(225,000)
Capital gain	$ 75,000
Inclusion rate	1/2
Taxable capital gain	$ 37,500

Exercise 9-10 Solution

ITA 73(1) applies   If Mary Sharp does not elect to avoid ITA 73(1), the results will be as follows:

- The deemed POD to Mary Sharp will be equal to the UCC of $110,000, resulting in no income tax consequences to her.
- For CCA and recapture purposes the cost to her spouse will be $110,000.
- Her spouse would be deemed (ITA 73(2)) to have the same capital cost as Mary of $175,000 with the difference between $175,000 and the $110,000 UCC balance considered to be deemed CCA of $65,000.
- ITA 13(7)(e) would not apply since it requires that either the POD to the transferor exceeds the capital cost such that there would be a capital gain to the transferor or that the POD to the transferor is less than the capital cost. This is equivalent to the two situations discussed in the chapter. Remember that the application of the rollover of ITA 73(1), particularly ITA 73(2), ensures that the transferee's capital cost is equal to the capital cost of the transferor; therefore ITA 13(7)(e) would not apply.

ITA 73(1) does not apply   If Mary Sharp elects to avoid ITA 73(1) then the transaction would take place at FMV of $225,000:

- For capital gains purposes, the ACB for Mary Sharp's spouse would be $225,000. However, for CCA and recapture purposes, ITA 13(7)(e) would deem the spouse's capital cost to be $200,000 [($175,000 + (1/2)($225,000 - $175,000)].
- She will include the following amounts in her net income:

POD	$ 225,000
ACB	(175,000)
Capital gain	$ 50,000
Inclusion rate	1/2
Taxable capital gain	$ 25,000

UCC	$ 110,000
Deduct lesser of:	
POD = $225,000	
Capital cost = $175,000	(175,000)
Negative ending balance = Recapture of CCA	($ 65,000)

Exercise 9-11 Solution

Ms. Lee The income tax consequence for Ms. Lee is as follows:

UCC	$ 37,200
Deduct lesser of:	
POD = $40,000	
Capital cost = $53,000	(40,000)
Negative ending balance = Recapture of CCA	($ 2,800)

Ms. Lee's Father Ms. Lee and her father are related persons and therefore deemed not to deal with each at arm's length. This means that ITA 69 potentially applies as does ITA 13(7)(e). ITA 69 does not apply to the transaction because it takes place at FMV. ITA 13(7)(e) applies where the transferor, Ms. Lee, either experiences a capital gain on the sale or the sale takes place at an amount below her capital cost. While she does not realize a capital gain on the sale to her father the sale price is below her capital cost, and therefore ITA 13(7)(e) applies. ITA 13(7)(e) deems the father's capital cost to be equal to Ms. Lee's capital cost of $53,000. The $13,000 difference between the deemed capital cost and his cost of $40,000 is deemed to be CCA, resulting in UCC of $40,000. When he subsequently sells the property for $44,000, the result will be as follows:

UCC	$40,000
Deduct lesser of:	
POD = $44,000	
Deemed capital cost = $53,000	(44,000)
Negative ending balance = Recapture of CCA	($ 4,000)

Exercise 9-12 Solution

With respect to the land, the $280,000 paid is between the $250,000 ACB, which is the lower limit, and the $325,000 FMV, which is the upper limit. Therefore, the POD would be $280,000, resulting in a taxable capital gain for Mr. Nobel of $15,000 [(1/2)(POD $280,000 - ACB $250,000]). The $280,000 would be the cost and therefore the ACB for his daughter.

With respect to the barn, the range in which the property can be transferred is from the UCC of $85,000 to the capital cost of $115,000 to the transferor. Where the actual proceeds are less than the lower limit of $85,000, it is that limit that becomes the POD to the transferor. With respect to his daughter, her cost would be that same $85,000 (ITA 73(3.1)(a)(iii)). Finally, because the capital cost of $115,000 exceeds the deemed POD of $85,000, the daughter inherits the tax attributes of the property of the transferor. The result is that she would be deemed to have a capital cost of $115,000 and deemed CCA of $30,000, resulting in a UCC of $85,000 (ITA 73(3.1)(h)).

Exercise 9-13 Solution

Truck A would be transferred to her spouse on a rollover basis as a result of ITA 70(6) at its capital cost amount or proportional UCC of $25,500 [$51,000/2 properties]. As a result, no income will be realized in Mrs. Lardner's final income tax return as a result of the disposition. The tax attributes of the truck will be the same capital cost of $42,000 with deemed CCA of $16,500, with the result that the UCC to Michel will be $25,500.

Truck B would be transferred to Melinda at the FMV of $33,000 as a result of ITA 70(5), since the rollover of ITA 70(6) is only available to spouses or common-law partners or trusts created for them. This means that the POD for the two trucks would be $58,500 ($25,500 + $33,000). This would result in recapture of $7,500 ($51,000 - $58,500) being included in Ms. Lardner's net income in her final income tax return. The $33,000 transfer price would be the UCC value to Melinda. Since Ms. Lardner's capital cost of $42,000 exceeds the $33,000 capital cost to Melinda she would retain Ms. Lardner's $42,000 capital cost with the difference of $9,000 treated as deemed CCA, leaving her with UCC of $33,000.

Exercise 9-14 Solution

ITA 73(1) provides for a tax-free rollover of capital property to a spouse or common-law partner. The income tax consequences for Mr. and Mrs. Moreau for the two years can be outlined as follows:

- 2020 for Mr. Moreau–none. He is deemed to acquire the shares for their ACB of $23,000.
- 2020 for Mrs. Moreau–none. She is deemed to have disposed of the shares for her ACB of $23,000, resulting in no capital gain or capital loss [POD $23,000 - ACB $23,000].
- 2021 for Mr. Moreau–none. While technically there is a taxable capital gain of $9,500 [(1/2)($42,000 - $23,000)], it is considered as that of Mrs. Moreau and not Mr. Moreau. The same occurs for the taxable dividend.
- 2021 for Mrs. Moreau–total increase in net income of $12,950 composed of a taxable capital gain of $9,500 plus taxable eligible dividends of $3,450.

Exercise 9-15 Solution

There is no provision for a rollover of shares to a child that are not farm or fishing property. The income tax consequences for Norah and Nicki Moreau for the two years can be outlined as follows:

- 2020 for Nicki–none. Nicki is deemed to have acquired the shares for $37,000 as a result of ITA 69(1)(c). That amount is her cost and ACB.
- 2020 for Norah–ITA 69(1)(b) deems Norah to have disposed of the shares by gift at POD equal to the FMV at that time. As a result, she will realize a taxable capital gain of $7,000 [(1/2)(POD $37,000 - ACB $23,000)].
- 2021 for Nicki–Nicki will realize a taxable capital gain of $2,500 [(1/2)(POD $42,000 - ACB $37,000)] as a result of a disposition at FMV. She will also have a taxable dividend that is deemed by ITA 74.1(2) to be attributed back to her mother.
- 2021 for Norah–taxable dividends of $3,450 are attributed to her and will be included in her net income.

Exercise 9-16 Solution

The property transfer between the spouses is eligible for the ITA 73(1) rollover. Since Mr. Bronski did not report the transfer as a disposition at FMV in his 2020 income tax return he is considered not to have elected to avoid the rollover. In other words, the ITA 73(1) rollover would apply to deem him to have received POD equal to the ACB of the bonds of $115,000, therefore there will be no capital gain or capital loss [POD $115,000 - ACB $115,000]. Mrs. Bronski will be considered to have acquired the bonds for the same amount of $115,000, which will be her cost and ACB.

To avoid the attribution rules Mr. Bronski would have had to (1) report the gift to his spouse as a disposition at FMV and (2) ensure that the promissory note from his spouse charged interest at a rate equal to the prescribed rate. Since the promissory note was interest free, the attribution rules cannot be avoided. The attribution rules will apply to attribute the bond interest of $6,100 back to Mr. Bronski.

In 2021 Mrs. Bronski will realize a taxable capital gain of $7,000 [(1/2)($129,000 - $115,000)], which would be attributed to Mr. Bronski. The total increase in Mr. Bronski's 2021 net income is $13,100 (interest $6,100 + taxable capital gain $7,000). There will be no income tax consequences for Mrs. Bronski in 2021.

Self-Study Problem Solutions

Self-Study Problems are available to download from MyLab Accounting.

SSP 9-1 Solution

Costs for food and lodging at or near an old or new residence are limited to a maximum period of 15 days. Note that the nine days spent travelling to Vancouver are not included in the 15-day total. Since the daily costs for her Montreal stay are higher than those for her Vancouver stay, she claims the 15-day maximum at the Montreal rate.

The deductible moving expenses can be calculated as follows:

House hunting trip hotel and food (not deductible)		Nil
Real estate commission–Montreal home		$27,500
Legal fees–Montreal home		800
Other Montreal home costs (not deductible)		Nil
Storage costs		2,200
Moving company charges		10,200
Hotel in Montreal (15 nights at $350)		5,250
Food–Maximum (15 days at $51 simplified rate)		765
Expenses of travel to Vancouver:		
Gas (using simplified method)	Nil	
Simplified mileage rate		
[(4,558 @ $0.58)	$2,644	
Hotel (9 nights–total)	1,575	
Food (9 days at $51 simplified rate)	459	4,678
Vancouver hotel		Nil
Moving expense deductions available		$51,393

Moving costs can only be deducted against income earned at the new work location. The income at the new work location includes the general moving allowance, compensation for house loss, and payment for higher housing costs. As a result, there will be sufficient income to allow a full deduction of the moving expenses. The total employment income at the new work location would be as follows:

Salary at new location (one month @ $15,000)	$15,000
General moving allowance	20,000
Compensation for loss on Montreal residence (Note 1)	30,000
Payment for higher housing costs (Note 2)	10,000
Total employment income at new location	$75,000

Note 1 Under ITA 6(20), one-half of any housing loss reimbursement in excess of $15,000 must be included in income. As the total reimbursement was $75,000 ($625,000 - $550,000), the inclusion would be $30,000 [(1/2)($75,000 - $15,000)].

Note 2 Any amounts paid to compensate an employee for higher housing costs must be included in income in full (ITA 6(23)).

As the deductible costs are less than the income at the new location, they are fully deductible in Michelle's 2021 income tax return. There would be no carry forward of moving costs.

SSP 9-2 Solution
Mrs. Fortin

Generally, the spouse with the lower net income must claim the deduction for child care expenses. However, under certain circumstances (e.g., if the spouse is hospitalized), the spouse with the higher net income can claim the deduction for the period of hospitalization. Note that in this case earned income is equal to net income. Thus Mrs. Fortin can claim the least of the following:

	Case A	Case B
Actual payments [($400)(48)]	$19,200	$19,200
2/3 of earned income [(2/3)($84,000)]	$56,000	$56,000
Annual expense limit:		
Case A [(2)($8,000)]	$16,000	
Case B [(2)($8,000) + (1)($5,000)]		$21,000
Periodic expense limit:		
Case A [(2)($200)(6 weeks)]	$ 2,400	
Case B {[(2)($200)(6 weeks)] + [(1)($125)(6 weeks)]}		$ 3,150

In Case A, the least of these figures is $2,400, the periodic expense limit. In Case B, the least of the figures is $3,150, also the periodic expense limit.

Mr. Fortin
The calculations for Mr. Fortin are as follows:

	Case A	Case B
Actual payments	$19,200	$ 19,200
2/3 of earned income [(2/3)($8,000)]	$ 5,333	$ 5,333
Annual expense limit:		
Case A [(2)($8,000)]	$16,000	
Case B [(2)($8,000) + (1)($5,000)]		$21,000

The lowest figure in both cases is $5,333, two-thirds of Mr. Fortin's earned income. Mr. Fortin's deduction for the current year will be reduced by the amount claimed by Mrs. Fortin. Mr. Fortin's deduction for the current year is $2,933 ($5,333 - $2,400) in Case A and $2,183 ($5,333 - $3,150) in Case B.

SSP 9-3 Solution
The deductible actual costs are as follows:

Actual costs excluding camp costs (48 weeks at $260)	$12,480
Periodic cost limit for camp weeks	
[($125)(1)(4 weeks) + ($200)(1)(4 weeks) + ($275)(1)(4 weeks)]	2,400
Deductible actual costs	$14,880

Generally, the common-law partner with the lower net income must claim the deduction for child care expenses. In this case, that would be Sue Brendal. However, under certain circumstances, the common-law partner with the higher net income can claim a deduction that is subject to a weekly limitation.

One of these circumstances is when the lower net income common-law partner is in attendance on a full-time basis at a designated educational institution. This means that for the five-week period that Sue is attending the accounting course, Maureen can deduct limited child care expenses.

The relevant calculations for determining the deductible costs for each individual are as follows:

	Maureen	**Sue**
Actual costs and limited camp costs	$ 14,880	$ 14,880
Annual expense limit [($5,000)(1) + ($8,000)(1) + ($11,000)(1)]	$ 24,000	$24,000
2/3 of earned income [(2/3)($216,000)] [(2/3)($24,000)]	$144,000	$ 16,000
Periodic expense limit [($125)(1)(5 weeks) + ($200)(1)(5 weeks) + ($275)(1)(5 weeks)]	$ 3,000	N/A

The least of these amounts for Maureen is $3,000. You should note that there is no requirement that actual payments be allocated on the basis of the time that Sue was attending the accounting course.

The lowest figure for Sue is $14,880, the actual child care costs. Sue's deduction for the current year of $11,880 ($14,880 - $3,000) has been reduced by the amount claimed by Maureen.

As Maureen is the higher net income common-law partner, her three-week stay in the hospital has no effect on the child care expense calculations.

SSP 9-4 Solution
Net and Taxable Income

John's income	**No Split**	**With Split**
Pension receipt	$64,000	$64,000
Net rental income	23,000	23,000
Pension income to Fatima	N/A	(32,000)
Net and taxable income	$ 87,000	$55,000

Fatima's income	**No Split**	**With Split**
Interest income	$8,400	$ 8,400
Pension income from John	N/A	32,000
Net and taxable income	$8,400	$40,400

Federal Tax Payable with No Pension Income Splitting

Fatima   Fatima's federal tax payable with no pension income splitting would be calculated as follows:

Tax before credits [(15%)($8,400)]	$1,260
Basic personal credit [(15%)($13,808)]	(2,071)
Federal tax payable–Fatima	Nil

John   Without pension income splitting, John's tax payable would be calculated as follows:

Tax on first $49,020		$ 7,353
Tax on next $37,980 ($87,000 - $49,020) at 20.5%		7,786
Total before credits		$15,139
Credits:		
Basic personal	($13,808)	
Spousal ($13,808 - $8,400)	(5,408)	
Pension	(2,000)	
Total	($ 21,216)	
Rate	15%	(3,182)
Federal tax payable–John		$11,957

Federal Tax Payable with Pension Income Splitting

Fatima   When pension income splitting is used, Fatima's tax payable would be as follows:

Tax before credits [(15%)($40,400)]		$6,060
Credits:		
Basic personal	($13,808)	
Pension	(2,000)	
Total	($15,808)	
Rate	15%	(2,371)
Federal tax payable–Fatima		$3,689

John   With pension income splitting, John's tax payable would be calculated as follows:

Tax on first $49,020		$7,353
Tax on next $5,980 ($55,000 - $49,020) at 20.5%		1,226
Tax before credits		$8,579
Credits:		
Basic personal	($13,808)	
Spousal	Nil	
Pension	(2,000)	
Total	($15,808)	
Rate	15%	(2,371)
Federal tax payable–John		$6,208

Comparison

Federal tax payable without income splitting (John only)	$11,957
Federal tax payable with income splitting ($3,689 + $6,208)	(9,897)
Savings with pension income splitting	$ 2,060

SSP 9-5 Solution
Part A–Net and Taxable Income

Martin's income	Scenario 1	Scenario 2
Pension receipt	$124,000	$124,000
Pension income to Sally	N/A	(62,000)
OAS	N/A	7,400
Net income before OAS clawback	$124,000	$ 69,400
OAS clawback (Notes 1 and 2)	N/A	N/A
Net and taxable income–Martin	$124,000	$ 69,400

Sally's income	Scenario 1	Scenario 2
OAS	$ 7,400	$ 7,400
Interest earned	43,000	43,000
Pension income from Martin	N/A	62,000
Net income before OAS clawback	$50,400	$ 112,400
OAS clawback (Note 3)	Nil	(4,883)
Net and taxable income–Sally	$50,400	$107,517

Note 1   As Martin did not apply for OAS in Scenario 1, there can be no clawback.

Note 2   In Scenario 2, Martin's net income is less than the clawback income threshold of $79,845, so there is no clawback.

Note 3   With pension income splitting, the OAS clawback for Sally would be $4,883 [(15%)($112,400 - $79,845)].

Part B–Scenario 1

Without pension income splitting, Martin's amount owing would be calculated as follows:

Tax on first $98,040		$ 17,402
Tax on next $25,960 ($124,000 - $98,040) at 26%		6,750
Tax before credits		$24,152
Credits:		
Basic personal	($13,808)	
Age [$7,713 - (15%)($124,000 - $38,893)]	Nil	
Pension	(2,000)	
Total	($ 15,808)	
Rate	15%	(2,371)
Total amount owing–Martin		$21,781

Without pension income splitting, Sally's amount owing would be calculated as follows:

Tax on first $49,020		$7,353
Tax on next $1,380 ($50,400 - $49,020) at 20.5%		283
Tax before credits		$7,636
Credits:		
Basic personal	($13,808)	
Age [$7,713 - (15%)($50,400 - $38,893)]	(5,987)	
Disability	(8,662)	
Total	($ 28,457)	
Rate	15%	(4,269)
Total amount owing (no clawback)–Sally		$3,367

Part B–Scenario 2

With pension income splitting and the OAS payments, Martin's amount owing would be calculated as follows:

Tax on first $49,020		$ 7,353
Tax on next $20,380 ($69,400 - $49,020) at 20.5%		4,178
Tax before credits		$11,531
Credits:		
Basic personal	($13,808)	
Age [$7,713 - (15%)($69,400 - $38,893)]	(3,137)	
Pension	(2,000)	
Total	($ 18,945)	
Rate	15%	(2,842)
Total amount owing (no clawback)–Martin		$ 8,689

With pension income splitting, Sally's amount owing would be calculated as follows:

Tax on first $98,040		$ 17,402
Tax on next $9,477 ($107,517 - $98,040) at 26%		2,464
Tax before credits		$19,866
Credits:		
Basic personal	($13,808)	
Age [$7,713 - (15%)($107,517 - $38,808)]	Nil	
Disability	(8,662)	
Pension	(2,000)	
Total	($ 24,470)	
Rate	15%	(3,671)
Federal tax payable		$ 16,195
OAS clawback		4,883
Total amount owing–Sally		$21,078

Part B–Comparison of After-Tax Income

This amount would be calculated as follows:

Amount owing–Scenario 1 ($21,781 + $3,367)		$25,148
Amount owing–Scenario 2 ($8,689 + $21,078)	($29,767)	
OAS benefits received–Scenario 2	7,400	(22,367)
Cash advantage–Scenario 2		$ 2,781

This problem illustrates the complexity associated with pension income splitting. Although Scenario 2 served to make the incomes more equal, it had several negative side effects (e.g., the clawback of a large part of Sally's OAS, as well as the elimination of her age credit). However, there is a definite cash advantage to Scenario 2.

The result would be improved if pension income splitting were limited to an amount that would give Martin a net income of the OAS clawback income threshold, as that would reduce Sally's OAS clawback without clawing back his OAS. However, that may not be the best solution. Finding the optimum solution is not an intuitive process, especially if there are other factors such as medical expenses, and would require the use of tax software.

SSP 9-6 Solution
Part A–Net Income
The minimum 2021 net income would be determined as follows:

Wages from summer employment		5,400
Moving costs to Pelican Lake (Note 1)		(350)
Scholarship received	$3,500	
Exempt portion of scholarship (100%)	(3,500)	Nil
Moving costs to Winnipeg (Note 1)		Nil
Eligible dividends received		2,000
Gross up of dividends (38%)		760
Child support received (Note 2)		Nil
Inheritance (not income)		Nil
TFSA contributions (Note 3)		Nil
TFSA withdrawal (Note 3)		Nil
2021 net income		$ 7,810

Note 1   The cost of the move to Pelican Lake is deductible against the income that was earned at that location as it is more than 40 kilometres from Winnipeg. Since there was no part of the scholarship that was required to be included in net income, he cannot claim any of the moving expenses back to Winnipeg.

Note 2   While spousal support is required to be included in net income of the recipient and is deductible to the payer, child support is not included in net income nor eligible for a deduction by the payer.

Note 3   TFSA contributions and withdrawals have no income tax consequences since the total $20,000 contributed is less than the maximum contribution allowable. There is also no income attribution as a result of the TFSA contribution by Mr. Masters' wife.

Part B–Registered Education Savings Plan
Payments into an RESP are not deductible. However, since a trust governed by an RESP is exempt from Part I tax (ITA 149(1)(u)), no income tax will be imposed on income earned within the RESP. Rather, the accumulated earnings of the RESP will be required to be included when ultimately paid to the recipient (presumably Mr. Masters' son). However, the child must be in full-time or part-time attendance at an educational institution in order to be entitled to receive these amounts.

Mr. Masters must obtain information regarding the contribution room available for the Canada Education Savings Grant (CESG). Since his parents have been contributing to the RESP, it is not possible to determine how much CESG his son has available without more information.

Given his wife's profession, the family income is well in excess of what is permitted to benefit from the Canada Learning Bonds program. As a result, that program would have no impact on any advice related to Mr. Masters' son's RESP.

SSP 9-7 Solution
Part A–Case 1: Arm's-length sale
The result for Martin would be as follows:

POD	$500,000
ACB	(360,000)
Capital gain	$140,000
Inclusion rate	1/2
Taxable capital gain	$ 70,000

With respect to the subsequent sale by the arm's-length purchaser, the results for that individual would be as follows:

POD	$500,000
ACB	(500,000)
Capital gain	Nil

Part A–Case 2: Non-arm's-length sale to sister

The result for Martin would be as follows:

Deemed POD–ITA 69(1)(b)	$500,000
ACB	(360,000)
Capital gain	$140,000
Inclusion rate	1/2
Taxable capital gain	$ 70,000

With respect to the subsequent sale by Martin's sister, the results for her would be as follows:

POD (actual)	$500,000
ACB	(360,000)
Capital gain	$140,000
Inclusion rate	1/2
Taxable capital gain	$ 70,000

Note that the punitive nature of ITA 69(1) is to subject the $140,000 gain to income tax to both Martin and his sister.

Part A–Case 3: Non-arm's-length disposition (gift) to son

The result for Martin would be as follows:

Deemed POD–ITA 69(1)(b)	$500,000
ACB	(360,000)
Capital gain	$140,000
Inclusion rate	1/2
Taxable capital gain	$ 70,000

With respect to the subsequent sale by Martin's son, the results for him would be as follows:

POD	$500,000
Deemed ACB–ITA 69(1)(c)	(500,000)
Capital gain	Nil

The fact that his son is younger than 18 years of age does not affect the results.

Part A–Case 4: Non-arm's-length sale to mother

The result for Martin would be as follows:

POD (Actual)	$600,000
ACB	(360,000)
Capital gain	$240,000
Inclusion rate	1/2
Taxable capital gain	$120,000

With respect to the subsequent sale by Martin's mother, the results for her would be as follows:

POD (actual)	$500,000
ACB–ITA 69(1)(a)	(500,000)
Capital gain	Nil

The one-sided nature of ITA 69(1) results in no change to Martin, therefore his POD remains at $600,000. Had it not been for ITA 69(1) Martin's mother would have realized a capital loss (POD $500,000 - actual cost $600,000), but the ITA 69(1) adjustment causes her to adjust her ACB based on the FMV of the land at $500,000. The effect is that Martin includes the $100,000 difference between $600,000 and $500,000 in his net income, but his mother receives no reduction for the fect that she did not recover her full $600,000 cost.

Part B

In case 2, the sale was for $360,000, less than the $500,000 FMV of the land. Motivation would include an attempt to shift the gain to a lower-income individual or to an individual who could shelter the gain with loss carry overs. Note that if the sister had been obligated to sell the land, then there would have been no disposition since Martin would have retained beneficial ownership with his sister simply acting on his instructions (on his behalf as his agent). In that case ITA 69(1) would not have applied.

In case 3 the motivation for the sale could be that Martin expects the land to greatly increase in value and as a result it would be preferable to have any future capital gain included in the minor's net income given his low income tax rate (15%).

In case 4, the sale was for $600,000, more than the $500,000 FMV of the land. The motivation for this type of transaction would typically be that Martin would not have been subject to income tax on the additional $100,000 of capital gain due to loss carry overs while his mother may have needed capital losses to offset her capital gains.

SSP 9-8 Solution
Scenario 1–FMV > Transferor's Capital Cost

The results of the disposition for Martin can be calculated as follows:

UCC balance	$36,000
Lesser of:	
POD = $87,000	
Capital cost = $52,000	(52,000)
Negative ending UCC balance = Recapture of CCA	($16,000)
POD	$87,000
ACB	(52,000)
Capital gain	$35,000
Inclusion rate	1/2
Taxable capital gain	$17,500

Martin's net income will increase by $33,500 ($16,000 + $17,500).

For his sister, the ACB will be the sale price of $87,000. However, because the FMV of the property exceeded the capital cost, ITA 13(7)(e) will limit the capital cost for CCA and recapture purposes to the following amount:

$$[\$52,000 + (1/2)(\$87,000 - \$52,000)] = \$69,500$$

Scenario 2–FMV < Transferor's Capital Cost
The results of this disposition for Marion can be calculated as follows:

UCC balance	$105,000
Lesser of:	
POD = $142,000	
Capital cost = $212,000	(142,000)
Negative ending UCC balance = Recapture of CCA	($ 37,000)

Marion's net income will increase by $37,000.

In this case, where the FMV of the property is less than its capital cost, there could be potential recapture if Martin continued to own the property and it increased in value. To ensure that any subsequent increase in value is included as recapture (up to the original capital cost of $212,000), ITA 13(7)(e) deems the non-arm's-length purchaser's capital cost to be equal to Martin's capital cost of $212,000. This capital cost will effectively be used for purposes of determining any capital gain and/or recapture on a future disposition.

The $70,000 ($212,000 - $142,000) difference between this capital cost and the sale price will be considered deemed CCA, resulting in a UCC balance of $142,000.

SSP 9-9 Solution
Case 1
Assuming that the transfer was to Margarette's spouse, the land would have been transferred at its ACB and the building would have been transferred at its UCC. As a consequence, there would have been no income tax consequences to be included in Margarette's net income on her final income tax return.

For CCA purposes, the building would have been transferred at Margarette's UCC of $363,000. Given this, maximum CCA would be $14,520 [(4%)($363,000)] for 2021, leaving a UCC of $348,480 at the beginning of 2022. Since the acquisition of the building is a non-arm's-length transaction, it was used and continues to be used to produce income, and was owned for more than one year by Margarette, the half-year rule does not apply to Gianni. The AccII does not apply for two separate reasons: (1) It was acquired on a rollover basis (ITA 70(6)) and (2) it was acquired in a non-arm's-length transaction.

Note, however, that after the transfer Gianni would inherit the tax characteristics of the building. Therefore, capital cost is $473,000, previously clamed CCA is $110,000 (capital cost of $473,000 - UCC $363,0000), and the UCC is $363,000 when acquired on his spouse's death. The income tax consequences of the 2021 sale would be determined as follows:

	Land	Building
POD	$160,000	$525,000
ACB	(150,000)	(473,000)
Capital gain	$ 10,000	$ 52,000
Inclusion rate	1/2	1/2
Taxable capital gain	$ 5,000	$ 26,000
UCC		$348,480
Deduct disposition–Lesser of:		
• Capital cost = $473,000		
• POD = $525,000		(473,000)
Negative closing UCC balance = Recaptured CCA		($ 124,520)

A total of $155,520 ($5,000 + $26,000 + $124,520) would be added to Gianni's net income for 2022. Since the attribution rules cease to apply on death, none of the increases in net income are attributed to Margarette.

Case 2

As the transfer was to her daughter, Ciara, ITA 70(5) applies to deem the POD to be equal to the FMV of the land and building. As a result, the following income tax consequences are determined for Margarette's net income for the year of death:

	Land	Building
Deemed POD–ITA 70(5)	$175,000	$571,000
ACB	(150,000)	(473,000)
Capital gain	$ 25,000	$ 98,000
Inclusion rate	1/2	1/2
Taxable capital gain	$ 12,500	$ 49,000
UCC		$363,000
Deduct disposition–Lesser of:		
• Capital cost = $473,000		
• Deemed POD = $571,000		(473,000)
Negative closing UCC balance = Recaptured CCA		($ 110,000)

A total of $171,500 ($12,500 + $49,000 + $110,000) would be added to Margarette's 2021 net income.

The costs and therefore ACB of the land to Ciara will be $175,000, and the building will be class 1 property with a capital cost and UCC of $571,000.

Maximum 2021 CCA is $22,840 [($571,000)(4%)], leaving a UCC of $548,160 ($571,000 - $22,840) at the beginning of 2022. Since the acquisition of the building is a non-arm's-length transaction, it was used and continues to be used for the purpose of earning income, and was owned for more than one year by Margarette, the half-year rule does not apply to Ciara. The AccII does not apply because the property was acquired in a non-arm's-length transaction. In addition, ITA 13(7)(e), which restricts the capital cost, does not apply to a disposition that occurs as a result of death.

Since there cannot be a capital loss on depreciable property (ITA 39(1)(b)) and the building is the only property in the class, the income tax consequences of the 2022 sale would be determined as follows:

	Land	Building
POD	$160,000	$525,000
ACB	(175,000)	(571,000)
Capital loss	($ 15,000)	N/A
Inclusion rate	1/2	N/A
Allowable capital loss	($ 7,500)	N/A
UCC		$548,160
Deduct disposition–Lesser of:		
• Capital cost = $571,000		
• POD = $525,000		(525,000)
Positive closing UCC balance = Terminal loss (ITA 20(16))		$ 23,160

A total of $30,660 ($23,160 + $7,500) would be deducted in determining net income for 2022. The $7,500 allowable capital loss is only deductible against net taxable capital gains for 2022. Any amount that cannot be deducted becomes a net capital loss for 2022 available to be applied in other taxation years.

Comparison of Case 1 vs. 2

The overall income tax consequences for the two years in the two cases are as shown in the following table:

	Case 1 Gianni	Case 2 Margarette	Case 2 Ciara
2021	Nil	$171,500	Nil
2021–CCA taken	($ 14,520)		($22,840)
2022	155,520		(30,660)
Net income (loss)	$141,000	$171,500	($ 53,500)

There is a difference in the case 1 and case 2 results of $23,000 [$141,000 - ($171,500 - $53,500)]. This reflects the fact that, in case 2, a portion of the amount that was taxed as a capital gain (50%) in Margarette's final return was deducted by Ciara as CCA and a terminal loss (100%). Had ITA 13(7)(e) applied there would have been no difference. ITA 13(7)(e), however, is clear that it does not apply as the consequence of the death of an individual.

This can be shown in the following calculation:

Actual sale price of building for Ciara	$525,000
Fair market value (deemed proceeds) at death	(571,000)
Amount deducted by Ciara as CCA and terminal loss*	($ 46,000)
Portion taxed as capital gain in final return [(1/2)($46,000)]	23,000
Difference	($ 23,000)

*$23,160 + $22,840 = $46,000

SSP 9-10 Solution
Alonso
At Transfer

As Alonso did not elect to avoid the ITA 73(1) spousal rollover, no income will result from the gift of shares to his spouse, Alice. However, there is no rollover for the transfer of public company shares to a related minor ,and as a result ITA 69(1) will apply to treat the gift as a disposition at FMV. This means there will be a taxable capital gain on the transfer of 10,000 shares to his son as follows:

Deemed POD [($17.00)(10,000)]	$170,000
ACB [($12.50)(10,000)]	(125,000)
Capital gain	$ 45,000
Inclusion rate	1/2
Taxable capital gain	$ 22,500

The cost and therefore ACB of the shares gifted to Alonso's spouse remain at $12.50 per share as a result of ITA 73(1), whereas the ACB to Alonso's son will be $17.00 as a result of ITA 69(1)(c).

Dividends

As all of the shares were gifted to a spouse and a related minor, all of the dividends would be attributed back to Alonso as a result of ITA 74.1. The increase in Alonso's net income for 2021 due to the dividends would be $16,560 [(15,000)(138%)($0.80)].

Sale of Shares

As there is no attribution of capital gains when shares are transferred to a related minor, the sale of shares by Alonso's son would have no effect on Alonso's 2021 net income. However, the gain on the sale of shares by his spouse would be attributed back to him. The attributed capital gain would be calculated as follows:

POD [($16.00)(5,000)]	$80,000
ACB [($12.50)(5,000)]	(62,500)
Capital gain	$ 17,500
Inclusion rate	1/2
Taxable capital gain	$ 8,750

Alice

None of these transactions would have any effect on Alice's net income for 2021.

Alonso Jr.

When Alonso Jr. sells his Lisgar Inc. shares, he will realize an allowable capital loss calculated as follows:

POD [($16.00)(10,000)]	$160,000
ACB [($17.00)(10,000)]	(170,000)
Capital loss	($ 10,000)
Inclusion rate	1/2
Allowable capital loss	($ 5,000)

The allowable capital loss can only be deducted in 2021 by Alonso Jr. to the extent there are net taxable capital gains available to apply it against. As a result, the sale will not affect his 2021 net income unless he has taxable capital gains.

SSP 9-11 Solution
Long Consulting Ltd.
1. Gift to Spouse–ITA 73(1) Rollover Applies

ITA 73(1) permits transfers of a capital property to a spouse at tax costs (i.e., ACB or UCC). This means that the shares in Long Consulting Ltd. could be gifted to Mr. Long with no immediate income tax consequences.

The ACB for these shares for the spouse would be the same ACB to Mrs. Long of $210,000.

The exception to avoid the attribution rules requires electing to avoid ITA 73(1) and actually paying FMV consideration, and where debt is used that the debt bear interest at the prescribed rate. Since the exception is not met, then the attribution rules apply and any dividends received by the spouse would be attributed back to Mrs. Long.

If Mr. Long subsequently sells these shares for $525,000 ($50,000 more than the $475,000 FMV at the time of the gift), the resulting taxable capital gain of $157,500, as calculated in the following table, would also be attributed to Mrs. Long.

POD	$525,000
ACB	(210,000)
Capital gain	$315,000
Inclusion rate	1/2
Taxable capital gain	$ 157,500

2. Gift to Spouse–Elect to Avoid the ITA 73(1) Rollover

The election to avoid the spousal rollover results in the application of the non-arm's-length gifting rule of ITA 69(1) that treats the gift as a disposition at FMV to both parties. The result is that the gift would result in POD of $475,000. Mrs. Long would have an immediate taxable capital gain of $132,500 [(1/2)($475,000 - $210,000)] and Mr. Long's ACB would be $475,000. However, since the transfer is a gift, and Mr. Long does not use his own funds to purchase the shares or incur a debt to his spouse at an interest rate at least equal to the prescribed rate, income attribution would apply to any dividends received by Mr. Long. In addition, if the property were subsequently sold by Mr. Long for $525,000, the resulting taxable capital gain of $25,000 [(1/2)(525,000 - $475,000)] would also be attributed to her.

3 and 4. Gift to Children

Under ITA 69(1), a gift to a non-arm's-length person (i.e., a related person) is treated as if it were a disposition at FMV. Given this, a taxable capital gain of $132,500 [(1/2)($475,000 - $210,000) would result from a gift of all of the shares to either one of the children.

The ACB to the children would be equal to the FMV of $475,000.

Under the attribution rules, any dividends received on the shares given to Mary, who is under 18, would be attributed back to Mrs. Long. Note that in this instance the attribution rules would not apply since the TOSI rules would apply.

As Barry is over 18, the gift would not result in attribution of dividends received.

There is no attribution of capital gains on capital property transferred to children, regardless of their age. This means that if the property were later sold for $525,000, the resulting taxable capital gain of $25,000 would be included in the net income of the child who owned the shares that were the subject of the gift.

Rental Property
1. Gift to Spouse–ITA 73(1) Rollover Applies

ITA 73(1) would allow a rollover at the tax costs of the property (ACB, capital cost, and UCC) to Mr. Long with no income tax consequences. Since ITA 73(1) applies, then ITA 69 cannot apply.

The tax attributes of the building to Mr. Long would be that he would inherit the same tax attributes as his spouse. Capital cost of the building would be $190,000, deemed CCA $65,000, and UCC $125,000. He would also retain the tax cost of the land with the result that his cost and ACB would be $100,000.

The exceptions to the attribution rules require an election to avoid the ITA 73(1) rollover and an actual payment at FMV for the rental property, which can be in the form of a promissory note bearing interest in an amount at least equal to the prescribed rate. Since these conditions are not met the attribution rules would apply. This means that any rental income or loss would be attributed to Mrs. Long.

If Mr. Long were to later sell the building for $325,000 ($50,000 more than its FMV at the time of the gift), the following amounts would be attributed to Mrs. Long:

Capital Cost	$190,000
UCC	(125,000)
Recaptured CCA	$ 65,000
POD	$325,000
ACB	(190,000)
Capital gain	$135,000
Inclusion rate	1/2
Taxable capital gain	$ 67,500

Since we are assuming the value of the land on which the building was situated has not changed, the sale of the land by Mr. Long would have no income tax consequences for Mrs. Long.

2. Gift to Spouse–Elect to Avoid the ITA 73(1) Rollover

The election to avoid the spousal rollover results in the application of the non-arm's-length gifting rule of ITA 69(1) that treats the gift as a disposition at FMV to both parties. The result is that the gift would result in POD of $275,000. Mrs. Long would have an immediate taxable capital gain of $42,500 [(1/2)($275,000 - $190,000)] and recapture of $65,000 [UCC $125,000 - capital cost $190,000]. Mr. Long's ACB would be $275,000. However, since the transfer is a gift, and Mr. Long does not use his own funds to purchase the shares or incur a debt to his spouse at an interest rate at least equal to the prescribed rate, income attribution would apply. There would be no income tax consequences related to the land as its ACB is equal to its FMV at the time of the gift.

Since the spousal rollover does not apply, ITA 13(7)(e) will apply to limit the capital cost of the building for CCA/UCC purposes. The capital cost would be limited to $232,500 [$190,000 + (1/2)($275,000 - $190,000)]. His cost and ACB for the land would both be $100,000.

Electing out of ITA 73(1) would not change the fact that the transfer is a gift to a spouse and, as a consequence, future rental income or loss would be attributed to Mrs. Long.

If Mr. Long subsequently sells the building for $325,000, the additional taxable capital gain of $25,000 [(1/2)($325,000 - $275,000)] would also be attributed back to Mrs. Long. As we are assuming the value of the land remains at $100,000 and that no CCA is taken prior to the sale, there are no further income tax consequences associated with the sale.

3 and 4. Gift to Children

Under ITA 69(1), a gift to a non-arm's-length person (e.g., a related person) is treated as if it were a disposition at FMV. As a consequence, Mrs. Long would be considered to have disposed of the building at its FMV of $275,000. This would result in a taxable capital gain of $42,500 [(1/2)($275,000 - $190,000)] as well as recapture of $65,000 (UCC $125,000 - capital cost $190,000). There would be no income tax consequences related to the sale of the land as the ACB and FMV are the same [POD $100,000 - ACB $100,000].

The ACB of the building to either of the children would be $275,000. The ACB of the land would be $100,000. The capital cost for CCA/UCC purposes would be limited to $232,500 [$190,000 + (1/2)($275,000 - $190,000)].

If the rental property were given to Mary, the income attribution rules of ITA 74.1 would apply to attribute any rental income or loss back to Mrs. Long because Mary is under 18 years of age. This attribution would continue until Mary reached 18 years of age. Alternatively, if the property were gifted to her son, Barry, none of the income or loss would be attributed to Mrs. Long because Barry is not under the age of 18.

There is no attribution of capital gains on gifts to related children regardless of their age. As a result, there would be no attribution of capital gains on a gift to either child. This means that if the property were later sold for $325,000 ($275,000 + $50,000), the $25,000 taxable capital gain would be included in the net income of the child who was the recipient of the gift.

Dynamics Inc.

1. Gift to Spouse–ITA 73(1) Rollover Applies

As with the other properties, these shares could be given to Mr. Long and, under the provisions of ITA 73(1), no immediate income tax consequences would arise.

The ACB to Mr. Long would be $212,000. The POD to Mr.s Long would also be $212,000.

Any dividends received by Mr. Long on the shares would be attributed back to Mrs. Long.

If Mr. Long were to subsequently sell the shares for $434,000 ($50,000 more that their $384,000 FMV at the time of the gift), the income attribution rules of ITA 74.2 would require that the following taxable capital gain be attributed back to Mrs. Long:

POD	$434,000
ACB	(212,000)
Capital gain	$222,000
Inclusion rate	1/2
Taxable capital gain	$ 111,000

2. Gift to Spouse–Elect to Avoid the ITA 73(1) Rollover

The election to avoid the spousal rollover results in the application of the non-arm's-length gifting rule of ITA 69(1) that treats the gift as a disposition at FMV to both parties. The result to Mrs. Long would be a taxable capital gain of $86,000 [(1/2)($384,000 - $212,000)].

The ACB to Mr. Long would be $384,000 as a result of ITA 69(1)(c).

However, since the shares were gifted, meaning that Mr. Long did not actually pay FMV consideration or issue a promissory note at the prescribed interest rate, the attribution would apply to any dividend he receives and to any further capital gains he may realize on a subsequent sale. If the property were subsequently sold for $434,000, Mr. Long would have a taxable capital gain of $25,000 [(1/2)(POD $434,000 - ACB $384,000)] that would be attributed back to Mrs. Long.

3 and 4. Gift to Children

In the case of a gift to either of her children, ITA 69(1) would treat the gift as a disposition at FMV to both parties. This would result in an immediate taxable capital gain of $86,000 [(1/2) (POD $384,000 - ACB $212,000)].

The cost and ACB to the children would be the FMV of $384,000.

A gift to Mary would result in the application of the income attribution rules of ITA 74.1 since she is under 18 and did not pay FMV consideration or pay by way of a promissory at the prescribed rate of interest. This would mean that subsequent dividends received would be attributed back to Mrs. Long until Mary reaches 18 years of age. If the shares were transferred to Barry, there would be no attribution of dividends because he is not under 18 years of age.

There is no attribution of capital gains on capital property gifted to children regardless of their age. This means that if the shares were later sold for $434,000 the resulting taxable capital gain of $25,000 [(1/2)(POD $434,000 - ACB $384,000)] would be included in the net income of the child who was gifted the shares.

Farm Land

1. Gift to Spouse–ITA 73(1) Rollover Applies

As with all of the other properties, Mrs. Long could gift the farm land to her spouse under ITA 73(1).

The ACB to Mr. Long would be the same as the ACB to Mr.s Long of $80,000.

As farm income is considered to be business income rather than property income, there would be no attribution of any farm income that arises while Mr. Long is the beneficial owner of the property.

In the event of a subsequent sale of the farm land for $225,000 ($50,000 more than the fair market value at the time of transfer), the following taxable capital gain would be attributed to Mrs. Long under ITA 74.2:

POD	$225,000
ACB	(80,000)
Capital gain	$145,000
Inclusion rate	1/2
Taxable capital gain	$ 72,500

2. Gift to Spouse–Elect to Avoid the ITA 73(1) Rollover

The election to avoid the spousal rollover results in the application of the non-arm's-length gifting rule of ITA 69(1) that treats the gift as a disposition at FMV to both parties. The result would be a taxable capital gain of $47,500 [(1/2)(POD $175,000 - ACB $80,000)].

In this case, the ACB to Mr. Long would be equal to the FMV of $175,000 as a result of ITA 69(1)(c).

A noted, farm income is business income, which would not be attributed back to Mrs. Long.

As the property was gifted, the attribution rules would apply to subsequent capital gains on the property since Mr. Long did not pay FMV consideration nor did he issue a promissory note at the prescribed rate of interest. If Mr. Long sells the property for $225,000, the resulting taxable capital gain of $25,000 [(1/2)(POD $225,000 - ACB $175,000)] would be attributed back to Mrs. Long.

3 and 4. Gift to Children

ITA 73(3.1) permits the inter vivos transfer of farm property used by an idnividual or her family to a child on a rollover basis. The deemed POD would be Mrs. Long's ACB, which means that Mrs. Long would not be required to include any amount in her net income with respect to the gift to either child [POD $80,000 - ACB $80,000].

The ACB to either child would be the same $80,000 that was deemed to be POD to Mrs. Long.

There will be no attribution of any income from either child on the presumption that it is business income since the attribution rules do not apply to business income.

While there is no attribution of capital gains from children of any age under ITA 74.2 it is a different story in the case of farm or fishing properties that benefit from the rollovers available as a result of ITA 73(3) and (4). ITA 75.1 requires that the realization of any gain resulting from a disposition by the transferee before they reach age 18 is to be attributed back to the transferor.

This means that if the farm property is transferred to Mary and she sells the property for $225,000 before she reaches age 18, a taxable capital gain of $72,500 [(1/2)($225,000 - $80,000)] will be attributed back to Mrs. Long. If the transfer was to Barry, this capital gain would not be attributed back to Mrs. Long and would be included in his net income.

SSP 9-12 Solution
Employment Income

Carolyn's employment income would be calculated as follows:

Salary [(10 months)($5,000)]	$50,000
RPP contributions (Note 1)	(2,600)
Automobile (Note 2)	6,047
Travel allowance (Note 3)	Nil
Moving cost allowance	10,000
Housing loss reimbursement (Note 4)	Nil
Housing cost allowance (Note 5)	7,500
Employment income	$70,947

Note 1 While Carolyn's RPP contributions can be deducted, the matching contribution by her employer does not create a taxable benefit.

Note 2 The automobile benefit would be calculated as follows:

Standby charge [(2%)($42,000)(9)(8,000 ÷ 15,003*)]	$4,031
Operating cost benefit–Lesser of:	
• [(1/2)($4,031)] = $2,016	
• [(8,000)($0.28)] = $2,240	2,016
Total benefit	$6,047

*[(9)(1,667)]

Note 3 As the allowance appears to be reasonable, it does not have to be included in employment income. Given this, Carolyn cannot deduct her actual costs.

Note 4 As the housing loss reimbursement is less than $15,000, it does not have to be included in employment income.

Note 5 Assistance with higher housing costs related to a required move must be included in an employee's income (ITA 6(23)).

Property Income

Carolyn's property income is calculated as follows:

Eligible dividends received	$ 5,800
Gross up at 38%	2,204
Recapture on rental property (Note 6)	20,000
Property income	$28,004

Note 6 The FMV of the rental building when it is bequeathed to Carolyn is $270,000. ITA 70(5)(c) establishes a rule to preserve subsequent recapture where the capital cost of the depreciable property to the deceased exceeds its FMV at the time of death. This rule is designed to ensure that should the value of depreciable property acquired on the death of an individual increase in value, a subsequent disposition will include recapture up to the capital cost of the deceased. In this case this means that the capital cost of the building to Carolyn is deemed to be $300,000, CCA of $30,000 is deemed to have been previously claimed, and the resulting UCC would then be $270,000.

Carolyn's POD from the sale of the building is $290,000 and, when she subtracts the lesser of the deemed capital cost ($300,000) and the POD of $290,000 from the $270,000 UCC, the result is recapture of $20,000 (UCC $270,000 - POD $290,000).

There is no capital gain or capital loss on the disposition of the land since the POD and ACB are both $50,000.

Taxable Capital Gains

Carolyn's only capital gains will arise on the sale of the shares that were gifted to her by her father. Note that when her father gifted her the investments the FMV at the time was $62,000. ITA 69(1) treats gifts of property between non-arm's-length individuals as a disposition at FMV, and as a result Carolyn's cost and ACB are deemed to be the same FMV of $62,000. Since Carolyn and her father are "related persons" ITA 251(1) deems them to be non-arm's length.

POD	$74,000
ACB	(62,000)
Capital gain	$12,000
Inclusion rate	1/2
Taxable capital gain	$ 6,000

Other Income and Deductions

Carolyn's other income and deductions amount is calculated as follows:

Spousal support (Note 7)	$ 500
Moving costs (Note 8)	(27,950)
Child care cost (Note 9)	(7,300)
Total other income and deductions	($34,750)

Note 7 When the full amount of support is not paid, the first payments are deemed to be for child support. Given the total payments of $12,500 and the required child support of $12,000 [(12)($1,000)], Carolyn will include only $500 in her net income.

Note 8 Costs for food and lodging at or near an old or new residence are limited to a maximum period of 15 days. Carolyn has a total of 23 eligible days: 14 days in Lethbridge and 9 days in Edmonton. Note that the 2 days spent travelling to Edmonton are not included in the 15-day total. As the hotel in Edmonton is the more expensive, she will deduct all 9 days spent there. Carolyn's deductible moving costs can be calculated as follows:

Selling cost of Lethbridge property	$12,500
Legal fees–Sale of Lethbridge property	600
Legal fees–Purchase of Edmonton property	450
Storage costs–February 15 through March 10	1,400
Cost of moving belongings	7,250
Lodging in Lethbridge and Edmonton (9 @ $200 + 6 @$175)	2,850
Simplified meal cost [(3)($51)(15 + 2 days)]	2,601
Simplified mileage [($.59)(506)]	299
Total deductible moving costs	$27,950

As this amount is less than her income at her new job, she will be able to deduct the full amount of these expenses. Note that the $785 of costs incurred for house hunting would not qualify as a moving expense.

Note 9 Carolyn's deductible child care costs would be the least of three amounts:

Actual costs plus deductible camp costs		
Edmonton cost [(38)(($175)]	$6,650	
Camp [(2)($200 + $125)]	650	$ 7,300
Annual limit ($8,000 + $5,000)		$13,000
Two-thirds earned income		
[(2/3)($70,947 + $2,600 RPP)]		$49,031

The least of these three amounts is the actual cost of $6,650 and the limited camp costs of $650.

Net Income

Carolyn's net income would be determined as follows:

Employment income	$70,947
Property income	28,004
Taxable capital gains	6,000
Other income and deductions	(34,750)
Deductible CPP contributions ($3,166 - $2,876)	(290)
Net income	$69,911

Taxable Income

As Carolyn has no Division C deductions, her taxable income would be equal to her net income.

Federal Income Tax Payable

Carolyn's tax payable would be determined as follows:

Tax on first $49,020		$ 7,353
Tax on next $20,891 ($69,911 - $49,020) at 20.5%		4,283
Tax before credits		$11,636
Tax credits:		
Basic personal	($13,808)	
Eligible dependant	(13,808)	
EI premiums	(890)	
CPP contributions	(2,876)	
Canada employment	(1,257)	
Medical expenses (Note 10)	(5,503)	
Total credit base	($ 38,142)	
Rate	15%	(5,721)
Dividend tax credit [(6/11)($2,204)]		(1,202)
Charitable donations (Note 11)		
[(15%)($200) + (29%)($600 - $200)]		(146)
Federal income tax payable		$ 4,567

Note 10   The medical expenses eligible for the credit are as follows:

Total medical costs	$7,600
Lesser of:	
• $2,097 [(3%)($69,911)]	
• 2021 threshold amount = $2,421	(2,097)
Medical expense tax credit base	$5,503

Note 11   As none of her income is taxed at 33%, this rate will not be applicable to the calculation of the charitable donations tax credit.

SSP 9-13 Solution
Part A–Net Income and Taxable Income for Mr. Winded

The 2021 net income for Mr. Winded would be calculated as follows:

Employment income

Salary [($84,000)(2/12)]	$14,000	
Standby charge [(2/3)($360)(2)]	480	
Operating cost benefit [(90%)(3,000)($0.27)]		
(alternate calculation not available)	729	
Taxable portion of gift ($700 - $500)	200	
Stock option benefit [(1,500)($11 - $8)]	4,500	
RPP contributions	(500)	$ 19,409
Business income (Note 1)		13,395

Property income

Interest income	$ 3,478	
Eligible dividends received	1,700	
Eligible dividends attributed from Mrs. Winded	1,400	
Gross up [(38%)($1,700 + $1,400)]	1,178	
Non-eligible dividends received from Sail	800	
Gross up [(15%)($800)]	120	
Net rental income (Note 2)	Nil	8,676

Net taxable capital gains

TCG on sale of Celebrate Ltd. shares			
[(1/2)(1,000)($17 - $11)]		$ 3,000	
Attributed TCG on sale of preferred shares			
[(1/2)(($31,000 - $27,000)]		2,000	
TCG on listed personal property			
Stamps ($5,000 - $8,000)	($3,000)		
Rare book ($4,200 - $1,000)	3,200		
Painting ($1,000 - $1,000)	Nil		
	$ 200		
Inclusion rate	1/2	100	
Loss on furniture (PUP) of $3,800			
($4,800 - $1,000 floor) not deductible		Nil	
TCG on sale of Sail shares			
[(1/2)($48,000 - $12,000)]		18,000	
TCG on sale of CNR shares (Note 3)		1,230	
ACL on sale of BCE shares (Note 4)		(400)	
TCG on sale of cottage (Note 5)		50,000	73,930

Other income and deductions

Old Age Security	$ 5,350	
CPP receipts	9,600	
Pension income from Celebrate Ltd. pension plan	44,000	
RRIF withdrawal	8,000	
Moving expenses (Note 6)	(23,000)	
CPP ($572 - $520) [(0.0545 - 0.0495)($14,000 - $3,500)]	(52)	
Pension income transferred to spouse		
[(1/2)($44,000 + $8,000)]	(26,000)	17,898

Income before clawback	$133,308
OAS clawback–Lesser of:	
• Amount received = $5,350	
• $8,024 [(15%)($133,335 - $79,845)]	(5,350)
2021 net income–Mr. Winded	**$ 127,958**

Note 1 Business income would be calculated as follows:

Revenues		$38,000
Expenses:		
Supplies		(16,000)
Advertising		(1,000)
Home office costs (see following calculation)		(3,060)
CCA		
Class 50 [(55%)(1.5)($3,800)]	($3,135)	
Class 8		
{[20%][$2,400 + (1.5)($1,600)]}	(960)	
Class 12 [(100%)($450)]*	(450)	(4,545)
Business income		$13,395

*As the two hand tools cost a total of $450, each must have cost less than $500. As a result, the first-year one-half rule is not applicable. In addition, the AccII does not apply to class 12 property.

The deductible home office costs can be calculated as follows:

Mortgage interest	$ 4,000
Utilities	3,600
Property taxes	4,500
Insurance	1,400
Maintenance	1,800
Total	$15,300
Floor space used	20%
Deductible amount	$ 3,060

Note 2 Rental income would be calculated as follows:

	Property A	Property B	Total
Rental revenues	$ 98,000	$62,000	$160,000
Operating expenses	(104,000)	(54,000)	(158,000)
Income (loss) before CCA	($ 6,000)	$ 8,000	$ 2,000
Class 8 CCA*			(2,000)
Rental income			Nil

*Maximum CCA on class 8 would have been $5,600 [(20%)($12,000 + $16,000)]. However, the actual deduction is limited to the amount that would reduce the rental income to nil. Note that the CCA was claimed on class 8 in order to preserve the class 1 UCC balances. This will result in a lower amount of recapture when the buildings are sold. The class 8 property would likely have little or no POD when they are disposed of. This means that recapture on these buildings would be unlikely.

Note 3 The taxable capital gain on the sale of CNR shares would be calculated as follows:

POD [($67.00)(300)]	$20,100
ACB [($58.80*)(300)]	(17,640)
Capital gain	$ 2,460
Inclusion rate	1/2
Taxable capital gain	$ 1,230

*The average cost of these shares would be calculated as follows:

	Shares	Total	Per Share
May 1, 2017, purchase at $52	200	$ 10,400	
May 1, 2018, purchase at $46	300	13,800	
Balance	500	$ 24,200	$48.40
May 1, 2019, sale at cost of $48.40			
($24,200 ÷ 500)	(400)	(19,360)	
Balance	100	$ 4,840	$48.40
May 1, 2020, purchase at $64	200	12,800	
Balance	300	$ 17,640	$ 58.80

Note 4 The allowable capital loss on the sale of BCE shares would be calculated as follows:

POD [(1,000)($36)]	$36,000
ACB [(1,000)($38)]	(38,000)
Capital loss	($ 2,000)
Capital loss per share ($2,000 ÷ 1,000)	$2 loss/share

As 600 of the shares, or 60%, were reacquired within 30 days of the sale, the capital loss is considered a superficial loss to the extent of $1,200 [(60%)($2,000)] and is disallowed, resulting in a revised capital loss of $800 [$2,000 - $1,200]. This will leave an allowable capital loss of $400 [(1/2)($800)]. The superficial loss amount of $1,200 will be added to the ACB of the remaining 600 shares.

Note 5 The taxable capital gain on the sale of the cottage would be calculated as follows:

	Winnipeg Home	Lake Winnipeg Cottage
POD	$313,000	$290,000
Selling costs	(13,000)	(10,000)
ACB	(140,000)	(80,000)
Capital gain	$160,000	$200,000
Exempt portion		
Home [($160,000)(9 + 1)] ÷ 10]	(160,000)	
Cottage [($200,000)(7 + 1)] ÷ 16]		(100,000)
Capital gain	Nil	$ 100,000
Inclusion rate		1/2
Taxable capital gain	Nil	$ 50,000

*The costs of selling a previously occupied residence that was ordinarily inhabited can be deducted as part of moving expenses. There is no restriction on claiming the selling costs to both reduce the capital gain on the old residence and also to increase moving expenses.

The annual gain on the two properties is as follows:

- Winnipeg home ($160,000 ÷ 10) = $16,000
- Lake Winnipeg cottage ($200,000 ÷ 16) = $12,500

Given this, maximum available years should be allocated to the Winnipeg property. These would be the nine years 2013 through 2021. This would leave the seven years 2006 through 2012 for the cottage.

Note 6 As there is no income in the Vancouver location during 2020, the moving expenses incurred in that year will have to be deducted in 2021. None of the costs of the house hunting trip are deductible. The eligible moving expenses that were incurred in 2020 and 2021 are as follows:

Legal fees–Purchase of new home	$ 4,800
January airfare	1,200
Selling costs–Sale of old home	13,000
Transport of household effects	4,000
Total available moving expenses	$23,000

These expenses can only be deducted to the extent of employment and business income earned during 2021. As these two amounts total $32,831 ($19,436 + $13,395), the full amount of eligible expenses can be deducted.

Part A–Taxable Income for Mr. Winded

Taxable income for Mr. Winded would be calculated as follows:

2021 net income	$ 127,958
Stock option deduction [($4,500)(1/2)]	(2,250)
2021 taxable income–Mr. Winded	$125,708

Part A–Net Income and Taxable Income for Mrs. Winded

Mrs. Winded has no taxable income deductions. This means that her net and taxable income will be the same, which would be calculated as follows:

Old Age Security	$ 7,400
Canada Pension Plan	3,100
Transferred pension income	26,000
Dividends (attributed back to Mr. Winded)	Nil
2021 net income & taxable income–Mrs. Winded	$36,500

Part B–Federal Income Tax Owing (Tax Payable) for Mrs. Winded

While the medical expenses can be claimed by either spouse, they are claimed on Mrs. Winded's return as she has the lowest net income. This results in a lesser reduction of the medical expenses claimed in the computation of the credit. She does have sufficient income tax payable to fully use this non-refundable credit.

Mrs. Winded's federal income tax payable would be calculated as follows:

Tax before credits [(15%)($36,500)]		$5,475
Tax credits:		
Basic	($13,808)	
Age (Note 7)	(7,713)	
Disability	(8,662)	
Pension amount	(2,000)	
Medical expenses (Note 8)	(2,455)	
Total credit base	$34,638	
Rate	15%	(5,196)
2021 federal income tax payable		$ 279

Note 7 Rachel's income is below the income threshold of $38,893 for the age credit. This means the full age amount is available to her.

Note 8 The base for the medical expense credit is calculated as follows:

Total medical expenses ($150 + $4,600 - $1,200)	$3,550
Reduced by the lesser of:	
• [(3%)($36,500)] = $1,095	
• 2021 threshold amount = $2,421	(1,095)
Base for medical expense credit	$2,455

Part B–Federal Income Tax Payable for Mr. Winded

As Mrs. Winded has fully used her credits, there are none available to be transferred to Mr. Winded. The federal income tax payable for Mr. Winded would be calculated as follows:

Tax on first $98,040		$ 17,402
Tax on next $27,668 ($125,708 - $98,040) at 26%		7,194
Tax before credits		$24,596
Tax credits:		
Basic	($13,808)	
Spousal (income exceeds $16,103)	Nil	
Age (income exceeds $90,313)	Nil	
Pension amount	(2,000)	
CPP	(520)	
EI	(221)	
Canada employment	(1,257)	
Total credit base	($ 17,806)	
Rate	15%	(2,671)
Charitable donations (Note 9)		
[(15%)($200) + (29%)($3,700 - $200)]		(1,045)
Dividend tax credits		
Eligible dividends [(6/11)($1,178)]		(643)
Sail Ltd. dividends [(9/13)($120)]		(83)
Federal tax payable		$20,154
OAS repayment		5,350
Total balance owing		$25,504

Note 9 As none of his income is taxed at 33%, this rate will not be applicable to the calculation of the charitable donations tax credit.

CHAPTER 10

Learning Objectives

After completing Chapter 10, you should be able to:

1. Explain the general procedures used to provide tax deferral on retirement savings (Paragraph [P hereafter] 10-1 to 10-17).
2. Describe the difference between a defined benefit pension plan and a defined contribution (a.k.a. money purchase) pension plan (P 10-18 to 10-20).
3. Describe the basic mechanism and operation of RRSPs (P 10-21 to 10-37).
4. Understand the terms RRSP deduction limit, unused RRSP deduction room, and RRSP dollar limit (P 10-38 to 10-46).
5. Calculate earned income for RRSP purposes (P 10-47 to 10-49).
6. Explain the concepts underlying pension adjustments (PAs) (P 10-50 to 10-60).
7. Explain the concepts underlying past service pension adjustments (PSPAs) (P 10-61 to 10-66).
8. Explain the concepts underlying pension adjustment reversals (PARs) (P 10-67 to 10-71).
9. Calculate an individual's maximum RRSP deduction and unused RRSP deduction room (P 10-72).
10. Apply the tax treatment for undeducted RRSP contributions (P 10-73 and 10-74).
11. Determine whether an individual has made "excess" contributions to an RRSP and identify associated tax planning issues, including the use of TFSAs (P 10-75 to 10-83).
12. Recall the tax treatment of RRSP and RRIF administration fees (P 10-84).
13. Apply the provisions relating to RRSP withdrawals and voluntary conversions of RRSPs (P 10-85 to 10-92).
14. Apply the provisions relating to RRSP terminations due to the age limitation (P 10-93 to 10-94).
15. Apply the provisions associated with spousal RRSPs and identify associated tax planning issues (P 10-95 to 10-103).
16. Describe and apply the provisions of the Home Buyers' Plan (HBP) (P 10-104 to 10-113).
17. Describe and apply the provisions of the Lifelong Learning Plan (LLP) (P 10-114 to 10-122).
18. Apply the RRSP provisions relating to ceasing to be a resident of Canada and death of an annuitant (P 10-123 to 10-136).
19. Explain the general provisions associated with registered pension plans (RPPs) (P 10-137 to 10-152).
20. Describe, in general terms, pooled registered pension plans (PRPPs) and target benefit plans (P 10-153 to 10-159).
21. Describe how an expanded CPP program could help the retirement savings problem (P 10-160 to 10-165).
22. Describe the basic operation of RRIFs and the role that RRIFs play in tax planning for retirement (P 10-166 to 10-184).
23. Explain the general rules for deferred profit-sharing plans (DPSPs) (P 10-185 to 10-190).
24. Describe, in general terms, employee profit-sharing plans (EPSPs) (P 10-191 to 10-194).
25. Describe the tax-free transfers that can be made between various types of plans (P 10-195 and 10-196).
26. Apply the special rules associated with RRSP contributions and retiring allowances (P 10-197 and 10-199).

27. Explain the general provisions related to retirement compensation arrangements (RCAs) (P 10-200 to 10-207).
28. Describe salary deferral arrangements (SDAs) (P 10-208 to 10-216).
29. Explain in your own words individual pension plans (IPP) and their purpose (P 10-217 to 10-219).

How to Work through Chapter 10

Visit pearsonmylabandmastering.com to access MyLab Accounting for this text. Once there, you can access student resources such as Self-Study Problems, Practice Exams, Flashcards, updates, and more.

We recommend the following approach in dealing with the material in this chapter:

Planning for Retirement
- Read paragraph 10-1 to 10-20 (in the text).

Registered Retirement Savings Plans (RRSPs)
- Read paragraph 10-21 to 10-37.
- Do Exercise 10-1 (in the text) and check the solution in this Study Guide.
- Read paragraph 10-38.

RRSP Deduction Limit
- Read paragraph 10-39 to 10-49.
- Do Exercises 10-2 and 10-3 and check the solutions in this Study Guide.

Pension Adjustments (PAs)
- Read paragraph 10-50 to 10-52.
- Do Exercise 10-4 and check the solution in this Study Guide.
- Read paragraph 10-533 to 10-59.
- Do Exercise 10-5 and check the solution in this Study Guide.
- Read paragraph 10-60.

Past Service Pension Adjustments (PSPAs) and Pension Adjustment Reversals (PARs)
- Read paragraph 10-61 to 10-71.
- Do Self-Study Problem 10-1, which is available on MyLab, and check the solution in this Study Guide.

Examples of RRSP Deduction Calculations
- Read paragraph 10-72.
- Do Exercises 10-6 and 10-7 and check the solutions in this Study Guide.

Undeducted and Excess RRSP Contributions, Including Tax Planning
- Read paragraph 10-73 to 10-79.
- Do Exercise 10-8 and check the solution in this Study Guide.
- Read paragraph 10-80 to 10-83.
- Do Self-Study Problem 10-2 to 10-5 and check the solutions in this Study Guide.

RRSP and RRIF Administration Fees
- Read paragraph 10-84.

RRSP Withdrawals, Voluntary Conversions, and Involuntary Termination (Age)
- Read paragraph 10-85 to 10-94.

Spousal RRSPs
- Read paragraph 10-95 to 10-103.
- Do Exercise 10-9 and check the solution in this Study Guide.

Home Buyers' Plan (HBP) and Lifelong Learning Plan (LLP)
- Read paragraph 10-104 to 10-113.
- Do Exercise 10-10 and check the solution in this Study Guide.
- Read paragraph 10-114 to 10-122.
- Do Exercise 10-11 and check the solution in this Study Guide.

RRSPs–Ceasing to Be a Resident of Canada and Death of the RRSP Annuitant
- Read paragraph 10-123 to 10-136.
- Do Self-Study Problem 10-6 and check the solution in this Study Guide.

Registered Pension Plans (RPPs)
- Read paragraph 10-137 to 10-152.

Pooled Registered Pension Plans (PRPPs), Target Benefit Plans (TBPs), and Expanded CPP
- Read paragraph 10-153 to 10-165.

Registered Retirement Income Funds (RRIFs)–General Rules
- Read paragraph 10-166 to 10-176.
- Do Exercise 10-12 and check the solution in this Study Guide.

RRIFs–Death of the RRIF Annuitant and Evaluation of RRIFs
- Read paragraph 10-177 to 10-184.

Deferred Profit-Sharing Plans (DPSPs) and Employee Profit-Sharing Plans (EPSPs)
- Read paragraph 10-185 to 10-194.

Transfers between Plans and Retiring Allowances
- Read paragraph 10-195 to 10-199.
- Do Exercise 10-13 and check the solution in this Study Guide.
- Do Self-Study Problem 10-7 and check the solution in this Study Guide.

Retirement Compensation Arrangements (RCAs), Salary Deferral Arrangements (SDAs), and Individual Pension Plans (IPPs)
- Read paragraph 10-200 to 10-219.
- Do Self-Study Problems 10-8 and 10-11 and check the solutions in this Study Guide.

To Complete This Chapter
- Visit MyLab Accounting for more practice problem material, and test yourself with the glossary flashcards.
- Review the Key Terms at the end of the chapter, and consult the glossary for definitions.
- Ensure you have achieved the Chapter 10 Learning Objectives listed in this Study Guide.
- As a review, view the PowerPoint presentations available on MyLab

Practice Examination
- Available on MyLab, write the Practice Examination for this chapter, and mark it using the solutions provided.

Exercise Solutions

Exercise 10-1 Solution

Invested through an RRSP

Deductible contribution	$20,000
Dividends received [(5 years)(5%)($20,000)]	5,000
Balance after five years	$25,000
Income tax on withdrawal [(40%)($25,000)]	(10,000)
Available for vacation	$15,000

Invested through a TFSA

Initial investment [($20,000)(1 - .40)]	$12,000
Tax-free dividends [(5 years)(5%)($12,000)]	3,000
Available for vacation	$15,000

Invested outside of an RRSP or TFSA

Initial investment [($20,000)(1 - .40)]	$20,000
After-tax dividends [(5 years)(5%)($12,000)(1 - .22)]	2,340
Available for vacation	$14,340

Investing outside the RRSP or TFSA is the worst alternative by $660 ($15,000 - $14,340).

Exercise 10-2 Solution
His earned income for RRSP purposes would be $70,500 (employment income $56,000 + rental income $2,500 + spousal support $12,000).

Exercise 10-3 Solution
Her earned income for RRSP purposes would be $54,500 (employment income before the RPP deduction $85,000 - business loss $12,500 - spousal support payments $18,000). The $4,200 taxable dividends are not included.

Exercise 10-4 Solution
The basic mechanism is the pension adjustment (PA). Individuals who accrue benefits in an RPP or a DPSP have their RRSP deduction limit reduced by the amount of their PA for the previous year. PAs are designed to reflect the amount of contributions or benefits that have been accumulated in employer-sponsored RPPs and DPSPs.

Exercise 10-5 Solution
The pension adjustment will be $7,200 (employer contribution to the DPSP $1,800 + RPP factor $5,400). The RPP defined benefit factor multiplies the accrued pension benefit of $600 per year on retirement by 9. With an RRSP dollar limit of $27,830 for 2021, additional contributions of $20,630 [$27,830 - PA of $7,200] could be made.

Exercise 10-6 Solution
The required calculations would be as follows:

Unused deduction room–End of 2020	$ 4,800
Lesser of:	
• 2021 RRSP dollar limit = $27,830	
• 18% of 2020 earned income of $38,000 = $6,840	6,840
2020 RRSP deduction limit	$11,640
RRSP deduction is least of:	
• RRSP deduction limit = $11,640	
• Available contributions = $6,000	
• Amount Mr. Haslich chooses to deduct = $4,500	(4,500)
Unused RRSP deduction room–End of 2021	$ 7,140

Assuming Mr. Haslich deducted only $4,500, he would have $1,500 ($6,000 - $4,500) in undeducted contributions that can be carried forward and deducted in a subsequent year.

If Mr. Haslich wanted to deduct his maximum RRSP deduction of $11,640, he would have to contribute an additional $5,640 ($11,640 - $6,000).

Exercise 10-7 Solution
The required calculations would be as follows:

Unused deduction room–End of 2020	$10,750
Lesser of:	
• 2021 RRSP dollar limit = $27,830	
• 18% of 2020 earned income of $66,530* = $11,975	11,975
Less 2020 PA	(4,800)
2021 RRSP deduction limit	$ 17,925
RRSP Deduction is lesser of:	
• RRSP deduction limit = $17,925	
• Available contributions = $19,760 ($6,560 + $13,200)	(17,925)
Unused RRSP deduction room–End of 2021	Nil

*Earned Income = $78,000 (after adding back the RPP deduction of $2,400) + $6,530 - $18,000.

Mr. Black's maximum RRSP deduction is $17,925. While he has no unused RRSP deduction room, he has $1,835 ($19,760 - $17,925) in undeducted contributions that can be carried forward and deducted in a subsequent year in which there is sufficient RRSP deduction room.

Exercise 10-8 Solution
In 2019 and 2020, 18% of Ms. Brownell's $160,000 in earned income, or $28,800, is more than the RRSP dollar limit for those years ($26,500 and $27,230, respectively). Her 2021 earned income is not relevant in this exercise as it will not be used until 2022. Given this, the calculation of the excess amount of contributions is as follows:

2020 contribution (July 1)	$28,350
2020 addition to deduction room = RRSP dollar limit	(27,230)
Excess contributions for 2020 (less than $2,000)	$ 1,120
2021 contribution (May 1)	30,000
2021 addition to deduction room = RRSP dollar limit	(27,830)
Permitted $2,000 cushion	(2,000)
Excess contributions subject to penalty	$ 1,290

As the excess contribution for 2020 was less than $2,000, there is no penalty for that year. There will be a 2021 penalty of $103.20 [(1%)($1,290)(8 months)]. The fact that no RRSP deduction was claimed is irrelevant to the penalty since its purpose is to guard against excess contributions that would earn income that would be exempt from Part I tax within the RRSP.

Exercise 10-9 Solution
ITA 146(8.3) first looks to whether a withdrawal has been made by an individual annuitant from an RRSP in which a spouse has made a contribution in the year or in one of the two preceding years. In this case Mr. Garveau withdrew $9,000 in 2021. This means that if Mrs. Garveau made a contribution to his RRSP in 2021 or either of 2019 or 2020 that she will be required to include the lesser of the amount withdrawn of $9,000 by her spouse or the amount of the total contributions she made to the spousal RRSP in the three-year period 2019 to 2021. Since she contributed $5,000 in 2019 (which is the lesser amount), she will include $5,000 in her net income and her spouse will include the remaining $4,000.

Exercise 10-10 Solution
Ms. DeBoo will have to repay $867 [(1/15)($18,000 - $5,000)] for 2021. Note that the voluntary advance payment that was made during 2020 did not reduce the fraction of the remaining balance that must be paid in 2021.

Exercise10-11 Solution

There are no income tax consequences associated with the withdrawal of $5,000. He is not enrolled in a qualifying education program in either 2020 or 2021 and, as a consequence, his repayment period begins in 2021. As he makes the required payments of $500 ($5,000 ÷ 10) within 60 days of the end of each of the years 2021 through 2030, there are no income tax consequences associated with his repayments.

Exercise 10-12 Solution

Minimum withdrawals are only required for the year following the year in which the RRIF was established. Since the RRIF was only established in 2021, no minimum withdrawals are required until 2022. His minimum withdrawal for 2022 will be $27,500 [$660,000 ÷ (90 - 66)].

Exercise 10-13 Solution

It would appear that Mr. Bartoli began working for his employer in 1977. Given this, he can contribute a total of $56,000 [($2,000)(19 years before 1996) + ($1,500)(12 years before 1989)] to his RRSP. The net impact of the retiring allowance is that his 2021 net income will increase by $44,000 [$100,000 - $56,000].

Self-Study Problem Solutions

Self-Study Problems are available to download from MyLab Accounting.

SSP 10-1 Solution

Case 1

The required 2021 PA would be calculated as follows:

Employer's contribution to DPSP	$2,500
Employer's contribution to RPP	1,000
Fredia's contribution to RPP	1,000
PA	$4,500

Case 2

The required 2021 PA would be calculated as follows:

$$[(0.0125 \text{ or } 1.25\%)(9)(\$71,000)] = \$7,988$$

Note that the contributions made by either the employer or employee have no influence on the PA for a defined benefit RPP.

Case 3

The required PSPA would be calculated as follows:

2019 amount [(0.011 or 1.1%)(9)($38,000)]	$3,762
2020 amount [(0.011 or 1.1%)(9)($42,000)]	4,158
2021 PSPA	$ 7,920

In addition to the PSPA calculated above, there would be a 2021 PA of $5,049 [(0.011 or 1.1%)(9)($51,000)].

Case 4

The required PAR would be calculated as follows:

2019 PA	$ 5,200
2020 PA	5,400
2021 PAR	$10,600

Case 5
The required PSPA would be calculated as follows:

2019 amount [(1.5% - 1.3%)(9)($58,000)]	$1,044
2020 amount [(1.5% - 1.3%)(9)($62,000)]	1,116
2021 PSPA	$2,160

There would also be a 2021 PA. However, this cannot be calculated as the problem does not provide the 2021 pensionable earnings.

SSP 10-2 Solution
Part A–Maximum RRSP Deduction
Deeta's maximum 2021 RRSP deduction would be calculated as follows:

Unused deduction room–January 1, 2020	$35,000
2020 addition (based on 2019 earned income of nil)	Nil
2021 addition (based on 2020 earned income of nil)	Nil
Maximum 2021 RRSP deduction	$35,000

Part B–Excess RRSP Contributions
At the beginning of 2020, Deeta's undeducted contributions of $37,000 are equal to her $35,000 unused deduction room, plus the permitted $2,000 cushion. As she withdraws $25,000 and made no further contributions during 2020, there are no excess contributions during the 2020 taxation year.

The excess contributions for 2021 would be calculated as follows:

Undeducted contributions	
January 1, 2021 ($37,000 - $25,000)	$12,000
Additional contribution on May 2, 2021	40,000
Total undeducted contributions	$52,000
Unused deduction room	(35,000)
Permitted cushion	(2,000)
Excess contributions subject to penalty	$15,000
Penalty rate	1%
Monthly penalty	$ 150
Months (May to December)	8
Total penalty for 2021	$ 1,200

Part C–Advice on Income Tax Planning
As the preceding calculation demonstrates, Deeta's excess contributions are attracting a significant penalty, based on a monthly charge of 1% of the excess amount.

As her earned income for 2021 will be $61,000, the addition to her 2022 deduction room will be $10,980 [(18%)($61,000)]. As her December 31, 2021, excess contributions are $15,000, she will need to withdraw $4,020 ($15,000 - $10,980) to avoid having an additional penalty in 2022. If the excess contributions are withdrawn from the RRSP prior to the end of the year following the year in which an assessment is received for the year in which the contribution is made, an offsetting deduction is available. If, however, any excess is not withdrawn within this specified timeframe, it will be included in income and subject to income tax on withdrawal, even though it was never deducted from income. Deeta should withdraw the $4,020 immediately to stop the assessment of the penalty.

Since she has never had a TFSA, she should open one. The withdrawn funds should be contributed to her TFSA, along with any other excess funds up to her TFSA contribution room. For 2021, the maximum total contributions are $75,500 (assuming that the individual was over

17 years of age when the TFSA was first introduced in 2009) and, while TFSA contributions are not deductible, earnings are not required to be included in net income. In addition, withdrawals can be made without income tax consequences.

Whether Deeta should withdraw the $2,000 cushion as well depends on future expectations. As there is no time limit on using contributions that are in the plan, it would make sense to simply leave the $2,000 in place, provided that she expects to have earned income in some future year.

In the future, she should ensure that she continues to contribute to her RRSP and TFSA, but should limit the amounts to the maximum permitted contribution.

SSP 10-3 Solution

Mr. Barnes' 2020 earned income for RRSP purposes would be calculated as follows:

Salary	$55,000
Taxable benefits	1,150
Union dues	(175)
Employment income	$55,975
Business income	4,150
Rental loss	(11,875)
Spousal support received	2,400
Earned income	$50,650

Note that CPP and EI contributions do not reduce earned income for RRSP purposes.

Since Mr. Barnes has no undeducted RRSP contributions, his maximum deductible RRSP contribution for 2021 is equal to his RRSP deduction limit.

This is calculated for Part A (not a member of RPP or DPSP) and Part B (member of RPP) as follows:

	Part A	Part B
Unused deduction room–End of 2020	Nil	Nil
Annual addition–Lesser of:		
• 2021 RRSP dollar limit = $27,830		
• 18% of 2020 earned income of $50,650 = $9,117	9,117	9,117
Less 2020 PA	N/A	(4,200)
Maximum deductible RRSP contribution	$9,117	$4,917

SSP 10-4 Solution

The annual addition for 2021 would be the lesser of $27,830 or 18% of earned income for 2020. The latter amount would be determined as follows:

Salary	$86,200
Taxable benefits	5,600
RPP contributions (Note 1)	Nil
Union dues	(450)
Employment income (RRSP figure)	$91,350
Business loss	(4,500)
Rental income	6,700
Common-law partner support paid	(12,000)
Eligible dividends (Note 2)	N/A
Interest (Note 2)	N/A
2020 earned income	$81,550
Rate	18%
Annual addition (less than $27,830)	$14,679

Note 1 While Ms. Storm's RPP contribution would be deducted in determining employment income for net income purposes, it is not deducted in calculating employment income for RRSP earned income purposes.

Note 2 Neither the eligible dividends nor the interest are part of earned income.

Ms. Storm's maximum deductible RRSP contribution would be calculated as follows:

Opening unused RRSP deduction room	$17,000
Annual addition	14,679
2020 pension adjustment [(2)($2,500)]	(5,000)
RRSP deduction limit for 2021	$26,679
Undeducted contributions from prior years	(8,000)
Maximum deductible contribution for 2021	$18,679

SSP 10-5 Solution
Part A
For purposes of determining her maximum 2021 RRSP contribution, 2020 earned income would be determined as follows:

Employment income*		
Salary	$150,000	
Automobile benefit	6,500	
Employee stock option benefit	3,000	
Benefit on interest-free loan	1,500	
Deductible employment expenses	(3,400)	$157,600
Business income		14,600
Royalty income (own invention)		6,600
Rental loss		(10,000)
Spousal support received		24,000
2020 earned encome		$192,800

*Note that, in calculating earned income for RRSP purposes, no deduction is made from employment income for contributions made to an RPP.

A listing of the items that are not included in the calculation of earned income is as follows:

- Registered pension plan contributions
- Interest income
- Taxable capital gains
- Eligible dividends

Part B
The calculation of Sherly's maximum deductible RRSP contribution for 2021 is as follows:

2019 RRSP dollar limit	$26,500
2020 RRSP dollar limit	27,230
Opening unused RRSP deduction room	$53,730
Annual addition–Lesser of:	
• 2021 RRSP dollar limit = $27,830	
• 18% of 2020 earned income	
[(18%)($192,800)] = $34,704	27,830
2020 PA	(15,000)
Maximum deductible RRSP contribution for 2021	$66,560

SSP 10-6 Solution
Part A

Mr. Sabatini's minimum 2021 employment income would be calculated as follows:

Salary	$ 58,000
Commissions	74,000
RPP contributions	(3,500)
Disability benefits (Note 1)	3,950
Life insurance premium paid by employer	1,500
Automobile benefit (Note 2)	6,671
Stock option benefit	
[($23.50 - $12.50)(1,000 shares)]	11,000
Golf and country club costs (Note 3)	(3,400)
Employment income	$148,221

Note 1 As Mr. Sabatini's employer has made contributions to the sickness and accident plan, the benefit of $4,500 is required to be included in employment income (ITA 6(1)(f)). This is reduced by the payments of $550 [($100)(12 - 1)/2] that were made by Mr. Sabatini during the year, leaving a net amount of $3,950.

Note 2 With respect to the standby charge, Mr. Sabatini's employment-related usage is over 50% of the total and, as a consequence, he can reduce his standby charge to the extent of personal usage that is less than 1,667 kilometres per month. Also note that because the car was not available during November, his standby charge would be based on 335 days of availability. This would be rounded to 11 months (335/30). Given this, the standby charge would be determined as follows:

$$[(\$68,000)(11 \text{ months})(2\%)(7,000/18,337)] = \$5,711$$

As Mr. Sabatini's employment-related use was over 50% of the total use, he can base his operating cost benefit on one-half of the standby charge. Given this, the benefit would be the lesser of:

- [($0.28)(7,000)] = $1,960; or
- [(1/2)($5,711)] = $2,856

Using the lesser figure of $1,960, the total benefit would be calculated as follows:

Standby charge	$5,711
Operating cost benefit	1,960
Payment to employer	(1,000)
Total automobile benefit	$6,671

Note 3 Only 50% of the $6,800 country club entertainment costs can be deducted by Mr. Sabatini (ITA 67.1). The $5,000 membership fee would not be a taxable benefit and would not be deductible by his employer.

Other Notes

- The travel costs that the corporation reimbursed to Mr. Sabatini have no income tax effect since they are expenses incurred by the employer for business purposes.

- The EI contributions are not deductible. They can be used to create credits against tax payable. The CPP contributions are partly allowed as both a non-refundable tax credit and a deduction under ITA 60(e) and (e.1), but this deduction does not affect employment income.

- Income taxes are not deductible.

- Donations to a registered charity will create a non-refundable income tax credit against income tax payable. Donations do not have any effect on employment income.

- Parking fees related to Mr. Sabatini's normal employment location are considered personal and therefore not deductible.

- Although he cannot deduct his share of the life insurance premiums of $1,500, any life insurance proceeds received in the future will generally not be included in net income.

- The use of frequent flyer points earned on employment-related travel does not usually create a taxable employment benefit unless they are used extensively enough to act as a form of income replacement.

- The discounts on merchandise provided by the employer do not generally create a taxable employment benefit provided that the discounted price paid by the employee is not below the employer's original cost.

Part B
Mr. Sabatini's 2020 earned income and maximum deductible 2021 RRSP contribution would be calculated as follows:

2020 earned income from employment (given)	$116,000
2020 business loss	(12,500)
2020 rental income	7,500
2020 earned income	$111,000
Unused deduction room–End of 2020	Nil
Annual addition–Lesser of:	
• 2021 RRSP dollar limit = $27,830	
• 18% of 2020 earned income of $111,000 = $19,980	$19,980
Less 2020 PA	(6,800)
2021 RRSP deduction limit	$13,180
RRSP deduction for 2021	$ 2,600

While Mr. Sabatini has deduction room of $13,180, only the $2,600 contribution to his spouse's plan can be deducted. His $10,000 contribution to his own RRSP in February 2021 was deducted in the 2020 year and therefore cannot be deducted in 2021.

Part C
Since the RRSP has no beneficiary specified, an amount equal to the FMV of all the property held in the RRSP at the time of death will have to be included in Mr. Sabatini's net income for 2021, the year of death.

Part D
Since Mr. Sabatini's spouse is the sole beneficiary, she can choose to transfer all the property within the RRSP to her own RRSP. If this is done, there will be no income tax consequences for either his spouse or Mr. Sabatini. This would generally be the most advantageous result for dealing with Mr. Sabatini's RRSP. The effect is that the ITA allows for a spousal or common-law partner rollover on death.

Note that there are also similar rollover provisions that allow RRSPs to be transferred to a financially dependent child. Given Mr. Sabatini is receiving child support for an 8-year-old son, this approach might also be advantageous.

SSP 10-7 Solution
Part A
Ms. Wheeler's employment income for 2020 would be $20,800, her gross salary of $22,000 reduced by her RPP contributions of $1,200.

Part B
The annual addition for 2021 would be the lesser of $27,830 and 18% of earned income for 2020. The latter amount would be calculated as follows:

Employment income (Part A–before RRP deduction)	$22,000
Spousal support received [(6)($1,200)]	7,200
Business loss	(2,500)
Earned income	$26,700
Percent	18%
Annual addition (less than $27,830)	$ 4,806

Ms. Wheeler's maximum deductible RRSP contribution would be calculated as follows:

Opening unused deduction room	Nil
Annual addition	$4,806
Less 2020 PA ($1,200 + $1,200)	(2,400)
Maximum deductible RRSP contribution	$2,406

Part C
As Ms. Wheeler has made no contributions prior to 2021, she has no undeducted contributions. In addition, she has interest income and dividends that are both subject to income tax. Given this, as well as the fact that her lump-sum payment of $80,000 and $50,000 inheritance leaves her with cash in excess of her needs, she should contribute the maximum deductible amount to her RRSP of $2,406 for 2021.

While she could deduct the $2,406 in 2021, it would be advantageous to defer this deduction until 2022 when she expects to be in a higher income tax bracket. At the federal level alone, the income tax savings will be $626 [(26%)($2,406)] in 2022, as compared to $361 [(15%)($2,406)] in 2021, a difference $265 [$626- $361].

Given her available funds, Ms. Wheeler should be advised to consider contributing the maximum allowable amount to a TFSA, as well as overcontributing up to $2,000 to her RRSP. Although she would not be able to deduct these contributions, they would enjoy the benefit of earning a return that would be exempt from Part I tax as long as the funds remain within the RRSP. In addition, the penalty tax for excess contributions would not apply because of a built-in cushion of $2,000.

All of these contributions should be made as soon as possible in order to maximize the earnings that will accrue within her RRSP and TFSA.

SSP 10-8 Solution
Part A
Jeff's 2020 net income would be determined as follows:

Income under ITA 3(a):		
Employment income	$59,000	
Interest	2,300	
Eligible dividends	1,400	
Gross up [(38%)($1,400)]	532	
Royalties	5,000	
Spousal support received	12,000	
Child support received (non-taxable)	N/A	$ 80,232
Income under ITA 3(b):		
Taxable capital gains	$62,000	
Allowable capital losses	(6,000)	56,000
Balance from ITA 3(a) and (b)		$136,232
Subdivision e deductions		
Spousal support paid	($24,000)	
Child care costs	(5,000)	(29,000)
Balance from ITA 3(c)		$107,232
Deductions under ITA 3(d):		
Rental loss		(27,200)
2020 net income		$ 80,032

The net capital loss carry forward would affect his taxable income only.

Part B
Jeff's 2020 earned income would be calculated as follows:

Employment income (before the RPP deduction)	$60,500
Royalties (Jeff's own work)	5,000
Spousal support received	12,000
Spousal support paid	(24,000)
Rental loss	(27,200)
2020 earned income	$26,300

Given this, his maximum 2021 RRSP contribution would be calculated as follows:

Unused deduction room–End of 2020	$18,000
Annual addition–Lesser of:	
• 2021 RRSP dollar limit = $27,830	
• 18% of 2020 earned income of $26,300 = $4,734	4,734
Less 2020 PA ($1,500 + $1,500 + $1,000)	(4,000)
2021 RRSP deduction limit	$18,734
Allowable excess amount	2,000
Non-penalty contribution limit	$20,734
Undeducted contributions from previous years	(20,000)
Maximum RRSP contribution	$ 734

If Jeff contributes this amount of $734, his deduction will be equal to $18,734 and he will carry forward undeducted RRSP contributions of $2,000 ($20,000 + $734 - $18,734).

Part C

With the additional $175,000 of business income, Jeff's earned income would be calculated as follows:

Employment income (before RPP deduction)	$ 60,500
Royalties	5,000
Spousal support received	12,000
Spousal support paid	(24,000)
Rental loss	(27,200)
Business income	175,000
2020 earned income	$201,300

Given this, his maximum 2021 contribution would be calculated as follows:

Unused deduction room–End of 2020	$18,000
Annual addition–Lesser of:	
• 2021 RRSP dollar limit = $27,830	
• 18% of 2020 earned income of $201,300 = $36,234	27,830
Less 2020 PA ($1,500 + $1,500 + $1,000)	(4,000)
2020 RRSP deduction limit	$41,830
Allowable excess amount	2,000
Non-penalty contribution limit	$43,830
Undeducted contributions from previous years	(20,000)
Maximum RRSP contribution	$23,830

If Jeff contributes the amount of $23,830, his deduction will be equal to $41,830 ($18,000 + $23,830) and he will carry forward undeducted RRSP contributions of $2,000 ($20,000 + $23,830 - $41,830).

SSP 10-9 Solution

General Income Tax Planning Goals

The most desirable solution would be to identify benefits the cost of which would be fully deductible to the company but would not be required to be included in his employment income. Examples of some of the items that fall into this category include the following:

- Payments for private health care plans (e.g., dental and medical plans)
- Payments for disability insurance
- Discounts on company merchandise
- Annual non-cash gifts with a value of $500 or less

Discounts on industrial engines are not likely to be of any value to Mr. Jones. However, Mr. Jones should arrange to have the company provide private health care coverage, including a dental plan. The company could also pay the premiums on a disability insurance plan without it becoming a taxable employment benefit to Mr. Jones at the time of payment (benefits received would be required to be included in employment income). Finally, an annual non-cash gift with a value of $500 or less would be deductible to the company and would be received with no amount being included in employment income.

Use of RPP, DPSP, RRSP, and Retiring Allowance

In terms of income tax deferral, Mr. Jones should be included in the company's RPP. Once he becomes a member of the plan, both he and the company should make the maximum contributions that are permitted under the terms of the plan. Contributions to the plan cannot create a PA that is in excess of the lesser of 18% of Mr. Jones' compensation for the year or the money purchase limit for the year under consideration ($29,210 for 2021).

While there is no indication that the company has such an arrangement, a DPSP might also be useful. Whether or not Mr. Jones would be able to use such an arrangement would depend on the total employee/employer contributions to the company's RPP. Contributions to a DPSP are included in the calculation of Mr. Jones' PA and, when combined with the RPP contributions, the total is subject to the same limitation as described in the preceding paragraph.

Housing Loan

The company could provide a loan to Mr. Jones to purchase his new residence. A low-interest or interest-free loan will result in imputed interest being added to Mr. Jones' employment income without an offsetting deduction. Note, however, that the prescribed rate for this purpose is at the low rate of 1%. At this rate, even if the loan is interest free, the imputed interest added to employment income is fairly small and could make a large interest-free loan desirable. On the $100,000 he requires to buy a residence, the benefit on an interest-free loan would only be $1,000 [(1%)(100,000)].

As there is an intent to compensate, arrangements would have to be made for forgiving the loan after Mr. Jones retires. While such forgiveness would result in the forgiven principal being added to his employment income, the addition could be structured to occur in the year he retires and is subject to a lower income tax rate.

Company Car

The company could provide Mr. Jones with an automobile. In this case, Mr. Jones will be assessed an employment benefit in the form of a standby charge (24% per year of the original cost or two-thirds of lease payments, if he is not eligible for a reduction) and for operating costs (one-half of the standby charge or $0.27 per kilometre of personal use). Whether or not this will be desirable depends on the use of the automobile. In some cases, especially if the car has a list price of more than $30,000, the employment benefit may exceed the actual benefit because of the restricted CCA or restricted lease deduction to the employer as a result of class 10.1 and comparable classes for zero-emission vehicles, making this an undesirable form of compensation.

Recreational Facilities

The company could pay the dues for any recreational facilities that Mr. Jones might wish to use. Without a business purpose, payment of dues could result in an employment benefit. The employer, however, would be unable to claim any of the dues as a deduction because of the restriction of ITA 18(1)(l). These factors make it unlikely the the company would agree to this.

Moving Costs

The company could provide assistance with the costs that will be incurred by Mr. Jones in moving to Hamilton. With respect to costs that Mr. Jones would be permitted to deduct, it makes little difference whether the company pays the costs or simply pays an equivalent amount in salary and lets Mr. Jones pay the costs and deduct them. However, certain types of moving costs that would not be deductible by Mr. Jones can be paid by the company without creating an employment benefit. An example of this would be compensation for a loss on a personal residence (see Chapter 9).

Bonus and/or Stock Options

Martin Manufacturing can declare a bonus in the third year, but not pay it until the following calendar year as long as it is paid within 179 days of the end of that year and that final day falls in the next calendar year. The result will be that the employer retains its deduction in the current year, but Mr. Jones would only be required to include the bonus in his net income in the following calendar year. At this time, he expects to be in a lower tax bracket.

As an incentive, the company could grant Mr. Jones options to purchase its stock. This would have no income tax cost to the company. The timing of the exercise of the options for Mr. Jones could be delayed until after retirement.

Services as a Self-Employed Contractor or through a Corporation

Since Mr. Jones has been operating as a consultant, it may be possible to structure the project so that he will be considered an independent contractor rather than an employee. This would considerably increase the amount and type of expenditures that would be deductible by him and also create an opportunity to income split with his wife, if she could assist him in the project by providing necessary services. Her assistance would have to have a business purpose (super-natural phenomena expertise would have questionable value) and any payments to her would have to be reasonable in the circumstances.

In considering this alternative it should be kept in mind that, if Mr. Jones is not an employee, some of the possibilities that have been previously discussed would no longer be feasible. For example, unless Mr. Jones is an employee, it would not be possible for him to be a member of the company's RPP.

Another possibility would be for Mr. Jones to provide his services through a corporation. However, this would probably not be helpful. Given his relationship with Martin Manufacturing Company, any corporation could potentially be viewed as a personal services business and subject to income tax at the maximum corporate income tax rates. (Personal services corporations are covered in Chapter 12, "Taxable Income and Tax Payable for Corporations.")

SSP 10-10 Solution
Part A–RRSP Contribution

In order to calculate the maximum deductible RRSP contribution, employment income and rental income must first be calculated.

Employment Income

The calculations required for 2020 (to be used in the RRSP earned income calculation) and 2021 would be as follows:

	2020	2021
Gross salary	$47,000	$53,000
Commissions	6,200	7,800
RPP contributions	(1,800)	(1,950)
Work space in home costs (Note 1)	(1,001)	(1,073)
Employment income	$50,399	$57,777

Note 1 As an employee, Kerri cannot deduct either the listed mortgage interest or CCA on this office space. Because she has commission income, Kerri can deduct all of the other listed costs, as long as they do not exceed her commission income. Given this, the 2020 and 2021 deductions are as follows:

	2020	2021
Utilities and maintenance	$1,850	$2,040
Insurance	625	715
Property taxes	4,200	4,400
Total	$6,675	$7,155
Percentage used	15%	15%
Deductible amount	$1,001	$1,073

Rental Income

The calculations required for 2020 and 2021 would be as follows:

	2020	**2021**
Rents	$ 8,400	$13,800
Expenses other than CCA	(10,300)	(11,100)
Income (loss) before CCA	($ 1,900)	$ 2,700
CCA (Note 2)	N/A	(2,700)
Rental income (loss)	($ 1,900)	Nil

Note 2 As CCA cannot be used to increase or create a rental loss, no CCA can be claimed for 2020. For 2021, the maximum available CCA deduction is $10,400 [(4%) ($260,000)]. However, the actual deduction is limited to the $2,700 of rental income prior to the deduction of CCA. The AccII adjustment does not apply since this is the second year the property is owned. The fact that no CCA was deducted in the first year is not relevant.

RRSP Calculations

Determining the RRSP deduction first requires determining the earned income for 2020. The calculation is as follows:

Employment income without the RPP deduction	$52,199
Spousal support received [(12)($500)]	6,000
Rental loss	(1,900)
2020 earned income	$56,299

Using this figure, Kerri's maximum 2021 deduction, along with the additional contribution required to make this deduction, would be determined as follows:

Opening unused deduction room	$ 6,200
Annual addition–Lesser of:	
• 2021 RRSP dollar limit = $27,830	
• 18% of 2020 earned income of $56,299 = $10,134	10,134
Less 2020 PA (employee and employer RPP contributions)	(3,600)
2021 maximum RRSP deduction	$12,734
Undeducted contributions in plan	(5,800)
Required additional contribution	$ 6,934

Part B–Net Income and Taxable Income
Other Required Information

While we can use several of the figures from Part A to calculate net income, two other items must first be determined.

Taxable Capital Gain and Dividends–Employer's Shares

The income tax consequences related to buying, holding, and selling her employer's shares are as follows:

POD [(5,000)($14.75)]	$73,750
ACB [(5,000)($12.00)]	(60,000)
Capital gain	$13,750
Inclusion rate	1/2
Taxable capital gain	$ 6,875
Eligible dividends [(5,000)($0.60)]	$ 3,000

Child Care Costs

Kerri's deductible child care costs are the least of three amounts:

Actual Costs   The actual costs were given as $8,600.

Annual Limit   The annual limit is $13,000 ($8,000 for Barry and $5,000 for Kim).

Income Limit   For this purpose, Kerri's "earned income" is her gross employment income of $60,800 ($53,000 + $7,800). Two-thirds of this amount is $40,533.

The least of these figures is the actual costs of $8,600.

As Kerri has no deductions from net income to taxable income, they are both the same. Net income is determined as follow:

Employment income (Part A)	$57,777
Rental income (Part A)	Nil
RRSP deduction (Part A)	(12,734)
Spousal support received	6,000
Taxable capital gains	6,875
Eligible dividends [(5,000)($0.60)]	3,000
Gross up [(38%)($3,000)]	1,140
Child care costs	(8,600)
Deductible CPP ($3,123 - $2,836) [$2,836 = ($60,800 - $3,500)(4.95%)]	(287)
2021 net income and taxable income	$53,171

Part B–Federal Income Tax Payable

The required calculations are as follows:

Tax on first $49,020		$ 7,353
Tax on next $4,151 ($53,171 - $49,020) at 20.5%		851
Tax before credits		$8,204
Tax credits:		
Basic personal amount	($13,808)	
Eligible dependant–Either child, but only one of them	(13,808)	
EI premiums	(890)	
CPP contributions	(2,836)	
Canada employment	(1,257)	
Medical expenses (Note 3)	(1,025)	
Total credit base	($33,624)	
Rate	15%	(5,044)
Dividend tax credit [(6/11)($1,140)]		(622)
2021 federal income tax payable		$2,538

Note 3   The base for Kerri's medical expense tax credit would be calculated as follows:

Eligible expenses	$2,620
Reduced by the lesser of:	
• [(3%)($53,171)] = $1,595	
• 2021 threshold amount = $2,421	(1,595)
Base for credit	$1,025

SSP 10-11 Solution
Part A–Spousal RRSP Contribution

As noted in the problem, we are to assume that Ahmed's 2020 earned income is equal to his 2021 earned income. In order to calculate the 2021 earned income, we need to calculate both employment income and rental income. These are the only components of Ahmed's earned income.

Employment Income

Even though Ahmed is no longer an employee, he has employment income related to the exercise of his stock option shares. The calculations are as follows:

Exercise date value [(5,000)($21)]	$105,000
Option price [(5,000)($15)]	(75,000)
Employment income (ITA 7(1))	$ 30,000

There will be a deduction in determining taxable income equal to one-half of the stock option benefit or $15,000 (ITA 110(1)(d)). There is also a taxable capital gain, which will be calculated separately below.

Rental Income

The required calculations here are as follows:

Revenues ($34,000 + $42,000 + $26,000)	$102,000
Recapture on property A (Note 1)	138,000
Expenses other than CCA	
($29,000 + $37,000 + $23,000)	(89,000)
CCA (Note 1)	(38,240)
Rental income	$112,760

Note 1   CCA on the rental properties would be calculated as follows:

	Property A	Property B	Property C
UCC on January 1	$422,000	$571,000	$385,000
Dispositions–Capital cost	(560,000)	N/A	N/A
Subtotal	($138,000)	$571,000	$385,000
Recapture	138,000	N/A	N/A
Balance subject to CCA	Nil	$571,000	$385,000
Rate N/A	4%	4%	4%
CCA	Nil	$ 22,840	$ 15,400

The total 2021 CCA would be $38,240 ($22,840 + $15,400).

RRSP Deduction

Since we are assuming that Ahmed's 2020 earned income is equal to his 2021 earned income, the required figure is calculated as follows:

Employment income	$ 30,000
Rental income	112,760
2020 earned income (assumed to be equal to 2021)	$142,760

The maximum deductible spousal RRSP contribution for 2021 would be the lesser of $25,697 [(18%)($142,760)] and the 2021 RRSP dollar limit of $27,830. Using the lesser figure, the maximum deductible contribution would be $25,697.

Part B–Net Income

While the employment income and rental income figures from Part A are components of net income, other amounts are needed to complete the determination of 2021 net income.

Taxable Capital Gains

There will be a taxable capital gain on the sale of the stock option shares, calculated as follows:

POD [(5,000)($23)]	$115,000
ACB [(5,000)($21)]	(105,000)
Capital gain	$ 10,000
Inclusion rate	1/2
Taxable capital gain	$ 5,000

In addition, there will be a capital gain on the sale of property A, calculated as follows:

	Land	**Building**
POD	$340,000	$620,000
ACB	(100,000)	(560,000)
Capital gain	$240,000	$ 60,000

The total capital gain is $300,000 ($240,000 + $60,000). However, as the total proceeds were not collected in the year of sale, Ahmed can reduce the capital gains to be included in his net income through the use of a capital gains reserve (ITAAT 40(1)(a)).

Total capital gain ($240,000 + $60,000)	$300,000
Reserve–Lesser of:	
• [($300,000)($864,000 ÷ $960,000)] = $270,000	
• [($300,000)(20%)(4 - 0)] = $240,000	(240,000)
Capital gain	$ 60,000
Inclusion rate	1/2
Taxable capital gain for 2021	$ 30,000

Minimum RRIF Withdrawal

A registrant can irrevocably elect to base the minimum RRIF withdrawal calculation on the age of his spouse rather than his own age. If the spouse is younger, this will minimize the required withdrawal. Adrianna is aged 66, which is five years younger than Ahmed.

For individuals under the age of 71, the minimum RRIF withdrawal is calculated by dividing the FMV of the RRIF at the beginning of the year by the number 90, less the registrant's age, or the spouse's age if elected.

The minimum RRIF withdrawal would be $52,083 [$1,250,000 ÷ (90 - 66)].

Pension Income Splitting

The election to split CPP benefits is provided for in the CPP legislation (CPP 65.1) and results in an actual split of the payments. The ITA 60.03 legislation allows certain other types of pension income to be split. Both payments of RPPs and withdrawals from RRIFs qualify for this split, which is implemented solely in the relevant income tax returns. The total qualifying pension income for Ahmed is $138,083 ($86,000 + $52,083), one-half of which is $69,042.

2021 Net Income

Based on the preceding calculations and the other information provided in the problem, Ahmed's minimum 2021 net income can be calculated as follows:

Employment income–Part A	$ 30,000
Rental income–Part A	112,760
Spousal RRSP deduction–Part A	(25,697)
RPP receipts (pension split)	86,000
CPP receipts after election to split with wife	5,500
Taxable capital gain–Option shares	5,000
Taxable capital gain–Rental property	30,000
Minimum RRIF withdrawal (pension split)	52,083
Interest from Canadian sources	18,000
Eligible dividends received	2,200
Gross up [(38%)($2,200)]	836
Foreign source interest	3,000
Net income before pension split	$319,682
Income split with spouse [(1/2)($86,000 + $52,083)]	(69,042)
2021 net income	$250,640

Part B–Taxable Income

Ahmed's taxable income would be calculated as follows:

Net income	$250,640
Stock option deduction–Part A	(15,000)
Taxable income	$235,640

Part B–Federal Income Tax Payable

As the problem requires the minimum federal income tax payable, Ahmed has claimed the credits for his son, the medical expenses, and charitable donations. These could have been claimed by Adrianna. The required calculations are as follows:

Tax on first $216,511		$50,141
Tax on next $19,129 ($235,640 - $216,511) at 33%		6,313
Tax before credits		$56,454
Tax credits:		
Basic personal amount	($12,421)	
Spousal (Note 2)	Nil	
Age (net income too high)	Nil	
Canada caregiver–Son	(7,348)	
Canada employment	(1,257)	
Pension income	(2,000)	
Transfer of disability from son	(8,662)	
Medical expenses (Note 3)	(12,979)	
Total credit base	($44,667)	
Rate	15%	(6,700)
Charitable donations (Note 4)		(1,284)
Dividend tax credit on eligible dividends [(6/11)($836)]		(456)
Foreign tax credit (amount withheld)		(300)
2021 federal income tax payable		$47,714

Note 2 While Adrianna has only $7,400 of OAS and the $5,500 in CPP benefits in her name, the added amounts resulting from the pension income splitting of more than $69,000 will be more than enough to eliminate the spousal tax credit. This additional income will use up all of her other tax credits (age and pension), preventing any transfers to Ahmed.

Note 3 The base for the medical expense tax credit is calculated as follows:

Ahmed and Adrianna ($2,500 + $3,100)		$ 5,600
Lesser of:		
• [(3%)($250,640)] = $7,519		
• 2021 threshold amount = $2,421		(2,421)
Subtotal		$ 3,179
Son's medical expenses	$9,800	
Reduced by the lesser of:		
• $2,421		
• [(3%)(nil)] = Nil	Nil	9,800
Allowable amount of medical expenses		$12,979

Note 4 Ahmed's charitable donations tax credit would be calculated as follows:

15% of $200		$ 30
33% of the lesser of:		
($4,000 - $200) = $3,800		
($235,640 - $216,511) = $19,129		1,254
Total credit		$1,284

Part C–Pension Income Splitting

Given Ahmed's high taxable income, even after pension splitting, more than $19,000 is subjected to the maximum federal income tax bracket of 33%. Despite splitting the maximum amount of pension income, none of Adrianna's taxable income is taxed at higher than 20.5% federally.

As a result, maximum pension income splitting appears to be advantageous if only federal income tax rates are considered.

What should also be considered is the effect of the pension income splitting on the OAS clawback for Adrianna and the effect of provincial income taxes on both Ahmed and Adrianna. The effect of the OAS clawback and provincial taxes could make it more advantageous to reduce the amount of income splitting so that Adrianna's net income is below the OAS clawback threshold of $79,845 for 2021.

While the ability to claim more medical expenses could be a factor in some pension income-splitting analyses, it would have very little influence in this case given the high levels of net income for both individuals.

CHAPTER 11

Learning Objectives

After completing Chapter 11, you should be able to:

1. Describe the four-step process used to determine net federal tax payable for individuals, the common taxable income deductions, and their place in that process (Paragraph [P hereafter] 11-1 to 11-8).
2. Describe the purpose of the rules related to lump-sum payments and how they apply (P 11-9 to 11-14).
3. Explain how transaction-based losses differ from source-based losses, the exceptions to transaction-based losses, how they fit into net income under ITA 3, and what happens when there is insufficient income to apply them in a year (P 11-15 to 11-29).
4. Explain how personal tax credits play a role in loss planning (P 11-30 to 11-31).
5. Explain and be able to apply how current-year losses become loss carry overs and the importance of ITA 3 in that process (P 11-32).
6. Describe the various types of loss carry overs, their carry over period, and their restrictions, if any (P 11-33).
7. Calculate and apply the loss carry over provisions applicable to non-capital losses (P 11-34 to 11-38).
8. Calculate and apply the loss carry over provisions applicable to net capital losses, including the conversion of a net capital loss carry over to a non-capital loss carry over (P 11-39 to 11-45).
9. Explain the special rules for applying net capital losses on the death of an individual (P 11-46 to 11-49).
10. Describe the circumstances under which an ABIL can occur, how it is treated in determining net and taxable income, and the interaction with the capital gains deduction (P 11-50 to 11-60).
11. Explain the difference between a restricted farm loss and a non-restricted farm loss and the loss carry overs that apply when there is insufficient net income to apply them in the year they arise (P 11-61 to 11-65).
12. Explain the purpose of the capital gains deduction together with the type of property to which it applies (P 11-66 to 11-73)
13. Apply the provisions of the capital gains deduction (P 11-74 to 11-89).
14. Explain the importance of selectively applying loss carry overs in the optimum way possible and describe some of the basic tax planning points to keep in mind when choosing which losses to apply (P 11-90 to 11-94).
15. Describe basic federal tax payable (P 11-95 to 11-100).
16. Explain why income splitting is such a concern to the federal government and the types of transactions that were identfied as problematic (P 11-101 to 11-105).
17. Describe the kiddy tax and how it applies (P 11-106 to 11-110).
18. Describe the TOSI and how it differs from the kiddy tax (P 11-111 to 11-114).
19. Describe and apply the TOSI analysis to a basic fact pattern (P 11-115 to 11-130).
20. Explain the circumstances under which dividends can be transferred between spouses or common-law partners. Apply the transfer and determine whether it is beneficial in specific cases (P 11-131).

21. Explain how the eligible amount of donation is determined, the impact of an "advantage," and how the legal concept of a donation differs from that of the ITA (P 11-132 to 11-140)
22. Explain how the ITA treats donations of property to registered charities, how it affects the 75% annual limit and any special treatment to certain property donations such as publicly listed shares, and calculate the charitable donations tax credit for donations of these various types of property (P 11-141 to 11-157).
23. Explain the purpose of the foreign tax credit, the tax treatment of the payment of foreign taxes, and be able to calculate both the foreign business and non-business income tax credits (P 11-158 to 11-168).
24. Explain the purpose and reasons for the AMT and the circumstances under which it is likely to apply (P 11-169 to 11-171).
25. Apply the provisions of the AMT (P 11-172 to 11-182)
26. Review a personal tax return completed using the ProFile T1 tax preparation software program.

How to Work through Chapter 11

Visit pearsonmylabandmastering.com to access MyLab Accounting for this text. Once there, you can access student resources such as Self-Study Problems, Practice Exams, Flashcards, updates, and more.

We recommend the following approach in dealing with the material in this chapter:

Introduction and Taxable Income Overview
- Read paragraph 11-1 to 11-8 (in the text).

Lump-Sum Payments—ITA 110.2
- Read paragraph 11-9 to 11-14.

Loss Basics
- Read paragraph 11-15 to 11-29.
- Do Exercise 11-1 (in the text) and check the solution in this Study Guide.
- Read paragraph 11-30 to 11-33.

Non-Capital Losses
- Read paragraph 11-34 to 11-38.
- Do Exercise 11-2 and check the solution in this Study Guide.

Net Capital Losses (Including Special Rules at Death)
- Read paragraph 11-39 to 11-45.
- Do Exercise 11-3 and check the solution in this Study Guide.
- Read paragraph 11-46 to 11-49.
- Do Exercise 11-4 and check the solution in this Study Guide.

Allowable Business Investment Losses (ABILs)
- Read paragraph 11-50 to 11-60.
- Do Exercise 11-5 and check the solution in this Study Guide.
- Do Self-Study Problem 11-1, which is available on MyLab, and check the solution in this Study Guide.

Farm Losses
- Read paragraph 11-61 to 11-65.
- Do Exercise 11-6 and check the solution in this Study Guide.
- Do Self-Study Problem 11-2 and check the solution in this Study Guide.

Capital Gains Deduction
- Read paragraph 11-66 to 11-81.
- Do Exercise 11-7 and check the solution in this Study Guide.

- Read paragraph 11-82 to 11-89.
- Do Exercise 11-8 and check the solution in this Study Guide.
- Do Self-Study Problem 11-3 and check the solution in this Study Guide.

Ordering of Deductions and Losses
- Read paragraph 11-90 to 11-94.
- Do Exercise 11-9 and check the solution in this Study Guide.

Tax Payable Overview and Tax on Split Income (TOSI)
- Read paragraph 11-95 to 11-100 [tax payable overview].
- Read paragraph 11-101 to 11-130 [kiddy tax & TOSI].
- Do Exercise 11-10 and check the solution in this Study Guide.
- Do Self-Study Problem 11-4 and check the solution in this Study Guide.

Transfer of Dividends to a Spouse or Common-Law Partner—ITA 82(3)
- Read paragraph 11-131.
- Do Exercise 11-11 and check the solution in this Study Guide.
- Do Self-Study Problems 11-5 and 11-6 and check the solutions in this Study Guide.

Charitable Donations Credit—Gifts of Capital Property
- Read paragraph 11-132 to 11-148.
- Do Exercise 11-12 and check the solution in this Study Guide.
- Read paragraph 11-149.
- Do Exercise 11-13 and check the solution in this Study Guide.
- Read paragraph 11-150 to 11-157.

Foreign Tax Credits Revisited
- Read paragraph 11-158 to 11-168.
- Do Exercise 11-14 and check the solution in this Study Guide.

Alternative Minimum Tax (AMT)
- Read paragraph 11-169 to 11-182.
- Do Exercise 11-15 and check the solution in this Study Guide.

Comprehensive Tax Payable and Sample Personal Tax Return for Chapter 11
- Read paragraph 11-183.
- Do Self-Study Problems 11-7 to 11-11 and check the solutions in this Study Guide.
- Read the Sample Personal Tax Return For Chapter 11 found in this chapter of the Study Guide. The complete tax returns are available on MyLab in two formats, a T1 ProFile return file and a .PDF file.

Tax Software Self-Study Problem
- Do Tax Software Self-Study Problem—Chapter 11 using the ProFile T1 Software. The Self-Study Problem is found in this chapter of the Study Guide. The complete tax return is available on MyLab.

To Complete This Chapter
- Visit MyLab Accounting for more practice problem material, and test yourself with the glossary flashcards.
- Review the Key Terms at the end of the chapter, and consult the glossary for definitions.
- Ensure you have achieved the Chapter 11 Learning Objectives listed in this Study Guide.
- As a review, view the PowerPoint presentations available on MyLab.

Practice Examination
- Available on MyLab, write the Practice Examination for this chapter, and mark it using the solutions provided.

Sample Personal Tax Return for Chapter 11

The following example contains a T1 individual income tax return completed using the ProFile T1 Personal Income Tax Program for 2020 tax returns from Intuit Canada. As software for 2020 is not yet available, this example contains 2020 rates and credits.

The updated 2021 filing version of the ProFile software will be available in January 2022. Non-filing versions will be available prior to that date but include a number of 2021 draft forms that have not yet been updated. On installation, the program defaults to check for updates, so non-filing versions may be installed automatically. In January 2022, after the first 2020 filing version is released, the updated 2021 version of this sample return will be available shortly thereafter on MyLab at:

http://www.pearsonmylabandmastering.com

This example was introduced in Chapter 4 and is expanded in Chapter 11 to contain other components of taxable income and tax payable. For comparison purposes, you might find it useful to review the Chapter 4 version of this example before proceeding with this version.

In the following example, the relevant T1 schedule or ProFile form name is provided in square brackets to indicate where the information is input.

Sample Problem Data

> **DISCLAIMER:** All characters appearing in this example are fictitious. Any resemblance to real persons, living or dead, is purely coincidental.

George Pilot (SIN 527-000-145) is a married, semi-retired air force pilot living in Banff, Alberta. His wife, Deborah (SIN 130-692-544), was mauled by a grizzly bear while hiking three years ago. The attack left her blind and limited her mobility. [Check appropriate box on the Info form on Deborah's return under Filing. Check Yes for the disability amount and the mentally or physically infirm box. Press F5 on the info tab to move to and from the spouse's info.]

They have been your clients for many years. George was born on February 24, 1969, and Deborah was born on April 10, 1973. They are both Canadian residents and citizens.

After some discussion with George and Deborah, you confirm that they have never owned any foreign property. They both authorize the CRA to provide information to Elections Canada and authorize you to e-file their returns. They are currently living at 69 BBB Street in Banff, Alberta, T9Z 0C0. Their home phone number is (403) 111-1111.

George and Deborah have three children who are all in good health:

- Bryan (SIN 527-000-947) was born on March 12, 2013, and had no income during the year.

- Janice (SIN 527-000-269) was born on June 6, 2007, and is in high school. She had income from babysitting totalling $400 during 2020.

- Willa (SIN 527-000-228) was born on January 22, 2001, and is attending university in Edmonton. Willa had net income of $3,300 during 2020.

George has a passion for flying and was hired in February to fly fire bombers from June 1 to September 30 for the provincial forest service fire control squad located in Banff.

George informs you that on February 12, 2020, he received $2 million from his mother's estate. Using some of these funds, George bought a house in Banff. The remainder of the funds were invested with his stockbroker, $$$$ Inc.

Deborah, a voice teacher, adapted to her blindness quickly and required no outside help to take care of the family last year or for the first eight months of 2020. She decided to move temporarily to Edmonton with Willa to attend the music program at the University of Alberta.

During 2020, Deborah made a $50,000 loan to her brother, Andrew, who used the funds to expand his business. On December 31, 2020, Andrew paid her $6,500, which included a principal payment of $5,000 and all interest accrued to that date in the amount of $1,500. Since the CRA administrative policy is not to require the preparation of a T5 ("Statement of Investment Income") for transactions between individuals, no T5 has been prepared. Include the interest income on Deborah's tax return on the form titled "Other Income" for line 12100, which can be accessed by right clicking that line. Also in 2020, Deborah provided teaching services, specifically private voice lessons, earning a gross total of $3,200. No expenses have been claimed. If you right click on line 13700 of her T1 you will see a reference to the T2125 ("Statement of Business and Professional Activities") that you must complete. The self-employment form will also be generated once you have completed the T2125.

George brings you the following receipts and documents:

1. A T4, T4A, and a T5 (included in this example). A statement from his bank stating that he paid $7,382 in interest on the mortgage on his house during 2020. (See Items 17 and 23.)

2. A T2202 "Tuition And Enrollment Certificate" for himself from Athabasca University. It showed he was a part-time student for six months and paid $591 in tuition for 2020. [T2202]

3. Two charitable donation receipts. One in George's name for $1,000 from the Canadian Wildlife Federation dated April 10, 2020. A second receipt in Deborah's name for $100 from the Canadian National Institute for the Blind (CNIB) dated December 3, 2020. [Donations]

4. A statement from the Banff Dental Clinic that George paid a total of $1,650 during 2020. This consisted of $850 for himself on November 24, and $200 each for Deborah, Bryan, Willa, and Janice on December 15. [Medical] None of the expenses are cosmetic and all are eligible.

5. An invoice from the CNIB in Deborah's name for $375 dated December 26, 2020, for computer peripherals designed exclusively for a person who is blind to use a computer. She had obtained a prescription from her doctor specifying her need for this equipment. [Medical]

6. George spent $14,700 during 2020 on various permanent modifications to the house. His goal for these changes was to allow Deborah to be more mobile inside and outside the house (e.g., outside ramps and railings in the halls and stairways) and to reduce the risk of harm to her (a walk-in bathtub). George has detailed invoices for the renovations. Since Deborah's mobility impairment is not severe, these expenditures do not qualify as allowable medical expenses.

7. An agreement of purchase and sale for a house at 69 BBB St. in Banff. The purchase price was $800,000 and the invoice for legal fees totalled $1,200. The deal closed March 31, 2020, and George paid the purchase price of the house in cash. George and his family had been living in a rented townhouse for the last five years. Prior to that George had owned a house, but it went to his ex-wife in the divorce settlement. Deborah has never owned a principal residence. [Other Credits for the Home Buyers' Credit.]

8. An instalment statement for 2020 showing that George had paid the CRA instalments of $1,500 on September 14 and December 14 ($3,000 in total). These were the instalments requested by the CRA for the year due to his self-employed income in the previous year. [Other Credits]

9. A T2202 "Tuition and Enrollment Certificate" for Deborah from the University of Alberta situated in Edmonton. It showed she was a full-time student for four months and paid $2,600 in tuition for 2020. [Schedule 2]. Deborah's Canada Training Limit is $250 for 2020, as indicated on her 2019 notice of assessment.

10. A T2202 "Tuition and Enrollment Certificate" for Willa from the University of Alberta. It showed she was a full-time student for eight months and paid $6,200 in tuition for 2020. She had signed the certificate authorizing the maximum transfer of her tuition amount to her father. [Dependant]

11. His 2019 notice of assessment showing that his 2020 RRSP deduction limit is $13,979. He has no undeducted RRSP contributions from previous years. [RRSP]

12. A contribution receipt to a spousal RRSP (George contributed to Deborah's RRSP) for $2,000 from $$$$ Inc. dated February 20, 2021. [RRSP]

13. A receipt for $2,000 from George's 40-year-old sister, Shirley Burns (SIN 527-000-582), for child care. She took care of Bryan after school during 2020 while Deborah was in Edmonton. [Input on Dependants, flows to T778]

14. A receipt for Janice, an accomplished trombone player, from the Peak Music Camp in Whistler, B.C. The receipt for $1,600 was for two weeks of intensive music instruction at the camp. This fee also included $400 in accommodations and $325 for meals. [Input on Dependants, flows to T778]

15. A receipt for $2,148 dated April 1, 2020, from the Mountain Moving Company. The invoice describes the charges as fees for packing, moving, and delivering George's household effects and furniture from his former rented home at 123 CCC Avenue in Calgary (the "old home") to his newly purchased home in Banff (the "new home") a distance of 125 kilometres. The distance between the old home and George's place of employment at Alberta Fire and Brimstone Control was 130 kilometres, whereas the distance between the new home and the place of employment is only 5 kilometres. George agrees to use the simplified method.

16. In July 2020, George asked you how much he could contribute to TFSAs for himself and Deborah. By accessing their accounts through the CRA's online Represent a Client service, you informed him that he could contribute $25,000 for both himself and Deborah. George brings in TFSA statements for himself and Deborah that shows he made the maximum contribution to each TFSA on October 20, 2020. It also shows that Deborah withdrew $3,000 from her TFSA on December 15, 2020.

17. George's new stockbroker, Mr. Ace Securities at $$$$ Inc., convinces him to take out a mortgage on his new home in order to invest the funds in various stocks. George assumes a $500,000 mortgage as of June 1, 2020. In the 2020 income tax package you will note that there are no Schedule 1 (previously federal tax), 4 (investment income), 10 (previously refundable medical supplement) and 12 (previously home accessibility expense). The information is either no longer relevant or is included elsewhere, such as the deduction of carrying charges, which is now included on the "worksheet for the return."

18. George's capital gain transaction summary statement for 2020 issued from $$$$ Inc. lists the details of 33 separate share sale transactions. The separate details of each transaction would be required to be entered in Schedule 3. The ProFile software requires that the form S3 Details be completed to record each transaction, which is then automatically entered into Schedule 3. Assume for this purpose that the details are combined into one transaction to be entered in S3 Details as follows:

Code 3a for Mutual Funds/Shares

Year of acquisition: 2018

Date of disposition: 12/12

Proceeds of disposition: $100,000

Adjusted cost base (ACB): $94,000

Outlays and expenses: $1,928.00

19. On January 8, 2020, George sold his 1971 Ford Mustang for $50,000. The car was driven only on sunny Sunday afternoons. Its original price in 2002 was $6,000, and George reconditioned it over the years at a cost of $12,000. [S3 Details]

20. At the beginning of 2020, George has a 2018 net capital loss carry forward of $2,580. [Loss Net Cap]

21. During 2020, he paid $6,000 in spousal support to his ex-wife, Marilyn (SIN 527-000-103), pursuant to a written agreement. [Support payments]

22. George owns a commercial property at 999 JJJ Avenue, Edmonton, Alberta, T9Z 0C0. The property was 10 years old when he purchased it on February 15, 2018, for $600,000, of which $160,000 was allocated to the land and $440,000 to the building. Shortly after George purchased the building, the major tenant went bankrupt and he had rental losses for 2018 and 2019. As a result no CCA claims were made in either year. No capital additions were made since the building's acquisition. The financial information for the property, for the year ended December 31, 2020, is as follows [Rental, T776, T776 Asset and T776 CCA will be completed]:

Rental income	$46,700
Mortgage interest	$19,500
Maintenance and repairs	5,100
Management and administration fees	8,200
Legal fees	1,000
Property taxes	11,750
Total expenses	$45,550
Net income before CCA	$ 1,150

23. In Calgary in prior years, George gave the occasional private flying lesson and found it very rewarding. After moving to Banff, he began to pursue private pilot training in earnest beginning April 1 through his business, Pilot's Flying School. A portion of his new house is used exclusively for various training activities, such as one-to-one ground instruction. He also writes and reviews practice pilot exams. George's fiscal year end for the business is December 31.

    The business area of the house occupies 420 square feet of the 2,100 square foot house. George does not intend to claim any CCA on the house. At your request he provides the following costs related to the house during the period April 1, 2020, through December 31, 2020 [T2125, T2125 Asset and T2125 CCA]:

Utilities	$1,500
Repairs and maintenance	4,325
Home insurance	700
Mortgage interest	7,382
Property paxes	2,600

24. On April 15, 2020, George purchased a laptop computer and various software that will be used solely for his business activities. The laptop cost $1,900 and the software costs totalled $800. Prior to this, George had not been using a computer for business purposes. [T2125]

25. George provides the following other information for Pilot's Flying School, for the fiscal period ended December 31, 2020:

Lesson and training fees received	$40,200
Plane rental fees expense	9,600
Business meals with clients	3,250
Licences and fees	1,650
Office expenses	550
Accounting fees	300

Completed Tax Returns and Related Notes

There are three sample tax returns available on MyLab in two versions, a T1 ProFile return file and a .PDF file. Notes to the returns are in a separate .PDF file.

A. A coupled return assuming George does not elect to split his pension income.

B. A coupled return assuming George elects to split his pension income with Deborah and she files a tax return as well. To split the pension, select the T1031 form from the search feature. When you have determined the maximum split, which is 50% of qualifying income, right click on that figure and select optimize the pension split from the drop-down menu.

Notes to the Chapter 11 Return—No Pension Splitting

Both George and Deborah are filing income tax returns. Deborah is eligible for the Canada training credit which, for 2020, provides her with a refund of $250.

General Notes

- Inheritances are not taxable.

- Willa's tuition fees total more than $5,000. As a result, her transfer to George is limited to the $5,000 maximum. Only Willa can claim the unused credits in the future. Willa should file a return to receive the GST credit and to help her keep track of her tuition credit carry forward. While transfers of tuition credits can be made federally, many provinces either restrict or do not allow such transfers. In its 2020 budget, Alberta discontinued the transfer of tuition and education credits beginning with the 2020 taxation year. Only unused amounts from years prior to 2020 are eligible to be used in 2020.

- Since Willa is over 17 years of age, her medical expenses are reduced by 3% of her net income.

- George is not eligible for the refundable medical expense supplement or the Canada Workers Benefit as his income is too high. Given 3% of his net income is greater than the medical expense threshold, the only allowable medical expenses are those of Willa.

- Given that the medical expenses do not exceed the net income limit (line 33099) it is best to carry forward the expenses to 2021, particularly as they were paid in November and December of 2020. They could be claimed in the following year if the 12-month limit is used.

- Deborah has interest income of $1,500 and professional fees of $3,200. As a result, the spousal credit base is decreased by this amount on Schedule 2. Note that the principal repayment of $5,000 is not income. Deborah's disability credit has been transferred to George, as well as $2,350 of her tuition tax credit of $2,600. The $250 difference is claimed by Deborah as a refund as a result of the Canada training credit See line 45350).

- As a resident of Alberta, George qualifies for the refundable Climate Action Incentive payment for 2020. This refundable credit is available to individuals who are residents of Ontario, Manitoba, Saskatchewan, and Alberta in 2020. The maximum credit for a family of four in Alberta for 2020 is $981.

- George's 2020 CPP contribution of $813.75 is calculated as 5.25% of insurable earnings, which are equal to his employment income of $19,000 minus a basic exemption of $3,500. There are two components to the CPP contribution rate of 5.25%. The first is a basic contribution rate of 4.95% and the second an additional amount of 0.30% referred to as an enhancement. The enhancement represents an effort by the federal government to provide increased CPP retirement pension benefits. The basic 4.95% or $767.25 [(0.0495)($19,000 - $3,500)] is treated as a non-refundable tax credit and the enhanced portion of $46.50 [(0.0525 - 0.0495)($19,000 - $3,500)] is allowed as a deduction (new line 22215). George is also required to contribute to the CPP on his income from self-employment (e.g., carrying on a business), which adds an additional $2,432.61 [(5.25% + 5.25%)($23,167.64)]. CPP contributions are double on self-employed earnings (Add lines 22200 and 31000).

Item Specific Notes

- (Item 3) For couples, the CRA's administrative practices permit either spouse or common-law partner to claim some or all of the donations made by the couple. George should claim both donations as combining them is advantageous given the 15% rate on the first $200 of donations. As a general rule, if one of the individuals has taxable income that is subject to the 33% rate then it is preferable that donations be claimed by that individual since the credit rate above $200 of donations would be 33% instead of 29%.

- (Item 5) Both ITA 118.2 and Income Tax Folio S1-F1-C1 clearly state that medical expenses can only be deducted by the individual who paid for them. However, the CRA provides an administrative concession that allows either spouse or common-law partner to claim the medical expense credit without regard to who actually paid for the expenses. As a result, George is claiming the amount Deborah paid for the computer peripherals. The general rule for claiming medical expenses is that they should be claimed by the individual with the lower net income because of the annual threshold, which is $2,397 for 2020.

- (Item 6) George's receipts for the expenses eligible for the home accessibility credit total more than the $10,000 maximum for the year on the "Other Credits" form. As a result, the maximum credit of $1,500 [(15%)($10,000)] is available.

- (Item 7) The home buyers' tax credit of $750 [(15%)($5,000)] is available since George had been living in a rented townhouse for five years and neither he nor Deborah had another principal residence. The credit is also claimed on the "Other Credits" form.

- (Items 13 and 14) Since Deborah was in full-time attendance at the University of Alberta, George can deduct child care costs of up to $4,000 [(2)($125)(16 weeks)]. The $2,000 paid to Shirley Burns is totally deductible. The deduction for child care costs is limited to $125 per week for overnight camp fees. This results in maximum deductible child care costs of $2,250.

- (Item 15) Form T1M, "Claim for Moving Expenses," should be filled out to calculate the deductible moving expenses. George cannot deduct the legal fees related to the purchase of his new home because he had been living in a rented townhouse in Calgary. Such expenses are only deductible if the old home was owned and sold as a result of the move. On Form T1M, since the "Simplified Method" box is checked, the program calculates the allowable deduction for mileage using the 2020 Alberta rate of $0.48 per kilometre.

- (Item 17) The house was purchased for cash and the mortgage was obtained for investment purposes only. As a result all of the interest is deductible on the "Other Deductions" form. Note that Schedule 4 no longer exists.

- (Item 20) George has claimed his net capital loss carry forward of $2,580 since his total taxable capital gains were well in excess of this amount.

- (Item 22) Since the rental property has been showing a loss since its acquisition, no CCA could have been taken prior to 2020. As a result, the beginning of the year UCC of the building will be George's original allocation of $440,000. The CCA for 2020 is limited to $1,150, the amount that reduces his rental income to nil, since CCA deductions are not allowed to create or increase a rental loss.

T2125 (Items 24 to 26)

- The Industry Code must be chosen from the list near the top right corner of the T2125. The appropriate choice is 611690, "All Other Schools and Instruction."

- Expenses for income tax purposes are applied against the source of income to which they relate. Since the mortgage interest of $7,382 is sourced to investment income, no part of it can be sourced to the professional income of the flying school as a business use-of-home expense. The interest expense is included on the "Other Deductions" form of the ProFile software.

- There are three CCA rules that affect the amount of CCA that can be claimed for 2020 with respect to the laptop and software. The three rules are (1) the short fiscal period rule (ITR 1100(3)), (2) the regular half-year rule (ITR 1100(2)), and (3) the Accelerated Investment Incentive rule or AccII (ITR 1104(4)). The laptop falls into class 50 (55%) and the software into class 12 (100%). The fiscal period of the business in its first year is short, beginning April 1, 2020, and ending December 31, 2020 (275 days). This results in a prorated CCA amount that is automatically calculated by ProFile. In the T2125 "Statement of Business or Professional Activities" for the flying school business, make sure to enter April 1, 2020, as the start of the fiscal period.

- The regular half-year rule applies to depreciable property that is not eligible for the AccII. Most depreciable property acquired in arm's-length transactions between November 21, 2018, and December 31, 2023, is eligible for a first-year accelerated CCA claim rather than a reduced claim under the historical half-year rule. Since class 12 property is eligible for a 100% rate, the government opted to exclude such property from the new AccII rules. As a result, the laptop is eligible for the AccII whereas the software is only subject to the half-year rule.

Tax Planning Points

- If he has sufficient funds, George should contribute the maximum deductible for 2020 of $13,979 [see RRSP Limit form] to a spousal RRSP as soon as possible. Since George is already getting a pension and Deborah appears to have little income, a spousal RRSP would offer more opportunity for future income splitting. Although the pension income splitting legislation allows for some flexibility, the maximum split is 50%. With a spousal RRSP, Deborah can be taxed on 100% of the funds from her RRSP.

- George should consider opening RESPs for Bryan and Janice if he has not already done so. How much he should contribute will depend on many factors (see the RESP coverage in the text), but it is probably advisable that he contribute enough to take advantage of the Canada Education Savings Plan each year if he has sufficient funds.

- Deborah has created some RRSP contribution room with her professional income. George should consider whether Deborah should contribute to her own RRSP. Funds for George's RRSP and the RESPs should probably have priority given George's higher tax bracket and the Canada Education Savings Plan, though with his inheritance there should be sufficient funds to contribute to all the plans.

- Since TFSA contributions are not deductible and withdrawals are not taxable, the TFSAs will not have an effect on any of the tax returns. George should try to contribute the maximum to both his and Deborah's TFSA on an ongoing basis if he has sufficient funds. He should replace Deborah's withdrawal as soon as possible as it was withdrawn in the preceding calendar year. As long as there are other funds available where related income would be taxable, it would be advisable not to make withdrawals from the TFSAs to take advantage of the tax-free earnings.

- George should consider a TFSA for Willa. If her income is earned income for RRSP purposes, he should also consider contributing to an RRSP in Willa's name.

Notes to the Chapter 11 Returns—With Pension Splitting
Both are filing income tax returns with pension income splitting

The notes to the return with no pension income splitting are also relevant in this scenario.

In creating Deborah's tax return, the following forms and schedules were filled in:

- T2202—Tuition slips
- T2125—Statement of Business or Professional Activities
- T1032—Joint Election to Split Income (originated from George's return)

Neither Deborah or George should claim the medical expenses, other than George claiming the medical expenses for Willa. Although 3% of Deborah's net income is less than the threshold, which would enable her to make a claim where George cannot, the tuition fee credit is calculated before consideration of medical expenses, so the claim for medical expenses has no effect on her tax payable and does not save her any taxes.

Willa's medical expenses could have been claimed by Deborah, but since it will make no difference to her federal tax payable, it is more advantageous to have George claim Willa's medical expenses.

In addition, although we do not cover provincial tax rules in the text, if you examine Deborah's Alberta tax credits [AB428], you will see that she does not use all of her non-refundable Alberta tax credits, even if she does not claim any medical expenses. Claiming Willa's medical credit will decrease George's Alberta and federal tax payable.

Since the couple has elected to split the pension income, the withholdings on the pension income must also be split (See line 43700 of Deborah's return).

The tax savings can be determined by using the "Optimize—split-pension income" function, which is accessed from the pension transferors' (George) tax return. In this case the optimum pension transfer is $12,384.89, which produces the following results:

Combined refund—With pension splitting	$3,002.45
Combined refund—No pension splitting	741.70
Tax savings	$2,260.75

T1032Opt

Optimize - Split-pension income

Calculation of the elected split-pension amount

		Zero transfer	Suggested transfer
Elected split-pension amount		0.00	12,066.04
Total payable (line 43500)	George - Chapter 11 NO SPLIT	8,964.05	6,983.62
	Deborah		
	Combined	8,964.05	6,983.62
Balance owing / refund	George - Chapter 11 NO SPLIT	(923.95)	(1,755.23)
	Deborah		(1,149.15)
	Combined	(923.95)	(2,904.38)
Combined net benefit (cost)			1,980.43

		Calculator			
		Scenario #1	Scenario #2	Scenario #3	Scenario #4
Elected split-pension amount		21,000.00	15,000.00		
Total payable (line 43500)	George - Chapter 11 NO SPLIT	7,198.51	7,262.36		
	Deborah	77.10			
	Combined	7,275.61	7,262.36		
Balance owing / refund	George - Chapter 11 NO SPLIT	(689.49)	(1,197.07)		
	Deborah	(1,922.90)	(1,428.57)		
	Combined	(2,612.39)	(2,625.64)		
Combined net benefit (cost)		1,688.44	1,701.69		

Summary of the elected split-pension amount

We have determined that transferring **$12,066.04** to Deborah's return will result in the lowest combined total payable. If you elect to transfer the suggested amount, the refund of $923.95 is increased to $2,904.38. This represents an overall savings of **$1,980.43**.

Maximum split-pension amount (from line F of your T1032) — 21,000.00 F

This amount will appear on line G on your T1032.   Elected split-pension amount — 12,066.04 G

Impact of electing a split-pension amount on your combined total payable

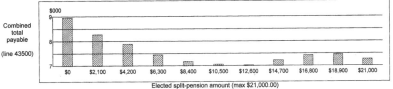

Elected split-pension amount (max $21,000.00)

Tax Software Self-Study Problem—Chapter 11

This problem is an expansion of the Tax Software Self-Study Problem—Chapter 4.

Note The following problem contains the 2020 updated version of the problem that was revised following the release of the 2020 Intuit ProFile software in early 2021.

DISCLAIMER: All characters appearing in this problem are fictitious. Any resemblance to real persons, living or dead, is purely coincidental.

Ms. Eleanor Victoria's husband died two years ago. After her husband died, she moved from her house in Prince George, B.C., to a rented house in Victoria, B.C.

Ms. Victoria's widowed mother, Marjorie Vancouver, lives with Ms. Victoria and takes care of the house, Ms. Victoria's younger daughter, Amy, and all of the household cooking. In addition to OAS benefits, Marjorie has a very small income from her deceased husband's life insurance policy. She has never filed an income tax return and she is not infirm.

Diane Victoria, Eleanor's older daughter, is studying psychology at McGill University in Montreal. Her field is addiction research with a special emphasis on gambling. She does volunteer work at a gambling addiction treatment centre in Montreal in the summers. As Eleanor has paid for her tuition and living costs, Diane has agreed that the maximum tuition amount should be transferred to her mother.

Diane has decided not to file a tax return this year as she knows she does not owe any taxes. Her income was earned driving for a client of the addiction treatment centre who had lost his licence after being charged with impaired driving.

Late in December 2019, Eleanor was notified that she had inherited $500,000 from an aunt. Eleanor loves her work and though she plans to travel more, she has no plans to retire.

Information concerning Ms. Victoria for 2020 is given on the following pages.

Required:

A. With the objective of minimizing Ms. Victoria's Tax Payable, prepare the 2020 income tax return of Eleanor Victoria using the ProFile tax software program. List any assumptions you have made, and any notes and tax planning issues you feel should be discussed with Ms. Victoria. Ignore GST/HST implications in your solution by assuming that Ms. Victoria does not qualify for the GST/HST rebate. Assume that Diane will not file an income tax return and will not take advantage of the Canada training credit for 2020.

B. Calculate the maximum deductible contribution Ms. Victoria can make to her RRSP for the 2020 taxation year. What advice would you give Ms. Victoria concerning the various deferred savings plans available to her given the funds from her inheritance?

Personal Information	
Title	Ms.
First Name	Eleanor
Last Name	Victoria
SIN	527-000-087
Date of birth (Y/M/D)	1973-05-15
Marital Status	Widowed
Canadian citizen?	Yes
Provide information to Elections Canada?	Yes
Own foreign property of more than $100,000 Canadian?	No

Taxpayer's Address	
111 VVV Street Victoria, B.C., V4H 3W4	
Phone number (250) 111-1111	

Dependants	Child 1	Child 2	Mother
First Name	Diane	Amy	Marjorie
Last Name	Victoria	Victoria	Vancouver
SIN	527-000-293	None	527-000-483
Date of birth (Y/M/D)	2000-05-14	2008-10-11	1948-05-21
Net income	$2,300	Nil	$8,000

T4	Box	Amount
Issuer—1750 Canada Inc.		
Employment income	14	60,201.80
Employee's CPP contributions	16	2,898.00
Employee's EI premiums	18	856.36
RPP contributions	20	2,406.16
Pension adjustment	52	7,829.00
Income tax deducted	22	6,408.00
Employment commissions	42	0
Union dues	44	748.59
Charitable donations	46	175.00

Eleanor has a signed T2200 from her employer specifying her work requires her to have an office in the home. She meets the conditions required to deduct work space in the home expenses. Of the 1,800 square feet in the house, her office, waiting area, and storage space totals 310 square feet. She doesn't qualify for the GST rebate.

During 2020 she paid the following:

Rent for the year (no GST charged)	$30,000
Utilities (hydro and gas) for the year	2,500
Cleaning services (no GST charged)	1,200
Insurance for household effects (no GST charged)	400
Car insurance (no GST charged)	700

T2202—(Diane)	Box	Amount
Tuition fees—for Diane Victoria (daughter)	A	7,000
Number of months in school—part time	B	2
Number of months in school—full time	C	8

Eleanor and her family had the following medical expenses, all of which Eleanor paid for:

Patient	(Y/M/D)	Medical Expenses	Description	Amount
Eleanor	2020-08-15	Grace Hospital	Ambulance charge	392
Eleanor	2020-08-18	Paramed Home Health	Nursing care	1,350
Marjorie	2020-05-20	Dr. Zhang (Optometrist)	Contact lenses	110
Marjorie	2020-07-06	Pharmacy	Prescription	75
Diane	2020-09-01	Dr. Glassman	Physiotherapist	100
Amy	2020-05-11	Walk Right Foot Clinic	Orthotics	450
Amy	2020-01-23	Dr. Tamo	Dental fees	1,120

Donor	Charitable Donation Receipts	Am't
Eleanor	Heart and Stroke Foundation (annual donation)	375
Eleanor	Terry Fox Foundation (annual donation)	50
Diane	Addiction Research Council of Canada (annual donation)	100

T3	Box	Amount
Issuer—Global Strategy Financial		
Foreign country—United States		
Capital gains (foreign)	21	982.22
Foreign non-business income	25	310.94

T4A	Box	Amount
Issuer—3601 Canada Inc. (survivor benefit from husband)		
Pension	16	22,249.44
Income tax deducted	22	3,510.78

T4A(P)	Box	Amount
Survivor benefit	15	4,823.28
Income tax deducted	22	Nil

T5	Box	Slip 1	Slip 2
Issuer		Scotiabank	Bank of Montreal
Actual amount of eligible dividends	24		1,603.00
Taxable amount of eligible dividends	25		2,212.14
Interest from Canadian sources	13	509.45	

RRSP information	(Y/M/D)	Amount
Issuer of receipt—Scotiabank	2021-02-10	2,620.00
Earned income for 2019		38,873.00
Pension adjustment for 2019		4,376.00
Unused deduction room at the end of 2019		1,666.00

Child	Child Care Expenses	No. of weeks	Amount
Amy	Croft Computer Camp (14 days overnight)	2	1,000
Amy	Y Day Camp (July)	3	400

Eleanor did not sell her house in Prince George when she moved to Victoria as it was her intention to move back into it within three years. It has been rented on a month-to-month lease since November 2018. She wishes to preserve the principal residence status throughout the years the home is rented. She claimed a rental loss of $4,250 in 2019.

Real Estate Rental	Amount
Address—222 PPP Street, Prince George, B.C., V4H 3W4	
Gross rents (12 months for 2020)	15,600.00
Property taxes	2,190.00
Insurance	1,093.27
Interest on mortgage	5,377.58
Payment on principal	3,688.95
Plumbing repairs	290.94
Snow plow annual contract	300.00
Lawyer's fees for new lease	172.54
Hydro (during vacancy)	288.34
Building purchased October 1, 2018, for $168,900—UCC beginning of year	168,900.00
Washer/dryer purchased May 9, 2019, for $921—UCC beginning of year	921.00
Stove and refrigerator purchased August 17, 2020—UCC beginning of year	1,500.00

Exercise Solutions

Exercise 11-1 Solution

In Chapter 9 we discussed ITA 69(1)(c), which is a rule that applies when property is gifted from one person to another. The gift is treated as a sale and purchase at FMV, meaning that Mr. Smothers' cost and therefore ACB will be equal to $100,000, which was the FMV at the time of the gift. As a result, Mr. Smothers will have a 2020 listed personal property loss of $5,500 [(1/2)($89,000 POD - $100,000 ACB)]. The loss carry over can only be claimed to the extent there are net listed personal property gains in the carry over period of three years back and seven years forward. This means that the 2020 loss could be claimed in 2017 to 2019 or 2021 to 2027. Since he has a $2,000 [(1/2)($5,000 POD - $1,000 ACB)] net listed personal property gain in 2021 (which is within the carry over period), $2,000 of the loss can be deducted. The 2021 results would be as follows:

Income under ITA 3(a)	$62,000
Income under ITA 3(b) ($2,000 - $2,000)	Nil
Net income and taxable income	$62,000

In this case, the listed personal property loss carry forward balance at the end of 2021 is $3,500 ($5,500 - $2,000).

If the sale had been of shares, Mr. Smothers would have had a 2020 net capital loss of $5,500 instead of a listed personal property loss. His 2021 net and taxable income would be calculated as follows:

Income under ITA 3(a)	$62,000
Income under ITA 3(b)	2,000
2021 net income ($2,000 higher)	$64,000
ITA 111(1)(b) net capital loss (limited to taxable capital gains)	(2,000)
2021 taxable income (same)	$62,000

In this case, the $3,500 net capital loss balance is available to be applied in any of the carry over years to the extent there are net taxable capital gains (e.g., an ITA 3(b) amount).

Exercise 11-2 Solution
Net income for 2021 would be determined as follows:

ITA 3(a) Employment income	$35,000
ITA 3(b)(i) Taxable capital gains	
ITA 3(b)(ii) Allowable capital losses	13,000
ITA 3(a) + 3(b)	$48,000
Subdivision e moving expenses	Nil
ITA 3(c)	$48,000
ITA 3(d) Business losses ($58,000 + $2,200)	(60,200)
2021 Net income	Nil

Amount E ITA 3(d) + nil adjustments	$60,200
Less: Amount F ITA 3(c)	(48,000)
Amount A (E-F)	12,200
Less: Amount D (farm loss)	(2,200)
2021 Non-capital loss (A-D)	$10,000

Note that without any component E adjustments the total loss carry overs would be $12,200 ($60,200 - $48,000). This amount is split between a farm loss of $2,200 and a non-capital loss of $10,000. The non-farm business loss of $58,000 is reduced by the ITA 3(c) amount of $48,000 before affecting the farm loss.

Exercise 11-3 Solution
If Laura makes no effort to minimize the net capital loss carry forward, her net income and taxable income would be calculated as follows:

Net taxable capital gain (ITA 3(b))	$40,000
ITA 3(c)	$40,000
Rental loss (ITA 3(d))	(30,000)
2021 Net Income	$10,000
Net capital loss (ITA 111(1)(b))	(10,000)
2021 Taxable income	Nil

This approach results in a 2020 net capital loss balance of $5,000 and no non-capital loss. (The E component would equal $30,000 + $10,000 and the F component would equal the ITA 3(c) amount of $40,000.)

Alternatively, if she chooses to claim the maximum net capital loss deduction of $15,000, the non-capital loss would be calculated as follows:

Amount E ($30,000 ITA 3(d) + $15,000 ITA 111(1(b))	$45,000
Amount F—ITA 3(c) amount	(40,000)
2021 Non-capital loss	$ 5,000

While taxable income remains unchanged at nil, the net capital loss carry forward has been reduced from $5,000 to nil, with the non-capital loss carry forward increased from nil to $5,000.

Exercise 11-4 Solution

If Derek had not died, his 2021 taxable capital gain would have restricted the deductibility of his 2017 net capital loss balance. The limitation, however, does not apply in the year of death as a result of ITA 111(2). To maximize income tax savings, his final return should indicate taxable income of $13,808, the 2021 basic personal amount. This means that only $9,992 ($23,800 - $13,808) of the net capital loss balance should be claimed as a deduction. This amount can be applied against any type of income in 2021. The $10,008 ($20,000 - $9,992) can be carried back to 2020 and applied against any type of income in that year.

Exercise 11-5 Solution

The ABIL for the year would be calculated as follows:

Actual capital loss	$50,000
ITA 39(9) reduction for previous capital gains deduction	(26,000)
BIL	$24,000
Inclusion rate	1/2
ABIL	$12,000

The $12,000 is deducted at ITA 3(d) and can be deducted against Mr. Latvik's employment income. Since only $24,000 of the capital loss qualified as a BIL, the remaining $26,000 is an ordinary capital loss, which becomes a $13,000 allowable capital loss that can be deducted at ITA 3(b)(ii). The net taxable capital gains or ITA 3(b) amount for the year would be nil (ITA 3(b)(i) $9,000 - ITA 3(b)(ii) $13,000). This leaves a 2021 net capital loss of $4,000 [ITA 3(b)(ii) $13,000 - ITA 3(b)(i) $9,000].

You will note that the ITA 39(9) reduction works with the full amount of the capital losses and not the 50% allowable capital losses. Since all ITA 39(9) calculations ignore the 50% amount, the capital gains deduction, which is based on the actual 50% taxable capital gain, must be doubled to adjust to 100% of the capital gains.

Exercise 11-6 Solution

It appears that Ms. Bodkin's farming activity is a source of income, although secondary to her employment. Given this, the farm loss would be subject to ITA 31. Since the farm loss exceeds $32,500 the unrestricted part of the loss will be $17,500 and the remaining $18,500 will be her 2020 restricted farm loss.

In 2021, $3,500 of the 2020 restricted farm loss can be deducted against 2021 taxable income, which is equal to the 2021 farm income. This leaves a 2020 restricted farm loss balance of $15,000 ($18,500 - $3,500). Ms. Bodkin's 2021 net income is $88,500 (ITA 3(a) $85,000 + $3,500) and her 2021 taxable income is $85,000 ($88,500 net income - $3,500 ITA 111(1)(c)).

Exercise 11-7 Solution

The AGL is $26,000 ($42,000 - $16,000). This is calculated using the ITA 110.6 formula of A – B where:

The A component of the formula would be equal to $42,000, the lesser of:

- ITA 3(b) (amount of $74,000 ($114,000 + $42,000 - $82,000); or
- modified ITA 3(b) amount $42,000

The B component would be $16,000, the sum of:

- $13,000* and
- $3,000 ABIL

   *The amount by which the net capital loss of $45,000 exceeds $32,000. The $32,000 amount is determined as the difference between the actual ITA 3(b) amount of $74,000 and the modified ITA 3(b) amount of $42,000.

Note that the net taxable capital gain on non-qualified property was $32,000 ($114,000 - $82,000). The mechanics of the B component of the formula are such that the first $32,000 of the $45,000 net capital loss deduction was applied against those net taxable capital gains that do not qualify for the capital gains deduction. Only the remaining $13,000 ($45,000 - $32,000) served to reduce the AGL.

To make maximum use of her capital gains deduction, it would be advisable for Ms. Slovena to deduct only $32,000 of the 2018 net capital loss. If she did this, the B component would be $3,000 and her annual gains limit would increase to $39,000 [$42,000 - (nil + $3,000)]. Although she would have used $13,000 ($39,000 - $26,000) more of her capital gains deduction, her taxable income and tax liability for 2021 would not change and she would have a net capital loss carry forward of $13,000 ($45,000 - $32,000) that could be applied against any positive ITA 3(b) amount over the carry over period. The trade-off in such a strategy is that her available capital gains deduction is reduced by $13,000 while her 2018 net capital loss balance is increased by $13,000.

Exercise 11-8 Solution

His maximum capital gains deduction is $223,500, the least of the following:

Available deduction   His remaining deduction would be $428,109 ($446,109 - $5,000 - $13,000).

AGL   In the absence of taxable capital gains that do not qualify for the capital gains deduction in any of the years under consideration, the simplified version of this calculation can be used. Given this, this limit would be calculated as follows:

Taxable capital gain on QSBC shares [(1/2)($510,000)]	$255,000
2020 Net capital loss deducted	(31,500)
AGL	$223,500

CGL   In the absence of taxable capital gains that do not qualify for the capital gains deduction in 2013 and 2015, the AGL for 2013 and 2015 would simply be the amount of the taxable capital gains on QSBC shares in those years. Given this, the required calculation would be as follows:

Sum of AGLs	
($5,000 + $13,000 + $223,500)	$241,500
Previous years' capital gains deduction ($5,000 + $13,000)	(18,000)
CNIL	Nil
CGL	$223,500

Exercise 11- 9 Solution

Alan's net income would be calculated as follows:

Income under ITA 3(a):		
Non-farming business income	$12,000	
Employment income	56,000	
Farming business income	3,500	$71,500
Income under ITA 3(b):		
Taxable capital gains		9,000
Net income		$80,500

Alan's taxable income is as follows:

Net income	$80,500
Loss carry forwards:	
2018 Restricted farm loss (limited to farming business income) (	3,500)
2015 Net capital loss (limited to taxable capital gains) (	9,000)
2020 Non-capital loss (	36,000)
Taxable income	$32,000

Loss carry over balances:

• 2018 Restricted farm loss balance ($8,000 - $3,500)	$ 4,500
• 2015 Net capital loss balance ($20,000 - $9,000)	$11,000
• 2020 Non-capital loss balance	Nil

Exercise 11-10 Solution

The regular tax payable would be calculated as follows:

Income sources:	
Taxable non-eligible dividends [(115%)($15,000)]	$ 17,250
Contract income	15,200
Taxable eligible dividends [(138%)($8,600)]	11,868
Deduction for split income—Taxable non-eligible dividends	(17,250)
Net income = Taxable income	$ 27,068
Rate	15%
Tax payable before credits	$ 4,060
Basic personal credit [(15%)($13,808)]	(2,071)
Dividend tax credit—Eligible dividends [(6/11)(38%)($8,600)]	(1,783)
Regular tax payable	$ 206

The tax payable on split income would be calculated as follows:

Split income—Taxable non-eligible dividends	$ 17,250
Rate	33%
Tax payable before dividend tax credit	$ 5,693
Dividend tax credit [(9/13)(15%)($15,000)]	(1,558)
Tax payable on split income	$ 4,135

The total tax payable would be $4,341 ($206 + $4,135).

Exercise 11-11 Solution

Without the transfer, Mr. Ho's spouse would have net income of $11,730 [(138%)($8,500)], $691 less than the base for the spousal credit of $12,421 available to individuals with taxable income of $216,511 or higher. This would result in a small spousal credit of $104 [(15%)($691)]. With the transfer, he would be eligible for the full $1,863 [(15%)($12,421)], an increase of $1,759 [($1,863 - $104). Given this, the analysis of his position at the federal level is as follows:

Additional taxes on dividends [(33%)(138%)($8,500)]	$3,871
Increase in spousal tax credit	(1,759)
Dividend tax credit [(6/11)(38%)($8,500)]	(1,762)
Tax increase (decrease)	$ 350

The election would not be beneficial since it would result in additional income tax to Mr. Ho. Mrs. Ho will have no federal income tax to pay whether or not the election is made.

Exercise 11-12 Solution

With the gift being designated at $85,000, Ms. Felder will have a taxable capital gain of $11,500 [(1/2)(POD $85,000 - ACB $62,000)], plus recapture of $34,000 [$62,000 (lesser of proceeds of $85,000 and capital cost of $62,000) - UCC of $28,000], for a total net income of $45,500. Given this, her maximum credit base would be calculated as follows:

75% of net income [(75%)($45,500)]	$34,125
25% of taxable capital gain [(25%)($11,500)]	2,875
25% of recaptured CCA [(25%)($34,000)]	8,500
2021 Charitable donations credit base limit	
(equals net income as a result of the donation)	$45,500

Note that, because Ms. Felder's taxable income is less than $216,511, the 33% tax rate is not relevant in calculating the charitable donations tax credit. This donation base results in a potential credit of $13,167 [(15%)($200) + (29%)($45,500 - $200)]. While this amount could be used, she does not have sufficient tax payable to use all of this potential credit. Her federal tax payable for the year would be calculated as follows:

Tax before credits [(15%)($45,500)]	$6,825
Basic personal credit [(15%)($13,808)]	(2,071)
Federal tax payable before donations credit	$4,754

To reduce her tax payable to nil, Ms. Felder should use a sufficient amount of her charitable donations credit base to produce a tax credit of $4,754. To determine the optimal amount to claim, first subtract the $30 credit for the first $200 of the donation. This equals $4,724 ($4,754 - $30). Next divide $4,724 by 29%. This equals $16,290. Finally, add the first $200 to the $16,290 for a total of $16,490. This is the optimal credit to claim, leaving a carry forward of $68,510 ($85,000 - $16,490).

Exercise 11-13 Solution

As a donation of publicly traded shares is involved, there will be no recognized taxable capital gain on the donation. This means that Mr. Radeem's net and taxable income for 2021 will consist only of his employment income of $90,000. The limit for the base of Mr. Radeem's charitable donations tax credit would be $67,500 [(75%)($90,000)]. If he were to use this full amount, his 2021 charitable donations tax credit would be $19,547 [(15%)($200) + (29%)($67,500 - $200)]. Note that, because Mr. Radeem's taxable income is less than $216,511, the 33% rate is not relevant in calculating the charitable donations tax credit.

As it would exceed his tax payable after other tax credits, Mr. Radeem will not want to deduct the maximum available charitable donations tax credit. Given this, he needs to determine the amount of the credit that will reduce his tax payable to nil. This is determined as follows:

Tax on first $49,020	$ 7,353
Tax on next $40,980 ($90,000 - $49,020) at 20.5%	8,401
Tax before credits	$15,754
Tax credits (given)	(4,000)
Federal tax payable before donations credit	$11,754

To reduce his tax payable to nil, Mr. Radeem should use a sufficient amount of his charitable donations credit base to produce a tax credit of $11,754. To determine the optimal amount to claim, first subtract the $30 credit for the first $200 of the donation. This equals $11,724 ($11,754 - $30). Next divide $11,724 by 29%. This equals $40,428. Finally, add the first $200 to the $40,428 for a total of $40,628. This is the optimal credit to claim, leaving a carry forward of $69,372 ($110,000 - $40,628).

Exercise 11-14 Solution

Ms. Cheung's 2021 net income and taxable income would be calculated as follows:

Rental income	$44,000
Net taxable capital gains (ITA 3(b))	2,500
Foreign non-business income	3,500
2021 Net income	$50,000
Net capital loss carry forward (ITA 111(1)(b))	(1,000)
Adjusted Division B income	$49,000
Non-capital loss carry forward (ITA 111(1)(a))	(4,000)
Taxable income	$45,000

Ms. Cheung's credit for foreign tax paid would be the lesser of the foreign tax withheld of $385 [(11%)($3,500)] and an amount determined by the following formula:

$$\left[\frac{\text{Foreign Non–Business Income}}{\text{Adjusted Division B Income}} \right] [\text{Tax Otherwise Payable}]$$

In this formula, the adjusted Division B income would be $49,000 (as shown in the preceding table). Note that, because the non-capital loss is not deducted here, this is not the same as her taxable income of $45,000.

Ms. Cheung's tax otherwise payable would be calculated as follows (note that the foreign tax credit is not subtracted in this calculation):

Tax before credits [(15%)($45,000)]	$6,750
Basic personal credit [(15%)($13,808)]	(2,071)
Tax otherwise payable	$4,679

Using this information, the formula amount would be $334 [($3,500 ÷ $49,000)($4,679)]. As this is less than the $385 withheld, this would be the foreign tax credit. Based on this, Ms. Cheung's actual federal tax payable would be calculated as follows:

Tax before credits [(15%)($45,000)]	$6,750
Basic personal credit	(2,071)
Foreign tax credit	(334)
Federal tax payable	$4,345

Note: In practice, the remaining $51 of unused credit [$385- $334] would be deducted under ITA 20(12), which would reduce net and taxable income to $44,949 [$45,000- $51]. Adjusted Division B income would be $48,949 [$49,000 - $51] and tax otherwise payable would be $4,671 [(15%)($45,000 - $51) - $2,071]. The foreign tax credit would be $334 [($3,500 ÷ $48,949)($4,672)].

Exercise 11-15 Solution

Mr. Blouson's regular tax payable would be calculated as follows:

Tax on first $49,020	$ 7,353
Tax on next $35,980 ($85,000 - $49,020) at 20.5%	7,376
Total	$14,729
Basic personal credit [(15%)($13,808)]	(2,071)
Dividend tax credit [(6/11)(38%)($20,000)]	(4,145)
Regular federal tax payable	$ 8,513

For AMT purposes, his adjusted taxable income would be calculated as follows:

Regular taxable income	$85,000
60% of taxable capital gains [(60%)($22,500)]	13,500
Dividend gross up [(38%)($20,000)]	(7,600)
Adjusted taxable income	$90,900

Calculation of the AMT would be as follows:

Adjusted taxable income	$90,900
Basic exemption	(40,000)
Amount subject to tax	$50,900
Rate	15%
Minimum tax before credit	$ 7,635
Basic personal credit [(15%)($13,808)]	(2,071)
AMT for 2021	$ 5,564

Mr. Blouson would not pay the AMT as it is less than the regular tax payable. Note that the $50,000 RRSP deduction does not affect the AMT calculation. Technically the retiring allowance is included in income at ITA 3(a) and the RRSP rollover causes a deduction of the same amount (ITA 3)(c)).

If the taxable capital gains increased by $200,000 to $222,500 but the additional $200,000 was claimed as a capital gains deduction, the taxable income would not have changed and the regular tax payable would remain unchanged at $8,513.

For AMT purposes, his adjusted taxable income would be calculated as follows:

Regular taxable income	$ 85,000
60% of taxable capital gains [(60%)($222,500)]	133,500
Dividend gross up [(38%)($20,000)]	(7,600)
Adjusted taxable income	$210,900

Calculation of the AMT would be as follows:

Adjusted taxable income	210,900
Basic exemption	(40,000)
Amount subject to tax	170,900
Rate	15%
Minimum tax before credit	25,635
Basic personal credit [(15%)($13,808)]	(2,071)
AMT for 2021	23,564

Since the AMT of $23,564 exceeds the regular tax payable of $8,513, the AMT must be paid. The excess amount of $15,051 can be recovered through a carry over to the next seven years (ITA 120.2) to the extent that regular tax payable exceeds the AMT for that year.

Self-Study Problem Solutions

Self-Study Problems are available to download from MyLab Accounting.

SSP 11-1 Solution

The calculation of Miss Atwater's taxable income for 2020 would be as follows:

Rental income	$34,200
Interest income	4,000
2020 Net income and taxable income	$38,200

The corresponding calculation for 2021 is as follows:

Rental income	$ 35,200	
Interest income	4,200	$39,400
ABIL ITA 50(1) election		
[(1/2)(POD nil - ACB $170,000)]		(85,000)
2021 Net income and taxable income		Nil

The bankrupt status of the company in 2021 allows Miss Atwater to file an election under ITA 50(1) to deem there to be a disposition of the shares for nil proceeds. As the capital loss relates to the shares of a small business corporation, it qualifies as a business investment loss. This means that, in contrast to other types of capital losses, the allowable portion can be deducted against any type of income. The ABIL that is available for deduction in 2021 is $85,000 [(1/2)($170,000)].

An ABIL is deducted at ITA 3(d) in determining net income. Any amount in ITA 3(d) (other than farming business losses) that cannot be fully deducted because of insufficient income under ITA 3(c) becomes a non-capital loss for that year equal to the difference between the ITA 3(d) and ITA 3(c) amount plus certain adjustments, none of which would apply in this case. Her 2021 non-capital loss is therefore $45,600 [ITA 3(d) $85,000 - ITA 3(c) $39,400].

In carrying the 2021 non-capital loss back to 2020, the optimum amount to deduct should leave $13,229 of taxable income so that Miss Atwater can use her basic personal tax credit.

This means that she needs a loss carry back deduction of $24,971 ($38,200 - $13,229) to 2020. This deduction will leave a taxable income of $13,229 [2020 net income $38,200 - ITA 111(1)(a) non-capital loss $24,971]. As planned, the gross federal tax payable will equal $1,984 [(15%) ($13,229)] and the net federal tax payable will be nil [gross federal tax $1,984 - personal tax credit of $1,984 [(15%)($13,229)].

A carry back of $24,971 to 2020 leaves a 2021 non-capital loss balance of $20,629 ($45,600 - $24,971) to be used in other carry over years.

The undeducted ABIL remains a part of the 2021 non-capital loss and can be deducted against other type of income in the next 10 years. Any unused portion would become a net capital loss in year 11.

SSP 11-2 Solution
2018 Analysis
The required information can be calculated as follows:

ITA 3(a)		
Business income	$19,800	
Taxable dividends [(138%)($1,870)]	2,581	$22,381
ITA 3(b)		
Taxable capital gains [(1/2)($1,320)]	$ 660	
Allowable capital losses [(1/2)($4,620)]	(2,310)	Nil
ITA 3(c)		$22,381
ITA 3(d)		
Farm loss (see note)		(6,750)
2018 Net income and taxable income		$15,631

Note Dale's farm losses are restricted as follows:

Total farm loss		$11,000
Deductible amount:		
First $2,500	($2,500)	
One-half of $8,500 ($11,000 - $2,500)	(4,250)	(6,750)
2018 Restricted farm loss carry forward		$ 4,250

As noted in the problem, none of the losses can be carried back before 2018. This would leave the following 2018 losses:

- 2018 Restricted farm loss $4,250
- 2018 Net capital loss ($2,310 - $660) $1,650

2019 Analysis
The required information can be calculated as follows:

ITA 3(a)		
Farm income	$2,200	
Taxable dividends [(138%)($2,351)]	3,244	$ 5,444
ITA 3(b)		
Taxable capital gains [(1/2)($2,200)]	$1,100	
Allowable capital losses	Nil	1,100
ITA 3(c)		$ 6,544
ITA 3(d)		
Business loss		(15,400)
2019 Net income		Nil
2018 Net capital loss carry forward		($ 1,100)
Taxable income		Nil

Since there are taxable capital gains this year, and the problem states that Dale would like to deduct the maximum amount of his net capital loss carry forwards, the net capital loss carry forward of $1,100 is added to the 2019 non-capital loss.

The non-capital loss carry over is calculated as follows:

Business loss	$15,400
2017 Net capital loss deducted	1,100
ITA 3(c) income	(6,544)
2019 Non-capital loss	$ 9,956

The entire non-capital loss carry over could be carried back to 2018, but since Dale requires $15,400 in taxable income to fully use his tax credits, the maximum carry back to 2018 is $231, calculated as follows:

2018 Taxable income (as reported)	$15,631
2019 Non-capital loss (ITA 111(1)(a))	(231)
2018 Amended taxable income (minimum)	$15,400

This carry back leaves Dale with his required $15,400 in taxable income. There would be the following carry forward balances at the end of 2019:

- 2018 Restricted farm loss (unchanged) — $4,250
- 2018 Net capital loss ($1,650 - $1,100)] — $ 550
- 2019 Non-capital loss ($9,956 - $231) — $9,725

2020 Analysis

The required information can be calculated as follows:

ITA 3(a)		
Business income	$33,000	
Farm income	3,465	
Taxable dividends [($3,160)(1.38)]	4,361	40,826
ITA 3(b)		
Taxable capital gains [(1/2)($4,400)]	$ 2,200	
Allowable capital losses	Nil	2,200
2020 Net income		$43,026
2018 Restricted farm loss (equal to farm income)		(3,465)
2018 Net capital loss (less than $2,200)		(550)
2019 Non-capital loss (All)		(9,725)
2020 Taxable income		$29,286

There would be the following carry forward balance at the end of 2020:

- 2018 Restricted farm loss ($4,250 - $3,465) — $785

2021 Analysis

The required information can be calculated as follows:

ITA 3(a)		
Taxable dividends [(138%)($5,140)]		$ 7,093
ITA 3(b)		
Taxable capital gains [(1/2)($4,950)]	$ 2,475	
Allowable capital losses [(1/2)($15,950)]	(7,975)	Nil
ITA 3(c)		$ 7,093
ITA 3(d)		
Non-farm business loss	($20,900)	
Farm loss	(2,200)	(23,100)
Net income and taxable income		Nil

The available non-capital loss can be calculated as follows:

Business loss	$20,900	
Farm loss (unrestricted)	2,200	$23,100
ITA 3(c) income		(7,093)
2021 Non-capital loss		$16,007

Although technically the farm loss carry over is accounted for separately from the non-capital loss, since the farm loss is less than $2,500 it is treated as an unrestricted farm loss and can be applied against all types of income. ITA 31 states that any loss allowed under that provision is considered an unrestricted loss from a farming business for the year for the purposes of calculating the non-capital loss carry over. As a result, the preceding loss carry over of $16,007 is available for carry back to 2020 to be applied against any type of income. Again, technically the 2021 farm loss carry over would be $2,200 and the 2021 non-capital loss would be $13,807.

With respect to the net capital loss of $5,500 [(ITA 3(b)(ii) $7,975 - ITA 3(b)(i) $2,475)], there are $1,650 ($2,200 - $550) in taxable capital gains remaining in 2020 as the basis for a carry back. This means that $1,650 of the 2021 net capital loss can be carried back, leaving $3,850 ($5,500 - $1,650) to be carried forward.

If both the $16,007 non-capital loss and the $1,650 net capital loss were carried back to 2019, the result would be taxable income of $11,629 ($29,286 - $16,007 - $1,650), less than the $15,400 that is required to fully use Dale's available tax credits. As the net capital loss can only be deducted to the extent of taxable capital gains, it would be advisable to claim the full amount of this loss carry back. Based on this view, the non-capital loss deduction will be limited to $12,236 ($29,286 - $15,400 - $1,650), an amount that will provide for full use of Dale's 2020 tax credits:

2020 Taxable income (as reported)	$29,286
2021 Non-capital loss	(12,236)
2021 Net capital loss	(1,650)
2020 Amended taxable income	$15,400

These carry backs leave Dale with his required $15,400 in 2020 taxable income. There would be the following carry forward balances at the end of 2021:

• 2018 Restricted farm loss (unchanged)	$ 785
• 2020 Net capital loss ($5,500 - $1,650)]	$3,850
• 2020 Non-capital loss (nil + $16,007 - $12,236)	$3,771

SSP 11-3 Solution

Capital losses only qualify as business investment losses (BIL) if they meet the conditions of ITA 39(1)(c). If the conditions are met a potential BIL is reduced to the extent that the capital gains deduction has been claimed in previous years. Any part of a capital loss that fails to meet these requirements remains a regular capital loss. Given this, the BIL would be calculated as follows:

2021 Capital loss (ACB $228,000 + selling cost $1,000 - POD $55,000)	$174,000
Reduction for previous capital gains deductions ($38,000 + $21,000)	(59,000)
BIL	$115,000
Inclusion rate	1/2
ABIL	$ 57,500

In effect the capital loss of $174,000 is equal to a BIL of $115,000 and a regular capital loss of $59,000.

Using this analysis, Mr. Barkin's minimum net income and taxable income would be calculated as follows:

Employment income		$115,000
ABIL		(57,500)
Net taxable capital gains:		
Taxable capital gain		
[(1/2)($328,000 - $153,000 - $2,000)]	$86,500	
Allowable capital loss (disallowed ABIL)		
[(1/2)($59,000)]	(29,500)	57,000
2021 Net income		$114,500
Capital gains deduction (Note 1)		Nil
2016 Net capital loss deducted (Note 2)		(13,700)
2021 Taxable income		$100,800

Note 1   As the only capital gains during 2021 are on qualified property, the simplified formula for the annual gains limit can be used. Given this, the lifetime capital gains deduction is nil, the least of:

Amount available [(1/2)($892,218)]*	$446,109
Amount used [(1/2)($38,000 + $21,000)]	(29,500)
Amount available	$416,609

*This is the 2021 limit for gains on dispositions of QSBC shares:

Net taxable capital gains ITA 3(b)	$57,000
ABIL realized	(57,500)
Annual gains limit prior to loss carry forward	Nil
Net capital loss deducted	(13,700)
Annual gains limit	Nil

Sum of annual gains limits ($19,000 + $10,500 + nil)	$29,500
Amounts deducted in previous years ($19,000 + $10,500)	(29,500)
CNIL	(4,800)
Cumulative gains limit	Nil

Note 2   Even without the deduction of the net capital loss carry forward, the annual gains limit was nil, preventing the deduction of any amount for the capital gains deduction. Given this, it is appropriate to deduct the 2016 net capital loss.

SSP 11-4 Solution
CASE A
There are multiple exclusions for Marty. The business is a related business to him since Miranda owns shares that are worth at least 10% of the value of the corporation's issued and outstanding shares. However, since he is actively engaged in the business on a regular, continuous, and substantial basis, the corporation is an excluded business to him. In addition, his shares are excluded shares, plus his past contributions to the business justify a reasonable return. Given all of these factors, Marty's dividends are not split income.

The business is a related business to Miranda both because of Marty's involvement in the corporate business and because Marty owns 10% or more of the FMV of the company's issued and outstanding shares. While Miranda is not actively engaged in the business the business would not be an excluded business. However, since she is 25 years of age or older and owns shares that represent 10% or more of both the number of voting rights and the FMV of the corporation's issued and outstanding shares the shares would be excluded shares. In addition, the company is not a professional corporation, less than 90% of its business involves performing services, and substantially all of its income is not from a related business. The dividends she received are therefore not split income.

CASE B

As Jerome is actively engaged in the business on a regular, continuous, and substantial basis, the corporation is an excluded business from his point of view. In addition, the business would not be a related business to Jerome. Finally, Jerome's contributions substantiate a reasonable return. Given all of these factors, Jerome's dividends are not split income.

While Jeff has not been active in the business in either 2020 or 2021, he worked full time in the business for more than the required five years (2014 through 2019). Given this, the corporation is an excluded business and Jeff's dividends will not be classified as split income. It is also arguable that Jeff may have an arm's-length capital and safe harbour capital return based on his past contributions, including the share purchase directly from the company.

CASE C

As Charles is actively engaged in the business on a regular, continuous, and substantial basis, the corporation is an excluded business to him. In addition, his shares would be excluded shares and past contributions are supportive of a reasonable return. Given these factors, Charles' dividends are not split income.

As Clifford has never been actively involved in Chill, it is not an excluded business from his point of view. However, Clifford is 25 years of age or older and owns more than 10% of the number of voting rights and the FMV of the Chill shares. In addition, Chill is not a professional corporation, less than 90% of its business involves performing services, and substantially all of its income is not from a related business. Given this, Clifford's shares would be excluded shares and the dividends he received would not be split income.

SSP 11-5 Solution
Part A—Taxable Income

Mr. and Mrs. Hanson's net income and taxable income would be calculated as follows:

	Mr. Hanson	Mrs. Hanson
Old Age Security benefits	$ 7,400	$ 7,400
RRIF income	50,000	Nil
Registered pension plan receipts	25,380	1,680
Dividends received ($800 + $180 ITA 82(3))	980	Nil
Gross up on dividends (38%)	372	Nil
Interest on government bonds	500	4,359
Net taxable capital gain	Nil	Nil
Net income before clawback	$84,632	$13,439
Social benefits repayment (see Note)	(718)	Nil
Net income and taxable income	$83,914	$13,439

> **Note** Mrs. Hanson would not have to repay any of her OAS benefits as her net income is well below the threshold income of $79,845. Mr. Hanson's social benefits repayment would be the lesser of:
>
> - $7,400, or
> - [(15%)($84,632 - $79,845)] = $718

Part A—Tax Credits

Mr. Hanson can claim a spousal credit in the amount of $121 [$13,808 - $13,687] prior to an ITA 82(3) election. The election under ITA 82(3) could be made since it would increase the spousal credit to $369 [$13,808 - ($13,687 - $180 - $68)]. The amount that can be transferred from Mrs. Hanson to Mr. Hanson is calculated as follows:

Age	$7,713
Pension (on RPP only)	1,680
Reduced by Mrs. Hanson's taxable income in excess of her basic personal tax credit ($13,439 - $13,808)	Nil
Credit base transferred to spouse	$9,393

Mr. Hanson's maximum tax credits would be as follows:

Basic personal amount	$13,808
Spousal credit [$13,808 - $13,439]	369
Age $7,713 - [(15%)($84,632 - $38,893)]	852
Pension	2,000
Transfers from Mrs. Hanson (see preceding calculations)	9,393
Total base	$26,422
Rate	15%
Total	$ 3,963
Dividend tax credit [(6/11)($372)]	203
Charitable donations [(15%)($200) + (29%)($600 + $200 - $200)]	204
Total credits	$ 4,370

Charitable donations can be claimed by either spouse, as long as the total donations are less than 75% of the claiming spouse's net income. As Mrs. Hanson has no tax payable, Mr. Hanson will claim her charitable donations. It is usually advantageous for one spouse to claim all the charitable donations if they total more than $200, as the low rate of credit is only applied once. Note that as none of Mr. Hanson's Ttxable income is subject to the 33% federal tax rate, that rate is not relevant to the calculation of charitable donations tax credit.

Part A—Loss Carry Overs
Mrs. Hanson's 2021 net capital loss of $175 [(1/2)($725 - $375)] can be carried back three years and forward indefinitely to be claimed against taxable capital gains.

Part B—Pension Income Splitting
The optimum use of pension income splitting would accomplish the following objectives:

- It would permit Mrs. Hanson to claim her dividend tax credit.
- It would permit Mrs. Hanson to fully use her pension income tax credit.
- It would eliminate Mr. Hanson's OAS clawback.
- It would enable both Mr. and Mrs. Hanson to be in the same 20.5% tax bracket.

SSP 11-6 Solution
Part A
Mr. and Mrs. Dalton's net income and taxable income would be calculated as follows:

	Mr. Dalton	Mrs. Dalton
Old Age Security benefits	$ 7,400	$ 7,400
Registered pension plan receipts	Nil	62,000
RRIF income	1,640	12,420
Interest on government bonds	1,420	2,580
Eligible dividends received	3,420	460
Gross up on dividends (38%)	1,300	175
Net income before clawback	$15,180	$85,035
Social benefits repayment (Note 1)	Nil	(779)
Net income and taxable income before any transfer of dividends	$15,180	$84,256

Note 1 Mr. Dalton would not have to repay any of his OAS benefits as his net income is less than the threshold income of $79,845. Mrs. Dalton's social benefits repayment would be the lesser of:

- $7,400, or
- [(15%)($85,035 - $79,845)] = $779.

Mr. Dalton's net federal tax payable would be calculated as follows:

Federal tax before credits [(15%)($15,180)]		$2,277
Tax credits		
Basic personal	($13,808)	
Other (transferred to Mrs. Dalton)	Nil	
Total base	($13,808)	
Rate	15%	(2,071)
Dividend tax credit [(6/11)($1,300)]		(709)
2021 Net federal tax payable		Nil

The transfer to Mrs. Dalton would be calculated as follows:

Credits available for transfer:		
Age		$ 7,713
Pension (limited to RRIF receipts)		1,640
Disability		8,662
Total available		$18,015
Reduced by excess of:		
Mr. Dalton's net income	($15,180)	
over basic personal credit amount	13,808	(1,372)
Available for transfer to Mrs. Dalton		$16,643

The amount owing for Mrs. Dalton would be calculated as follows:

Tax on first $49,020	$ 7,353	
Tax on next $35,236 ($84,256 - $49,020) at 20.5%	7,223	$14,576
Tax credits		
Basic personal	($13,808)	
Spousal including extra infirm amount		
($13,808 + $2,295 - $15,180)	(923)	
Additional caregiver amount (Note 2)	(6,425)	
Age {$7,713 - [(15%)($84,256 - $38,893)]}	(909)	
Pension	(2,000)	
Transfer from spouse (preceding calculation)	(16,643)	
Credit base	($40,708)	
Rate	15%	(6,106)
Charitable donations		
[(15%)($200) +(29%)($350 + $960 - $200)] (Note 3)		(352)
Dividend tax credit [(6/11)($175)]		(95)
Federal tax payable		$ 8,023
OAS clawback (Note 1)		779
Amount owing—Mrs. Dalton		$ 8,802

Note 2 Mr. Dalton's net income of $15,180 was below the Canada caregiver income threshold of $17,256. In the absence of the spousal credit, the Canada caregiver amount would have been $7,348. Given this, the additional Canada caregiver amount would be $6,425 ($7,348 - 923).

Note 3 Charitable donations can be claimed by either spouse, as long as the total donations are less than 75% of the claiming spouse's net income. As Mr. Dalton has no net federal tax payable, Mrs. Dalton will claim his charitable donations. It is usually advantageous for one spouse to claim all the charitable donations if they total more than $200, as the low rate of credit is only applied once. Note that as none of Mrs. Dalton's taxable income is subject to the 33% federal tax rate, that rate is not relevant to the calculation of her charitable donations tax credit.

Part B — Eligibility for Transfer

If Mr. Dalton transfers his dividends to Mrs. Dalton as a result of an election under ITA 82(3), the transfer would leave Mr. Dalton with a net income of $10,460 ($15,180 - $3,420 - $1,300). Based on this, her spousal credit would be $5,643 [($13,808 + $2,295 - $10,460)], an increase from the pre-transfer credit of $923. Given this, the elective transfer would be allowed.

Part C

If all of Mr. Dalton's dividends are transferred to Mrs. Dalton, the revised net income and taxable income amount would be calculated as follows:

	Mr. Dalton	Mrs. Dalton
Net income before clawback as per Part A	$15,180	$85,035
Dividend transfer	(3,420)	3,420
Gross up transfer	(1,300)	1,300
Net income after dividend transfer before clawback	$10,460	$89,755
Social benefits repayment (Note 4)	Nil	(1,487)
Revised net income and taxable income	$10,460	$88,268

Note 4 Mr. Dalton would not have to repay any of his OAS benefits as his net income is less than the threshold income of $79,845. Mrs. Dalton's social benefits repayment would be the lesser of:

- $7,400, or
- [(15%)($89,755 - $79,845)] = $1,487.

As Mr. Dalton's revised income figure is below the basic personal credit of $13,808, his net federal tax payable would continue to be nil. The transfer to Mrs. Dalton would be calculated as follows:

Credits available for transfer:		
Age		$ 7,713
Pension (limited to RRIF receipts)		1,640
Disability		8,662
Total available		$18,015
Reduced by excess of:		
Mr. Dalton's net income	($10,460)	
over basic personal credit amount	13,808	(Nil)
Available for transfer		$18,015

With respect to Mrs. Dalton, her amount owing would be calculated as follows:

Tax on first $49,020	$7,353	
Tax on next $39,248 ($88,268 - $49,020) at 20.5%	8,046	$15,399
Tax credits		
Basic personal	($13,808)	
Spousal including infirm amount		
($13,808 + $2,295 - $10,460)	(5,643)	
Additional caregiver amount (Note 5)	(1,705)	
Age {$7,713 - [(15%)($88,268 - $38,893)]}	(307)	
Pension	(2,000)	
Transfer from spouse (preceding calculation)	(18,015)	
Credit base	($41,478)	
Rate	15%	(6,222)
Charitable donations [(15%)($200) +		
(29%)($350 + $960 - $200)]		(352)
Dividend tax credit [(6/11)($175 + $1,300)]		(805)
Federal tax payable		$ 8,020
OAS clawback (Note 4)		1,487
Amount owing—Mrs. Dalton		$ 9,507

Note 5 As was the case before the transfer of dividends, Mr. Dalton's net income of $10,460 is below the Canada caregiver income threshold of $17,256. In the absence of the spousal credit, the Canada caregiver amount would have been $7,348. Given this, the additional Canada caregiver amount would be $1,705 ($7,348 - $5,643).

Conclusion

The use of the ITA 82(3) dividend transfer has decreased Mrs. Dalton's federal tax payable by $3 ($8,023 - $8,020). However, it has increased her OAS clawback by $708 ($1,487 - $779). Since the net effect is an increase in the amount owing of $705 ($9,507 - $8,802), the dividend transfer should not be done.

SSP 11-7 Solution

The regular net federal tax payable calculations would be as follows:

	Walter	Wendel	Winston
Employment and business income	$ 52,100	$42,300	$ 41,300
Eligible dividends received	82,300	Nil	12,300
Dividend gross up (38%)	31,274	Nil	4,674
RRSP deduction	Nil	(27,000)	Nil
Taxable capital gains	36,400	Nil	226,550
Net income	$202,074	$15,300	$284,824
Lifetime capital gains deduction	(36,400)	Nil	(221,500)
Taxable income	$165,674	$15,300	$ 63,324
Federal tax (Note 2)	$ 35,398	$ 2,295	$ 10,285
Basic personal credit	(1,910)	(2,071)	(1,863)
Dividend tax credit (6/11 of gross up)	(17,059)	Nil	(2,549)
Regular federal tax payable	$ 16,429	$ 224	$ 5,873

Note 1 Walter's basic personal amount would be calculated as follows:

$13,808 - [($1,387][($202,074 - $151,978) ÷ $64,533] = $12,731

Walter's credit would be $1,910 [(15%)($12,731)]. Since Wendel's net income is less than $151,978 his basic personal credit is equal to $13,808, or $2,071 when the 15% tax credit rate is applied. Since Winston's net income exceeds $216,511 his basic personal credit is equal to $12,421, or $1,863 when the 15% tax credit rate is applied.

Note 2 The federal tax payable, before the dividend tax credit, is as follows:

	Taxable Income	Federal Tax Calculations	Federal Tax
Walter	$165,674	$31,426 + (29%)($13,696)	$35,398
Wendel	$ 15,300	(15%)($15,300)	$ 2,295
Winston	$ 63,324	$7,353 + (20.5%)($14,304)	$10,285

The alternative minimum tax (AMT) calculations would be as follows:

	Walter	Wendel	Winston
Regular taxable income	$165,674	$15,300	$ 63,324
60% of taxable capital gains	21,840	Nil	135,930
Dividend gross up	(31,274)	Nil	(4,674)
Adjusted taxable income	$156,240	$15,300	$194,580
AMT exemption	(40,000)	(40,000)	(40,000)
AMT base	$116,240	$ Nil	$154,580
Rate	15%	15%	15%
Federal AMT before credit	$ 17,436	$ Nil	$ 23,187
Basic personal credit	(1,910)	(2,071)	(1,863)
Federal AMT	$ 15,526	Nil	$ 21,324
Regular federal tax payable	(16,429)	(224)	(5,873)
Additional tax required (Note 3)	Nil	Nil	$ 15,451

Note 3 The excess AMT over regular tax payable for Winston of $15,451 can be carried forward for seven years and applied against any future excess of regular tax payable over the AMT.

SSP 11-8 Solution
Part A—Net Income
Ms. Worthmore's minimum taxable income is calculated as follows:

Employment income		
Gross salary—Intra Graphics	$73,532	
Gross salary—Lindworth Inc.	2,500	
RPP contributions	(1,233)	$74,799
Income from property		
Eligible dividend attribution (Note One)	$ 182	
Gross up [(38%)($182)]	69	
Non-eligible dividends from Lindworth	4,325	
Gross up [(15%)($4,325)]	649	5,225
Taxable capital gains		
Attribution from husband (Note Two)	$ 1,144	
Transfer to Jayne (Note Three)	122	
Lackmere shares (Note Four)	394	
Agricultural land (Note Five)	9,000	10,660
Other income and deductions		
Spousal support payments [($225)(12)]	($ 2,700)	
RRSP deduction (Note Six)	(6,849)	(9,549)
Deductible CPP ($3,166 - $2,876)	(290)	(9,839)
2021 Net income		$80,845

Note One   There would be income attribution for the $182 [($3.50)(52)] in dividends received by Mr. Dalton on the shares received as a gift.

Note Two   In the case of transfers to a spouse, unless an election is made to avoid the rollover of ITA 73(1), capital property is transferred at the ACB to the transferor. As a result, no capital gains were recognized at the time of the transfer. However, when Mr. Dalton sells the shares on August 31, 2021, there would be attribution of taxable capital gains in the amount of $1,144 [($56 - $12)(52)(1/2)].

Note Three   In the case of a gift to a minor child, it is treated as a deemed disposition at FMV. This results in a taxable capital gain at the time of transfer in the amount of $122 [($27 - $18)(27)(1/2)].

Note Four   The taxable capital gain on the Lackmere Ltd. shares would be computed using the average value for the shares as a result of ITA 47(1). The average value would be calculated as follows:

122 shares at $92	$11,224
178 shares at $71	12,638
Total cost	$23,862
Average cost ($23,862 ÷ 300 shares)	$ 79.54

Based on this, the gain would be calculated as follows:

POD [(122)($86)]	$10,492
ACB [(122)($79.54)]	(9,704)
Capital gain	$788
Inclusion rate	1/2
Taxable capital gain	$ 394

Note Five   When there is a non-arm's-length transfer of property for consideration of less than FMV, ITA 69(1) deems that, for the transferor, the transfer takes place at FMV. Given this, the taxable capital gain would be calculated as follows:

Deemed POD (FMV)	$28,000
ACB	(10,000)
Capital gain	$18,000
Inclusion rate	1/2
Taxable capital gain	$ 9,000

Note Six   Ms. Worthmore's 2020 earned income (assumed to be equal to the 2021 figure) is as follows:

Gross salary—Intra	$73,532
Gross salary—Lindworth	2,500
Spousal support paid and deducted [(12)($225)]	(2,700)
Earned income	$73,332

Ms. Worthmore's maximum deductible 2021 RRSP contribution is calculated as follows:

Unused deduction room—End of 2020	Nil
Lesser of:	
• 2021 RRSP dollar limit = $27,830	
• [(18%)($73,332)] = $13,200	$13,200
Less 2020 PA	(6,351)
2021 Maximum deductible RRSP contribution	$ 6,849

This means the excess contribution of $651 ($7,500 - $6,849) can be carried forward and deducted in future years.

Part B — Taxable Income
As Ms. Worthmore has no taxable income deductions, her net income and taxable income are both the same at $80,845.

Part C — Tax Payable
Ms. Worthmore's federal tax payable can be calculated as follows:

Tax on first $49,020		$ 7,353
Tax on next $31,825 ($80,845 - $49,020) at 20.5%		6,524
Gross federal tax payable		$13,877
Basic personal amount	($13,808)	
Spousal $13,808 - $1,065	(12,743)	
CPP contribution	(2,876)	
EI premiums	(890)	
Canada employment	(1,257)	
Transfer of spouse's tuition credit—Lesser of:		
• Absolute limit of $5,000		
• Tuition paid of $2,300	(2,300)	
Medical expenses (Note Seven)	(10,685)	
Credit base	($44,559)	
Rate	15%	(6,684)
Eligible dividend tax credit [(6/11)($69)]		(38)
Non-eligible dividend tax credit [(9/13)($649)]		(449)
Charitable donations (Note Eight)		
[(15%)($200) + (29%)($342 - $200)]		(71)
Political contributions [(3/4)($100)]		(75)
2021 Net federal tax payable		$ 6,560

Note Seven Ms. Worthmore can claim all of the medical expenses of her husband and daughters, Joyce and June, without taking into consideration June's income, as she is under 18 years of age. Allowable medical expenses are as follows:

John Dalton, Joyce, and June medical expenses	
($1,056 + $2,200 + $9,850)	$13,106
Threshold—Lesser of:	
[(3%)($80,845)] = $2,425	
2021 Limit of $2,421	(2,421)
Allowable medical expenses	$10,685

Note Eight As none of her taxable income is subject to the 33% tax rate, this rate does not apply to the calculation of the charitable donations tax credit.

SSP 11-9 Solution
Taxable Income

Mr. Slater's net income and taxable income would be calculated as follows:

Employment income—Salary		$ 35,000
Non-farming business income ($28,300 - $2,300—Note One)		26,000
Property income:		
Interest on savings account	$ 4,450	
Interest on loans to friends	12,000	
Eligible Canadian dividends	44,000	
Gross up [($44,000)(38%)]	16,720	
Dividends from U.S. corporations		
(before withholding, no gross up)	10,000	87,170
Taxable capital gain [(1/2)($111,500 - $23,000)]		44,250
CPP benefits		5,100
OAS benefits (Note One)		7,400
Farm loss (Note Two)		(5,750)
Net income before OAS repayment		$199,170
OAS repayment (Note Three)—Lesser of:		
• $7,400		
• $17,899 [(15%)($199,170 - $79,845)]		(7,400)
2021 Net income and taxable income		$191,770

Note One Drawings from any business carried on as a sole proprietorship have no impact on net income since the funds belong to the sole proprietor. This would be different if the business were incorporated, as the funds would belong to the corporation. Personal funds represent a capital investment and would not be deductible (ITA 18(1)(b)). The $2,300 in interest, however, would be deductible (ITA 20(1)(c) since the loan proceeds were used to capitalize the business.

Note Two Since Mr. Slater's farming business is not a chief source of income, his farm loss would be subject to ITA 31 and restricted as follows:

Farm revenues	$36,000
Farm expenses	(45,000)
Total farm loss	($ 9,000)
Unrestricted loss [$2,500 + (1/2)($9,000 - $2,500)]	5,750
2021 Restricted farm loss	($ 3,250)

The $3,250 restricted farm loss could be carried back to the preceding three years (2018 to 2020) and forward for 20 years (to 2041) to be deducted against farming income only.

Note Three Technically Mr. Slater was entitled to the OAS of $7,400, but it was withheld because of the OAS clawback. ITA 153(3) deems the amount to have been received in this circumstance, therefore it must be included in net income.

Tax Payable

Mr. Slater's federal tax payable would be calculated as follows:

Tax on first $151,978		$31,426
Tax on next $39,792 ($191,770 - $151,978) at 29%		11,540
Gross federal tax		$42,966
Tax credits:		
Basic personal amount (Note Four)	($12,953)	
Spousal, including extra amount for infirmity		
($12,953 + $2,295)	(15,248)	
Mr. Slater's age		
{$7,713 - [(15%)($191,770 - $38,893)]}	Nil	
Spouse's disability	(8,662)	
Canada employment	(1,257)	
Credit base	($38,120)	
Rate	15%	(5,718)
Charitable donations (Note Five)		
[(15%)($200) + (29%)($2,700 - $200)]		(755)
Subtotal = Tax otherwise payable for foreign tax credit		$36,493
Dividend tax credit [(6/11)($16,720)]		(9,120)
Foreign tax credit (Note Six)		(1,500)
Federal political contributions tax credit (Note Seven)		(350)
OAS clawback		7,400
OAS withheld		(7,400)
2021 Net federal tax payable		$25,523

Note Four   The basic personal amount would be calculated as follows:

$$\$13,808 - [\$1,387][(\$191,770 - \$151,978) \div \$64,533] = \$12,953$$

Note Five   As none of his taxable income is subject to the 33% tax rate, this rate will not aply to the calculation of the charitable donations tax credit.

Note Six   The federal foreign tax credit will be the lesser of the foreign tax actually paid of $1,500 and an amount determined by the following formula:

$$\left[\frac{\text{Foreign Non–Business Income}}{\text{Adjusted Division B Income}} \right] [\text{Tax Otherwise Payable}]$$

The tax otherwise payable is equal to federal tax payable before the dividend tax credit and political contributions tax credit is deducted (the subtotal in the preceding table). This amount would be $1,903 [($10,000 ÷ $191,770)($36,493)], leaving the actual taxes of $1,500 as the lesser amount.

Note Seven   The political contributions tax credit can be calculated as follows:

3/4 of first $400	$300
1/2 of the next $100	50
Total credit	$350

Other Notes

- The net gambling wins would not be a source of income given the facts.
- Inheritances are not a source of income nor are they required to be included in income.

- The life insurance premiums are personal expenditures and therefore not deductible (ITA 18(1)(a) and (h)).
- The mortgage payments on his personal residence are also not deductible (ITA 18(1)(a) and (h)).

SSP 11-10 Solution
Deemed Dispositions Immediately before Death
Immediately before the time of Mrs. Steele's death, there is a deemed disposition of all of her capital property. If the beneficiary is a spouse, the deemed POD will, in general, be equal to the tax cost of the property (ACB or UCC). If Andrea's representatives choose to do so, they can elect out of this rollover and treat the disposition at POD equal to the FMV.

Principal Residence to Daughter
The bequest of the family home to her daughter would normally result in a capital gain of $134,600 ($544,000 - $409,400). As it appears to have been Mrs. Steele's principal residence throughout the years of ownership, the principal residence exemption would reduce the gain to nil (ITA 40(2)(b)).

Other Properties at Death
Under ITA 70(6), capital property may be transferred at death to a spouse on the basis of ACB for non-depreciable capital property or its UCC in the case of depreciable property. This means that the Rolston Inc. shares, the painting, and the depreciable property of the boutique can be transferred to Mr. Steele with no income tax consequences in Mrs. Steele's final income tax return. Mr. Steele will inherit the tax values of the transferred properties immediately prior to Mrs. Steele's death.

Although the AGF Industries shares would also be eligible for the spousal rollover, it would not be advantageous to do so as there is an unrealized capital loss on these shares. It would be preferable for the legal representative of Mrs. Steele to elect in the final return to have the AGF Industries shares transferred to Mr. Steele at FMV in order to use the capital loss. Electing out of ITA 70(6) is implemented in the final tax return and does not require filing a form.

There is no rollover available for the rental property as that is being transferred to her daughter. There is a taxable capital gain for the rental property on both the building and the land and recaptured CCA on the building.

The allowable capital loss resulting from the election on the shares and the taxable capital gains and recaptured CCA on the deemed disposition of the rental property can be calculated as follows:

	AGF Shares	Land	Building
FMV deemed POD	$ 7,900	$164,000	$235,000
ACB	(10,600)	(92,000)	(183,000)
Capital gain (loss)	($ 2,700)	$ 72,000	$ 52,000
Inclusion rate	1/2	1/2	1/2
Taxable capital gain (allowable capital loss)	($ 1,350)	$ 36,000	$ 26,000

	Building
Lesser of capital cost and deemed POD	$183,000
UCC	(144,800)
Recapture of CCA	$ 38,200

Mortgage Interest—Attribution
With respect to the mortgage interest received by Mr. Steele, it was earned on mortgages given to him by Mrs. Steele and, as a consequence, it would be attributed to her up until her death on

June 3, 2021. This means that $886 [(154/365)($2,100)] of the $2,100 would be included in her net income. As attribution from a spouse ceases when the transferor spouse dies, the remaining $1,214 ($2,100 - $886) would be included in Mr. Steele's net income. When this is combined with his $425 boutique salary, his net income for the year is $1,639. His net income for the whole year, not just prior to Mrs. Steele's death, will decrease the spousal credit available on Mrs. Steele's final return.

Net Income and Taxable Income

Mrs. Steele's minimum taxable income (ignoring CPP) would be calculated as follows:

Business income		$ 55,200
Property income:		
Eligible dividends received	$ 1,090	
Gross up [(38%)($1,090)]	414	
Interest	2,025	
Attributed mortgage interest (Note One)	886	
Rent revenues	41,200	
Rental expenses (Note Two)	(24,650)	
Recaptured CCA on rental property	38,200	59,165
Net taxable capital gains:		
Taxable capital gains on rental property		
($26,000 + $36,000)	$62,000	
Allowable capital loss on AGF Industries shares	(1,350)	60,650
Net income		$175,015
2018 Net capital loss (Note Three)		(76,500)
Taxable income		$ 98,515

Note One Income attribution would cease with Ms. Steele's death on June 3, 154 days into 2021. Given this, the amount of mortgage interest attribution would be $886 [(2,100)(154/365)].

Note Two As there was a deemed disposition of the rental property immediately before the time of Mrs. Steele's death, no CCA can be taken for 2021 since the UCC at year end would be nil.

Note Three In the year of death, any allowable capital losses can be deducted against the total taxable capital gains and then any net capital losses can be deducted against any type of income, not just capital gains, as long as the capital gains deduction has not been claimed. As a result, although she has net taxable capital gains of only $60,650, she can deduct her total 2018 net capital loss carry forward of $76,500 (ITA 111(2)).

Tax Payable

Mrs. Steele's minimum net federal tax payable would be calculated as follows:

Tax on first $98,040		$17,402
Tax on remaining $475 ($98,515 - $98,040) at 26%		124
Gross federal tax		$17,526
Basic personal amount	($13,808)	
Spousal ($13,808 - $1,639)	(12,169)	
Credit base	($25,977)	
Rate	15%	(3,897)
Dividend tax credit [(6/11)($414)]		(226)
Net federal tax payable		$13,403

SSP 11-11 Solution
Part A—Taxable Income

Daniel Tong's employment income would be calculated as follows:

Inclusions:		
Salary	$78,000	
2020 bonus (cash basis)	6,000	
Home office allowance	2,400	
Standby charge—No reduction [($5,200)(2/3)]	3,467	
Automobile operating benefit [(14,000 km)($0.27)]	3,780	
Group term life insurance premium	650	
Dental insurance	N/A	
Stock option benefit [(2,500)($15 - $12)]	7,500	$101,797
Deductions:		
Company pension contributions	($ 3,900)	
Home office [(30/300)($2,100 + $750)]	(285)	
Office supplies	(230)	(4,415)
Employment income		**$ 97,382**

Notes

- In general, the only home office costs that can be deducted are utilities and maintenance (ITA 8(1)(i)). In the case of employees with commission income, a pro rata share of insurance and property taxes would also be deductible (ITA 8(1)(f)). However, it does not appear that Mr. Tong has any commission income.
- As the only capital costs that are deductible by an employee are those related to an automobile, aircraft, or musical instrument, the cost of the computer and peripherals are not deductible (ITA 8(2)).
- The use of employment-related frequent flyer points is typically not considered a taxable benefit by the CRA.

Mr. Tong's net income and taxable income would be calculated as follows:

Employment income (see preceding calculations)		$ 97,382
Business income—Sale of automobile		
[$14,500 - ($2,500 + $8,100)]		3,900
Property income:		
Portus dividends received	$4,500	
Gross up [(38%)($4,500)]	1,710	
Less interest expense	(1,200)	5,010
Spousal RRSP withdrawal (attributed to Mr. Tong)		1,000
Net taxable capital gain:		
Taxable capital gain on Portus shares (Note 1)	$3,581	
Allowable capital loss on global shares (Note 2)	Nil	3,581
RRSP contribution (Note 3)		(10,200)
Deductible CPP ($3,166 - $2,876)		(290)
2021 Net income		**$100,383**
Stock option benefit [(1/2)($7,500)]		(3,750)
Net capital loss carry forward (Note 4)		(3,581)
2021 Taxable income		**$ 93,052**

Note 1 For shares acquired through the exercise of stock options, the ACB is the FMV of the shares at the time of exercise. Based on this, the average cost of his Portus Ltd. shares is calculated as follows:

2,500 shares at $15	$37,500
250 shares at $18	4,500
Total ACB	$42,000

Based on this total, the average cost per share is $15.27 ($42,000 ÷ 2,750) (ITA 47(1)). Using this figure, the taxable capital gain would be calculated as follows:

POD [(1,250)($21)]	$26,250
Adjusted cost base [(1,250)($15.27)]	(19,088)
Capital gain	$ 7,162
Inclusion rate	1/2
Taxable capital gain	$ 3,581

Note 2 The $2,400 loss ($8,600 - $11,000) is deemed to be superficial, as Mr. Tong repurchased more than 800 Global shares within 30 days of the original disposition. This means that the loss will be disallowed. However, it will be added to the ACB of the replacement shares, giving a total ACB of $8,200 ($5,800 + $2,400).

Note 3 Mr. Tong's 2021 RRSP deduction room would be calculated as follows:

Lesser of:	
2021 RRSP limit = $27,830	
18% of $61,500 = $11,070	$11,070
2020 pension adjustment	Nil
Total 2021 deduction room	$11,070

While he has $11,070 in deduction room, his actual deduction is limited to $10,200, his $2,200 in undeducted contributions from the beginning of the year, plus his $8,000 contribution to his wife's RRSP.

Note 4 Mr. Tong has a net capital loss balance of $11,500 ($2,500 + $6,000 + $3,000). However, the amount that can be deducted is limited to the 2021 net taxable capital gains of $3,581. ITA 111(3) requires that the oldest loss carry overs be applied first. As a result, the 2014 net capital loss is nil , the 2016 net capital loss balance is $4,919 [$6,000 - ($3,581 deducted - 2014 net capital loss $2,500)], and the 2017 net capital loss balance is unchanged at $3,000. This will leave a net capital loss balance of $7,919 ($11,500 - $3,581).

Part B—Tax Payable

Mr. Tong's minimum net federal tax payable is calculated as follows:

Tax on first $49,020		$ 7,353
Tax on next $44,032 ($93,052 - $49,020) at 20.5%		9,027
Gross federal tax		$16,380
Basic personal amount	($13,808)	
Spousal	(13,808)	
CPP	(2,876)	
EI	(890)	
Canada employment	(1,257)	
Transfer of tuition (Note 5)	(5,000)	
Credit base	($37,639)	
Rate	15%	(5,646)
Dividend tax credit [(6/11)($1,710)]		(933)
2021 Net federal tax payable		$ 9,801

Note 5 Marion's net federal tax payable is nil as the scholarship is eligible for the scholarship exemption and therefore no amount is included in net and taxable income.

Interest income	$ 3,000
Scholarship ($10,000 - $10,000)	Nil
Taxable income	$ 3,000
Basic personal amount	(13,808)
2021 Net federal tax payable	Nil

As Marion is unable to use any of her tuition credit, the transfer is the lesser of:

- the absolute limit of $5,000; or
- the actual tuition cost of $7,150.

Given this, the maximum transfer is $5,000. However, the $2,150 ($7,150 - $5,000) excess can be carried forward indefinitely, but can only be used by Marion.

Part B — Carry Forwards

- From Note 4, there is a 2016 net capital loss of $4,919 and a 2017 net capital loss of $3,000.
- From Note 5, Marion has a $2,150 tuition amount available for carry forward to subsequent years.

Solution to Tax Software Self-Study Problem — Chapter 11

The complete 2020 tax return is available on the MyLab in two versions, a T1 ProFile return file and a .PDF file.

For more information on how to use the ProFile tax program, refer to the Chapter 4 sample tax return in this Study Guide.

Notes to Tax Return

- Diane transfers the $5,000 maximum tuition amount to Eleanor and carries forward the remaining $2,000 [$7,000 - $5,000]. The carry forward can only be used by Diane.

- Eleanor cannot claim the charitable donation made by Diane, but Diane can carry it forward for up to five years.

- Since Amy is under 18 and wholly dependent, Eleanor claimed the eligible dependant credit for Amy.

- Note that, because Marjorie is not infirm, Eleanor can claim no credit for her.

- Since Diane and Marjorie are over 17 years of age, their medical expenses are reduced by 3% of their net income. This means that none of Marjorie's medical expenses can be claimed by Eleanor.

- In calculating work space in the home costs, the home insurance is not deductible as the T4 information shows she has no commission income. The car insurance is not relevant as there is no information that Eleanor uses her car for employment-related purposes.

- The Croft Computer Camp was an overnight camp, which means that the deductible costs are limited to $125 per week, a total of $250 [(2)($125)]. In contrast, there is no limit on the costs of day camps. This provides for the deduction of the entire $400 cost of the Y Day Camp.

- Since Eleanor is currently renting out her house, but plans to move back into it, no CCA is taken on the class 1 building to preserve her principal residence status. Since she had a rental loss in the previous year, and the cost is equal to the UCC, no CCA has been taken on the building nor on the washer/dryer. Her CCA on the class 8 property would not affect her principal residence election and should be taken. The payments on principal are not deductible as they are capital expenditures disallowed by ITA 18(1)(b) but allowed as a CCA claim.

  The purchase of the appliances in 2020 is eligible for the AccII, which applies to depreciable property acquired in arm's-length transactions between November 21, 2018, and December 31, 2023. The appliances were acquired within this period and are therefore eligible for enhanced CCA under the AccII rules for the year of purchase. The CCA would be calculated as [(20%)($921) + (20%)(1.5)(1,500)], which equals $634.20.

  Given her inheritance, she should have more than sufficient funds to pay her income taxes without taking CCA on her rental property.

Tax Planning Points

- Since Marjorie is taking care of Amy and is over 18 years old, Eleanor could pay her for child care costs and deduct them. Given Marjorie's low income, it is probable that Eleanor is already providing some funds to her. The amount should be calculated on a basis that is no more than the going rate per hour for similar services for the time when Amy is home and Eleanor is not. As long as Marjorie's income remains below the basic personal credit plus the age credit, it would not result in any income tax liability for Marjorie. Since she is over 80 years old, there would be no CPP liability.

- Although she is not required to file, Marjorie should file a tax return, otherwise she will not be eligible for the GST credit. If Eleanor pays her for child care in the future, filing a tax return could also reduce the probability that Eleanor will be asked for proof of payment.

- Although she is not required to file, Diane should file a tax return, otherwise she will not be eligible for the GST credit and she will not benefit from the RRSP deduction room created during the year. Filing a tax return will also make her tuition tax credit and charitable donation tax credit easier to keep track of for carry forward purposes.

- With the inflow of funds from the inheritance, Eleanor should review her debt outstanding and pay off any balances that have non-deductible interest, such as credit card balances. Although it is not exactly a tax planning point, Eleanor should compare the after-tax cost of the interest she is paying on her rental property mortgage with the after-tax yields that she can obtain on her investments to determine whether she should pay off her mortgage.

Part B

The maximum deductible RRSP contribution that Eleanor can make for 2021 is calculated as $4,440 by the program on the form "RRSP Limit." To access the form, press <F4> and type "rrsplimit" in the form box.

Note that if Eleanor chooses to deduct CCA on her rental building and reduce her net rental income to nil, her maximum deductible RRSP contribution will be reduced by $946 [(18%) ($5,253)] since rental income is earned income for RRSP purposes. This is another reason she should not take CCA on the rental building.

Given her inheritance, Eleanor should contribute the maximum deductible RRSP contribution as early in 2021 as possible. For the 2020 year Eleanor could have made an additional contribution of $1,667 equal to her unused deduction room at the end of 2019.

Eleanor should open an RESP for Amy if she has not already done so. How much she should contribute will depend on many factors (see the text coverage of RESPs), but she should request that her accountant create a contribution schedule that will maximize Canada Education Savings Plan contributions and optimize RESP contributions.

Eleanor should open TFSAs for herself, Diane, and possibly Marjorie and determine how much she should contribute to each. This would involve many investment and budgeting factors, as well as her future financial plans. Since the contributions are not deductible and the withdrawals are not taxable, the TFSAs will not have an effect on any of the tax returns.

Given her inheritance she should also consider overcontributing up to $2,000 to her RRSP, which would allow her to take advantage of the tax-free earnings in the RRSP without penalty. This would only be advantageous as long as she plans to have earned income for RRSP purposes sufficient to deduct the $2,000 in the future.

CHAPTER 12

Learning Objectives

After completing Chapter 12, you should be able to:

1. Explain the basic differences or similarities in determining net income, taxable income, and taxes payable for corporations and individuals (Paragraph [P hereafter] 12-1 to 12-7).
2. Briefly describe the four general tax payable deductions available to Canadian corporations and how these deductions contribute toward identfying general corporate tax rates by type of income and corporation (P 12-8 to 12-13)
3. Calculate a corporation's net income for ITA purposes (P 12-14 to 12-17).
4. List the deductions that are available to corporations in calculating taxable income (P 12-18 to 12-19).
5. Explain the purpose of ITA 112 in terms of integration and the impact on a corporation's net income and taxable income (P 12-20 to 12-24).
6. Explain the purpose of ITA 112(3), how it applies, and the circumstances under which it would not apply (P 12-25 to 12-28).
7. Describe the general income tax treatment when foreign dividends are received (P 12-29).
8. Apply and calculate the non-capital losses rules to a corporation (P 12-30 to 12-36).
9. Explain the factors that are relevant in deciding the optimum ordering of the taxable income deductions (P 12-37 to 12-42).
10. Describe and apply the rules that allocate corporate income to specific provinces (P 12-43 to 12-50).
11. Apply the basic corporate tax rate and explain the effect of the federal tax abatement and the general rate reduction (P 12-51 to 12-57).
12. Calculate provincial tax payable for a corporation using a supplied schedule of rates and other data (P 12-58 to 12-68).
13. List the important non-revenue-raising goals of the corporate tax system (P 12-69 and 12-70).
14. Explain the rules for determining which corporations and what amounts of income are eligible for the small business deduction (P 12-71 to 12-80).
15. Describe the main characteristics of a CCPC and the circumstances where CCPC status could change (P 12-81 to 12-84).
16. Explain the meaning of an "active business," including the interaction with income from property and the meaning and implications of a "specified investment business" (P 12-85 to 12-98).
17. Describe and calculate the amount of the small business deduction (P 12-99 to 12-109).
18. Explain why the government introduced the TCEC and AAII grinds to the small business limit. Calculate and apply the reduction to the small business deduction (P 12-110 to 12-127).
19. Describe a personal services business, explain why the concept was added to the ITA, and describe the tax treatment (P 12-128 to 12-137).
20. Explain the meaning of a professional corporation and why corporations are created to provide management services (P 12-138 and 12-139).

21. Calculate the M&P deduction for all types of corporations and explain whether the M&P deduction is still relevant and why (P 12-140 to 12-157).
22. Calculate the general rate reduction that is available to all corporations and the specific application of the general rate reduction to CCPCs (P 12-158 to 12-171).
23. Calculate the foreign non-business (property) and business income tax credits for corporations and explain and apply the rules that deal with any excess of foreign tax withheld over the allowable foreign tax credit (P 12-172 to 12-182).
24. Describe the basic concept of the refundable journalism labour tax credit (P 12-183 to 12-186).

How to Work through Chapter 12

Visit pearsonmylabandmastering.com to access MyLab Accounting for this text. Once there, you can access student resources such as Self-Study Problems, Practice Exams, Flashcards, updates, and more.

We recommend the following approach in dealing with the material in this chapter:

Introduction
- Read paragraph 12-1 to 12-7.

Corporate Income Tax Payable — The Basics
- Read paragraph 12-8 to 12-13.

Computation of Net Income
- Read paragraph 12-14 to 12-17.
- Do Exercise 12-1 (in the text) and check the solution in this Study Guide.
- Do Self-Study Problem 12-1, which is available on MyLab, and check the solution in this Study Guide.

Computation of Taxable Income
- Read paragraph 12-18 to 12-19.

Taxable Dividends from Taxable Canadian Corporations
- Read paragraph 12-20 to 12-22.
- Do Exercise 12-2 and check the solution in this Study Guide.
- Read paragraph 12-23 to 12-24.

Dividend Stop Loss Rule — ITA 112(3)
- Read paragraph 12-25 to 12-28.
- Do Exercise 12-3 and check the solution in this Study Guide.
- Do Self-Study Problem 12-2 and check the solution in this Study Guide.
- Read paragraph 12-29.

Non-Capital Loss Carry Over for a Corporation
- Read paragraph 12-30 to 12-36.
- Do Exercises 12-4 and 12-5 and check the solutions in this Study Guide.

Ordering of Taxable Income Deductions
- Read paragraph 12-37 to 12-42.
- Do Self-Study Problems 12-3 and 12-4 and check the solutions in this Study Guide.

Geographical Allocation of Income
- Read paragraph 12-43 to 12-50.
- Do Self-Study Problem 12-5 and check the solution in this Study Guide.

Federal Tax Payable
- Read paragraph 12-51 to 12-57.
- Do Exercise 12-6 and check the solution in this Study Guide.

Provincial Tax Payable
- Read paragraph 12-58 to 12-68.

Other Goals of the Corporate Tax System
- Read paragraph 12-69 to 12-70.

Small Business Deduction—ITA 125
- Read paragraph 12-71 to 12-109.
- Do Exercise 12-7 and check the solution in this Study Guide.

Small Business Deduction—ITA 125(5.1)
- Read paragraph 12-110 to 12-121.
- Do Exercise 12-8 and check the solution in this Study Guide.
- Read paragraph 12-122 to 12-124.
- Do Exercise 12-9 and check the solution in this Study Guide.
- Read paragraph 12-125 to 12-127.
- Do Exercise 12-10 and check the solution in this Study Guide.

Personal Services Businesses and Professional and Management Companies
- Read paragraph 12-128 to 12-139.

Manufacturing and Processing Profits Deduction—ITA 125.1
- Read paragraph 12-140 to 12-157.
- Do Exercise 12-11 and check the solution in this Study Guide.

General Rate Reduction—ITA 123.4
- Read paragraph 12-158 to 12-165.
- Do Exercise 12-12 and check the solution in this Study Guide.
- Read paragraph 12-166 to 12-171.
- Do Exercise 12-13 and check the solution in this Study Guide.
- Do Self-Study Problems 12-6 to 12-9 and check the solutions in this Study Guide.

Foreign Income Tax Credits for Corporations—ITA 126
- Read paragraph 12-172 to 12-182.
- Do Exercise 12-14 and check the solution in this Study Guide.
- Do Self-Study Problem 12-10 and check the solution in this Study Guide.

Refundable Journalism Labour Tax Credit—ITA 125.6
- Read paragraph 12-183 to 12-186.

To Complete This Chapter
- Visit MyLab Accounting for more practice problem material, and test yourself with the glossary flashcards.
- Review the Key Terms at the end of the chapter, and consult the glossary for definitions.
- Ensure you have achieved the Chapter 12 Learning Objectives listed in this Study Guide.
- As a review, view the PowerPoint presentations available on MyLab.

Practice Examination
- Available on MyLab, write the Practice Examination for this chapter, and mark it using the solutions provided.

Exercise Solutions

Exercise 12-1 Solution

Item 1   Add back the accounting loss of $5,600 ($48,300 - $53,900), which would have been deducted for accounting purposes. Add the recapture of CCA of $13,700 [UCC $34,600 - $48,300 (lesser of POD of $48,300 and capital cost of $120,700)], for a total addition of $19,300 ($5,600 + $13,700). There are no capital losses allowed on depreciable property.

Item 2   As goodwill is not amortized for accounting purposes and there was no impairment during the year, no adjustment is required. However, since the goodwill is added to class 14.1, it would be subject to the AccII adjustment and a maximum CCA rate of 5%. This means that there would be a CCA deduction of $13,500 ($180,000)(1.5)(5%)].

Item 3   You would add the charitable donations of $15,000 since they are not an allowable expense for net income purposes of a corporation. The corporation would be entitled to a taxable income deduction, however.

Item 4   The premium amortization of $4,500 would have reduced the interest expense that could have been claimed for income tax purposes, therefore it can be deducted.

Exercise 12-2 Solution

Net income for tax purposes	$263,000
Taxable dividends received	(14,200)
Charitable donations	(8,600)
2018 Non-capital loss carry forward	(82,000)
2019 Net capital loss*	(14,250)
Taxable income for 2021	$143,950

*While there is a net capital loss of $18,000 available, the actual deduction is limited to the current year's net taxable capital gains of $14,250 (the ITA 3(b) amount). The remaining 2019 net capital loss carry forward is $3,750 ($18,000 - $14,250).

Exercise 12-3 Solution

Although Loren Ltd. owned the shares for more than 365 days when the dividend was received, it owned more than 5% of the shares of any class of Manon Inc. As a result, the capital loss is subject to the dividend stop loss rule. The revised capital loss would be calculated as follows:

POD [($21.15)(1,000)]	$21,150
ACB [($25.30)(1,000)]	(25,300)
Total loss	($ 4,150)
Taxable dividend [($2.16)(1,000)]	2,160
Capital loss	($ 1,990)
Inclusion rate	1/2
Allowable capital loss	($ 995)

Exercise 12-4 Solution

Hacker's 2021 net income would be nil, the business and property income of $63,500 less the ABIL of $75,750.

The 2021 net capital loss would be $7,650 [($19,200 - $11,550)].

The 2021 non-capital loss would be calculated as follows:

Amount E (the ABIL)	$75,750
Amount F—ITA 3(c) income	(63,500)
2021 Non-capital loss	$12,250

Exercise 12-5 Solution

The 2021 non-capital loss would be calculated as follows:

Amount E:		
Business loss		$273,000
ABIL		5,250
Dividends received and deducted ITA 112(1)		48,000
2020 Net capital loss claimed		
(limited to net taxable capital gains for the year)		13,500
Total for amount E		$339,750
Amount F—ITA 3(c) income:		
Interest	($27,200)	
Dividends	(48,000)	
Net taxable capital gains	(13,500)	(88,700)
Non-capital loss at end of year		$251,050
Net capital loss carry forward ($19,000 - $13,500)		$ 5,500

TIP: Of the ITA 3(c) amounts, $48,000 of dividends does not make it through to taxable income because of the ITA 112(1) taxable income deduction. In addition, the $13,500 of net taxable capital gains does not make it to taxable income because of the net capital loss deduction under ITA 111(1)(b). This means that only the interest of $27,200 flows through to taxable income. As a result, the non-capital loss for 2021 should be $251,050, calculated as the business loss and ABIL combined of $278,250 minus $27,200. This method can be used as a double check on the calculations.

Exercise 12-6 Solution

The percentage of taxable income earned in each province would be calculated as follows:

	Gross Revenues		Wages and Salaries	
	Amount	**Percent**	**Amount**	**Percent**
Ontario	$1,303,000	44.6%	$ 52,000	31.5%
Manitoba	896,000	30.7%	94,000	57.0%
Not related to a province	724,000	24.7%	19,000	11.5%
Total	$2,923,000	100.0%	$165,000	100.0%

The average of the two percentages applicable for income not related to a province is 18.1% [(24.7% + 11.5%)/2], leaving an average for income related to a province of 81.9% [100% - 18.1%]. Given this, federal tax payable can be calculated as follows:

Base amount of Part I tax [(38%)($226,000)]	$85,880
Federal tax abatement [(10%)(81.9%)($226,000)]	(18,509)
General rate reduction [(13%)($226,000)]	(29,380)
Federal income tax payable	$ 37,991

Exercise 12-7 Solution

As a CCPC throughout the year, with no associated companies and a full taxation year (365 days), Kartoom's business limit for 2021 is $500,000. The amount eligible for the SBD will be the least of the following amounts:

• Net active business income—ITA 125(1)(a)	$425,000
• Adjusted taxable income (see following calculation)—ITA 125(1)(b)	$292,857
• Annual business limit—ITA 125(1)(c)	$500,000

2021 Net income	$570,000
Dividends received—ITA 112(1)	(85,000)
2019 Non-capital loss—ITA 111(1)(a)	(160,000)
2021 Taxable income	$325,000
100/28 times foreign non-business tax credit	
[(100/28)($9,000)]	(32,143)
Adjusted taxable income—ITA 125(1)(b) amount	$292,857

The least of these figures is the adjusted taxable income of $292,857. The small business deduction for 2021 would equal $55,643 [(19%)($292,857)]. Canadian income tax on the foreign non-business income of $60,000 would have equalled $16,800 [(28%)($60,000)]. Net Canadian corporate income tax on the foreign non-business income after the $9,000 foreign tax credit would equal $7,800 [$16,800 - $9,000]. The taxable income adjustment of $32,143 leaves $27,857 [$60,000 - $32,143], which when taxed at a rate of 28% results in Canadian corporate income tax of $7,800 [(28%)($27,857)].

Exercise 12-8 Solution

The B component of the ITA 125(5.1)(a) reduction formula is $2,925 [(.00225)($11,300,000 - $10,000,000)]. Given this, the required reduction would be calculated as follows:

$$[(\$500,000)(\$2,925 \div \$11,250)] = \underline{\$130,000}\ \textbf{Reduction}$$

This reduction leaves the 2021 business limit at $370,000 ($500,000 - $130,000).

The foreign non-business income tax credit is equal to $5,400 [(15%)($36,000)]. The small business deduction for Largely Small Inc. is equal to 19% of the least of:

• Net active business income		$1,197,000
• Taxable income ($1,233,000 - $914,000)	$319,000	
Less 100/28 times non-business income FTC		
of $5,400	(19,286)	$ 299,714
• Reduced annual business limit ($500,000 - $130,000)		$ 370,000

The small business deduction is equal to $56,946 [(19%)($299,714)]. There is no AAII grind for 2021 since the AAII for the preceding year (2020) was nil. The foreign non-business income of $36,000 will be included in the AAII for 2021 and will only impact the business limit for 2022. However, since it is less than $50,000, there would be no AAII grind in 2022.

TIP: The TCEC grind of $130,000 can be verified by noting that the TCEC for 2020 of $11,300,000 is 26% of the way between $10 and $15 million. This means that the small business limit reduction would be 26% of $500,000, or $130,000.

Exercise 12-9 Solution

The TCEC of Investco for 2020 was only $9.0 million and that of the associated corporation Subco for 2020 was only $200,000. Since the TCEC of Investco for purposes of the TCEC grind is only $9.2 million there is no TCEC grind since the TCEC is $10 million or less.

The AAII grind, however, applies since the 2020 AAII of Investco for purposes of the grind is between $50,000 and $150,000 at $105,000 [$95,000 for Investco plus $10,000 for Subco]. The required reduction in the business limit would be calculated as follows:

$$[(\$300,000/\$500,000)][(5)(\$105,000 - \$50,000)] = \underline{\$165,000}\ \textbf{Reduction}$$

This reduction would leave the company's business limit at $135,000 ($300,000 - $165,000).

- Active business income—ITA 125(1)(a) $350,000
- Taxable income—ITA 125(1)(b) $475,000
- Reduced business limit—ITA 125(1)(c) $135,000

The small business deduction is equal to $25,650 [(19%)($135,000)].

TIP: You can double check the reduced business limit again by noting that AAII of $105,000 is 55% of the way between $50,000 and $150,000. The result is that the reduction to the business limit equals $165,000 [(55%)($300,000)], resulting in a business limit of $135,000 [$300,000 - $165,000].

Exercise 12-10 Solution

Case 1 Since the 2020 combined AAII is between $50,000 and $150,000 at $72,000, the AAII grind will have to be determined. In addition, since the combined TCEC for 2020 is between $10 and $15 million, the TCEC grind will also have to be determined.

The B component of the TCEC reduction formula is $7,875 [(.00225)($13,500,000 - $10,000,000)]. Given this, the required reduction would be calculated as follows:

$$[(\$350,000)(\$7,875 \div \$11,250)] = \underline{\$245,000}\ \textbf{Reduction}$$

The calculation of the AAII grind would be calculated as follows:

$$[(\$350,000/\$500,000)][(5)(\$72,000 - \$50,000)] = \underline{\$77,000}\ \textbf{Reduction}$$

The greater of these reductions is the TCEC grind amount of $245,000. This leaves a reduced business limit of $105,000 ($350,000 - $245,000). Using this, the 2021 small business deduction for Reduco would be 19 % of the least of:

- Active business income—ITA 125(1)(a) $450,000
- Taxable income ($540,000 - $60,000)—ITA 125(1)(b) $480,000
- Reduced business limit—ITA 125(1)(c) $105,000

The small business deduction in Case 1 is equal to $19,950 [(19%)($105,000)].

TIP: The TCEC grind can be double checked by noting that the 2020 TCEC of $13.5 million is 70% of the way between $10 and $15 million. As a result, the reduction would be 70% of $350,000, or $245,000. In a similar manner, the 2020 AAII of $72,000 is 22% of the way between $50,000 and $150,000, resulting in an AAII reduction of 22% of $350,000, or $77,000.

Case 2 Since the 2020 combined AAII is between $50,000 and $150,000 at $72,000, the AAII grind will have to be determined. In addition, since the combined TCEC for 2020 is between $10 and $15 million, the TCEC grind will also have to be determined.

The B component of the TCEC reduction formula is $2,250 [(.00225)($11,000,000 - $10,000,000)]. Given this, the required reduction would be calculated as follows:

$$[(\$350,000)(\$2,250 \div \$11,250)] = \underline{\$70,000} \textbf{ Reduction}$$

The AAII reduction would be the same $77,000 that was determined in Case 1. This would also be the greater of the two reductions, resulting in a 2021 business limit of $273,000 ($350,000 - $77,000). Given this, the small business deduction for Reduco is equal to 19% of the least of:

- Active business income—ITA 125(1)(a) $450,000
- Taxable income ($540,000 - $60,000)—ITA 125(1)(b) $480,000
- Reduced business limit—ITA 125(1)(c) $273,000

The small business deduction in Case 2 is equal to $51,870 [(19%)($273,000)].

TIP: The TCEC grind can be double checked by noting that the 2020 TCEC of $11.0 million is 20% of the way between $10 and $15 million. As a result, the reduction would be 20% of $350,000, or $70,000. In a similar manner, the 2020 AAII of $72,000 is 22% of the way between $50,000 and $150,000, resulting in an AAII reduction of 22% of $350,000, or $77,000.

Exercise 12-11 Solution
The M&P deduction can only be determined once the small business deduction has been calculated, and as a result the small business deduction should always be determined before the M&P deduction.

The small business deduction for Marion Manufacturing would be equal to 19% of the least of:

- Canadian active business income $411,000
- Taxable income ($462,000 - $310,000) $152,000
  Less 4 times business income FTC of $3,150   (12,600) $139,400
- Business limit $500,000

Based on this, the small business deduction would be $26,486 [(19%)($139,400)].

The M&P deduction would be equal to 13% of the lesser of:

- M&P profits $411,000
  Less amount eligible for small business deduction   (139,400) $271,600
- Taxable income ($462,000 - $310,000) $152,000
  Less:
  Amount eligible for small business deduction   (139,400)
  4 times business FTC of $3,150   (12,600)
  Aggregate investment income (taxable capital gain)   (30,000) $ Nil

The M&P profits deduction would be equal to nil.

It would have been possible to increase the small business deduction to the full $411,000 of active business income by increasing taxable income to $423,600 ($411,000 + $12,600 FTC adjustment that will be deducted). This could be accomplished by limiting the deduction for charitable donations to $38,400 ($462,000 - $423,600). The remaining unclaimed donations of $271,600 ($310,000 - $38,400) could be carried forward for up to five years.

Although this increases taxable income and the total tax payable for the year, there could still be an ultimate tax savings with this approach, as the small business deduction cannot be carried forward while charitable donations can be. As the exercise states that Marion expects large increases in income in the future, this approach would be advantageous if Marion's expectations turn out to be correct. The revised numbers would be as follows:

The small business deduction for Marion Manufacturing would be equal to 19% of the least of:

• Canadian active business income		$411,000
• Taxable income ($462,000 - $38,400)	$423,600	
Less 4 times business income FTC of $3,150	(12,600)	$411,000
• Business limit		$500,000

Based on this, the small business deduction would be $78,090 [(19%)($411,000)].

The M&P deduction would be equal to 13% of the lesser of:

• M&P profits	$411,000		
Less amount eligible for small business deduction	(411,000)	$	Nil
• Taxable income ($462,000 - $38,400)	$423,600		
Less:			
Amount eligible for small business deduction	(411,000)		
4 times business FTC of $3,150	(12,600)		
Aggregate investment income (taxable capital gain)	(30,000)	$	Nil

The M&P profits deduction would be equal to nil.

The downside is that with taxable income increasing by $271,600 from $152,000 to $423,600 there would be additional income taxes of $76,048 [(38% - 10%)($271,600)], which exceeds the additional small business deduction of $51,604 [$78,090 = $26,486] by $24,444. This will be offset by tax savings on the donation deduction of $271,600 in future years, but this strategy would result in additional tax in 2021.

Exercise 12-12 Solution

The federal tax payable for Marchand Inc. would be calculated as follows:

Base amount of Part I tax [(38%)($320,000)]	$121,600
Federal tax abatement [(10%)($320,000)]	(32,000)
M&P deduction [(13%)($180,000)]	(23,400)
General rate reduction [(13%)($320,000 - $180,000)]	(18,200)
Federal tax payable	$ 48,000

As you would expect, the overall tax rate is equal to 15% ($48,000 ÷ $320,000).

Exercise 12-13 Solution

The federal tax payable for Redux Ltd. would be calculated as follows:

Base amount of Part I tax [(38%)($200,000)]	$76,000
Federal tax abatement [(10%)($200,000)]	(20,000)
Small business deduction (Note One)	(26,600)
M&P deduction (Note Two)	(650)
General rate reduction (Note Three)	(7,150)
Federal tax payable	$21,600

Note One The small business deduction would be equal to $26,600, 19% of $140,000, the least of:

Active business income	200,000
Taxable income	200,000
Business limit	140,000

Note Two The M&P deduction would be equal to $650, 13% of $5,000, the lesser of:

- M&P profits $145,000
  Amount eligible for small business deduction (140,000) $ 5,000

- Taxable income $200,000
  Amount eligible for small business deduction (140,000) $60,000

Note Three The general rate reduction would be calculated as follows:

Taxable income	$200,000
Amount eligible for the small business deduction	(140,000)
Amount eligible for the M&P deduction	(5,000)
Full rate taxable income	$ 55,000
Rate	13%
General rate reduction	$ 7,150

TIP: It is possible to verify the tax payable of $21,600 by recognizing that the 9% small business rate applied to $140,000 and the general business rate of 15% applied to the remaining $60,000 of taxable income equals (9%)($140,000) + (15%)($60,000) = $21,600.

Exercise 12-14 Solution

The taxable income figure would be calculated as follows:

Net income	$146,000
Dividends—ITA 112(1)	(30,000)
2018 Non-capital loss—ITA 111(1)(a)	(75,000)
2019 Net capital loss—ITA 111(1)(b)	(25,000)
Taxable income	$ 16,000

Starting with this figure, the required calculation of Part I tax payable would be as follows:

Base amount of Part I tax [(38%)($16,000)]	$6,080
Federal tax abatement [(88%)(10%)($16,000)]	(1,408)
General rate reduction [(13%)($16,000)]	(2,080)
Foreign business income tax credit (see Note)	(879)
Part I tax payable	$1,713

Note The foreign business income tax credit would be $879, the least of:

- The amount withheld $3,000

- $$\left[\frac{\$20,000}{\$146,000 - 30,000 - 25,000} \right] [\$6,080 - \$2,080]$$ $ 879

- $6,080 - $2,080 $4,000

The unused foreign business tax amount of $2,121 ($3,000 - $879) can be carried back three years or forward for 10 years. In calculating the allowable tax credit for such carry overs, these unused amounts will be added to the foreign tax paid factor in the calculation of the foreign business income tax credit.

Self-Study Problem Solutions

Self-Study Problems are available to download from MyLab Accounting.

SSP 12-1 Solution

1. The required adjustments would be:

   - Add: Amortization expense of $254,000
   - Deduct: CCA of $223,000

2. The required adjustment would be:

   - Deduct: Premium amortization of $2,000

3. The capital gain on this sale is $40,000 ($120,000 - $80,000). Because $48,000 ($120,000 - $72,000) of the proceeds are outstanding at the end of the current year, a reserve can be deducted. The reserve will be the lesser of:

   - $16,000 [($40,000)($48,000 ÷ $120,000)]
   - $32,000 [($40,000)(20%)(4 - 0)]

   The deduction of the lesser value of $16,000 will leave a capital gain of $24,000 ($40,000 - $16,000). Based on this, the required adjustments are:

   - Deduct: Accounting gain of $67,000 ($120,000 - $53,000)
   - Add: Taxable capital gain of $12,000[(1/2)($24,000)]

   There is no recapture on this disposition as property remains in the class at the end of the year.

4. The required adjustments would be:

   - Add: Membership fees of $8,000
   - Add: Non-deductible entertainment expenses of $6,000[(50%)($12,000)]

5. The required adjustment would be:

   - Add: Charitable donations of $11,000

6. The required adjustments would be:

   - Add: Accounting loss of $16,000 ($23,000 - $39,000)
   - Add: Recapture of $23,000 (Nil - $23,000)
   - Note: There are no capital losses allowed on depreciable property.

SSP 12-2 Solution

1. The adjustments here would be as follows:

   - Add the donation of $45,000.
   - Deduct the accounting gain of $7,000 ($45,000 - $38,000).
   - Add the taxable capital gain of $1,500 [(1/2)($45,000 - $42,000)].
   - Add the recapture of $5,500 ($42,000 - $36,500).

2. The adjustments here would be as follows:

   - Add the amortization expense of $32,450.
   - Deduct the CCA of $27,650.

3. The adjustment here would be as follows:

   - Add the increase in the warranty liability of $2,010 ($10,470 - $8,460).

4. Since item 1 created a taxable capital gain of $1,500, the adjustments here would be as follows:

   - Add the accounting loss of $550 ($12,870 - $12,320).
   - Deduct the allowable capital loss of $275 [(1/2)($12,870 - $12,320)].

5. The adjustment here would be as follows:

   - Add the $2,600 in bond discount amortization.

6. The adjustments here would be as follows:

   - Add the accounting loss of $14,810 ($107,000 - $92,190).
   - Deduct the terminal loss of $9,580 ($92,190 - $101,770).
   - Note that there are no capital losses on depreciable property.

SSP 12-3 Solution

The required calculation of net income and taxable income is as follows:

ITA 3(a) Dividends		$ 22,300
ITA 3(b) Taxable capital gains	$15,600	
Allowable capital losses	(3,450)	12,150
ITA 3(c)		$ 34,450
ITA 3(d) Business loss		(126,000)
Net income		Nil
Taxable dividends—ITA 112(1)		($ 22,300)
2018 Net capital loss—ITA 111(1)(b)		
(limited to net taxable capital gains)		(12,150)
Charitable donations		Nil
Taxable income		Nil

The carry forward balances available at the end of the year are as follows:

2018 Net Capital Loss Balance

Beginning balance	$ 42,300
Used during year	(12,150)
2018 Net capital loss balance	$ 30,150

Charitable Donations Carry Forward

2020 Donations	$3,500
2021 Donations	2,600
Used during year	Nil
Available and unused donations	$6,100

Non-Capital Loss

Balance under E	
Dividends	$ 22,300
Business loss	126,000
Net capital loss carry forward deducted	12,150
Subtotal	$160,450
Balance under F—Income under ITA 3(c)	(34,450)
2021 Non-capital loss	$126,000

Non-Capital Loss Carry Forward Balances

2019 Non-capital loss	$ 33,500
2021 Non-capital loss	126,000
Used during year	Nil
Available non-capital loss balances	$159,500

As per the policy of the company, this solution minimizes the net capital loss carry forward. In the absence of this policy, an alternative solution could minimize the non-capital loss balance.

SSP 12-4 Solution
2018 Analysis
Net and Taxable Income

Net income and taxable income would be calculated as follows:

Business income	$ 95,000
Dividends	12,000
Net income	**$107,000**
Dividends	(12,000)
Charitable donations	(21,400)
Taxable income	**$ 73,600**

There would be a 2018 net capital loss of $5,000 [(1/2)($10,000)].

Loss Carry Forward

At the end of 2018, there would be a 2018 net capital loss of $5,000 [(1/2)($10,000)].

2019 Analysis
Net and Taxable Income

Both net **income** and taxable **income** would be nil, as shown in the following calculation:

Business loss	($205,000)
Dividends	42,000
Net income	**Nil**
Dividends	(42,000)
Taxable income	**Nil**

This would leave a 2019 non-capital loss of $205,000, calculated as follows:

Amount E ($205,000 + $42,000)	$ 247,000
Income under ITA 3(c)—Dividends	(42,000)
2019 Non-capital loss	$205,000

There would also be a 2019 net capital loss of $7,000 [(1/2)($14,000)].

Carry Back Request and Reassessment of 2018

Of the total non-capital loss of $205,000, $73,600 can be carried back to 2018, resulting in the following reassessed taxable income for 2018:

Taxable income as previously reported	$73,600
2019 Non-capital loss	(73,600)
Reassessed 2018 taxable income	Nil

Carry Forwards

After the carry back, the following carry forward balances would be available at the end of 2018:

- 2019 Charitable donations — $ 4,600
- 2019 Non-capital loss balance ($205,000 - $73,600) — $131,400
- 2018 Net capital loss balance — $ 5,000
- 2019 Net capital loss balance — $ 7,000

2020 Analysis
Net and Taxable Income

Net income and taxable income would be calculated as follows:

Business income	$ 69,500
Taxable capital gains [(1/2)($9,000)]	4,500
Dividends	28,000
Net income	**$102,000**
Dividends	(28,000)
Charitable donations	(8,000)
Taxable income before carry forwards	$ 66,000
2018 Net capital loss carry forward	
(limited to taxable capital gains)	(4,500)
2019 Charitable donations carry forward (all)	(4,600)
2019 Non-capital loss carry forward (Note)	(56,900)
Taxable income	**Nil**

Note The amount of the non-capital loss carry forward that was deducted was the amount required to reduce the 2020 taxable income to nil.

While the various balances carried forward from 2018 and 2019 could be used in any order that Linden chooses, it is the policy of the company to minimize its net capital loss balance. Also, since the charitable donations can only be carried forward for five years, it is more advantageous to deduct the charitable donations rather than more of the non-capital loss carry forward as the non-capital loss carry forward has a 20-year carry forward period.

Loss Carry Forwards

After the preceding allocation of losses, the following balances remain:

- 2019 Non-capital loss carry forward ($131,400 - $56,900) — $74,500
- 2018 Net capital loss balance — $ 500
- 2019 Net capital loss balance — $ 7,000

2021 Analysis
Net and Taxable Income

Net income and taxable income would be calculated as follows:

Business income	$ 90,000
Taxable capital gains [(1/2)($10,000)]	5,000
Dividends	32,000
Net income	**$ 127,000**
Dividends	(32,000)
Charitable donations	(22,000)
Taxable income before carry forwards	$ 73,000
Net capital loss—ITA 111(1)(b)	
($500 for 2018 and $4,500 for 2019)	(5,000)
2019 Non-capital loss—ITA 111(1)(a)	
(amount that reduces taxable income to nil)	(68,000)
Taxable income	**Nil**

Loss Carry Forwards

After the preceding allocation of losses, the following balances remain:

• 2019 Non-capital loss balance ($74,500 - $68,000)	$6,500
• 2019 Net capital loss balance ($7,000 - $4,500)	$2,500

SSP 12-5 Solution

The allocation to each of these provinces and the United States would be based on the following calculations:

Province	Salaries and Wages		Gross Revenues	
	Amount	Percent	Amount	Percent
Manitoba	$ 369,750	15%	$1,252,000	20%
Ontario	616,250	25%	1,565,000	25%
Quebec	986,000	40%	2,191,000	35%
United States	493,000	20%	1,252,000	20%
Total	$2,465,000	100%	$6,260,000	100%

The province-by-province average of the two percentages, calculated above, would be used to allocate the total taxable income of $1,467,000 as follows:

Province	Wages	Revenues	Average	Taxable Income
Manitoba	15%	20%	17.5%	$ 256,725
Ontario	25%	25%	25.0%	366,750
Quebec	40%	35%	37.5%	550,125
United States	20%	20%	20.0%	293,400
Total	100%	100%	100.0%	$1,467,000

SSP 12-6 Solution

Jordu's Part I tax payable for the year would be calculated as follows:

Base amount of Part I tax [(38%)($1,265,000)]	480,700
Federal tax abatement [(10%)(95.5%)($1,265,000)] (Note One)	(120,808)
Foreign business tax credit	
(assumed to be equal to taxes withheld)	(19,500)
Small business deduction (Note Two)	(8,326)
General rate reduction (Note Three)	(158,753)
Part I tax payable	$ 173,313

Note One The federal tax abatement must be reduced because of the foreign business income. The percentage would be calculated as follows:

• Canadian gross revenues as a percentage of total (28% + 63%)	91%
• Canadian wages and salaries as percentage of total	100%

Using these figures, the average percent would be 95.5%.

Note Two Since Jordu and its associated companies have combined TCEC for 2020 that was greater than $10 million and less than $15 million, its small business deduction is proportionally reduced. The B component of the ITA 125(5.1) reduction formula is $7,306 [(.00225)($13,246,900 - $10,000,000)]. In addition, because of Jordu's association with other companies, the A component of the formula would be reduced to $125,000 ($500,000 ÷ 4). Given these considerations, the reduction would be calculated as follows:

$$[(\$125,000)(\$7,306 \div \$11,250)] = \$81,178$$

Using this information, Jordu's small business deduction is equal to 19% of the least of:

- Canadian active business income ($1,265,000 - $130,000) $1,135,000
- Taxable income $1,265,000
  Less: Foreign tax credit adjusted [(4)($19,500)]   (78,000)
                                                        $1,187,000
- Reduced annual business limit ($125,000 - $81,178) $ 43,822

You can verify the TCEC reduction by noting that $13,246,900 is 64.938% between $10 and $15 million. Applying this percentage to the business limit of $125,000 equals a reduction of $81,172.50 (slight rounding difference).

The small business deduction would be $8,326 [(19%)($43,822)].

Note Three The general rate reduction would be calculated as follows:

Taxable income	$1,265,000
Amount eligible for small business deduction	(43,822)
Full rate taxable income	$1,221,178
Rate	(13%)
General rate reduction	$ 158,753

SSP 12-7 Solution

The taxable income and tax payable for the Serendipity Shop Corp. for the year would be calculated as follows:

Net income		$240,000
Deductions:		
Dividends	($20,000)	
Donations	(48,000)	(68,000)
Taxable income		$ 172,000

Base amount of Part I tax [(38%)($172,000)]	$ 65,360
Federal tax abatement [(10%)($172,000)]	(17,200)
Small business deduction (Note)	(25,650)
General rate reduction [(13%)($172,000 - $135,000)]	(4,810)
Part I federal tax payable	$ 17,700

Note The small business deduction is based on the least of the following:

Active business income	$220,000
Taxable income	172,000
Business limit	135,000

The small business deduction is equal to $25,650 [(19%)($135,000)].

TIP: The Part I tax liability can be verified by recognizing that the small business rate of 9% is applied to the first $135,000 of taxable income and the general business rate of 15% is applied to the remaining $37,000. Part I tax therefore equals $17,700 [(9%)($135,000) + (15%)($37,000)].

SSP 12-8 Solution
Part A—Net Income

The minimum net income for Borscan Inc. would be calculated as follows:

Accounting income before taxes		$1,275,000
Additions:		
Taxable capital gain—Building		
[(1/2)(POD bldg $525,000 - ACB bldg $500,000)]	$ 12,500	
Taxable capital gain—Land ($100,000 - $100,000)	Nil	
Recaptured CCA ($500,000 - $350,000)	150,000	
Amortization expense	255,000	
Interest and penalties—Late payment	500	
Charitable donations	13,500	431,500
		$1,706,500
Deductions:		
Capital cost allowance	($287,000)	
Gain on expropriated building		
(from income statement)	(25,000)	(312,000)
Net income for ITA purposes		$1,394,500

Part B—Taxable Income

The minimum taxable income for Borscan Inc. would be calculated as follows:

Net income for ITA purposes	$1,394,500
Taxable dividends—ITA 112(1)	(25,000)
Charitable donations—ITA 110.1	(13,500)
2020 Net capital loss (Note)—ITA 111(1)(b)	(12,500)
2019 Non-capital loss—ITA 111(1)(a)	(35,000)
Taxable income	$1,308,500

Note   The 2020 net capital loss can only be claimed to the extent of the net taxable capital gain for the year, resulting in a deduction of $12,500. This leaves a 2020 net capital loss balance of $17,500 ($30,000 - $12,500).

Part C—Tax Payable

The minimum federal tax payable for Borscan Inc. is as follows:

Base amount of Part I tax [(38%)($1,308,500)]	$ 497,230
Federal tax abatement [(10%)($1,308,500)]	(130,850)
General rate reduction [(13%)($1,308,500)]	(170,105)
Federal tax payable	$ 196,275

SSP 12-9 Solution
Part A—Net Income
Net income for ITA purposes for Industrial Tools Ltd. would be calculated as follows:

Accounting income before taxes		$2,305,000
Additions:		
Taxable capital gain on building (Note)	$ 37,500	
Taxable capital gain on land		
($200,000 - $200,000)	Nil	
Recaptured CCA ($875,000 - $625,000)	250,000	
Charitable donations	28,000	
Interest and penalties	2,500	
Warranty reserve	20,000	
Amortization expense	478,000	816,000
		$3,121,000
Deductions:		
Accounting gain on building (given)	($225,000)	
CCA	(523,000)	(748,000)
Net income for ITA purposes		$2,373,000

Note The taxable capital gain on the building would be calculated as follows:

Proceeds of disposition ($1,150,000 - $200,000)	$950,000
Adjusted cost base ($1,075,000 - $200,000)	(875,000)
Capital gain	$ 75,000
Inclusion rate	1/2
Taxable capital gain	$ 37,500

As its value has not changed, there is no capital gain on the land.

Part B—Taxable Income
Taxable income for Industrial Tools Ltd. would be calculated as follows:

Net income for ITA purposes	$ 2,373,000
Dividends received	(42,000)
Charitable donations	(28,000)
Net capital loss carry forward (Note)	(37,500)
Taxable income	$ 2,265,500

Note The 2019 net capital loss can only be used to the extent of net taxable capital gains for the year, resulting in a maximum deduction of $37,500. This leaves a 2019 net capital loss balance of $52,500 ($90,000 - $37,500).

Part C—Tax Payable
Federal tax payable for Industrial Tools Ltd. would be calculated as follows:

Base amount of Part I tax [(38%)($2,265,500)]	$ 860,890
Federal tax abatement [(10%)($2,265,500)]	(226,550)
General rate reduction [(13%)($2,265,500)]	(294,515)
Federal Part I tax payable	$ 339,825

SSP 12-10 Solution

Note to Instructor As the ART is not covered until Chapter 13, this problem does not require the calculation of the ART. However, given the capital loss carry forward applied during the year, it would be nil.

Part A—Net Income for ITA Purposes

The calculation of Mamora's net income for ITA purposes would be as follows:

Accounting net income before taxes			$1,115,050
Additions, including relevant problem part:			
1	Amortization expense	$405,525	
2	Taxable capital gain on building (Note 1)	25,000	
2	Taxable capital gain on building land (Note 1)	12,500	
3	Taxable capital gain on vacant land (Note 2)	15,918	
2	Recapture on building (Note 3)	250,000	
2	Accounting loss on vehicles (given)	63,000	
6	Foreign tax withheld	2,700	
7	Articles of incorporation amendment costs	21,000	
8	Bond discount amortization	4,600	
8	Donations to registered charities	12,500	
8	Interest on late income tax instalments	1,400	
8	Interest on late municipal taxes	Nil	
9	Non-deductible meals and entertainment (50% of $42,000)	21,000	
9	Golf club membership fees	23,000	858,143
			$1,973,193
Deductions:			
2	Accounting gain on building (given)	($175,000)	
2	Capital cost allowance (Note 3)	(628,575)	
2	Terminal loss (Note 3)	(20,000)	
3	Accounting gain on vacant land (given)	(75,000)	
4	Landscaping	(53,000)	(951,575)
	Net income for ITA purposes		$1,021,618

Note 1 While the accounting gain on the building of $175,000 is calculated on the combined value of the land and building, separate income tax calculations are required for each property disposition. The taxable capital gains on the building and land are separately calculated as follows:

Proceeds of disposition	$1,350,000
ACB (equal to capital cost)	(1,300,000)
Capital gain	$ 50,000
Inclusion rate	1/2
Taxable capital gain—Building	$ 25,000

Proceeds of disposition	$ 375,000
ACB	(350,000)
Capital gain	$ 25,000
Inclusion rate	1/2
Taxable capital gain—Land	$ 12,500

Note 2 There is a capital gain and accounting gain on the vacant land of $75,000 ($695,000 - $620,000). However, as not all of the proceeds of disposition were received in 2021, a reserve can be deducted for income tax purposes. The reserve will be the lesser of the following two amounts:

- [($75,000)($400,000 ÷ $695,000)] =$43,165
- [($75,000)(20%)(4 - 0)] = $60,000

Deducting the lesser amount leaves a capital gain of $31,835 ($75,000 - $43,165) and a taxable capital gain of $15,918 [(1/2)($31,835)].

Note 3 Maximum CCA and other related inclusions and deductions are found in the tables that follow. Note that the new building was added to a separate class in order to qualify for the enhanced CCA rate of 10% for M&P buildings. This resulted in recapture on the old building that was disposed of.

Class 1—Old Building

January 1, 2021, class 1 balance	$1,050,000
Disposition—Lesser of:	
• Proceeds = $1,350,000	
• Capital cost = $1,300,000	(1,300,000)
Negative ending UCC balance	($ 250,000)
Recapture	250,000
January 1, 2022, UCC balance	Nil

Class 1—New Building

New class 1 addition	$1,700,000
AccII adjustment	850,000
Balance	$2,550,000
CCA [(10%)($2,550,000)]	(255,000)
AccII adjustment reversal	(850,000)
January 1, 2022, UCC balance	$1,445,000

Class 8

January 1, 2021, class 8 balance	$1,460,000
Additions	150,000
AccII adjustment	(75,000)
CCA base	($1,685,000)
CCA [(20%)($1,685,000)]	(337,000)
AccII adjustment reversal	(75,000)
January 1, 2022, UCC balance	1,273,000

Class 10

January 1, 2021, class 10 balance	$142,000
Disposition—Lesser of:	
• Proceeds = $122,000	
• Capital cost = $285,000	(122,000)
Positive balance at year end with no property remaining in class	($ 20,000)
Terminal loss	(20,000)
January 1, 2022, UCC balance	Nil

Class 13

January 1, 2021, class 13 balance	$175,000
2021 CCA:	
2016 Expenditures ($250,000 ÷ 10 years)	(25,000)
2020 Expenditures ($60,000 ÷ 6 years)	(10,000)
January 1, 2022, UCC balance	140,000

Class 14.1

January 1, 2021, class 14.1 balance	Nil
2021 Additions	$21,000
AccII adjustment	10,500
CCA base	$31,500
CCA [(5%)($31,500)]	(1,575)
AccII adjustment reversal	(10,500)
January 1, 2022, UCC balance	$19,425

The cost of amending the articles of incorporation does not qualify for the $3,000 deduction under ITA 20(1)(b) as the costs were not incurred for incorporation.

Summary of CCA and UCC Results

Class	Maximum CCA	UCC
Class 1—Old (recapture = $250,000)	Nil	Nil
Class 1—New	$255,000	$1,445,000
Class 8	337,000	1,273,000
Class 10 (terminal Loss = $20,000)	Nil	Nil
Class 13	35,000	140,000
Class 14.1	1,575	19,425
Total	$628,575	

Part B—Taxable Income

Mamora's taxable income would be calculated as follows:

Net income	$1,021,618
14 Dividends from taxable Canadian corporations	(22,000)
8 Contributions to registered charities	(12,500)
10 2018 Net capital loss (Note 4)	(53,418)
10 2018 Non-capital loss (all)	(95,000)
Taxable income	$ 838,700

Note 4 Mamora's net income contained net taxable capital gains calculated as follows:

Taxable capital gain on building (Note 1)	$25,000
Taxable capital gain on building land (Note 1)	12,500
Taxable capital gain on vacant land (Note 2)	15,918
Total taxable capital gains	$53,418

While there is a 2018 net capital loss balance of $210,000, the amount to be used is limited to the $53,418 in net taxable capital gains for the year.

Part B—Loss Carry Forwards

At the end of 2021, there would be a 2018 net capital loss balance of $156,582 ($210,000 - $53,418). There is no remaining 2019 non-capital loss balance.

Part C—Federal Tax Payable

Mamora's federal tax payable would be calculated as follows:

Base amount of Part I tax [(38%)($838,700)]	$318,706
Federal tax abatement [(10%)(88%)($838,700)]	(73,806)
Small business deduction (Note 5)	(33,250)
M&P deduction (Note 6)	(32,500)
General rate reduction (Note 7)	(53,781)
Foreign business tax credit (given)	(2,700)
Part I tax payable	$122,669

Note 5 The amount eligible for the small business deduction would be the least of the following amounts:

Canadian source active business income (given)	$976,380
Taxable income	$838,700
Less: 4 times the foreign business tax credit [(4)($2,700)]	(10,800)
Adjusted taxable income	**$ 827,900**
Annual business limit (given)	$ 175,000

The least of these figures is $175,000, resulting in a small business deduction of $33,250 [(19%)($175,000)].

Note 6 The base for the M&P deduction would be the lesser of:

M&P profits (given)	$ 425,000
Less: Amount eligible for the small business deduction	(175,000)
Balance	$ 250,000
Taxable income	$ 838,700
Less:	
Amount eligible for the small business deduction	(175,000)
4 times the foreign business tax credit [(4)($2,700)]	(10,800)
Aggregate investment income ($53,418 - $53,418)	Nil
Adjusted taxable income	$ 652,900

The lesser of these two figures is $250,000, resulting in an M&P deduction of $32,500 [(13%)($250,000)]. The aggregate investment income is reduced to nil by the deduction of the 2018 net capital loss.

Note 7 The general rate reduction would be calculated as follows:

Taxable income	$838,700
Amount eligible for the small business deduction	(175,000)
Amount eligible for the M&P deduction	(250,000)
Full rate taxable income	$413,700
Rate	13%
General rate reduction	$ 53,781

CHAPTER 13

Learning Objectives

After completing Chapter 13, you should be able to:

1. Explain the goal of integration in the design of the Canadian taxation of investment and describe the four steps that are required to analyze the integrated flow of that investment income when taxable dividends are paid to individual shareholders (Paragraph [P hereafter] 13-1 to 13-11).
2. Explain the difference between eligible and non-eligible dividends, their purpose in terms of integration, and how to calculate their after-tax returns (P 13-12 to 13-19).
3. Demonstrate how the dividend gross up and tax credit procedures work to implement integration with respect to business income (P 13-20 to 13-26).
4. List the components of aggregate investment income as it is defined in ITA 129(4) and describe the basic concept of refundable taxes (P 13-27 to 13-36).
5. Calculate the additional refundable tax (ART) on the investment income of a CCPC (P 13-37 to 13-40). Note that additional information is provided in the appendix at the end of the chapter concerning the interaction of the ART with foreign tax credits.
6. Explain the Part I refundable tax concept and calculate Part I refundable tax on the investment income of a CCPC (P 13-41 to 13-53).
7. Explain the Part IV refundable concept and apply the provisions related to portfolio dividends (P 13-54 to 13-65).
8. Explain and apply the connected corporation Part IV concept (P 13-66 to 13-68).
9. Explain how Part IV applies when there are connected corporations and the general analysis to determine the circumstances under which Part IV applies (P 13-69 to 13-75).
10. Explain the eligible dividend designation concept and explain and calculate the GRIP of a CCPC (P 13-76 to 13-85).
11. Explain the relevance of the LRIP concept for corporations that are not CCPCs and apply the general provision (P 13-86 to 13-89).
12. Explain the purpose of Part III.1 and calculate the Part III.1 tax on excessive eligible dividend designations (EEDD) (P 13-90 to 13-98).
13. Explain in terms of integration why the RDTOH system was changed (P 13-99 to 13-104).
14. Calculate the Part I refundable tax (P 13-105 to 13-114).
15. Calculate the balance in the eligible and non-eligible RDTOH accounts (P 13-115 to 13-118).
16. Calculate the dividend refund on the payment of eligible and non-eligible dividends (P 13-119 to 13-122).
17. Describe the economic impact of the new RDTOH system and any tax planning considerations (P 13-123 to 13-137).
18. Briefly describe the systematic approach when dealing with the taxation of corporations (P 13-138 to 13-139).
19. Review a simple corporate income tax return completed using the ProFile T2 tax preparation software program.

How to Work through Chapter 13

Visit pearsonmylabandmastering.com to access MyLab Accounting for this text. Once there, you can access student resources such as Self-Study Problems, Practice Exams, Flashcards, updates, and more.

We recommend the following approach in dealing with the material in this chapter:

Introduction
- Read paragraph 13-1 to 13-6, with emphasis on the analysis mentioned in Paragraph 13-6.

Integration
- Read paragraph 13-7 to 13-24.
- Do Exercises 13-1 and 13-2 (in the text) and check the solutions in this Study Guide.
- Do Self-Study Problem 13-1, which is available on MyLab, and check the solution in this Study Guide.
- Read paragraph 13-25 to 13-26.

Refundable Taxes on Investment Income
- Read paragraph 13-27 to 13-36.

Additional Refundable Tax on Investment Income (ART)
- Read paragraph 13-37 to 13-40.
- Do Exercise 13-3 and check the solution in this Study Guide.

Refundable Part I Tax Basics
- Read paragraph 13-41 to 13-53.
- Do Exercise 13-4 and check the solution in this Study Guide.

Refundable Part IV Tax Basics
- Read paragraph 13-54 to 13-65.
- Read paragraph 13-66 to 13-68 on connected corporations.
- Read paragraph 13-69 to 13-73 on the Part IV flowchart.
- Do Exercise 13-5 and check the solution in this Study Guide.
- Read paragraph 13-74 to 13-75.

Designation of Eligible Dividends
- Read paragraph 13-76 to 13-81.

CCPCs—The General Rate Income Pool (GRIP)
- Read paragraph 13-82 to 13-85.
- Do Exercise 13-6 and check the solution in this Study Guide.

Other Corporations—The Low Rate Income Pool (LRIP)
- Read paragraph 13-86 to 13-89.

Part III.1 Tax—Excessive Eligible Dividend Designations (EEDDs)
- Read paragraph 13-90 to 13-98.

Refundable Dividend Tax on Hand (RDTOH)
- Read paragraph 13-99 to 13-114.
- Do Exercise 13-7 and check the solution in this Study Guide.

Eligible and Non-Eligible RDTOH Accounts
- Read paragraph 13-115 to 13-122.
- Do Exercise 13-8 and check the solution in this Study Guide.
- Do Self-Study Problems 13-2 to 13-5 and check the solutions in this Study Guide.

Economic Impact of Changes
- Read paragraph 13-123 to 13-125.

Example of the Taxation of Corporate Investment Income
- Read paragraph 13-126 to 13-137

Working through Corporate Tax Problems
- Read paragraph 13-138 to 13-139.
- Do Self-Study Problems 13-6 to 13-8 and check the solutions in this Study Guide.

Sample Corporate Tax Return
- Read the Sample Corporate Tax Return found in this Study Guide. The complete tax return is available on MyLab in two formats, a T2 ProFile return file and a .PDF file.

To Complete This Chapter
- Visit MyLab Accounting for more practice problem material, and test yourself with the glossary flashcards.
- Review the Key Terms at the end of the chapter, and consult the glossary for definitions.
- Ensure you have achieved the Chapter 13 Learning Objectives listed in this Study Guide.
- As a review, view the PowerPoint presentations available on MyLab.

Practice Examination
- Available on MyLab, write the Practice Examination for this chapter, and mark it using the solutions provided.

Sample Corporate Tax Return

Note The following simplified example contains the 2020 updated version of the T2 corporate income tax return completed using the 2020 ProFile T2 corporate tax preparation program from Intuit Canada released in early 2021. The updated version of this problem will be available on MyLab at:

http://www.pearsonmylabandmastering.com

As this example is designed to illustrate corporate tax return calculations, limited GIFI (General Index of Financial Information) data has been included. The relevant T2 schedule or form name is provided in square brackets to make it easier for users to find where the information is input. Note that capital dividends are covered in detail in Chapter 14.

Sample Files on MyLab
To View the Tax Return Files
The complete sample tax return is available on MyLab in two versions, a T2 ProFile return file and a .PDF file.

To view the ProFile return file (with a .GT2 extension), you must have the ProFile program installed. For information on how to obtain the program for free, see MyLab.

To view the .PDF files, you must have the Adobe Reader program installed. This program can be installed for free from the Adobe website (www.adobe.com).

Sample Problem Data

Note: The government's Crown copyright does not permit us to use fabricated business numbers in software examples. To reduce the number of ProFile error messages, we have used NR (for not registered) in the business number field.

On the ProFile schedule titled "Info," the filing question "Complete return from GIFI?" is answered Yes by default. Click the No box and you can ignore the GIFI requirements.

MetroFaux Inc. is a Canadian controlled private corporation based in Saskatoon that manufactures metal and composite office furniture. Its head office is located at 123 ABC Avenue, Saskatoon, SK S7G 1A1, phone number (306)111-1111. The signing officer and contact person is the president of the company, Jack Saskatoon. MetroFaux Inc. was incorporated on August 28, 1977.

Most of its income is earned from active business in Canada. The company has no associated corporations. Although the company has a sophisticated website, it is only for information purposes. It has no income from a webpage or website. [Schedule 88 is not applicable.]

As at December 31, 2019, the following information applied to MetroFaux Inc:

Taxable capital employed in Canada [Info]	$1,590,000
RDTOH [T2, line 520 & 535]	Nil
Dividends declared and paid during 2019	Nil
GRIP balance [Schedule 53]	276,000

During the taxation year ending December 31, 2020, the condensed before tax income statement of MetroFaux Inc. was prepared in accordance with international financial reporting standards (IFRS). In condensed form it is as follows:

MetroFaux Inc.
Condensed Income Statement
Year Ending December 31, 2020

Sales	$ 3,847,000	
Interest on bonds	97,000	
Eligible dividends	36,000	
Gain on building sale	160,000	$4,140,000
Amortization expense	$ 607,000	
Other expenses excluding taxes	1,773,000	2,380,000
Accounting income before taxes		$1,760,000

Preliminary GIFI Procedures

On the ProFile schedule titled "Info," the Filing question "Complete return from GIFI?" is answered Yes by default. Click the No box. Ignore the GIFI requirements except as follows:

- On GIFI Schedule 125 (Income Statement), input the total sales as "Trade sales of goods and services" (Code 8000) and the Gain on Building Sale as "Realized gains/losses on disposal of assets" (Code 8210) from the drop-down menu under Revenues. Input the Amortization Expense as "Amortization of tangible assets" (Code 8670) and the Other Expenses as "Other expenses" (Code 9270) from the drop-down menu under Operating Expenses.
- On GIFI Schedule 100 (Balance Sheet), input the net income figure as "Cash and deposits" (Code 1000) in order to make the total assets equal to the total liabilities and equity.

Although this will not properly complete the GIFI statements, it will eliminate the warning messages that would otherwise be generated when the net income figure and Amortization Expense are input on Schedule 1. These GIFI entries will have no effect on the calculations in the tax return. To prevent audit warnings, S141, "Notes Checklist," has to be completed. Assume there are no notes to the financial statements and answer "No" to any other relevant questions.

Other Information:

1. Expenses include interest and penalties of $2,300 resulting from late income tax instalments and a failure to file the 2019 tax return within the prescribed time period. [Schedule 1]

2. Expenses include a deduction for charitable donations to the Cancer Research Society in the amount of $15,000. [Schedule 2]

3. Accounting income before taxes includes eligible dividends of $36,000 from Canadian Tax Save Inc., a taxable Canadian corporation. MetroFaux Inc. is not associated with Canadian Tax Save Inc. and considers the dividends portfolio dividends. [Schedule 3. Note that under the "Column F deduction type" = s. 112 and $36,000 must be placed in the "Indicate eligible dividends" column G.]

4. The company paid $100,000 in taxable dividends during 2020. Maximize the eligible dividends, ensuring the largest dividend refund possible. [Lines 450 and 455 of Schedule 3]

5. The company has available a 2019 non-capital loss of $56,000 [S4Supp] and a 2017 net capital loss balance of $22,500 (1/2 of $45,000). [Schedule 4—note 100% figures are used for the capital loss]

6. During 2020, the company earned $97,000 of interest income on bonds purchased in 2019 that mature in 2023. [Schedule 7]

7. Amortization expense on the income statement amounts to $607,000. The opening UCC balance was $905,000 for class 8, $800,000 for class 10, and $429,000 for class 53. The only depreciable property acquisition was $100,000 in class 53 manufacturing equipment on May 1, 2020, which was acquired from an arm's-length person. There were no dispositions in classes 8 or 10. [Schedule 8 flows to Schedule 1]

8. The Gain on Building Sale resulted from the sale of a building for proceeds of $792,000, of which $120,000 was allocated to the land and the remaining $672,000 allocated to the building. The building at 456 DEF Street, Regina, Saskatchewan S7G 1A1, was acquired on August 28, 2010, for $764,000, of which $100,000 was allocated to the land and the remaining $664,000 allocated to the building. The sales office of the company had been located in this building and the sales office has subsequently moved to leased space in Saskatoon. As the company leases all of its other buildings and equipment, the building was the only property in class 1. The UCC of this class prior to the disposition of the building was $514,000. [Schedules 1, 6, and 8]

9. Information related to Canadian manufacturing and processing activities for the year is as follows: [Schedule 27]

Cost of capital [(10% of $6,000,000) + ($200,000 in rental costs)]	$ 800,000
Portion of capital used in M&P activities	500,000
Cost of labour	1,000,000
Portion of labour used in M&P activities	760,000

10. All of the common shares of MetroFaux Inc. are held by the president, Jack Saskatoon (SIN 527-000-582). [Schedule 50]

11. The beginning balance in the company's capital dividend account is nil [CDA]. Note that capital dividends are covered in detail in Chapter 14. The CDA balance at December 31, 2020, is shown on Schedule 89 (Form S89)

12. The company paid one federal income tax instalment of $212,000 on September 1, 2018 [TaxPaid].

13. Assume that the adjusted aggregate investment income (AAII) in the preceding year (2019) is equal to the bond interest of $97,000. Enter this amount on the T2 for the Small Business Deduction for amount F. You should see a reduction to the small business limit of $485,000.

Completed Tax Return

The complete sample tax return is available on MyLab in two versions, a T2 ProFile return file and a .PDF file.

Notes on Sample Corporate Tax Return

Loss Carry Forwards

The losses of prior taxation years deducted in the calculation of taxable income consist of the 2019 non-capital loss of $56,000 and $14,000 of the 2017 net capital loss. As calculated on Schedule 4, the net capital loss carry forward deduction is limited by the $28,000 capital gain for the year and leaves a capital loss carry forward of $17,000 or a net capital loss balance of $8,500. Note Schedule 4 uses the 100% amounts. There is no non-capital loss carry forward remaining.

Building Sale

The $160,000 Gain on Building Sale is deducted on Schedule 1 as the tax effects of the disposition are included in net income. As calculated on Schedule 6, the taxable capital gain on the building sale is $14,000 [(1/2)($792,000 - $764,000)].

As calculated on Schedule 8, the recapture of CCA on the building is equal to $150,000 ($664,000 - $514,000). This is shown as an addition on Schedule 1, separate from the CCA.

Aggregate Investment Income

As calculated on Schedule 7, Part 1, the aggregate investment income of $97,000 consists of:

- the taxable capital gains of $14,000, less
- the $14,000 net capital loss carry forward claimed, plus
- net property income of $133,000 (dividends received of $36,000 plus interest income of $97,000), less
- taxable dividends deductible of $36,000.

This figure is used in calculating the refundable portion of Part I tax.

Active Business Income

As calculated on Schedule 7, Part 6, income eligible for the small business deduction of $1,505,800 is net income for tax purposes of $1,652,800 less the sum of:

- the taxable capital gains of $14,000, plus
- net property income of $133,000 (eligible dividends of $36,000 plus interest on five-year bonds of $97,000).

This amount is used in both the small business deduction calculation of Schedule 7 and the T2 together with the calculation of the M&P tax credit in Schedule 27.

The small business limit of $500,000 is reduced as a result of adjusted aggregate investment income (AAII) of $97,000 in 2019. The reduction occurs when the preceding year's AAII exceeds $50,000 and is less than $150,000. The small business limit is not reduced if AAII is $50,000 or less but is reduced to zero if AAII is $150,000 or more. In this instance the AAII for 2019 is 47% of the way between $50,000 and $150,000, which equals the reduction. As a result, the small business limit of $500,000 is reduced by $235,000 [(47%)($500,000)], or $265,000. This is shown on line 428 of the T2.

The AAII for 2020 of $133,000 will reduce the small business limit for 2021.

M&P

Manufacturing and processing profits are determined by formula and set out in Schedule 27. As the grossed up M&P labour of $1,013,333 [(100/75)($760,000)] is greater than the $1,000,000 cost of labour, M&P labour in the Schedule 27, Part 7, calculation is limited to $1,000,000.

As mentioned in the text, although the effect of the federal M&P deduction has been negated by the general rate reduction, there are still provincial M&P tax reductions available. In this example, MetroFaux Inc. is eligible for the Saskatchewan M&P tax reduction (see Schedule 404). You will note that the federal amount upon which the M&P credit is based of $1,063,647 as shown in Schedule 27 is different than the amount of $1,010,647 used to calculate the Saskatchewan M&P credit as shown in the provincial form S404. The $53,000 difference is attributable to different corporate tax rates in Saskatchewan, including the fact that starting January 1, 2018, Saskatchewan increased the small business limit by an additional $100,000, from $500,000 to $600,000.

CCA—Class 53 & Schedule 8

Most depreciable property acquired in arm's-length transactions between November 21, 2018, and December 31, 2023, are eligible for a first-year accelerated CCA claim rather than a reduced claim under the historical half-year rule. The corporation acquired class 53 manufacturing depreciable property on May 1, 2019, for $100,000. This acquisition qualifies for the Accelerated Investment Incentive (AccII). Column 4 of Schedule 8 requires identifying and including any qualifying depreciable property. Once identified, most qualifying property is eligible for CCA equal to three times the CCA that would have been determined under the regular half-year rules. Class 53, however, is given special treatment, the result of which is to ensure that 100% of the cost can be claimed as CCA in the year of acquisition. In this case, CCA for class 53 is calculated as [(50%)($429,000) + (50%)(2.0)($100,000)], which equals $314,500.

Capital Dividend Account

The balance in the capital dividend account is $14,000 [(1/2)($692,000 - $664,000)]. A tax-free capital dividend of $14,000 could have been paid if form T2054 had been filed (see Chapter 14). The year-end balance is shown in Schedule 89.

Adjusted Aggregate Investment Income (AAII) and the New Passive Investment Rules (ITA 125(5.1))

The above rules, with the exception of GRIP, become effective for corporate taxation years that begin after December 31, 2018. In our case the first taxation year to which these rules apply is January 1, 2019, to December 31, 2019.

AAII starts with aggregate investment income (AII) and makes certain adjustments. Both AII and AAII are found in Schedule 7 in Parts 1 and 2, respectively. While AII includes all taxable capital gains, AAII excludes taxable capital gains from "active assets," which are typically property actually used in a business that generates active business income. Our objective is not to explain the legislation, which can be found in the text, but rather to point out this new information, which is now contained within the ProFile and other tax software. In this case you will note that we have left the taxable capital gain line 705 blank. The reason is that the taxable capital gains relate to the sale of land and building that were used in the business and are therefore active assets. The interest on five-year bonds, however, is another matter and is included. The 2019 AAII of $97,000 only becomes relevant for the 2020 taxation year of the company. The 2020 impact would be to reduce the small business limit of $500,000 in 2020 by $235,000 to $265,000. The reduction is calculated as [(500,000/500,000)(5)(97,000 - 50,000)]. This was discussed under "Active Business Income" above.

GRIP, Dividend Refunds, and Eligible and Non-Eligible RDTOH

Schedule 53 is used to determine the GRIP for the year. It begins with an opening balance of $276,000 and makes adjustments based on the income received including the receipt of eligible dividends.

The T2 corporate tax return includes the calculations for the opening RDTOH balance (lines 460, 465, & 480). The corporation is subject to a new set of RDTOH rules beginning with its 2019 taxation year that divides the RDTOH into two new accounts referred to as eligible RDTOH or

ERDTOH (line 530) and non-eligible RDTOH or NERDTOH (line 545). We refer you to the text for the details, but the general rule is that the designation and payment of eligible dividends will not trigger a dividend refund unless the corporation has an ERDTOH account at year end. In this case the corporation paid a taxable eligible dividend of $36,000, which was sufficient to refund the year-end balance of $13,800 [($36,000)(38 1/3%)]. The remaining dividend of $64,000 is a non-eligible dividend, which entitles the corporation to a dividend refund of $24,533 [($64,000) (38 1/3%)]. The ERDTOH balance for 2021 is nil and $5,214 [$29,747 - $24,533]. These amounts are shown as carry forward amounts in the ProFile Form "Summary."

Exercise Solutions

Exercise 13-1 Solution

If Ms. Teason incorporates her business, the corporation will pay income taxes of $15,000 [(15%) ($100,000)], leaving $85,000 to be distributed as taxable dividends. Her individual income tax payable on these non-eligible dividends would be calculated as follows:

Non-eligible dividends received	$85,000
Gross up [(15%)($85,000)]	12,750
Grossed up dividends	$ 97,750
Personal tax rate	45%
Tax before credit	$43,988
Dividend tax credit [(9/13 + 30%)($12,750)]	(12,652)
Tax payable on dividends	$ 31,336

The net after-tax retention would be $53,664 ($85,000 - $31,336). This compares to $55,000 [($100,000)(1 − .45)] retained if she continues to carry on her business as a sole proprietor. In this case there is a tax cost of $1,336 [$55,000 - $53,664] of incorporating the business. This results from two integration factors. The first is that the provincial corporate tax rate of 15% exceeds the 13.04% rate required for perfect integration, and second, the provincial dividend tax credit of 30% is below the required provincial dividend tax credit for perfect integration of 30.8%.

Exercise 13-2 Solution

If John incorporates his business, the corporation will pay income taxes of $30,000 [(30%) ($100,000)], leaving $70,000 to be distributed as taxable dividends. His individual income tax payable on the receipt of eligible dividends would be calculated as follows:

Eligible dividends received	$ 70,000
Gross up [(38%)($70,000)]	26,600
Grossed up dividends	$ 96,600
Personal tax rate	42%
Tax before credit	$ 40,572
Dividend tax credit [(6/11 + 28%)($26,600)]	(21,957)
Tax payable on dividends	$ 18,615

The net after-tax retention would be $51,385 ($70,000 - $18,615). This compares to $58,000 [($100,000)(1 - .42)] if he continues to carry on his business as a sole proprietor. In this case there is a tax cost of $6,615 [$58,000 - $51,385] of incorporating the business. This results from two integration factors. The first is that the provincial corporate tax rate of 30% exceeds the 27.54% rate required for perfect integration, and second, the provincial dividend tax credit of 28% is significantly below the required provincial dividend tax credit rate of 45.5%.

Exercise 13-3 Solution

Zircon's taxable income would be calculated as follows:

Net income	$281,000
Dividends from taxable Canadian corporations—ITA 112(1)	(22,000)
2018 Net capital loss—ITA 111(1)(b)	(26,000)
2019 Non-capital loss—ITA 111(1)(a)	(23,000)
Taxable income	$210,000

Zircon's amount eligible for the small business deduction of $198,000 is the least of active business income of $198,000, taxable income of $210,000, and the annual business limit of $500,000. There are no business limit reductions since adjusted aggregate investment income in 2020 was not more than $50,000 and the taxable capital employed in Canada in 2020 was not more than $10 million.

Given these calculations, Zircon's ART on investment income would be calculated using the lesser of:

Aggregate investment income		
Taxable capital gains	$ 46,000	
Net capital loss deducted	(26,000)	
Interest income	15,000	$35,000
Taxable income	$210,000	
Amount eligible for SBD	(198,000)	$12,000

The additional refundable tax on investment income would be $1,280 [(10 2/3%)($12,000)]. Note that the taxable income limit is $23,000 ($35,000 - $12,000) less than the aggregate investment income. This difference is the result of the deduction of the $23,000 2019 non-capital loss. The effect of the calculations is that taxable income of $210,000 is composed of $198,000 of active business income eligible for the small business deduction and the remaining $12,000 is considered investment income. Total corporate taxes would equal $22,460 [(9% small business rate)($198,000) + (38 2/3% investment rate)($12,000)].

Exercise 13-4 Solution

If Ms. Nicastro does not incorporate the investments and continues to own them personally she will pay $51,000 of income tax and retain $49,000. Alternatively, if the investments are incorporated, the results would be as follows:

Corporate investment income	$100,000
Corporate tax at 52%	(52,000)
After-tax income	$ 48,000
Dividend refund [($48,000 ÷ .61667) - $48,000]	29,837
Non-eligible dividends paid to Ms. Nicastro	$ 77,837
Non-eligible dividends received	$ 77,837
Gross up of 15%	11,676
Personal taxable income	$ 89,513
Personal tax rate	51%
Tax payable before dividend tax credit	$ 45,652
Dividend tax credit [(9/13 + 30%)($11,676)]	(11,586)
Personal tax payable with corporation	$ 34,066
Non-eligible dividends received	$ 77,837
Personal tax payable	(34,066)
After-tax cash retained with a corporation	$ 43,771

There would be no tax deferral if the investments are incorporated since the corporate tax rate of 52% exceeds her personal tax rate of 51%. In addition, incorporating the investments would result in a tax cost of $5,229 ($43,771 vs. $49,000). She should not incorporate the investments.

Exercise 13-5 Solution

The amount of Part IV tax payable by Opal Ltd. for its 2021 taxation year would be calculated as follows:

Tax on portfolio dividends [(38 1/3%)($14,000)]	$5,367
Tax on Emerald Inc. dividends	Nil
Tax on Ruby Inc. dividends [(30%)($15,000)]	4,500
Part IV tax payable	$9,867

Exercise 13-6 Solution

Since taxable income is greater than aggregate investment income (comparison used in D in the following table), the 2021 ending balance in GRIP will be calculated as follows:

C—GRIP balance at end of 2020		$ 35,000
D—Taxable income	$960,000	
Income eligible for SBD ($42,750 ÷ 19%)	(225,000)	
Aggregate investment income		
($65,000 + $23,000 - $14,000)	(74,000)	
Adjusted taxable income	$661,000	
Rate	72%	475,920
E—Eligible dividends received in 2021		85,000
G—Eligible dividends paid in 2020		(25,000)
GRIP at end of 2021		$570,920

The eligible dividends paid during 2021 will be deducted from the GRIP in 2022.

Note that, in this exercise, there is no adjusted aggregate investment income grind to the annual business limit for the small business deduction. This is because the 2021 business limit grind would be based on the 2020 adjusted aggregate investment income of $35,000, which was less than the $50,000 threshold.

Exercise 13-7 Solution

The refundable Part I tax of Debut Inc. would be the least of the following three amounts:

Foreign non-business income		$ 15,000
Taxable capital gains		19,125
Rental income		6,500
Interest income		9,200
2017 Net capital loss deducted		(9,000)
Aggregate investment income under ITA 129(4)		$ 40,825
Rate		30 2/3%
Amount before foreign income adjustment		$ 12,520
Deduct excess of: (cannot be negative)		
Foreign non-business tax credit minus	($ 750)	
8% of foreign non-business		
income [(8%)($15,000)]	1,200	Nil
Amount under ITA 129(4)(a)(i)		$ 12,520

Taxable income ($121,825 - $22,000 ITA 112(1) - $9,000 ITA 111(1)(b))	$ 90,825
Deduct:	
Amount eligible for the small business deduction	(50,000)
[(100 ÷ 38 2/3)($750)]* Foreign non-business tax credit	(1,940)
Adjusted taxable income	$ 38,885
Rate	30 2/3%
Amount under ITA 129(4)(a)(ii)	$ 11,925
Amount under ITA 129(4)(a)(iii) = Part I tax payable (given)	$ 19,536

The least of these three amounts is $11,925, and this would be the refundable portion of Part I tax for the year that would be added to the non-eligible RDTOH.

*Can be shortened to $750 ÷ 0.38667

Exercise 13-8 Solution
Dividend Refund on Eligible Dividends The dividend refund on eligible dividends would be $76,667, the lesser of:

- **$76,667** (38 1/3% of the $200,000 of eligible dividends paid in 2021)

- $134,167 (the balance in the eligible RDTOH on December 31, 2021)

Dividend Refund on Non-Eligible Dividends Component 1 of the dividend refund on non-eligible dividends would be $95,833, the lesser of:

- $153,333 (38 1/3% of the $400,000 of non-eligible dividends paid in 2021)

- **$95,833** (the balance in the non-eligible RDTOH on December 31, 2021)

With respect to component 2, 38 1/3% of the $400,000 of non-eligible dividends paid during 2021, or $ 153,333, exceeds the balance in the non-eligible RDTOH by $57,500 ($153,333 - $95,833). Given this, component 2 would be equal to the lesser of:

- the excess of $57,500; o r
- $57,500 ($134,167 - $76,667), the balance left in the eligible RDTOH after the refund on eligible dividends paid.

Self-Study Problem Solutions

Self-Study Problems are available to download from MyLab Accounting.

SSP 13-1 Solution
The required calculations would be as follows:

Corporate Taxes

Income for the year	$50,000
Corporate taxes (17%)	(8,500)
Income available for dividends	$41,500

Personal Taxes on Dividends

Dividend income	$41,500
Gross up (15%)	6,225)
Taxable dividends	$47,725

Tax Payable before dividend tax credit [(33% + 16%)($47,725)]	$23,385
Dividend tax credit [(9/13 + 4/13)($6,225)]	(6,225)
Personal tax payable	$ 17,160

Total Income Taxes

Corporate taxes	$ 8,500
Personal taxes	17,160)
Total taxes	$25,660

Total Taxes on Income Earned Directly

Income for the year	$50,000
Combined federal/provincial tax rate (33% + 16%)	49%)
Personal tax payable	$24,500

While the provincial dividend tax credit is at the rate required for perfect integration, the combined corporate federal/provincial tax rate of 17% is well above the 13.04% that is required to achieve perfect integration. The result is that taxes on $50,000 of income flowed through a corporation are $1,160 ($25,660 - $24,500) higher than the taxes on the same $50,000 had the income been earned by the individual. The conclusion is that it is not advisable to incorporate in this case. There is an argument, however, that because there is significant tax deferral incorporating the business income would provide the business with additional funds to grow as long as there is no immediate need for the individual to access these funds. The deferral amount would be $16,000 [(49% - 17%)($50,000)].

SSP 13-2 Solution

Dividend Refund on Eligible Dividends   The refund on eligible dividends would be the lesser of:

- **$115,000** (38 1/3% of the $300,000 of eligible dividends paid in 2021)

- $201,250 (the balance in the eligible RDTOH on December 31, 2021)

Dividend Refund on Non-Eligible Dividends   Component 1 of the refund on non-eligible dividends would be the lesser of:

- $230,000 (38 1/3% of the $600,000 of non-eligible dividends paid in 2021)

- **$143,750** (the balance in the non-eligible RDTOH on December 31, 2021)

Component 2 would be equal to $86,250, the excess of $230,000, 38 1/3% of the $600,000 of non-eligible dividends paid during 2021, over $143,750, the balance in the non-eligible RDTOH on December 31, 2021. Note that this component of the refund will have to be taken out of the corporation's eligible RDTOH.

The total refund resulting from the payment of non-eligible dividends is $230,000 ($143,750 + $86,250). Note that $230,000 is equal to 38 1/3% of the $600,000 in non-eligible dividends paid.

You should also be aware that the combined refund of $345,000 ($115,000 + $230,000) is equal to the combined balances ($201,250 + $143,750) in the two RDTOH accounts.

When taxable dividends are paid that are non-eligible, dividend refunds can be taken from both RDTOH accounts; however, the non-eligible RDTOH account must first be reduced to nil before the eligible RDTOH can be drawn upon.

SSP 13-3 Solution
Part A—Required Balances for FOL
For FOL, the only refundable taxes paid in 2021 would be on the $7,000 of Canadian interest income. This amount would be added to the non-eligible RDTOH for this corporation. Given this, the December 31, 2021, non-eligible RDTOH balance for FOL would be as follows:

Opening non-eligible RDTOH	$2,000
Refundable portion of Part I tax [(30 2/3%)($7,000)]*	2,147
December 31, 2021, non-eligible RDTOH	$4,147

*While the full calculation of the refundable portion of Part I tax would require selecting the least of the amounts described in ITA 129(4)(a)(i), (ii), and (iii), the problem asks you to assume that the refundable portion of Part I tax is equal to 30 2/3% of aggregate investment income.

Based on this information, FOL's 2021 dividend refund would be $4,147, the lesser of:

- $28,750 [(38 1/3%)($75,000)]; or
- $4,147, the balance in the non-eligible RDTOH.

Part B—Required Balances for SHI
For 2021, SHI would pay Part IV tax as follows:

Part IV tax payable on eligible dividends from Royal Bank [(38 1/3%)($8,000)]	$3,067
Part IV tax payable on SHI's share of FOL's dividend refund on payment of non-eligible dividends (100%)—Part B	4,147
Part IV tax payable	$7,214

SHI's Part I refundable taxes would be as follows:

Interest income	$ 12,000
Taxable capital gain	23,625
Aggregate investment income	$ 35,625
Rate	30 2/3%
Refundable portion of SHI's Part I tax payable	$ 10,925

The December 31, 2021, balances in SHI's RDTOH accounts would be as follows:

Opening eligible RDTOH	Nil
Part IV tax on Royal Bank eligible dividends	$3,067
December 31, 2021, eligible RDTOH	$3,067

Opening non-eligible RDTOH	$10,000
Part IV tax on FOL's non-eligible dividends	4,147
Part I refundable tax on aggregate investment income	10,925
December 31, 2021, non-eligible RDTOH	$25,072

Part C—SHI's Dividend Refund
The amount of taxable dividends that can be designated as eligible is limited by the corporation's GRIP. The balance in this account is $8,000, the initial balance of nil plus the $8,000 in eligible

dividends received from Royal Bank. This means that the maximum amount of dividends that can be designated as eligible is $8,000 and the dividend refund on these dividends would be $3,067, the lesser of:

- $3,067 [(38 1/3%)($8,000)]; or
- $3,067, the balance in SHI's eligible RDTOH.

With $8,000 of the dividends paid designated as eligible, the remaining $42,000 ($50,000 - $8,000) would be non-eligible. The dividend refund on these dividends would be $16,100, the lesser of:

- $16,100 [(38 1/3%)($42,000)]; and
- $25,072, the balance in SHI's non-eligible RDTOH.

SHI's total dividend refund would be as follows:

Dividend refund on eligible dividends	$ 3,067
Dividend refund on non-eligible dividends	16,100)
Total dividend refund	$19,167

SSP 13-4 Solution

Note to Students The assumed tax payable of $23,960 cannot be verified based on the information in the problem. It is, however, a reasonable figure given the information that is available.

Part A—Part IV Tax Payable

The Part IV tax payable for Insal Ltd. would be calculated as follows:

Dividend refund received by Dorne Inc.	$8,400
Insal's percentage of ownership	45%
Part IV tax payable on Dorne's non-eligible dividends	$3,780
Part IV tax payable on public company eligible dividends	
[(38 1/3%)($6,200)]	2,377
Part IV tax payable	$6,157

Part B—Part I Refundable Tax

The refundable portion of the Part I tax would be the least of the following amounts:

Taxable capital gain	$ 12,300
Rental income	4,200
Aggregate investment income	$ 16,500
Rate	30 2/3%
ITA 129(4)(a)(i)	$ 5,060

Taxable income	$ 123,400
Amount eligible for small business deduction	
(see Note)	(45,000)
Total	$ 78,400
Rate	30 2/3%
ITA 129(4)(a)(ii)	$ 24,043

ITA 129(4)(a)(iii) Part I tax payable (given)	$ 23,960

Note As the problem indicates that Insal's tax payable was reduced by a small business deduction of $8,550, the amount eligible for this deduction must have been $45,000 ($8,550 ÷ 19%).

The refundable portion of Part I tax is equal to $5,060, which is the least of the preceding three amounts.

Part C—Eligible RDTOH

The December 31, 2021, the eligible RDTOH balance would be as follows:

Opening eligible RDTOH	$ Nil
Part IV taxes paid on Enbridge's eligible dividends	2,377
December 31, 2021, eligible RDTOH	$2,377

The taxable dividends paid by Dorne were non-eligible. Part IV tax paid by Insal on these dividends can be added to Insal's eligible RDTOH where Dorne, the connected corporation, has drawn upon its eligible RDTOH for its dividend refund; however, this was not the case in this problem.

While the $6,200 of eligible dividends received by Insal from a Canadian public company can be added to Insal's GRIP, the non-eligible dividends received from Dorne cannot be.

Part C—Non-Eligible RDTOH

Insal's December 31, 2021, non-eligible RDTOH would be calculated as follows:

Opening non-eligible RDTOH	$ 4,150
Part IV tax payable on Dorne's non-eligible dividends	3,780
Refundable Part I tax	5,060
December 31, 2021, non-eligible RDTOH	$12,990

Part D—Dividend Refund

The maximum amount of dividends that can be designated as eligible is limited by Insal's GRIP. We know that the initial 2021 balance was nil and that the $6,200 of eligible dividends received from Enbridge would be added. There is also the possibility that a further amount would be added as a result of some of the corporation's income not being eligible for the small business deduction. (This amount cannot be determined based on the information given in the problem.)

However, given Insal's policy of designating dividends as eligible only when a dividend refund is available, a further addition to the GRIP would not be relevant in this problem. This is because a dividend refund will only be available for the balance in the eligible RDTOH, an amount of $2,377. Based on this, the eligible dividend designation will be for $6,200, the amount of the eligible dividends received. The refund on these dividends will be sufficient to pay out all of the eligible RDTOH account of $2,377 [($6,200)(38 1/3%)].

The remaining dividends of $12,050 ($18,250 - $6,200) will be non-eligible.

The refund on these non-eligible dividends would be $4,619, the lesser of:

- $4,619 [(38 1/3%)($12,050)]; and
- $12,990, the balance in the non-eligible RDTOH.

The total dividend refund would be as follows:

Dividend refund on eligible dividends	$2,377
Dividend refund on non-eligible dividends	4,619
Total dividend refund	$6,996

SSP 13-5 Solution
Part A—Part I Tax Payable

The required calculations to determine Part I federal tax payable are as follows:

Net income	$473,900
Dividends ($108,000 + $56,000)—ITA 112(1)	(164,000)
Taxable income	$309,900

Base amount of Part I tax [(38%)($309,900)]	$117,762
Federal tax abatement [(10%)($309,900)]	(30,990)
Small business deduction (Note One)	(41,097)
Additional refundable tax on investment income (Note Two)	9,984
General rate reduction (Note Three)	Nil
Part I federal tax payable	$ 55,659

Note One The small business deduction is 19% of the least of the following three amounts:

1.	Active business income	$216,300
2.	Taxable income (no foreign tax credit adjustment)	$309,900
3.	Business limit	$300,000

The lowest of these figures is the active business income of $216,300, and this gives a small business deduction of $41,097 [(19%)($216,300)].

Note Two The aggregate investment income of $93,600 is calculated as follows:

Interest on government bonds	$36,300
Taxable capital gains	57,300
Aggregate investment income	$93,600

The ITA 123.3 refundable tax (ART) is 10 2/3% of the lesser of:

1.	Aggregate investment income		$93,600
2.	Taxable income	$309,900	
	Deduct: Amount eligible for the SBD	(216,300)	$93,600

The ITA 123.3 tax on aggregate investment income is $9,984 [(10 2/3%)($93,600)].

Note Three The general rate reduction would be calculated as follows:

Taxable income	$309,900
Amount eligible for the small business deduction	(216,300)
Aggregate investment income (Note Two)	(93,600)
Full rate taxable income	Nil
Rate	13%
General rate reduction	Nil

Part B—Refundable Part I Tax Payable

The refundable portion of Part I tax payable would be the least of:

- Amount under ITA 129(4)(a)(i) [(30 2/3%)($93,600)] $28,704
- Amount under ITA 129(4)(a)(ii) [(30 2/3%)($309,900 - $216,300)] $28,704
- Amount under ITA 129(4)(a)(iii) Part I tax payable (Part A) $55,659

The Part I refundable tax payable would be $28,704.

Part C—Part IV tax payable

The required calculation of the Part IV tax payable is as follows:

Part IV tax on portfolio investments [($56,000)(38 1/3%)]	$21,467
Part IV tax on subsidiary dividends*	Nil
Total Part IV tax	$21,467

*The subsidiary is a connected corporation. As it did not receive a dividend refund as a result of paying the dividends, Part IV tax does not apply to the corporate recipient Vader.

Part D—GRIP Balance

Since taxable income is greater than aggregate investment income, the December 31, 2021, GRIP balance would be calculated as follows:

GRIP balance at end of 2020		$ 59,000
Taxable income	$309,900	
Income eligible for SBD	(216,300)	
Aggregate investment income	(93,600)	
Adjusted taxable income	Nil	
Rate	72%	Nil
Eligible dividends received		56,000
Eligible dividends designated in 2020		Nil
GRIP balance at end of 2021		$115,000

Part E—RDTOH Balances—December 31, 2021

The December 31, 2021, balance in the eligible RDTOH would be as follows:

Opening balance	$ Nil
Part IV tax on portfolio investments	21,467
Eligible RDTOH—December 31, 2021	$21,467

The December 31, 2021, balance in the non-eligible RDTOH would be as follows:

Opening balance	$ Nil
Part I refundable tax	28,704
Non-eligible RDTOH—December 31, 2021	$28,704

Part F—Dividend Refunds

The corporation's GRIP balance at the end of 2021 is $115,000. As this is greater than the $32,400 of dividends paid in the year, all of these dividends can be designated as eligible.

The eligible RDTOH of $21,467 is sufficient to support a full dividend refund on $56,000 ($21,467 ÷ 38 1/3%). This is also greater than the $32,400 of eligible dividends paid and means that the dividend refund on eligible dividends paid in 2021 would be equal to $12,420 [(38 1/3%)($32,400)].

No dividend refund would be claimed for 2021 on non-eligible dividends because no non-eligible dividends were paid in 2021.

Part G—Total Federal Tax Payable

The required calculation to determine federal tax payable is as follows:

Part I tax (Part A)	$55,659
Part IV tax (Part C)	21,467
Dividend refund (Part F)	(12,420)
Federal tax payable	$64,706

Part H—RDTOH Balances—January 1, 2022

The January 1, 2022, balance in the eligible RDTOH would be as follows:

Eligible RDTOH—December 31, 2021	$21,467
Dividend refund on 2021 eligible dividends paid	(12,420)
Eligible RDTOH—January 1, 2022	$ 9,047

The January 1, 2022, balance in the non-eligible RDTOH would be as follows:

Non-eligible RDTOH—December 31, 2021	$28,704
Dividend refund on 2021 non-eligible dividends paid	Nil
Non-eligible RDTOH—January 1, 2022	$28,704

SSP 13-6 Solution
Part A—Part I Tax Payable

The Part I tax payable is calculated as follows:

Base amount of Part I tax [(38%)($503,500)]	$191,330
Federal tax abatement [(10%)(72.95%)($503,500)]	(36,730)
Small business deduction [(19%)($200,000, given)]	(38,000)
Additional refundable tax on investment income (Note One)	11,782
General rate reduction (Note Three)	(25,097)
Foreign non-business income tax credit (given)	(8,250)
Foreign business income tax credit (given)	(34,300)
Part I tax payable	$ 60,735

Note One The aggregate investment income of $110,450 is calculated as follows:

Interest on loan to subsidiary	$ 43,250
Foreign investment income	55,000
Taxable capital gains	24,500
Net capital losses claimed	(12,300)
Aggregate investment income (Note Two)	$110,450

The ITA 123.3 refundable tax (ART) is 10 2/3% of the lesser of:

1. Aggregate investment income		$ 110,450
2. Taxable income	$503,500	
Deduct: Amount eligible for the SBD	(200,000)	$303,500

The ITA 123.3 tax on aggregate investment income is $11,782 [(10 2/3%)($110,450)].

Note Two   The definition contained in ITA 129(4.1) excludes income from property that is incidental to carrying on an active business and, as a consequence, we have left out the $5,050 of term deposit interest. With respect to the interest on the loan to the subsidiary, if the subsidiary had deducted the $43,250 in computing active business income eligible for the small business deduction, ITA 129(6) would have deemed this interest to be active business income rather than investment income. However, the problem notes that the subsidiary was not carrying on an active business of its own and therefore would not have claimed the interest expense as a business expense. As a consequence, the interest from the subsidiary remains income from property and is included in its calculation of aggregate investment income.

Note Three   The general rate reduction is based on the amount of taxable income that is not subject to other types of favourable tax treatment. The reduction would be calculated as follows:

Taxable income	$503,500
Amount eligible for the small business deduction (given)	(200,000)
Aggregate investment income (Note One)	(110,450)
Full rate taxable income	$ 193,050)
Rate	13%
General rate reduction	$ 25,097

Part B—Refundable Portion of Part I Tax Payable

The refundable portion of Part I tax would be the least of the following three amounts:

Aggregate investment income (see Note One)		$ 110,450
Rate		30 2/3%
Total		$ 33,872
Deduct excess of:		
Foreign non-business tax credit	($8,250)	
Over 8% of foreign non-business income		
[(8%)($55,000)]	4,400	(3,850)
Amount under ITA 129(4)(a)(i)		$ 30,022

Taxable income	$ 503,500
Deduct:	
Amount eligible for the small business deduction	(200,000)
[(100 ÷ 38 2/3)($8,250)] Foreign non-business tax credit	(21,336)
[(4)($34,300)] Foreign business tax credit	(137,200)
Total	$ 144,964
Rate	30 2/3%
Amount under ITA 129(4)(a)(ii)	$ 44,456

Amount under ITA 129(4)(a)(iii) = Part I tax payable (Part A)	$ 60,735

The least of these three amounts is $30,022, the amount calculated under ITA 129(4)(a)(i).

Part C—Part IV Tax Payable

The Part IV tax payable would be calculated as follows:

On eligible portfolio dividends received [(38 1/3%)($19,600)]	$ 7,513
Share of dividend refund included in non-eligible dividends from subsidiary [(75%)($12,750)]	9,563
Part IV tax payable	$17,076

Part D—GRIP Balance

Since taxable income is greater than aggregate investment income, the December 31, 2021, GRIP balance would be calculated as follows:

GRIP balance at end of 2020		$ Nil
Taxable income	$503,500	
Income eligible for SBD	(200,000)	
Aggregate investment income	(110,450)	
Adjusted taxable income	$193,050	
Rate	72%	138,996
Eligible dividends received		19,600
Eligible dividends designated in 2020		Nil
GRIP balance at end of 2021		$158,596

Part E—RDTOH Balances

The December 31, 2021, balance in the eligible RDTOH would be as follows:

Opening nalance	$ Nil
Part IV tax on eligible dividends—Portfolio investments	7,513
Eligible RDTOH—December 31, 2021	$7,513

The December 31, 2021, balance in the non-eligible RDTOH would be as follows:

Opening balance ($23,500 - $9,600)	$13,900
Part I refundable tax	30,022
Part IV tax on non-eligible subsidiary dividends	9,563
Non-eligible RDTOH—December 31, 2021	$53,485

Part F—Dividend Refund

Dividend refunds are calculated on the basis of dividends paid, not dividends declared. The relevant total here is $109,000 [$25,000 + (3)($28,000)].

As the corporation's GRIP balance of $158,596 is larger than this total of $109,000, the corporation's policy would require that the full amount of the dividend be designated as eligible. The eligible RDTOH of $7,513 is only sufficient to support a full dividend refund on $19,600 ($7,513 ÷ 38 1/3%). If $109,000 of dividends paid are designated eligible, the refund on these eligible dividends would be $7,513, the lesser of:

- $41,783 [(38 1/3%)($109,000)]; or
- $7,513, the balance in the eligible RDTOH.

The non-eligible RDTOH of $53,485 is sufficient to support a full dividend refund on $139,527 ($53,485 ÷ 38 1/3%). If all of the taxable dividends paid are designated eligible a dividend refund is only possible from the eligible RDTOH account at year end, which is only $7,513.

Part G—Total Federal Tax Payable

The required calculation to determine federal tax payable is as follows:

Part I tax (Part A)	$60,735
Part IV tax (Part C)	17,076
Dividend refund (Part F)	(7,513)
Federal tax payable	**$70,298**

Part H—Advice on Dividend Policy

Sinzer's dividend policy to maximize eligible dividends, which was beneficial to the individual shareholder, limits the dividend refund that can be claimed. This is because eligible dividends are only permitted to trigger a dividend refund to the extent there exists an eligible RDTOH balance at the end of the year. The dividend policy should optimize the dividend refund while maximizing eligible dividends.

The eligible RDTOH of $7,513 would all be refunded on the payment of $19,600 in eligible dividends [(38 1/3%)($19,600) = $7,513]. The remaining $89,400 would be non-eligible dividends, which would enable the company to claim a dividend refund of $34,270 [(38 1/3%)($89,400)] because it is less than the balance of $53,485 in the non-eligible RDTOH. The total dividend refund for 2021 would be $41,783 [$7,513 + $34,270], which would reduce federal tax payable to $36,028 [$70,298 - $41,783] from $70,298, a difference of $34,270, which is the dividend refund attributable to the non-eligible RDTOH account.

The increase in the personal tax rate going from eligible to non-eligible dividends is about 8.4 percentage points higher in 2021. This means that additional income taxes of $7,510 [(8.4%)($89,400)] will be payable versus a dividend refund to the company of $34,270.

SSP 13-7 Solution
Part A—Net and Taxable Income

The calculation of Acme Imports' net income for tax purposes and taxable income would be as follows:

Accounting income before taxes		$232,300
Additions:		
Amortization expense	$29,500	
Charitable donations	25,000	
Taxable capital gain on sale of equipment [(1/2)($84,500 - $62,000)]	11,250	
Golf club membership	2,800	
50% of business meals and entertainment	3,360	
Share issue costs [(80%)($950)]	760	
Costs of supplementary letters patent	7,000	
Interest on mortgage for the land	12,300	91,970
Deductions:		
CCA (Note One)	($53,050)	
Gain on sale of equipment ($84,500 - $27,500)	(57,000)	(110,050)
Net income for tax purposes		**$214,220**
Charitable donations		(25,000)
Dividends from Sarco Ltd.		(24,000)
Taxable income		**$165,220**

Note One The maximum CCA on the class 8 equipment would be calculated as follows:

Opening UCC	$256,000
Disposition—Lesser of:	
Proceeds of disposition = $84,500	
Capital cost = $62,000	(62,000)
CCA base	$194,000
Rate	20%
CCA—Class 8	$ 38,800

The customer list, as well as the cost of the supplementary letters patent, would be added to class 14.1. The maximum CCA for this class would be as follows:

Opening UCC	Nil
Additions ($183,000 + $7,000)	$190,000
AccII adjustment [(1/2)($190,000)]	95,000
CCA base	$285,000
Rate	5%
CCA—Class 14.1	$ 14,250

Based on this, the maximum total CCA would be $53,050 ($38,800 + $14,250).

Several of the items in this problem need further comment. These are as follows:

- **Item 4** With respect to the costs of issuing shares, such amounts have to be deducted over at least five years at a maximum rate of 20% per year (Ref: ITA 20(1)(e)).

- **Item 6** Only 50% of the $6,720 in charges at the local golf and country club are deductible (Ref: ITA 67.1)).

- **Item 7** The cars provided to the principal shareholder and to the manager of the company will result in their being assessed a taxable benefit. However, these employment-related costs are fully deductible to the company.

- **Item 10** The fees paid to the site consultant are deductible as indicated in ITA 20(1)(dd). ITA 18(3.1) disallows the deduction of interest on financing related to land during construction. The $12,300 interest on the $244,000 mortgage on the land would be added to the cost of the land and is not deductible.

Part B—Active Business Income

The active business income of Acme is as follows:

Net income for tax purposes		$214,220
Dividends		(24,000)
Aggregate investment income:		
Interest revenue	($10,000)	
Taxable capital gain	(11,250)	(21,250)
Active business income		$168,970

Part C—Federal Tax Payable

The calculation of Acme Ltd.'s federal tax payable would be as follows:

Base amount of Part I tax [(38%)($165,220)]	$62,784
Federal tax abatement [(10%)($165,220)]	(16,522)
Small business deduction (Note Two)	(31,392)
Additional refundable tax on investment income (Note Three)	Nil
General rate reduction (Note Four)	Nil
Part I tax payable	$14,870
Part IV tax payable (Note Five)	3,000
Dividend refund (no taxable dividends paid)	Nil
Federal tax payable	$17,870

Note Two As Acme and Sarco's combined adjusted aggregate investment income exceeds $50,000, there will be a grind of the annual business limit. The amount of the grind is as follows:

$$[(\$500,000/\$500,000)][(5)(\$110,000 - \$50,000)] = \$300,000$$

You can also calculate the business limit grind of $300,000 be recognizing that $110,000 of adjusted aggregate investment income is 60% of the way between $50,000 and $150,000, which is the range in which the limit is reduced. Sixty percent of $500,000 equals $300,000.

Applying this grind, the small business deduction is 19% of the least of the following three amounts:

1.	Active business income (Part B)	$168,970
2.	Taxable income (no foreign tax credit adjustment)	$165,220
3.	Reduced annual business limit ($500,000 - $300,000)	$200,000

This gives a small business deduction of $31,392 [(19%)($165,220)].

Note Three The ITA 123.3 refundable tax (ART) is 10 2/3% of the lesser of:

1.	Aggregate investment income (Part B)		$21,250
2.	Taxable income	$165,220	
	Deduct: Amount eligible for the SBD	(165,220)	Nil

Since the income eligible for the small business deduction is equal to taxable income, there is no ART.

Note Four The general rate reduction would be nil, calculated as follows:

Taxable income	$165,220
Amount eligible for the small business deduction	(165,220)
Aggregate investment income (Part B)	(21,250)
Full rate taxable income	Nil
Rate	13%
General rate reduction	Nil

Note Five The Part IV tax on Sarco's non-eligible dividends would be as follows:

Sarco's dividend refund	$5,000
Acme's ownership percentage	60%
Acme's share of refund = Part IV tax payable	$3,000

Part D—RDTOH Balances

The amount of refundable Part I tax will be the least of the following three amounts. In this problem, the calculation of these amounts is greatly simplified by the absence of foreign non-business income. The calculations are as follows:

ITA 129(4)(a)(i) $6,517—This amount would be 30 2/3% of aggregate investment income of $21,250 ($10,000 + $11,250).

ITA 129(4)(a)(ii) Nil—This amount would be 30 2/3% of taxable income, reduced by the amount of income that is eligible for the small business deduction [(30 2/3%) ($165,220 - $165,220)].

ITA 129(4)(a)(iii) $14,870—This amount would be the Part I tax payable.

The least of these amounts is nil, so there would be no refundable portion of Part I tax.

At the beginning of 2021, both the eligible RDTOH and the non-eligible RDTOH were nil. As there is no addition to the eligible RDTOH for the year, the December 31, 2021, balance in the eligible RDTOH is nil.

The December 31, 2021, balance in the non-eligible RDTOH would be as follows:

Opening non-eligible RDTOH	$ Nil
Part IV tax payable on Sarco's non-eligible dividend	3,000
Non-eligible RDTOH—December 31, 2021	$3,000

The December 31, 2021, GRIP would be as follows:

GRIP balance at end of 2020		Nil
Taxable income	$165,220	
Income eligible for SBD	(165,220)	
Aggregate investment income	(21,250)	
Adjusted taxable income	$ Nil	
Rate	72%	Nil
Eligible dividends received		Nil
Eligible dividends designated in 2020		Nil
GRIP balance at end of 2021		Nil

SSP 13-8 Solution
Part A—Net and Taxable Income

Brasco's minimum net income for tax purposes and taxable income would be calculated as follows:

Active business income (given)		$ 171,000
Net taxable capital gains (given)		36,000
Canadian source interest income		2,200
Eligible portfolio dividends		15,800
Foreign source investment income (gross amount)		4,500
Non-eligible dividends from subsidiary		37,800
Net income for tax purposes		**$ 267,300**
Dividends received:		
Portfolio	($ 15,800)	
Subsidiary	(37,800)	(53,600)
Charitable donations		(11,900)
2019 Non-capital loss		(25,800)
2019 Net capital loss (Note One)		(36,000)
Taxable income		**$140,000**

Note One   Note that the net capital loss carry forward is limited to the net taxable capital gains. This will leave a 2019 net capital loss balance of $28,500 ($64,500 - $36,000) to claim against other taxation years.

Part B—Part I Tax Payable (FTC = Amount Withheld)

Assuming the foreign non-business tax credit is equal to the amount withheld, Brasco's tax payable would be calculated as follows:

Base amount of Part I tax [(38%)($140,000)]	$ 53,200
Federal tax abatement [(10%)($140,000)]	(14,000)
Small business deduction (Note Two)	(23,750)
Additional refundable tax on investment income (Note Three)	715
General rate reduction (Note Four)	(1,079)
Foreign non-business tax credit (given as amount withheld)	(675)
Part I tax payable	$ 14,411

Note Two   The small business deduction is 19% of the least of the following three amounts:

1. Active business income (given)		$171,000
2. Taxable income	$140,000	
Deduct:		
[(100/28)($675)] Foreign non-business tax credit	(2,411)	$137,589
3. Allocated annual business limit (given)		$125,000

The lowest of these figures is the allocated annual limit of $125,000, and this gives a small business deduction of $23,750 [(19%)($125,000)].

Note Three   The aggregate investment income of $6,700 is calculated as follows:

Taxable capital gains	$ 36,000
Net capital loss carry forward deducted	(36,000)
Canadian interest	2,200
Foreign investment income	4,500
Aggregate investment income	$ 6,700

The ITA 123.3 refundable tax (ART) is 10 2/3% of the lesser of:

1. Aggregate investment income		$ 6,700
2. Taxable income	$140,000	
Deduct: Amount eligible for the SBD	(125,000)	$15,000

The ITA 123.3 tax on aggregate investment income is $715 [(10 2/3%)($6,700)].

Note Four   The general rate reduction is based on the amount of taxable income that is not subject to other types of favourable tax treatment. The reduction would be calculated as follows:

Taxable income	$ 140,000
Amount eligible for the small business deduction (Note Two)	(125,000)
Aggregate investment income (Note Three)	(6,700)
Full rate taxable income	$ 8,300
Rate	13%
General rate reduction	$ 1,079

Part C—Refundable Part I Tax Payable

The refundable portion of Part I tax will be the least of the following three amounts:

Aggregate investment income (Note Three)		$ 6,700
Rate		30 2/3%
		$ 2,055
Deduct excess of:		
Foreign non-business tax credit	($675)	
Over 8% of foreign non-business income		
[(8%)($4,500)]	360	(315)
Amount under ITA 129(4)(a)(i)		$ 1,740

Taxable income		$ 140,000
Deduct:		
Amount eligible for the small business deduction		(125,000)
[(100 ÷ 38 2/3)($675)] Foreign non-business tax credit		(1,746)
Adjusted taxable income		$ 13,254
Rate		30 2/3%
Amount under ITA 129(4)(a)(ii)		$ 4,065

Amount under ITA 129(4)(a)(iii) = Part I tax payable	$ 14,411

The least of these three amounts would be $1,740, the amount calculated under ITA 129(4)(a)(i).

Part D—Part IV Tax Payable

The calculation of Part IV tax payable would be as follows:

Part IV tax on Masco's non-eligible dividends [(60%)($24,1520)]	$14,490
Part IV tax on eligible dividends from portfolio investments	
[(38 1/3%)($15,800)]	6,057
Part IV tax payable	$20,547

Part E—GRIP Balance

The 2021 ending balance in GRIP will be calculated as follows:

GRIP balance at beginning of 2021		$ 126,000
Taxable income	$140,000	
Income eligible for SBD	(125,000)	
Aggregate investment income	(6,700)	
Adjusted taxable income	$ 8,300	
Rate	72%	5,976
Eligible dividends received		15,800
Eligible dividends designated in 2020		Nil
GRIP balance at end of 2021		$ 147,776

Any eligible dividends paid during 2021 will be deducted from the GRIP in 2022.

Part F—RDTOH Balances

The December 31, 2021, eligible RDTOH balances would be as follows:

Opening balance	$ 7,000
Part IV tax on eligible dividends—Portfolio investments	6,057
Eligible RDTOH—December 31, 2021	$13,057

The December 31, 2021, balance in the non-eligible RDTOH would be as follows:

Opening balance	$ Nil
Part I refundable tax	1,740
Part IV tax on Masco's non-eligible dividends	14,490
Non-eligible RDTOH—December 31, 2021	$ 16,230

Part G—Dividend Refund

Brasco paid $39,000 in taxable dividends, creating a potential refund of $14,950 [(38 1/3%) ($39,000)]. Given Brasco's GRIP balance of $147,776, the entire $39,000 dividend could be designated as eligible. However, the eligible RDTOH balance is only $13,057. Given this, the maximum designation on which a full refund would be available would be $34,062 ($13,057 ÷ 38 1/3%).

If $34,062 of the dividends paid are designated eligible, the dividend refund on these eligible dividends would be $13,057, the lesser of:

- $13,057 [(38 1/3%)($34,062)]; or
- $13,057, the balance in the eligible RDTOH.

This would leave $4,938 ($39,000 - $34,062) as non-eligible dividends. The dividend refund on these non-eligible dividends would be $1,893, the lesser of:

- $1,893 [(38 1/3%)($4,938)]; or
- $16,230, the balance in the non-eligible RDTOH.

Based on this, the total dividend refund would be as follows:

Dividend refund on eligible dividends	$ 13,057
Dividend refund on non-eligible dividends	1,893
Total dividend refund	$ 14,950

CHAPTER 14

Learning Objectives

After completing Chapter 14, you should be able to:

1. Explain why the acquisition of control legislation was added to the ITA and what the rules are desined to accomplish (Paragraph [P hereafter] 14-1 to 14-10).
2. Describe the importance of a loss restriction event and explain, with a few examples, situations in which it would apply (P 14-11 to 14-14).
3. Explain the impact on an acquired corporation when its control has been acquired in terms of its year end and any impact on donation carry forward amounts and non-capital and net capital losses (P 14-15 to 14-27).
4. Describe and apply the income tax consequences to a corporation that has been subject to an acquisition of control in terms of accrued and unrealized losses on its property including elective options that may be available if there are accrued but unrealized gains (P 14-28 to 14-35).
5. Explain the purpose of the associated corporation rules (P 14-36 to 14-41).
6. Apply the associated corporation rules (P 14-42 to 14-62).
7. Explain the purpose of investment tax credits and how the rules apply when CCPCs incur qualifying capital and current expenditures (P 14-63 to 14-77).
8. Determine the refundable investment tax credits available to individuals and CCPCs (P 14-78 to 14-82).
9. Explain how the acquisition of control rules apply to investment tax credits (P 14-83 to 14-85).
10. Describe the type of distributions that a corporation can make to its shareholders (P 14-86 to 14-87).
11. Describe the parallel between financial statement accounts and income tax accounts (P 14-88 to 14-90).
12. Describe the three tax attributes of shares and explain how the tax concept of PUC is determined and how it differs from the ACB of shares (P 14-91 to 14-96).
13. Explain the purpose of a capital dividend account (CDA) and how it is calculated (P 14-97 to 14-100).
14. Describe the different types of dividends contemplated by the ITA and the impact of corporate law (P 14-101 to 14-107).
15. Describe a stock dividend, its general treatment under corporate law, and the income tax implications (P 14-108 to 14-112).
16. Explain how the payment of dividends with corporate property is treated for income tax purposes (P 14-113 to 14-117).
17. Describe the procedures necessary to elect capital dividend treatment and the income tax treatment when capital dividends are received, including the consequences of overpaying the CDA (P 14-118 to 14-123).
18. Describe the circumstances under which ITA 84(1) applies to create a deemed dividend, including any exceptions to the rule. Calculate the deemed dividend and determine the post-dividend ACB and PUC for one shareholder (P 14-124 to 14-132).

19. Describe the reporting requirements when there is a deemed dividend (P 14-133).
20. Explain the general circumstances that cause deemed dividend treatment under ITA 84(2). In addition, calculate the deemed dividend and determine the impact on the ACB and PUC of one shareholder (P 14-134 to 14-139).
21. Explain the circumstances that would result in a deemed dividend under ITA 84(3) and determine the resulting income tax consequences (P 14-140 to 14-144).
22. Explain the circumstances that cause ITA 84(4) and (4.1) to apply, including why the treatment is different. In addition, calculate the income tax consequences, including the impact on PUC and ACB of one shareholder (P 14-145 to 14-149).
23. Summarize and compare the income tax consequences of each of the five deemed dividend provisions of ITA 84 (P 14-150).

How to Work through Chapter 14

Visit pearsonmylabandmastering.com to access MyLab Accounting for this text. Once there, you can access student resources such as Self-Study Problems, Practice Exams, Flashcards, updates, and more.

We recommend the following approach in dealing with the material in this chapter:

Chapter Introduction
- Read paragraph 14-1 to 14-3 (in the text).

Acquisition of Control Rules
- Read paragraph 14-4 to 14-27.
- Do Exercise 14-1 (in the text) and check the solution in this Study Guide.
- Read paragraph 14-28 to 14-29.
- Do Exercise 14-2 and check the solution in this Study Guide.
- Read paragraph 14-30 to 14-35.
- Do Exercise 14-3 and check the solution in this Study Guide.
- Do Self-Study Problems 14-1 and 14-2, which are available on MyLab, and check the solutions in this Study Guide.

Associated Corporations—ITA 256
- Read paragraph 14-36 to 14-62.
- Do Exercise 14-4 and check the solution in this Study Guide.
- Do Self-Study Problems 14-3 and 14-4 and check the solutions in this Study Guide.

Investment Tax Credits—ITA 127(5)
- Read paragraph 14-63 to 14-74.
- Do Exercise 14-5 and check the solution in this Study Guide.
- Read paragraph 14-75 to 14-77.
- Do Exercise 14-6 and check the solution in this Study Guide.

Refundable Investment Tax Credits—ITA 127.1
- Read paragraph 14-78 to 14-83.
- Do Exercise 14-7 and check the solution in this Study Guide.
- Do Self-Study Problem 14-5 and check the solution in this Study Guide.
- Read paragraph 14-84 to 14-85.

Corporate Distribution Principles
- Read paragraph 14-86 to 14-87.

Tax Basis Equity Concepts (Including PUC and ACB)
- Read paragraph 14-88 to 14-96.
- Do Exercise 14-8 and check the solution in this Study Guide.

Capital Dividend Account—ITA 89(1)
- Read paragraph 14-97 to 14-100.
- Do Exercise 14-9 and check the solution in this Study Guide.
- Do Self-Study Problems 14-6 and 14-7 and check the solutions in this Study Guide.

Corporate Distributions (Stock Dividends and Dividends in Kind)
- Read paragraph 14-101 to 14-112.
- Do Exercise 14-10 and check the solution in this Study Guide.
- Read paragraph 14-113 to 14-117.
- Do Exercise 14-11 and check the solution in this Study Guide.

Capital Dividends—ITA 83(2)
- Read paragraph 14-118 to 14-123.

ITA 84(1) Deemed Dividends—Increase in PUC
- Read paragraph 14-124 to 14-131.
- Do Exercise 14-12 and check the solution in this Study Guide.
- Read paragraph 14-132.

A Word on Reporting Deemed Dividends
- Read paragraph 14-133.

ITA 84(2) Deemed Dividends—Reorganization
- Read paragraph 14-134 to 14-139.
- Do Exercise 14-13 and check the solution in this Study Guide.

ITA 84(3) Deemed Dividends—Share Redemption
- Read paragraph 14-140 to 14-144.
- Do Exercise 14-14 and check the solution in this Study Guide.

ITA 84(4) and ITA 84(4.1) Deemed Dividends
- Read paragraph 14-145 to 14-150.
- Do Exercise 14-15 and check the solution in this Study Guide.
- Do Self-Study Problem 14-8 and check the solution in this Study Guide.

To Complete This Chapter
- Visit MyLab Accounting for more practice problem material, and test yourself with the glossary flashcards.
- Review the Key Terms at the end of the chapter, and consult the glossary for definitions.
- Ensure you have achieved the Chapter 14 Learning Objectives listed in this Study Guide.
- As a review, view the PowerPoint presentations available on MyLab.

Practice Examination
- Available on MyLab, write the Practice Examination for this chapter, and mark it using the solutions provided.

Exercise Solutions

Exercise 14-1 Solution
No Acquisition of Control Net income for 2021 is $289,000 ($42,000 + $247,000) and, if there was no acquisition of control, the total 2020 non-capital loss of $135,000 could be deducted. This would result in a 2021 taxable income of $154,000 ($289,000 - $135,000).

Acquisition of Control If there was an acquisition of control on January 1, 2021, net income would be unchanged at $289,000. However, in this case the 2020 non-capital loss of $135,000 could only be used to the extent of the income from the pen business of $42,000. This means that taxable income would be $247,000 ($289,000 - $42,000) with a 2020 non-capital balance of $93,000 ($135,000 - $42,000).

Exercise 14-2 Solution

The income tax consequences of the AOC with respect to the two properties are as follows:

Land Since there is an unrealized loss of $78,000, the provisions of ITA 111(4)(c) and (d) apply to treat the loss as a capital loss, which becomes an allowable capital loss of $39,000 [($293,000 - $215,000)(50%)] and potentially a net capital loss unless there are any taxable capital gains in the deemed taxation year. In addition, the ACB of the land is reduced by $78,000, from $293,000 to $215,000.

Class 8 property If all of the class 8 property were sold for FMV of $184,000 there would be a terminal loss of $92,000, therefore ITA 111(5.1) applies to cause the terminal loss to be deducted. In addition, the $92,000 is deemed to be CCA such that the UCC at the beginning of the next taxation year is reduced to $184,000. The capital cost and ACB of the depreciable property are not changed.

Exercise 14-3 Solution

Based on the facts, the company would need to trigger $220,000 of capital gains, which would equate to $110,000 of taxable capital gains. This would offset the $110,000 of net capital losses from 2019 and prevent the AOC rules from tainting those net capital losses. In addition, the company can afford to trigger up to an additional $45,000 in income, which would be offset with the business loss of $45,000.

It would clearly be desirable to elect to have a deemed disposition of the non-depreciable property. The elected amount can be between $500,000 and $650,000. Electing the maximum amount of $650,000 would be advisable. This would result in a $75,000 taxable capital gain [(1/2)($650,000 - $500,000)]. This will leave a net capital loss balance of $35,000 ($110,000 - $75,000).

The $35,000 balance could be eliminated by electing to have a deemed disposition of the depreciable property at an elected value of $470,000, which is within the allowable elective range of $400,000 to $500,000. This election would produce the required taxable capital gain of $35,000 [(1/2)($470,000 - $400,000)].

The election would also result in recapture of $50,000 ($400,000 - $350,000). As this is $5,000 ($50,000 - $45,000) greater than the current-year business loss, this would result in some taxable income and tax payable. However, the ability to use the remaining $35,000 net capital loss carry forward is probably worth the cost of the tax payable on the extra $5,000 of income. In addition, the election would result in increased future CCA based on a new capital cost, for CCA purposes only, of $435,000 [$400,000 + (1/2)($470,000 - $400,000)].

Exercise 14-4 Solution

Top and Middle Top and Middle are associated under ITA 256(1)(a) as Top controls Middle with 65%. ITA 256(1)(b) would also have applied since both Top and Middle are controlled by Mr. Top.

Top and Bottom Top and Bottom are associated under ITA 256(1)(b) as they are both controlled by the same person, Mr. Top. He controls Top directly with 100%. In addition, he controls Bottom through a combination of direct ownership, indirect ownership, and deemed ownership. His majority interest would be calculated as follows:

Direct interest in Bottom	5%
Deemed ownership through Top Company [(100%)(10%)]	10%
Indirect interest through control of Middle Company	35%
Deemed ownership through son—ITA 256(1.3)	15%
Deemed ownership through options—ITA 256(1.4)	10%
Controlling interest	75%

Middle and Bottom   Middle and Bottom are associated under ITA 256(1)(b) as they are both controlled by the same person, Mr. Top. Mr. Top controls Middle indirectly through Top. He controls Bottom through a combination of direct and indirect control, as described in the discussion of Top and Bottom.

Exercise 14-5 Solution

With respect to the $125,000 in apprentice salaries, the investment tax credit is limited to eligible salaries of $20,000 per apprentice. As a result, the 2021 investment tax credit is $10,000 [(5 employees)(10%)(eligible salary of $20,000 each)]. This $10,000 credit will be added to income in 2022 as a result of ITA 12(1)(t).

With respect to the $3,000,000 in capital expenditures, there will be a 2021 investment tax credit of $300,000 [(10%)($3,000,000)]. The $300,000 credit will not affect the calculation of CCA for 2021, which will be $900,000 [(20%)(1.5)($3,000,000)].

In 2022, the $300,000 investment tax credit claimed in 2021 will reduce the capital cost of the class 8 property by $300,000, from $3,000,000 to $2,700,000. As a result, the January 1, 2022, UCC will be $1,800,000 (reduced capital cost $2,700,000 - 2021 CCA $900,000). CCA for 2022 will be $360,000 [(20%)($1,800,000)].

Exercise 14-6 Solution

For 2021, the A value in the reduction formula would be $2,500,000 ($12,500,000 - $10,000,000). Based on this, the amount that would be available for the enhanced 35% investment tax credit would be calculated as follows:

$$[\$3,000,000][(\$40,000,000 - \$2,500,000) \div \$40,000,000] = \$2,812,500$$

TIP: Legislative calculations are often cumbersome and can be determined in other ways. You can double check the results by using a shortcut calculation. The expenditure limit is reduced where the taxable capital employed in Canada is between $10 and $50 million. Determine the percentage distance between these two points of the taxable capital. That amount is the reduction. In this case, the taxable capital is $2.5 million above the $10 million limit. This represents 6.25% between the two points [$2.5/$40 million] of $10 and $50 million and is the reduction. This leaves 93.75% of the $3 million expenditure limit, or $2,812,500 [($3 million)(0.9375)].

Exercise 14-7 Solution

As Sci-Tech has taxable income of less than $500,000 in the previous year, and its taxable capital employed in Canada is less than $10 million, it is a qualifying company and its expenditure limit for the year is not reduced.

Given the $3,000,000 expenditure limit for the 35% rate, the total amount of investment tax credits available can be calculated as follows:

Qualified property [(10%)($123,000)]	$ 12,300
SRED current expenditures [(35%)($1,200,000)]	420,000
Total available amount	$432,300

The refund available would be as follows:

Qualified property [(40%)($12,300)]	$ 4,920
SRED current expenditures [(100%)($420,000)]	420,000
Total refund available	$424,920

The non-refunded investment tax credit of $7,380 ($432,300 - $424,920) can be carried forward 20 years to be applied against tax payable. There was no tax payable in the last three years, so it cannot be carried back.

The cost of the qualified property will be reduced in the following year by the refundable investment tax credit claimed of $4,920. The $420,000 tax credit on current SRED expenditures will be added to income in the following taxation year under ITA 12(1)(t).

Exercise 14-8 Solution

The ACB of the shares to the individual investor would be determined as follows:

	Number of Shares	Cost/Share	Total Cost
First purchase	2,400	$1.10	$2,640
Second purchase	3,850	$1.82	7,007
Totals	6,250		$9,647

The ACB for all of the investor's shares is $9,647. The ACB per share would be $1.54 ($9,647 ÷ 6,250). The ACB is determined under ITA 47 (discussed in Chapter 8) using a weighted average calculation.

The PUC for the investor's shares would be calculated as follows:

	Number of Shares	PUC/Share	Total PUC
First sale	100,000	$1.10	$110,000
Second sale	50,000	$1.35	67,500
Third sale	30,000	$1.82	54,600
Total PUC of the class of shares	180,000		$232,100

Number of shares (from first table)	6,250
PUC per share [$232,100 ÷ 180,000 shares]	$ 1.29
Total PUC for the investor	$8,063

Exercise 14-9 Solution

The balance in the capital dividend account on November 1, 2021, would be as follows:

2019 Capital gain on land [(1/2)($22,000)]	$ 11,000
2020 Capital dividend received	8,200
2021 Sale of goodwill [(1/2)($43,000 - ACB nil)]	21,500
2021 ABIL	(6,000)
2021 Capital dividend paid	(16,000)
Balance—November 1, 2021	$18,700

Note that goodwill can only have a tax cost or ACB if the goodwill is actually purchased. Internally generated goodwill has no such cost and therefore the cost and ACB would be nil.

Exercise 14-10 Solution

The required calculations are as follows:

FMV per share	$ 25.00
Stock dividend shares received [(5%)(1,000)]	50
Non-eligible dividend received	$1,250.00
Gross up [(15%)($1,250.00)]	187.50
Taxable dividend	$ 1,437.50
Dividend tax credit [(9/13)($187.50)]	$ 129.81

Jean's 2021 net income would be increased by the taxable dividend of $1,437.50. His federal income tax payable would be decreased by the dividend tax credit of $129.81.

	Number of Shares	ACB/Share	Total ACB
Pre-dividend shares	1,000	$18	$18,000
Stock dividend addition—ITA 52(3)(a)	50	$25	1,250
Totals	1,050		$19,250

The per share ACB of Jean's shares would be $18.33 ($19,250 ÷ 1,050).

The number of shares issued and outstanding after the stock dividend equals 24,570 [(105%)(23,400 shares)].

The addition to the PUC of the shares equals the declared dividend of $29,250 [(5%)(23,400)($25)] such that the total PUC after the stock dividend equals $380,250 [$351,000 + $29,250].

The PUC per share would be $15.48 ($380,250 ÷ 24,570).

Exercise 14-11 Solution

The income tax consequences to the corporation are as follows:

POD [($51)(150,000)]	$ 7,650,000
ACB [($42)(150,000)]	(6,300,000)
Capital gain	$ 1,350,000
Inclusion rate	1/2
Taxable capital gain	$ 675,000

The income tax consequences for Sandrine are as follows:

Non-eligible dividend received [(15%)($51)(150,000)]	$ 1,147,500
Gross up [(15%)($1,147,500)]	172,125
Taxable dividend	$1,319,625
Dividend tax credit [(9/13)($172,125)]	$ 119,163

Cloutier Ltd.'s 2021 net income would be increased by the $675,000 taxable capital gain. In addition, its CDA would increase by the same amount. Sandrine's 2021 net income would be increased by the taxable dividend of $1,319,625. Her federal tax payable would be decreased by the dividend tax credit of $119,163. The cost and therefore ACB of the shares received as a dividend in kind are $1,147,500, which is the FMV of those shares at the time of the dividend (ITA 52(2)).

Exercise 14-12 Solution

This transaction will result in an ITA 84(1) deemed dividend for all shareholders, calculated as follows:

PUC of new shares [(40,000)($12.70)]	$508,000
Increase in net assets (debt reduction)	(450,000)
ITA 84(1) Deemed dividend	$ 58,000

The deemed dividend is would be allocated proprtionally to all 166,000 (126,000 + 40,000) shares outstanding, on the basis of $0.35 per share (deemed dividend $58,000 ÷ 166,000 shares).

Absent a capital dividend election there would be an eligible or non-eligible dividend. The $0.35 per share dividend would also be added to the ACB of all 166,000 shares as a result of ITA 53(1)(b).

With the addition of $0.35 resulting from the ITA 84(1) deemed dividend to the original issue price of $10.50, the ACB of the shares would be $10.85 per share. Mr. Uni's sale of 5,000 shares at $13.42 per share would result in a taxable capital gain calculated as follows:

POD [($13.42)(5,000)]	$ 67,100
ACB [($10.85)(5,000)]	(54,250)
Capital gain	$ 12,850
Inclusion rate	1/2
Taxable capital gain	$ 6,425

Exercise 14-13 Solution

The analysis of the $2,350,000 distribution would be as follows:

Cash distributed	$2,350,000
PUC reduction	(180,000)
ITA 84(2) Deemed dividend	$2,170,000

To the extent the company has a balance in its GRIP account, some amount of the $2,170,000 dividend could be designated as eligible. Any remainder will be taxed as a non-eligible dividend.

There is no disposition of shares as the corporation continues to exist. The PUC of the shares to the sole shareholder is $70,000 [$250,000 - $180,000 PUC reduction], and the ACB is also the same $70,000 [cost $250,000 - ACB adjustment ITA 53(2)(a)(ii) $180,000].

Exercise 14-14 Solution

The redemption transaction would have no income tax consequences to Ms. Tandy. The income tax consequences to Ms. Tandy 's brother, however, would be as follows:

Redemption amount [(15,000)($11.75)]	$176,250
PUC [(15,000)($8.25)]	(123,750)
ITA 84(3) Deemed dividend	$ 52,500
Gross up of 15%	7,875
Taxable dividend	$ 60,375
Dividend tax credit [(9/13)($7,875)]	$ 5,452
Redemption amount [(15,000)($11.75)]	$176,250
ITA 84(3) Deemed dividend	(52,500)
Modified POD	$123,750
ACB [(15,000)($7.90)]	(118,500)
Capital gain	$ 5,250
Inclusion rate	1/2
Taxable capital gain	$ 2,625

Both the taxable dividend and the taxable capital gain would increase the net income of Ms. Tandy's brother by a total of $63,000 ($60,375 + $2,625). The federal dividend tax credit would decrease federal tax payable by $5,452.

Exercise 14-15 Solution

ITA 84(4) deems there to be a dividend to the extent that the payment of $330,000 exceeds the reduction in the PUC of $225,000. As a result, there will be a deemed dividend of $105,000 and the remaining $225,000 is considered a tax-free distribution. The PUC of the shares will be reduced from $450,000 to $225,000 as a result. In addition, there will be a reduction in the ACB from $625,000 to $400,000 as a result of ITA 53(2)(a)(ii). The deemed dividend, absent a capital dividend election, will be either an eligible or non-eligible dividend.

Self-Study Problem Solutions

Self-Study Problems are available to download from MyLab Accounting.

SSP 14-1 Solution
Part A—Non-Capital and Net Capital Losses
Business Loss   The business loss for the period January 1, 2021, to March 31, 2021, would be as follows:

Reported business loss	($23,000)
Accounts receivable adjustment ($45,000 - $33,000)—ITA 111(5.3)	(12,000)
Building election—Recaptured CCA ($285,000 - $270,000)	15,000
Fixtures and equipment—Deemed CCA ($95,000 - $90,000)	(5,000)
Vehicles election—Recaptured CCA ($87,000 - $80,000)	7,000
Business loss for taxation year ending March 31, 2021	($18,000)

Net and Taxable Income   Net income and taxable income for the period ending March 31, 2021, would be as follows:

ITA 3(a)—Sources of income		Nil
ITA 3(b)—Net taxable capital gains (losses):		
Elections under ITA 111(4)(e):		
Gain on land [(1/2)($420,000 - $275,000)]	$72,500	
Gain on building [(1/2)($320,000 - $285,000)]	17,500	
Required write-down—ITA 111(4)(c) and (d)		
Loss on temporary investments		
[(1/2)($53,000 - $23,000)]	(15,000)	75,000
ITA 3(c)—Total		$75,000
ITA 3(d)—Business loss		(18,000)
Net income		$ 57,000
Net capital losses = 2019 loss of $34,000 + 2020 loss of $41.000		
(limited to amount included under ITA 3(b))		(75,000)
Taxable income		Nil

Net Capital Loss   The net capital loss that cannot be claimed in a taxation year subsequent to the March 31, 2021, taxation year would be as follows:

From 2019	$34,000
From 2020	42,500
Net capital loss balance at March 31, 2021	$76,500
Amount deducted in 2021	(75,000)
2020 Net capital loss lost balance	$ 1,500

March 31, 2021 Taxation Year Non-Capital Loss   The non-capital loss carry forward would be calculated as follows:

Business loss	$ 18,000
Net capital loss deducted	75,000
Subtotal	$ 93,000
Income under ITA 3(c)	(75,000)
Non-capital loss for the taxation year ending March 31, 2021	$ 18,000
2019 Non-capital loss balance	63,500
2020 Non-capital loss balance	78,500
Total non-capital losses available after March 31, 2021	$ 160,000

Part B—Loss Carry Forward in 2021

The April 1 to December 31, 2021, net income would be $78,000 ($123,000 - $45,000). Note that there is no restriction against deducting the current-year loss on bread operations against other sources of income. However, none of the non-capital losses to March 31, 2021, can be claimed since those losses are restricted by ITA 111(5) and can only be claimed against income from the loss business in subsequent taxation years. This leaves the December 31, 2021, taxation year results as $78,000 for both net income and taxable income. The non-capital losses available to be claimed in taxation years after December 31, 2021, are unchanged at $160,000.

Part C—Loss Carry Forward In 2021

The $40,000 business loss on the figurines must first be applied against the business income from the bread business. As a result, net income will be $171,000 ($211,000 - $40,000). As this income is entirely from the loss business, all of the $160,000 of non-capital losses for the three taxation years can be claimed, resulting in taxable income of $11,000. There are no non-capital loss balances remaining for taxation years after December 31, 2022.

SSP 14-2 Solution
Part A

As a result of the acquisition of control, LF will have a deemed taxation year end on April 30, 2021. This results in a short January 1, 2021, through April 30, 2021, taxation year for LF. The effects of this include the following:

- An additional taxation year will be counted toward the expiry of the non-capital losses.
- If CCA is to be taken, it will have to be prorated for a short fiscal period.
- All of the usual year-end procedures (timing of bonuses, inclusion of reserves, etc.) will have to be carried out.
- For the first year after the acquisition of control, LF can choose a new fiscal year end on any date up to 53 weeks after the deemed year end.

Other implications are as follows:

- Any net capital loss balance that remains cannot be used in a taxation year ending after the deemed year end.
- Any non-capital loss balance that is carried forward can only be used against income from the loss business and other businesses that are the same or similar.
- The manufacturing equipment, because its FMV is less than its UCC, will have to be written down to the $285,000 UCC value. The $90,000 ($375,000 - $285,000) amount of the write-down will be treated as deemed CCA. This amount is not subject to proration for a short fiscal period.

Part B

The land, class 1 property, and class 8 property all have an FMV in excess of their tax costs. If the deemed disposition election is made and the FMV of these properties is used as the elected value, the results would be as follows:

Asset	Recapture	Capital Gain
Land ($925,000 - $450,000)	N/A	$475,000
Class 1 ($650,000 - $515,000)	$135,000	Nil
Class 8 ($15,000 - $10,000)	5,000	Nil
Total income	$140,000	$475,000

Part C

If the companies believe they will be able to generate sufficient income to claim the non-capital losses in subsequent taxation years, they will not want to make elections that will result in any unneccessary income for the deemed taxation year. If the elections are made, adjustments will be made to the ACB or UCC balances of the properties that were the subject of the elective treatment. In the case of the land, the increased cost will not be of benefit until the land is sold. In the case of the depreciable property, the increased UCC will only be deductible at the applicable rates of 4% or 20%. Alternatively, a non-capital loss balance can be claimed in full for the taxation year in which there is income against which the losses can be applied.

The situation with net capital losses is different. If such losses are not used during the deemed taxation year they cannot be claimed in any taxation year subsequent to the deemed year end. As a result it would be recommended to make an election that would absorb the 2019 $65,000 net capital loss. This will require capital gains of $130,000 [(2)($65,000)], which can be created by electing a deemed disposition on the land at a value of $580,000. This election will create a taxable capital gain of $65,000 [(1/2)($580,000 - $450,000)], which is sufficient to use the net capital loss in full.

Given the required write-down of the manufacturing equipment, the business loss would be calculated as follows:

Reported business loss to April 30, 2021 (given)	($ 55,000)
Deemed CCA on class 53 ($375,000 - $285,000)	(90,000)
Business loss for the taxation year ending April 30, 2021	($ 145,000)

Using this figure, along with the results of the election on the land, net income and taxable income would be calculated as follows:

ITA 3(a) sources of income	Nil
ITA 3(b) net taxable capital gains	
Election under ITA 111(4)(e) on land	$ 65,000
ITA 3(c) total	$ 65,000
ITA 3(d) business loss	(145,000)
Net income	Nil
2019 Net capital loss (limited to ITA 3(b) amount)	($ 65,000)
Taxable income for the taxation year ending April 30, 2021	Nil

The non-capital loss for the taxation year ending April 30, 2021, would be calculated (ITA 111(8)) as follows:

Business loss	$ 145,000
Net capital loss deducted	65,000
Subtotal	$ 210,000
Income under ITA 3(c)	(65,000)
Non-capital loss—Taxation year April 30, 2021	$ 145,000
2019 Non-capital loss	180,000
2020 Non-capital loss	140,000
Total non-capital losses	$ 465,000

The 2019 net capital loss balance would be reduced to nil by the claim for the taxation year ending April 30, 2021.

Part D

If there is uncertainty with respect to the ability of LF to generate sufficient business income in the loss business or in another business that is the same or similar, additional elections should be made to absorb as much of the non-capital losses as possible. This would require elections on all of the properties with capital gains or recapture. Under this approach, business income would be recalculated as follows:

Reported business loss to April 30, 2021 (given)	($ 55,000)
Deemed CCA on class 53 ($375,000 - $285,000)	(90,000)
Class 1—Recaptured CCA	135,000
Class 8—Recaptured CCA	5,000
Business loss for the taxation year ending April 30, 2021	($ 5,000)

The resulting net and taxable income would be determined as follows:

ITA 3(a)—Sources of income	Nil
ITA 3(b)—Net taxable capital gains (losses):	
Capital gain on land [(1/2)($925,000 - $450,000)]	$ 237,500
ITA 3(c)—Total	$ 237,500
ITA 3(d)—Business loss	(5,000)
Net income	$ 232,500
2019 Net capital loss	(65,000)
Subtotal	$ 167,500
2019 Non-capital loss	
(maximum needed to reduce income to nil)	(167,500)
Taxable income	Nil

Under this Part D approach, the non-capital loss carry forward at April 30, 2021, would be calculated as follows:

Net business loss for the period	$ 5,000
Net capital loss deducted	65,000
Subtotal	$ 70,000
Income under ITA 3(c)	(237,500)
Non-capital loss for the taxation year ending April 30, 2021	Nil

2019 Non-capital loss balance	$ 12,500
2020 Non-capital loss balance	140,000
Total non-capital losses available	$ 152,500

SSP 14-3 Solution
Part A

John Fleming and Eric Flame are related persons by the fact that they are married to individuals who are connected by a blood relationship (their wives). In addition, under ITA 256(1.5) a person who owns shares in two or more corporations shall be, as a shareholder of one of the corporations, deemed to be related to himself or herself as a shareholder of the other corporation(s).

Given this, Fleming Ltd. and Lartch Inc. are associated under ITA 256(1)(d). John Fleming controls Fleming Ltd., is a member of a related group (John Fleming and Eric Flame) that controls Lartch Inc., and John owns more than 25% of the voting shares of Lartch Inc.

In a similar fashion, Flame Ltd. is associated with Lartch Inc. under ITA 256(1)(d), as Eric Flame controls Flame Ltd., is a member of a related group (John Fleming and Eric Flame) that controls Lartch Inc., and Eric owns more than 25% of the voting shares of Lartch Inc.

Based on these associations, Fleming Ltd. and Flame Ltd. are associated under ITA 256(2), as they are both associated with a third corporation, Lartch Inc., and the two corporations would not otherwise be associated as a result of ITA 256(1). If it were desirable, Lartch Inc. could make the appropriate election under ITA 256(2) to break the association between Fleming Ltd. and Flame Ltd. The business limit for Lartch Inc. would be reduced to nil. Lartch Inc. would continue to be separately associated with each of Fleming Ltd. and Flame Ltd.

Part B

Mr. and Mrs. Cuso are a group with respect to both Male Ltd. and Female Inc. because they are shareholders of each corporation. The group of persons concept allows the formation of a group of persons with any shareholders as long as the group owns more than 50% of the shares of each corporation. Therefore, the two companies are associated under ITA 256 (1)(b). The fact that Mr. and Mrs. Cuso are related is not relevant.

Part C

Ms. Jones and Miss Lange are a group that controls Alliance Ltd. However, they do not control Breaker Inc., as Mrs. Kelly (not a member of the group that controls Alliance Ltd.) owns 50% of the shares. Therefore, Alliance Ltd. and Breaker Inc. are not associated.

Part D

While they are not related, Mr. Martin and Mr. Oakley constitute a group [ITA 256(1.2)(a)] with respect to both Martin Inc. and Oakley Ltd. As both Martin Inc. and Oakley Ltd. are controlled by the same group, the two companies are associated under ITA 256(1)(b). Groups can be formed from related or unrelated individuals as long as each individual owns shares in each corporation and the combined share total for each corporation exceeds 50%.

Part E

The two companies are not associated. While Lily and James are related, they are not a group with respect to the two companies and there is no cross-ownership of shares. Note that if one of the two individuals has de facto control of both corporations, then the two companies would be associated, although we have not provided sufficient information to make that determination. In addition, ITA 256(2.1) applies to associate two corporations if there is no valid reason to carry on a single business through two corporations.

SSP 14-4 Solution
Case 1

As a group, Mr. Jones and Mr. Twitty control both Jones Ltd. with 55% and Twitty Inc. with 60%. As a consequence, these two companies would be associated under ITA 256(1)(b).

Case 2

Ms. Wynette controls Wynette Enterprises Ltd. and is related to each member of the group that controls Lynn Inc. In addition, Ms. Wynette has the necessary 25% cross-ownership in Lynn Inc. As a consequence, Wynette Enterprises Ltd. and Lynn Inc. are associated under ITA 256(1)(d).

Case 3

A group, consisting of Mr. Travis and Mr. Cash has control of both Cowboys Ltd. with 67% and Horses Inc. with 100%. Therefore, Cowboys Ltd. and Horses Inc. are associated under ITA 256(1)(b).

Case 4

As Randy's Boots Inc. controls Hill Inc., those two companies are associated under ITA 256(1)(a).

As Mr. Nelson owns 80% of the shares of Willie's Hits Ltd., he controls that company. This gives him control over the 20% of Hill Inc. shares that are owned by Willie's Hits.

However, Mr. Nelson does not control Randy's Boots, and this means that his indirect interest in Hill Inc. through Randy's Boots of 24% [(30%)(80%)] is the product of the two ownership percentages.

As a result, his overall interest in Hill Inc. is only 44% (20% + 24%), which is not sufficient to give him control over Hill. Therefore, Willie's Hits Ltd. and Hill Inc. are not associated and Willie's Hits Ltd. and Randy's Boots Inc. are not associated.

Case 5

Ms. Parton controls Alpha Company, is related to each member of the group (Ms. Parton and her spouse) that control Beta Company, and has cross-ownership of at least 25% of Beta Company. This means that these two companies are associated under ITA 256(1)(d).

Her spouse controls Centra Company, is related to each member of the group (the spouse and Ms. Parton) that controls Beta Company, and has the necessary cross-ownership of at least 25% of Beta Company shares. This means that these two companies are also associated under ITA 256(1)(d).

As they are not controlled by the same individual or group, Alpha Company and Centra Company are not associated under ITA 256(1). However, as they are both associated with the same third corporation (Beta Company), Alpha and Centra would be associated under ITA 256(2). Note that ITA 256(2) allows Alpha and Centra to avoid association provided Beta elects not to be associated with either company. This will mean, however, that Beta will have a business limit for the period of nil. While the election breaks the association between Alpha and Centra, both corporations remain separately associated with Beta.

Case 6

For the purposes of association, Ms. Gale is deemed to own the 30% interest in Norton Music Inc. owned by her minor child [ITA 256(1.3)] and the 20% interest in Norton Music Inc. for which she holds an option [ITA 256(1.4)]. When this is combined with her own interest of 10%, she would be considered to control Norton Music Inc. As she controls both Kristal Enterprises Ltd. and Norton Music Inc., these companies are associated as a result of ITA 256(1)(b).

SSP 14-5 Solution

Case A

Luxor's 2021 expenditure limit would be $2,887,500. This amount is calculated as follows:

$$[\$3,000,000][(\$40,000,000 - \$1,500,000) \div \$40,000,000]$$

TIP: $1.5 million (the amount in excess of $10 million) is 3.75% of the distance between $10 and $50 million (1.5 ÷ $40 million). Therefore, 3.75% would be the reduction in the $3 million expenditure limit of $112,500.

Case B

Gargle's 2021 expenditure limit would be $2,827,500, calculated as follows:

$$[\$3,000,000][(\$40,000,000 - \$2,300,000) \div \$40,000,000]$$

TIP: $2.3 million (the amount in excess of $10 million) is 5.75% of the distance between $10 and $50 million (2.3 ÷ $40 million). Therefore, 5.75% would be the reduction in the $3 million expenditure limit of $172,500.

As the eligible SRED current expenditures exceed this limit, some of the expenditures will only be eligible for the 15% rate:

Total current SRED expenditures	$ 3,200,000
2021 Expenditure limit (eligible for 35% rate)	(2,827,500)
Limited to 15% rate	$ 372,500

The total amount of investment tax credits available can be calculated as follows:

Qualified property [(10%)($86,000)]	$ 8,600
SRED current expenditures:	
At 35% rate [(35%)($2,827,500)]	989,625
At 15% rate [(15%)($372,500)]	55,875
Total available amount	$1,054,100

Gargle is a qualifying corporation, therefore the refund available would be as follows:

	Rate	ITC	Refund
Qualified property	40%	$ 8,600	$ 3,440
SRED current expenditures	100%	989,625	989,625
SRED current expenditures	40%	55,875	22,350
Total available		$1,054,100	$1,015,415

The non-refunded investment tax credit of $38,685 ($1,054,100 - $1,015,415) can be carried forward 20 years to be applied against tax payable. There was no tax payable in the last three years, so it cannot be carried back.

The cost of the qualified property will be reduced in 2022 by the refundable investment tax credit of $3,440. The $1,011,975 ($989,625 + $22,350) refundable tax credit on current SRED expenditures will be added to income in 2022.

Case C

With respect to the $250,000 in apprentice salaries, the investment tax credit is available on an annual salary maximum of $20,000 per apprentice. As a result, there will be a $17,500 [(5)(10%)($15,000) + (5)(10%)($20,000 maximum)] credit against 2020 federal tax payable. This $17,500 credit will be added to income in 2021.

With respect to the $800,000 in capital expenditures, there will be a 2021 credit against federal tax payable of $80,000 [(10%)($800,000)].

The $80,000 credit will not influence the calculation of 2020 CCA. This amount will be $360,000 [(30%)(150%)($800,000)].

In 2021, the $80,000 credit will reduce the capital cost of the property to which it relates, which will indirectly reduce the UCC of the class (ITA 13(7.1)). UCC at December 31, 2021, would be $360,000 ($720,000 - 2020 CCA $360,000). Given this, 2021 CCA will be $108,000 [(30%)($360,000)].

SSP 14-6 Solution

The December 31, 2021, balance in the capital dividend account is calculated as follows:

2010 Capital gain [(1/2)($343,500 - $225,000)]	$ 59,250
2011 Life insurance proceeds	162,000
2013 Capital loss [(1/2)($150,000 - $220,000)]	(35,000)
2015 Capital dividend received	26,000
2019 Capital gain [(1/2)($80,000 - $50,000)]	15,000
2019 Capital loss [(1/2)($45,000 - $100,000)]	(27,500)
2019 to 2021 Capital dividends paid [(3)($45,000)]	(135,000)
Balance—December 31, 2021	$ 64,750

SSP 14-7 Solution
The December 31, 2021, balance in the capital dividend account is calculated as follows:

2010 Life insurance proceeds	$186,000
2012 Capital dividend received	26,300
2017 Capital dividend paid	(45,200)
2018 Capital gain [(1/2)($226,100 - $184,300)]	20,900
2020 Capital gain [(1/2)($93,400 - $48,600)]	22,400
2020 Capital loss [(1/2)($108,300 - $112,600)]	(2,150)
2021 Capital dividend paid	(16,400)
Balance—December 31, 2021	$191,850

SSP 14-8 Solution
Case 1
The corporation in this case has made a distribution that includes a return of PUC. Of the five deemed dividend provisions there are three deemed dividends that relate to a return of PUC—ITA 84(2), (4), and (4.1). Since ITA 84(4.1) only applies to public companies it can be excluded. ITA 84(2) applies on a reorganization of a company's business, which would include a discontinued business and winding-up of a business. The facts indicate this is not the reason for the return of capital. This leaves ITA 84(4), which is applicable in this case.

ITA 84(4) deems there to be a dividend to the extent that the distribution exceeds and reduction of PUC. The result is that there is a deemed dividend of $97,000 ($260,000 - $163,000). The dividend would be prorated among shareholders of the class of shares that resulted in a reduction of PUC. Since there is only one shareholder, all of the deemed dividend will be attributable to that individual. The amount to be included in net income will be $111,550 [(115%)($97,000)]. The inidvidual will be entitled to a federal dividend tax credit of $10,073 [(9/13)(gross up of $14,550)].

The part of the distribution represented by the PUC reduction of $163,000 is tax free. The PUC and ACB of outstanding shares would be as follows:

- The PUC of Mr. Farnsworth's shares will be reduced to $160,000 ($323,000 - $163,000).
- The ACB of Mr. Farnsworth's shares will be reduced to $299,000 ($462,000 - $163,000) (ITA 53(2)(a)(ii)).

Case 2
Technically there are two deemed dividend provisions that result in a corporation redeeming or cancelling its shares. The first is ITA 84(2) that applies when a corporation's business is wound up as a result of the winding-up of the corporation. The facts indicate this not to be the case, and therefore ITA 84(2) does not apply. This leaves ITA 84(3), which applies when ITA 84(2) does not apply to this type of redemption transaction.

The income tax consequences to Ms. Chawla resulting from the redemption of her shares would be as follows:

Redemption amount [($20.80)(125,000)]	$2,600,000
PUC [($20)(125,000)]	(2,500,000)
ITA 84(3) Deemed dividend	$ 100,000

Redemption amount [($20.80)(125,000)]	$2,600,000
ITA 84(3) Deemed dividend	(100,000)
Proceeds of disposition	$2,500,000
ACB [($16.80)($125,000)]	(2,100,000)
Capital gain	$ 400,000
Inclusion rate	1/2
Taxable capital gain	$ 200,000

For purposes of determining net income, the ITA 84(3) dividend will be grossed up by 15% to $115,000 [(115%)($100,000)], resulting in a total increase in net income of $315,000 ($115,000 + $200,000). Ms. Chawla will also be entitled to a federal dividend tax credit of $10,385 [(9/13) ($15,000)]. There are no ACB adjustments. The PUC of the remaining shares will have decreased from $5,000,000 to $2,500,000.

Case 3

The debt settlement transaction results in an increase in the legal capital and therefore PUC of the shares of the corporation without a matching increase in net assets. ITA 84(1) is the only deemed dividend provision that applies where the PUC of a corporation is increased in these circumstances.

This transaction will result in an ITA 84(1) deemed dividend for all shareholders of the class of shares, calculated as follows:

PUC of new shares [(42,000)($24.10)]	$1,012,200
Increase in net assets (liability eliminated)	(900,000)
ITA 84(1) Deemed dividend	$ 112,200

This would be allocated to all 275,000 (233,000 + 42,000) shares outstanding, on the basis of $0.408 per share ($112,200 ÷ 275,000).

Sue's share of the dividend would be $9,506 [(23,300)($0.408)] and her net income will increase by $10,932 [(115%)($9,506)].

The deemed dividend will be added to the ACB of her shares as a result of ITA 53(1)(b), resulting in an ACB of $22.908 ($22.50 + $0.408)] per share. She will be entitled to a federal dividend tax credit of $987 [(9/13)($1,426)].

The income tax consequences of selling her shares would be as follows:

POD [(23,300)($24.85)]	$579,005
ACB [(23,300)($22.908)]	(533,756)
Capital gain	$ 45,249
Inclusion rate	1/2
Taxable capital gain	$ 22,625

This will result in a total increase in net income of $33,557 ($22,625 + $10,932).

Instructor Note: This is not covered in the chapter text and the problem, but is for information purposes only. Note that she will also realize a capital gain of $102,694 [(POD of debt $1,012,200 - ACB of debt $900,000) - $9,506 representing part of the difference that was included in her income as a dividend].

Case 4

The reduction of PUC in this case is as a result of the reorganization of the corporation's business (i.e., the liquidation of a part of its business). The result is that ITA 84(2) applies to the transaction. In this case, however, there is also a disposition given that the return of capital occurs as part of the cancellation of shares. In addition, there is an election to treat the deemed dividend as a capital dividend.

The initial analysis of the $1,175,000 distribution would be as follows:

Cash distributed	$1,175,000
PUC of shares cancelled [(40%)($800,000)]	(320,000)
ITA 84(2) Deemed dividend	$ 855,000
ITA 83(2) Capital dividend	(855,000)
Taxable dividend	$ Nil

The capital dividend is distributed tax free. Since there is no taxable dividend there is no gross up or dividend tax credit.

The transaction would also result in an allowable capital loss calculated as follows:

Cash distributed	$ 1,175,000
ITA 84(2) Deemed dividend	(855,000)
Proceeds of disposition	$ 320,000
ACB [(40%)($1,450,000)]	(580,000)
Capital loss	($ 260,000)
Inclusion rate	1/2
Allowable capital loss	($ 130,000)

The capital loss of $260,000 is disallowed since the sole shareholder is affiliated to the corporation after the share transaction. An individual is affiliated with a corporation if she controls the company. The $260,000 capital loss will be added to the ACB of her remaining shares. The new ACB will be $1,130,000 [(60%)($1,450,000) + $260,000)].

CHAPTER 15

Learning Objectives

After completing Chapter 15, you should be able to:

1. Explain how a corporation can be used to reduce income tax, defer income tax, and facilitate income splitting (Paragraph [P hereafter] 15-1 to 15-11).
2. Describe other non-tax advantages and disadvantages of incorporation (P 15-12 and 15-13).
3. Use various individual and corporate income tax rates to determine post-tax retention of an individual where sources of income have been incorporated with after-tax corporate distributions made to individual shareholders (P 15-14 to 15-26).
4. Calculate the amount of tax reduction and tax deferral that is available when sources of income are incorporated within a public corporation (P 15-27 to 15-35).
5. Calculate the amount of tax reduction and tax deferral that is available through the use of a CCPC earning active business income (P 15-36 to 15-41).
6. Explain why bonusing down is contemplated and the advantages to individual shareholders of a CCPC eligible for the small business deduction (P 15-42 to 15-46).
7. Calculate the amount of tax reduction and tax deferral that is available through the use of a CCPC earning investment income other than dividends (P 15-47 to 15-49).
8. Calculate the amount of tax reduction and tax deferral that is available through the use of a CCPC earning dividend income (P 15-50 to 15-54).
9. Summarize the tax reduction and tax deferral conclusions available through the use of various types of corporations earning different types of income (P 15-55 to 15-57).
10. Identify the impact of provincial income taxes on the decision to incorporate (P 15-58 to 15-74).
11. Explain why significant amounts of taxable dividends can be received tax free by individuals with no other sources of income (P 15-75 to 15-86).
12. Describe and calculate the benefits that can be achieved by using a corporation for income splitting purposes (P 15-87 to 15-88).
13. Describe how shareholder benefits are determined and explain the income tax consequences (P 15-89 to 15-103).
14. Describe the purpose of the shareholder loan rules, how they apply, and the exceptions (P 15-104 to 15-124).
15. Explain the income tax principles of management compensation in the context of a closely held CCPC (P 15-125 to 15-129).
16. Describe the basic trade-off between the payment of salary and the payment of dividends (P 15-130 to 15-135).
17. Calculate the appropriate choice between salary and dividends, taking into consideration factors other than federal income tax savings (P 15-136 to 15-158).
18. Optimize the salary/dividend mix when all tax credits are not used or there is a limited amount of cash in the corporation (P 15-159 to 15-174).
19. Summarize the various non-tax factors that must be taken into consideration in making salary vs. dividend decisions (P 15-175 to 15-176).

How to Work through Chapter 15

Visit pearsonmylabandmastering.com to access MyLab Accounting for this text. Once there, you can access student resources such as Self-Study Problems, Practice Exams, Flashcards, updates, and more.

We recommend the following approach in dealing with the material in this chapter:

The Decision to Incorporate—Basic Tax Considerations
- Read paragraph 15-1 to 15-11 (in the text).

Other Advantages and Disadvantages of Incorporation
- Read paragraph 15-12 to 15-13.
- Do Self-Study Problems 15-1 and 15-2, which are available on MyLab, and check the solutions in this Study Guide.

Basic Example Data—Tax Reduction and Deferral
- Read paragraph 15-14 to 15-26.

Public Corporations—Tax Reduction and Deferral
- Read paragraph 15-27 to 15-35.
- Do Exercise 15-1 (in the text) and check the solution in this Study Guide.

CCPCs—Active Business Income—Tax Reduction and Deferral
- Read paragraph 15-36 to 15-41.
- Do Exercise 15-2 and check the solution in this Study Guide.
- Read paragraph 15-42 to 15-46.

CCPCs—Non-Dividend Investment Income—Tax Reduction and Deferral
- Read paragraph 15-47 to 15-49.
- Do Exercise 15-3 and check the solution in this Study Guide.
- Do Self-Study Problem 15-3 and check the solution in this Study Guide.

CCPCs—Dividend Income—Tax Reduction and Deferral
- Read paragraph 15-50 to 15-54.

Conclusions on Tax Reductions and Deferrals
- Read paragraph 15-55 to 15-57.
- Do Exercises 15-4 and 15-5 and check the solutions in this Study Guide.
- Do Self-Study Problem 15-4 and check the solution in this Study Guide.

Provincial Taxes and Integration
- Read paragraph 15-58 to 15-74.
- Do Self-Study Problem 15-5 and check the solution in this Study Guide.

Tax-Free Taxable Dividends
- Read paragraph 15-75 to 15-86.

Income Splitting
- Read paragraph 15-87 to 15-88.
- Do Self-Study Problem 15-6 and check the solution in this Study Guide.

Shareholder Benefits
- Read paragraph 15-89 to 15-92.
- Do Exercises 15-6 and check the solutions in this Study Guide.
- Read paragraph 15-93 to 15-103.

Shareholder Loans
- Read paragraph 15-104 to 15-124.
- Do Exercises 15-7 to 15-9 and check the solutions in this Study Guide.
- Do Self-Study Problems 15-7 and 15-8 and check the solutions in this Study Guide.

Management Compensation—General Principles
- Read paragraph 15-125 to 15-129.

Salary vs. Dividend Decisions
- Read paragraph 15-130 to 15-158.
- Do Exercise 15-10 and check the solution in this Study Guide.

Salary vs. Dividends—Use of Tax Credits
- Read paragraph 15-159 to 15-174.
- Do Exercises 15-11 and 15-12 and check the solutions in this Study Guide.

Salary vs. Dividends—Conclusion
- Read paragraph 15-175 to 15-176.
- Do Self-Study Problems 15-9 to 15-11 and check the solutions in this Study Guide.

To Complete This Chapter
- Visit MyLab Accounting for more practice problem material, and test yourself with the glossary flashcards.
- Review the Key Terms at the end of the chapter, and consult the glossary for definitions.
- Ensure you have achieved the Chapter 15 Learning Objectives listed in this Study Guide.
- As a review, view the PowerPoint presentations available on MyLab.

Practice Examination
- Available on MyLab, write the Practice Examination for this chapter, and mark it using the solutions provided.

Exercise Solutions

Exercise 15-1 Solution

As the new corporation would not be allocated any part of the business limit, all of the $100,000 would be taxed at full corporate rates:

Corporate income	$100,000
Corporate taxes [(26.5%)($100,000)]	(26,500)
Available for dividends	$ 73,500
Eligible dividends received by Ms. Ashley	$ 72,000
Gross up at 38%	27,360
Non-eligible dividends	1,500
Gross up at 15%	225
Taxable dividends	$101,085
Ms. Ashley's tax rate	45%
Tax payable before dividend tax credit	$ 45,488
Dividend tax credit [(6/11 + 47.1%)($27,360)]	(27,810)
Dividend tax credit [(9/13 + 31.0%)($225)]	(226)
Personal tax payable	$ 17,452
Taxable dividends received	$ 73,500
Tax payable	(17,452)
After-tax retention	$ 56,048

This exercise uses a below-average corporate tax rate and an above-average provincial dividend tax credit, both of which are favourable to the use of a corporation. Even with these favourable rates, use of a corporation only improves the after-tax retention by $1,048 ($56,048 - $55,000). GRIP is calculated as 72% of active business income that was not eligible for the small business deduction, and as a result the GRIP is $72,000. This limits the amount that can be paid as an eligible dividend. The remaining $1,500 can only be paid as a non-eligible dividend.

Exercise 15-2 Solution

Mr. Slater's combined tax rate on income earned from the business is 49% (33% + 16%). If the business is incorporated, all of the $126,000 of business profits will be eligible for the small business deduction. This means it will be taxed at a combined corporate income tax rate of 12% (basis rate 38% - abatement 10% - small business deduction 19% + 3% provincial corporate income tax rate). Mr. Slater's effective tax rate on non-eligible dividend income is 41.92% [(115%)(49%) - (9/13 + 27%)(15%)].

Using these tax rates, a comparison of the income retained with and without a corporation is as follows:

	With Corporation	**Without Corporation**
Business income	$126,000	$ 126,000
Tax rate	12%	49%
Tax payable	$ 15,120	$ 61,740
Business income	$126,000	$126,000
Tax payable	(15,120)	(61,740)
Maximum non-eligible dividend payable	$110,880	N/A
Personal tax on dividends [(41.92%)($110,880)]	(46,481)	N/A
After-tax income retained by Mr. Slater	$ 64,399	$ 64,260

There is clearly a significant amount of tax deferral with respect to income left in the corporation. The tax payable on direct receipt of the $126,000 of business income would be $61,740, far higher than the $15,120 that would be paid by the corporation. There would also be a small tax savings as the $64,399 in income retained using the corporation is $139 greater than the $64,260 in income retained without the use of the corporation.

Exercise 15-3 Solution

Mr. Slater's combined tax rate on interest income earned outside the corporation is 51% (33% + 18%). Income tax on the direct receipt of $126,000 of interest income, therefore, would be $64,260.

If he incorporates the source of the interest, the interest income will not be eligible for the small business deduction or the general rate reduction, but will be subject to the ART. This means that if the investments are transferred to a CCPC, the interest will be taxed at a rate of 50 2/3% (38% - 10% + 10 2/3% + 12%). Mr. Slater's effective income tax rate on non-eligible dividends received is 44.2% [(115%)(51%) - (9/13 + 27%)(15%)].

Using these tax rates, a comparison of the income retained with and without the use of a corporation is as follows:

	With Corporation	Without Corporation
Interest income	$ 126,000	$ 126,000
Tax rate	50-2/3%	51%
Tax payable	$ 63,840	$ 64,260
Interest income	$ 126,000	$126,000
Tax payable	(63,840)	(64,260)
Net corporate income before dividend refund	$ 62,160	N/A
Maximum dividend refund (see Note)	38,640	
Maximum dividend payable	$ 100,800	
Personal tax on dividends [(44.2%)($100,800)]	(44,554)	
After-tax income retained by Mr. Slater	$ 56,246	$ 61,740

The balance in the non-eligible RDTOH would as follows:

Non-eligible RDTOH balance [(30 2/3%)($126,000)]	$ 38,640

Note   The refund is the lesser of 38 1/3% of taxable dividends paid and the balance in the non-eligible RDTOH account. The available cash of $62,160 would support a dividend of $100,800 ($62,160 ÷ .61667), which includes a potential dividend refund of $38,640 [(38 1/3%)($100,800)]. In this case the two amounts are both equal to $38,640.

With Mr. Slater's individual tax rate at 51% and the corporate tax rate at 50 2/3%, there is a very small amount of deferral. The amount would be $420 ($64,260 - $63,840), not enough to justify the tax cost associated with the use of a corporation.

The after-tax retention results with a corporation are significantly worse than when the income is received directly. After-tax retention is reduced from $61,740 to $56,246, a reduction of $5,494. There is clearly a tax cost as a result of incorporating the investments.

Exercise 15-4 Solution
Direct Receipt   If the income is received directly, the tax payable will be determined as follows:

Eligible dividends received	$46,000	
Gross up at 38%	17,480	$ 63,480
Non-eligible dividends received	$87,000	
Gross up at 15%	13,050	100,050
Taxable dividends		$163,530
Interest income		32,000
Taxable income		$195,530
Personal tax rate (33% + 18%)		51%
Tax payable before dividend tax credit		$ 99,720
Dividend tax credit		
[(6/11 + 5/11)($17,480)]	($17,480)	
[(9/13 + 4/13)($13,050)]	(13,050)	(30,530)
Personal tax payable		$ 69,190

The after-tax retention can be calculated as follows:

Cash received ($46,000 + $87,000 + $32,000)	$165,000
Tax payable	(69,190)
After-tax retention—Direct receipt	$ 95,810

Incorporate the Investments If the investments are incorporated, the income tax rate on the interest income is 50 2/3% (38% - 10% + 10-2/3% + 12%). Given this, the corporate taxes will be as follows:

Part IV tax on eligible dividends received [(38 1/3%)($46,000)]	$17,633
Part IV tax on non-eligible dividends received	
(100% of the dividend refund received from the subsidiary)	29,000
Tax On Interest Income [(50-2/3%)($32,000)]	16,213
Corporate tax payable before refund	$62,846

Since the corporate tax payable of $62,846 is less than the personal income tax of $69,190, the use of a corporation provides significant tax deferral (the deferral is only on the interest and non-eligible dividends). However, as the client needs all of the investment income, this advantage will not be beneficial.

As a newly incorporated CCPC there would be no opening RDTOH account balance. Given this, the balance in the eligible RDTOH would equal the Part IV tax on the eligible dividends received and would as follows:

Eligible RDTOH balance [(38 1/3%)($46,000)]	$17,633

The balance in the non-eligible RDTOH would be as follows:

Part IV tax on non-eligible dividends received	$29,000
Part I addition [(30 2/3%)($32,000)]	9,813
Non-eligible RDTOH balance	$38,813

The cash available to pay taxable dividends would be $102,154 ($165,000 - $62,846). This amount would support a taxable dividend of $165,654 ($102,154 + 0.61667). Paying a dividend of $165,654 would result in a dividend refund of $63,500 [(38 1/3%)($165,654). However, this exceeds the combined sum of the RDTOH balances of $56,446 ($17,633 + $38,813). This means that the total dividend refund would be limited to $56,446, resulting in the payment of a taxable dividend of $158,600 ($102,154 + $56,446).

The eligible dividends received by the corporation will be added to the GRIP balance, leaving $46,000 in this account. This means that $46,000 in dividends could be designated as eligible. The remainder of the dividends paid of $112,600 ($158,600 - $46,000) would be non-eligible.

This would result in personal taxes as follows:

Eligible dividends received	$ 46,000	
Gross up at 38%	17,480	$ 63,480
Non-eligible dividends received	$112,600	
Gross up at 15%	16,890	129,490
Taxable dividends		$192,970
Personal tax rate		51%
Tax payable before dividend tax credit		$ 98,415
Dividend tax credit		
[(6/11 + 5/11)($17,480)]	($ 17,480)	
[(9/13 + 4/13)($16,890)]	(16,890)	(34,370)
Personal tax payable		$ 64,045
Dividends received ($46,000 + $112,600)		$158,600
Personal tax payable		(64,045)
After-tax retention—With corporation		$ 94,555

As this is less than the $95,810 that would be retained without the use of a corporation, there is no tax advantage in going to the trouble and expense of incorporating the client's investments.

Exercise 15-5 Solution

The client's combined income tax rate on any additional income is 49% (33% + 16%). Based on this, the personal post-tax retention is calculated as follows:

Capital gain	$ 92,000
Personal taxes on taxable capital gain [(49%)(1/2)($92,000)]	(22,540)
After-tax retention—Without a corporation	$69,460

If the investments are incorporated within a CCPC, the aggregate investment income will be $46,000 [(1/2)($92,000)]. The applicable tax rate will be 50 2/3% (38% basic corporate rate - 10% abatement + 10 2/3% ART + 12% provincial tax rate). As this rate is higher than the client's personal tax rate of 49%, there would be no deferral of income tax through the use of a corporation. However, even if the rate was such that there was some tax deferral it would not be relevant to this case since the client requires all of the post-tax funds.

Based on this corporate tax rate, the maximum distribution that can be made would be calculated as follows:

Available cash	$92,000
Corporate tax payable [(50 2/3%)($46,000)]	(23,307)
Capital dividend [(1/2)($92,000)]—ITA 83(2)	(46,000)
Available for non-eligible dividend	$22,693
Dividend refund (see Note)	14,107
Non-eligible dividend received	$36,800

Part I refundable taxes with respect to aggregate investment income is a component of the non-eligible RDTOH and not the eligible RDTOH. The balance in the non-eligible RDTOH would as follows:

Non-eligible RDTOH balance [(30 2/3%)($46,000)]	$14,107

Note The refund is the lesser of 38 1/3% of taxable dividends paid and the balance in the non-eligible RDTOH account. The available cash of $22,693 would support a dividend of $36,800 ($22,693 ÷ .61667), which includes a potential dividend refund of $14,107 [(38 1/3%)($36,800)]. In this case, the two amounts are both equal to $14,107.

The client's tax rate on non-eligible dividend income is 41.35% [(115%)(49%) - (9/13 + 4/13)(15%)]. Based on this, the net after-tax retention when a corporation is used would be as follows:

Tax-free capital dividend received	$46,000
Non-eligible dividend received	36,800
Tax payable on non-eligible dividend received [(41.35%)($36,800)]	(15,217)
After-tax retention—With corporation	$67,583

As this is less than the $69,460 that would be retained on direct receipt of the income, there is no income tax advantage in going to the trouble and expense of incorporating the investments.

Exercise 15-6 Solution

Case 1 Since the plan benefits Ms. Clarke because of her shareholding and is unavailable to any other employees, it would be a shareholder benefit. $15,000 would be added to her income as income from property.

Case 2 The facts indicate that Ms. Clarke appropriated the sale proceeds of $40,000 and therefore is a shareholder benefit to be included in her income as a result of ITA 15(1). The $40,000 amount also must be added to the corporation's income.

Case 3 Ms. Clarke has received a benefit equal to the FMV of what it would cost to stay at equivalent accomodations in Florda at that time of year. Had Ms. Clarke paid some amount it would have reduced the benefit. The portion of expenses for that six-week period would not be allowed as an expense to the corporation.

Case 4 Ms. Clarke has received a shareholder benefit equivalent to the $8,000 of premiums paid by the company on her behalf. Had the insurance been a requirement of a financial institution as collateral security for a loan, then there would have been no shareholder benefit since the primary beneficiary of the payment would have been the corporation.

Case 5 Ms. Clarke has received a shareholder benefit because she has used the corporation to her economic advantage. Had the corporation not signed a guarantee she would not have received financing from the bank. The value of the benefit is equal to what it would have cost her to acquire such a guarantee from an arm's-length person.

Exercise 15-7 Solution
Since Ms. Rourke is a shareholder of a corporation that provided her with a loan, ITA 15(2) applies subject to any available exceptions. The two-year limitation is not relevant since no part of the loan was repaid by December 31, 2022. The minority shareholder exception is also not relevant since a related person, her spouse, owns 10% or more of the issued shares of any class of the capital stock of the corporation. The only possible exception that would apply is the loan for a motor vehicle to be used in her employment duties. This specific loan exception requires meeting two other conditions. The first is that there is a time when it is known that the loan will be repaid. This condition is met since there is a set repayment date of June 30, 2025. The second condition, however, is problematic as it requires that the loan was not received as a result of anyone's shareholding. The fact that her spouse controls the company and the loan is sizable suggests that the loan was received because of a shareholder capacity.

This means that she would not qualify for the motor vehicle exception. In that case, the $50,000 loan would be included in her income as income from property for 2021. She will be entitled to a $50,000 deduction under ITA 20(1)(j) when she repays the loan in 2025.

Exercise 15-8 Solution
The only possible exception in this case is the two-year limitation. Since the corporation made a loan in its taxation year ending June 30, 2021, the deadline for the repayment is one full year (365 days) from June 30, 2021, which is June 30, 2022.

If the loan is repaid on January 1, 2022, it will be paid within the two-year limitation period. As a consequence, the principal amount will not have to be included in Ms. Fisk's income under ITA 15(2). However, as it is an interest-free loan, she will be required to include an interest benefit in her income. The amount for 2021 would be $1,890 [($162,000)(2% - nil)(7/12)]. The interest benefit will be income from property as a result of ITA 80.4(2) since the facts suggest that the loan was received in a shareholder capacity.

If the loan is repaid in full on December 31, 2022, the two-year limitation exception will not apply since the loan was not paid by June 30, 2022. This means the $162,000 will be included in Ms. Fisk's 2021 income as income from property. Since the loan is included in her income there will be no interest benefit (ITA 80.4(3)(b)). The repayment of the loan in 2022 will entitle her to a deduction under ITA 20(1)(j) for that year.

Exercise 15-9 Solution
Since the loan was made in the 2021 taxation year of the corporation the two-year limitation deadline is one year from the last day of the corporation's 2021 taxation year, which is December 31, 2022.

Mr. Hasid will repay one-quarter of the loan, or $30,750, on October 31, 2022, which is within the two-year limitation. This will leave an outstanding balance of $92,250 ($123,000 - $30,750), which will be outside the two-year limitation.

If in an Employment Capacity   If the housing loan is received as a result of employment and not anyone's shareholdings, then the housing loan exception will apply. The exception prevents the application of ITA 15(2) to any part of the loan. However, as the loan is interest free, there will be an interest benefit that will be required to be included in employment income as a result of ITA 80.4(1).

The interest benefit for 2021 would be $410 [($123,000)(2%)(2/12)] and $2,358 {[($123,000)(2%)(10/12)] + [($92,250)(2%)(2/12)]} for 2022. The interest benefit calculations for 2023 to 2025 would be calculated in a similar manner. In addition, Mr. Hasid would be eligible for the five-year interest benefit cap that would limit the prescribed rate to the 2% rate in effect when the loan was received.

If in a Shareholder Capacity   If the housing loan is received as a result of a shareholder capacity the housing loan exception cannot apply. The only exception that would apply in this case is the two-year limitation. Since part of the loan ($30,750) is repaid within the two-year limitation it is only the remaining amount of $92,250 that will be included in his income as income from property for 2021. The remaining $30,750 would not be included in income as it will have been repaid before the deadline. However, this amount will result in an interest benefit of $102.50 [($30,750)(2%)(2/12)] in 2021 and $512.50 [($30,750)(2%)(10/12)] in 2022.

Repayments made for 2023 to 2025 entitle Mr. Hasid to a deduction under ITA 20(1)(j) in the year of repayment.

TIP: To understand the mechanics of how ITA 15(2) and ITA 80.4 interact where only part of a loan is repaid within the deadline, think of the loan as two separate loans—one of $30,750 that is repaid within the deadline and another of $92,250 that is not paid within that same deadline.

Exercise 15-10 Solution
(1) All Salary
If the full $550,000 is paid out as salary, it will be deductible and will reduce the company's net and taxable income to nil. This means that no corporate income taxes will be payable. Ms. Broad's taxable income will be $550,000. Given this, her income tax payable will be calculated as follows:

Tax on first $216,511 (given)	$ 75,000
Tax on remaining	
$333,489 ($550,000 - $216,511) at 51%	170,079
Tax payable before credits	$245,079
Personal tax credits (given)	(5,000)
Total income tax payable	$240,079

Ms. Broad's after-tax retention would be $309,921 ($550,000 - $240,079).

(2) All Dividends
As dividends paid are not a deductible expense for income tax purposes, corporate income taxes will be payable before the payment of any taxable dividends. While the $50,000 of income in excess of the annual business limit of $500,000 would not be entitled to the small business deduction, it would be eligible for the general rate reduction of 13%. Given this, the corporate rate on this income would be 29% (38% - 10% - 13% + 14%). On income eligible for the small business deduction, the rate would be 12% (38% - 10% - 19% + 3%). Using these rates, corporate income taxes would be calculated as follows:

Income not eligible for SBD [(29%)($50,000)]	$14,500
Income eligible for SBD [(12%)($500,000)]	60,000
Corporate tax payable	$74,500

Post-tax earnings available for the payment of taxable dividends would be $475,500 ($550,000 - $74,500). The fact that the corporation's income was in excess of the annual business limit of $500,000 will create an addition to the GRIP of $36,000 [(72%)($550,000 - $500,000)]. Given this, $36,000 of the dividend can be designated as eligible, leaving a non-eligible dividend of $439,500 ($475,500 - $36,000). The grossed up taxable dividends would be calculated as follows:

Total eligible and non-eligible dividends received	$475,500
Gross up:	
Eligible dividends [(38%)($36,000)]	13,680
Non-eligible dividends [(15%)($439,500)]	65,925
Taxable income	$555,105

Personal income taxes are calculated as follows:

Tax on first $216,511 (given)	$ 75,000
Federal tax on remaining	
$338,594 ($555,105 - $216,511) at 51%	172,683
Taxes payable before credits	$ 247,683
Personal tax credits (given)	(5,000)
Dividend tax credit:	
Eligible dividends [(6/11 + 30%)($13,680)]	(11,566)
Non-eligible dividends [(9/13 + 30%)($65,925)]	(65,418)
Personal tax payable	$165,699

The after-tax retention would be equal to $309,801 ($475,500 - $165,699). This is $120 less than the after-tax retention in the salary option of $309,921.

Exercise 15-11 Solution
Required Salary Ms. Mortell's combined tax rate on additional salary is 45%. In order to have $30,000 in after-tax funds, she would have to receive salary of $54,545 [$30,000 ÷ (1 - .45)].

Required Dividend Ms. Mortell's income tax rate on non-eligible dividends is 37.6% [(115%) (45%) - (9/13 + 25%)(15%)]. In order to have $30,000 in after-tax funds, she would have to receive dividends of $48,077 [$30,000 ÷ (1 - .376)].

Tax Cost of Salary The net tax cost of paying salary can be calculated as follows:

Personal tax on receipt of salary [(45%)($54,545)]	$24,545
Tax savings to corporation [(12%)($54,545)]	(6,545)
Net tax cost of salary alternative	$18,000

Tax Cost of Dividend As the dividend payment is not deductible, it would not change the corporate income tax. This means that the only tax cost would be the $18,077 [($48,077)(37.6%)] in personal taxes that Ms. Mortell would pay on the dividends received.

Conclusion As the tax cost associated with the payment of dividends is slightly larger, the salary alternative would be marginally preferable.

Exercise 15-12 Solution
Salary Alternative As the available cash is less than the income, some corporate income taxes will have to be paid since there is insufficient cash to pay a salary that would reduce taxable income to nil. To determine the maximum salary that can be paid (X), it is necessary to solve the following algebraic equation:

$$X = \$18,500 - [(12\%)(\$21,500 - X)]$$
$$X - 0.12X = [\$18,500 - (12\%)(\$21,500)] = \$18,091$$

Corporate cash before taxes		$18,500
Corporate taxes [(12%)($21,500 - $18,091)]		(409)
Corporate cash available for salary		$18,091
Salary received		$18,091
Personal tax payable:		
Personal tax on salary [(25%)(18,091)]	($4,523)	
Personal tax credits (given)	3,950	(573)
After-tax cash retained		$ 17,518

Dividend Alternative After-tax cash retained with the dividend alternative would be calculated as follows:

Corporate cash before taxes	$18,500
Corporate taxes [(12%)($21,500)]	(2,580)
Corporate cash available for dividends	$15,920
Non-eligible dividend received	$15,920
Individual taxes*	Nil
After-tax cash retained	$15,920

*No taxes would be paid on this amount of dividends (see Paragraph 15-84 of the text).

Given these calculations, it is clear that the preferred approach is to pay the maximum salary.

Self-Study Problem Solutions

Self-Study Problems are available to download from MyLab Accounting.

SSP 15-1 Solution
Part A—Goal of Integration
The goal of integration is to ensure that the amount of after-tax income that an individual receives from a given income source should be the same regardless of whether that income is earned directly or whether it is first earned by a corporation with any after-tax funds distributed to the individual as a taxable dividend.

Part B—Tax Payable without Corporation
Personal tax payable without the corporation would be calculated as follows:

	Business Income	Eligible Dividends
Income	$80,000	$ 96,000
Gross up (38% of $96,000)	N/A	36,480
Taxable income	$80,000	$132,480
Tax rate (33% + 18%)	51%	51%
Tax payable before dividend tax credit	$40,800	$ 67,565
Dividend tax credit [(6/11 + 5/11)($36,480)]	N/A	(36,480)
Personal tax payable	$40,800	$ 31,085

The personal tax payable if the income is received directly totals $71,885 ($40,800 + $31,085). The after-tax income would be $104,115 [$80,000 + $96,000 - $71,885].

Part C—Corporate Tax Payable

The portfolio dividends would result in Part IV tax of $36,800 [(38 1/3%)($96,000)]. However, this tax would be fully refunded on the payment of dividends. As a result, the portfolio dividends received of $96,000 would all be available for distribution.

The after-tax corporate income available for distribution would be calculated as follows:

	Business Income	Dividends
Income	$80,000	$96,000
Part I tax [(28% - 19% + 2%)($80,000)]	(8,800)	
Part IV tax [(38 1/3%)($96,000)]		(36,800)
Available for dividends	$71,200	$59,200
Dividend refund [($59,200 ÷ .61667) - $59,200]	N/A	36,800
Total distributable income	$71,200	$96,000

The amount of the dividend refund would be limited by the balance in the RDTOH accounts. The balance here would reflect the Part IV taxes paid on the portfolio dividends, all of which would be added to the eligible RDTOH.

At this point, Slater Ltd. has the cash to support a dividend of $167,200 ($71,200 + $96,000), which includes the dividend refund of $36,800. As all of the $96,000 of portfolio dividends received were allocated to the company's GRIP account, this amount of dividends can be designated as eligible. The remaining dividends of $71,200 ($167,200 - $96,000) will be non-eligible.

The $36,800 refund would leave the balance in the company's eligible RDTOH at nil for the next taxation year.

Part C—Personal Tax Payable

Keith Slater's personal tax payable on receipt of the dividend distribution would be calculated as follows:

	Non-Eligible Dividends	Eligible Dividends
Eligible dividends	N/A	$ 96,000
Gross up at 38%	N/A	36,480
After-tax ABI as non-eligible dividends	$71,200	N/A
Gross up at 15%	10,680	N/A
Taxable dividends	$81,880	$132,480
Tax rate (33% + 18%)	51%	51%
Tax payable before dividend tax credits	$41,759	$ 67,565
Dividend tax credits:		
Eligible dividends [(6/11 + 5/11)($36,480)]	N/A	(36,480)
Non-eligible dividends [(9/13 + 4/13)($10,680)]	(10,680)	N/A
Personal tax payable	$31,079	$ 31,085

The corporate and personal tax payable if Slater Ltd. is used totals $70,964 (Part I corporate tax of $8,800 + $31,079 + $31,085). The after-tax cash to Mr. Slater would be $105,036 [$71,200 + $96,000 - $31,079 - $31,085]

Part D—Comparison of Results

Comparing the total tax payable under the two alternatives provides the following result:

Tax payable—Without corporation	$71,885
Tax payable—With corporation	(70,964)
Tax savings with corporation	$ 921

The tax savings can also be seen by measuring the after-tax retention as $921 [$105,036 with a corporation - $104,115 without a corporation].

Flowing the income through Slater Ltd. results in a tax savings of $921. By calculating the tax burden on the active business income separately from the dividends, it is clear that there is perfect integration on the portfolio dividends. The Part IV tax paid at the corporate level is totally refunded, and the personal taxes paid on the dividends are the same with or without the corporation.

In this example, the Part I corporate rate of 11% on the active business income is lower than the 13.04% level that is required for perfect integration (see Figure 13-2). In addition, the combined federal/provincial dividend tax credit is equal to the rate required for perfect integration. As a result, there is a tax savings of $921 when the income is flowed through the corporation.

SSP 15-2 Solution
Advantages of Incorporation
Among the more commonly cited advantages of incorporation would be the following:

Tax Deferral   It would appear that, if he incorporates the business, all of the income earned by the corporation will be eligible for the small business deduction. The corporate rate on the business income is only 11% compared to a personal rate that is likely close to 50%. As a result, the tax deferral would be significant.

Tax Reduction   For CCPCs earning active business income, the tax rate required for perfect integration is 13.04%. As the relevant corporate rate in his province is 11%, this suggests that there would be a tax savings on income flowed through a corporation. However, the provincial dividend tax credit must also be considered. Since the CCPC's income would all be eligible for the small business deduction there would be no GRIP and therefore no possibility of designating taxable dividends as eligible. As a result, all taxable dividends would be non-eligible. The required rate for perfect integration is 4/13 of the non-eligible dividend gross up. If the rate in Gerald's province is below this, the savings resulting from the low corporate rate could be reduced or even eliminated.

Income Splitting   With a proper structuring of the corporation, income could be directed to family members. This can be in the form of either salary or dividends and will be subject to what we would assume to be significantly lower rates of tax. Salary would be feasible as long as the children are actually employed in the business. The amount of the salary would need to be commensurate with their skills, experience, and expertise given the services they would provide. The payment of taxable dividends to children, however, would only be tax efficient if the TOSI did not apply, which is dependent on many factors, including the age of the children, the circumstances under which they acquired shares, and the contributions previously made to the business.

Capital Gains Deduction   For 2021, this provision allows for the deduction of up to $892,218 in capital gains. It is available on the disposition of shares in a qualified small business corporation. Properly structured, incorporation could permit all members of Gerald's family access to the capital gains deduction. To qualify, the corporation must be a CCPC and have at least 90% of the FMV of its assets being used in an active business in Canada. In addition, the shares:

- must not have been owned by anyone other than the taxpayer or a related party for at least 24 months preceding the disposition; and

- throughout this 24-month period, more than 50% of the FMV of the corporation's assets must be used in an active business carried on primarily in Canada.

This deduction could represent a significant advantage of incorporating the business.

Employee Benefits   While the business may be somewhat small to make this feasible, the corporation can be used to establish various retirement programs, as well as group life and health insurance packages (e.g., dental and medical plans).

Estate Planning A corporation provides many estate planning advantages, including business succession plans.

Limited Liability An investor in a corporation is, in general, not personally liable to creditors and lenders for the debts of the corporation. In the case of large publicly traded corporations this is a very real and important consideration. However, in the case of a small owner-managed business such as Mr. Copley's, it is unlikely that creditors and lenders would extend significant amounts without personal guarantees.

However, limited liability could be important if the business was potentially exposed to any type of product liability risk.

Liquidation Losses If the corporation is unsuccessful and must be dissolved, any resulting loss on the shares would potentially be deductible as an allowable business investment loss. This means that one-half of the total amount could be deducted against any other income. There are often additional legal and accounting costs associated with liquidating a business and dissolving a corporation then there would be if the business was not incorporated.

Disadvantages of Incorporation
A list of the disadvantages associated with incorporation would include the following:

Administrative Costs There will be higher legal, accounting, and other costs associated with meeting the various annual reporting requirements that are necessary for the startup and maintenance of a corporation.

Losses No corporate losses cannot be used by shareholders.

Higher Taxes Under advantages we noted that there could be a tax reduction associated with a corporation earning income that is eligible for the small business deduction. On the other hand, if the corporation earns income that is not eligible for the small business deduction, there will be some additional income tax. Certain actions can be taken in this circumstance, such as declaring bonuses at year end to reduce corporate taxable income to an amount that qualifies for the small business deduction.

Winding-Up and Dissolution Procedures Because of its status as a separate legal entity, the procedures associated with winding-up and dissolving a corporation and its business are significantly more complex than those associated with terminating a business carried on as a sole proprietor.

Conclusions on Incorporation
In evaluating the preceding advantages and disadvantages, a recommendation that Mr. Copley incorporate his business seems to be appropriate. He does not appear to need all of the income produced by the business for personal needs and, as a consequence, the ability to defer income within the corporation is attractive. Further, his eligibility for the small business deduction could result in a reduction in taxes, even on amounts that are withdrawn from the corporation. Other advantages related to incorporating the business are the opportunities that may be available to split income between the various members of his family and for estate planning and business succession purposes.

SSP 15-3 Solution
Part A—Direct Personal Investment
Mrs. Martin's marginal tax rate is 46% (29% + 17%). If Mrs. Martin invests the $200,000 as an individual, the after-tax return can be calculated as follows:

Interest income (all taxable)	$14,000
Interest received	$14,000
Personal tax payable at 46%	(6,440)
After-tax retention—Direct receipt	$ 7,560

Part B—Investment Incorporated with a CCPC

If Mrs. Martin invests the $200,000 through her CCPC, any dividends paid will be non-eligible. The after-tax return would be as follows:

Interest income	$14,000
Corporate taxes at 52%	(7,280)
Net corporate income before dividend refund	$ 6,720
Maximum dividend refund (see Note)	4,177
Maximum non-eligible dividend payable	$10,897
Gross up at 15%	1,635
Taxable dividend	$12,532
Personal tax rate	46%
Personal tax payable before dividend tax credit	$ 5,765
Dividend tax credit [(9/13 + 25%)($1,635)]	(1,541)
Personal tax payable	$ 4,224
Dividends received	$10,897
Personal tax payable	(4,224)
After-tax retention—With corporation	$ 6,673

Note The Part I refundable taxes on the interest income would be $4,293 [(30 2/3%)($14,000)]. This full amount would be added to the non-eligible RDTOH account.

The available corporate cash would support a dividend of $10,897 ($6,720 ÷ .61667), including a dividend refund of $4,177 [(38 1/3%)($10,897)]. As this refund is less than the balance in the non-eligible RDTOH, the refund would be limited to $4,177, for a total dividend of $10,897. The refund will leave a balance in the non-eligible RDTOH of $116 ($4,293 - $4,177) in the next taxation year.

The difference between the two alternatives is $887 ($7,560 - $6,673) in favour of direct personal investment. Using a corporation is therefore not recommended.

SSP 15-4 Solution
Part A—Investment Owned Personally (No Corporation)

Mr. Martin's tax rate on additional income is 46% (29% + 17%). If he invests the $200,000 personally, any dividends received will be eligible given they are paid by a public company that does not have an LRIP account. The after-tax return can be calculated as follows:

Eligible dividends received	$14,000
38% gross up	5,320
Taxable dividend	$19,320
Personal tax rate	46%
Personal tax payable before dividend tax credit	$ 8,887
Dividend tax credit [(6/11 + 25%)($5,320)]	(4,232)
Personal tax payable	$ 4,655
Dividends received	$14,000
Personal tax payable	(4,655)
After-tax retention—No corporation	$ 9,345

Part B—Investment Incorporated within a CCPC

If Mr. Martin incorporates the preferred share investments in a CCPC, the eligible dividends received would be considered portfolio dividends, subject to Part IV tax at a rate of 38 1/3%. There would also be an addition to the corporation's GRIP account of $14,000 (notice that eligible dividends are not multiplied by 72% for this GRIP addition). The after-tax retention with the use of a CCPC would be as follows:

Eligible dividends received	$14,000
Part IV tax at 38 1/3% (portfolio dividends)	(5,367)
Earnings retained by corporation	$ 8,633
Refund when dividends paid (see Note)	5,367
Eligible dividends paid	$14,000

Note The available cash would support a dividend of $14,000 ($8,633 ÷ .61667), including a dividend refund of $5,367 [(38 1/3%)($14,000)]. This dividend refund is equal to the lesser of the eligible RDTOH of $5,367 and 38 1/3% of the taxable dividends paid of $14,000, which also equals $5,367.

At this point, the CCPC has no income tax liabailty as its Part IV tax is fully recovered. The result is that Mr. Martin receives the same $14,000 eligible dividend either directly when the preferred shares are owned personally or indirectly when his own CCPC pays him that same eligible dividend. The income tax consequences to him are therefore exactly the same. In addition, there is no tax deferral since his personal taxes of $4,655 were not less than the Part IV corporate taxes of $5,367.

SSP 15-5 Solution
Approach 1 (becomes a member of the partnership)

Cora's share of the partnership income would be $70,000 [(10%)($700,000)]. Cora's tax payable resulting from this approach would be calculated as follows:

Tax on first $49,020 at 23% (15% + 8%)	$11,275
Tax on next $20,980 ($70,000 - $49,020)	
at 32.5% (20.5% + 12%)	6,819
Tax payable before credits	$18,094
Personal tax credits (given)	(3,342)
Personal tax payable	$14,752
Business income	$70,000
Personal tax payable	(14,752)
After-tax retention—Alternative 1	$55,248

Approach 2 (all dividends)

The total corporate taxes would be calculated as follows:

First $50,000 at 12%	$ 6,000
Remaining $20,000 at 27%	5,400
Corporate tax payable	$11,400

If all of the after-tax income is distributed, the resulting taxable dividend will be $58,600 ($70,000 - $11,400).

As $20,000 of the corporation's income was taxed at the general rate, there would be a GRIP balance of $14,400 [(72%)($20,000)]. This means that of the total dividend of $58,600, $14,400 could be designated as eligible, with the remaining $44,200 ($58,600 - $14,400) being non-eligible. Based on this, Cora's taxable income would be as follows:

Eligible dividend	$14,400
Gross up on eligible dividend at 38%	5,472
Non-eligible dividend	44,200
Gross up on non-eligible dividend at 15%	6,630
Taxable income	$70,702

Based on this taxable income, her tax payable would be as follows:

Tax on first $49,020 at 23% (15% + 8%)	$ 11,275
Tax on remaining $21,682 ($70,702 - $49,020)	
at 32.5% (20.5% + 12%)	7,047
Tax payable before credits	$18,322
Personal tax credits (given)	(3,342)
Dividend tax credit = Gross up ($5,472 + $6,630)	(12,102)
Personal tax payable	$ 2,878

Business income	$70,000
Corporate tax payable	(11,400)
Personal tax payable	(2,878)
After-tax retention—Alternative 2	$55,722

Approach 3 (salary and dividends)

With the payment of $20,000 in salary to reduce corporate income to her $50,000 share of the small business deduction, corporate taxes would be $6,000 [(12%)($50,000)]. This would leave $44,000 ($70,000 - $20,000 - $6,000) for the payment of dividends.

Since no income was taxed at the general rate, the GRIP balance would be nil. This means that the total dividend of $44,000 would be non-eligible. Cora's taxable income would be calculated as follows:

Salary	$ 20,000
Non-eligible dividend	44,000
Gross up on non-eligible dividend at 15%	6,600
Taxable income	$70,600

Her tax payable would be calculated as follows:

Tax on first $49,020 at 23% (15% + 8%)	$ 11,275
Tax on next $22,065 ($70,600 - $49,020)	
at 32.5% (20.5% + 12%)	7,014
Tax payable before credits	$ 18,289
Personal tax credits (given)	(3,342)
Dividend tax credit = Gross up	(6,600)
Personal tax payable	$ 8,347

Business income	$ 70,000
Corporate tax payable after salary [(12%)($70,000 - $20,000)]	(6,000)
Personal tax payable	(8,347)
After-tax retention—Alternative 3	$ 55,653

Evaluation

The after-tax amount retained for each of the three approaches is as follows:

Approach 1 (joins partnership as individual)	$55,248
Approach 2 (all dividends)	55,722
Approach 3 (salary and dividends)	55,653

If only after-tax cash flows are considered, Approach 2 provides the highest retention and would be the best choice.

Other factors to consider:

- While Approach 2 provides the largest after-tax retention, it does not take into consideration CPP contributions. If the effect of CPP were considered, she would pay two times the annual maximum in Approach 1, no CPP in Approach 2, and in Approach 3 both Cora and her corporation would pay less than the annual maximum. Paying CPP contributions would allow her to receive CPP payments in the future, but would incur a liability at the present time. Without going through the required calculations, Approach 2 would remain the best if the required CPP contributions were considered.

- If the Canada employment credit were considered, it would only be applicable in Approach 3.

- If Cora wanted to participate in the Employment Insurance program on a voluntary basis, it would only be available to her in Approach 1 where she would be considered to be carrying on a business as a member of the partnership.

- If she wanted to contribute to an RRSP or deduct child care costs, she would need earned income. Dividends are not a component of earned income for either purpose. Earned income would be $70,000 in Approach 1 and $20,000 in Approach 3.

- Depending on the province, there could be additional payroll costs that her corporation would have to pay in Approach 3 as a result of the salary.

- The opportunity for income splitting may be easier with a corporation given that family members could buy shares that entitle them to dividends. This, however, is likely to be limited by the application of the tax on split income (TOSI). Income splitting through the partnership would be much more difficult.

- Although an advantage of incorporation is the availability of the capital gains deduction, given the current situation it is questionable whether the shares of the CCPC could be sold for much of a gain given how important her personal services are to its value.

SSP 15-6 Solution
Part A—Tax Payable with Corporation

The business income of the corporation would be calculated as follows:

Management fees		$82,900
Expenses:		
Mr. Ashley's salary	($18,400)	
Office salaries	(25,400)	
Office rent	(8,180)	
CCA on office and dental equipment	(5,700)	
Other business expenses	(2,170)	(59,850)
Business income		$23,050
Rate on active business income		11%
Tax payable on active business income		$ 2,536

Tax payable on the dividends and investment income would be calculated as follows:

Interest income	$ 21,600
Net rental income ($34,600 - $27,800)	6,800
Aggregate investment income	$ 28,400
Rate on investment income	51-2/3%
Part I tax on investment income	$ 14,673
Part IV tax on dividends received [(38 1/3%)($13,900)]	5,328
Tax payable on property income	$ 20,001

The refundable portion of the Part I tax payable would be the least of the following amounts:

- $8,709 = 30 2/3% of aggregate investment income [(30 2/3%)($28,400)]

- $8,709 = 30 2/3% of taxable income less amount eligible for
  small business deduction [(30 2/3%)($23,050 + $28,400 - $23,050)]

- $17,209 = Part I tax payable ($2,536 + $14,673)

The balances in the two RDTOH accounts would be as follows:

Non-eligible RDTOH (Part I refundable tax)	$8,709
Eligible RDTOH (Part IV tax payable)	$5,328

The eligible dividends received by the corporation will be added to the GRIP balance, leaving $13,900 in this account (note that the amount received is added, not the amount received multiplied by 72%). This means that $13,900 in dividends could be designated as eligible.

Given the preceding calculations, the maximum eligible and non-eligible dividend that could be paid is as follows:

Business income	$23,050
Taxes on business income	(2,536)
Interest income	21,600
Net rental income	6,800
Taxes on property income	(20,001)
Eligible dividends	13,900
Balance before refund	$42,813
Dividend refund (see Note)	14,037
Available for dividends	$56,850
Eligible dividends (GRIP balance)	(13,900)
Non-eligible dividends (remainder)	$42,950

Note The available cash of $42,813 would support a dividend of $69,426 ($42,813 ÷ 0.61667), including a refund of $26,613 ([(38 1/3%)($69,426)]). However, the actual refund is the lesser of this amount and the $14,037 ($8,709 + $5,328) total of the two RDTOH accounts. Given this, the total dividend is limited to $56,850 ($42,813 + $14,037).

The refund will be deducted from the two RDTOH accounts, leaving each with a balance of nil for the next taxation year.

With respect to the eligible dividends, $8,340 [(60%)($13,900)] would go to Mr. Ashley and $5,560 [(40%)($13,900)] would go to Dr. Ashley. With respect to the non-eligible dividends,

$25,770 [(60\%)($42,950)] would go to Mr. Ashley, and $17,180 [40\%)($42,950)] would go to Dr. Ashley. The resulting tax payable would be as follows:

	Dr. Ashley	Mr. Ashley
Salary	Nil	$18,400
Eligible dividends ($13,900)	$ 5,560	8,340
Gross up at 38%	2,113	3,169
Non-eligible dividends ($42,950)	17,180	25,770
Gross up at 15%	2,577	3,866
Taxable income	$ 27,430	$59,545
Tax rate	47%	30%
Tax payable before dividend tax credit	$12,892	$ 17,864
Dividend tax credits:		
Eligible dividends [(6/11 + 25%)(gross up)]	(1,681)	(2,521)
Non-eligible dividends [(9/13 + 25%)(gross up)]	(2,428)	(3,643)
Tax payable	$ 8,783	$ 11,700

This would leave after-tax balances available to Dr. and Mr. Ashley as follows:

Ashley Management Services	Nil
Dr. Ashley ($5,560 + $17,180 - $8,783)	$ 13,957
Mr. Ashley ($18,400 + $8,340 + $25,770 - $11,700)	40,810
After-tax retention—Dr. and Mr. Ashley	$54,767

Part B—Balances with No Corporation

If Dr. Ashley had earned all of the income personally, her tax payable and net retention would be calculated as follows:

Business income ($23,050 + $18,400 salary to husband)	$41,450
Interest income	21,600
Rental income (net)	6,800
Eligible dividends	13,900
Gross up at 38%	5,282
Taxable income	$89,032
Tax rate	47%
Tax before dividend tax credit	$41,845
Dividend tax credit [(6/11 + 25%)($5,282)]	(4,202)
Tax payable	$ 37,643

Income received ($41,450 + $21,600 + $6,800 + $13,900)	$ 83,750
Tax payable	(37,643)
After-tax retention—Dr. Ashley only	$46,107

It is clear from these calculations that the use of the management company has had a positive effect on after-tax retention of income. Without the corporation, Dr. Ashley would have ended up with only $46,107. This compares to a total of $54,767 for Mr. and Dr. Ashley when the corporation is used, an improvement of $8,660.

You should note, however, that Dr. Ashley could have paid a salary to her husband without using a corporation. This would have significantly improved the results in Part B.

The problem asked you to ignore personal tax credits, the Canada employment tax credit, CPP contributions, and GST/HST. Personal tax credits would have made only a small difference, as Dr. Ashley would be able to claim the spousal credit in full if Mr. Ashley had no income.

While it is clear the Canada employment tax credit would favour paying Mr. Ashley a salary, the advantage or disadvantage of CPP contributions is less clear cut. Although GST/HST is not covered in detail until Chapter 21, we noted in Chapter 12 that the GST/HST legislation has made management companies for GST-exempt services such as dentistry less attractive.

SSP 15-7 Solution
Housing Loan

As such loans are available to all employees, Ms. Lord can claim that she has received the loan in an employment capacity. This means that ITA 15(2) does not apply to require the $200,000 loan to be included in her income as income from property for 2021. However, as the rate on the loan is below the prescribed interest rate rate of 2%, there will be an interest benefit that will be included in her income as income from employment as long as the loan is outstanding.

The amount of the interest benefit for 2021 is $1,000 [($200,000)(2% - 1%)(6/12)]. For 2022 the interest benefit is $1,600 [($200,000 - $40,000)(2% - 1%)(12/12)], and for 2023 the interest benefit is $1,200 [($200,000 - $80,000)(2% - 1%)(12/12)].

NOTE: While not part of the solution, the 1% charged on the loan by the employer represents indebtedness in each year the amount accrues. This accrual would be treated as a separate debt for purposes of ITA 15(2) and ITA 80.4.

Automobile Loan

The motor vehicle exception would apply except for the fact that there appears to be no repayment date that can be identified. As a result, the only possible exception would be the two-year limitation, which establishes August 31, 2023, as the deadline. The deadline is determined by taking the last day of the taxation year of the corporation in which the loan was made and adding one year. The loan was made September 1, 2021, which is the first day of the corporate taxation year ending August 31, 2022. Any amounts repaid by August 31, 2023, will not be required to be included in income but will be subject to an interest benefit through ITA 80.4(1) as employment income. Any amounts repaid after August 31, 2023, will be included in her income as income from property under ITA 15(2) in 2021. Subsequent repayments related to amounts included in her income would then be eligible for a deduction under ITA 20(1)(j) in the year of repayment.

Other Loans

- **February 1, 2021** As this loan is not repaid prior to August 31, 2022 (the two-year limitation), it has to be included in Ms. Lord's 2021 income as income from property as a result of ITA 15(2). The repayment of $35,000 in 2023 entitled Ms. Lord to a deduction under ITA 20(1)(j). There will be no interest benefit since the loan was included in her income.

- **July 1, 2021** As the loan is repaid by August 31, 2022 (the two-year limitation), it does not have to be included in Ms. Lord's income for 2021. However, as it is interest free, there will be an interest for 2021 of $250 [(2%)($25,000)(6/12)] and $333 [(2%)($25,000)(8/12)] for 2022.

- **December 10, 2021** Since the loan is repaid by the two-year limitation date of August 31, 2023, the loan is not required to be included in her income. In addition, since the prescribed interest rate of 2% does not exceed the interest rate charged on the loan there will be no interest benefit. If, however, the prescribed rate increases while the loan is outstanding there will be an interest benefit attributable to that time. NOTE: Technically any interest payable on a loan or indebtedness must be paid within 30 days of the end of the year (by January 29 of the following year) for individuals to be allowed an offset to the prescribed interest rate. This would mean that even though the actual interest rate and prescribed interest rate are equal there would still be an interest benefit if the interest was not paid within the 30-day period.

SSP 15-8 Solution
Overview
The receipt of a loan from a corporation in which an individual is a shareholder is subject to ITA 15(2), with the result that the full amount of the loan may be required to be included in the individual's income subject to any exceptions. There is an exception for a housing loan that will exclude the application of ITA 15(2) if the borrower is an employee, the house will be acquired for the borrower's habitation (or that of a spouse or common-law partner), there is an identifiable period of time in which the loan will be fully repaid, and the loan is received as a result of an employment capacity and not because of a shareholder capacity of anyone. The troubling condition is the employment capacity. It may be difficult for a manager of a small business to argue that the loan is not received because of Mr. Blaine's controlling shareholder interest.

Shareholder Capacity Loan
If the loan is considered received because of the shares Mr. Blaine owns in the company (shareholder capacaity), the housing loan exception will not be available. As a result, he will only be able to rely on the two-year limitation, which only excludes part of the loan from being included in income under ITA 15(2) for the year the loan is received. Subsequent repayments related to the amount required to be included in income would be eligible for a deduction in the year of the repayment. The result would be that a significant part of the loan would be included in income with a smaller amount of an interest benefit for the first two years.

In this situation, having the company make the loan has the same income tax consequences for Mr. Blaine as having the company pay a similar amount of salary. There are, however, several differences:

- When the loan is repaid, the repayment can be deducted under ITA 20(1)(j). In contrast, salary repayments would not be deductible under these circumstances.

- Mr. Blaine's salary of $77,000 does not provide sufficient earned income to allow him to make maximum RRSP contributions. Paying salary would increase his earned income and allow him to make additional RRSP contributions. Amounts added to income because of ITA 15(2) are not earned income.

- Additional salary reduces net and taxable income, which would reduce corporate income tax. Lending money interest free would not have an effect on the corporation's net and taxable income.

Note that since Arthur is receiving a salary of $77,000, he is already eligible for the Canada employment tax credit and paying the maximum CPP contributions, so these factors are not relevant to a marginal comparative analysis.

Employee Capacity Loan
If an argument could be made that the loan is received in an employment capacity and not because of anyone's shareholding, then the housing loan exception would be available. The result would be that no amount of the loan would be included in income because of ITA 15(2). However, an interest benefit would apply to the interest-free loan based on the prescribed rate applied to the the balance outstanding during each year.

Evaluation
If Mr. Blaine can successfully argue that the loan was made in an employment capacity, then the only income tax concern will be the interest benefit under ITA 80.4. Generally, the prescribed interest rate tends to be several percentage points below the going rate for mortgages. Based on this, it would appear that if ITA 15(2) can be avoided, having his company provide the loan would be an effective form of income tax planning.

If ITA 15(2) applies to Mr. Blaine because he has received the loan in a shareholder capacity the income tax implications would mean that income tax would have to be paid, reducing the amount he would need. In this situation it may be preferable for the company to pay additional salary instead for the reasons listed above.

The case law weighs heavily in favour of making it difficult to argue that housing loans are not the result of a shareholder capacity. Caution should also be exercised to ensure that all terms and conditions of a loan are respected. In one case an individual shareholder's housing loan was considered a shareholder capacity because the terms and conditions were not respected, which was a point raised by the judge. In that case, not all payments were made on time or for the full amount, leading the judge to conclude that this situation would not have been acceptable had the borrower been an employee with no shares and no relation to any existing shareholders.

SSP 15-9 Solution
Tax Reduction
Bonus Down

Since salary is deductible to the corporation, an additional $250,000 of salary avoids the high corporate rate of 27% on this amount by reducing taxable income from $750,000 to $500,000. The receipt of an additional $250,000 in salary would leave Mrs. Litvak's with the following after-tax cash:

Salary payment	$250,000
Personal taxes on salary [(52%)($250,000)]	(130,000)
After-tax cash retained after bonus down (2021)	$120,000

No Bonus Down

If Morcan Inc. does not pay the additional $250,000 in salary, the additional $250,000 in taxable income will be subject to the high corporate tax rate of 27%, resulting in additional corporate tax of $67,500 [(27%)($250,000)]. There would also be an addition to the GRIP of $180,000 [(72%)($750,000 - $500,000)].

The after-tax retention of funds with respect to the additional $250,000 of taxable income subject to the high corporate rate would be $182,500 ($250,000 - $67,500). If this amount is paid out as dividends in 2025, $180,000 (the balance in the GRIP account) could be designated as eligible, with the remaining $2,500 paid as a non-eligible dividend. Given this, the income tax consequences of paying out these dividends would be as follows:

Eligible dividends received	$180,000
Gross up at 38%	68,400
Non-eligible dividends received	2,500
Gross up at 15%	375
Taxable dividend paid in 2025	$251,275

Tax at 52% [(52%)($251,275)]	$130,663
Dividend tax credits:	
Eligible [(6/11 + 5/11)($68,400)] +	
Non-eligible [(9/13 + 4/13)($375)]	(68,775)
Personal tax cost of dividends	$ 61,888

Dividends received ($180,000 + $2,500)	$182,500
Personal tax cost	(61,888)
After-tax cash retained—No bonus down	$120,612

Conclusion

The difference in after-tax retention between the two alternatives is only $612 ($120,612 - $120,000). While this is slightly in favour of bonusing down, the difference is not significant.

Tax Deferral

If Morcan Inc. pays the additional salary, there will be an immediate personal tax cost of $130,000. This is more than the $129,388 ($67,500 + $61,888) in taxes that would be paid if she did not bonus down and instead paid high corporate income tax on the $250,000 with the remaining funds paid out as dividends in the future. However, Ms. Litvak has indicated that she does not need the additional income and, as a consequence, the payment of the personal taxes can be deferred until 2025. This means the current income tax obligation would be limited to the $67,500 in corporate income tax and would represent a significant tax deferral.

A potential problem with this is the question of whether the corporation can use the additional funds in its business. If not, any income earned would be considered aggregate investment income and would be subject to an income tax rate that could exceed the 52% marginal tax rate applicable to Ms. Litvak.

Conclusion

In terms of tax reduction, there is no significant advantage resulting from bonusing down. However, if the retained funds are not paid out as dividends until 2025, there is a significant tax deferral. This would favour not bonusing down. This conclusion is dependent on whether the funds can be used within the corporation's business.

Whether bonusing down will be advantageous will also depend on the use of the funds by Mrs. Litvak. If, for example, she has not contributed fully to her RRSP and TFSA and/or her daughter's, bonusing down could be more advantageous.

SSP 15-10 Solution
Required Salary
Given Miss Morgan's personal tax rate of 51% (33% + 18%), a salary of $40,816 [$20,000 ÷ (1 - .51)] would be required to provide an additional $20,000 of after-tax funds.

Tax Cost of Salary
The net tax cost of this alternative would be calculated as follows:

Personal taxes on salary [(51%)($40,816)]	$20,816
Tax savings to corporation [(12%)($40,816)]	(4,898)
Net tax cost of salary	$15,918

Required Dividend
Miss Morgan's tax rate on non-eligible dividends would be as follows:

$$[(115\%)(51\%) - (9/13 + 25\%)(15\%)] = 44.52\%$$

This gives after-tax retention of dividend income in the amount of 55.48% (1 - 44.52%). This means a dividend of $36,049 ($20,000 ÷ 55.48%) will be required to provide an additional $20,000 of after-tax funds.

Tax Cost of Dividend Alternative
The personal tax payable on the dividend would be calculated as follows:

Non-eligible dividends received	$36,049
Gross up at 15%	5,407
Taxable income	$41,456
Tax rate (33% + 18%)	51%
Tax payable before dividend tax credit	$21,143
Dividend tax credit [(9/13 + 25%)($5,407)]	(5,095)
Personal tax payable on dividend alternative	$16,048

Subtracting the tax payable of $16,048 from the dividends received of $36,049 gives $20,001 in after-tax funds. (The extra $1 is a rounding issue).

As the dividend payment would not be deductible, its payment would not change corporate taxes. This means that the only tax cost would be the $16,048 in personal taxes that Miss Morgan would pay on the dividends received.

Conclusion

The salary alternative has a net tax cost that is $130 ($16,048 - $15,918) lower than the additional tax cost of paying dividends. Given this, the salary alternative would have a marginally lower tax cost.

Since Miss Morgan has already received a salary of $84,000, CPP contributions and the Canada employment credit are not relevant to this analysis as they would have already been accounted for and would not affect the conclusion.

SSP 15-11 Solution
Part A — Taxes and Salary

The combined federal/provincial tax rate applicable to Speelburg Films Ltd. would be 11% (38% - 10% - 19% + 2%).

As the corporation's taxable income exceeds the amount of cash available, the maximum amount of salary that can be paid (X) must be determined using the following simple equation:

$$X = \$49,000 - [(11\%)(\$123,000 - X)]$$
$$X = \$49,000 - \$13,530 + 0.11X$$
$$0.89X = \$35,470$$
$$X = \$35,470 \div 0.89)$$

Solving this equation for X indicates that the maximum salary that can be paid is $39,854. This can be verified by the following calculation:

Corporate taxable income before salary	$ 123,000
Maximum salary	(39,854)
Corporate taxable income after salary	$ 83,146
Corporate rate	11%
Corporate tax payable	$ 9,146

This will leave cash of $39,854 ($49,000 - $9,146) for the payment of salary.

With this amount of salary, Mr. Lucas would have the following amount of after-tax cash:

Salary payment	$39,854
Rate (15% + 6%)	21%
Tax before credits	$ 8,369
Personal tax credits (given)	(3,900)
Personal tax payable	$ 4,469
Salary received	$39,854
Personal tax payable	(4,469)
After-tax cash retained (all salary)	$35,385

Part B — All Dividends

As dividends paid by a corporation are not a deductible expense to the company, income tax of $13,530 [(11%)($123,000)] will be required. This will leave a cash balance of $35,470 ($49,000 -

$13,530) that can be used to pay non-eligible dividends. When this amount is paid, the after-tax retention by Mr. Lucas will be as follows:

Non-eligible dividends received	$35,470
Gross up [(15%)($35,470)]	5,321
Taxable dividends	$40,791
Personal tax rate (15% + 6%)	21%
Tax payable before credits	$ 8,566
Personal tax credits (given)	(3,900)
Dividend tax credit [(9/13 + 30%)($5,321)]	(5,280)
Tax payable (unused credits = $614)	Nil

Mr. Lucas will retain all of the $35,470 in dividends since there is no income tax payable.

Part C—Possible Improvement
The existence of $614 in unused tax credits suggests that there may be a better solution than either all salary or all dividends.

Part D—Salary/Dividend Combination
To examine the possibility of a better solution using a combination of salary and dividends, consider the impact that occurs when $1,000 in salary is substituted for $1,000 in dividends. Because the deductible salary payment would reduce corporate taxes, dividends would only have to be decreased by $890 [($1,000)(1 - 0.11)]. The income tax effects can be calculated as follows:

Increase in salary	$ 1,000.00
Decrease in dividend [($1,000)(1 - .11)]	(890.00)
Decrease in dividend gross up [(15%)($890)]	(133.50)
Decrease in Mr. Lucas' taxable income	($ 23.50)
Personal tax rate	21%
Decrease in tax payable before dividend tax credit	($ 4.935)
Decrease in dividend tax credit	
= Increase in tax payable [(9/13 + 30%)($133.50)]	132.473
Net increase in personal tax payable	$ 127.538

The rate on a $1,000 increase in salary is 12.7538% ($127.538 ÷ $1,000). Applying this rate to the unused credits of $614 (see Part C) results in a required increase in salary of $4,814 ($614 ÷ 0.127538).

Payment of salary of $4,814 would result in the following corporate income tax:

Corporate taxable income before salary	$123,000
Salary	(4,814)
Corporate taxable income after salary	$ 118,186
Corporate rate	11%
Corporate income tax	$ 13,000

Based on available cash of $49,000, dividends in the following amount could be paid:

Cash available	$49,000
Corporate income tax	(13,000)
Salary payment	(4,814)
Available for dividends	$31,186

The after-tax retention of the payment of $31,186 in non-eligible dividends would be as follows:

Non-eligible dividends received	$31,186
Gross up [(15%)($31,186)]	4,678
Taxable dividends	$35,864
Salary	4,814
Mr. Lucas' taxable income	$40,678
Personal tax rate (15% + 6%)	21%
Tax payable before credits	$ 8,542
Personal tax credits (given)	(3,900)
Dividend tax credit [(9/13 + 30%)($4,678)]	(4,642)
Tax payable	Nil
Amounts received ($31,186 + $4,814)	$36,000
Personal tax payable	Nil
After-tax cash retained (salary and dividends)	$36,000

The comparative results for the three alternatives are as follows:

All salary	$35,385
All dividends	$35,470
Salary/Dividend combination	$36,000

The combination of salary and dividends maximizes post-tax cash for Mr. Lucas. It is a $615 ($36,000 - $35,385) improvement over all salary and a $530 ($36,000 - $35,470) improvement over all dividends.

Part E—Other Factors

Other factors that might be considered include the following:

- The Canada employment tax credit was ignored in the calculations as it is not a credit against provincial taxes. The tax reduction value would be $189 [(15%)($1,257)].
- If the effect of CPP were considered, both Mr. Lucas and Speelburg Films Ltd. would pay CPP contributions. The all salary alternative would require employee and employer contributions of $1,738 each [($35,385 - $3,500)(5.45%)]. The salary/dividend combination would require equal CPP contributions from both employee and employer of $72 each [($4,814 - $3,500)(5.45%)].
- If Speelburg Films Ltd. has benefits for employees, such as a private health services plan, this could make being an employee (by taking salary) more advantageous.
- Dividend income is not earned income for purposes of making RRSP contributions or for purposes of claiming child care expenses.
- If Mr. Lucas has a CNIL, dividend payments will reduce the balance and increase access to the capital gains deduction.
- Mr. Lucas should consider declaring a bonus (a form of salary) to be paid after the end of the calendar year if he does not require the cash immediately. This would defer any individual income tax to the following calendar year without affecting corporate income tax as long as the bonus was paid within 180 days of December 31 (by June 28).
- Though not relevant in this problem, some provinces have payroll taxes that would affect the outcome.

CHAPTER 16

Learning Objectives

After completing Chapter 16, you should be able to:

1. Describe the purpose of ITA 85(1) and the common situations in which it is used (Paragraph [P hereafter] 16-1 to 16-14).
2. Explain the general rules that are applicable to the persons participating in the rollover, including the type of property that is eligible for rollover treatment (P 16-15 to 16-22).
3. Describe the types of consideration that can be received and the importance of FMV and mismatches of value (P 16-23 to 16-29).
4. Describe the procedures required for making the election, including filing on time, when penalties could apply, and some important features of the T2057 election form (P 16-30 to 16-34).
5. Determine the acceptable range of elected amounts that can be used with respect to eligible property (P 16-35 to 16-40).
6. Apply the general rules that apply to all eligible property that determine the range of elected amounts that can be used (P 16-41 to 16-47).
7. Apply the detailed rules for determining elected amounts for eligible property that is accounts receivable, inventories, and non-depreciable capital property (P 16-48 to 16-61).
8. Describe the rules related to the transfer of non-depreciable capital property, including identifying superficial losses and their income tax consequences (P 16-62 to 16-70).
9. Explain the rules used for determining elected amounts for depreciable property, including options when depreciable properties are sold at the same time (P 16-71 to 16-75).
10. Explain the consequences to a rollover under ITA 85(1) when a sale of depreciable property to an affiliated person would result in a terminal loss (P 16-76 to 16-77).
11. Summarize the rules for determining the elected amount for all eligible property (P 16-78 and Figure 16-3).
12. Calculate the allocation of the elected amount to all consideration received on the sale of eligible property to a corporation (P 16-79 and 16-83).
13. Determine the tax cost of eligible property acquired by a corporation, including the impact of the AccII, ITA 85(5), and ITA 13(7)(e) (P 16-84 to 16-92).
14. Calculate the PUC of share consideration received, including where multiple classes of shares are issued (P 16-93 to 16-105).
15. Analyze and apply the rules of ITA 85(1) where a business carried on as a sole proprietorship is incorporated (P 16-106 to 16-120).
16. Explain the reasons for the gifting rule of ITA 85(1)(e.2), including the income tax consequences to the person responsible for the gift and the person who benefits from the gift. In addition, explain what changes in terms of the tax cost and PUC of consideration received (P 16-121 to 16-136).
17. Explain and calculate the income tax consequences when a shareholder receives too much consideration on a rollover transaction under ITA 85(1) and whether the result may be influenced by certain corporations (P 16-137 to 16-143).

18. Explain the purpose of ITA 84.1 and the standard type of tax planning to which it applies (P 16-144 to 16-148).
19. Calculate the income tax consequences when ITA 84.1 is applicable and determine the best way to minimize any income tax consequences (P 16-149 to 16-164).
20. Explain the purpose of ITA 55(2), the conditions necessary for its application, and the exceptions that limit or prevent its application (P 16-165 to 16-170).
21. Calculate the income tax consequences when ITA 55(2) applies and discuss the relevance of safe income and its impact (P 16-171 to 16-185).

How to Work through Chapter 16

Visit pearsonmylabandmastering.com to access MyLab Accounting for this text. Once there, you can access student resources such as Self-Study Problems, Practice Exams, Flashcards, updates, and more.

We recommend the following approach in dealing with the material in this chapter:

Rollovers under Section 85—Overview
- Read paragraph 16-1 to 16-40 (in the text).

The Elected Amount—Rules Applicable to All Eligible Property
- Read paragraph 16-41 to 16-47.

The Elected Amount—Accounts Receivable
- Read paragraph 16-48 to 16-50.

The Elected Amount—Inventories and Non-Depreciable Capital Property
- Read paragraph 16-51 to 16-61.
- Do Exercise 16-1 (in the text) and check the solution in this Study Guide.

The Elected Amount—Losses on Non-Depreciable Capital Property
- Read paragraph 16-62 to 16-70.

The Elected Amount—Depreciable Property
- Read paragraph 16-71 to 16-75.
- Do Exercise 16-2 and check the solution in this Study Guide.

The Elected Amount—Depreciable Property and Disallowed Terminal Losses
- Read paragraph 16-76 to 16-77.

The Elected Amount—Summary of Acceptable Elected Amounts
- Read paragraph 16-78 and Figure 16-3.
- Do Self-Study Problems 16-1 and 16-2 and check the solutions in this Study Guide.

Allocating the Elected Amount
- Read paragraph 16-79 to 16-83.
- Do Exercise 16-3 and check the solution in this Study Guide.

Tax Cost of Eligible Property to the Corporate Purchaser
- Read paragraph 16-84 to 16-92.

Share Consideration—PUC ITA 85(2.1) [Overview]
- Read paragraph 16-93 to 16-96.

PUC Reduction—ITA 85(2.1)
- Read paragraph 16-97 to 16-101.

Share Consideration—Multiple Classes of Shares
- Read paragraph 16-102 to 16-105.
- Do Exercise 16-4 and check the solution in this Study Guide.
- Do Self-Study Problem 16-3 and check the solution in this Study Guide.

Comprehensive Example—Section 85 Rollovers
- Read paragraph 16-106 to 16-120.
- Do Exercise 16-5 and check the solution in this Study Guide.
- Do Self-Study Problems 16-4, 16-5, 16-6, and 16-7 and check the solutions in this Study Guide.

Gift to a Related Person—ITA 85(1)(e.2)
- Read paragraph 16-121 to 16-136.
- Do Exercise 16-6 and check the solution in this Study Guide.
- Do Self-Study Problem 16-8 and check the solution in this Study Guide.

Excess Consideration—ITA 15(1)
- Read paragraph 16-137 to 16-143.
- Do Exercise 16-7 and check the solution in this Study Guide.
- Do Self-Study Problem 16-9 and check the solution in this Study Guide.

Dividend/Surplus Stripping—ITA 84.1
- Read paragraph 16-144 to 16-164.
- Do Exercise 16-8 and check the solution in this Study Guide.
- Do Self-Study Problem 16-10 and check the solution in this Study Guide.

Capital Gains Stripping—ITA 55(2)
- Read paragraph 16-165 to 16-185.
- Do Exercise 16-9 and check the solution in this Study Guide.
- Do Self-Study Problem 16-11 and check the solution in this Study Guide.

To Complete This Chapter
- Visit MyLab Accounting for more practice problem material, and test yourself with the glossary flashcards.
- Review the Key Terms at the end of the chapter, and consult the glossary for definitions.
- Ensure you have achieved the Chapter 16 Learning Objectives listed in this Study Guide.
- As a review, view the PowerPoint presentations available on MyLab.

Practice Examination
- Available on MyLab, write the Practice Examination for this chapter, and mark it using the solutions provided.

Exercise Solutions

Exercise 16-1 Solution
Inventories The first step is to determine the acceptable range of elected amounts. Since there is an accrued loss, the elected amount must be the FMV of $125,000. The next step is to determine the consideration paid by the corporation. It is important that the total consideration paid by the corporation match the FMV of the eligible property to avoid any mismatches of value. In addition, since shares must be issued there should be nominal share consideration that can be a fraction of a share. This would mean that the election should indicate share consideration of a nominal amount, such as $1, but can be less (e.g., $0.01). The balance of the consideration will be NSC represented by a promissory note. With nominal share consideration we will round the promissory note to $125,000, although technically if $1 is chosen for the

shares the promissory note would be $124,999. The transfer would result in a loss of $15,000 ($140,000 - $125,000) that would decrease business profits or increase a business loss (ITA 23). As a final point, Mr. Doan may want to avoid ITA 85(1) with respect to the inventories since the same result is achieved with a sale without the use of the rollover.

Land   The first step is to again determine the acceptable range of elected amounts. Since there is an accrued gain and the FMV of the NSC exceeds the ACB of the land the range will be between $150,000 and $350,000. It is also important to ensure that there are no mismatches of value, which means that the FMV of the land of $350,000 is equal to the total consideration paid by the company for the land. Based on the facts, Mr. Doan will receive a promssiory note of $150,000 and share consideration of $200,000. The result of the rollover selecting the lowest possible amount of $150,000 is that the corporation will be considered to have acquired the land for $150,000 and Mr. Doan will be considered to have sold the land for the same $150,000. Electing the minimum amount would result in a taxable capital gain of $20,000 [($150,000 - $110,000)(50%)].

Exercise 16-2 Solution
Class 1 Property   Since there are accrued capital gains and recapture, the range of acceptable elected amounts is initially between $150,000 (the least of the capital cost of $220,000 and the UCC of $150,000) and $475,000 (the FMV of the property). Since the FMV of the NSC falls within that initial range it resets the range to between $250,000 and $475,000. Electing the minimum amount of $250,000 would result in recapture of $70,000 (UCC of $150,000 minus the elected amount of $220,000) and a taxable capital gain of $15,000 [(POD $250,000 - ACB $220,000)(1/2)].

Class 10 property   Since there is a potential recapture, the range of acceptable elected amount is initially between $8,000 (the least of the capital cost of $28,000 and the UCC of $8,000) and $12,000 (the FMV of the property). Since the FMV of the NSC falls within that initial range it resets the range to between $10,000 and $12,000. Electing the minimum amount of $10,000 would result in recapture of $2,000 (UCC of $8,000 minus the elected amount of $10,000).

Exercise 16-3 Solution
The ACB of the consideration received would be calculated as follows:

Elected amount	$62,000
Less: FMV of NSC	(51,000)
Balance available for shares	$11,000
ACB of preferred shares*	(11,000)
ACB of common shares (residual)	Nil

*The maximum amount that can be allocated to the preferred shares is the FMV of $53,000.

Exercise 16-4 Solution
The ACB of the consideration would be determined as follows:

Elected amount	$114,000
Less: FMV of NSC	(83,000)
Balance available for shares	$ 31,000
ACB of preferred shares*	(31,000)
ACB of common shares	Nil

*Balance available as it is less than the FMV of $97,000.

The total PUC reduction would be calculated as follows:

Increase in legal capital ($97,000 + $54,000)		$ 151,000
Less the excess of:		
Elected amount	($114,000)	
Less: FMV of NSC	83,000	(31,000)
PUC reduction		$ 120,000

Note that this reduction is equal to the deferred gain on the election ($234,000 - $114,000). The PUC reduction would be allocated on the basis of the relative FMV of the two classes of shares as follows:

Preferred shares [($120,000)($97,000 ÷ $151,000)]	$ 77,086
Common shares [($120,000)($54,000 ÷ $151,000)]	42,914
Total PUC reduction	$ 120,000

The PUC of the two classes of shares would be as follows:

	Preferred Shares	Common Shares
Legal capital	$ 97,000	$ 54,000
PUC reduction (from preceding)	(77,086)	(42,914)
PUC	$ 19,914	$ 11,086

The FMV of the preferred shares is $97,000, the ACB is $31,000, and the PUC is $19,914, whereas the FMV of the common shares is $54,000, the ACB is nil, and the PUC is $11,086. Note that if both classes of shares were sold for their FMV the capital gain would equal $120,000, which equals the deferred capital gain on the eligible property of $120,000 ($234,000 - $114,000).

Exercise 16-5 Solution

Part 1 The tax cost of the consideration received will total the elected amount of $275,000. It will be determined as follows:

Elected amount	$ 275,000
Less: FMV of NSC ($83,000 + $17,000)	(100,000)
Balance available for shares	$ 175,000
Less: FMV of preferred shares (maximum)	(125,000)
Tax cost of common shares	$ 50,000

Part 2 The PUC of the shares issued must be reduced as follows:

Increase in legal capital ($125,000 + $925,000)		$1,050,000
Less the excess of:		
Elected value	($275,000)	
Less: FMV of NSC	100,000	(175,000)
PUC reduction		$ 875,000

This PUC reduction would be split between the preferred and common shares on the basis of their FMV:

Preferred shares [($125,000/$1,050,000)($875,000)]	$104,167
Common shares [($925,000/$1,050,000)($875,000)]	770,833
Total PUC reduction	$875,000

The PUC of the two classes of shares would be as follows:

	Preferred Shares	Common Shares
Legal capital	$125,000	$925,000
PUC reduction (from preceding)	(104,167)	(770,833)
Total PUC	$ 20,833	$ 154,167

Part 3 The income tax consequences of the preferred share redemption would be as follows:

Proceeds of redemption	$ 125,000
PUC	(20,833)
ITA 84(3) deemed dividend (non-eligible)	$ 104,167

Proceeds of redemption	$ 125,000
ITA 84(3) deemed dividend	(104,167)
ITA 54 deemed POD	$ 20,833
ACB	(125,000)
Capital loss—Disallowed (ITA 40(3.6))	($ 104,167)

The grossed up non-eligible dividend of $119,792 [(115%)($104,167)] would qualify for a federal dividend tax credit of $10,817 [(9/13)(15%)($104,167)]. The capital loss would be disallowed because the shareholder is affiliated with the corporation immediately after the redemption. The disallowed loss of $104,167 will be added to the tax cost (ACB) of the common shares with the result that their ACB would be $154,167 [$50,000 + $104,167].

Exercise 16-6 Solution

Using the reassessed FMV of $110,000, the calculation of the gift is as follows:

FMV of investments (CRA value)	$110,000
Less the greater of:	
• FMV of all consideration received = $65,000	
($50,000 + $15,000)	
• Elected mmount = $50,000	(65,000)
Excess = Gift to daughter	$ 45,000

Given this gift, the income tax consequences of the sale of the investments to the corporation to Ms. Bellows would be as follows:

Revised elected amount = POD	
($50,000 + $45,000 gift)	$95,000
ACB	(50,000)
Capital gain	$45,000
Inclusion rate	1/2
Taxable capital gain	$22,500

The ACB of the preferred share consideration would be calculated as follows:

Elected amount (initial)	$ 50,000
Less: FMV of NSC	(50,000)
ACB of the preferred shares	Nil

The PUC of the preferred shares. based on the revised elected amount, would be:

Increase in legal capital (based on FMV)		$ 15,000
Less excess, if any, of:		
Revised elected amount	($95,000)	
Less: FMV of NSC	50,000	(45,000)
PUC reduction		$ 15,000
PUC of preferred shares ($15,000 - $15,000)		$ Nil

The FMV of the common shares issued to the daughter as a result of the rollover is $46,000 ($110,000 reassessed value + $1,000 - $50,000 - $15,000).

The sale of the shares for their FMV would result in the following taxable capital gains:

	Preferred	Common
POD (FMV)	$15,000	$46,000
ACB	Nil	(1,000)
Capital gain	$15,000	$45,000
Inclusion rate	1/2	1/2
Taxable capital gain	$ 7,500	$22,500

If the investments had simply been sold for the $110,000 post-reassessment FMV, there would have been a $60,000 [($110,000 - $50,000) capital gain to Ms. Bellows. The result of ITA 85(1)(e.2), however, is that Ms. Bellows is immediately subject to income tax on the $45,000 gift, which is treated as a capital gain. The sale of Ms. Bellows' preferred shares and her daughter's common shares totals $60,000 in capital gains. The $45,000 gift was subject to income tax to Ms. Bellows and to her daughter on the sale of the common shares. This reflects the fact that the $45,000 amount of the gift has effectively been subject to income tax twice.

Exercise 16-7 Solution
On the original sale in 2020, Mr. Custer would have recognized a capital gain of nil [(1/2)(POD $123,000 - ACB $123,000)].

With the lower value required by the reassessment, there is excess consideration and an ITA 15(1) benefit.

FMV of consideration received	$270,000
FMV of property given in exchange	(217,000)
ITA 15(1) shareholder benefit	$ 53,000

With the value of the property transferred reassessed at $217,000, the original elected amount of $123,000 remains valid and the revised capital gain of nil would not change. The acceptable range for ITA 85(1) would be between $123,000 and $217,000.

Elected amount after reassessment (unchanged)		$123,000
ACB		(123,000)
Capital gain	$	Nil
Inclusion rate		1/2
Taxable capital gain on property after reassessment	$	Nil

As a result of the reassessment, net income for 2020 is increased by $53,000 as shown in the following table:

Taxable capital gain after reassessment	$	Nil
Shareholder benefit after reassessment		53,000
Revised taxable capital gain		Nil
Total change in net income		$53,000

The ACB of the note remains unchanged at $123,000 and the PUC of the preferred shares also remain unchanged at nil. ITA 52(1) contains an ACB adjustment where the excess consideration results in a shareholder benefit under ITA 15(1). Had the corporation known that the FMV of the investments was only $217,000 it would have only issued $94,000 in share consideration instead of $147,000. Therefore, it is the additional $53,000 in shares that represents the excess consideration. As a result the ACB of the preferred shares is increased from nil to $53,000.

ACB of the preferred shares—ITA 85(1)	$ Nil
ITA 52(1) ACB adjustment	53,000
ACB of the preferred shares	$ 53,000

The PUC of the preferred shares would be nil. The revised amounts can be reconciled. When Mr. Custer sold investments to his company for $270,000 he would have recognized a gain of $147,000 since the ACB was only $123,000. Of that gain, $53,000 was included in income as a shareholder benefit, leaving $94,000 that has yet to be included in income. The FMV of the preferred shares is $147,000 with a revised ACB of $53,000; therefore, if he sells the preferred shares he will recognize the remaining gain of $94,000.

Exercise 16-8 Solution

Ms. Cole (an individual) has sold shares of a resident corporation to a second corporation. She is non-arm's length with the second company (SHL) at the time of the share sale because she controls the company. Finally, the two corporations are connected immediately after the sale because SHL owns more than 10% of the shares of Cole Inc. As a result, all of the conditions of ITA 84.1 have been met. The income tax consequences of the share sale by Ms. Cole to SHL are as follows:

Increase in legal capital		$ 317,000
Less excess, if any, of:		
PUC and ACB of Cole Inc. shares	($125,000)	
Less: FMV of NSC	450,000	Nil
PUC reduction		$ 317,000
PUC of SHL shares ($317,000 - $317,000)		Nil
Increase in legal capital		$ 317,000
Add: FMV of NSC		450,000
Total		$ 767,000
Less the sum of:		
PUC and ACB of Cole Inc. shares	($125,000)	
PUC reduction	(317,000)	(442,000)
ITA 84.1 deemed dividend (non-eligible)		$ 325,000
POD		$ 767,000
Less: ITA 84.1 deemed dividend		(325,000)
Adjusted POD—ITA 54 "POD"		$ 442,000
ACB of Cole Inc. shares		(125,000)
Capital gain		$ 317,000
Inclusion rate		1/2
Taxable capital gain		$ 158,500
ACB of SHL shares ($767,000 - $450,000)		$ 317,000

The grossed up non-eligible dividend of $373,750 [(115%)($325,000)] would be included in her net income and there would be a federal dividend tax credit of $33,750 [(9/13)(15%)($325,000)] to reduce her federal income tax payable. In addition, there would be a taxable capital gain of $158,500 that would be eligible for the capital gains deduction.

Ms. Cole is attempting to realize a capital gain of $642,000 ($767,000 - $125,000). However, her NSC was $450,000, $325,000 more than the ITA 84.1 limit. She could have avoided the deemed dividend consequences of ITA 84.1 by limiting the NSC to $125,000.

Exercise 16-9 Solution

Markem Ltd. has received a taxable dividend on the Larkin Ltd. shares for which it is entitled to a taxable income deduction under ITA 112(1). In addition, the taxable dividend is part of the series of transactions that includes a sale to an arm's-length person. Had Markem Ltd. sold the shares there would have been a capital gain of $765,000 (POD $840,000 - ACB $75,000). The actual capital gain is only $15,000 [POD $90,000 - ACB $75,000). The $750,000 reduction ($765,000 - $15,000) in the capital gain is attributable to the $750,000 taxable dividend. The only exception would be for the safe income of $225,000, which would leave $525,000 ($750,000 - $225,000), which would be caught by ITA 55(2). The income tax consequences of ITA 55(2) that reflect this conclusion are as follows:

Taxable dividends received	$750,000
Dividends attributable to safe income	(225,000)
Amount deemed by ITA 55(2)(a) not to be a dividend and by ITA 55(2)(c) to be a capital gain	$525,000
Capital gain on sale of shares (POD $90,000 - ACB $75,000)	15,000
Total capital gain	$540,000
Inclusion rate	1/2
Taxable capital gain	$270,000

The $225,000 of dividends paid from safe income will retain its status as a taxable dividend and will be a taxable income deduction under ITA 112(1).

Self-Study Problem Solutions

Self-Study Problems are available to download from MyLab Accounting.

SSP 16-1 Solution
Part A—No Elections

Inventories sold as part of the disposition of a business are treated as if they were sold in the ordinary course of carrying on the business (ITA 23(1)). This means that any gain is treated as business income and any loss would either reduce business profits or increase a business loss. As a result, there would be $15,000 added to business income as a result of the sale of the inventories to the new corporation.

The sale of accounts receivables would be treated as a capital gain or capital loss since they are non-depreciable capital property. A sale for $45,000 would therefore result in a $6,000 capital loss, one-half of which ($3,000) would be an allowable capital loss. However, it is a superficial loss in that the property is sold to an affiliated person (the new corporation). ITA 40(2)(g) deems such losses to be nil. This loss would be added to the tax cost of the accounts receivable to the corporation (ITA 53(1)(f)).

The sale of furniture and fixtures at FMV would not result in any capital gain since the FMV of $45,000 does not exceed the ACB (capital cost) of $62,000. There would, however, be a recapture of $7,000 given that the FMV exceeds the UCC of $38,000. There would also be no capital loss since the ITA does not allow capital losses on the sale of depreciable property.

Since the goodwill was not purchased but internally generated there would be no cost and therefore no ACB. As a result there would be a capital gain of $150,000 as indicated, 50% of which ($75,000) would be included in income as a taxable capital gain.

The addition to net and taxable income as a result of a sale at FMV can be calculated as follows:

Inventories—Business income ($88,000 - $73,000)	$15,000
Furniture and fixtures—Recaptured CCA ($45,000 - $38,000)	7,000
Capital gain on goodwill [(1/2)($150,000 - nil)]	75,000
Additional income	$ 97,000

Part B—ITA 22 and ITA 85 Elections

The cash would not qualify as eligible property for ITA 85(1) purposes. The preferable method of handling cash is to loan the amount to the corporation, which creates a credit balance in a shareholder loan account that can be drawn down without any income tax consequences.

All of the other property can be sold using ITA 85(1). The income tax consequences would be as follows:

Accounts Receivable If the accounts receivable are sold using ITA 85(1), the only elected amount is the FMV of $45,000 since there is an accrued loss on the receivables. There would be a capital loss of $6,000 (allowable capital loss of $3,000). However, this loss will be disallowed under ITA 40(2)(g) because the transfer is to a corporation that will be controlled by Ms. Flack. ITA 22, however, provides a better solution as it allows the $6,000 capital loss to be treated as fully deductible for business purposes that reduces business profits or increases a business loss. The downside is that the same $6,000 amount has to be included in the business income of the purchaser corporation. An ITA 22 election would allow the corporation to claim doubtful debt reserves (ITA 20(1)(l)) and bad debt deductions (ITA 20(1)(p)), which would not be available in the absence of the election. A further benefit of an election under ITA 22 is that the superficial loss rules would not apply since the fully deductible loss is not a capital loss.

Inventories Since there is an accrued gain, the acceptable ITA 85(1) amounts for inventories is between the tax cost of $73,000 and the FMV of $88,000. Electing the minimum amount of $73,000 eliminates any income on the sale to the corporation.

Furniture and Fixtures Since there is accrued recapture on the furniture and fixtures, the acceptable ITA 85(1) amounts are between the UCC of $38,000 and the FMV of $45,000. Electing the minimum amount avoids any recapture on the sale to the new corporation.

Goodwill Since there is an accrued gain on the goodwill, the acceptable range for purposes of ITA 85(1) is between $1 and $150,000. Electing the minimum amount avoids any income tax on the sale to the corporation. Note that technically the ACB of the goodwill is nil, however ITA 85(1) requires selecting an "amount," which is a term defined in ITA 248(1). An amount is not an amount unless it is positive, meaning there is no such thing as a negative or nil amount. This is the reason that the CRA requires choosing a nominal amount. While $1.00 is common, $0.01 would be acceptable.

SSP 16-2 Solution
Part A—Eligible Property to Be Incorporated

Of the assets in the balance sheet, cash does not qualify as eligible property listed. Cash is generally loaned to the company and represents a credit balance in a shareholder loan account.

The sale of accounts receivable to the corporation could be elected using either ITA 22 or ITA 85(1). Since the FMV and tax cost of the receivables are the same there is no accrued gain or accrued loss. There is, therefore, no justification for electing ITA 85(1) in this case. ITA 22, on the other hand, has advantages to the corporation that will permit the claiming of subsequent doubtful debt reserves and bad debt deductions with respect to the purchased receivables. The reserves and deduction would not be available to the company unless a joint election is filed under ITA 22.

The inventories, land, building, and goodwill all have accrued gains, meaning that the acceptable range for the elected amounts will be between the tax cost and the FMV. The FMV of NSC, however, could reset the range.

There is an accrued loss (i.e., terminal loss) on the equipment as its FMV $32,500 is less than the UCC of the class of $67,000. Since the result of a sale to a controlled corporation (an affiliated person) would result in a terminal loss, ITA 13(21.2) prevents the property from qualifying for ITA 85(1) treatment. The terminal loss would be disallowed as part of the stop loss rules in the ITA on a sale of the equipment to the corporation at FMV.

Part B—Minimum Elected Amounts

The shareholder has only authorized use of ITA 85(1) where there is an income tax advantage to using the rollover. This leaves inventories, land, the building, and goodwill as the only eligible property that would meet that objective.

The minimum elected amounts for the eligible properties to be sold to the corporation would be as follows:

Inventories (cost)	$261,000
Land (adjusted cost base)	196,000
Building (UCC)	103,600
Goodwill (nominal value)	1

Note   The amount elected for goodwill must be a positive amount, such as $1. Using a nil amount would not be considered as having elected an "amount," which would disqualify the goodwill from the election. A disqualification of the goodwill for rollover treatments would mean the FMV rule would apply.

Part C—Income Tax Consequences

The income tax consequences of the ITA 85(1) rollover with respect to the elected eligible property to both Ms. Speaks and Speaks Inc. can be described as follows:

Inventories   The cost of the inventories to Speaks Inc. would be $261,000. As this was the cost of the inventories, there would be no income tax consequence to Ms. Speaks.

Land   The cost of the land to Speaks Inc. would be $196,000. As this was the ACB of the land, there would be no income tax consequence to Ms. Speaks.

Building   The UCC of the building to Speaks Inc. would be $103,600 (capital cost $155,6500 - deemed CCA $51,900). A sale at the UCC amount would not create and income tax consequence for Ms. Speaks.

Goodwill   The cost of the goodwill to Speaks Inc. will be $0.50 (ITA 13(7)(e)) and will be added to class 14.1. Ms. Speaks will include a taxable capital gain of $0.50 (POD $1.00 - ACB nil) in her income.

SSP 16-3 Solution

Alternative 1

Immediate Income Tax Consequences   The $230,000 elected amount becomes the POD to the seller, Mr. Sindren. As this amount is equal to the ACB of the land, there are no immediate tax consequences resulting from the transfer.

ACB of the Land   The ACB of the land to the corporation would be equal to the elected amount of $230,000.

ACB of Shares   The ACB of the shares issued by the corporation would be calculated as follows:

Elected amount	$230,000
FMV of NSC	Nil
ACB of shares	$230,000

PUC of Shares   The required PUC reduction and resulting PUC would be calculated as follows:

Legal capital of shares		$ 660,000
Less excess, if any, of:		
Elected amount	($230,000)	
Less: FMV of NSC	Nil	(230,000)
PUC reduction		$ 430,000
PUC of shares ($660,000 - $430,000)		$ 230,000

Alternative 2

Immediate Income Tax Consequences   The elected amount of $500,000 becomes the POD to Mr. Sindren. As this amount exceeds the $230,000 ACB of the land, there is a taxable capital gain of $135,000 [(1/2)($500,000 - $230,000)].

ACB of the Land   The ACB of the land to the corporation will be equal to the elected amount of $500,000.

ACB of Shares   The ACB of the shares issued by the corporation would be calculated as follows:

Elected amount	$500,000
Less: FMV of NSC	Nil
ACB of shares	$500,000

PUC of Shares   The required PUC reduction and resulting PUC would be calculated as follows:

Legal capital of shares		$ 660,000
Less excess, if any, of:		
Elected amount	($500,000)	
Less: FMV of NSC	Nil	(500,000)
PUC reduction		$ 160,000
PUC of shares ($660,000 - $160,000)		$ 500,000

Alternative 3

Immediate Income Tax Consequences   The elected amount of $500,000 becomes the POD to Mr. Sindren. As this amount exceeds the $230,000 ACB of the land, there is a taxable capital gain of $135,000 [(1/2)($500,000 - $230,000)].

ACB of the Land   The ACB of the land to the corporation will be equal to the elected amount of $500,000.

ACB of Shares The ACB of the shares issued by the corporation would be calculated as follows:

Elected amount	$500,000
Less: FMV of NSC	(500,000)
ACB of shares	Nil

PUC of Shares The required PUC reduction and resulting PUC would be calculated as follows:

Legal capital of shares		$160.000
Less excess, if any, of:		
Elected amount	($500,000)	
Less FMV of NSC	500,000	Nil
PUC reduction		$160,000
PUC of shares ($160,000 - $160,000)		Nil

SSP 16-4 Solution
Part A—Tax Cost (ACB) of Consideration

The tax cost for each type of consideration, under the three alternatives, would be determined as follows:

	Alternative		
	One	**Two**	**Three**
Elected amount	$225,000	$225,000	$225,000
Less FMV of NSC	(150,000)	(175,000)	(210,000)
Available for shares	$ 75,000	$ 50,000	$ 15,000
Less: FMV preferred shares	(50,000)	(50,000)	N/A
Tax cost of common shares	$ 25,000	N/A	$ 15,000

Part B—Legal Capital and PUC

The legal capital for the share consideration would be as follows:

	Alternative		
	One	**Two**	**Three**
Preferred shares	$ 50,000	$450,000	Nil
Common shares	425,000	Nil	$415,000
Total legal capital	$475,000	$450,000	$415,000

The required PUC reduction would be calculated as follows:

	Alternative		
	One	**Two**	**Three**
Increase in legal capital—			
All shares (A)	$475,000	$450,000	$415,000
Elected amount	$225,000	$225,000	$225,000
Less: FMV of NSC	(150,000)	(175,000)	(210,000)
Elected amount, less boot (B)	$ 75,000	$ 50,000	$ 15,000
Required PUC reduction (A - B)	$400,000	$400,000	$400,000

Alternative One   In Alternative One, the PUC reduction would have to be split between the two classes of shares on the basis of their relative FMV. The relevant calculation would be as follows:

Preferred shares: [($400,000)($50,000 ÷ $475,000)] = $42,105

Common shares: [($400,000)($425,000 ÷ $475,000)] = $357,895

This would leave a PUC of $7,895 for the preferred shares ($50,000 - $42,105) and a PUC of $67,105 for the common shares ($425,000 - $357,895).

Alternative Two   In Alternative Two, the entire PUC reduction of $400,000 would be allocated to the preferred shares, leaving a PUC of $50,000 ($450,000 - $400,000).

Alternative Three   In Alternative Three, the entire PUC reduction of $400,000 would be allocated to the common shares, leaving a PUC of $15,000 ($415,000 - $400,000).

SSP 16-5 Solution
Part A—ACB of the Share Consideration
The ACB of the shares would be as follows:

Elected amount	$ 467,000
Less: FMV of NSC ($122,000 + $128,000)	(250,000)
Available for shares	$ 217,000
Less preferred shares (FMV)	(150,000)
ACB of common shares	$ 67,000

Part B—PUC of the Share Consideration
The legal capital of the preferred and common shares would be their respective FMV of $150,000 and $326,000. The PUC reduction required under ITA 85(2.1) would be calculated as follows:

Increase in legal capital ($150,000 + $326,000)		$476,000
Less excess of:		
Elected amount	($ 467,000)	
Less: FMV of NSC	250,000	(217,000)
Reduction in PUC		$259,000

Note that this total reduction is equal to the deferred gain on the election ($726,000 - $467,000). The PUC reduction would be allocated on the basis of relative FMV as follows:

Preferred shares [($259,000)($150,000 ÷ $476,000)]	$ 81,618
Common shares [($259,000)($326,000 ÷ $476,000)]	177,382
Total PUC reduction	$259,000

The PUC of the two classes of shares would be as follows:

	Preferred Shares	Common Shares
Legal capital	$150,000	$326,000
PUC reduction	(81,618)	(177,382)
PUC	$ 68,382	$148,618

Since the FMV of the NSC is less than the elected amount, the difference of $217,000 remains available to be filled with PUC. The combined PUC of the two classes of shares confirms this amount once the PUC reduction has been considered.

Part C—Tax Consequences of a Redemption of Each Class

The income tax consequences to Mr. Lardner, if the corporation redeems all of the shares issued as consideration, would be calculated as follows:

	Preferred Shares	**Common Shares**
Redemption proceeds	$150,000	$326,000
PUC (see preceding calculations)	(68,382)	(148,618)
ITA 84(3) deemed dividend	$ 81,618	$ 177,382
Redemption proceeds	$150,000	$326,000
ITA 84(3) deemed dividend	(81,618)	(177,382)
Deemed POD (ITA 54 "POD")	$ 68,382	$ 148,618
ACB (Part A)	(150,000)	(67,000)
Capital gain (loss)	($ 81,618)	$ 81,618

Mr. Lardner would have a deemed non-eligible dividend of $259,000 ($81,618 + $177,382). The grossed up non-eligible dividend of $297,850 [(115%)($259,000)] would qualify for a federal dividend tax credit of $26,896 [(9/13)($38,850)]. He has a net capital gain of nil ($81,618 - $81,618).

SSP 16-6 Solution

Part A—Income Tax Consequences of Incorporating the Land and Building

The $250,000 elected amount for the land will become the POD to Mr. Bodin and the ACB to the corporation. Since the elected amount equals Mr. Bodin's ACB, there will be no capital gain or capital loss as a result of the sale.

The elected amount for the building of $750,000 becomes the POD to Mr. Bodin and the initial cost to the company. Since the POD does not exceed the ACB (equal to the capital cost) of $1,100,000 there is no capital gain on the sale; however, since the POD exceeds the UCC Mr. Bodin will be required to include recapture of $116,400 ($750,000 - $633,600) in his income for 2021. In addition, since less than 100% of the potential recapture on the building was included in income the corporation will be subject to ITA 85(5). The result is that the corporation will be deemed to have a capital cost equal to Mr. Bodin's capital cost of $1,100,000 with the difference between that amount and $750,000 considered as deemed CCA of $350,000. Therefore, the UCC to the company of the building will be $750,000 [Deemed capital cost $1,100,000 - deemed CCA $350,000].

Part B—Tax Cost (ACB) of the Consideration

The tax cost of all consideration received by Mr. Bodin will be equal to the elected amount of $1,000,000 ($250,000 + $750,000). It will be allocated as follow:

Elected amount	$1,000,000
Less: FMV of NSC	
($450,000 assumed mortgage + $400,000 new debt)	(850,000)
Tax cost of preferred shares	$ 150,000

Part C—PUC of the Preferred Shares

The calculation of PUC would be as follows:

Increase in legal capital		$950,000
Less excess of:		
Elected amount	($1,000,000)	
Less: FMV of NSC	850,000	(150,000)
Reduction in PUC		$800,000

The PUC of the preferred shares would be $150,000 ($950,000 - $800,000).

Part D—Sale of All of the Preferred Shares

The increase in net income from a sale of the preferred shares for POD of $950,000 would be as follows:

POD	$950,000
ACB	(150,000)
Capital gain	$800,000
Inclusion rate	1/2
Taxable capital gain	$400,000

Part E—Redemption of All of the Preferred Shares

The income tax consequences of a redemption for $950,000 would be as follows:

Proceeds from redemption	$950,000
PUC	(150,000)
ITA 84(3) deemed dividend (non-eligible)	$800,000

There would be no capital gain on this redemption as shown in the following calculation:

Redemption proceeds	$950,000
ITA 84(3) deemed dividend	(800,000)
Deemed POD (ITA 54 "POD")	$150,000
ACB	(150,000)
Capital gain	Nil

The amount to be included in Mr. Bodin's net income for 2021 would be $920,000, the $800,000 deemed non-eligible dividend grossed up by 15%.

There would also be a federal dividend tax credit of $83,077 [(9/13)($120,000)].

SSP 16-7 Solution

Part A—Balance Sheet Assets to Be Included in the Rollover and the Elected Amounts

Cash and prepayments are not "property" for income tax purposes and therefore they cannot qualify as eligible property within the meaning of ITA 85(1.1). As a result, they cannot be included in the rollover. It is best for Mr. Danforth to lend the cash to the company, which will create a credit balance in his shareholder loan account.

The FMV of the accounts receivable is $1,250 ($13,750 - $12,500) less than the amount owing. This accrued loss would be considered a capital loss, which would be denied to Mr. Danforth if the receivables were included in the rollover. This is because the capital loss would be a super-ficial loss since the sale would be between affiliated persons as Mr. Danforth controls the company. In addition, the company would be unable to claim any doubtful debt reserves or deduct any bad debts with respect to the purchased receivables. This result, however, can be improved with a joint election under ITA 22. Mr. Danforth would be able to deduct the $1,250 accrued loss as a business deduction, although the company would have to add that same amount to its income. In addition, the stop loss rule that would deny the loss to Mr. Danforth would not apply. Finally, the company would then be able to claim doubtful debt reserves and deduct any bad debts. As a result, a joint election will be filed under ITA 22 with respect to the receivables, which precludes the receivables from being included in an ITA 85(1) rollover.

With respect to the inventory, there is no accrued gain or accrued loss and therefore there would be no advantage to including inventories in the rollover.

The land has an accrued loss, which would also be disallowed as a superficial loss because of the affiliated person relationship between Mr. Danforth and his company. As a result, there is also no advantage to including the land in the rollover. It is important to note that when incorporating a business carried on as a sole proprietorship an individual is selling business properties to a corporation. That fact does not change because of ITA 85(1). ITA 85(1) applies to eligible property selected among the business properties being sold to obtain an income tax advantage, specifically to avoid the income tax consequences that would normally occur because of a sale at FMV.

There is also an accrued terminal loss on the equipment. Since the sale between Mr. Danforth and the company are between affiliated persons, ITA 13(21.2) would apply that precludes the rules in ITA 85 from applying. As a result, there is no advantage to including the equipment in the rollover. Mr. Danforth will be denied the terminal loss on the sale of the equipment to the company whether or not the equipment is included in the rollover.

In summary, the following business assets will not be included in the rollover:

Cash (not eligible property)	$ 2,500
Accounts receivable (ITA 22 election filed)	12,500
Inventories (no accrued gain or loss)	17,500
Prepayments (not eligible property)	7,500
Land (accrued loss subject to stop loss rules)	77,500
Equipment (accrued terminal loss ITA 13(21.2))	7,500
Total FMV	$125,000

The remaining properties, the investments, building, and goodwill, all have accrued gains and therefore the elected amount for each property is between the tax cost (ACB for the investments and goodwill and UCC for the building) and FMV. Limiting the FMV of NSC will achieve the objective of deferring any income tax on the sale of these three properties to the corporation.

	Tax Cost	FMV	Elected Amount
Temporary investments	$27,500	$ 37,500	$27,500
Buildings	70,000	125,000	70,000
Goodwill (see Note)	Nil	117,500	1
Total assets transferred	$97,500	$280,000	$97,501

Part B—Maximum Non-Share Consideration
The liabilities of $20,000 that are assumed by the corporation are considered NSC to Mr. Danforth. The maximum amount of non-share consideration that can be received by Mr. Danforth to defer all accrued gains and recapture is $97,501. The NSC would therefore consist of the assumed debt of $20,000 plus the issuance of a promissory note in the amount of $77,501.

Part C—Sale of the Shares
The ACB of the preferred share consideration determined as follows:

Elected amount	$97,501
Less: FMV of NSC	97,501
ACB of preferred shares	Nil

Given this, the taxable capital gain on the sale of the preferred shares would be calculated as follows:

POD	$208,000
ACB	Nil
Capital gain	$208,000
Inclusion rate	1/2
Taxable capital gain	$ 104,000

Since the shares qualify as QSBC shares the capital gain is eligible for the capital gains deduction. This means that he will be able to claim a taxable income deduction of $104,000, reducing taxable income to nil with respect to the sale of the shares. However, use of his capital gains deduction could result in a liability for alternative minimum tax (AMT).

SSP 16-8 Solution
Part A
The following table shows that the post-reassessment FMV of the business properties sold to the corporation exceeds the FMV of the consideration received:

FMV of eligible property	
($1,578,000 + $430,000 - $350,000)	$1,658,000
Less the greater of:	
• FMV of all consideration received	
($160,000 + $947,000 + $471,000) = $1,578,000	
• Elected amount = $1,107,000	(1,578,000)
Excess = Gift	$ 80,000

As Sarah Cheng is the only common shareholder of the new corporation, it is clear that Mr. Cheng has made a gift to his daughter. As a consequence, the amount of the gift must be added to the elected amount, which revises the POD. As the reassessment was on the land, the result will be a capital gain. This results in the following income tax consequences for Mr. Cheng:

Revised elected amount of the land = Revised POD	
($350,000 + $80,000)	$430,000
ACB of the land	(350,000)
Capital gain	$ 80,000
Inclusion rate	1/2
Taxable capital gain	$ 40,000

The ACB of the preferred shares received by Mr. Cheng would be calculated as follows:

Elected amount (Initial)	$1,107,000
Less: FMV of NSC ($160,000 + $947,000)	(1,107,000)
ACB of the preferred shares	Nil

The required PUC reduction and resulting PUC would be calculated as follows:

Increase in legal capital ($471,000)		$471,000
Excess, if any, of:		
Revised elected amount		
($1,107,000 + $80,000)	($1,187,000)	
Less: FMV of NSC	1,107,000	(80,000)
PUC reduction		$391,000
PUC of preferred shares ($471,000 - $391,000)		$ 80,000

Part B

The income tax consequences to Mr. Cheng of having his shares redeemed would be as follows:

Proceeds of redemption	$471,000
PUC of shares	(80,000)
ITA 84(3) deemed dividend	$391,000

Redemption proceeds	$471,000
ITA 84(3) deemed dividend	(391,000)
Adjusted POD	$ 80,000
ACB	Nil
Capital gain (loss)	$ 80,000
Inclusion rate	1/2
Taxable capital gain	$ 40,000

This non-eligible deemed dividend would be grossed up to $449,650 [(115%)($391,000)] and will generate a federal dividend tax credit of $40,604 [(9/13)(15%)($391,000)].

Part C

The income tax consequences of Sarah selling her shares would be as follows:

POD	$90,000
ACB	(10,000)
Capital gain	$80,000
Inclusion rate	1/2
Taxable capital gain	$40,000

Economic Analysis (Not Required)

If Mr. Cheng had simply sold the business properties for their post-reassessment FMV, he would have the following income:

FMV after reassessment	
($1,578,000 + $80,000)	$1,658,000
Tax cost of business properties sold	(1,107,000)
Income (capital gains and recapture)	$ 551,000

The comparable tax consequences of the application of the gifting rule and a subsequent redemption of all of the share consideration would be as follows:

Capital gain as a result of the gift	$ 80,000
ITA 84(3) deemed dividend	391,000
Capital gain on redemption	80,000
Total	$551,000

While the composition of the income is different, the overall result is the same $551,000 that would have resulted from a simple sale.

However, there is an impact on Sarah. The $80,000 gift increased the FMV of her shares with no corresponding increase in the ACB of the shares. As a result, when she disposes of the shares, there will be a capital gain equal to the gift amount, which was already included in her father's income. In effect, the $80,000 amount of the gift will be subject to income tax twice.

SSP 16-9 Solution
Part A

The original elected amount remains valid, therefore the original capital gain remains unchanged at nil. However, the revised FMV of $650,000 results in the following ITA 15(1) shareholder benefit:

FMV of consideration received	$800,000
FMV of property given in exchange	(650,000)
ITA 15(1) shareholder benefit	$ 150,000

The reassessed FMV of $650,000 changes the acceptable range for ITA 85(1) purposes from $475,000 to $650,000. Since the original elected amount of $475,000 remains within an acceptable range the reassessment does not change the initial results, which resulted in a nil capital gain as follows:

Elected amount after reassessment (unchanged)	$475,000
ACB	(475,000)
Capital gain	$ Nil
Inclusion rate	1/2
Taxable capital gain on property after reassessment	$ Nil

The net effect of the reassessment would be calculated as follows

Initial taxable capital gain	$ Nil
Shareholder benefit	150,000
Revised taxable capital gain	Nil
Total change to net income	$ 150,000

Part B

The ACB of the note remains unchanged at $475,000 and the PUC of the preferred shares also remains unchanged at nil. ITA 52(1) contains an ACB adjustment where the excess consideration results in a shareholder benefit under ITA 15(1). Had the corporation known that the FMV of the land was only $650,000 it would have only issued $175,000 in share consideration instead of $325,000. Therefore, it is the additional $150,000 in shares that represents the excess consideration. As a result, the ACB of the preferred shares is increased from nil to $150,000.

ACB of the preferred shares—ITA 85(1)	$ Nil
ITA 15(1) shareholder benefit—ITA 52(1)	150,000
ACB of the preferred shares	$ 150,000

The revised amounts can be reconciled. When Mr. Gibber sold the land to his company for $800,000 he would have recognized a gain of $325,000 since the ACB was only $475,000. Of that gain, $150,000 was included in income as a shareholder benefit, leaving $175,000 to be included in his income. The FMV of the preferred shares are $325,000 with a revised ACB of $150,000; therefore, if he sells the shares he will realize the $175,000 capital gain at that time. Note that the PUC of the preferred shares remains unchanged at nil. A redemption of the shares for $325,000 would result in a deemed dividend of $325,000 and a capital loss of $150,000 that would be disallowed as a result of ITA 40(3.6). The net difference between the deemed dividend of $325,000 and the capital loss of $150,000 also equals $175,000.

SSP 16-10 Solution
Part A—Income Tax Consequences of Proposed Plan

Ms. Chadwick's plan involves the sale of shares of a corporation resident in Canada to another corporation with which she does not deal at arm's length. Subsequent to the transaction, the two corporations are connected (Borque Inc. controls Norton Ltd.). Given these facts, ITA 84.1 applies to this transaction.

The required calculations begin with the PUC reduction under ITA 84.1(1)(a):

Increase in legal capital of Borque Inc.		$1,590,000
Less the excess, if any, of:		
ITA 84.1 limit	($225,000)	
Over the FMV of NSC	875,000	Nil
PUC reduction		$1,590,000
PUC ($1,590,000 - $1,590,000)		Nil

The nil PUC reflects the fact that all of the PUC of the Norton Ltd. shares was taken out as NSC.

The deemed non-eligible dividend under ITA 84.1(1)(b) and federal dividend tax credit would be calculated as follows:

Increase in legal capital of Borque Inc.		$1,590,000
Add: FMV of NSC		875,000
Total		$2,465,000
ITA 84.1 limit	($ 225,000)	
PUC reduction under ITA 84.1(1)(a)	(1,590,000)	(1,815,000)
Deemed dividend—ITA 84.1(1)(b)		$ 650,000
Gross up 15%		97,500
Taxable non-eligible dividend		$ 747,500
Federal dividend tax credit [(9/13)($97,500)]		$ 67,500

You will note that, because of the application of ITA 84.1, there is no capital gain eligible for the lifetime capital gains deduction. The revised capital gain is determined as:

POD—ITA 85(1) elected amount	$875,000
Less: ITA 84.1(1)(b) deemed dividend	(650,000)
Adjusted POD (ITA 54)	$225,000
ACB	(225,000)
Capital gain or capital loss	Nil

Part B—An Improved Solution

The approach suggested by Ms. Chadwick will not be successful in producing the required $650,000 capital gain. To avoid the ITA 84.1 deemed dividend she would be required to limit the FMV of NSC to the ITA 84.1 limit of $225,000 and take the remaining value of $2,240,000 as share consideration. Using this revised consideration the required PUC reduction under ITA 84.1(1)(b) would be as follows:

Increase in legal capital of Borque Inc.		$2,240,000
Less the excess, if any, of:		
ITA 84.1 limit	($225,000)	
Over FMV of NSC	225,000	Nil
PUC reduction		$2,240,000
PUC ($2,240,000 - $2,240,000)		Nil

The deemed non-eligible dividend under ITA 84.1(1)(b) would be calculated as follows:

Increase in legal capital of Borque Inc.		$2,240,000
Add: FMV of NSC		225,000
Total consideration		$2,465,000
ITA 84.1 limit	($ 225,000)	
PUC reduction under 84.1(1)(b)	(2,240,000)	(2,465,000)
Deemed dividend under ITA 84.1(1)(b)		Nil

Given the preceding, the capital gain resulting from this transaction is calculated as follows:

POD (elected amount—ITA 85(1))	$875,000
Less: ITA 84.1(1)(b) deemed dividend	Nil
Adjusted POD—ITA 54 "POD"	$875,000
ACB	(225,000)
Capital gain	$650,000

There would be no income tax consequences using this approach, except for the possibility that the alternative minimum tax (AMT) may be payable. While there would be a $650,000 capital gain, it could be completely offset by Ms. Chadwick's available capital gains deduction of the same amount.

Part C—Sale of Shares (No ITA 85(1) Election)

Since the basic facts have not changed, the conditions of ITA 84.1 are met. This means that ITA 84.1 is still applicable.

As no Borque Inc. shares are issued as consideration, no PUC reduction is required. Technically ITA 84.1(1)(a) only applies if there is share consideration and ITA 84.1(1)(b) only applies if there is NSC.

The ITA 84.1(1)(b) deemed non-eligible dividend would be calculated as follows:

Increase in legal capital of Borque Inc.		N/A
FMV of NSC		
[(6,530 shares)($2,465,000 ÷ 22,500)]		$715,398
Total		$715,398
ITA 84.1 limit [(6,530 shares)($10)]	($65,300)	
PUC reduction under ITA 84.1(1)(a)	N/A	(65,300)
Deemed dividend under ITA 84.1(1)(b)		$650,098

The taxable non-eligible dividend of $747,613 [(115%)($650,098)] would qualify for a federal dividend tax credit of $67,510 [(9/13)(15%)($650,098)]. Given the deemed dividend, the sale of shares will not result in any capital gain. This can be seen in the following calculation:

POD	
[(6,530 shares)($2,465,000 ÷ 22,500)]	$715,398
Less: Deemed dividend under ITA 84.1(1)(b)	(650,098)
Adjusted POD—ITA 54 "POD"	$ 65,300
ACB [(6,530 shares)($10)]	(65,300)
Capital gain or capital loss	Nil

SSP 16-11 Solution
Part A

Since Largely Ltd. received a taxable dividend that was not taxable under Part I because of the taxable income deduction of ITA 112(1), it is within the conditions of ITA 55(2). Had Largely Ltd.

sold the Dardley shares for FMV without the dividend there would have been a hypothetical capital gain of $2,000,000 (POD $2,300,000 - ACB $300,000). The actual capital gain, however, was nil after the payment of the dividend (POD $300,000 - ACB $300,000). The difference of $2,000,000 represents a significant reduction in a capital gain that is attributable to the taxable dividend. As a result, ITA 55(2) will apply subject to any exceptions.

The one exception is for safe income of $565,000. This means that only the remaining part of the dividend of $1,435,000 would be subject to ITA 55(2). This is reflected in the following calculations:

Taxable dividends received	$ 2,000,000
Dividend attributable to safe income	(565,000)
Amount deemed by ITA 55(2)(a) not to be a dividend and by ITA 55(2)(c) to be a capital gain	$ 1,435,000
Inclusion rate	1/2
Taxable capital gain	$ 717,500

As shown, $565,000 of the funds would be received by Lardley as a taxable dividend, which is deductible under ITA 112(1). However, the remainder is deemed to be a capital gain.

Part B

In the absence of ITA 55(2), the results for Lardley would be as follows:

Proceeds of redemption	$ 2,300,000
PUC	(300,000)
ITA 84(3) deemed dividend	$ 2,000,000
Redemption amount	$ 2,300,000
Less: ITA 84(3) dividend	(2,000,000)
Adjusted POD—ITA 54 "POD"	$ 300,000
ACB	(300,000)
Capital gain	Nil

ITA 55(2) would apply for the same reasons as in Part A.

ITA 55(2)(a) would deem $1,435,000 ($2,000,000 less the safe income of $565,000) of the ITA 84(3) dividend to not be a dividend. ITA 55(2)(b) would then adjust the POD. The result would be a capital gain determined as follows:

Adjusted POD	$ 300,000
Add: Adjustment—ITA 55(2)(b)	1,435,000
POD	$ 1,735,000
ACB	(300,000)
Capital gain	$ 1,435,000
Inclusion rate	1/2
Taxable capital gain	$ 717,500

The overall result would be the same as in Part A. That is, a $565,000 taxable dividend and a taxable capital gain of $717,500.

CHAPTER 17

Learning Objectives

After completing Chapter 17, you should be able to:

1. Explain the purpose and tax policy reasons why certain corporate-based rollovers are permitted (Paragraph [P hereafter] 17-1 to 17-5).
2. Explain the purpose of ITA 85.1, the basic situation in which it applies, situations in which it does not apply, and the income tax consequences of its application (P 17-6 to 17-17).
3. Explain the purpose of ITA 86, how it applies, and some of the most common practical uses for it (P 17-18 to 17-21).
4. Explain the basic functions of the application of ITA 86 to a standard estate freeze (P 17-22).
5. Describe the conditions that must be met to use the ITA 86 rollover, including characteristics of preferred shares received on the exchange (P 17-23 to 17-25).
6. Apply the tax calculations required of ITA 86 and explain how to avoid any immediate income tax consequences (P 17-26 to 17-35).
7. Explain the circumstances that lead to the gifting rule and determine the income tax consequences when gifting applies (P 17-36 to 17-47).
8. Explain the different tax planning considerations in share exchange reorganizations between ITA 85 and ITA 86, including how these rules can be used in key employee estate freezes (P 17-48 to 17-53).
9. Explain the nature of an amalgamation and the role of corporate law (P 17-54 to 17-58).
10. Explain the purpose of ITA 87, specifically what it is expressly designed to accomplish and its effect on shareholders of predecessor corporations (P 17-59 to 17-64).
11. Describe some of the advantages and disadvantages of an amalgamation and some of the practical reasons why it is used (P 17-65 to 17-69).
12. Explain the nature of the winding-up of a corporation, the wind-up process, and the role of corporate law (P 17-70 to 17-72).
13. Describe the three types of wind-up situations contemplated by the ITA (P 17-73 to 17-74).
14. Explain the impact of ITA 88(1) to both the subsidiary and the parent company, including the treatment of subsidiary losses once the wind-up is complete (P 17-75 and 17-79).
15. Explain the purpose of the bump and when and how it applies (P 17-80 to 17-85).
16. Describe the legal and income tax difference between an amalgamation and a subsidiary dissolution, including any preferences for one over the other (P 17-86 to 17-91).
17. Describe the common situations in which ITA 88(2) is used and the income tax consequences when it applies (P 17-92 to 17-95).
18. Apply the income tax consequences when a corporation is dissolved, including final corporate distributions to shareholders (P 17-96 to 17-104).
19. Describe the income tax consequences when a corporation is involuntarily dissolved without the knowledge of the shareholders (P 17-105 to 17-108).
20. Explain the rollover rule of ITA 51, including the conditions that cause it to apply and the income tax consequences of its application (P 17-109 to 17-115).
21. Explain the purpose of ITA 51.1 (P 17-116).

22. Briefly explain how the gifting rule applies in a rollover under ITA 51 (P 17-117).
23. Compare the differences between selling the shares of a corporation versus selling its assets, including the advantages and disadvantages of each to the purchaser and seller (P 17-118 to 17-123).
24. Explain the meaning of a restrictive covenant, its purpose, and the income tax consequences to both the payor and recipient (P 17-124 to 17-129).
25. Describe the income tax consequences and process when a corporation sells its assets and distributes all of its property in the course of winding-up (P 17-130 to 17-134).
26. Describe the income tax consequences of selling a corporation by selling its shares and some tax planning considerations that may minimize income tax to shareholders (P 17-135 to 17-137).
27. Apply the ITA provisions and analyze the results when comparing a sale of corporate assets versus a sale of shares (P 17-138 to 17-149).

How to Work through Chapter 17

Visit pearsonmylabandmastering.com to access MyLab Accounting for this text. Once there, you can access student resources such as Self-Study Problems, Practice Exams, Flashcards, updates, and more.

We recommend the following approach in dealing with the material in this chapter:

Introduction
- Read paragraph 17-1 to 17-5 (in the text).

Share-for-Share Exchanges—ITA 85.1
- Read paragraph 17-6 to 17-17.
- Do Exercise 17-1 (in the text) and check the solution in this Study Guide.
- Do Self-Study Problems 17-1 and 17-2, which are available on MyLab, and check the solutions in this Study Guide.

Share Exchange in a Capital Reorganization—ITA 86
- Read paragraph 17-18 to 17-35.
- Do Exercises 17-2 to 17-4 and check the solutions in this Study Guide.
- Do Self-Study Problem 17-3 and check the solution in this Study Guide.

Gifting to a Related Person—ITA 86(2)
- Read paragraph 17-36 to 17-47.
- Do Exercise 17-5 and check the solution in this Study Guide.

ITA 86 vs. ITA 85(1)—Tax Planning Considerations
- Read paragraph 17-48 to 17-53.
- Do Self-Study Problems 17-4 and 17-5 and check the solutions in this Study Guide.

Amalgamations—ITA 87
- Read paragraph 17-54 to 17-69.
- Do Exercise 17-6 and check the solution in this Study Guide.

Winding-Up a 90% Owned Subsidiary
- Read paragraph 17-70 to 17-79.
- Do Exercise 17-7 and check the solution in this Study Guide.
- Read paragraph 17-80 to 17-85.
- Do Exercise 17-8 and check the solution in this Study Guide.
- Read paragraph 17-86.

Tax Planning Considerations—Amalgamation vs. Winding-Up
- Read paragraph 17-87 to 17-91.
- Do Self-Study Problem 17-6 and check the solution in this Study Guide.

Winding-Up a Canadian Corporation—ITA 88(2)
- Read paragraph 17-92 to 17-104.
- Do Exercise 17-9 and check the solution in this Study Guide.
- Do Self-Study Problem 17-7 and check the solution in this Study Guide.
- Read paragraph 17-105 to 17-108.

Convertible Properties—ITA 51
- Read paragraph 17-109 to 17-117.

Sale of an Incorporated Business
- Read paragraph 17-118 to 17-149.
- Do Self-Study Problem 17-8 and check the solution in this Study Guide.

To Complete This Chapter
- Visit MyLab Accounting for more practice problem material, and test yourself with the glossary flashcards.
- Review the Key Terms at the end of the chapter, and consult the glossary for definitions.
- Ensure you have achieved the Chapter 17 Learning Objectives listed in this Study Guide.
- As a review, view the PowerPoint presentations available on MyLab.

Practice Examination
- Available on MyLab, write the Practice Examination for this chapter, and mark it using the solutions provided.

Exercise Solutions

Exercise 17-1 Solution
The share-for-share exchange meets the conditions of ITA 85.1(1) and (2). Unless Ms. Alee opts out of this rollover provision by reporting any part of the capital gain in her income tax return for the year of the exchange, the income tax consequences for both Ms. Alee and Global Outreach Inc. would be as follows:

- Ms. Alee would be deemed to have received POD on the disposition of her shares in an amount equal to the ACB of $450,000. As a consequence, there would be no capital gain or capital loss on the exchange (deemed POD $450,000 - ACB $450,000).
- Ms. Alee would be deemed to have acquired her Global Outreach Inc. shares at a cost equal to the ACB of the Aayee Ltd. shares, or $450,000.
- The cost and therefore the ACB of the Aayee Ltd. shares that have been acquired by Global Outreach Inc. would be deemed to be the lesser of their FMV of $2,450,000 [($49)(50,000)] and their PUC of $450,000. As a result, the cost to Global Outreach Inc. is $450,000.
- The PUC of the Global Outreach Inc. shares that have been issued to Ms. Alee would be equal to $450,000—their legal capital of $2,450,000 minus a PUC reduction of $2,000,000 (ITA 85.1(2.1)). The PUC reduction is designed to ensure that the PUC of the newly issued shares equals the PUC of the exchanged shares.

Exercise 17-2 Solution
The first thing to keep in mind is that since the NSC of $1,000,000 does not exceed either the ACB or PUC of the old shares, there will be no immediate income tax consequences as a result of the application of ITA 86.

The required PUC reduction for the redeemable preferred shares would be calculated as follows:

Increase in legal capital		$ 1,300,000
Less the excess, if any, of:		
PUC of common shares (old shares)	($1,000,000)	
Less: FMV of NSC	1,000,000	Nil
PUC reduction		$ 1,300,000

This means that the redeemable preferred shares would have a PUC of nil ($1,300,000 - $1,300,000).

The ACB of the redeemable preferred shares would be calculated as follows:

ACB of common shares (old shares)	$1,000,000
Less: FMV of NSC	(1,000,000)
ACB of preferred shares (new shares)	Nil

Because Mr. Samson did not receive NSC in excess of either the PUC or ACB of the old shares, there would be no ITA 84(3) deemed dividend and no capital gain or capital loss. The calculations in support of that initial conclusion would be as follows:

PUC of the new shares	Nil
Plus: FMV of NSC	$1,000,000
Proceeds of redemption under ITA 84(5)(d)	$1,000,000
Less: PUC of old shares	(1,000,000)
ITA 84(3) deemed dividend	Nil
ACB of new shares	Nil
Plus: FMV of NSC	$1,000,000
POD under ITA 86(1)(c)	$1,000,000
Less: ITA 84(3) deemed dividend	Nil
Adjusted POD	$1,000,000
ACB of old shares	(1,000,000)
Capital gain (loss)	Nil

Exercise 17-3 Solution

The first thing to keep in mind is that since the NSC of $1,000,000 does not exceed either the ACB or PUC of the old shares, there will be no immediate income tax consequences as a result of the application of ITA 86.

The required PUC reduction for the redeemable preferred shares would be calculated as follows:

Increase in legal capital		$1,300,000
Less: The excess, if any, of:		
PUC of common shares (old shares)	($1,000,000)	
Less: FMV of NSC	1,000,000	Nil
PUC reduction		$1,300,000

This means that the redeemable preferred shares would have a PUC of nil ($1,300,000 - $1,300,000).

The ACB of the redeemable preferred shares would be calculated as follows:

ACB of common shares (old shares)	$1,250,000
Less: FMV of NSC	(1,000,000)
ACB of redeemable preferred shares (new shares)	$ 250,000

The deemed dividend and capital gain/loss calculations would be as follows:

PUC of preferred shares (new shares)	Nil
Plus: FMV of NSC	$1,000,000
Proceeds of redemption under ITA 84(5)(d)	$1,000,000
Less: PUC of common shares (old shares)	(1,000,000)
ITA 84(3) deemed dividend	Nil

ACB of preferred shares (new shares)	$ 250,000
Plus: FMV of NSC	1,000,000
POD under ITA 86(1)(c)	$1,250,000
Less: ITA 84(3) deemed dividend	Nil
Adjusted POD	$1,250,000
Less: ACB of common shares (old shares)	(1,250,000)
Capital gain (loss)	Nil

Exercise 17-4 Solution

The first thing to keep in mind is that since the NSC of $1,200,000 exceeds the PUC of the old shares there will be immediate income tax consequences as a result of the application of ITA 86.

The required PUC reduction on the redeemable preferred shares would be calculated as follows:

Increase in legal capital		$1,100,000
Less the excess, if any, of:		
PUC of common shares (old shares)	($1,000,000)	
Less: FMV of NSC	1,200,000	Nil
PUC reduction		$1,100,000

This means that the redeemable preferred shares would have a PUC of nil ($1,100,000 - $1,100,000).

The ACB of the redeemable preferred shares would be calculated as follows:

ACB of common shares (old shares)	$1,250,000
Less: FMV of NSC	(1,200,000)
ACB of redeemable preferred shares (new shares)	$ 50,000

The deemed dividend and capital gain/loss calculations would be as follows:

PUC of preferred shares (new shares)	Nil
Plus: FMV of NSC	$1,200,000
Proceeds of redemption under ITA 84(5)(d)	$1,200,000
Less: PUC of common shares (old shares)	(1,000,000)
ITA 84(3) deemed dividend (non-eligible)	$ 200,000
ACB of preferred shares (new shares)	$ 50,000
Plus: FMV of NSC	1,200,000
POD under ITA 86(1)(c)	$1,250,000
ITA 84(3) deemed dividend	(200,000)
Adjusted POD	$1,050,000
Less: ACB of common shares (old shares)	(1,250,000)
Capital loss	($ 200,000)
Inclusion rate	1/2
Allowable capital loss	($ 100,000)

The taxable amount of the non-eligible dividend would be $230,000 [(115%)($200,000)]. It would qualify for a federal dividend tax credit of $20,769 [(9/13)(15%)($200,000)]. The capital loss of $200,000 would be disallowed under ITA 40(3.6) and would be added to the ACB of the preferred shares, resulting in an ACB of $250,000 ($50,000 (ITA 86(1)(b)) + $200,000 (ITA 53(1)(f.2)).

Exercise 17-5 Solution

The gift portion can be determined as follows:

FMV of the common shares [(80%)($1,600,000)]	$1,280,000
Less: FMV of NSC & preferred shares ($300,000 + $800,000)	(1,100,000)
Gift portion	$ 180,000

The presence of a gift and the connection to a related person results in the application of ITA 86(2).

The PUC reduction on the preferred shares would be calculated as follows:

Increase in legal capital		$800,000
Less the excess, if any, of:		
PUC of common shares [(80%)($250,000)]	($200,000)	
Over the FMV of NSC	300,000	Nil
PUC reduction		$800,000

This means that the redeemable preferred shares would have a PUC of nil ($800,000 - $800,000).

Under ITA 86(2)(e), the ACB of the redeemable preferred shares would be calculated as follows:

ACB of the common shares (old shares)		$200,000
Deduct:		
FMV of NSC	($300,000)	
Gift portion	(180,000)	(480,000)
ACB of the preferred shares		Nil

Given the $180,000 gift, the ITA 84(3) deemed dividend and the taxable capital gain would be calculated as follows:

PUC of the preferred shares	Nil
Plus: FMV of NSC	$300,000
Proceeds of redemption—ITA 84(5)(d)	$300,000
Less: PUC of common shares (old shares)	(200,000)
ITA 84(3) deemed dividend (non-eligible)	$ 100,000

POD—ITA 86(2)(c)—Lesser of:	
• FMV of common shares = $1,280,000	
• FMV of NSC + gift portion	
($300,000 + $180,000) = $480,000	$480,000
Less: ITA 84(3) deemed dividend	(100,000)
Adjusted POD	$380,000
ACB of the common shares (old shares)	(200,000)
Capital gain	$ 180,000
Inclusion rate	1/2
Taxable capital gain	$ 90,000

The taxable amount of the non-eligible dividend would be $115,000 [(115%)($100,000)]. It would qualify for a federal dividend tax credit of $10,385 [(9/13)(15%)($100,000)].

The total gain is $280,000 (deemed dividend $100,000 + capital gain $180,000). In economic terms this reflects the $100,000 excess of the NSC over the PUC and ACB of the old shares ($300,000 - $200,000) plus the $180,000 gift. Ms. Reviser would also have a deferred gain of $800,000, the excess of the $800,000 FMV of the preferred shares over their PUC and ACB of nil.

The combination of the current and deferred gains is $1,080,000 ($800,000 + $280,000). This is the same gain that would have arisen had Ms. Reviser sold her shares for their FMV of $1,280,000 (POD $1,280,000 - ACB $200,000 = $1,080,000).

While this transaction has not changed Ms. Reviser's economic position, it has created an additional gain for her daughter. Before this transaction, the FMV of the daughter's shares was $320,000 [(20%)($1,600,000)]. The FMV of the shares has increased to $500,000. This is the $1,600,000 total pre-share exchange value of the company less the cash of $300,000, less the FMV of the preferred shares of $800,000. As there is no increase in the ACB of her shares, the extra $180,000 ($500,000 - $320,000) in value represents a deferred gain that will be subject to income tax when she subsequently disposes of the shares.

Exercise 17-6 Solution
The shareholders of predecessor Upton Inc. have a controlling interest in Amalgo Inc. on the amalgamation, and the two predecessor corporations were not related. As a result, the control of Downer Ltd. will be considered to have been acquired prior to the amalgamation (ITA 256(7)(b)). The acquisition of control means that the non-capital and net capital losses of Downer Ltd. are tainted, meaning that while they still flow through to Amalgo Inc. (ITA 87(2.1)) the tainting features also flow through. The result is that Amalgo will be unable to claim any of the net capital loss (ITA 111(4)) but that the non-capital losses may be claimable (ITA 111(5)) as long as the conditions for their use are met, which would require that the loss business of Downer Ltd. is carried on for profit by Amalgo Ltd. If this is the case, Amalgo will be able to claim the non-capital loss flowed from Downer Ltd. but only to the extent of any profits from that loss business or any other business that is virtually identical to Downer Ltd.'s loss business.

Exercise 17-7 Solution
The non-capital loss of the subsidiary Side Ltd. flows through to the parent Park Inc. as a result of ITA 88(1.1). The non-capital loss, however, can only be claimed by the parent for the first taxation that starts after the commencement of the wind-up. Since the wind-up process began on June 1, 2021, the parent can claim the loss for its next taxation that starts October 1, 2021.

The 2018 non-capital loss of the subsidiary is deemed to be a 2019 non-capital loss of the parent because the last day of the 2018 taxation year of the subsidiary, October 31, 2018, falls in the 2019 taxation year of the parent (October 1, 2018, to September 30, 2019). The non-capital loss would expire in 20 years, which would generally mean 2039, however ITA 88(1.1)(b) changes the expiry date based on the expiry to the subsidiary, which in this case would mean that the non-capital loss would expire in 2038.

Exercise 17-8 Solution
Under ITA 88(1), the parent company (Procul) can increase the tax cost of non-depreciable capital property acquired from a subsidiary on its dissolution. The first step is to determine the maximum available bump, which is determined as follows:

ACB of Lorne Inc. shares	$1,200,000
Less: Tax costs of Lorne Inc.'s property minus any debt at winding-up ($500,000 - $75,000)	(425,000)
Less: Dividends paid to Procul	Nil
Maximum available bump	$ 775,000

The maximum bump can only be applied to non-depreciable capital property that was owned at the time Procul acquired control of Lorne and was distributed to the parent Procul in the winding-up process. The maximum bump that can be applied is limited to the difference between the FMV of the land (the only non-depreciable capital property) of $270,000 at the time Procul acquired control of Lorne in 2017 and the tax cost of $140,000 at that time. Therefore, the maximum bump that can be applied to the land is $130,000 (2017 FMV $270,000 - 2017 ACB $140,000). The bump in the land value is limited to that amount, resulting in the following tax costs for property acquired by Procul on the winding-up of Lorne:

Cash	$120,000
Land	270,000
Depreciable property—UCC	240,000
Total tax costs to Procul	$630,000

The unapplied maximum bump of $645,000 (maximum bump $775,000 - $130,000 applied to the land) is lost.

Exercise 17-9 Solution

The amount of the proceeds is sufficient to trigger a full dividend refund of $47,000, and as a result the distribution to the shareholders will be $912,000 (cash $865,000 + dividend refund $47,000).

The taxable dividend component of the total distribution to the shareholders is calculated as follows:

Total distribution ($865,000 + $47,000)	$912,000
Less: PUC	(88,000)
ITA 84(2) deemed dividend	$824,000
Less: CDA—ITA 88(2)(b)	(26,000)
Taxable non-eligible dividend*	$798,000

*As the company's GRIP balance is nil, all of the dividends will be non-eligible. Non-eligible dividends qualify for a dividend refund from a corporation's eligible RDTOH once the non-eligible RDTOH has been completely refunded.

The non-eligible dividend will be grossed up to $917,700 [(115%)($798,000)]. The shareholders will also have a federal dividend tax credit of $82,869 [(9/13)(15%)($798,000)], which can be applied to reduce federal income tax payable.

The capital gain consequences of the cancellation of the shares as a result of the dissolution of the corporation is determined as follows:

Total distribution to shareholders	$912,000
Less: ITA 84(2) deemed dividend	(824,000)
Adjusted POD	$ 88,000
ACB	(88,000)
Capital gain	Nil

Self-Study Problem Solutions

Self-Study Problems are available to download from MyLab.

SSP 17-1 Solution
Part A—ITA 85.1 Applies

Jerry elected to use ITA 85(1) to defer any immediate income tax when incorporating his business and chose elected amounts equal to the combined tax costs of his business properties of $986,000. Given that he took back NSC of $500,000, the tax attributes (ACB and PUC) of Jerry's Flowers common shares would therefore be calculated as follows:

Elected amount	$986,000
Less: FMV of NSC	(500,000)
ACB of the common shares issued	$486,000

The PUC of the shares would be calculated as follows:

Increase in legal capital		$1,840,000
Less excess, if any, of:		
Elected amount	($986,000)	
Less: FMV of NSC	500,000	(486,000)
PUC reduction		$1,354,000
PUC of common shares ($1,840,000 - $1,354,000)		$ 486,000

The ACB and PUC of the common shares of Jerry's Flowers would be $486,000 and the FMV $3,750,000 [($75)(50,000 shares)]. If Jerry does not opt out of ITA 85.1, the income tax consequences would be as follows:

- Jerry would be deemed to have received POD equal to the ACB of $486,000. Given this, there would be no capital gain on the disposition (deemed POD $486,000 - ACB $486,000).
- Jerry would be deemed to have acquired his Large Flowers Inc. shares at a cost equal to the same amount of $486,000.
- The PUC of the Large Flowers Inc. shares that have been issued to Jerry would be $486,000, the PUC of the Jerry's Flowers shares that were given up (legal capital $3,750,000 - PUC reduction $3,264,000). The PUC reduction would be calculated as the difference between the legal capital of $3,750,000 and the PUC of the exchanged shares of $486,000.

Part A—Opting Out of ITA 85.1

The FMV of the Large Flowers shares is $3,750,000. In order to opt out of ITA 85.1, Jerry will have to include a taxable capital gain of $1,632,000 [(1/2)(POD $3,750,000 - ACB $486,000)] in his 2021 income tax return. This has the advantage of allowing a deduction of the 2016 net capital loss balance of $800,000. However, it will result in his being required to pay income taxes on the remaining $832,000 (taxable capital gain $1,632,000 - net capital loss $800,000). This option is an all-or-nothing option and does not provide Jerry with any flexibility.

Part B—ACB for Large Flowers Inc.

The cost and therefore ACB of the Jerry's Flowers common shares to Large Flowers Inc. would be the lesser of the FMV of $3,750,000 and their PUC of $486,000. As a result, the ACB and PUC of the shares to Large Flowers Inc. are both $486,000.

Part C—Alternative Solutions

There are two possible solutions that would optimize the use of the $800,000 net capital loss balance while minimizing any immediate income tax.

Alternative One   Jerry could use ITA 85(1) to exchange the shares at an elected amount of $2,086,000. The resulting taxable capital gain would be equal to $800,000 [(1/2)(deemed POD $2,086,000 - ACB $486,000)]. The ACB of the exchanged shares to Large Flowers Inc. would be $2,086,000, which is much more favourable than the $486,000 cost determined under ITA 85.1(1)(b).

Alternative Two (allocation of consideration)   The FMV of the common shares of Jerry's Flowers Ltd. is $3,750 ($3,750,000 ÷ 1,000) and the ACB is $486 ($486,000 ÷ 1,000). This means that each share that is sold to Large Flowers would result in a taxable capital gain of $1,632 [(1/2)($3,750 - $486)]. Given this, selling 490 of these shares ($800,000 ÷ 1,632) to Large Flowers would result in a taxable capital gain of $799,680 [(490)($1,632)]. This would be completely offset by the 2016 net capital loss balance. The remaining 510 (1,000 - 490) shares of Jerry's Flowers could then be exchanged for Large Flowers Inc. shares on a rollover basis under ITA 85.1.

SSP 17-2 Solution
Part A—ITA 85.1 applies

Sarah elected to use ITA 85(1) to defer any immediate income tax when incorporating her business and chose elected amounts equal to the combined tax costs of her business properties of $842,000. Given that she took back NSC of $360,000, the tax attributes of her Hartman shares (ACB and PUC) would be calculated as follows:

Elected amount	$842,000
Less: FMV of NSC	(360,000)
ACB of the common shares issued	$482,000

The PUC of these shares would be calculated as follows:

Increase in legal capital		$1,200,000
Less excess, if any, of:		
Elected amount	($842,000)	
Less: FMV of NSC	360,000	(482,000)
PUC reduction		$ 718,000
PUC of common shares ($1,200,000 - $718,000)		$ 482,000

The ACB and PUC of the Hartman shares would both be $482,000 and the FMV $2,700,000 [($18)(150,000 shares)]. If Sarah does not opt out of ITA 85.1, the income tax consequences would be as follows:

- Sarah would be deemed to have received POD equal to the ACB of her Hartman shares of $482,000. Given this, there would be no capital gain on the disposition (deemed POD $482,000 - ACB $482,000).

- Sarah would be deemed to have acquired her Grande Ltd. shares at a cost equal to the same amount of $482,000.

- The PUC of the Grande Ltd. shares issued to Sarah would be $482,000, the PUC of the Hartman shares that were given up (legal capital of $2,700,000 - PUC reduction of $2,218,000). The PUC reduction would be calculated as the difference between the legal capital of $2,700,000 and the PUC of the exchanged shares of $482,000.

Part A—Opting Out of ITA 85.1

The FMV of the Hartman shares is $2,700,000. In order to opt out of ITA 85.1, Sarah will have to include a taxable capital gain of $1,109,000 [(1/2)(POD $2,700,000 - ACB $482,000)] in her 2021 income tax return. This has the advantage of allowing a deduction of the 2017 net capital loss balance of $625,000. However, it will result in her being required to pay income taxes on the remaining $484,000 ($1,109,000 - $625,000). This option is an all-or-nothing option and does not provide her with any flexibility.

Part B—ACB for Grande Ltd.

The cost and therefore the ACB of the Hartman shares to Grande would be the lesser of the FMV of $2,700,000 and their PUC of $482,000. As a result, the ACB and PUC of the shares to Grande are both $482,000.

Part C—Alternative Solutions

There are two possible solutions that would optimize the use of the $625,000 net capital loss balance while minimizing any immediate income tax.

Alternative One Sarah could use ITA 85(1) to exchange the shares at an elected amount of $1,732,000. The resulting taxable capital gain would be equal to $625,000 [(1/2)(deemed POD $1,732,000 - ACB $482,000)]. The ACB of the exchanged shares to Grande would be $1,732,000, which is much more favourable than the $482,000 cost determined under ITA 85.1(1)(b).

Alternative Two (allocation of consideration) The FMV of each of the shares of Hartman Inc. is $450 ($2,700,000 ÷ 6,000) and the ACB is $80.33 ($482,000 ÷ 6,000). This means that each share that is sold to Grande would result in a taxable capital gain of $184.84 [(1/2)($450 - $80.33)]. Given this, selling 3,381 ($625,000 ÷ $184.84) of these shares to Grande would result in a taxable capital gain of $624,944 [(3,381) ($184.84)]. This would be completely offset by the 2017 net capital loss balance. The remaining 2,619 (6,000 - 3,381) shares of Hartman could then be exchanged for Grande Ltd. shares on a rollover basis under ITA 85.1.

SSP 17-3 Solution

The FMV of Ms. Boswick's common shares are $10,985,000, which is composed of tangible assets of $12,450,000 plus goodwill of $2,000,000 less the bank loan of $3,465,000. The ACB and PUC of her common shares are both $250,000.

The first step is to reorganize the capital of the corporation by obtaining the necessary approvals and amending the articles of incorporation to add a new class of shares. The corporation will add the ability to issue fixed value preferred shares. On approval, Ms. Boswick can exchange all of her common shares for newly issued preferred shares that are redeemable for $10,985,000. Once the exchange is complete her two sons can each invest $10,000 in exchange for common shares of BIL.

The share exchange by Ms. Boswick will not result in any deemed dividend or capital gain or capital loss since there is no NSC. The ACB and PUC of the newly issued preferred shares would be determined as follows:

ACB of the common shares (old shares)		$ 250,000
Less: FMV of NSC		Nil
ACB of the preferred shares (new shares)		$ 250,000
Legal capital—Preferred shares (new shares)		$10,985,000
Less excess, if any, of:		
PUC—Common shares (old shares)	($250,000)	
Less: FMV of NSC	Nil	(250,000)
Required PUC reduction		$10,735,000
PUC—Preferred shares ($10,985,000 - $10,735,000)		$ 250,000

Ms. Boswick's preferred shares will not participate in the future growth of the company. This means that all of the future growth in Boswick Industries will accrue to her sons, the only two common shareholders.

In order for Ms. Boswick to retain control of the company, she should consider ensuring that the preferred shares have full voting rights.

Subsequent to reorganization, the July 1, 2021, balance sheet would be as follows:

Boswick Industries Ltd.
Shareholders' Equity
as at July 1, 2021

Tangible assets at tax costs	
($12,450,000 + $10,000 + $10,000)	$12,470,000
Bank loan	$ 3,465,000
Preferred shares	250,000
Common shares ($10,000 + $10,000)	20,000
Retained earnings	8,735,000
Total	$12,470,000

SSP 17-4 Solution
Part A

Gift to Jack The exchange results in a gift of $320,000 to Mr. Mark's son, Jack, calculated as follows:

FMV of common shares (old shares)		
[(80%)($2,400,000)]		$1,920,000
FMV of preferred shares (new shares)		(1,600,000)
Gift		$ 320,000

The benefit of the gift is conferred on Jack as the only remaining common shareholder. Jack's shares would have increased in value by $320,000.

PUC of the Preferred Shares The PUC reduction required under ITA 86(2.1) would be calculated as follows:

Legal capital of the preferred shares		$8,000
Deduct:		
PUC of common shares	($8,000)	
Less: FMV of NSC	Nil	(8,000)
PUC reduction		Nil
PUC of the preferred shares ($8,000 - nil)		$8,000

As the required PUC reduction is nil, the PUC of the new shares would be equal to the $8,000 PUC of the old shares.

ACB of the Preferred Shares This amount would be calculated as follows:

ACB of the common shares (old shares)		$ 8,000
Deduct:		
FMV of NSC	$ Nil	
Gift	(320,000)	(320,000)
ACB of preferred shares (new shares)		Nil

Proceeds of Redemption of the Common Shares—ITA 84(5)(d) For purposes of determining any ITA 84(3) deemed dividend on the redemption of the old shares, the proceeds of redemption would be as follows:

PUC of the preferred shares	$8,000
FMV of NSC	Nil
Proceeds of redemption	$8,000

As this amount is equal to the old PUC, there is no ITA 84(3) deemed dividend on the transaction.

POD of the Common Shares—ITA 86(2)(c) For purposes of determining any capital gain or capital loss on the redemption of the common shares, the POD would be the lesser of the FMV of $1,920,000 of the common shares and the following amount:

FMV of NSC	$ Nil
Gift	320,000
POD	$320,000

The taxable capital gain would be determined as follows:

POD	$320,000
ITA 84(3) deemed dividend	Nil
Adjusted POD	$320,000
ACB	(8,000)
Capital gain	$312,000
Inclusion rate	1/2
Taxable capital gain	$156,000

The total unrealized gain on Mr. Mark's common shares is $1,912,000 ($1,920,000 - $8,000). Because there was a gift to his son, $312,000 of this amount must be recognized at the time of the share exchange. The remaining $1,600,000 is deferred until the preferred shares are sold or otherwise disposed of. In the absence of the gift, all of the gain would have been deferred.

Part B

The share exchange does not alter the FMV of the company, which remains at $2,400,000. The share exchange, however, does reallocate that value. Initially Mr. Mark's shares were valued at $1,920,000 and Jack's at $480,000. After the exchange Mr. Mark's share value has dropped by $320,000 to $1,600,000 and Jack's has increased by $320,000 from $480,000 to $800,000. There will be no corresponding increase in the amount of the tax cost of Jack's shares to recognize that the $320,000 gift portion has already been included in Mr. Mark's income. As a result, that difference will be included in Jack's income when he disposes of his shares.

Part C

If Mr. Mark's preferred shares were redeemed at their FMV of $1,600,000, the income tax consequences would be as follows:

Redemption proceeds	$1,600,000
PUC	(8,000)
ITA 84(3) deemed dividend (non-eligible)	$1,592,000

Redemption proceeds	$1,600,000
Deemed ITA 84(3) dividend	(1,592,000)
Adjusted POD	$ 8,000
ACB	(Nil)
Capital gain	$ 8,000
Inclusion rate	1/2
Taxable capital gain	$ 4,000

The overall income tax consequences of the redemption would be as follows:

Taxable dividend [($1,592,000)(115%)]	$1,830,800
Taxable capital gain	4,000
Income inclusion	$1,834,800

The deemed non-eligible dividend would qualify for a federal dividend tax credit of $165,323 [(9/13)(15%)($1,592,000)].

Note that Mr. Mark's dividends and capital gains from the rollover total $1,912,000 ($312,000 + $1,592,000 + $8,000). This is equal to the $1,912,000 [(80%)($2,400,000) - $8,000] capital gain that would have resulted from a sale of his shares at FMV. From his point of view, the redemption result is less favourable in that part of the gain is in the form of more heavily taxed non-eligible dividends. In addition, if his son were to sell his shares, the $320,000 that he included in his income will also be included in the income of his son.

SSP 17-5 Solution
Approach One—No Gift
Part A

Since the FMV of the cash and preferred shares ($50,000 + $1,300,000) received by Ms. Platt on the exchange equal the FMV of the common shares there is no gift portion.

Part B

The PUC of the preferred shares would be subject to the following reduction:

Increase in legal capital—Preferred shares		$90,000
Less the excess, if any, of:		
PUC—Old shares [(75%)($120,000)]	($90,000)	
Over FMV of NSC	50,000	(40,000)
PUC reduction—Preferred shares		$50,000

Given this reduction, the PUC of the preferred shares would be:

Increase in legal capital—Preferred shares	$90,000
Less: PUC reduction	(50,000)
PUC—Preferred shares	$40,000

Part C

The ACB of the preferred shares would be calculated as:

ACB—Common shares (old shares) [(75%)($120,000)]	$90,000
Less: FMV of NSC	(50,000)
ACB—Preferred shares	$40,000

Part D

The proceeds of redemption would be calculated as follows:

PUC—New shares	$40,000
Plus: FMV of NSC	50,000
Proceeds of redemption (POR) [ITA 84(5)(d)]	$90,000

The POD would be calculated as follows:

ACB—New shares	$40,000
Plus: FMV of NSC	50,000
POD [ITA 86(1)(c)]	$90,000

Part E   Immediate Tax Consequences

The ACB and PUC of the common shares are both $90,000 [(75%)($120,000)]. The deemed dividend on the redemption of common shares as a result of the share exchange would therefore be nil (POR $90,000 - PUC $90,000). In addition, since the POD of the common shares on the exchange is also $90,000 there would be no capital gain or capital loss (POD $90,000 - ACB $90,000). As a result, there are no immediate income tax consequences. You can indirectly verify this result of a nil deemed dividend and capital gain by recognizing that the FMV of the NSC of $50,000 did not exceed either the ACB or PUC of the common shares, both of which were $90,000.

Part F

The income tax consequences of the redemption of the preferred shares would be as follows:

Redemption proceeds	$1,300,000
PUC	(40,000)
ITA 84(3) deemed dividend (non-eligible)	$1,260,000
POD	$1,300,000
Less: ITA 84(3) deemed dividend	(1,260,000)
Adjusted POD—ITA 54 ("POD")	$ 40,000
ACB—Preferred shares	(40,000)
Capital gain	Nil

The income tax consequence would be an income of $1,449,000 [(115%)($1,260,000)] for the non-eligible dividend and the availability of a federal dividend tax credit of $130,846 [(9/13)(15%)($1,260,000)] that would reduce the federal tax payable.

Approach Two—Gift
Part A

Under this approach, the FMV of the cash and preferred shares received by Ms. Platt on the exchange of her common shares of $1,320,000 ($50,000 + $1,270,000) is less than the FMV of the common shares of $1,350,000. The $30,000 difference represents the gift portion, all of which increases the FMV of the common shares owned by her son. ITA 86(2) applies as a result.

Part B

The PUC of the preferred shares would be subject to the following reduction:

Increase in legal capital—Preferred shares		$1,270,000
Less the excess, if any, of:		
PUC—Common shares [(75%)($120,000)]	($90,000)	
Over FMV of NSC	50,000	(40,000)
PUC reduction—Preferred shares		$1,230,000
Increase in legal capital—Preferred shares		$1,270,000
Less: PUC reduction		(1,230,000)
PUC—Preferred shares		$ 40,000

Part C

The ACB of the preferred shares would be calculated as:

ACB—Common shares		$90,000
Deduct:		
FMV of NSC	($50,000)	
Gift portion	(30,000)	(80,000)
ACB—Preferred shares		$ 10,000

Part D

The proceeds of redemption (POR) would be calculated as follows:

PUC—Preferred shares	$40,000
Plus: FMV of NSC	50,000
POR— ITA 84(5)(d)	$90,000

The POD would be calculated as follows:

FMV of NSC	$50,000
Plus: Gift portion	30,000
POD— ITA 86(2)(c)	$80,000

Part E   Immediate Tax Consequences

As the ITA 84(5)(d) proceeds of redemption of $90,000 are equal to the PUC of the common shares, there is no deemed dividend. However, the POD determined under ITA 86(2)(c) are less than the ACB of the common shares, resulting in a capital loss of $10,000 (POD $80,000 - ACB $90,000). This loss is disallowed by ITA 86(2)(d).

Part F

The income tax consequences of the redemption of the preferred shares is as follows:

Redemption proceeds	$1,270,000
PUC	(40,000)
ITA 84(3) deemed dividend (non-eligible)	$1,230,000
POD	$1,270,000
Less: ITA 84(3) deemed dividend	(1,230,000)
Adjusted POD—ITA 54 "POD"	$ 40,000
ACB	(10,000)
Capital gain	$ 30,000
Inclusion rate	1/2
Taxable capital gain	$ 15,000

The overall income tax consequences of the redemption are:

Taxable dividend [(115%)($1,230,000)]	$1,414,500
Taxable capital gain	15,000
Income inclusion	$1,429,500

The deemed non-eligible dividend would qualify for a federal dividend tax credit of $127,731 [(9/13)(15%)($1,230,000)].

Additional Analysis

While this analysis is not required, the total unadjusted income accruing to Ms. Platt is $1,260,000 (deemed dividend $1,230,000 + capital gain $30,000). This is the same amount that would have been realized had she sold her shares [(FMV $1,350,000 - ACB $90,000) = gain $1,260,000]. The income tax liability would have been far less with a capital gain of $1,260,000 as opposed to a non-eligible dividend of $1,230,000 and a $30,000 capital gain. In addition, increase in the FMV of the common shares of her son of $30,000 will be subject to income tax when the shares are subsequently disposed of.

SSP 17-6 Solution
Income Tax Perspective
Vertical Short Form Amalgamation (Parent/Subsidiary)—ITA 87(11)

The income tax consequences would be as follows:

- The subsidiary will be deemed to have received POD for the land equal to its ACB of $175,000 (ITA 88(1)(a)). As a result, there will be no capital gain or capital loss.

- The amalgamation qualifies for the bump since the subsidiary is 100% owned by the parent. The only property eligible for the bump is the land, which is non-depreciable capital property. The maximum bump is equal to the lesser of:

ACB of Lynn shares		$390,000
Deduct:		
Lynn's NTV—Tax cost of the land minus liabilities	($175,000)	
Dividends received from Lynn	Nil	(175,000)
Maximum available bump		$215,000

FMV of the land when Ricon Ltd. acquired control of Lynn Inc.		$390,000
Less: ACB of land		(175,000)
Maximum bump that can be applied to the land		$215,000

The ACB of the land to Ricon Ltd is $390,000 (original cost $175,000 + bump $215,000).

ITA 88(1)

The application of ITA 88(1) results in the following income tax consequences:

- The result to Lynn Inc. is identical to that of the amalgamation.

- The bump results are also the same as that of the amalgamation.

Conclusion

Both approaches result in a bump of $215,000 and an ACB of the land to Ricon Ltd. of $390,000. From an income tax perspective the income tax results are the same.

Non-Income Tax Considerations

From the point of view of non-tax considerations there would be clearance procedures involved if Lynn Inc. were dissolved. In addition, the land ownership would have to be changed with the possibility that there could be provincial transfer taxes on a dissolution of the company. Amalgamations are generally exempt from transfer pricing concerns. In general, it would be more cost efficient to amalgamate the two corporations rather than dissolving Lynn Inc.

SSP 17-7 Solution
Part A—Funds Available for Distribution to Shareholders

The taxable capital gains and active business income (recapture) of the corporation can be calculated as follows:

Property	Taxable Capital Gains	Active Business Income
Inventories	Nil	Nil
Taxable capital gains:		
On land [(1/2)($1,243,000 - $623,000)]	$310,000	Nil
On building [(1/2)($1,173,000 - $775,000)]	199,000	
Recapture on building ($775,000 - $586,000)		$189,000
Totals	$509,000	$189,000

As the active business income is less than the $500,000 annual business limit, there will be no 2021 addition to the GRIP. The taxable capital gains (e.g., aggregate investment income) do not increase the GRIP balance.

Taxable income for 2021 is $698,000 ($509,000 + $189,000). Income tax payable is calculated as follows:

Federal income tax on business income [(38% - 10% - 19%)($189,000)]	$ 17,010
Federal income tax on taxable capital gains [(38% - 10% + 10 2/3%)($509,000)]	196,815
Part I tax payable	$213,825
Provincial income tax on business income [(3%)($189,000)]	5,670
Provincial income tax on taxable capital gains [(13%)($509,000)]	66,170
Corporate income tax payable	$285,665

Non-Eligible RDTOH Balance

The refundable portion of the Part I tax would be $156,093, the least of:

- 30 2/3% of investment income [(30 2/3%)($509,000)] $156,095
- 30 2/3% of taxable income less the amount eligible for the small business deduction [(30 2/3%)($698,000 - $189,000)] $156,095
- Part I tax payable $213,825

The Part I refundable tax is added to the non-eligible RDTOH resulting in the following balance:

Opening non-eligible RDTOH	$ 27,000
Refundable Part I tax	156,095
Ending non-eligible RDTOH	$183,095

The amount available for distribution to the shareholders can be calculated as follows:

FMV (sales proceeds):	
Inventories	$ 35,000
Land	1,243,000
Building	1,173,000
Sale proceeds	$2,451,000
Corporate income tax payable	(285,665)
Dividend refund (Note)	183,095
Funds available for distribution	$2,348,430

Note Technically, the dividend refund is the lesser of the $183,095 balance in the RDTOH account and 38 1/3% of taxable dividends paid. A taxable dividend of only $296,909 is required to obtain a full dividend refund. Since the actual taxable dividend will far exceed that amount, all of the RDTOH is refunded.

The CDA balance is determined as follows:

Initial balance	$215,000
Capital gain on the land	310,000
Capital gain on the building	199,000
Ending balance	$724,000

Part B—Components of Distribution

Assuming an election has been filed under ITA 83(2) to claim all of the CDA balance, the taxable dividend component of the total distribution to the shareholders can be determined as follows:

Distribution to shareholders	$2,348,430
Less: PUC	(447,000)
ITA 84(2) deemed dividend	$1,901,430
Less: Capital dividend—ITA 88(2)(b)	(724,000)
Taxable non-eligible dividend	$ 1,177,430

The grossed up taxable dividend to individual shareholders will be $1,354,045 [(115%)($1,177,430)]. This dividend will qualify for a federal dividend tax credit of $122,272 [(9/13)(15%)($1,177,430)], which will be applied to reduce federal income tax payable.

Part B—Capital Gain

The capital gain consequences of the cancellation of the shares as a result of the dissolution of the corporation is determined as follows:

Distribution to shareholders	$2,348,430
Less: ITA 84(2) deemed dividend	(1,901,430)
Adjusted POD	$ 447,000
Less: ACB	(447,000)
Capital gain	Nil

SSP 17-8 Solution

Offer #1: Purchase Corporate Assets for $2,416,000

The analysis of this offer first requires determining the income tax consequences of selling the corporate assets, paying the requisite income tax, and determining the amount available for a final distribution to the sole shareholder. The second and final stage is determining the income tax impact to the sole shareholder of the liquidating dividend on the dissolution of the company.

Sale Proceeds, Capital Gains, and Active Business Income

The sale of the assets would have the following income tax consequences:

Asset	Sale Proceeds	Taxable Capital Gains	Active Business Income
Accounts receivable			
($91,000 - $83,000)	$ 91,000		$ 8,000
Inventory ($298,000 - $237,000)	298,000	Nil	61,000
Land [(1/2)($656,000 - $167,000)]	656,000	244,500	
Building:			
[(1/2)($652,000 - $582,000)]		35,000	
($582,000 - $176,000)	652,000		406,000
Goodwill	719,000	359,500	Nil
Total	$ 2,416,000	$ 639,000	$475,000
Cash	529,000	N/A	N/A
Totals	$ 2,945,000	$ 639,000	$475,000

Taxable Income and Corporate Income Tax Payable

Taxable income equals $1,114,000 ($639,000 + $475,000). Corporate income tax would be calculated as follows:

Federal income tax:	
Business income [(38% - 10% - 19%)($475,000)]	$ 42,750
Investment income [(38% - 10% + 10 2/3%)($639,000)]	247,082
Part I tax payable	$289,832
Provincial tax on business income [(3%)($475,000)]	14,250
Provincial tax on investment income [(14%)($639,000)]	89,460
Corporate income tax	$393,542

Non-Eligible RDTOH Balance

The only addition for 2021 would be the refundable portion of Part I tax. This amount would be the least of:

• 30 2/3% of investment income [(30 2/3%)($639,000)]	$195,962
• 30 2/3% of taxable income, less the amount eligible for the small business deduction [(30 2/3%)($1,114,000 - $475,000)]	$195,962
• Part I tax payable	$289,832

The least of these items is $195,962. This amount would be added to the non-eligible RDTOH and this would be the ending balance in that account.

Funds Available for Distribution

The amount available for distribution would be calculated as follows:

Gross sale proceeds + cash	$2,945,000
Payment of liabilities	(355,000)
Tax payable	(393,542)
Dividend refund (Note)	195,962
Total available for distribution	$2,392,420

Note Technically, the dividend refund is the lesser of the $195,960 balance in the non-eligible RDTOH account and 38 1/3% of taxable dividends paid. The large amount of the distribution is more than sufficient to result in a full recovery of the RDTOH.

Capital Dividend Account (CDA)

The balance in the CDA would be calculated as follows:

Opening balance	Nil
Non-taxable one-half of capital gains (from table calculating corporate income on asset dispositions)	$639,000
CDA	$639,000

Taxable Dividend Consequence to Mr. Lange

Assuming an election has been made with respect to the CDA, the taxable dividend component of the total distribution to Mr. Lange can be determined as follows:

Funds available for distribution	$2,392,420
Less: PUC	(135,000)
ITA 84(2) deemed dividend	$ 2,257,420
Less: ITA 83(2) capital dividend (ITA 88(2)(b))	(639,000)
Non-eligible dividend	$1,618,420

There would be no capital gain on the disposition that results from the cancellation of the shares on the dissolution of the company, as demonstrated in the following calculation:

Redemption proceeds	$2,392,420
Less: ITA 84(2) deemed dividend	(2,257,420)
Adjusted POD (ITA 54 "POD")	$ 135,000
Less: ACB	(135,000)
Capital gain	Nil

Personal Income Tax

As there is no capital gain and the capital dividend is received tax free, the personal tax payable on the non-eligible dividend would be calculated as follows:

Non-eligible dividend	$1,618,420
15% gross up	242,763
Taxable amount of dividends	$1,861,183
Combined tax rate (33% + 18%)	51%
Tax before dividend tax credit	$ 949,203
Dividend tax credit [(9/13 + 4/13)($242,763)]	(242,763)
Personal income tax	$ 706,440

Sale of Shares for $2,380,000

The income tax resulting from a sale of the shares would be calculated as follows:

POD	$2,380,000
Less: ACB	(135,000)
Capital gain	$2,245,000
Inclusion rate	1/2
Taxable capital gain	$1,122,500
Tax rate (33% + 18%)	51%
Personal tax payable	$ 572,475

Note   This capital gain would not qualify for the capital gains deduction because the shares of Alcove are not QSBC shares. This is because at least 90% of the FMV of the assets must be attributable to the active business assets. The FMV of the assets together with the cash total $2,945,000 ($2,416,000 + cash $529,000). Ninety percent of that amount equals $2,650,500 which exceeds the active business assets of $2,416,000. Had a purification taken place prior to the sale to move the cash out of the company the shares would have qualified for the capital gains deduction. Two simple purification strategies would have been to use the cash to pay the liabilities of $355,000 or using the cash to pay a capital dividend.

Conclusion

Given the preceding calculations, the after-tax, personal cash retention under both alternatives would be as follows:

	Asset Sale	Share Sale
Sale proceeds + cash	$2,392,420	$2,380,000
Personal income tax	(706,440)	(572,475)
After-tax retention	$1,685,980	$1,807,525

As the after-tax retention is $121,545 ($1,807,525 - $1,685,980) larger when shares are sold, this would be the preferable alternative. If the capital gains deduction were available, this alternative would have been even more favourable. The income tax savings for the capital gains deduction in 2021 would have been $455,031 in this problem [(51%)($892,218)].

CHAPTER 18

Learning Objectives

After completing Chapter 18, you should be able to:

1. Explain the basic approach to the taxation of partnerships (Paragraph [P hereafter] 18-1 to 18-6).
2. Describe, for income tax purposes, the meaning of a partnership and the common-law features necessary to establish the existence of a partnership (P 18-7 to 18-12).
3. Identify the three types of partnerships used in Canada and their differences (P 18-13 to 18-20).
4. Describe the difference between partnerships and co-ownership, joint ventures, and syndicates (P 18-21 to 18-31).
5. Explain the basic rules set out in ITA 96(1) that are used in the determination of partnership income and the impact on members of partnerships (P 18-32 to 18-47).
6. Reconcile accounting business income to business income for income tax purposes (P 18-48 to 18-49).
7. Explain the allocation of other types of income from a partnership to partners, specifically capital gains, dividends, foreign source income, and charitable donations (P 18-50 to 18-56).
8. Explain the concept of a partnership interest and its relevance (P 18-57 to 18-60).
9. Determine the income tax consequences when a partner is admitted to a partnership (P 18-61 to 18-69).
10. Calculate the ACB of a partnership interest on the first and last day of a fiscal period (P 18-70 to 18-77).
11. Explain what is meant by a negative ACB, when it applies, and its consequences (P 18-78 to 18-80).
12. Determine the income tax consequences when a partner disposes of his or her partnership interest (P 18-81 to 18-82).
13. Explain the meaning of a limited partner for income tax purposes (P 18-83 to 18-85).
14. Explain the at-risk concept and determine the at-risk amount and limited partnership losses (P 18-86 to 18-94).
15. Explain the meaning of a Canadian partnership and its relevance (P 18-95 to 18-97).
16. Explain and apply the basic default rules of the ITA when property is sold between partners and a partnership (P 18-98 to 18-100).
17. Explain the purpose and basic application of the rollover under ITA 97(2) (P 18-101 to 18-103).
18. Explain the purpose and basic application of the rollover under ITA 98(5) & 98(6) (P 18-104 to 18-108).
19. Explain how the ITA accommodates the incorporation of a partnership on a rollover basis (P 18-109 to 18-116).

How to Work through Chapter 18

Visit pearsonmylabandmastering.com to access MyLab Accounting for this text. Once there, you can access student resources such as Self-Study Problems, Practice Exams, Flashcards, updates, and more.

We recommend the following approach in dealing with the material in this chapter:

Introduction—Taxable Entities in Canada
- Read paragraph 18-1 to 18-6 (in the text).

Partnerships Defined
- Read paragraph 18-7 to 18-20.
- Do Self-Study Problem 18-1, which is available on MyLab, and check the solution in this Study Guide.

Co-Ownership, Joint Ventures, and Syndicates
- Read paragraph 18-21 to 18-31.
- Do Self-Study Problem 18-2 and check the solution in this Study Guide.

Determining Partnership Income, Losses, and Tax Credits
- Read paragraph 18-32 to 18-47.
- Do Exercise 18-1 (in the text) and check the solution in this Study Guide.
- Read paragraph 18-48 to 18-50.
- Do Exercise 18-2 and check the solution in this Study Guide.
- Read paragraph 18-51 to 18-52.
- Do Exercise 18-3 and check the solution in this Study Guide.

Allocations of Related Tax Credits and Methods of Allocation
- Read paragraph 18-53.
- Do Exercise 18-4 and check the solution in this Study Guide.
- Read paragraph 18-54 to 18-56.
- Do Self-Study Problems 18-3 and 18-4 and check the solutions in this Study Guide.

The Partnership Interest
- Read paragraph 18-57 to 18-69.
- Do Exercise 18-5 and check the solution in this Study Guide.

Adjusted Cost Base—Partnership Interest
- Read paragraph 18-70 to 18-80.
- Do Exercise 18-6 and check the solution in this Study Guide.
- Read paragraph 18-81 to 18-82.
- Do Self-Study Problems 18-5 and 18-6 and check the solutions in this Study Guide.

Limited Partnerships and Limited Partners
- Read paragraph 18-83 to 18-94.
- Do Exercise 18-7 and check the solution in this Study Guide.
- Do Self-Study Problem 18-7 and check the solution in this Study Guide.

Dispositions of Property to and from a Partnership—No Rollover
- Read paragraph 18-95 to 18-99.
- Do Exercise 18-8 and check the solution in this Study Guide.
- Read paragraph 18-100.
- Do Exercise 18-9 and check the solution in this Study Guide.

Common Partnership Rollovers
- Read paragraph 18-101 to 18-103.
- Do Exercise 18-10 and check the solution in this Study Guide.

- Read paragraph 18-104 to 18-116.
- Do Self-Study Problem 18-8 and check the solution in this Study Guide.

To Complete This Chapter
- Visit MyLab Accounting for more practice problem material, and test yourself with the glossary flashcards.
- Review the Key Terms at the end of the chapter, and consult the glossary for definitions.
- Ensure you have achieved the Chapter 18 Learning Objectives listed in this Study Guide.
- As a review, view the PowerPoint presentations available on MyLab.

Practice Examination
- Available on MyLab, write the Practice Examination for this chapter, and mark it using the solutions provided.

Exercise Solutions

Exercise 18-1 Solution
The following amounts would be added to Norm's 2021 net income:

Business income [(50%)($55,000)]	$27,500
Taxable capital gains [(50%)(1/2)($40,000)]	10,000
Eligible dividends [(50%)($10,000)]	5,000
Gross up [(38%)($5,000)]	1,900
Total partnership income—ITA 12(1)(l)	$44,400

In addition, Norm would be eligible for a federal dividend tax credit of $1,036 [(6/11)($1,900)] that would reduce his 2021 federal income tax payable. The drawings made during 2021 have no impact on his 2021 net income.

Exercise 18-2 Solution
The JL Partnership's business income would be calculated as follows:

Accounting net income		$262,000
Add:		
Salary to J	$45,000	
Interest to L	22,000	
Amortization expense	26,000	
Donations	2,500	95,500
Subtotal		$357,500
Deduct:		
Maximum CCA	($42,000)	
Accounting gain on sale of land	(24,000)	(66,000)
Net business income		$291,500
Priority allocations for salary and interest		(67,000)
Residual to be split 60-40		$224,500

The allocation of the business income to the two partners would be as follows:

	Partner J	Partner L
Priority allocation for salary	$ 45,000	N/A
Priority allocation for interest	N/A	$ 22,000
Allocation of residual		
[(60%)($224,500)]	134,700	
[(40%)($224,500)]		89,800
Total business income allocation	$ 179,700	$111,800

While not required, you might note that a taxable capital gain of $12,000 [(1/2)($24,000)] would be allocated to the partners on a 60-40 basis. With respect to the donations, the amount of the charitable donations of $2,500 would also be allocated on a 60-40 basis, leaving the individual partners to calculate the available credit.

Exercise 18-3 Solution

The ST Partnership's business income would be calculated as follows:

Accounting net income	$146,000
Amortization expense = CCA (no adjustment necessary)	Nil
Eligible dividends	(12,000)
Accounting gain on sale of land	(31,000)
Business income	$103,000

The net income addition for each of the two partners would be calculated as follows:

	Partner S	Partner T
Net business income [(50%)($103,000)]	$51,500	$51,500
Eligible dividends [(50%)($12,000)]	6,000	6,000
Gross up [(38%)($6,000)]	2,280	2,280
Taxable capital gain [(50%)(1/2)($31,000)]	7,750	7,750
2021 Net income	$ 67,530	$ 67,530

While not required, you might note that each partner would be eligible for a federal dividend tax credit of $1,244 [(6/11)($2,280)].

Exercise 18-4 Solution

The tax credits that would be available to each of the partners as a result of partnership allocations would be calculated as follows:

Charitable donations ($1,750 each) [(15%)($200) + (29%)($1,750 - $200)]	$ 480
Eligible dividends ($2,100 each) [(6/11)(38%)($2,100)]	435
Total tax credit available to each partner	$ 915

These amounts would serve to reduce the federal tax payable of each of the two partners for the year ending December 31, 2021.

Exercise 18-5 Solution

After the admission of Caitlan, Alan, and Balan will each have a one-third interest in the partnership, down from the previous interest of one-half. They are each, in effect, selling one-third of their partnership interest [(1/2 - 1/3) ÷ 1/2]. The ACB of their distribution to Caitlan is $16,000 [(1/3)($48,000)], resulting in a capital gain of $24,000 (POD $40,000 - ACB of part interest $16,000). The taxable capital gain is one-half of this amount, or $12,000.

The partner capital account transactions and ending balances will be:

	Alan	Balan	Caitlin
Opening capital accounts	$48,000	$48,000	Nil
Adjustment for Caitlin's admission	(16,000)	(16,000)	$32,000
Ending capital accounts (accounting amounts only)	$32,000	$32,000	$32,000
ACB of partnership interest	$32,000	$32,000	$80,000

Exercise 18-6 Solution

The ACB of Robert's partnership interest on December 31, 2021, and January 1, 2022, would be determined as follows:

Initial capital contribution	$12,500
Additional capital contribution	7,200
Drawing	(4,000)
ACB—December 31, 2021	$15,700
Adjustment for 2021 income	
[(40%)($11,600 + $3,100 + $46,700)]	24,560
ACB—January 1, 2022	$40,260

The addition to Robert's 2021 net income would be as follows:

Taxable capital gain [(40%)(1/2)($11,600)]	$ 2,320
Dividends received [(40%)($3,100)]	1,240
Gross up on dividends [(38%)($1,240)]	471
Business income [(40%)($46,700)]	18,680
Addition to 2021 net income	$ 22,711

Note that this $22,711 addition to Robert's 2021 net income is not the same amount as the $24,560 that was added to the ACB of Robert's partnership interest. Robert can also claim a federal dividend tax credit of $257 [(6/11)($471)], which will reduce his 2021 federal tax payable.

Exercise 18-7 Solution

ACB of partnership interest		$200,000
Share of partnership income (not losses) for 2021		Nil
Subtotal		$200,000
Amount owing to the partnership	($ 150,000)	
Other amounts intended to		
reduce investment risk		
(general partner guarantee)	(50,000)	(200,000)
ARA—December 31, 2021		Nil

As the at-risk amount is nil, none of the loss can be claimed in 2021. The 2021 LPL is therefore $75,000.

Exercise 18-8 Solution

Part A Charles is considered to have disposed of the land for $100,000 (ITA 97(1)), resulting in a $33,500 [(1/2)($100,000 - $33,000)] taxable capital gain. LIU will be considered to have acquired the land for $100,000. Charles is considered to have made a capital contribution of $100,000 that will be added to the ACB of his partnership interest.

Part B Charles will have the same $33,500 taxable capital gain as in Part A and LIU will be considered to have acquired the land for $100,000. The capital contribution and the addition to the ACB of the partnership interest is equal to $75,000. This is the difference between the FMV of the land contributed to LIU of $100,000 and the $25,000 in other consideration received by Charles. In effect, Charles received $25,000 in cash and an increased partnership interest for $75,000.

Part C Charles will have the same $33,500 taxable capital gain as in Part A and LIU will be considered to have acquired the land for $100,000. There is no capital contribution, however, since the net effect is that Charles withdrew $12,000 ($112,000 - $100,000). The ACB of his partnership interest will be reduced by the net withdrawal of $12,000.

Exercise 18-9 Solution

ITA 98(2) deems DG to have disposed of the share investments for the FMV of $94,000, resulting in a $55,000 ($94,000 - $39,000) capital gain. One-fifth of the capital gain, or $11,000, will be allocated to Darlene. One-half of this amount, or $5,500, will be a taxable capital gain that she will include in her income for 2021.

Darlene's ACB for the share investments is $18,800 [(20%)($94,000)].

The ACB of her partnership interest on December 31, 2021, and on January 1, 2022, is calculated as follows:

ACB prior to distribution	$30,000
Drawings [(20%)($94,000)]	(18,800)
ACB—December 31, 2021	$ 11,200
Allocated capital gain [(20%)($94,000 - $39,000)]	11,000
ACB—January 1, 2022	$22,200

Exercise 18-10 Solution

Applying the use of the ITA 85(1) rollover together with ITA 97(2), the property would be deemed to be disposed of at an elected amount of $156,000. As a result, there would be no income tax as a result of the contribution (POD $156,000 - ACB $156,000). The cost of the land to the partnership would be the same $156,000 elected amount. Since the only consideration is the interest in the partnership, $156,000 would be added to the its ACB.

Self-Study Problem Solutions

Self-Study Problems are available to download from MyLab.

SSP 18-1 Solution

The determination of the existence of a partnership is a mixed question of fact and law based on the intention of the parties, which may be expressed clearly through a valid written partnership agreement or inferred from actions. In Canada, the relevant provincial partnership legislation is applicable to answering this question.

In this case, an analysis of the three elements of a partnership is as follows:

1. **Was the business carried on in common by two or more persons?**

   The details of the partnership agreement contain many of the factors that the courts will look to in support of this element. Accordingly, it appears that this element has been met.

2. **Was a business carried on by the partnership?**

   A business has a beginning and an end. Ongoing profitable activity within the business may actually only occur between these two extremes, but the activity remains a business throughout the period. In other words, profitability is generally irrelevant to a finding that a business exists. In this case, the selling off of store property will likely occur as part of the wind-up process of the two stores. Accordingly, there are arguments that support the carrying on of a business.

3. **Was there a view to profit?**

   This element will be satisfied if there is a potential for profit even though one may never be realized. The facts clearly lead to a conclusion that there is no hope of profit. The additional fact that the partnership will be terminated once the property is sold and that losses are not only expected but anticipated speaks for itself. A tax motivation that predominates, such as this, will not invalidate a partnership as long as there is a profit potential and the other elements are met. This is not the case.

Conclusion: A partnership will not be created. As a result, any losses remain the losses of Wayout and cannot be allocated to any of the investors.

SSP 18-2 Solution
Part A—Partnership Results

As the original intention when the land was purchased was to develop and sell lots, the income from the sale of the lots would be reported as business income and not as a capital gain.

Using the rollover provisions of ITA 97(2), Mr. Marrazzo could sell the land to the partnership at its ACB of $400,000. There would be no income tax consequences with respect to his 2021 net income. His partnership income for the two years would be calculated as follows:

2021 Addition to net income	Nil

The total business income resulting from the 2022 sale of the property would be as follows:

Proceeds from lot sales	$4,400,000
Cost of land	(400,000)
Site servicing costs	(1,200,000)
Business income	$2,800,000

Mr. Marrazzo's 2022 addition to his net income would be calculated as follows:

Priority claim of accrued gain ($1,300,000 - $400,000)	$ 900,000
Allocation of remaining business income [(50%)($2,800,000 - $900,000)]	950,000
2022 Increase in net income	$1,850,000

Part B—Joint Venture Results

No rollover under ITA 85(1) could take place because land inventory is not eligible property. As a result, Mr. Marrazzo would recognize a 2021 gain on the transfer to Digger Inc. of $900,000 ($1,300,000 - $400,000). As previously noted, this gain would be business income. His partnership income inclusion for the two years would be calculated as follows:

2021 Addition to net income	$ 900,000

POD—Digger's sale of the land	$4,400,000
ACB	(1,300,000)
Site servicing costs	(1,200,000)
Business income	$1,900,000
Mr. Marrazzo's share	50%
2022 Addition to net income	$ 950,000

The addition to his net income over the two-year period is $1,850,000 ($900,000 + $950,000), the same total as in Part A.

Part C—Comparison

In total, Mr. Marrazzo will report the same increase in additional net income regardless of the form of the organization. However, with the joint venture, he would have to include $900,000 in 2021 and $950,000 in 2022. With the partnership, the entire $1,850,000 in income would be reported in 2022. Given that this approach provides significant tax deferral, the partnership approach appears preferable.

SSP 18-3 Solution
Partnership Income

The business income of the partnership is calculated as follows:

Net accounting income		$ 192,100
Additions:		
Partners' salaries [(2)($44,000)]	$88,000	
Amortization	12,500	
Charitable donations	7,200	
Closing accounts receivable (Note One)	56,000	163,700
Deductions:		
Opening accounts receivable (Note One)	($ 27,000)	
Capital gains on securities (Note Two)	(14,000)	
Taxable dividends received (Note Three)	(48,000)	
CCA:		
Class 8 [(20%)($26,000)]	(5,200)	
Class 50 [(55%)(150%)($8,500)]	(7,013)	(101,213)
Business income		$ 254,587

Note One The addition of closing accounts receivable and the deduction of the opening accounts receivable are required to adjust the accounting income to accrual-based income.

Note Two The total capital gain is deducted in the calculation of business income since capital gains are not part of business income. The taxable one-half of these gains is included in the income of the partners as a taxable capital gain.

Note Three The taxable dividends received are deducted in the calculation of business income because they are not part of business income. They are flowed through as eligible dividends to the partners.

Mr. Caldwell's Net Income

Mr. Caldwell's 2021 partnership income would be calculated as follows:

Partnership business income	$254,587	
Mr. Caldwell's share	50%	$ 127,294
Partner expenses: Automobile costs		
CCA [($13,500)(30%)(75%)]		(3,038)
Operating costs [($4,000)(75%)]		(3,000)
Business income		$121,256
Other partnership income:		
Taxable capital gains [(1/2)($14,000)]	$ 7,000	
Eligible dividends	48,000	
Gross up [(38%)($48,000)]	18,240	
Subtotal	$ 73,240	
Mr. Caldwell's share	50%	36,620
Addition to net income		$ 157,876

Mr. Caldwell's $3,600 [(50%)($7,200)] share of the charitable donations can be used as the basis for a credit against his federal tax payable. The amount of the credit would be $1,016 [(15%)($200) + (29%)($3,600- $200)].

He is also entitled to a federal dividend tax credit of $4,975 [(50%)(6/11)($18,240)].

SSP 18-4 Solution
Part A—Income Inclusions

CCC has three types of income. These are business income, property income (dividends), and taxable capital gains.

The calculation of the partnership's business income is as follows:

Net accounting income		$ 37,200
Add:		
Salaries to partners [(3)($2,400)]	$7,200	
Interest on capital contributions	2,000	
Personal partner expenses	1,100	
Charitable donations	1,000	
Accounting amortization	1,450	12,750
Deduct:		
CCA		(2,000)
Business income		$ 47,950
Priority allocations for salaries and interest ($7,200 + $2,000)		(9,200)
Residual to be allocated		$38,750

This amount would be allocated to the three partners as follows:

	Christine	Jennifer and Danny (Each)
Priority allocation for salaries	$ 2,400	$ 2,400
Priority allocation for interest	2,000	N/A
Allocation of residual on equal basis		
[(1/3)($38,750)]	12,917	12,917
Business income allocation	$17,317	$15,317

Other non-business income inclusions for each partner related to partnership activities would be as follows:

Eligible dividends received	$ 3,440
Gross up [(38%)($3,440)]	1,307
Taxable capital gains [(1/2)($6,000)]	3,000
Total to be allocated	$ 7,747
Each partner's share	1/3
Non-business income allocation	$ 2,582

This results in an addition to net income for Jennifer and Danny of $17,899 ($15,317 + $2,582). For Christine, the increase would include the $2,000 in interest and would equal $19,899 ($17,317 + $2,582).

Part B—Tax Credits

Charitable Donations   Each partner would be allocated $333 ($1,000 ÷ 3) in charitable donations. This would provide a federal tax credit of $69 [(15%)($200) + (29%)($133)].

Dividends   Each of the partners would be eligible for a federal dividend tax credit of $238 [(1/3)(6/11)(38%)($3,440)].

SSP 18-5 Solution
Barry's Federal Tax Payable
The business income of the partnership would be calculated as follows:

Operating income		$458,668
Additions:		
Amortization expense	$ 17,466	
One-half meals and entertainment		
[(1/2)($9,740)]	4,870	
Charitable donations	8,658	30,994
Deductions:		
CCA	(23,562)	(23,562)
Business income		$466,100

Barry's taxable income and share of charitable donations for the year ending December 31, 2021, would be calculated as follows:

	Partnership	Share	Taxable Income
Partnership business income	$466,100	60%	$279,660
Taxable capital gain [(1/2)($18,660)]	9,330	Nil	Nil
Eligible dividends received	12,390	50%	6,195
38% gross up on eligible dividends	N/A		2,354
2021 net and taxable income			$288,209
Charitable donations	$8,658	50%	$4,329

Based on the preceding calculation, Barry's 2021 federal income tax payable would be calculated as follows:

Tax on the first $216,511	$50,141
Tax on additional	
$71,698 ($288,209 - $216,511) at 33%	23,660
Tax payable before credits	$73,801
Basic personal credit [(15%)($12,421)]	(1,863)
Dividend tax credit [(6/11)($2,354)]	(1,284)
Charitable donations credit (see Note)	(1,393)
2021 federal tax payable	$69,261

Note The charitable donations tax credit would be calculated as follows:

$$[(15\%)(A)] + [(33\%)(B)] + [(29\%)(C)], \text{ where}$$

A = $200
B = Lesser of:
  • $4,329 - $200 = $4,129
  • $288,209 - $216,511 = $71,698
C = Nil [$4,329 - ($200 + $4,129)]

The charitable donations credit would be equal to $1,393, calculated as [(15%)($200) + (33%)($4,129)].

Taxable Capital Gain from Sale of Partnership Interest

The ACB of Barry's partnership interest on January 1, 2022, would be calculated as follows:

	Partnership	**Share**	**ACB**
Capital contribution	N/A		$275,000
2020 Partnership business income	$372,466	60%	223,480
2020 Drawings	N/A		(114,000)
2021 Drawings	N/A		(142,000)
December 31, 2021			$242,480
2021 Business income	$466,100	60%	279,660
2021 Capital gain	9,330	Nil	Nil
2021 Dividends received	12,390	50%	6,195
2021 Charitable donations	(8,658)	50%	(4,329)
ACB January 1, 2022			$524,006

Given this calculation, the taxable capital gain on Barry's sale of the partnership interest would be calculated as follows:

POD	$656,000
ACB	(524,006)
Capital gain	$ 131,994
Inclusion rate	1/2
Taxable capital gain	$ 65,997

SSP 18-6 Solution
Part A—Adjusted Cost Base (ACB)

The ACB of John Mathis' partnership interest on January 1, 2022, would be calculated as follows:

Initial capital contribution	$200,000
Additional capital contribution	75,000
Total capital contribution	$275,000
Drawings	(55,000)
Business income [(1/3)($233,460)]	77,820
Capital gains to Monroe and Mathis [(50%)($18,464)]	9,232
Dividends to Darin	Nil
Charitable donations [(1/3)($8,460)]	(2,820)
ACB—January 1, 2022	$304,232

Note Only the taxable one-half of the capital gain is included in the partner's income on the flow through of capital gains realized by a partnership. However, the full amount of John's share of realized capital gains is added to the ACB of his partnership interest.

Part B—Taxable Capital Gain on Disposition

Given the preceding calculation, the gain on the disposition of the partnership interest can be calculated as follows:

POD		$320,000
ACB	($304,232)	
Outlays and expenses	(1,800)	(306,032)
Capital gain		$ 13,968
Inclusion rate		1/2
Taxable capital gain		$ 6,984

This amount would be included in John Mathis' 2021 net income as a taxable capital gain. He would not include any partnership income for January since he was not a partner during the month.

Part C—Effect on Other Partners
The fact that each partner paid $160,000 to John in return for one-half of his interest means that both Bob Darin and Matt Monroe would have a $160,000 increase in the ACB of each of their partnership interest.

SSP 18-7 Solution
Limited Partnership Loss Allocations, the ACB, ARA, and LPL
The addition of the share of the partnership income amounts to the ARA at December 31 is intended to ensure that this amount is taken into consideration in determining the amount that is actually at risk on that date.

2021 Results

The required amounts would be calculated as follows:

ACB of partnership interest—December 31, 2021	$ 50,000
Add: Share of 2021 partnership income (not loss)	Nil
Subtotal	$ 50,000
Amount owing to the partnership	(20,000)
ARA—December 31, 2021	$ 30,000

Share of 2021 business loss [(10%)($400,000)]	($ 40,000)
ARA—December 31, 2021	30,000
2021 LPL	($ 10,000)

Share of 2021 business loss [(10%)($400,000)]	($ 40,000)
2021 LPL	10,000
Deductible loss for 2021	($ 30,000)

2022 Results

ACB of partnership interest—December 31, 2021	$50,000
Loss deducted for 2021	(30,000)
ACB of partnership interest—December 31, 2022	$20,000
Add: Share of 2022 partnership income (not loss)	Nil
Subtotal	$20,000
Amounts owing to the partnership	Nil
ARA—December 31, 2022	$20,000

Share of 2022 business loss [(10%)($70,000)]	($ 7,000)
2021 LPL	(10,000)
ARA—December 31, 2022	20,000
2022 LPL	N/A

Share of 2022 business loss [(10%)($70,000)]	($ 7,000)
2021 LPL	(10,000)
Deductible business loss for 2022	($ 17,000)

The $10,000 2021 LPL balance can be deducted as it is less than $13,000, the December 31, 2022, ARA of $20,000 reduced by the allocated share of the 2022 partnership business loss of $7,000. As a result, there is no 2022 LPL.

2023 Results

ACB of partnership interest—December 31, 2022	$20,000
Losses deducted for 2022	(17,000)
ACB of partnership interest—December 31, 2023	$ 3,000
Add: Share of 2023 partnership income	Nil
Subtotal	$ 3,000
Amounts owing to the partnership	Nil
ARA—December 31, 2023	$ 3,000

There is no LPL for 2022 and no balance remaining in the 2021 LPL.

Summary of Results

The results are summarized in the following table:

	2021	2022	2023
ACB of the partnership interest—December 31	$50,000	$20,000	$3,000
ARA—December 31	30,000	20,000	3,000
LPL	10,000	Nil	Nil
Deductible loss	30,000	17,000	Nil
LPL balance at December 31	10,000	Nil	Nil

SSP 18-8 Solution
Part A—ACB of Preferred Shares
With respect to the preferred shares received by each partner, ITA 85(3)(e) deems the ACB to be equal to the lesser of:

- the FMV, which would be $180,000 for each of the three partners; or
- the ACB of each partnership interest, reduced by the FMV of NSC received by each partner.

This latter amount would be calculated as follows for each of the three partners:

	Porter	Quinn	Roberts
ACB of the partnership interest	$382,000	$526,000	$726,000
Less: FMV of NSC (cash)	(78,000)	(222,000)	(422,000)
Balance	$304,000	$304,000	$304,000

For each of the three partners, the lesser amount would be the FMV of $180,000 and, as a consequence, this would be the ACB of the preferred shares to each partner.

Part A—ACB of Common Shares
Under ITA 85(3)(f), the ACB of the common shares received by each partner would be the ACB of their partnership interest less the sum of the FMV of the NSC and the ACB of the preferred shares. The ACB of the common shares is therefore determined as follows:

	Porter	Quinn	Roberts
ACB—Partnership interest	$382,000	$526,000	$726,000
Less: FMV of NSC (cash)	(78,000)	(222,000)	(422,000)
Less: ACB—Preferred shares	(180,000)	(180,000)	(180,000)
ACB—Common shares	$ 124,000	$ 124,000	$ 124,000

Part B—Capital Gain or Capital Loss

The rules of ITA 85(3) do not permit a capital loss, and a capital gain is only possible if the FMV of the NSC exceeds the ACB of a partners' partnership interest. Since that is not the case there can be no capital gain. ITA 85(3)(g) determines the POD of the partnership interest of each partner as shown below:

	Porter	Quinn	Roberts
Proceeds of disposition:			
FMV of NSC (cash)	$ 78,000	$222,000	$422,000
ACB of preferred shares	180,000	180,000	180,000
ACB of common shares	124,000	124,000	124,000
POD	$382,000	$526,000	$726,000
ACB	(382,000)	(526,000)	(726,000)
Capital gain	Nil	Nil	Nil

From an economic point of view, the deferred gain is built into the common shares, which are valued at $1,080,000. The combined ACB of the common shares is $372,000 [(3)($124,000)], which is $708,000 less than their FMV ($1,080,000 - $372,000). This is also the difference between the $2,342,000 FMV of the partnership property and the tax cost of $1,634,000.

CHAPTER 19

Learning Objectives

After completing Chapter 19, you should be able to:

1. Explain the basic concepts of trusts from an income tax and legal perspective (Paragraph [P hereafter] 19-1 to 19-15).
2. Explain the difference between a trust and an estate, including the concept of a GRE (P 19-16 to 19-20).
3. Describe what is required to establish a trust (P 19-21 to 19-23).
4. Describe the tax return filing requirement for trusts and when taxes owing must be paid and whether instalments are required (P 19-24 to 19-25).
5. List the major non-tax reasons for using trusts (P 19-26).
6. Describe the different classifications and types of trusts (P 19-27 to 19-46).
7. Explain the basic model for the taxation of trusts (P 19-47 and 19-49).
8. Describe the type of situations that allow rollovers for contributions of property to a trust (P 19-50 to 19-61).
9. Describe the circumstances in which the ITA allows trust property to be distributed tax free to beneficiaries (P 19-62 to 19-66).
10. Describe the reasons for the 21-year rule and the basic concept (P 19-67 to 19-69).
11. Describe some alternatives offered by the ITA that shift income between a trust and beneficiaries, and describe how net income and taxable income are determined for a trust and how it differs from other taxpayers (P 19-70 to 19-81).
12. Describe the treatment of income allocations to beneficiaries (P 19-82 to 19-102).
13. Explain the calculation of federal income tax payable for testamentary and inter vivos trusts (P 19-103 to 19-111).
14. Explain how the attribution rules apply to trusts and any related tax planning considerations (P 19-112 to 19-117).
15. Explain the concept of an income and capital interest in a trust and the income tax implications of each (P 19-118 to 19-123).
16. Describe the major tax planning considerations when evaluating various types of trusts such as family, spousal, and alter ego (P 19-124 to 19-135).
17. List the non-tax and tax factors that should be considered in an evaluation of an estate plan (P 19-136 to 19-138).
18. Explain the general objectives of an estate freeze (P 19-139 and 19-140).
19. Describe the estate freeze techniques that do not involve the use of a rollover (P 19-141 to 19-148).
20. Describe the use of the rollover of ITA 86(1) to implement an estate freeze involving a family trust (P 19-149 to 19-157).
21. Describe the considerations involved in choosing between a rollover under ITA 85 and 86 when implementing an estate freeze (P 19-158 to 19-159).

How to Work through Chapter 19

Visit pearsonmylabandmastering.com to access MyLab Accounting for this text. Once there, you can access student resources such as Self-Study Problems, Practice Exams, Flashcards, updates, and more.

We recommend the following approach in dealing with the material in this chapter:

Introduction to Trusts and Estate Planning
- Read paragraph 19-1 to 19-5 (in the text).

Basic Concepts
- Read paragraph 19-6 to 19-20.

Establishing a Trust
- Read paragraph 19-21 to 19-23.
- Do Exercise 19-1 (in the text) and check the solution in this Study Guide.

Returns and Payments—Trusts
- Read paragraph 19-24 to 19-25.

Non-Tax Reasons for Using Trusts
- Read paragraph 19-26.

Classification of Trusts (Personal, Testamentary, and Inter Vivos)
- Read paragraph 19-27 to 19-46.

Taxation of Trusts—The Basic Model
- Read paragraph 19-47 to 19-49.
- Do Exercise 19-2 and check the solution in this Study Guide.

Rollovers to a Trust
- Read paragraph 19-50 to 19-57.
- Do Exercise 19-3 and check the solution in this Study Guide.
- Read paragraph 19-58 to 19-61.
- Do Exercise 19-4 and check the solution in this Study Guide.

Rollovers to Capital Beneficiaries
- Read paragraph 19-62 to 19-66.
- Do Self-Study Problem 19-1, which is available on MyLab, and check the solution in this Study Guide.

21-Year Deemed Disposition Rule and Other Deemed Dispositions
- Read paragraph 19-67 to 19-70.

Net Income and Taxable Income of a Trust
- Read paragraph 19-71 to 19-81.
- Do Exercise 19-5 and check the solution in this Study Guide.

Income Allocations to Beneficiaries
- Read paragraph 19-82 to 19-99.
- Do Exercise 19-6 and check the solution in this Study Guide.

Allocation of Business Income, CCA, Recapture of CCA, and Terminal Losses
- Read paragraph 19-100 to 19-101.
- Do Exercise 19-7 and check the solution in this Study Guide.

Principal Residence Exemption
- Read paragraph 19-102.

Tax Payable of Personal Trusts
- Read paragraph 19-103 to 19-111.
- Do Exercise 19-8 and check the solution in this Study Guide.
- Do Self-Study Problems 19-2 to 19-4 and check the solutions in this Study Guide.

Income Attribution—Trusts
- Read paragraph 19-112 to 19-114.
- Do Exercise 19-9 and check the solution in this Study Guide.
- Do Self-Study Problems 19-5 and 19-6 and check the solutions in this Study Guide.
- Read paragraph 19-115 to 19-117.

Purchase or Sale of an Interest in a Trust
- Read paragraph 19-118 to 19-123.
- Do Exercise 19-10 and check the solution in this Study Guide.

Tax Planning Using Trusts (Family, Spousal, and Alter Ego Trusts)
- Read paragraph 19-124 to 19-130.
- Do Exercise 19-11 and check the solution in this Study Guide.
- Read paragraph 19-131 to 19-135.

Estate Planning—Tax and Non-Tax Considerations
- Read paragraph 19-136 to 19-138.

Estate Freeze—Objectives and Techniques, Including ITA 86 Share Exchange
- Read paragraph 19-139 to 19-159.

To Complete This Chapter
- Visit MyLab Accounting for more practice problem material, and test yourself with the glossary flashcards.
- Review the Key Terms at the end of the chapter, and consult the glossary for definitions.
- Ensure you have achieved the Chapter 19 Learning Objectives listed in this Study Guide.
- As a review, view the PowerPoint presentations available on MyLab.

Practice Examination
- Available on MyLab, write the Practice Examination for this chapter, and mark it using the solutions provided.

Exercise Solutions

Exercise 19-1 Solution
Case A   While Mr. Black has transferred property (i.e., cash), it is not clear that there is an intention to create a trust. No trust would be created.

Case B   Jane's "friends" cannot be considered to be an ascertainable class of persons. As a consequence, there is no certainty as to beneficiaries with the result that no trust would be created.

Case C   Robert's "children" would be an ascertainable class of persons. It would appear that a trust has been created.

Case D   While Suzanne has signed the agreement, it does not appear that the property has actually been transferred. A promise to transfer property ownership at some point in time would not fulfill the transfer requirements and, as a result, no trust has been created.

Exercise 19-2 Solution

The transfer of the ownership of the investments on the establishment of the trust would constitute a disposition of property at proceeds equal to the FMV at that time. This would result in a taxable capital gain to Joanne of $10,000 [(1/2)(POD $220,000 - ACB $200,000)]. There would be no income tax consequences to the beneficiary. The trust will be deemed to have acquired the investments for $220,000.

The trust would include $15,000 in its income but would be entitled to a deduction in determining net income of the same amount of $15,000 since all of the income was distributed. As a result, net income and taxable income of the trust for 2021 would both be nil. The interest income would be included in the income of the beneficiary for 2021 and would not be subject to attribution since the beneficiary is not a minor child.

The distribution of the investments to the beneficiary would be a disposition of property that would normally be deemed to have been disposed of for the FMV of the property, however ITA 107(2) allows a rollover at the tax cost of the property to the trust where the distribution is to a capital beneficiary in settlement of a capital interest. The result is that there would be no income tax implications to the trust [(1/2)(POD $220,000 - ACB $220,000)]. The beneficiary would be deemed to have acquired the investments for $220,000, and therefore when they are sold for $230,000 a few days later the result is a taxable capital gain of $5,000 [(1/2)(POD $230,000 - ACB $220,000)].

Exercise 19-3 Solution

As there is a rollover available on transfers to a qualifying spousal trust, the accrued $30,000 capital gain ($90,000 - $60,000) will not be realized until the surviving spouse or the spousal trust sells the shares. The spousal trust acquires the shares (a non-depreciable capital property) at Louise's ACB of $60,000. When the shares are distributed by the trust to the surviving spouse beneficiary, the POD will be deemed to occur at the tax cost to the trust of $60,000, resulting in no income tax implications to the trust or the surviving spouse.

Exercise 19-4 Solution

In scenarios 1, 2, and 3, the settlor has a taxable capital gain of $300 [(1/2)(POD $1,600 - ACB $1,000)] and the ACB to the trust is the FMV of $1,600. In scenarios 4 to 7, rollover treatment is available. The results can be summarized as follows:

Scenario	Taxable Capital Gain (Settlor)	Adjusted Cost Base (Trust)
1. Inter vivos trust for an adult child	$300	$1,600
2. Inter vivos trust for a minor child	300	1,600
3. Testamentary trust for a friend	300	1,600
4. Inter vivos qualifying spousal trust	Nil	1,000
5. Testamentary qualifying spousal trust	Nil	1,000
6. Joint spousal trust	Nil	1,000
7. Alter ego trust	Nil	1,000

Exercise 19-5 Solution

The required calculations are as follows:

Business Iicome	$ 220,000
Preferred beneficiary election	(50,000)
Distributions to other beneficiaries	(170,000)
Designation under ITA 104(13.1) amounts deemed not paid	35,000
Net income	$ 35,000
Less: Non-capital loss	(35,000)
Taxable income	Nil

The preferred beneficiary election would mean that the $50,000 would be included in the income of the beneficiary with a disability even though the funds remain in the trust. Since this is an inter vivos trust, without the election the $50,000 would be taxed at the maximum federal income tax rate of 33%, resulting in federal income tax of $16,500 [(33%)($50,000)]. As the beneficiary with a disability has no other source of income, the $50,000 would be subject to federal income tax at lower rates than would be the case if it were taxed in the trust. In addition, the individual would be able to claim, for 2021, a basic personal tax credit of $13,808 plus a disability tax credit of $8,662. Based on 2021 income tax rates, the net federal income tax would be $4,183 [($7,353 (first $49,020) + $201 (tax at 20.5% on $980) - (15%)($13,808 + $8,662)] before considering any additional credits such as the medical expense tax credit.

By designating $35,000 as amounts not paid, the trust can increase its net income to an amount that is sufficient to offset its non-capital loss. As a result, the beneficiaries will not pay any income tax on this amount even though it has been distributed to them. The $35,000 amount can subsequently be distributed tax free.

Exercise 19-6 Solution
The income allocation would be as follows:

	Received by Trust	Paid to Bryan	Retained by Trust
Eligible dividends	$ 100,000	$ 60,000	$40,000
Non-eligible dividends	30,000	30,000	Nil
Capital gain	20,000	20,000	Nil
Totals	$ 150,000	$110,000	$40,000

The net income of the trust would be calculated as follows:

Eligible dividends	$ 40,000
Gross up at 38%	15,200
2021 net income—Trust	$ 55,200

The corresponding calculation for Bryan would be as follows:

Eligible dividends	$ 60,000
Gross up at 38%	22,800
Non-eligible dividends	30,000
Gross up at 15%	4,500
Taxable capital gains [(1/2)($20,000)]	10,000
2021 net income—Bryan	$127,300

Note that the non-taxable one-half of the capital gain would be received by Bryan on a tax-free basis. Both the trust and Bryan will be able to claim a federal dividend tax credit in calculating federal income tax payable.

Exercise 19-7 Solution
If the property is sold in December 2021, CCA cannot be claimed since the UCC balance would be nil. This means that the total amount of income to be distributed to Martin as property income is $97,000 ($32,000 of rental income plus $65,000 of recapture). The net income of the trust would be nil (income of $97,000 - $97,000 payable to the beneficiary).

Alternatively, if the rental property is not sold and all of the income is distributed to Martin, he will include $6,000 ($32,000 - $26,000) in his 2021 net income. The trust's 2021 net income would be nil (income of $6,000 - $6,000 payable to the beneficiary).

As an additional point it is important to bear in mind that Martin would have received $32,000 in cash but his net income only reflects the post-CCA claim of $6,000. In trust law terms he would have received an income allocation of $6,000 and a capital distribution of $26,000.

Exercise 19-8 Solution

The total taxable income in Parts A, B, and C is the same and would be calculated as follows:

Eligible dividends received	$100,000
Gross up at 38%	38,000
Taxable income	$138,000

Part A   As all of its 2021 income has been distributed, there would be no net income, taxable income, or tax payable for the trust. The beneficiary's federal income tax payable on taxable income of $138,000 is calculated in the table below.

Part B   As none of the dividends are distributed by the trust to the beneficiary, there would be no net income, taxable income, or tax payable for the beneficiary. The trust's federal income tax payable on taxable income of $138,000 is shown in the table below.

The federal income tax payable for Parts A and B would be calculated as follows:

	Part A	Part B
Tax on first $98,040	$ 17,402	$ 17,402
Tax on next $39,960 ($138,000 - $98,040) at 26%	10,390	10,390
Total federal income tax before credits	$ 27,792	$ 27,792
Personal tax credit [(15%)($13,808)]	(2,071)	N/A
Federal dividend tax credit [(6/11)($38,000)]	(20,727)	(20,727)
Federal income tax payable	$ 4,994	$ 7,065

Notice that the difference between the income tax payable in Part A and Part B is $2,071 ($7,065 - $4,994). This amount is equal to the basic personal tax credit.

Part C   With no distributions to the beneficiary, the trust's net income and taxable income would be $138,000. There would be no net income, taxable income, or income tax payable for the beneficiary. The income tax payable for the inter vivos trust would be calculated as follows:

Tax on $138,000 at 33%	$45,540
Federal dividend tax credit [(6/11)($38,000)]	(20,727)
Federal income tax payable	$24,813

Comparison   As a comparison of these examples makes clear, if a trust has beneficiaries with no other sources of income, overall tax payments will be reduced by distributing eligible dividends to beneficiaries (Part A). While these examples do not illustrate this possibility, the conclusion would be the same if non-eligible dividends were involved. Note that the results in Part C would be the same for a non-GRE testamentary trust. In Parts B and C, where the trust has paid the tax, the after-tax amount would be distributed to the beneficiary on a tax-free basis. However, in Part C, if the beneficiary has a marginal federal tax rate that is less than 33%, there will be a tax cost to taxing the income in the trust.

Exercise 19-9 Solution

Income on the bonds is income from property and therefore subject to the attribution rules to the extent that the income is allocated to Trevor's spouse, Carmen, and to their minor son, Mitch. This means that two-thirds of the interest will be attributed back to Trevor. With respect to the capital gain, the attribution rules do not apply on transfers to minors. This means that only Carmen's share of the capital gain will be attributed back to Trevor. The increase in net and taxable income for Trevor and the trust's beneficiaries are as follows:

	Carmen	Mitch	Rhonda	Attributed to Trevor
Interest income ($27,000 ÷ 3)	$9,000	$9,000	$ 9,000	
Interest attribution to Trevor	(9,000)	(9,000)	Nil	$18,000
Taxable capital gain [(1/2)($6,000) ÷ 3]	1,000	1,000	1,000	
Capital gain attribution to Trevor	(1,000)	Nil	Nil	1,000
Net and taxable income	Nil	$1,000	$10,000	$19,000

If Trevor had died on January 1 of the current year, there would be no income attribution for the year. Each of the beneficiaries would have taxable income of $10,000, composed of $9,000 in interest income and $1,000 of a taxable capital gain.

Exercise 19-10 Solution

With respect to Sam, he has acquired a capital interest for $190,000. This will be his cost and therefore the ACB of his interest. With respect to Mehrdad, he has disposed of capital property for proceeds of disposition of $190,000. Since he did not purchase the interest in the trust, his ACB is the greater of nil and the cost amount as determined under ITA 108(1). The cost amount would be $125,000, one-half of the $250,000 tax cost of the trust property. The result would be a taxable capital gain of $32,500 [(1/2)(POD $190,000 - ACB $125,000)].

Exercise 19-11 Solution

As Sarah's other income places her in the maximum federal income tax bracket of 33%, her federal income tax savings resulting from transferring ownership of the investments to a non-discretionary family trust would equal $36,300 [($110,000)(33%)]. The federal income tax payable on an income distribution of $55,000 to Jerri would be as follows:

Tax on first $49,020	$ 7,353
Tax on additional $5,980 ($55,000 - $49,020) at 20.5%	1,226
Tax before credit	$8,579
Personal tax credit [(15%)($13,808)]	(2,071)
Federal income tax payable—Jerri	$6,508

The AMT is not relevant to Jerri because the income is in the form of interest. As Mark would be in a position to use all of his tax credits prior to receiving the additional $55,000 in income, they are not relevant to the determination of his marginal increase in taxes. The federal income tax that would be payable on the additional $55,000 received by Mark is as follows:

Tax at 15% ($49,020 - $48,000 = $1,020 at 15%)	$ 153
Tax at 20.5% ($98,040 - $49,020 = $49,020 at 20.5%)	$10,049
Tax at 26% ($55,000 + $48,000 - $98,040 = $4,960 at 26%)	1,290
Additional federal income tax payable—Mark	$11,492

The total federal income tax paid by the two adult children would be $18,000 ($6,508 + $11,492). This is $18,300 ($36,300 - $18,000) per year less than the amount that would be paid by Sarah without the trust. When combined with a reduction in provincial income taxes, the total tax savings could be significantly larger. This should be more than enough to cover the costs of establishing and maintaining a trust.

One tax planning consideration would be to include Mark's spouse as a beneficiary and include discretionary authority that would allow the trustee to make distributions of income to Mark's spouse rather than to Mark. Since Mark's spouse has no income, her federal income tax payable would be equivalent to that of Jerri. Although Mark would lose the benefit of the spousal credit, the basic personal credit would be available to the spouse. Despite the fact that having Mark's spouse as a beneficiary would result in less income taxes being paid, whether this would be advantageous for Mark (and his mother) would also depend on non-tax considerations such as the state of the marriage.

Self-Study Problem Solutions

Self-Study Problems are available to download from MyLab Accounting.

SSP 19-1 Solution
Case A

1. The settlor has deemed proceeds of disposition equal to the FMV of $26,400, resulting in a taxable capital gain of $1,550 [(1/2)(POD $26,400 - ACB $23,300)]. In addition, there will be recapture of $7,900 (capital cost $23,300 - UCC $15,400).

2. The trust acquires the property at a deemed ACB of $26,400. However, for purposes of calculating CCA and recapture, ITA 13(7)(e) only allows capital cost to equal $24,850 [$23,300 + (1/2)($26,400 - $23,300)].

Case B

1. The settlor has deemed proceeds of disposition equal to the FMV of $15,200. This would result in the settlor having recapture of $2,800 (capital cost $15,200 - UCC $12,400). Since the FMV does not exceed the capital cost there are no capital gains. In addition, no capital losses are recognized on depreciable property.

2. The tax attributes to the trust would be capital cost of $19,500 with deemed CCA of $4,300, resulting in a UCC of $15,200.

3. When the depreciable property is distributed to the capital beneficiary, the deemed POD is equal to the UCC of $13,600, resulting in no gain or loss to the trust. The beneficiary will be deemed to have acquired the property for the UCC of $13,600. However, the beneficiary will have a deemed capital cost of $19,500 and deemed CCA of $5,900 for subsequent recapture purposes and an ACB of $19,500 for capital gains purposes.

Case C

1. Under the general ITA 70(6) rollover provision, the deemed POD to the deceased is equal to the ACB of $18,200, resulting in no capital gain or capital loss on the contribution. As the deceased has a net capital loss balance, a preferable alternative would be to elect to avoid the rollover of ITA 70(6) and transfer the property for proceeds equal to FMV of $76,400. The net capital losses available could then be used to offset the taxable capital gain of $29,100 [(1/2)(POD $76,400 - ACB $18,200)].

2. In the year of death, net capital loss balances can generally be deducted against any type of income. If the deceased has other income that could offset all of the net capital loss balance it may not be advantageous to elect out of the rollover.

3. The cost to the trust if the rollover is used would be $18,200 and equal to the FMV of $76,400 if an election is made by the legal representative to avoid the rollover. This higher value will reduce any future capital gain on the property when it is sold.

Case D

1. The settlor has deemed proceeds of disposition equal to the FMV of $123,200 resulting in a taxable capital gain of $18,900 [(1/2)(POD $123,200 - ACB $85,400)].

2. The cost to the trust equals the FMV of $123,200.

Case E

1. The settlor has deemed proceeds of disposition equal to the FMV of $51,600, resulting in a taxable capital gain of $4,200 [(1/2)(POD $51,600 - ACB $43,200)].

2. The cost to the trust equals the FMV of $51,600.

3. When the property is distributed to the capital beneficiary, the deemed proceeds of disposition to the trust will equal the tax cost of $51,600, resulting in no capital gain or capital loss as a result of ITA 107(2). The beneficiary will be deemed to have acquired the property at a cost of $51,600.

Case F

1. The deemed POD to the settlor would be the tax cost or ACB of $14,200, resulting in no capital gain or capital loss on the contribution.

2. The ACB to the trust would equal the same $14,200.

SSP 19-2 Solution
Part A—Net and Taxable Income for the GRE and Its Beneficiaries
The payments made by the GRE executor will result in the following net and taxable income for the GRE and the two children:

	Daughter (30%)	Son (50%)	GRE (20%)
Eligible dividends received	$ 26,100	$ 43,500	$ 17,400
Gross up of 38%	9,918	16,530	6,612
British interest (gross amount of $110,000)	33,000	55,000	22,000
Net rental income ($21,000)	6,300	10,500	4,200
Net and taxable income	$ 75,318	$ 125,530	$ 50,212
British taxes paid* ($16,500)	$ 4,950	$ 8,250	$ 3,300

*The net interest receipt of $93,500 equals 85% of $110,000 ($93,500 ÷ 0.85). This means that the taxes withheld totalled $16,500 [(15%)($110,000)].

Part B—Federal Income Tax Payable for the GRE
Income that remains in a GRE is taxed using the same income tax rates as would apply to an individual. However, the GRE would not be able to claim personal tax credits under ITA 118 to reduce the amount of federal income tax payable.

The after-tax income of the GRE can be distributed tax free to the beneficiaries of the GRE as a capital distribution.

Federal income tax payable for the GRE would be calculated as follows:

Federal income tax payable:	
On first $49,020	$ 7,353
On remaining $1,192 ($50,212 - $49,020) at 20.5%	244
Federal income tax payable before credits	$ 7,597
Federal dividend tax credit [(6/11)($6,612)]	(3,607)
Foreign tax credit (see Note)	(3,300)
Federal income tax payable	$ 690

Note The amount that can be deducted for the foreign tax credit is the lesser of the $3,300 of foreign taxes withheld and an amount determined by the following formula:

[(Foreign Non-Business Income ÷ Adjusted Net Income)(Tax Payable before Credits)]

= [($22,000 ÷ $50,212)($7,597)]

= $3,329

As this amount is more than the actual foreign taxes of $3,300 allocated to the GRE, the actual foreign taxes paid would be the lesser amount and would be the foreign tax credit.

Note that if the foreign taxes withheld had exceeded 15% of the foreign income, the excess would have been deductible under ITA 20(11), rather than added to the amount of foreign income tax withheld in the formula.

SSP 19-3 Solution
Parts A and B—Alternative One
The following tables assume that one-half of the dividend income will remain in the GRE. They provide the required information on net income, taxable income, and federal income tax payable for the relevant taxation years.

Income Allocation	GRE	Rowena	Roger
Business income	$ Nil	$12,000	$ 8,000
Interest	Nil	1,800	1,200
Non-eligible dividends received	25,000	15,000	10,000
Dividend gross up (15%)	3,750	2,250	1,500
Net rental income (Note)	Nil	2,400	1,600
Net income and taxable income	$28,750	$33,450	$22,300
Federal income tax at 15%	$ 4,313	$ 5,018	$ 3,345
Basic personal credit [(15%)($13,808)]	N/A	(2,071)	(2,071)
Federal dividend tax credit			
[(9/13)(gross up)]	(2,596)	(1,558)	(1,038)
Federal income tax payable (total = $3,342)	$ 1,717	$ 1,389	$ 236

Note The $4,000 net rental income is calculated as the rent receipts of $12,000 less the operating expenses of $6,000 and CCA of $2,000.

Parts A and B—Alternative Two
The following income allocation assumes that all of the GRE's income will be allocated to Rowena and Roger. This means that the net income, taxable income, and federal income tax payable of

the GRE will be nil. The calculations for Rowena and Roger for the year ending December 31, 2021, are as follows:

Income Allocation	Rowena	Roger
Business income	$ 12,000	$ 8,000
Interest	1,800	1,200
Non-eligible dividends received	30,000	20,000
Dividend gross up (15%)	4,500	3,000
Net rental income	2,400	1,600
Net and taxable income	$50,700	$33,800

Federal income tax:		
Roger: [(15%)($33,800)]		$ 5,070
Rowena: On first $49,020 at 15%	$ 7,353	
Rowena: On remaining $1,680		
($50,700 - $49,020) at 20.5%	344	
Basic personal credit [(15%)($13,808)]	(2,071)	(2,071)
Federal dividend tax credit [(9/13)(gross up)]	(3,115)	(2,077)
Federal income tax payable (total = $3,433)	$ 2,511	$ 922

Part C—Comparison
The total federal income tax payable in Alternative Two is $91 ($3,433 - $3,342) higher than the total in Alternative One. This difference reflects the fact that in Alternative Two, $1,680 of the total income was taxed at 20.5%, while in Alternative One, all of the income was taxed at 15% [(20.5% - 15%)($1,680)] = $91 ($1 rounding difference.)

SSP 19-4 Solution
Part A—Calculation of Net and Taxable Income
All amounts are allocated 45% to Jessica, 40% to Joseph, and 15% to the trust. The net and taxable income of the two beneficiaries and the trust would be calculated as follows:

	Jessica (45%)	Joseph (40%)	Trust (15%)
Interest on GICs	$ 56,700	$ 50,400	$ 18,900
Eligible dividends received	207,900	184,800	69,300
Gross up of 38%	79,002	70,224	26,334
Taxable capital gain on land			
[(1/2)($250,000 - $85,000)]	37,125	33,000	12,375
Taxable capital gain on building			
[(1/2)($962,000 - $725,000)]	53,325	47,400	17,775
Net rental income (Note)	63,000	56,000	21,000
Net and taxable income	$497,052	$441,824	$165,684

Note The rental income, including the recapture of CCA, can be calculated as follows:

Revenues from rental property		$125,000
Cash expenses on rental property		(83,000)
Recapture of CCA:		
Capital cost of the building	$725,000	
UCC	(627,000)	98,000
Rental income, including recapture		$140,000

Part B—Federal Income Tax Payable for the Trust

The federal income tax payable for the trust is as follows:

Federal tax before credits [(33%)($165,684)]	$54,676
Federal dividend tax credit [(6/11)($26,334)]	(14,364)
Federal income tax payable	$40,312

As this trust is an inter vivos trust, all of its income is subject to federal income tax of 33% [ITA 122(1)].

SSP 19-5 Solution

A. The trust is a personal trust that is an inter vivos trust. In common usage the trust could also be described as a family trust in that all of the beneficiaries are family members. In addition, it could be referred to as partially discretionary in that the trustee determines the timing of the distributions of income.

B. As the trust is an inter vivos trust, the taxation year end must be December 31.

C. All of the income that is allocated to Mr. Dion will be subject to the income attribution rules. As a consequence, it will be included in Mrs. Dion's net income. No amount will be included in the net income of Mr. Dion.

As the twins are over the age of 17, the attribution rules will not apply to their share of the trust's income. This means that the income that is allocated to them will only be included in their net income.

As all of the trust's income is either attributed back to Mrs. Dion or allocated to beneficiaries, the trust's net income will be nil.

D. The answer here will depend on the terms of the loan to the trust since the rules for non-arm's-length loans apply. If the loan is interest free, the results will be the same as in Part C. This would also be the result if the interest rate on the loan was less than the prescribed rate.

Alternatively, if the loan paid interest at the prescribed rate or higher, the income attribution rules would not apply and the trust income allocated to Mr. Dion would be included in his net income. Note that the loan would have to have bona fide repayment terms and the interest would have to be paid within 30 days of the end of each calendar year.

E. The attribution rules do not apply to any income or loss from property that relates to the period throughout which the individuals are living separate and apart because of a breakdown of their marriage or common-law partnership. The attribution rules do not apply to income that accrues subsequent to a separation (ITA 74.5(3)).

SSP 19-6 Solution
Part A—Trust for Daughter

The first trust created is a testamentary trust for the benefit of Mrs. Turner's daughter, Melanie. When there is a transfer of property at death to any person other than a spouse or a spousal trust, there is a deemed disposition at FMV resulting in the realization of capital gains with recapture of CCA on the warehouse building.

The principal residence exemption could be used to eliminate the $165,000 [(POD $265,000 - ACB $100,000)] capital gain on the principal residence. There is no taxable benefit with respect to the use of the residence by Melanie. However, the costs for the upkeep and maintenance of the residence represent an income distribution to Melanie and a net income deduction to the trust.

The capital gain and recapture on the disposition of the warehouse building would be included in Mrs. Turner's final income tax return. The taxable capital gain on the warehouse land is $10,000 [(1/2)(POD $75,000 - ACB $55,000)]. There is no capital gain on the warehouse building since FMV and ACB are both $85,000. However, there would be $40,000 ($85,000 - $45,000) of recaptured CCA. This amount would also be included in Mrs. Turner's final income tax return.

The trust will be deemed to acquire all of the properties at a cost equal to their respective FMVs. In the case of the warehouse land, the ACB to the trust is $75,000 and the ACB and capital cost of the warehouse building are both $85,000.

Part A—Trust for Spouse

The second trust is a qualifying spousal trust. Where there is a transfer at death to a qualifying spousal trust, the proceeds of disposition are deemed to equal the deceased's tax cost. This would be $152,000 for the cottage and $220,000 for the investment portfolio. and, as a consequence, there are no immediate income tax consequences for Mrs. Turner's final income tax return.

The trust will be deemed to have acquired the cottage and investment portfolio at the same amounts.

Part B—Death of Husband

The death of Mr. West results in a deemed disposition of the property of the trust (i.e., the cottage and investments) for proceeds equal to FMV. In the case of the cottage, there is a taxable capital gain of $85,000 [(1/2)(POD $322,000 - ACB $152,000)] and a taxable capital gain of $30,000 [(1/2)(POD $280,000 - ACB $220,000)] on the investments.

Part C—Graduated Rate Estate (GRE)

The principal advantage of a GRE is that any income that is not distributed to beneficiaries is subject to income tax within the trust at graduated rates, rather than at the maximum federal rate of 33%. If the marginal income tax rates of the beneficiaries exceed 15%, it may be advantageous to prolong the settlement of the estate.

CHAPTER 20

Learning Objectives

After completing Chapter 20, you should be able to:

1. Provide some practical examples of the importance of international tax issues to Canadians (Paragraph [P hereafter] P 20-1 to 20-6).
2. Explain the purpose of tax treaties (P 20-7 to 20-8).
3. Describe the circumstances under which non-residents could be subject to Part I income tax, including the general impact of the Canada/U.S. tax treaty (P 20-9 to 20-37).
4. Explain the purpose of Part XIII tax to non-residents, how it applies, and the impact of the Canada/U.S. treaty with respect to payments from Canada to U.S. residents for interest, dividends, royalties, rents, and pensions (P 20-38 to 20-65).
5. Describe how non-resident shareholders of Canadian corporations are treated when there are shareholder loans or other shareholder benefits (P 20-66 to 20-69).
6. Explain the purpose of the thin capitalization rules and their impact on the Canadian corporation and relevant non-resident shareholders (P 20-70 to 20-71).
7. Explain the purpose, the impact, and the exceptions to the immigration tax rules (P 20-72 to 20-73).
8. Describe the purpose of the emigration rules, their impact on departing Canadian residents, and any elective options available and the circumstances under which they would be used (P 20-74 to 20-83).
9. Explain the reason for legislation that allows the emigration rules to be reversed (P 20-84 to 20-87).
10. Explain how the immigration rules may benefit short-term residents (P 20-88 to 20-90).
11. Describe the foreign investment reporting requirements of form T1135 and explain the reason for these rules (P 20-91 to 20-100).
12. Explain how Canadian residents are taxed in both Canada and the U.S. when they are employed in the U.S., carry on business in the U.S., or dispose of U.S.-based property (P 20-101 to 20-109).
13. Explain the income tax consequences when Canadian resident individuals receive dividends from the U.S. (P 20-110 to 20-117).
14. Describe the Canadian income tax consequences when Canadian resident corporations receive dividends from U.S. corporations that are not foreign affiliates (P 20-118).
15. Explain the concept of a foreign affiliate in your own words and its purpose (P 20-119 to 20-121).
16. Describe the income tax treatment of dividends received from FAs that are not CFAs, including an explanation of both exempt and taxable surplus, the circumstances under which they apply, and their impact on Canadian income tax (P 20-122 to 20-136).
17. Explain the meaning of a controlled foreign affiliate (CFA) and how it differs from an FA (P 20-137 to 20-140).
18. Explain the purpose and meaning of FAPI and how it applies (P 20-141 to 20-147).
19. Describe the income tax treatment when dividends are paid from FAPI (P 20-148 to 20-149).

How to Work through Chapter 20

Visit pearsonmylabandmastering.com to access MyLab Accounting for this text. Once there, you can access student resources such as Self-Study Problems, Practice Exams, Flashcards, updates, and more.

We recommend the following approach in dealing with the material in this chapter:

Introduction—Overview
- Read paragraph 20-1 to 20-8 (in the text).

Canadian Income Tax and Non-Residents—Introduction
- Read paragraph 20-9 to 20-19.

Carrying on Business in Canada—General Rules
- Read paragraph 20-20 to 20-27.
- Do Exercise 20-1 (in the text) and check the solution in this Study Guide.

Canadian Source Employment Income—General Rules
- Read paragraph 20-28 to 20-32.
- Do Exercises 20-2 and 20-3 and check the solutions in this Study Guide.

Dispositions of Taxable Canadian Property—General Rules
- Read paragraph 20-33 to 20-37.
- Do Exercise 20-4 and check the solution in this Study Guide.
- Do Self-Study Problem 20-1, which is available on MyLab, and check the solution in this Study Guide.

Part XIII Tax on Non-Residents—Introduction and Applicability
- Read paragraph 20-38 to 20-44.

Interest Payments—ITA 212(1)(b)
- Read paragraph 20-45 to 20-48.
- Do Exercise 20-5 and check the solution in this Study Guide.

Dividend, Royalty, and Rental Income—ITA 212(1)(d) & 212(2)
- Read paragraph 20-49 to 20-59.
- Do Exercise 20-6 and check the solution in this Study Guide.

Pension Benefits, Shareholder Loans/Benefits, and Thin Capitalization—ITA 18(4), 214(3)(a), & 217
- Read paragraph 20-69 to 20-69.
- Do Self-Study Problem 20-2 and check the solution in this Study Guide.
- Read paragraph 20-70 to 20-71.
- Do Exercise 20-7 and check the solution in this Study Guide.

Entering Canada—Becoming a Resident of Canada
- Read paragraph 20-72 to 20-73.

Ceasing to Be a Resident of Canada—Emigration
- Read paragraph 20-74.
- Do Exercises 20-8 and 20-9 and check the solutions in this Study Guide.
- Read paragraph 20-75 to 20-78.
- Do Exercise 20-10 and check the solution in this Study Guide.
- Read paragraph 20-79 to 20-83.
- Do Self-Study Problem 20-3 and check the solution in this Study Guide.
- Read paragraph 20-84 to 20-90.
- Do Exercise 20-11 and check the solution in this Study Guide.

Foreign Source Income of Canadian Residents—Foreign Property Reporting Requirements (T1135)
- Read paragraph 20-91 to 20-100.
- Do Exercise 20-12 and check the solution in this Study Guide.
- Do Self-Study Problem 20-4 and check the solution in this Study Guide.

Foreign Employment Income
- Read paragraph 20-101 to 20-102.
- Do Self-Study Problem 20-5 and check the solution in this Study Guide.

Foreign Source Business Income of Canadian Residents
- Read paragraph 20-103 to 20-105.
- Do Exercise 20-13 and check the solution in this Study Guide.

Foreign Interest Income and Foreign Source Capital Gains
- Read paragraph 20-106 to 20-109.

Foreign Dividends—Including from FAs and CFAs
- Read paragraph 20-110 to 20-117.
- Do Self-Study Problem 20-6 and check the solution in this Study Guide.
- Read paragraph 20-118 to 20-121.
- Do Exercise 20-14 and check the solution in this Study Guide.
- Read paragraph 20-122 to 20-147.
- Do Exercise 20-15 and check the solution in this Study Guide.
- Read paragraph 20-148 and 20-149.
- Do Exercise 20-16 and check the solution in this Study Guide.
- Do Self-Study Problem 20-7 and check the solution in this Study Guide.

To Complete This Chapter
- Visit MyLab Accounting for more practice problem material, and test yourself with the glossary flashcards.
- Review the Key Terms at the end of the chapter, and consult the glossary for definitions.
- Ensure you have achieved the Chapter 20 Learning Objectives listed in this Study Guide.
- As a review, view the PowerPoint presentations available on MyLab.

Practice Examination
- Available on MyLab, write the Practice Examination for this chapter, and mark it using the solutions provided.

Exercise Solutions

Exercise 20-1 Solution
Case 1 Jazzco is not carrying on business in Canada through a permanent establishment and therefore would not be subject to Canadian income tax.

Case 2 Jazzco is carrying on business in Canada through a permanent establishment located in Toronto. Therefore, Jazzco is taxable in Canada under ITA 2(3) on the business profits attributable to the Canadian factory.

Case 3 The tax treaty allows Canada to tax business income of a non-resident only if such income is attributable to a permanent establishment in Canada. The warehouse constitutes a fixed place of business regardless of whether it is owned or leased. However, since it appears to be used exclusively to maintain an inventory for delivery, under the Canada/U.S. tax treaty it would be an excluded facility and would not be considered to be a permanent establishment. Jazzco would not be taxable under ITA 2(3) on its Canadian profits. The fact that the employee acts on behalf of the non-resident employer would not alter the conclusion since the employee does not have the authority to conclude contracts.

Case 4   In this case, because the employee has authority to conclude contracts on behalf of the non-resident employer, the employee is deemed to be a permanent establishment. This means that Jazzco is subject to income tax in Canada under ITA 2(3) on its business profits attributable to the permanent establishment (i.e., the employee).

Case 5   Since the warehouse is not used exclusively for maintaining an inventory, the permanent establishment exception in the tax treaty would not apply with the result that profits attributable to that warehouse would be subject to income tax in Canada.

Exercise 20-2 Solution
Dawn is an individual who has become a resident of another country but continues to receive remuneration from a resident Canadian taxpayer. Given that the tax treaty exempts her salary from taxation in Egypt, ITA 115(2)(c) deems her to be employed in Canada and, as a consequence, she would be subject to Canadian income tax on the salary.

Exercise 20-3 Solution
Case 1   The employment income is subject to income tax in Canada. The Canada/U.S. tax treaty allows Canada to tax employment income earned in Canada unless one of two exceptions applies. The first exception is when the total remuneration is $10,000 or less in Canadian currency. This exception does not apply, since David earned C$11,200 in 2021 [($2,800)(4 months)]. The second exception is the 183-day rule. Although David was in Canada for only 122 days during 2021 and therefore met the first part of the test, he failed the remaining part of the test since the employer was a Canadian resident with a permanent establishment in Canada and could deduct the payments.

Case 2   The employment income is not subject to income tax in Canada. The 183-day rule exempts the income from Canadian taxation because the employer was not resident in Canada, did not have a permanent establishment in Canada, and could not deduct the payments for Canadian income tax purposes.

Case 3   The employment income is subject to income tax in Canada. The Canada/U.S. tax treaty would exempt the income from Canadian tax if the amount was less than C$10,000 or if Sandra spent less than 183 days in Canada in any 12-month period beginning or ending in 2021. As she earned C$50,000 and spent 238 days at her job in Canada, neither of these exceptions are applicable.

Exercise 20-4 Solution
Case 1   Nancy is not subject to Canadian income tax on the gain. As a non-resident, Nancy is only taxable in Canada on gains from the disposition of taxable Canadian property. Shares of a Canadian resident public company are only taxable Canadian property if Nancy and non-arm's-length persons had together owned 25% or more of the issued shares of any class of the company in the 60 months preceding the disposition.

Case 2   Joe is subject to Canadian income tax on the gain. The condo is taxable Canadian property since it is real property (e.g., land and buildings) situated in Canada. The Canada/U.S. tax treaty gives Canada the right to impose income tax on U.S. residents with respect to such gains. The property is not exempt from Canadian tax as a principal residence since Joe did not purchase the condo for his own habitation.

Case 3   Joe would be subject to Canadian income tax on the gain on the sale of the shares. Shares of an unlisted corporation are taxable Canadian property if at any time within the preceding 60 months more than 50% of the FMV of the company is derived from Canadian real property. In addition, the Canada/U.S. treaty allows Canada to impose income tax on the gain on the disposition of shares if the corporation is resident in Canada and the value of the shares is derived principally from real property situated in Canada.

Case 4 Joe would not be taxable on the gain on the shares. The shares are taxable Canadian property because they represent shares of an unlisted corporation that, at some time in the 60 months preceding the disposition, derived more than 50% of their value from taxable Canadian property. This basic rule applies irrespective of the residency status of the corporation. The Canada/U.S. treaty, however, only allows Canada to impose income tax if the corporation is resident in Canada, and as a result the gain would not be subject to Canadian income tax. As a rule, corporations are considered resident in the country in which they are incorporated (Canada/U.S. tax treaty article IV(3)).

Exercise 20-5 Solution
Case 1 As Jason is at arm's length with the bank and the interest is not participating debt interest, Part XIII would not apply.

Case 2 As Janice is at arm's length with the Canadian government and the interest is not participating debt interest, the interest would not be subject to Part XIII tax. Note that interest on Government of Canada bonds is also fully exempt interest, but this fact does not affect the result in this case.

Case 3 As Julian is at arm's length from the bank and the interest is not participating debt interest, he would not have to withhold Part XIII tax.

Case 4 Part XIII applies to impose withholding tax on the $5,000 payment to Jasmine's U.S. resident brother because the interest is not fully exempt interest. The Canada/U.S. tax treaty, however, overrides Part XIII and exempts U.S. residents from Part XIII tax. This means that Jasmine does not have to withhold any Part XIII tax despite the fact that her brother is a non-arm's-length person.

Exercise 20-6 Solution
Case 1 Rentco appears to be carrying on business in Canada through a permanent establishment. As a result, no Part XIII tax is payable. However, Rentco would be subject to Part I tax on its income attributable to the permanent establishment in Saskatchewan.

Case 2 Jack would be subject to Part XIII tax of $10,500 [(25%)($42,000)]. This represents an effective tax rate of 37.5% on his net rental income of $28,000 ($10,500 ÷ $28,000). Alternatively, Jack could elect under ITA 216 to be taxed under Part I on the net rental income of $28,000 ($42,000 - $14,000). Whether this is would be a good alternative depends on Jack's Canadian marginal income tax rate. The break-even rate would be 37.5% ($10,500 ÷ $28,000). If his marginal rate is below this, Part I tax would be the better alternative. If his marginal rate exceeds 37.5%, Part XIII tax would be preferable. If Jack's only Canadian income is from the rental property then his Canadian tax rate would be 22.2% [15% + (48%)(15%) ITA 120(1)].

Case 3 Jack would be subject to Part XIII tax on the gross rents received for the boats unless he would be considered to be carrying on a business. However, the Canada/U.S. tax treaty reduces the withholding tax to 10% of the gross rents received, or $800. Note that Jack would not be eligible to elect under ITA 216 to be taxed under Part I on the boat rents, since this election is generally restricted to real property.

Exercise 20-7 Solution
As Ms. Johnson owns 30% of the common shares, she is a specified non-resident shareholder. Her relevant equity balance would be $1,620,000 [(30%)($2,400,000) + (100%)($900,000)]. Given this, the disallowed interest would be calculated as follows:

Total interest paid to Ms. Johnson [(9%)($4,500,000)]	$405,000
Maximum deductible interest [(9%)(1.5)($1,620,000)]	(218,700)
Disallowed interest	$186,300

The disallowed interest would be re-characterized as a deemed dividend (ITA 214(16)) and would not be deductible to the resident Canadian company. In addition, the withholding rates to Ms. Johnson would have increased from 10% on interest to a resident of Mexico or $40,500 to \$49,815 [(10%)(\$218,700 of interest) + (15%)(deemed dividend of \$186,300)]. Note: You can determine the impact of the Canada/Mexico tax treaty by accessing the non-resident calculator on the CRA website (see Paragraph 20-44 for the URL).

Exercise 20-8 Solution

There would be a deemed disposition of her shares at FMV immediately before the time she gave up her Canadian residency. She would be required to report a taxable capital gain of \$10,500 [(1/2)(\$49,000 - \$28,000)].

Exercise 20-9 Solution

Real property situated in Canada is exempt from the deemed disposition mechanism and, as a result, there would be no income tax consequences associated with him ceasing to be a resident of Canada with respect to the rental property at the time of Mr. Chrysler's departure. However, real property situated in Canada is taxable Canadian property and therefore, as a non-resident, he would remain liable for Canadian income taxes on both recapture and capital gains resulting from a subsequent disposition of the property.

Exercise 20-10 Solution

The shares of the Canadian private company would be deemed to have been disposed of for POD at FMV of \$235,000, resulting in a taxable capital gain of \$57,500 [(1/2)(deemed POD \$235,000-ACB \$120,000)]. In the absence of an election on the rental property, this would represent the only income tax consequence resulting from the termination of her Canadian residency.

However, if Ms. Lopez elects under ITA 128.1(4)(d) (Form T2061A) a deemed disposition on her rental property, the results will be as follows:

Deemed POD for the land	\$ 30,000
ACB	(60,000)
Capital loss on the land	(\$ 30,000)

UCC of building	\$142,000
Lesser of:	
Capital cost = \$160,000	
Deemed POD = \$100,000	(100,000)
Terminal loss	\$ 42,000

The net result would be as follows:

Taxable capital gain on shares	\$57,500
Allowable capital loss on land [(1/2)(\$30,000)]	(15,000)
Terminal loss on building	(42,000)
Additional net income	\$ 500

Exercise 20-11 Solution

In the absence of ITA 128.1(4)(b)(iv), there would be a deemed disposition of both the U.K. shares and the Canadian shares at the time Mr. Brookings' ceased to be a resident of Canada. As he has been in Canada for less than 60 months in the last 10 years, there will be no deemed disposition of the U.K. shares that he owned prior to becoming a resident of Canada. There will, however, be a deemed disposition of the Canadian shares that he acquired during his residency in Canada. This will result in a taxable capital gain of \$8,500 [(1/2)(\$92,000 - \$75,000)].

There will be no deemed disposition of the vacant Canadian land because real property situated in Canada is specifically excluded from the deemed disposition/reacquisition rules of ITA 128.1(4)(b). Note, however, that land situated in Canada is taxable Canadian property, and therefore a subsequent disposition by Mr. Brooking, while non-resident, would cause him to be liable for Canadian income tax under Part I with respect to any capital gain.

Exercise 20-12 Solution

The cost of Simon's foreign property total £197,000 (£52,000 + £145,000), which puts him over the $100,000 Canadian reporting limit [(£197,000)($1.70) = $334,900] for filing Form T1135 and over the $250,000 limit for the simplified method. He is required to report the following information on the T1135:

Funds held outside Canada:
- The name of the bank that holds the funds—Bank of Scotland
- The country code for the country of residence of the bank (Scotland)—GBR (available from the CRA website)
- The maximum amount of funds held during the year—$88,400 [(£52,000)($1.70)]
- The funds held at year end—$69,700 [(£41,000)($1.70)]
- Income from the property—$1,700 [(£1,000)($1.70)]

Indebtedness owed by a non-resident:
- A description of the indebtedness—Interest-free loan to brother-in-law
- The country code for the non-resident issuer's country of residence (Scotland)—GBR (available from the CRA website)
- The maximum cost amount during the year—$246,500 [(£145,000)($1.70)]
- The year-end cost amount—$246,500 [(£145,000)($1.70)]
- The income or loss—Nil
- The gain or loss on disposition—N/A

Exercise 20-13 Solution

The $18,000 in business profits will be subject to income tax in Canada. Jason's foreign business income tax credit is $1,800, the lesser of the $1,800 foreign tax withheld and $3,780 [($18,000 ÷ $100,000)($21,000)].

The required solution would be as follows:

Foreign business profits	$18,000
Canadian tax rate	44%
Canadian income tax payable before credit	$ 7,920
Foreign tax credit	(1,800)
Net Canadian income tax payable	$ 6,120
Foreign income tax	1,800
Total income tax payable	$ 7,920

Based on these amounts, his after-tax retention and overall tax rate on his foreign source income would be as follows:

After-tax retention ($18,000 - $7,920)	$10,080
Overall tax rate ($7,920 ÷ $18,000)	44%

Exercise 20-14 Solution

Forco 1 Canvest has the required 1% ownership and, with its related subsidiary, has the required 10% share ownership. Forco 1 is an FA of Canvest.

Forco 2 Canvest has the required 1% ownership. However, as it is not related to any other shareholders, the 10% ownership test has not been met. This means that Forco 2 is not an FA of Canvest.

Forco 3 Canvest has the required 1% ownership and, with the controlling shareholder's spouse (a related person), has the required 10% ownership. Forco 3 is an FA of Canvest.

Exercise 20-15 Solution

Since Forco is a CFA of Canco, Canco must accrue its proportionate share (100%) of Forco's FAPI. The required calculations are as follows:

FAPI [ITA 91(1)]	$100,000
Deduct lesser of:	
• FAPI = $100,000	
• ITA 91(4) deduction [(4)(18%)($100,000)]	(72,000)
Addition to net income	$ 28,000

Exercise 20-16 Solution

Foreign dividend—ITA 90(1)	$82,000
Deduct lesser of:	
• Previous FAPI after ITA 91(4) deduction = $28,000	
• Dividend received = $82,000	(28,000)
Addition to net income for 2022	$54,000

Note that the additions to net income for the two years total $82,000 ($28,000 + $54,000). This is equal to the $100,000 less the $18,000 in income taxes paid to the foreign country. Had there been any withholding taxes on the dividend, they would not have been eligible for a foreign tax credit.

While this is not a required part of the problem, you should note that taxable income would be nil in this example. There would be a taxable income deduction under ITA 113(1)(b) equal to $54,000 [($18,000)(4 - 1)]. The resulting taxable income of nil reflects the fact that on Forco's income of $100,000, taxes at the usual Canadian rate of 25% have already been paid. This $25,000 [(25%)($100,000)] is made up of the $18,000 [(18%)($100,000)] paid by Forco in the foreign country plus the $7,000 [(25%)($28,000)] of Canadian income taxes on the addition to Canco's 2021 net income.

Self-Study Problem Solutions

Self-Study Problems are available to download from MyLab Accounting.

SSP 20-1 Solution
Case A

As Sharon is earning employment income in Canada, she would generally be subject to Part I income tax as a result of ITA 2(3). Article XV of the Canada/U.S. tax treaty denies Canada the right to impose income tax on Canadian employment income in two situations. The first is where the employment income does not exceed $10,000 in Canadian dollars. The second is if her stay in Canada is less than 183 days and the remuneration is not paid by a Canadian resident with a permanent establishment in Canada. Since neither of these two exceptions are met, she would be subject to Canadian income tax on the employment income earned in Canada.

Case B

As Mariah is earning employment income in Canada, she would generally be subject to Part I income tax as a result of ITA 2(3). Article XV of the Canada/U.S. tax treaty denies Canada the right to impose income tax on Canadian employment income in two situations. The first is where the employment income does not exceed $10,000 in Canadian dollars. The second is if her stay in Canada is less than 183 days and the remuneration is not paid by a Canadian resident with a permanent establishment in Canada. While her employment income exceeds $10,000, her stay in Canada is less than 183 days. In addition, the payor is not a resident of Canada that will be able to deduct the payments against Canadian income tax. As a result, the second exception is met and the employment income is not subject to Canadian income tax.

Case C

Non-residents are subject to Canadian income tax under Part I if they dispose of taxable Canadian property at a gain. Shares of a private corporation qualify as taxable Canadian property if, within 60 months of the disposition, more than 50% of the FMV of the shares is derived from Canadian real property. Article XIII of the Canada/U.S. tax treaty limits Canada's ability to impose income tax on gains of a U.S. resident to certain types of taxable Canadian property, such as shares of corporations resident in Canada that derive more than 50% of their value from Canadian real property. As a result, the tax treaty does not prevent Canada from imposing income tax under Part I on the gain. The gain is subject to Part I income tax.

Case D

Shares of unlisted companies are taxable Canadian property if at any time within the preceding 60 months more than 50% of their value is derived from Canadian real property. This means that Rae's shares would be considered taxable Canadian property and the gain would be subject to Canadian income tax as a result of ITA 2(3). The Canada/U.S. tax treaty, however, limits Canada's ability to impose income tax on gains on the disposition of shares to shares of resident corporations. Therefore, the gain would not be subject to Canadian income tax under Part I as a result of article XIII of the Canada/U.S. treaty.

Case E

Under the Canada/U.S. tax treaty (articles V and VII), Part I tax is applicable to a U.S. resident only when the business is carried on through a permanent establishment. While the U.S. company in this case is carrying on business, it is not through a permanent establishment. The treaty specifically exempts the warehouse as it is used exclusively for holding inventories. In addition, Martha Faulk could not be viewed as a permanent establishment as she does not have authority to conclude individual sales contracts. Part I tax would not apply to any business profits of Olex in this case.

Case F

This case differs from Case E in that the warehouse is used for more than holding inventories. This means that it is not an excluded facility under the Canada/U.S. tax treaty. Further, as Martha Faulk has the authority to conclude contracts, she, as a person, would be viewed as a permanent establishment. This means that Olex would be considered to be carrying on business in Canada through a permanent establishment (article V(5)). Therefore, Part I tax would apply with respect to the business profits attributable to the permanent establishment (article VII(1)).

SSP 20-2 Solution
Case A

Part XIII applies to arm's-length interest where the debt to which the interest relates is participating debt. As a result, Part XIII would apply. Article XI of the Canada/U.S. tax treaty, however, prevents Canada from charging any tax on interest payments from Canada to U.S. residents. As a result, there will be no Canadian taxes on the interest received by Martha.

Case B

As a non-resident of Canada he would be subject to Part XIII tax at a rate of 25% of gross rents received. This would require a payment of $23,500 [(25%)($94,000)]. Alternatively, he could elect under ITA 216 to be subject to Canadian income tax under Part I instead of Part XIII. His Part I liability would be $16,338 [(148%)($7,353 on the first $49,020 + (20.5% of the next $17,980))calculated on net income of $67,000 ($94,000 - $27,000). Assuming the individual had no other Canadian income, the savings would be $7,162 ($23,500- $16,338). There would be no treaty impact given that the individual resides in a country with which Canada does not have a tax treaty.

Case C

As a non-resident of Canada, Barry would be subject to Part XIII tax at a rate of 25% of the interest received since it is participating debt interest. There would be no treaty impact given that Barry resides in a country with which Canada does not have a tax treaty. Given these facts, the interest would be subject to Part XIII tax of $1,170 [(25%)($4,680)].

Case D

Part XIII tax applies to interest only if (1) the interest is paid on participating debt or (2) the interest is paid to a non-arm's-length non-resident where the interest is not fully exempt interest. The debt is not participating, and Terence is at arm's length with the Canadian bank. Given this, Part XIII tax would not apply. There would be no treaty impact given that the individual resides in a country with which Canada does not have a tax treaty.

Case E

While the Canada/U.S. tax treaty reduces the Part XIII rate on dividends, Karl is a resident of a country that does not have a tax treaty with Canada. Given this, the $8,462 in dividends would be subject to Part XIII tax, which would equal $2,115.50 [(25%)($8,462)].

SSP 20-3 Solution

When an individual ceases to be a resident of Canada, there is a deemed disposition/reacquisition of property owned at that time for POD equal to FMV. Certain types of property are excluded from this treatment. For each of the listed properties, the income tax consequences are as follows:

City home and cottage*   Real property situated in Canada is exempt from the deemed disposition/reacquisition rule. As a result, there would be no income tax consequences for this property at the time residency ceased. However, the city home is taxable Canadian property and, as a result, any subsequent gain on the disposition of the property would be subject to Canadian income tax even though Mr. Rankin would no longer be a resident of Canada.

> *Either the city home and/or the cottage could qualify for the principal residence exemption. However, this would require a deemed disposition election.

Automobile   While capital gains or personal-use property are required to be included in income, capital losses are not recognized and therefore not deductible. As a result, there would be no income tax consequences associated with the deemed disposition of the automobile.

RRSP   An interest in an RRSP is an excluded interest, which is exempt from the deemed disposition/reacquisition rules. As a result, there are no income tax consequences to Jonathan when he terminates his Canadian residency. Future periodic payments from the RRSP while a non-resident will be subject to a 15% withholding tax. Had he cashed out the RRSP in a lump sum the withholding tax would have been 25%.

Shares of a CCPC   There is no exemption from the deemed disposition/reacquisition rules for any type of shares. There would be a deemed disposition of these shares resulting in a taxable capital gain of $7,500 [(1/2)($80,000 - $65,000)].

Shares in public companies   There would be a deemed disposition of these shares, resulting in a taxable capital gain of $39,000 [(1/2)($120,000 - $42,000)].

SSP 20-4 Solution

1. Foreign investment reporting is not required as the cottage is personal-use property. The cost amount would be $365,000 and not net of the mortgage. If the property were a rental property then foreign reporting would be required.

2. No foreign property reporting is required when property is used in an active business.

3. Foreign property reporting is only required for the shares held outside of the RRSP. The cost of one-half of the shares is greater than $100,000 [(1/2)($286,000) = $143,000]. The fact that the current FMV is less than $100,000 is not relevant since the foreign reporting is based on the ACB (cost amount). Specified foreign property held in an RRSP is excluded from the foreign reporting requirements.

4. Foreign investment reporting is not required. The total of the amount owing on the mortgage for the current year ($68,000) and the highest balance in the U.S. bank account for the year ($12,000) total less than $100,000.

5. Foreign property reporting is not required since the yacht is personal-use property.

6. Foreign property reporting is not required for personal-use property. If this property were used primarily for personal use (50% or more), it would not have to be reported. However, as the information in the problem states that it is used primarily as a rental property, it would be subject to the foreign property reporting rules.

SSP 20-5 Solution

A. As a resident of Canada, the individual will earn US$14,000 of employment income, which is subject to income tax in Canada. Although employed by a U.S. resident, only half of the income, or US$7,000, relates to employment in the U.S. with the other half for employment provided in Canada. While the U.S.-based employment income would be subject to income tax in the U.S., it is prevented from taxing the U.S. income since it is less than the tax treaty limit of $10,000.

B. Because the employee is a resident of Canada, the $150,000 of employment income would be subject to income tax in Canada. The individual would not be subject to income tax in the U.S. because the provisions of the Canada/U.S. tax treaty exempt Canadian residents from U.S. income tax provided they are in the U.S. less than 183 days, their employer does not have a permanent establishment in the U.S., and their employer does not deduct the remuneration in computing U.S. taxes. The expert was in the U.S. for only 180 days [(3)(60)], and his compensation is paid by a Canadian company; therefore the treaty exemption applies to exclude the U.S. employment income from U.S. income tax.

SSP 20-6 Solution

The Hispanic Ltd. income tax withholding rate is 25% ($5,750 ÷ $23,000) of the dividend. The Deutsch Inc. income tax withholding rate is 10% ($1,400 ÷ $14,000) of the dividend. As the foreign non-business tax credit for individuals is limited to 15%, the additional 10% ($2,300) withheld by Foreign Country 1 will have to be claimed as a deduction in the determination of Mona's net income.

Employment income	$ 87,000
Hispanic Ltd. dividends	23,000
Deutsch Inc. dividends	14,000
CPP deduction	(290)
Excess withholding [(25% - 15%)($23,000)]	(2,300)
2021 net and taxable income	$ 121,410

Using this result, her federal income tax payable would be calculated as follows:

Tax on first $98,040		$ 17,402
Tax on next $23,370 ($121,410 - $98,040) at 26%		6,076
Tax payable before credits		$23,478
Basic personal credit	($13,808)	
EI	(890)	
CPP	(2,876)	
Canada employment	(1,257)	
Total credit amount	($18,831)	
Applicable rate	15%	(2,825)
Tax otherwise payable		$20,653
Foreign tax credits (see Note)		
Hispanic Ltd.		(3,450)
Deutsch Inc.		(1,400)
2021 federal income tax payable		$15,803

Note The foreign non-business tax credits are calculated on a country-by-country basis (see Chapter 11).

The tax credit on the Hispanic Ltd. shares would be the lesser of:

- Amount withheld (limited to 15%) = [(15%)($23,000)] = $3,450

- $\left[\dfrac{\text{Foreign Non - Business Income}}{\text{Adjusted Division B Income}}\right]$ (Tax Otherwise Payable)

$= \left[\dfrac{\$23,000}{\$121,410}\right]$ ($20,653) = $3,913

The tax credit on the Deutsch Inc. shares would be the lesser of:

- Amount withheld (less than 15%) = $1,400

- $\left[\dfrac{\text{Foreign Non - Business Income}}{\text{Adjusted Division B Income}}\right]$ (Tax Otherwise Payable)

$= \left[\dfrac{\$14,000}{\$121,410}\right]$ ($20,653) = $2,382

SSP 20-7 Solution
Alta Inc. Dividends

As BK Inc. owns more than 10% of the Alta Inc. shares, Alta Inc. is an FA of BK Inc. Alta Inc. is resident in a country with which Canada has a tax treaty. In addition, all of its income is from an active business. Given this, all of the dividend represent exempt surplus dividends. This means that the $34,000 of dividends paid are included in BK's 2021 net income but that a taxable income deduction of $34,000 can be claimed under ITA 113(1)(a). The result is that the 2021 taxable income is nil and therefore there are no corporate income taxes payable in Canada.

Bolt Ltd. Dividends

While all of Bolt Ltd. income is from an active business, it is not resident in a country with which Canada has a tax treaty or a TIEA. Given this, the dividend will be paid from taxable surplus. It will be included in BK's net income for 2021 and not deductible as an exempt surplus dividend as a result of ITA 113(1)(a). However, it will be eligible for a deduction under ITA 113(1)(b) for income taxes paid by Bolt Ltd. in the foreign coiuntry, as well as a deduction under ITA 113(1)(c) for dividend withholding taxes.

Below are the taxable income and federal income tax payable calculations:

Alta Inc. dividends	$ 34,000
Bolt Ltd. dividends	76,000
Addition to 2021 net income	$110,000
Deductions:	
ITA 113(1)(a) Alta dividends	(34,000)
ITA 113(1)(b)—Note 1	(12,000)
ITA 113(1)(c)—Note 2	(45,600)
Taxable income	$ 18,400
Rate	25%
2021 federal income tax payable	$ 4,600

Note 1 Given Bolt's foreign income tax rate of 5%, the pre-tax income that formed the base for the dividend to BK Inc. was $80,000 [$76,000 ÷ (1 - 5%)]. This means that the underlying foreign income tax atributable to Bolt was $4,000 [(5%)($80,000)] and

that the ITA 113(1)(b) deduction would be $12,000 [($4,000)(3)]. See the text for an explanation of the relevant factor of 3.

Note 2 Taxes withheld were $11,400. Given this, the ITA 113(1)(c) deduction is equal to $45,600 [($11,400)(4)]. See the text for an explanation of the relevant factor of 4.

Verification

In terms of the tax policy objective of taxable surplus, the goal is that the total Canadian and foreign income taxes should equal 25% as long as the foreign combined income taxes do not exceed 25%. In this instance we can reconcile the policy objective with the following calculations:

Bolt's pre-tax income [$76,000 ÷ (1 - 5%)]	$80,000
Rate	25%
Total required income tax	$20,000

Foreign income tax paid on Bolt's income [(5%)($80,000)]	$ 4,000
Foreign dividend withholding taxes	11,400
Canadian income taxes	4,600
Total income tax	$20,000

CHAPTER 21

Learning Objectives

After completing Chapter 21, you should be able to:

1. Describe, in general terms, the GST and HST and how it applies across Canada in all provinces and territories (Paragraph [P hereafter] 21-1 to 21-17).
2. Describe the different ways in which transaction-based sales taxes can be applied and the approach used by the GST/HST (P 21-18 to 21-38).
3. Explain the basic charging provision for GST/HST, who is liable for the tax, and the concept of a supply (P 21-39 to 21-43).
4. Outline the difference between fully taxable supplies, zero-rated supplies, and exempt supplies (P 21-44 to 21-58).
5. Explain the place of supply rules and how the GST/HST is applied to tangible goods, real property, and services (P 21-59 to 21-67).
6. Explain who is responsible for collecting and remitting the GST/HST (P 21-68 to 21-71).
7. Determine whether an entity is required to register for GST/HST and, if so, at what point in time registration is required. Explain the concept of a small supplier and its impact on registration (P 21-72 to 21-90).
8. Apply the rules for calculating input tax credits (ITCs) on current and capital expenditures (P 21-91 to 21-97).
9. Explain some of the basic restrictions on claiming ITCs (P 21-98 to 21-99).
10. Explain how the ITC concept applies to vendors of exempt supplies (P 21-100).
11. Explain some of the differences and similarities as to how amounts are accounted for accounting, income tax, and GST/HST purposes (P 21-101 to 21-105).
12. Determine the GST/HST payable or refund when fully taxable, zero-rated, and exempt supplies are provided (P 21-106 to 21-109).
13. Describe and apply the quick method of accounting for GST/HST and compare it to the regular method to determine the optimum choice (P 21-110 to 21-121).
14. Determine the income tax consequences of claiming ITCs and the use of the quick method (P 21-122).
15. Describe and apply the simplified method of accounting for ITCs (P 21-123 to 21-127).
16. Outline the basic compliance and administration of the GST/HST, including reporting periods, filing returns, payments and instalment obligations, the assessment of penalties and interest, and general resolution of disputes with the CRA (P 21-128 to 21-151).
17. Explain the purpose of the employee and partner GST/HST rebate and calculate the rebate for an employee (P 21-152 to 21-160).
18. Explain how the GST/HST applies when residential homes are purchased and the circumstances where a new housing rebate is available, including a general description as to how the rebate is calculated in a non-HST province or territory (P 21-161 to 21-167).
19. Describe the possible GST/HST implications resulting from the sale of a business as either a sale of assets or a sale of shares (P 21-168 to 21-171).
20. Briefly explain the GST/HST implications when rollovers under ITA 85, 87, and 88(1) apply (P 21-172 to 21-175).

21. Briefly describe how the GST/HST applies to holding companies, to intercompany transactions between members of a closely held corporate group, and the general implications when a GST/HST registrant ceases to carry on a business (P 21-176 to 21-179).

22. Briefly describe how the GST/HST applies to certain types of organizations, such as charities, NPOs, and governmental organizations (P 21-180).

23. Describe the GST/HST implications related to partner expenses, dispositions of partnership interests, transfers between a partnership and its partners, and the reorganization of partnerships (P 21-181 to 21-188).

24. Briefly explain how GST/HST applies to trusts (P 21-189 to 21-192).

How to Work through Chapter 21

Visit pearsonmylabandmastering.com to access MyLab Accounting for this text. Once there, you can access student resources such as Self-Study Problems, Practice Exams, Flashcards, updates, and more.

We recommend the following approach in dealing with the material in this chapter:

Introduction to the GST/HST
- Read paragraph 21-1 to 21-8 (in the text).

Current Sales Tax Tates in Canada and How This Text Deals with the Complexity
- Read paragraph 21-9 to 21-17.

Transaction Tax Concepts, Including VATs
- Read paragraph 21-18 to 21-38.
- Do Exercise 21-1 (in the text) and check the solution in this Study Guide.
- Do Self0Study Problem 21-1, which is available on MyLab, and check the solution in this Study Guide.

Liability for GST/HST and the Concept of Supply
- Read paragraph 21-39 to 21-43.

Supply Categories (Fully Taxable, Zero-Rated, and Exempt)
- Read from the Note before paragraph 21-44 to 21-58.

Applying the GST/HST Rate Using the Place of Supply Rules
- Read paragraph 21-59 to 21-67.

Responsibility for Collection and Remittance of GST/HST
- Read paragraph 21-68 to 21-71.

Registration, Including the Small Supplier Exemption
- Read paragraph 21-72 to 21-86.
- Do Exercise 21-2 and check the solution in this Study Guide.
- Read paragraph 21-87 to 21-90.
- Do Self-Study Problem 21-2 and check the solution in this Study Guide.

Input Tax Credits
- Read paragraph 21-91 to 21-109.
- Do Exercises 21-3 to 21-5 and check the solutions in this Study Guide.
- Do Self-Study Problems 21-3 and 21-4 and check the solutions in this Study Guide.

Relief for Small Businesses (Quick Method and Simplified ITC Method)
- Read paragraph 21-110 to 21-122.
- Do Exercises 21-6 and 21-7 and check the solutions in this Study Guide.

- Do Self-Study Problems 21-5 and 21-6 and check the solutions in this Study Guide.
- Read paragraph 21-123 to 21-127.
- Do Exercise 21-8 and check the solution in this Study Guide.

GST/HST Compliance and Administration, Including GST/HST Returns and Payments
- Read paragraph 21-128 to 21-151.

Employee and Partner GST/HST Rebate
- Read paragraph 21-152 to 21-160.
- Do Self-Study Problem 21-7 and check the solution in this Study Guide.

Residential Property and New Housing Rebate
- Read paragraph 21-161 to 21-167.
- Do Self-Study Problems 21-8 and 21-9 and check the solutions in this Study Guide.

Sale of a Business
- Read paragraph 21-168 to 21-179.

Specific Applications, Including Charities, Non-Profits, and MUSH
- Read paragraph 21-180.

Partnerships and GST/HST
- Read paragraph 21-181 to 21-188.

Trusts and GST/HST
- Read paragraph 21-189 to 21-192.

To Complete This Chapter
- Visit MyLab Accounting for more practice problem material, and test yourself with the glossary flashcards.
- Review the Key Terms at the end of the chapter, and consult the glossary for definitions.
- Ensure you have achieved the Chapter 21 Learning Objectives listed in this Study Guide.
- As a review, view the PowerPoint presentations available on MyLab.

Practice Examination
- Available on MyLab, write the Practice Examination for this chapter, and mark it using the solutions provided.

Exercise Solutions

Exercise 21-1 Solution
Accounts-Based System   Under an accounts-based system, the 5% would be applied to the value added, resulting in a tax of $7,600 [(5%)($416,000 - $264,000)].

Invoice-Credit System   Alternatively, under an invoice-credit system, $20,800 [(5%)($416,000)] would be owing on sales but would be offset by an input tax credit (ITC) of $11,650 [(5%) ($233,000)] on purchases. The net tax difference in this case would be $9,150, $1,550 larger than the $7,600 tax using the accounts-based system. While this suggests that the accounts-based system is preferable in terms of cash flow, the opposite is true given that ITCs would have been provided in previous years with respect to the opening inventory. In other words, the $1,550 difference would have already been refunded in a previous year when the goods were purchased.

Exercise 21-2 Solution
As Ms. Salome's sales *exceed* $30,000 in the October to December 2021 calendar quarter, she will be required to begin collecting GST/HST on the first sale in that quarter that causes her to exceed the $30,000 threshold. This means she will have to begin collecting GST/HST

sometime between October 1 and December 31. She will be required to register within 29 days of that date.

As Mr. Laughton's sales *accumulate* to more than $30,000 ($8,000 + $13,000 + $4,000 + $17,000 = $42,000) by the end of the January to March 2022 calendar quarter, he is required to start collecting GST/HST on the first sale on or after May 1, 2022, one month after the quarter in which the $30,000 threshold is reached. Registration is required within 29 days of the first sale on which GST is collected.

Exercise 21-3 Solution
The HST payable for the period would be calculated as follows:

HST on sales [(13%)($1,223,000)]	$158,990
Input tax credits:	
Purchases [(13%)($969,000)]	(125,970)
Salaries	N/A
Interest	N/A
Amortization	N/A
HST payable for the period	$ 33,020

Exercise 21-4 Solution
The HST payable would be calculated as follows:

HST on sales [(15%)($224,000)]	$33,600
Input tax credits:	
Rent [(15%)($25,800)]	(3,870)
Assistant's salary	N/A
Capital expenditures [(15%)($36,000 + $20,000)]	(8,400)
HST payable for the year	$21,330

Exercise 21-5 Solution
The ITC for the land and building would be $24,000 [(5%)(40%)($1,200,000)]. There would be no ITC for the office equipment as it is not used more than 50% for taxable supplies. See Figure 21-3.

Exercise 21-6 Solution
The purchases made are current expenditures and are not eligible for an ITC when using the quick method. The GST payable under the quick method would be calculated as follows:

Basic tax [(1.8%)(105%)($42,500)]	$803.25
Less: Credit on first $30,000 [(1%)($30,000)]	(300.00)
GST payable for the first quarter	$503.25

Exercise 21-7 Solution
There would be a HST refund under the regular method determined as follows:

HST on sales [(13%)($56,100)]	$ 7,293.00
ITCs:	
Current expenditures [(13%)($23,400)]	(3,042.00)
Capital expenditures [(13%)($42,000)]	(5,460.00)
HST refund for the first quarter—Regular method	($ 1,209.00)

The HST refund under the quick method would be as follows:

Basic tax [(4.4%)(113%)($56,100)]	$2,789.29
Credit on first $30,000 [(1%)($30,000)]	(300.00)
Subtotal	$2,489.29
ITCs:	
Current expenditures	Nil
Capital expenditures [(13%)($42,000)]	(5,460.00)
HST refund for the first quarter—Quick method	($2,970.71)

The quick method is preferable since it results in a larger refund.

Exercise 21-8 Solution

To apply the simplified method, we need to know the tax-inclusive amounts of current expenditures as well as the tax-inclusive amounts of capital personal property expenditures. The tax-inclusive amount of current expenditures is $189,000 and the tax-inclusive amount of capital personal property expenditures is $52,500 [(105%)($50,000)]. Using the simplified method, the GST payable or GST refund would be calculated as follows:

GST sales [($315,000)(5/105)]	$15,000
ITCs on purchases and capital personal property	
[(5/105)($189,000 + $52,500)]	(11,500)
ITCs on capital real property [(5%)($150,000)]	(7,500)
GST refund	($ 4,000)

Self-Study Problem Solutions

Self-Study Problems are available to download from MyLab.

SSP 21-1 Solution
GST Calculation

Under the GST system, a 5% rate is applied on the selling price at each stage, and the business is eligible for an ITC for any GST paid on purchases. The net result is that, in the production and distribution stages, all payments of GST by sellers are refunded as ITCs by purchasers with the exception of the end consumer. As a result, there is no net out-of-pocket cost (other than administration) to sellers from the GST.

Seller	Cost	Selling Price	GST Charged	ITC Claimed
Raw materials supplier		$ 100	$ 5.00	Nil
Manufacturer	$100	150	7.50	$ 5.00
Wholesaler	150	225	11.25	7.50
Distributor	225	338	16.90	11.25
Retailer	338	507	25.35	16.90
Totals		$1,320	$66.00	$40.65

The net GST for all stages is $25.35 ($66.00 - $40.65), which is the GST that would be paid by the end consumer without the benefit of any ITC.

Turnover Tax Calculation

A strict turnover tax is similar to the GST, as it would apply to each selling price but without any ITCs. The turnover tax would simply be passed on to the ultimate consumer. Raising the same amount of net tax revenue of $25.35 would require a turnover tax rate of 1.92% ($25.35 ÷ $1,320).

SSP 21-2 Solution
Calendar Quarter Test
Under this test, persons are required to register for the GST/HST if revenues from taxable supplies before expenses exceed $30,000 in any single calendar quarter. Chantelle is not required to register as a result of this test since the limit is not exceeded in any calendar quarter.

Last Four Consecutive Calendar Quarters Test (Cumulative)
Under this test, persons are required to register for the GST/HST if revenues from taxable supplies before expenses total more than $30,000 in any four consecutive calendar quarters. In this problem four quarters of sales accumulate to $36,500 ($6,500 + $9,000 + $9,500 + $11,500) by the end of the calendar quarter ending December 31, 2021.

As a result, Chantelle Chance is required to start collecting GST/HST beginning with the first taxable supply made on or after February 1, 2022. Registration is officially required within 29 days of that first sale.

SSP 21-3 Solution
The HST refund for Sheila Norton for the current year would be calculated as follows:

HST collected [(13%)($250,000)]	$32,500
Input tax credits—Current expenditures:	
Purchases of fully taxable goods	
[(13%)($185,000)]	(24,050)
Purchases of zero-rated goods (Note 1)	Nil
Amortization expense (Note 2)	Nil
Salaries and wages (Note 3)	Nil
Interest expense (Note 3)	Nil
Other expenses [(13%)(100%)($10,000)] (Note 4)	(1,300)
Input tax credits—Capital expenditures:	
Building [(13%)(40%)($480,000)] (Note 5)	(24,960)
Equipment (Note 6)	Nil
HST payable (refund)	($17,810)

Note 1 HST is not payable on purchases of zero-rated goods. As a consequence, there are no ITCs.

Note 2 Amortization expense does not result in an ITC.

Note 3 No HST is payable on salaries and wages or interest. As a result, there are no ITCs.

Note 4 As more than 90% of the other expenses are attributable to taxable supplies, Sheila Norton is eligible for a 100% ITC.

Note 5 ITCs on real property are available based on the portion of use attributable to either fully taxable or zero-rated supplies.

Note 6 ITCs are not available on capital expenditures other than real property unless more than 50% of the use is attributable to fully taxable and zero-rated supplies.

SSP 21-4 Solution

The GST refund for Lassen Ltd. for the current year would be calculated as follows:

GST collected [(5%)($$2,100,000)]	$ 105,000
Input tax credits:	
Purchases [(5%)($2,400,000)]	(120,000)
Amortization expense	N/A
Salaries and wages	N/A
Interest expense	N/A
Other expenses {[5%][$370,000 - (50%)($40,000)]}	(17,500)
Income tax	N/A
Building [(5%)(40%)($3,000,000)]	(60,000)
Equipment	N/A
GST refund	($ 92,500)

Notes:

- The fact that GST is paid on all purchases is not unreasonable, despite the fact that the company provides both zero-rated and exempt supplies to its customers. Some zero-rated supplies, for example exports, involve selling items on which GST is paid. Exempt supplies could include the provision of certain types of services for which no purchases are required.

- Amortization expense is not entitled to an ITC.

- No GST is payable on salaries and wages, interest, or income taxes. As a result no ITCs are available.

- An ITC is only available with respect to meals and entertainment expenses to the extent of the deduction allowed for income tax purposes, which in this case is 50% of the actual expense.

- ITCs on real property equal the percentage use attributable to either fully taxable or zero-rated supplies if that usage is greater than 10% and less than 90%.

- ITCs are only available on capital expenditures such as equipment if the usage attributable to fully taxable and zero-rated supplies exceeds 50%. If that test is met the ITC is equal to 100% of the GST/HST.

SSP 21-5 Solution

The following recommendations are based solely on minimizing the GST payment. No consideration has been given to any cost savings, such as reduced accounting costs, that would generally be available with the use of the quick method.

Claire—Service Business

The quick method would be preferable in this case.

Regular Method

Net GST [($150,000 - $35,000)(5 ÷ 105)]	$5,476

Quick Method

Basic tax [($150,000)(3.6%)]	$5,400
Credit on first $30,000 [(1%)($30,000)]	(300)
Net GST	$5,100

Barbara—Retailer

The regular method is preferable in this case.

Regular Method

Net GST [($150,000 - $100,000)(5 ÷ 105)]	$2,381

Quick Method

Basic tax [($150,000)(1.8%)]	$2,700
Credit on first $30,000 [(1%)($30,000)]	(300)
Net GST	$2,400

Nicole—Service Business

The quick method would be preferable in this case.

Regular Method

Net GST [($120,000 - $35,000)(5 ÷ 105)]	$4,048

Quick Method

Basic tax [($120,000)(3.6%)]	$4,320
Credit on first $30,000 [(1%)($30,000)]	(300)
Net GST	$4,020

Elizabeth—Retailer

The quick method would be preferable in this case.

Regular Method

Net GST [($120,000 - $75,000)(5 ÷ 105)]	$2,143

Quick Method

Basic tax [($120,000)(1.8%)]	$2,160
Credit on first $30,000 [(1%)($30,000)]	(300)
Net GST	$1,860

SSP 21-6 Solution
Part A

The HST refund for Larkin Ltd. using the regular method for the current year would be calculated as follows:

HST collected [(13%)($103,000)]	$13,390
Input tax credits on current expenditures:	
Purchases [(13%)($69,000)]	(8,970)
Amortization expense	N/A
Salaries and wages	N/A
Rent [(13%)($24,000)]	(3,120)
Interest expense	N/A
Other expenses [(13%)($12,000)]	(1,560)
Input tax credits on capital expenditures	
[(100%)($36,160)(13 ÷ 113)]	(4,160)
HST refund	($ 4,420)

Notes:

- Amortization expense does not affect the HST calculation.

- No HST is paid on salaries and wages or interest. As a result no input tax credits are available.

- Full input tax credits are available on capital expenditures other than real property and passenger vehicles if the property is used more than 50% of the time to provide taxable or zero-rated supplies. Since the taxable supply use is 60%, a full 100% ITC is available.

Part B

As Larkin's HST-included taxable sales of $116,390 [(113%)($103,000)] is less than $400,000 and it is not engaged in an ineligible business such as accounting, Larkin is eligible to use the quick method.

Part C

The HST payable using the quick method would be as follows:

Basic tax [(4.4%)(113%)($103,000)]	$5,121
Credit on first $30,000 [(1%)($30,000)]	(300)
Total before capital expenditures	$4,821
Input tax credits on capital expenditures	
[(100%)($36,160)(13 ÷ 113)]	(4,160)
HST payable	$ 661

In this case, the regular method for determining HST is preferable as it results in a refund rather than a payable.

SSP 21-7 Solution

The maximum CCA that George can claim is as follows:

Opening UCC ($27,750 - $12,488)	$15,262
Less: GST rebate claimed on CCA in 2020	(595)
Adjusted UCC	14,667
Class 10 rate	30%
Maximum CCA	$ 4,400

The employee GST rebate for George in 2021 would be calculated as follows:

Total expenses other than CCA	$28,220	
Less: GST exempt expenses:		
Interest	(2,600)	
Insurance	(1,200)	
Eligible expenses other than CCA	$24,420	
Rate	5/105	$1,163
Eligible CCA	$ 4,400	
Rate	5/105	210
Employee GST rebate		$1,373

In 2022 George will add the 2021 GST rebate related to current expenses of $1,163 to his employment income and reduce the capital cost and therefore the UCC of the car by a further $210 for the GST rebate on the car.

SSP 21-8 Solution

The calculation of the new housing GST rebate is as follows:

$$[A][(\$450{,}000 - B) \div \$100{,}000], \text{ where}$$

A = The lesser of 36% of the GST paid and $6,300; and
B = The greater of $350,000 and the cost of the home.

The GST and total cost of each purchase would be as follows.

Property A

The renovations involve more than 90% of the interior and therefore are considered substantial. Since the renovations would be done by the vendor prior to the sale, the purchase would be deemed to be that of a "new" home. As a result, the total purchase price would be subject to GST and a new housing rebate could be claimed on the total, as follows:

GST payable [($370,000)(5%)]	$ 18,500
Less new housing rebate, where	
A = the lesser of [(36%)($18,500)] = $6,660 and $6,300	
B = the greater of $350,000 and $370,000	
[$6,300][($450,000 - $370,000) ÷ $100,000]	(5,040)
Net GST payable	$ 13,460
Purchase price	370,000
Total cost	$383,460

Property B

As this property is a used residential unit, no GST will be payable. This means that the total cost will be $387,000.

Property C

GST will be paid on the purchase price of $323,000 plus all of the improvements. However, the new housing rebate is only available on the $10,000 cost of the improvements done by the builder in addition to the purchase price. It is not available on the additional $12,000 of costs incurred by Martin.

GST payable [($323,000 + $10,000 + $12,000)(5%)]	$ 17,250
Less new housing rebate, where	
A = the lesser of [(36%)(5%)($323,000 + $10,000)] = $5,994 and $6,300	
B = the greater of $350,000 and $345,000	
[$5,994][($450,000 - $350,000) ÷ $100,000]	(5,994)
Net GST payable	$ 11,256
Purchase price ($323,000 + $10,000 + $12,000)	345,000
Total cost	$356,256

SSP 21-9 Solution

Since in all three cases the purchase price is less than $350,000, the new housing rebate is calculated at 36% of the GST paid.

Case A

The total GST included in the purchase price is $9,524 [(5/105)($200,000)].

The new housing GST rebate would be $3,429 [($9,524)(36%)].

As it appears that the purchaser will be paying the GST, that individual would be entitled to the rebate.

The net GST paid would be $6,095 ($9,524 - $3,429).

Case B

The total GST that would be charged is $10,000 [(5%)($200,000)].

The new housing rebate would be $3,600 [($10,000)(36%)].

As it appears that the purchaser will be paying the GST, that individual would be entitled to the rebate.

The net GST paid would be $6,400 ($10,000 - $3,600).

Case C

Since $200,000 is equal to the price of the house including GST net of the new housing rebate, the GST-excluded price can be calculated by solving the following equation for x:

$$\$200,000 = [(105\%)(x) - (36\%)(5\%)(x)]$$

The GST-excluded price of the new house would be $193,798 {$200,000 ÷ [105% - (36%)(5%)]}. The total GST amount is $9,690 [($193,798)(5%)].

The new housing rebate would be $3,488 [($9,690)(36%)].

A verification of these numbers is as follows: $193,798 + $9,690 - $3,488 = $200,000.

The only GST that will be remitted is being paid by the vendor, so it can be assumed that the vendor has been assigned the rights to the GST rebate. As a consequence, the $3,488 rebate would be claimed by the vendor.

The net GST paid would be $6,202 ($9,690 - $3,488).

GLOSSARY

A

Accelerated investment Incentive (AccII) A temporary program that encourages investments in capital assets by providing an accelerated CCA deduction on net acquisitions during the year of acquisition.

Accounting Income The net of revenues plus gains, less expenses plus losses, with all amounts determined by accounting standards and principles such as ASPE and IFRS. (See also Net Income for Tax Purposes.)

Accrual Basis A method of accounting for income based on recording assets when the right to receive them is established and liabilities when the obligation to pay them arises.

Acquisition of Control Acquisition of sufficient voting shares of a corporation, by a person, or group of persons, that they have the right to elect a majority of the board of directors of the corporation.

Active Business A business carried on by a taxpayer, other than a specified investment business or a personal services business.

Active Business Income Income earned by an active business.

Additional Refundable Tax (ART) A 10 2/3% tax on the aggregate investment income of a CCPC.

Adjusted Active Business Income A term used in calculating the M&P deduction, defined as the excess of a corporation's income from active business, less a corporation's losses from active business. It does not appear to be a different concept than active business income of a corporation.

Adjusted Aggregate Investment Income (AAII) A modified version of aggregate investment income that is used to calculate a possible grind of the annual business limit for the small business deduction.

Adjusted Cost Base For depreciable capital property it is the cost of the property to the taxpayer. For non-depreciable capital property it is the cost of the property to the taxpayer subject to ITA 53 adjustments (e.g., deduction of government grants on land purchase).

Adjusted Taxable Income Regular taxable income, adjusted to remove certain tax preferences. Used to calculate the alternative minimum tax.

Adoption Expenses Tax Credit A credit against tax payable that is available to individuals with eligible adoption expenses.

Advance Tax Ruling Interpretations provided, at the request of a taxpayer, by the income tax Rulings Directorate as to how a particular transaction will be treated for tax purposes. Such interpretations are not binding on the CRA.

Affiliated Group of Persons A group of persons, each member of which is affiliated with every other member.

Affiliated Person—ITA 251.1(1) For an individual, an affiliated person is that individual's spouse or common-law partner. For a corporation, an affiliated person is a person or an affiliated group of persons who controls the corporation, or the spouse or common-law partner of either the person who controls, or a member of the group that controls. More complex rules apply to determine affiliation between two corporations.

Age Tax Credit A credit against tax payable that is available to individuals who are 65 years of age or older.

Aggregate Investment Income As defined in ITA 129(4), this concept of investment income includes net taxable capital gains for the year reduced by any net capital loss carry overs deducted in the year, interest income, rents, and royalties.

Alimony A term that was used at an earlier point in time to refer to both spousal support and child support.

Allowable Business Investment Loss (ABIL) The deductible portion (currently one-half) of a business investment loss.

Allowable Capital Loss The deductible portion (currently one-half) of a capital Loss.

Allowance An amount paid by an employer to an employee to provide for certain types of costs incurred by the employee, usually travel costs or automobile costs.

Alter Ego Trust An inter vivos trust established by an individual aged 65 years or more, subject to the conditions that the individual must be entitled to all of the trust's income during his or her lifetime, and the individual must be the only person who can access the capital of the trust during his or her lifetime.

Alternative Minimum Tax (AMT)   A tax, calculated at the minimum federal rate on adjusted taxable income, less a basic $40,000 exemption.

Amalgamation   A rollover provision that allows two taxable Canadian corporations to be combined into a single taxable Canadian corporation, without tax consequences.

Annual Business Limit   The maximum amount of active business income that is eligible for the small businss deduction in a particular taxation year (currently $500,000).

Annual Child Care Expense Amount   The annual per child limit for deductible child care expense. The amount is $5,000, $8,000, or $11,000, depending on the age and health of the child.

Annual Gains Limit (AGL)   Taxable capital gains for the current year on qualified assets, less the sum of allowable capital losses and net capital loss carry overs deducted during the current year, plus allowable business investment losses realized during the current year. Used to determine the lifetime capital gains deduction for the current year.

Annuitant   This term is used to describe a person who is receiving an annuity. However, in tax publications this term is often (and incorrectly) used to refer to the beneficiary of an RRSP or RPP.

Annuity   A series of periodic payments that continues for a specified period of time, or until the occurrence of some event (e.g., the death of the annuitant).

Anti-Avoidance Provision   A provision in the *Income Tax Act* that is designed to prevent a taxpayer from taking some action that would allow him or her to avoid taxes.

Apprenticeship Job Creation Tax Credit   An investment tax credit that is available to eligible employers (individuals and corporations) for salaries and wages paid to qualifying apprentices.

Arm's Length   ITA 251(1) indicates that related persons (see definition) do not deal with each other at arm's length. Also, a taxpayer and a personal trust do not deal with each other at arm's length. In other cases, it is a question of fact as to whether an arm's-length relation exists.

ART   An acronym for "additional refundable tax on investment income."

Assessment   A formal determination of taxes to be paid or refunded. A reassessment is a form of assessment.

Associated Corporations   Two or more corporations that have an ownership/control arrangement that falls into one of the categories described in ITA 256(1) (e.g., two corporations controlled by the same person).

At-Risk Amount (ARA)   A defined measure that limits the amount of deductions that can be flowed through to a limited partner.

At-Risk Rules   A set of rules, directed largely at limited partners, designed to prevent an investment from creating tax deductions that exceed the amount invested (the at-risk amount).

B

Beneficiary   The person who will receive the benefits from a trust.

Billed Basis   A method of determining net business income based on recording inclusions when the relevant amounts are billed. Can only be used by certain specified types of professionals (e.g., accountants).

Bonus Arrangement   As used in this material, a tax planning arrangement for employees. A corporation declares and deducts a bonus near the end of its fiscal year. It is usually designed to be paid to the employee early in the following calendar year. As employment income is taxed on a cash basis, the bonus will not be taxed in the employee's hands until that year.

Bonusing Down   A process of paying deductible salary to the owner-manager of a CCPC, or related parties, in order to eliminate corporate taxable income that is not eligible for the small business deduction.

Boot   A colloquial term used by tax practitioners to refer to non-share consideration.

Business   A business is a self-sustaining integrated set of activities and assets conducted and managed for the purpose of providing a return to investors. A business consists of (a) inputs, (b) processes applied to those inputs, and (c) resulting outputs that are used to generate revenues.

Business Combination   A transaction in which an enterprise acquires net assets that constitute a business, or acquires an equity interest in a corporation that gives the enterprise control over the operating, financing, and investing decisions of that corporation.

Business Income   Income that is earned through active business activity. This would include amounts earned by producing goods, selling goods or services, or delivering services. While usage is not always consistent, this term usually refers to a net amount (i.e., inclusions less deductions, or revenues less expenses).

Business Investment Loss (BIL)   A loss resulting from the disposition of shares or debt of a small business corporation.

Business Limit   An expression defined in the *Income Tax Act* that represents the maximum amount of the active business income of A CCPC that is eligible for the small business deduction. The current limit is $500,000, which must be share among associated corporations.

C

Canada Caregiver Amount for Child   A credit against tax payable that is available to an individual who provides care and/or support for a child under 18 years of age who has a mental or physical infirmity.

Canada Caregiver Tax Credit A credit against tax payable that is available to an individual who provides care and/or support for certain specified dependants who have a mental or physical infirmity.

Canada Disability Savings Bonds A system of grants under which the federal government makes contributions to an individual's RDSP based on family net income.

Canada Disability Savings Grants A system of grants under which the federal government makes contributions to an individual's RDSP based on a percentage of the contributions to that individual's RDSP that have been made by others.

Canada Education Savings Grants (CESG) A system of grants under which the federal government makes contributions to an individual's RESP based on a percentage of the contributions to that individual's RESP that have been made by others.

Canada Employment Credit A credit against tax payable that is available to individuals with employment income.

Canada Learning Bonds A system of grants under which the federal government makes contributions to an individual's RESP based on the number of years in which the individual's family is eligible for the National Child Benefit supplement.

Canada Pension Plan (CPP) A pension plan sponsored by the federal government. Individuals with employment or business income must make contributions based on their income and, in return, they receive benefits in future years.

Canada Pension Plan Tax Credit A credit against tax payable that is available to individuals making contributions to the Canada Pension Plan.

Canada Training Credit A refundable credit that provides a refund to eligible individuals for a portion of training-related costs.

Canada Workers Benefit A refundable credit available to low-income individuals who are earning employment and business income (formerly Working Income Tax Benefit).

Canadian controlled private corporation (CCPC) A corporation that is controlled by persons resident in Canada and that does not have any of its shares listed on a designated stock exchange.

Canadian corporation A corporation that is resident in Canada.

Canadian Partnership A partnership, all of the members of which are residents of Canada at the time the term is relevant.

Capital Cost The amount paid to acquire a depreciable asset. The tax equivalent of acquisition cost in accounting.

Capital Cost Allowance (CCA) A deduction in the determination of business or property income based on the capital cost of capital assets. The tax equivalent of accounting amortization.

Capital Dividend A dividend paid out of a private corporation's capital dividend account. It is received on a tax-free basis.

Capital Dividend Account (CDA) An account that tracks a group of items, defined in ITA 89(1), that can be distributed by private corporations to shareholders as a tax-free capital dividend (e.g., the non-taxable portion of realized capital gains).

Capital Gain The excess of proceeds resulting from the disposition of a capital asset over the sum of the adjusted cost base of the asset plus any costs of disposition.

Capital Gains Deduction A deduction in the calculation of the taxable income of an individual. It permits the deduction of a cumulative lifetime amount of capital gains resulting from the disposition of qualified small business corporation shares or qualified farm or fishing property.

Capital Gain Reserve A reserve that is deductible against capital gains. It is available when some part of the proceeds of disposition is not collected in the period of disposition.

Capital Gains Stripping Procedures designed to allow a corporation to convert a taxable capital gain resulting from the disposition of investment shares to an arm's-length party into a tax-free intercorporate dividend.

Capital Interest (in a trust) All rights of the taxpayer as a beneficiary under the trust, other than those that are an income interest in the trust.

Capital Loss The excess of the sum of the adjusted cost base of a capital asset plus any costs of disposition over the proceeds resulting from the disposition of the asset.

Capital Property For GST purposes, any capital property other than real property.

Capital Tax A tax assessed on the capital of a corporation, without regard to its income.

Carry Over As used in tax work, the ability to apply current-year losses against income in earlier or later years.

Cash Basis A method of accounting for income based on cash receipts and cash disbursements.

Charitable Donations Tax Credit A credit against tax payable that is available to individuals making donations to qualifying charitable organizations.

Charitable Gifts Donations to a registered charity, a registered Canadian amateur athletic association, a housing corporation resident in Canada that is exempt from tax under ITA 149(1)(i), a Canadian municipality, the United

Nations or an agency thereof, a university outside of Canada that normally enrolls Canadian students, or a charitable organization outside of Canada to which Her Majesty in right of Canada has made a gift in the year or in the immediately preceding year.

Child Care Expenses Costs associated with caring for an eligible child.

Child Support A support amount that is not identified as being for the benefit of a spouse or common-law partner or a former spouse or common-Law partner.

Class As used in tax work, a defined group of depreciable assets for which the *Income Tax Regulations* specify the CCA rate to be applied, as well as the method to be used in applying the rate.

Clawback An income tested taxing back, or reduction, in the payment of Old Age Security benefits and Employment Insurance benefits.

Climate Action Incentive Payments A refundable credit based on family size that is available to the residents of four provinces and two territories, specifically Manitoba, New Brunswick, Ontario, Saskatchewan, Nunavut, and Yukon.

Commercial Activity This is a GST term that refers to any business or trade carried on by a person or any supply of real property made by a person. Commercial activity does not include any activity involved with making an exempt supply or any activity engaged in by an individual without a reasonable expectation of profit.

Commodity Tax A type of transaction tax that is applied to the sale of certain types of commodities (e.g., taxes on the sale of tobacco products).

Common Shares Corporate shares that normally have all of the rights that are provided for under the relevant corporate enabling legislation. While there may be variations in the rights of such shares, at a minimum voting rights would have to be present for the shares to be considered common shares.

Common-Law Partner A person who cohabits in a conjugal relationship with the taxpayer and (a) has so cohabited with the taxpayer for a continuous period of at least one year, or (b) is a parent of a child of whom the taxpayer is also a parent.

Connected Corporation Corporation A is connected with corporation B if corporation B controls corporation A, or if corporation B owns more than 10% of the voting shares of corporation A and more than 10% of the fair market value of all issued shares of corporation A.

Consumption Tax A tax levied on the consumption of some product or service. This type of tax is also called a sales tax.

Contributed Capital In accounting usage, the amount of a corporation's shareholders' equity that was received in return for issuing the shares that are currently outstanding.

Control Owning a sufficient number of shares (typically more than 50%) to entitle one to elect the majority of the members of the board of directors.

Controlled—ITA 251.1(3) Under ITA 251.1(3), controlled means controlled, directly or indirectly, in any manner whatever. (The reference here is to de facto control, which does not necessarily require majority ownership of shares.)

Controlled Foreign Affiliate (CFA) A foreign affiliate of the taxpayer that was controlled by (a) the taxpayer, (b) the taxpayer and not more than four other persons resident in Canada, (c) not more than four persons resident in Canada, other than the taxpayer, (d) a person or persons with whom the taxpayer does not deal at arm's length, or (e) the taxpayer and a person or persons with whom the taxpayer does not deal at arm's length.

Convertible Property A debt or equity financial instrument of a corporation that can be exchanged for an equity financial instrument of the same corporation without the payment of additional consideration.

Co-ownership Ownership of a single real or personal property by two or more persons.

Corporation An artificial legal entity created through either federal or provincial legislation.

Crowdfunding Funding a project, venture, or business by raising funds from a large number of people, usually in small amounts and usually via the internet.

Crown gifts Gifts made to Her Majesty in right of Canada or to Her Majesty in right of a province.

Cultural gifts Gifts of objects that the Canadian Cultural Property Export Review Board has determined meet the criteria of the *Cultural Property and Import Act*.

Cumulative Gains Limit (CGL) Taxable capital gains on qualified assets that have been realized since 1984, less the sum of allowable capital losses and net capital loss carry overs deducted after 1984, plus allowable business investment losses realized after 1984, capital gains deductions claimed in previous taxation years, and the cumulative net investment loss at the end of the year. Used to determine the lifetime capital gains deduction for the current year.

Cumulative Net Investment Loss (CNIL) The amount by which the aggregate of investment expenses for the current year and prior years ending after 1987 exceed the aggregate of investment income for that period.

Customs Duties A tax imposed on the importation or exportation of certain goods or services.

D

Death Benefit All amounts in excess of $10,000 that are received by a taxpayer in a taxation year, on or after the death of an employee, in recognition of the employee's service in an office or employment.

Declining Balance Method   A method of calculating CCA in which a specified rate is applied to the ending UCC balance in a depreciable asset class to determine the CCA for the period.

Deemed Disposition   A requirement to assume that a disposition has taken place when, in fact, a disposition transaction has not occurred (e.g., a change in use is deemed to be a disposition).

Deemed Dividends   A group of capital transactions and distributions, as specified in ITA 84(1), that are deemed to be dividend payments.

Deemed Resident   An individual who is considered a resident of Canada because of some factor other than physical presence in Canada (e.g., members of the Canadian Armed Forces are deemed to be Canadian residents under ITA 250 without regard to where they are physically located).

Deeming Rules   Rules that are used to require that an item or event be given a treatment for tax purposes that is not consistent with the actual nature of the item or event (e.g., members of the Canadian Armed Forces are deemed to be Canadian residents even if they are not present in Canada at any time during the year).

Deferred Income Plans   A group of plans that allow individuals to receive income on a tax-deferred basis. These include registered pension plans, deferred profit-sharing plans, registered retirement savings plans, and registered retirement income funds.

Deferred Profit-Sharing Plan (DPSP)   A trusteed plan to which employers can make deductible contributions, the amount of which is related to the profits of the enterprise, and which do not create a taxable benefit for the recipient employees. Earnings accumulate tax free within the plan. Withdrawals from the plan are subject to tax.

Defined Benefit Plan   A retirement savings plan in which the plan sponsor (usually an employer) promises a known or determinable retirement benefit and assumes financial responsibility for providing that benefit.

Defined Contribution Plan   A retirement savings plan in which the plan sponsor (employer or individual) makes known or determinable contributions. The retirement benefit is based on the accumulated contributions and earnings on investments within the plan.

Dependant   As defined in ITA 118(6), an individual who, at any time during the year, is dependent on the taxpayer for support and is the child or grandchild of the individual or of the individual's spouse or common-law partner, the parent, grandparent, brother, sister, uncle, aunt, niece, or nephew, if resident in Canada at any time in the year, of the individual or of the individual's spouse or common-law partner.

Depreciable Property   Capital property, such as equipment or furniture and fixtures, that is subject to depreciation or amortization.

Designated Stock Exchange   A stock exchange that has been designated as such by the minister of Finance. Replaces the term "prescribed stock exchange."

Digital News Subscriptions Credit   A non-refundable tax credit for individuals based on their expenditures for digital subscriptions with a qualifying Canadian journalism organization.

Disability Supports Deduction   A deduction available to individuals for attendant care and other disability support expenses incurred to allow the disabled individual to work or to attend a designated educational institution.

Disability Tax Credit   A credit against tax payable that is available to individuals with a doctor-certified severe mental or physical disability. Can be transferred to a supporting individual.

Disability Tax Credit Supplement   A supplement to the disability tax credit available to individuals who are under 18 years of age at the end of the year.

Disappearing Source Rule   Rules designed to provide relief to investors who have borrowed money to make an investment and subsequently sold the investment for less than the related borrowings. These rules provide that any amount of debt that remains after the proceeds of the sale used to pay off a portion of the total balance are deemed to be debt that is used to produce income.

Discretionary Trust   A trust for which the settlor has given the trustee discretion to decide the amounts of income or capital to be allocated to each beneficiary.

Disposition   The disposal of an asset through sale, gift, physical destruction, conversion, expropriation, or other means.

Dividend Gross Up   An amount that is based on a percentage of the dividends from taxable Canadian corporations that have been received by an individual or trust. This amount must be included in the net income of the individual or trust.

Dividend Stripping   Procedures designed to allow an individual to remove accumulated income from a corporation in the form of tax-free capital gains while still retaining control of the corporation.

Dividend Tax Credit   A credit against the tax payable of an individual or trust. The amount is based on a fraction of the dividend gross up that has been included in net income.

Dividends   Amounts declared and paid, at the discretion of management, as a return on equity investments.

Dividends in Kind   Dividends, other than stock dividends, paid in corporate assets other than cash.

Division B Income   An alternative name for net income.

Double Taxation   A reference to situations in which the same stream of income is subject to tax a second time.

Dual Resident   A taxpayer who is considered to be a resident of two countries.

E

Earned Capital   See Retained Earnings.

Earned Income (Child Care Expenses)   For purposes of determining the deductible amount of child care expenses, earned income is defined as employment income (gross), business income (not losses), and income from scholarships, training allowances, and research grants.

Earned Income (RRSP Limit)   The sum of employment income (without the RPP deduction), business income (losses), royalties (if the taxpayer is the author, inventor, or composer), taxable (deductible) support payments, supplementary unemployment benefits, income (loss) as an active partner, net rental income (loss), research grants (net of certain expenses), and CPP disability benefits.

Earned Surplus   An archaic accounting description of what now is called retained earnings. However, the term continues to be found in the *Income Tax Act*.

Ecological Gifts   Gifts of land certified by the minister of the Environment to be ecologically sensitive land, the conservation and protection of which is important to the preservation of Canada's environmental heritage.

Election   A choice that is available to a taxpayer with respect to a particular tax outcome (e.g., a taxpayer can elect to have the spousal rollover provision not be applicable).

Eligible Capital Expenditure   This term was used to refer to an amount expended to acquire an intangible asset that was not eligible for CCA or deduction. No longer available after 2016.

Eligible Capital Property   An intangible asset that results from making an eligible capital expenditure.

Eligible Child   With respect to the deductibility of child care expenses, a child of the taxpayer, his or her spouse, or a child who is dependent on the taxpayer or his or her spouse, and whose income does not exceed the basic personal tax credit base amount. An eligible child must either be under 16 years of age at some time during the year or dependent on the taxpayer or his or her spouse by reason of physical or mental infirmity.

Eligible Dependant Tax Credit   A credit against tax payable that is available to a single individual supporting a dependant in a self-contained domestic establishment.

Eligible Dividends   Dividends that have been designated by the payor as eligible for the enhanced gross up and tax credit procedure.

Eligible Newsroom Employee   An individual who is employed by a qualifying Canadian news organization and who spends at least 75% of his or her time engaged in the production of news content, including researching, collecting information, verifying facts, photographing, writing, editing, designing, and otherwise preparing content.

Eligible RDTOH   A balance containing refundable taxes that are available for dividend refunds on eligible dividends paid.

Emigration   Leaving a country, usually to establish permanent residency in another country.

Employee   An individual who has an employment relationship with an entity that provides remuneration. Whether or not an individual is working as an employee or a self-employed individual is dependent on factors such as control, ownership of tools, chance of profit or risk of loss, and the ability to subcontract or hire an assistant.

Employee and Partner GST/HST Rebate   A provision that allows employees and partners to recover the GST paid on their employment or partnership related expenses.

Employee Profit-Sharing Plans (EPSP)   A trusteed plan to which employers can make deductible contributions, the amount of which is related to the profits of the enterprise. Both the contributions and the earnings resulting from their investment are taxed in the hands of the employees as they occur. Payments from the plan are received by the employees on a tax-free basis.

Employer/Employee Relationship   A written, verbal, or tacit agreement in which an employee agrees to work on a full-time or part-time basis for an employer for a specified or indeterminate period of time in return for salary or wages. The employer has the right to decide where, when, and how the work will be done. In this type of relationship, a contract of services exists.

Employment Income   The salary, wages, and other remuneration, including gratuities, received by an employee in the year (see Employer/Employee Relationship).

Employment Insurance (EI)   A federal insurance plan designed to provide benefits to unemployed individuals. In order to receive benefits, employees must make contributions when they are employed.

Employment Insurance Tax Credit   A credit against tax payable that is available to employees making payments to the federal Employment Insurance plan.

Estate   As the term is used in the *Income Tax Act*, the property of a deceased individual.

Estate Freeze   Procedures undertaken by an individual to fix a tax value for all or part of the individual's property and to transfer future growth in the value of this property to other individuals.

Estate Planning   Tax planning directed toward the distribution of an individual's property at death.

Excessive Eligible Dividend Designation (EEDD)   A balance, subject to Part III.1 tax, that reflects an inappropriate designation of an amount of dividends paid as an eligible dividend.

Exchange of Shares in a Reorganization (ITA 86) A rollover provision that allows one class of shares in a corporation to be exchanged for a different class of shares without tax consequences.

Excluded Business A business is an excluded business of a specified individual if that individual is actively engaged in its activities on a regular, continuous, and substantial basis, either in the current taxation year or, alternatively, in any five prior taxation years.

Excluded Shares For shares to be classified as excluded shares, the specified individual must be aged 25 or older and must own, in terms of both fair market value and voting rights, at least 10% of the outstanding shares of the corporation. In addition, the corporation must not be a professional corporation, less than 90% of its business in the previous taxation year is from services, and less than 10% of its income in the previous year is from a related business.

Executor A person appointed by an individual in his or her will to oversee the administration of the estate on his or her death in accordance with the terms of that will.

Exempt Goods and Services Goods and services that are not subject to the GST. Registrants who sell exempt goods and services are not eligible for input tax credits for GST paid. Examples include sales of used residential housing, most medical services, and most financial services.

Exempt Surplus A surplus account that tracks certain sources of income of a foreign affiliate.

F

Fairness Package Replaced by the taxpayer relief provisions.

Family Trust An inter vivos trust, established by an individual, with family members as beneficiaries.

Farm Property Farm property includes real estate and property that is used in farming activities, a share of a corporation that is carrying on a farming business, or an interest in a partnership that is carrying on a farming business.

Federal Tax Abatement A 10 percentage point reduction in the federal tax rate on corporations, applicable to income earned in a province.

First-Time Home Buyers' Tax Credit A credit against tax payable equal to 15% of $5,000 of the cost of an individual's first principal residence.

First-Year Rules See Half-Year Rules.

Fiscal Period A taxation year that does not exceed 53 weeks.

Fishing Property Fishing property includes real estate and property that is used in fishing activities, a share of a corporation that is carrying on a fishing business, or an interest in a partnership that is carrying on a fishing business.

Fixed Term Annuity An annuity that is paid for a specified number of periods.

Flat-Tax System A tax on income that is applied at the same rate to all taxpayers, without regard to the level of their income.

Foreign Accrual Property Income (FAPI) Income of a controlled foreign affiliate from property (interest, dividends, rents, royalties), inactive businesses, taxable capital gains from properties not used in an active business, and income from an investment business, defined as a business the principal purpose of which is to earn property income.

Foreign Affiliate (FA) A non-resident corporation in which a Canadian taxpayer has an equity percentage of at least 1%. As well, the aggregate equity percentages of the taxpayer and each person related to the taxpayer must be at least 10%.

Foreign Tax Credit A credit against tax payable based on taxes withheld by a foreign taxing authority on foreign source income.

Former Business Property Real property that is used in the operation of a business.

Fringe Benefits Non-cash benefits provided to employees by an employer (e.g., contributions to an employee's registered pension plan).

Full Rate Taxable Income For purposes of calculating the general rate reduction, taxable income reduced by amounts that have received preferential treatment under some other provision (e.g., the small businss deduction).

Fully Taxable Goods and Services Goods and services that are taxable at the full 5% GST rate. Registrants who sell fully taxable goods and services are entitled to input tax credits for GST paid. Examples include clothing, furniture, legal fees, hydro services, building materials, and restaurant meals.

G

GAAP An acronym for generally accepted accounting principles.

GAAR An acronym for General Anti-avoidance Rule. This ITA 245 provision attempts, in a very generalized manner, to limit the ability of taxpayers to avoid tax through certain types of transactions that have no bona fide purpose other than to obtain a tax benefit.

General Partner A partner whose personal liability for the debts and obligations of the partnership are not limited.

General Partnership A partnership all of the members of which are general partners.

General Rate Income Pool (GRIP) A notional account that tracks amounts of a CCPC's income that can be used for the payment of eligible dividends.

General Rate Reduction A percentage point deduction in the calculation of corporate tax payable that is designed to reduce the general corporate tax rate of 38%.

Gift A voluntary transfer of goods or services without remuneration.

Goods and Services tax (GST) A type of transaction tax that is assessed on the sale of goods and services. As it is assessed at all stages of the production/distribution chain, the tax that an enterprise must collect and pay to the government is offset by input tax credits for the tax paid on the various inputs required to produce or distribute the goods and services.

Goodwill The excess, if any, of the total fair value of a business enterprise over the sum of the fair values of its identifiable tangible and intangible assets.

Graduated Rate Estate A testamentary trust that is designated as a graduated rate estate. Its special features include the ability to use graduated tax rates and a non-calendar fiscal period for the 36-month period following an individual's death.

Grind A programmed reduction in some specified tax variable (e.g., the spousal tax credit is ground down by the spouse's net income).

Group of Persons For purposes of determining control of a corporation, a group of persons is any two or more persons each of whom owns shares in the corporation.

GST/HST Tax Credit A refundable tax credit that is available to all resident individuals aged 19 or older who file a T1 tax return. May be reduced or eliminated by a deduction of income in excess of a threshold amount.

H

Half-Year Rules (a.k.a. First-Year Rules) A group of rules that require the subtraction of one-half of the year's net additions (additions less the amount subtracted from the class because of disposals) from the class prior to calculating the CCA for the year. The great majority of post-2018 capital asset acquisitions are eligible for the Accelerated Investment Incentive (AccII), so the half-year rules don't apply to those acquisitions.

Harmonized Sales Tax (HST) A combined federal/provincial sales tax that is generally assessed on the same basis as the federal goods and services tax (GST). The combined rate varies across the provinces and is notionally a combination of the 5% GST plus a provincial sales tax ranging from 7% to 10%.

Hobby Farmer A part-time farmer who does not have a reasonable expectation of profit.

Home Accessibility Tax Credit A tax credit that is available on expenditures made for renovations that will allow seniors and disabled individuals to gain access to or be more mobile within a dwelling.

Home Buyers' Plan (HBP) A provision that allows individuals to make a temporary non-taxable withdrawal from their RRSP for purposes of acquiring a residence.

I

Identical Property Rules Rules that require that, for a group of identical capital assets (e.g., common shares) acquired at different prices, the adjusted cost base used to determine the gain or loss will be the average cost of the group. The rules are used when there is a partial disposition of the group.

Imputed Interest Interest on outstanding debt calculated at a specified interest rate without regard to the actual interest rate being paid. This concept is used to determine the taxable benefit on loans to employees and shareholders.

Inadequate Consideration A term used to refer to a situation where a non-arm's-length transfer of property has been made and the proceeds of disposition are not equal to the fair market value.

Income A measure of either how much an entity has earned during a period or, alternatively, how much its net worth has increased during a period. As the term is used in accounting and tax, it is a rules-based calculation. In the case of accounting, the rules are referred to as generally accepted accounting principles (GAAP), while in tax the rules are found in the *Income Tax Act* and other sources.

Income Attribution The allocation of some types of income, on assets that have been transferred to a spouse or related minors, back to the transferor for inclusion in the transferor's net income.

Income Interest (in a trust) A right of the taxpayer as a beneficiary under a personal trust to receive all or any part of the income of the trust.

Income Splitting A group of tax planning techniques designed to divide a given stream of income among family members or other related parties. The value of these techniques is based on progressive tax rates, which means that if a stream of income can be divided into a group of smaller streams, a larger portion of it will be taxed at lower rates, resulting in aggregate tax savings.

Income Tax A tax on the income of certain defined entities.

Income Tax Application Rules A set of rules designed to deal with transitional problems associated with the introduction of capital gains taxation in 1972. While these rules were important in the years immediately after 1971, they are of declining importance at this point in time.

Income Tax Folios A CRA publication providing their interpretation of various technical issues related to income taxes. These will gradually replace the CRA's Interpretation Bulletins.

Income Tax Regulations A set of rules concerning administration and enforcement of the *Income Tax Act*. One of the major issues covered here is capital cost allowance rates and procedures.

Income Tax Technical News An irregularly published newsletter prepared by the Income Tax Rulings Directorate.

Indexation The process of adjusting tax brackets and some tax credits to reflect changes in the Consumer Price Index.

Individual A single human being.

Individual Pension Plan (IPP) A defined benefit pension plan established for one individual.

Information Circulars A group of separate publications that provide information regarding procedural matters that relate to both the *Income Tax Act* and the provisions of the Canada Pension Plan.

Information Return ITA 221(1)(d) gives the CRA the right to require any class of taxpayer to file a return providing any class of information that it would like to have. A common example of an information return would be the T4, which employers are required to file to provide information on their employees' earnings and withholdings.

Input Tax Credit (ITC) An amount, claimable by a registrant, for GST paid or payable on goods or services that were acquired or imported for consumption, use, or supply in the course of the registrant's commercial activity.

Instalment Threshold An amount, currently $3,000 of net tax owing for individuals or taxes payable for corporations, that is used to determine the need to make instalment payments (i.e., individuals are required to make instalment payments if their net tax owing in the current year and one of the two preceding years exceeds the instalment threshold of $3,000).

Instalments Payments made during a taxation year by both individuals and corporations. They are designed to accumulate to an amount sufficient to cover the tax liability for the year. Individuals and small CCPCs make quarterly instalments. Corporations that are not small CCPCs are required to remit monthly.

Integration An approach to the taxation of corporations that attempts to ensure that amounts of income that are flowed through a corporation to its individual shareholders are subject to the same amount of tax as would be the case if the individuals had received the income directly from its source.

Inter Vivos Transfer A transfer made by a living individual, as opposed to a transfer made subsequent to that individual's death.

Inter Vivos Trust A trust that is not a testamentary trust.

Interest Income An amount that represents compensation for the use of money, is calculated with reference to a principal sum, and that accrues on a continuous basis.

International Tax Treaty (a.k.a., International Tax Convention) A bilateral agreement between two countries that establishes rules for dealing with cross-jurisdictional tax issues.

International Taxation Income and other types of taxation related to transactions and events that take place in multiple jurisdictions.

Interpretation Bulletins A group of over 500 individual publications that provide the CRA's interpretation of the various laws that they administer. Gradually being replaced by Income Tax Folios.

In-the-Money A term used to describe stock options in situations where the fair market value of the stock exceeds the option price.

Inventory Property, the cost or value of which is relevant in computing a taxpayer's income from a business for a taxation year. The property is being held for resale as opposed to being held to produce income.

Investment Tax Credit A credit against tax payable, calculated as a percentage of some specified type of expenditure made by the taxpayer.

Involuntary Disposition A disposition of a capital property resulting from theft, destruction through natural causes, or expropriation by a statutory authority.

J

Joint Spousal or Common-Law Partner Trust An inter vivos trust established by an individual aged 65 years or more, subject to the conditions that the individual and his or her spouse or common-law partner must be entitled to all of the trust's income during their lifetimes, and the individual and his or her spouse or common-law partner must be the only individuals who can access the capital of the trust during his or her lifetime.

Joint Tenancy A holding of property, either real or personal, by two or more persons with each sharing the undivided interest that cannot be sold without the consent of all joint tenants.

Joint Venture An arrangement in which two or more persons work together in a limited and defined business undertaking, which does not constitute a partnership, a trust, or a corporation, the expenses and revenues of which will be distributed in mutually agreed portions.

L

Labour Sponsored Funds Tax Credit A credit against tax payable that is available to individuals making investments in prescribed labour sponsored venture capital corporations.

Legal Capital An amount that is specified in corporate enabling legislation. In general, it is equal to the amount of consideration received for the issuance of shares.

Life Annuity An annuity that continues until the death of the annuitant.

Lifelong Learning Plan (LLP) A provision that allows individuals to make temporary, non-taxable withdrawals from their RRSP when they are enrolled in a qualifying education program at a qualifying educational institution.

Limited Liability   A reference to the fact that the liability of investors in equity shares of a corporation is limited to the amount of their invested capital.

Limited Liability Partnerships   A partnership, all of the members of which are legislatively specified professionals. The members of such partnerships are relieved of any personal liability arising from the wrongful or negligent action of their professional partners, as well as employees, agents, or representatives of the partnership who conduct partnership business.

Limited Partner   As defined in most provincial legislation, a partner whose liabilities for partnership debts is limited to the amount of his or her contribution to the partnership and who is not permitted to participate in the management of the partnership.

Limited Partnership   A partnership composed of at least one general partner and at least one limited partner. To be considered a limited partnership, the partnership has to be registered as such under the appropriate provincial registry.

Limited Partnership Loss (LPL)   The excess of losses allocated to a limited partner (other than farming or capital losses) over his or her at-risk amount.

Liquidating Dividend   A dividend that represents a return of invested capital as opposed to a distribution from earnings.

Listed Personal Property   A defined subset of personal-use property. The included items are works of art, jewellery, rare books, stamps, and coins.

Loss Carry Back   The application of a loss incurred in the current taxation year against the income reported in a previous taxation year resulting in a refund of taxes paid in that previous year.

Loss Carry Forward   The application of a loss incurred in the current taxation year against income reported in a subsequent taxation year resulting in a reduction of tax payable in that subsequent year.

Low Rate Income Pool (LRIP)   A notional account that tracks amounts of a non-CCPC's income that cannot be used for the payment of eligible dividends.

Lump-Sum Payments   Retroactive payments for spousal or child support, pension benefits, EI benefits, and employment income (including payments for termination) that relate to prior years. Qualifying amounts of such payments are eligible for an alternative tax payable calculation.

M

M&P   An acronym for "manufacturing and processing" that is usually used in connection with the calculation of the manufacturing and processing profits deduction.

Manufacturing and Processing Profits Deduction (M&P Deduction)   A deduction in the calculation of corporate tax payable. It is equal to the general rate reduction applied to M&P profits.

Medical Expense Tax Credit   A credit against tax payable that is available to individuals with qualifying medical expenses.

Merger   A combination of two or more business enterprises. While widely used in the *Income Tax Act*, this term does not have a formal definition in that legislation.

Money Purchase Limit   An amount specified in tax legislation that represents the maximum amount of employee and employer contributions that can be added for the benefit of a given employee to an RPP in the specified taxation year.

Money Purchase Plan   A retirement savings plan in which the plan sponsor (employer or individual) makes known or determinable contributions. The retirement benefit is based on the accumulated contributions and earnings on investments within the plan.

Moving Expenses   Costs, as described in ITA 62(3), that can be deducted when an individual is moving to a new work location, to commence full-time attendance at a post-secondary institution, to a new work location after ceasing to be a full-time student at a post-secondary institution, or to a new location to take up employment if unemployed prior to the move.

MUSH   An acronym for "municipalities, universities, schools, and hospitals," It is used in GST work to refer to the special rules applicable to these organizations.

Mutual Fund   A taxable entity, either a trust or a corporation, that manages a portfolio of investments on behalf of its unitholders or shareholders.

N

"Negative" Adjusted Cost Base (ACB)   A term used to refer to situations where negative adjustments to the adjusted cost base of a capital asset exceed its original cost plus positive adjustments. While in general such amounts must be taken into income, an exception is made for partnership Interests, for which such amounts can be carried forward.

Net Business Income   As used in this text, the net of inclusions less deductions related to business income, with all amounts determined as per Division B, Subdivision b, of the *Income Tax Act*.

Net Capital Loss   The excess of allowable capital losses over taxable capital gains for the current year.

Net Income   This expression relates to a specific taxation year and means all sources of income (employment, business, and property) plus net taxable capital gains minus deductions in Subdivision e minus current-year losses. The expression "net income" is used in income tax returns but not in the ITA, where it is simply referred to as "income" (defined in ITA 3).

Net Income for Tax Purposes An expression used to differentiate accounting income from net income. We limit the use of the term in the text to discussions and problem material where the focus is on reconciliations of income from accounting to income tax.

Net Tax Owing A term applicable to taxpayers who are individuals used to describe the sum of federal and provincial taxes owing for the year less amounts withheld for the year.

New Housing GST/HST Rebate A provision that allows an individual to recover a portion of the GST paid on the acquisition of a new residence.

Non-Arm's Length ITA 251(1) indicates that related persons (see definition) do not deal with each other at arm's length. Also, a taxpayer and a personal trust do not deal with each other at arm's length. In other cases, it is a question of fact as to whether an arm's-length relation exists.

Non-Capital Loss The sum of employment losses (for individuals), business losses, property losses, net capital losses deducted, and deductible dividends received (for corporations) less income as calculated under ITA 3(c).

Non-Depreciable Capital Property Capital property, such as land or holdings of securities, that is not subject to depreciation or amortization.

Non-Discretionary trust A trust for which the trust documents have specified the amounts of income and capital to be allocated to each beneficiary.

Non-Eligible Dividends Dividends that have not been designated by the payor as eligible for the enhanced gross up and tax credit procedure.

Non-Eligible RDTOH A balance containing refundable taxes that are available for dividend refunds on non-eligible dividends paid.

Non-Refundable Tax Credit A tax credit that can only be used against the tax payable of an individual. It will not be "refunded" to individuals without sufficient tax payable to make use of it.

Non-Resident A corporation, trust, or any other type of entity that exists, was formed or organized, or was last continued under the laws of a country or a political subdivision of a country other than Canada.

Non-Share Consideration Consideration received by a taxpayer from a corporation that is in the form of assets other than shares of the corporation.

Northern Residents Deductions Deductions from the taxable income of residents of prescribed areas in northern Canada that are designed to compensate them for the higher costs of living in these regions.

Notice of Assessment A form that the CRA sends to all taxpayers after they process their returns. It tells taxpayers whether there were any changes made to the returns and, if so, what they are. It also informs taxpayers of the amount of their additional tax payable or their refund.

Notice of Objection A statement made to the CRA providing a statement of facts and reasons detailing why a taxpayer or GST registrant disagrees with an assessment. The notice can be filed using Form T400A or by simply writing a letter to the CRA.

O

OAS Clawback A taxing back, or reduction, in the payment of Old Age Security benefits. The federal government taxes back, or retains, an amount of these payments equal to 15% of the individual's income in excess of an indexed threshold amount.

Old Age Security (OAS) Benefits A monthly payment to residents of Canada who are 65 years of age or older (see also OAS Clawback).

Operating Cost Benefit A taxable benefit assessed to employees whose employers pay the operating costs of an automobile provided to the employee. It is designed to reflect, on a notional basis, the value of these operating costs.

Ordering Rule Rules that establish the sequence or order in which a group of deductions must be made.

Overintegration An application of integration procedures (e.g., gross up and dividend tax credit rates) that results in a situation where income flowed through a corporation is subject to less tax payable than the same income received directly by an individual.

P

Paid-Up Capital (PUC) A balance that is, in general, equal to legal stated capital as determined under the legislation governing the particular corporation. The equivalent of contributed capital in accounting usage.

Parent Company A corporation that controls one or more subsidiaries.

Part IV tax A refundable tax, applicable to private corporations and subject corporations, and assessed on portfolio dividends received as well as some dividends received from connected corporations.

Part-Year Resident An individual who either enters Canada during the year and becomes a resident or, alternatively, an individual who departs from Canada during the year and gives up resident status. In either case, the individual will be taxed on their worldwide income for the part of the year they were considered to be a resident of Canada.

Partner A person who is a member of a partnership.

Partnership Two or more persons who combine forces to carry on a business together for the purpose of making a profit by contributing their skills, knowledge, labour, experience, time, or capital.

Partnership Interest　A non-depreciable capital property that reflects the partner's original cost, adjusted for earnings, withdrawals, and other factors.

Past Service Cost　The cost of starting a pension plan and extending the benefits/contributions to years of service prior to the inception of the plan or, alternatively, amending the benefit/contribution formula of an existing plan and extending the change retroactively to years of service prior to the amendment.

Past Service Pension Adjustment (PSPA)　An adjustment to reflect the past service benefits/contributions allocated to an employee for years of service prior to the current year.

Penalties　Amounts taxpayers or GST registrants must pay if they fail to file returns or remit or pay amounts owing on time, or if they try to evade paying or remitting tax by not filing returns. Penalties must also be paid by people who knowingly, or under circumstances amounting to gross negligence, participate in or make false statements or omissions in their returns, and by those who do not provide the information required on a prescribed form.

Pension Adjustment (PA)　An adjustment reported by employers that reflects, for an individual employee, the employee and employer contributions to RPPs and DPSPs for the previous year (in the case of defined benefit RPPs, benefits are converted to an equivalent amount of contributions).

Pension Adjustment Reversal (PAR)　An adjustment for amounts of benefits/contributions that were included in previously issued pension adjustments but have subsequently been lost to the individual (e.g., benefits earned during a pre-vesting period that did not ultimately vest).

Pension Income Tax Credit　A credit against tax payable that is available to individuals with qualifying pension income.

Periodic Child Care Expense Amount　A weekly limit on deductible child care costs, defined as 1/40 of the annual child care expense amount.

Permanent Establishment　A fixed place of business of a corporation, including an office, a branch, a mine, an oil well, a farm, a timberland, a factory, a workshop, or a warehouse.

Person　A term used in the *Income Tax Act* to refer to taxable entities. For income tax purposes, the three taxable entities are individuals, corporations, and trusts.

Personal Services Business　A corporation that provides the services of a specified shareholder [ITA 248(1)] who could reasonably be regarded as an officer or employee of the business, and that does not have five or more other full-time employees throughout the year.

Personal Tax Credits　A group of credits against tax payable that are specified in ITA 118(1). They include credits for individuals, spouses, common-law partners, and various dependants, as well as credits for types of income such as pension or employment.

Personal Trust　A testamentary or inter vivos trust in which no beneficial interest was acquired for consideration paid to the trust or to a person who contributed property to the trust.

Personal-Use Property　Any property that is owned by the taxpayer and used primarily for his or her enjoyment, or for the enjoyment of one or more individuals related to the taxpayer.

Phased Retirement　A term used to refer to situations where an individual over 55 years of age continues to earn partial pension benefits despite the fact that he or she has started to receive pension benefits from that employer.

Political Contributions Tax Credit　A credit against tax payable that is available to individuals who have made contributions to a registered federal political party or to a candidate at the time of a federal election.

Pooled Registered Pension Plan　A registered pension plan established by a financial institution. Eligible registrants would be employees and other individuals who are not members of a registered pension plan established by an employer.

Portfolio Dividend　A dividend received from a corporation to which the recipient is not connected (see connected corporation). Usually applicable if 10% or less of the voting shares are owned.

Preferred Beneficiary　An individual who is a beneficiary of a trust and who is either eligible for the disability tax credit or, alternatively, 18 years of age or older and can be claimed by another individual for purposes of the dependent tax credit for individuals who are dependent because of mental or physical infirmity.

Preferred Beneficiary Election　An election that allows trust income to be allocated to a preferred beneficiary without being distributed to that beneficiary by the trust.

Preferred Shares　Shares that do not have all the rights that are provided for under the relevant corporate enabling legislation. While there are many variations in the rights that such securities have, preferred shares would normally have a fixed or determinable dividend and would not have voting rights.

Prescribed Rate　An interest rate that, as described in ITR 4301, changes quarterly and is based on the average interest rate paid on 90-day Treasury Bills during the first month of the preceding quarter. The basic rate is used for a variety of purposes (e.g., calculation of the taxable benefits on interest-free loans to employees). The basic rate plus 2 percentage points is used to calculate interest owing from the government to taxpayers (e.g., interest on late payment of a tax refund). The basic rate plus 4 percentage points is used to calculate interest owed by taxpayers to the government (e.g., interest on late instalments).

Prescribed Stock Exchange This term has been replaced by "designated stock exchange."

Principal Residence Any accommodation owned by the taxpayer that was ordinarily inhabited in the year by the taxpayer, his or her spouse, a former spouse, or a dependent child, and is designated by the taxpayer as a principal residence.

Private Corporation A corporation that is a resident of Canada but is not a public corporation.

Proceeds of Disposition (POD) Amounts received as the result of a disposition. Usually related to a capital property disposition.

Professional Corporation ITA 248(1) defines a professional corporation as a corporation that carries on the professional practice of an accountant, dentist, lawyer, medical doctor, veterinarian, or chiropractor. Corporations carrying on the practice of other professionals, for example architects, do not fall within this definition.

Progressive Tax System A tax system that applies higher effective rates for individuals with higher incomes and lower effective rates for individuals with lower incomes (e.g., personal income taxes).

Property Income Income that is earned through the passive ownership of property. It would include rents, interest, dividends, and some royalties (i.e., royalties paid on assets that have been purchased). While usage is not always consistent, this term usually refers to a net amount (i.e., inclusions less deductions, or revenues less expenses).

Property Tax A tax on the ownership of some particular set of goods.

Public Corporation A corporation that has at least one class of its shares listed on a designated stock exchange in Canada.

Purification of a Small Business Corporation A process of disposing of corporate assets that are not being used to produce active business income so that the corporation meets the 90% of assets test required to qualify as a small business corporation.

Q

Qualified Farm Property A farm property that, prior to its disposition, was owned by the taxpayer, his or her spouse or common-law partner, or their children for a period of 24 months or more.

Qualified Fishing Property A fishing property that, prior to its disposition, was owned by the taxpayer, his or her spouse or common-law partner, or their children for a period of 24 months or more.

Qualified Property Certain specified types of property that, when acquired, qualify the taxpayer for an investment tax credit.

Qualified Small Business Corporation (QSBC) A small business corporation that, at the time of its disposition, has been owned by no one other than the taxpayer or a related party during the preceding 24 months, and during that 24-month period more than 50% of the fair market value of its assets were used in an active business carried on primarily in Canada.

Qualifying Canadian Journalism Organization A Canadian organization that is primarily involved in the production of written news content.

Qualifying Corporation A CCPC throughout the year with taxable income in the immediately preceding year of no more than $500,000 and previous year taxable capital employed in Canada of $10 million or less, thereby qualifying for the additional 15% tax credit on the first $3,000,000 of qualified scientific research and development expenditures.

Qualifying Spousal or Common-Law Partner Trust A spousal or common-law partner trust that qualifies for the rollover of assets into the trust under ITA 73(1.01) for inter vivos trusts or ITA 70(6) for testamentary trusts.

Qualitative Characteristics This term is used in our text to refer to non-quantitative characteristics of a tax system that are considered to be desirable (e.g., fairness).

Quick Method A method of determining GST amounts payable or receivable that is available to registrants with annual GST taxable sales, including those of associated businesses, of $400,000 or less. Specified percentages are applied to the GST-inclusive sales figures to determine the GST payable or the refund. Accounting for input tax credits on non-capital expenditures is not required. Input tax credits on capital expenditures are tracked separately.

R

RDTOH An acronym for refundable dividend tax on hand.

Real Property Land and all appurtenances to it, including buildings, crops, and mineral rights—a.k.a., real estate.

Reassessment A revision of an original assessment (see Assessment and Notice of Assessment).

Recapture of CCA An inclusion in business and property income that arises when deductions from a CCA class, engendered by disposals, leave a negative balance in that class at the end of the taxation year.

Redemption of Shares A transaction in which a corporation purchases some of its own outstanding shares, either in the open market or through a direct purchase from shareholders.

Refundable Dividend Tax On Hand (RDTOH) A balance made up of refundable taxes paid, less refunds received as the result of paying dividends. There are two separate RDTOH balances: eligible RDTOH and non-eligible RDTOH.

Refundable Investment Tax Credit An investment tax credit that will be paid to the taxpayer even if the amount resulting from the investment tax credit exceeds the taxpayer's tax payable.

Refundable Journalism Labour Tax Credit A refundable credit for salaries and wages paid to eligible newsroom employees of a qualifying Canadian journalism organization.

Refundable Medical Expense Supplement A refundable credit against tax payable that increases the amount available to certain low-income individuals for their eligible medical expenses.

Refundable Part I tax The portion of Part I tax that is applicable to a notional amount of aggregate investment income earned by a CCPC.

Refundable Part XI.3 tax A 50% tax that is assessed on contributions to a retirement Compensation Arrangement and on the earnings of amounts invested in the plan. It is fully refundable when amounts are distributed from the arrangement and taxed in the hands of the recipient employees.

Refundable tax credit An amount, based on a tax credit calculation, that will be paid to an individual even if the amount resulting from the tax credit calculation exceeds the individual's tax payable.

Registered Disability Savings Plan (RDSP) A trusteed arrangement that allows individuals to make non-deductible contributions that will be invested on a tax-free basis, with the accumulated funds being used to make distributions to an individual who qualifies for the disability tax credit.

Registered Education Savings Plan (RESP) A trusteed arrangement that allows individuals to make non-deductible contributions that will be invested on a tax-free basis, with the accumulated funds being used to provide for the post-secondary education of a child.

Registered Pension Plan (RPP) A retirement savings plan sponsored by an employer to which the employer will make contributions that are not taxable to the employee, and the employee may make contributions that are deductible. Earnings accumulate tax free within the plan. Withdrawals from the plan are subject to tax.

Registered Retirement Income Fund (RRIF) A trusteed plan to which a resident individual can transfer balances from retirement savings plans on a tax-free basis. Earnings accumulate tax free within the plan. Withdrawals from the plan are subject to tax. Unlike RRSPs, a minimum withdrawal is required each year.

Registered Retirement Savings Plan (RRSP) A trusteed plan to which a resident individual can make deductible contributions. Earnings accumulate tax free within the plan. Withdrawals from the plan are generally subject to tax.

Registrant An entity who is registered to collect and remit the GST.

Regressive Tax System A tax system that applies higher effective rates for individuals with lower incomes and lower effective rates for individuals with higher incomes (e.g., most sales taxes).

Related Persons ITA 251(2)(a) indicates that two individuals are related if they are connected by blood relationship, marriage or common-law partnership, or adoption. ITA 251(2)(b) describes various situations in which a corporation would be related to other persons (e.g., a corporation is related to the person who controls it). ITA 251(2)(c) describes various situations in which two corporations would be related to each other (e.g., the two corporations are controlled by the same person).

Reorganization of Capital (ITA 86) A rollover provision that allows one class of shares in a corporation to be exchanged for a different class of shares, without tax consequences.

Replacement Property Rules A set of rules that provide for the deferral of both recapture and capital gains on involuntary dispositions and some voluntary dispositions of capital property. Deferral is conditional on replacing the property within a specified period after the proceeds of disposition are received.

Reserve A deduction in the calculation of net business income or net taxable capital gains.

Resident A person who is located in a place. This is the basis on which Canadian income taxes are assessed. That is, Canadian resident persons are liable for the payment of Canadian income tax, without regard to their citizenship or the source of their income. While not defined in the *Income Tax Act*, Folio S5-F1-C1 provides guidance on the determination of residency for individuals and IT-447 provides similar guidance for trusts.

Residential Ties Factors that will be considered in determining whether or not an individual is a resident of Canada. While there are many such ties, Folio S5-F1-C1 indicates that the most commonly used would be the maintenance of a dwelling in Canada, having one's spouse or common-law partner remain in Canada, and having one's dependants remain in Canada.

Restricted Farm Loss A farmer whose chief source of income is not farming or a combination of farming and some other source of income, but who has a reasonable expectation of long-run profitability, can only deduct losses to the extent of the first $2,500, plus one-half of the next $12,500. Losses in excess of this deductible amount are referred to as restricted farm losses.

Restrictive Covenant An agreement entered into, an undertaking made, or a waiver of an advantage or right by the taxpayer. This would include, but would not be limited to, non-competition agreements.

Retained Earnings In accounting usage, the amount of a corporation's shareholders' equity that resulted from the retention of earnings in the corporation.

Retirement Compensation Arrangement (RCA) An unregistered plan to which employers make deductible contributions to provide employees with benefits subsequent to their retirement. Both contributions and earnings are subject to a refundable Part XI.3 tax.

Retiring Allowance Amounts received at retirement as recognition for long service or as the result of loss of employment.

Reversionary trust A trust agreement under which the property held by the trustee can revert to the settlor.

Rollover As this term is used in tax work, it refers to a tax-free transfer of assets under circumstances that, in the absence of a special rollover provision, would be considered a taxable transfer.

RRSP Dollar Limit Generally, the money purchase limit for the preceding year.

RRSP Deduction Room The excess of the RRSP deduction limit over the amount of RRSP contributions that have been deducted.

S

Safe Income For purposes of applying ITA 55(2) to capital gains stripping, safe income is made up of amounts earned by a corporation after 1971, or if the investment shares in that corporation were acquired after that date, amounts earned after the acquisition.

Salary The amount an employer pays an employee for work done. An employer records this type of employment income on a T4. A common component of employment income.

Salary Deferral Arrangement (SDA) An arrangement, whether funded or not, under which an individual who has the right to receive compensation postpones the receipt of that compensation, and it is reasonable to assume that one of the main purposes of this postponement was to defer the payment of taxes.

Scientific Research and Experimental Development (SRED) Activities related to basic or applied research and for the development of new products and processes.

Self-Employed Individual An individual who has a business relationship with an entity. Whether or not an individual is working as an employee or a self-employed individual is dependent on factors such as control, ownership of tools, chance of profit or risk of loss, and the ability to subcontract or hire an assistant.

Separate Class Rules Rules that require certain types of assets that would, in the absence of these special rules, be included in a single class, be allocated to a separate balance for that class (e.g., each rental property with a cost greater than $50,000 must be placed in a different class 1).

Settlor The individual who creates a trust by contributing property to be managed and administered by a trustee for the beneficiaries.

Share-for-Share Exchange (ITA 85.1) A rollover provision that allows one corporation to acquire shares in another corporation by issuing its own shares without tax consequences to either of the corporations or their shareholders.

Shareholders' Equity The residual interest of the shareholders of a corporation in the net assets of the corporation.

Short Fiscal Year A taxation year that is less than 12 months in duration. Can occur in the first and last years of operation, as well as certain other situations.

Simplified ITC Accounting A method of determining input tax credits available to small businesses, charities, not-for-profit organizations, and certain public service bodies. The organization must have annual GST taxable sales, including those of associated businesses, of $1,000,000 or less and annual GST taxable purchases of $4,000,000 or less. Input tax credits are determined by multiplying all GST-inclusive purchases, except real property purchases, by 5/105 rather than using the actual GST paid. Input tax credits on real property are tracked separately.

Small Business Corporation A corporation that is a Canadian controlled private corporation that uses all or substantially all (90% or more) of the fair market value of its assets in an active business that is carried on primarily (more than 50%) in Canada.

Small Business Deduction A deduction in the calculation of corporate tax payable equal to 17.5 percentage points on the first $500,000 of active business income earned by a CCPC.

Small CCPC A Canadian controlled private corporation that has (1) taxable income in the current or previous year of $500,000 or less, (2) has taxable capital employed in Canada in the current or previous year of $10 million or less, (3) is able to claim some amount of the small business deduction in the current or previous year, and (4) has a perfect payment compliance record for the last 12 months.

Small Suppliers Exemption An exemption from the requirement to register for the collection and remittance of GST for those entities with less than $30,000 in taxable supplies.

Social Benefits Repayment An income tested taxing back, or reduction, in the payment of Old Age Security benefits and Employment Insurance benefits.

Soft Costs Costs, such as interest and property tax, on land and buildings that are incurred prior to the capital asset being used for business or income producing purposes.

Sojourner An individual who is deemed under ITA 250 to be a Canadian resident for the full taxation year as the result of having sojourned (i.e., been temporarily present) in Canada for 183 days or more.

Source Deductions Amounts that are withheld by an employer from the income of employees. The withholdings for income taxes, Canada Pension Plan contributions, and Employment Insurance premiums must be remitted to the government.

Source Individual A source individual (with respect to a specified individual) is a resident of Canada who is related to the specified individual.

Specified Class ITA 256(1.1) A class of shares that has certain specified terms and conditions, including a fixed or determinable dividend and an absence of voting rights. Would generally be referred to as preferred shares.

Specified Employee An employee who owns 10% or more of the shares of the corporation or who does not deal at arm's length with the corporation.

Specified Individual Under the tax on split income (TOSI) legislation a specified individual is an individual who is a resident of Canada and, if the individual is under 18, has a parent who is also a resident of Canada.

Specified Investment Business A corporation that does not have five or more full-time employees throughout the year whose principal purpose is to derive income from property.

Specified Non-Resident Shareholder A specified shareholder who is a non-resident person or non-resident investment company.

Specified Shareholder [(ITA 18(5)] A shareholder of a corporation who owns, either alone or together with other related persons, more than 25% of the voting shares of a corporation or, alternatively, shares that have more than 25% of the market value of all of the corporation's shares.

Specified Shareholder [ITA 248(1)] A shareholder of a corporation who owns, directly or indirectly, at any time in the year, not less than 10% of the issued shares of any class of the capital stock of the corporation, or of any other corporation that is related to the corporation.

Split Income Certain types of income received by a specified individual from non-arm's-length sources that will be taxed at the maximum federal rate.

Spousal or Common-Law Partner Trust An inter vivos or testamentary trust that has an individual's spouse or common-law partner as a beneficiary (see also Qualifying Spousal or Common-Law Partner Trust).

Spousal RRSP An RRSP to which the spouse or common-law partner of the annuitant (i.e., beneficiary of the RRSP) has made contributions that the spouse or common-law partner can deduct in calculating net income.

Spousal Support A support amount that is for the benefit of a spouse or common-law partner or a former spouse or common-law partner.

Spousal tax credit A credit against tax payable that is available to individuals who have a spouse or common-law partner.

Spouse An individual to whom a taxpayer is legally married.

Standby Charge A taxable benefit assessed to employees who have been provided with an automobile by their employer. It is designed to reflect, on a notional basis, the value of having the car available on a standby basis for personal usage.

Stock Dividend A pro rata distribution of a corporation's shares to existing shareholders of the corporation.

Stock Option A contractual arrangement that gives the holder the right to purchase a specified number of shares for a specified period of time at a specified acquisition price.

Stop Loss Rules A group of rules that, under specified conditions, prevent the deduction of a loss.

Straight-Line Method A method of calculating CCA in which a specified or determinable rate is applied to the capital cost of acquired assets in order to determine the CCA for the period.

Student Loan Interest Credit A credit against tax payable that is based on the amount of interest on a loan under the *Canada Student Loans Act* or the *Canada Student Financial Assistance Act*.

Subject Corporation For purposes of the Part IV tax, a public corporation that is controlled by, or is for the benefit of, an individual or a related group of individuals. Also used in the determination of dividend stripping (ITA 84.1) and share sales to non-residents (ITA 212.1) to describe a corporation whose shares have been sold.

Subsidiary An enterprise that is controlled by another enterprise (the parent company). The parent company has the right and ability to obtain future economic benefits from the resources of the subsidiary and is exposed to the related risks.

Superficial Loss—ITA 54 A loss on the disposition of property that is disallowed for tax purposes because the taxpayer has acquired an identical property, either 30 days before the disposition or, alternatively, 30 days after the disposition.

Supply A broad range of transactions between persons. To "make a supply of property or a service" means to provide it in any way, including sale, transfer, barter, exchange, licence, rental, lease, gift, or disposition.

Support Amount Amounts paid as the result of the separation or divorce of two individuals who were spouses or common-law partners. Can be divided into spousal support and child support.

Surtax An additional or extra tax on something already taxed.

Syndicates A group of persons combined or making a joint effort to undertake some specific project or to carry out a specific transaction.

T

Target Benefit Plan A hybrid pension plan that is based on defined contributions combined with a target or proposed benefit for retirees. However, unlike defined benefit plans, these plans also allow the benefit to be reduced if funding is not adequate to produce the target benefit.

Tariffs A tax imposed on the importation or exportation of certain goods or services.

Tax Avoidance The undertaking of transactions or arrangements with a view to avoiding or minimizing the payment of taxes. As the term is generally used, it refers to legitimate procedures that could also be described as tax planning.

Tax Base The income source, class of transaction, type of property, or other factor on which tax is assessed (e.g., sales tax is assessed on sales).

Tax Court of Canada A court that hears appeals about income tax and GST/HST assessments. In addition, the court has jurisdiction to hear appeals under the Canada Pension Plan Act, Employment Insurance Act, and several other acts. The tax court maintains four offices (Vancouver, Ottawa, Toronto, and Montreal) and regularly conducts hearings in major centres across Canada.

Tax Credit A credit against tax payable.

Tax Deferral An important type of tax planning. The basic idea here is to find procedures that will put off the payment of taxes until a later taxation year. The value of these procedures reflects the time value of money. That is, there is a value associated with making a payment later rather than sooner.

Tax Evasion This typically involves deliberately ignoring a specific part of the law or wilfully refusing to comply with legislated reporting requirements. Tax evasion, unlike tax avoidance, has criminal consequences.

Tax Expenditure Forgone tax revenues due to special exemptions, rate reductions, rebates, and credits that reduce the amount of tax that would otherwise be payable. Often designed to encourage certain kinds of activities or to serve other objectives, such as providing assistance to lower-income Canadians.

Tax-Free Savings Accounts (TFSA) A trusteed arrangement that allows individuals to make non-deductible contributions that will be invested in qualified assets. Earnings accumulate on a tax-free basis within the plan and can be distributed to the Individual who established the plan on a tax-free basis.

Tax Haven A foreign country used to avoid or reduce income taxes, especially by investors from another country.

Tax Incidence The person who ultimately pays a tax, regardless of the legal basis of assessment (e.g., taxes paid by corporations may be passed on to either employees or customers).

Tax Planning The undertaking of legitimate transactions or arrangements with a view to avoiding or minimizing the payment of taxes. Some or all of such efforts could also be referred to as tax avoidance.

Taxable Allowance An allowance provided by an employer to an employee that must be included in the employee's employment income. The amount is included on the employee's T4.

Taxable Benefit An amount of money, or the value of goods or services, that an employer pays or provides in addition to salary.

Taxable Canadian Corporation A Canadian corporation that is not exempt from Canadian income tax by way of a statutory provision.

Taxable Canadian Property A group of assets that are listed under the definition of taxable Canadian property in ITA 248(1). These assets are distinguished by the fact that gains on their disposition are taxable without regard to the residence of the selling taxpayer. For example, if a U.S. resident sells Canadian real estate, Canadian income tax will be assessed on any gain resulting from the sale.

Taxable Capital Employed in Canada (TCEC) This amount is the GAAP-determined capital of the corporation, less the allowance for investments in other corporations, multiplied by the percentage of the corporation's activity at permanent establishments in Canada as determined under ITR 402. It is used in a number of calculations, including the determination of a small CCPC and the calculation of the reduction of the small businss deduction.

Taxable Capital Gain The taxable portion (currently one-half) of a capital gain.

Taxable Entity A defined organization or individual that is subject to tax (e.g., corporations are taxable entities for income tax purposes).

Taxable Income Net income less certain deductions that are largely specified in Division C of Part I of the *Income Tax Act*. These deductions include loss carry overs, the lifetime capital gains deduction, and for corporations, dividends and charitable gifts.

Taxable Surplus A surplus account that tracks certain sources of income of a foreign affiliate.

Taxation Year The period that is covered by a taxpayer's return. As defined in ITA 249, it is equal to a calendar year for individuals and inter vivos trusts, and a fiscal period for corporations and testamentary trusts.

Taxpayer An entity that is required to file a tax return and pay taxes. For income tax purposes, a taxpayer is an individual, a corporation, or a trust.

Taxpayer Relief Provisions Information Circular 07-01 contains guidelines on the discretionary authority the minister has to grant relief based on a taxpayer's situation. An example would be a waiver of late filing interest and penalties because the individual suffered a serious illness. It replaces the fairness provisions.

Teacher School Supply Tax Credit A refundable tax credit available to eligible educators for up to $1,000 of eligible expenditures.

Tenancy in Common A holding of property, either real or personal, by two or more persons, with each having a divisible interest that can be sold.

Term Preferred Shares Preferred shares that have a provision allowing them to be redeemed by the issuer or redeemed at the request of the holder.

Terminal Loss A deduction in the calculation of business and property income that arises when the last asset in a CCA class is retired and a positive balance is left in the class.

Testamentary Trust A trust that arises on, and as a consequence of, the death of an individual.

Thin Capitalization A reference to situations where a non-resident specified shareholder is receiving interest on an amount of debt that exceeds two times the sum of his or her share of contributed capital plus 100% of retained earnings.

Tie-Breaker Rules Provisions in international tax treaties that are designed to prevent the double taxation of dual residents.

TOSI An acronym for tax on split income. (See Split Income.)

Transaction Tax A tax that is assessed on specified types of transactions. Such taxes are most commonly applied to transactions involving the sale of goods or services.

Transfer To convey or move from one taxpayer to a different taxpayer.

Transfer Tax A tax on the transfer of property from one owner to another.

Transferee A taxpayer to whom a transfer is made.

Transferor A taxpayer who makes a transfer.

Trust A relationship in which one person holds the title to property for the benefit of another person.

Trustee An individual or trust institution that holds legal title to property in trust for the benefit of the trust beneficiaries.

Tuition Fees Tax Credit A credit against tax payable that is available to individuals making qualifying tuition payments. The base includes specified ancillary fees and fees and ancillary costs associated with writing university examinations and required examinations in professional programs.

21-Year Deemed Disposition Rule A requirement, applicable to some types of personal trusts, that requires a deemed disposition of the trust's capital property at the end of every 21 years.

U

Undepreciated Capital Cost (UCC) The capital cost of a depreciable asset class less the cumulative CCA that has been taken to date. The tax equivalent of net book value in accounting.

Underintegration An application of integration procedures (e.g., gross up and dividend tax credit rates) that results in a situation where income flowed through a corporation is subject to more tax payable than the same income received directly by an individual.

Unused RRSP Deduction Room The cumulative total of all RRSP deduction limits less amounts deducted in those years. The end of the preceding-year balance is used when calculating the RRSP deduction limit.

V

Value Added Tax (VAT) A tax based on the value added to a product at each stage of production or distribution by a particular entity. It is generally based on some accounting measurement of income.

Vertical Amalgamation An amalgamation of a parent company and one or more of its subsidiaries.

Vested Benefit A benefit is vested if the beneficiary has an irrevocable right to receive it.

Vested Contribution A contribution is vested if the individual making the contribution has an irrevocable right to either the amount of the contribution or a benefit of equivalent value.

Volunteer Firefighters Tax Credit A credit against tax payable that is available to volunteer firefighters who perform at least 200 hours of volunteer firefighting services during a taxation year.

Volunteer Search and Rescue Tax Credit A credit against tax payable that is available to volunteer search and rescue workers who perform at least 200 hours of volunteer search and rescue services during a taxation year.

W–Z

Wholly Dependent Person A dependant who lives with the taxpayer (this requirement is not applicable if the dependant is the taxpayer's child) in a self-contained domestic establishment and is eligible for the eligible dependant tax credit.

Will A document that is a legal declaration of an individual's wishes as to the disposition of his or her property after death.

Winding-Up of a 90% Owned Subsidiary A rollover provision that allows the assets of a 90% or more owned subsidiary to be combined with the assets of its parent company without tax consequences.

Winding-Up of a Canadian Corporation A series of transactions that result in substantially all of the assets of a Canadian corporation being distributed to the shareholders of that corporation.

Zero-Emission Passenger Vehicles A motor vehicle that is fully powered by electricity or hydrogen, or partially powered by electricity with a minimum battery capacity of 15 kwh.

Zero-Rated Goods and Services Goods and services that are taxable at a zero GST rate. The fact that they are designated as "taxable" means that registrants who sell such goods and services are eligible for input tax credits for the GST that they pay. Examples include basic groceries (e.g., milk, bread, and vegetables), prescription drugs, and exports.